Revised Edition

Irasshai: Welcome to Japanese
Volume 2

An Interactive, Multimedia Course
in Beginning Japanese

Cliff Walker and Ellen Jones-Walker
K. Negrelli, K. Suzuki and S. Suzuki

Irasshai is produced and operated by Georgia Public Broadcasting.

Published by Booksurge Publishing, 7290-B Investment Dr., Charleston, SC 29418.

First edition, 1997, by Cliff Walker and Ellen Jones-Walker.

Printed in the U.S.A.

ISBN: 1-4196-8557-0
Library of Congress Card No. 9781419685576

INTRODUCTION

What is *Irasshai*?
Irasshai is a nationally acclaimed Japanese language and culture distance learning program designed for high school students but enjoyed by people of all ages. The program is performance-based in both instruction and assessment, and its curriculum was designed to mirror national foreign language standards. This textbook, Volume 2 of two volumes, and its corresponding workbook, was designed to be used in conjunction with *Irasshai*'s **Video Lessons** -- 138 interactive video lessons that can be viewed from the *Irasshai* website, Georgia Public Broadcasting's Digital Library, or can be delivered as a complete DVD media set.

What You'll Learn in *Irasshai*
The purpose of the *Irasshai* program is to help you develop a beginning level of proficiency in listening, speaking, reading and writing Japanese. You will also develop an understanding of Japanese culture. *Irasshai* is a performance-based curriculum, meaning the development team has:
- identified what you should be able to do as a result of instructional experience with the program,
- created activities and materials that help you develop those skills, and
- determined how you can demonstrate acquisition of those skills.

Irasshai materials are aligned to state standards for foreign language, Levels I and II. The curriculum consists of useful language functions (asking, stating, describing, etc.) and vocabulary organized around topics such as school, family, leisure activities, food, and more. You will learn language that is useful in everyday situations with speakers of Japanese in this country and in Japan. Specific objectives of each lesson are listed at the beginning of the lesson.

Organization of the Textbook
The format of each lesson of Volume 2 is generally organized as follows:
Objectives - state what you should be able to do by the end of the lesson;
Vocabulary - lists Words, Phrases and expressions, and Other words and expressions you will hear in this lesson, all intended to facilitate oral and written communication;
Key Grammar Points - include brief explanations of the grammar introduced in the lesson with examples;
Culture Notes - provide information on Japanese culture that is pertinent to the lesson;
Kanji Notes - provide information on the reading and writing of *kanji*, as well as lists of words and phrases in *kanji* and examples in sentences;
Yomimashoo! - provides practice reading of words, phrases and sentences introduced in the lesson;
Interactive Activities - reinforce the language skills of the lesson;
Denwa de Hanashimashoo （電話で話しましょう） - illustration pages that can be used in conversation practice with an instructor of Japanese.

Review lessons are found interspersed throughout the textbook, and appendices, a glossary, a topical index, and a *kanji* index are located in the back of this book.

Irasshai Textbook-Specific Conventions

Certain conventions and references are used in *Irasshai*: Welcome to Japanese. Some of these are:

- references to JPN I and JPN II indicate Vol. 1 and Vol. 2 of the textbook respectively;
- references made to Tim-*sensei* indicate the instructor in the video lessons;
- symbols such as (✐) and (📄 & ✐) that can be found in the Interactive Activities signify activities for which pens, pencils and paper are recommended;
- suggestions to practice with a partner, a classmate or in a group are often found in the Interactive Activities;
- references to the *Irasshai* website and to the assignment section of the workbook.

Irasshai Course Curriculum

Irasshai: Welcome to Japanese, Volumes 1 and 2 are recommended for use as a three-year high school foreign language program. The breakdown of the lessons for each year is as follows:

Year 1	Vol. 1, Lessons 1 ~ 49
Year 2	Vol. 1, Lessons 50 ~73 Vol. 2, Lessons 1 ~ 20
Year 3	Vol. 2, Lessons 21 ~ 63

A series of review lessons is located at the start of the second and third year lesson groupings.

Acknowledgements

We would like to express deep gratitude to Mr. Cliff Walker and Ms. Ellen Jones-Walker, authors of the original *Irasshai* textbook, whose dedication and long hours at the inception of the *Irasshai* program in 1995-1996 have laid the foundation for this revised edition. We are also grateful for the individual contributions of Ms. Tomoko Aeba, Ms. Akiko Davis, Ms. Masayo Nishioka and Ms. Yoko Takeuchi, whose input and insight have provided valuable additions to the original text. Reformatting of the textbook and workbook has truly been a cooperative endeavor, and we would like to give special thanks for the collective efforts of Ms. Jennifer Barclay, multimedia designer, whose artwork and design has brought fun, freshness, and a contemporary look in celebration of the 10th anniversary of *Irasshai*; Mr. Nick Bess, whose expertise has allowed for the eye-catching arrangement of the textbook and workbook covers; Ms. Lisa Hannabach, editor extraordinaire, whose keen sense of detail and unending efforts have provided us with new-and-improved tables of contents, glossaries, topical indices and a whole lot more; and last but not least, Mr. Danny Hong, graphic designer, whose optimism, speed, technical skills and patience have miraculously pulled the many pieces of the puzzle together.

Hiragana Chart

ん	わ	ら	や	ま	は	な	た	さ	か	あ
n	wa	ra	ya	ma	ha	na	ta	sa	ka	a
		り		み	ひ	に	ち	し	き	い
		ri		mi	hi	ni	chi	shi	ki	i
		る	ゆ	む	ふ	ぬ	つ	す	く	う
		ru	yu	mu	fu	nu	tsu	su	ku	u
		れ		め	へ	ね	て	せ	け	え
		re		me	he	ne	te	se	ke	e
	を	ろ	よ	も	ほ	の	と	そ	こ	お
	(w)o	ro	yo	mo	ho	no	to	so	ko	o

Katakana Chart

ン	ワ	ラ	ヤ	マ	ハ	ナ	タ	サ	カ	ア
n	wa	ra	ya	ma	ha	na	ta	sa	ka	a
		リ		ミ	ヒ	ニ	チ	シ	キ	イ
		ri		mi	hi	ni	chi	shi	ki	i
		ル	ユ	ム	フ	ヌ	ツ	ス	ク	ウ
		ru	yu	mu	fu	nu	tsu	su	ku	u
		レ		メ	ヘ	ネ	テ	セ	ケ	エ
		re		me	he	ne	te	se	ke	e
	ヲ	ロ	ヨ	モ	ホ	ノ	ト	ソ	コ	オ
	(w)o	ro	yo	mo	ho	no	to	so	ko	o

Table of Contents

PRELIMINARY LESSON 1
Review (Volume 1, Part 1)

This lesson provides you with an opportunity to review the following objectives from Volume 1:

- ☑ Greet someone for the first time
- ☑ Introduce yourself
- ☑ Greet others at different times of day
- ☑ Ask about and state ages
- ☑ Use the numbers 1-99
- ☑ Ask about and state grade designation
- ☑ Ask for and state the date
- ☑ Ask and tell when birthdays are
- ☑ Ask for and tell the time
- ☑ Ask about and express wants
- ☑ Read and write the *hiragana*: あいうえお、かきくけこ、さしすせそ、たちつてと、なにぬねの

VOCABULARY   たんご

Hajimemashite.	How do you do?
Doozo yoroshiku.	Pleased to meet you.
Ohayoo-gozaimasu.	Good morning.
Konnichi-wa.	Hello.
Doozo.	Please; Go ahead.
Doomo.	Thanks.
Nan-sai desu-ka?	How old are you/they?
	How old is he/she?
Nan-nen-sei desu-ka?	What grade are you/they (is he/she) in?
Nan-ji desu-ka?	What time is it?
Kyoo-wa nan-gatsu nan-nichi desu-ka?	What is the date today?
O-tanjoobi-wa itsu desu-ka?	When is your birthday?
Yasumi-wa itsu-kara itsu-made desu-ka?	When does the vacation start and end?
Yoofuku-to kutsu-ga hoshii desu.	I want clothes and shoes.

KEY GRAMMAR POINTS   ぶんぽうポイント

This lesson reviews a number of important grammar points from Volume 1. Following each grammar point is the lesson in which it was first presented. Most of these – grades, ages, clock times, dates, and counting people – involve the use of numbers and counters. Let's begin by reviewing the numbers from 1 to 99. Mask the Japanese number words and look only at the numerals. Say each Japanese number and then uncover it to check your answer.

THE NUMBERS 1-99						
1	ichi	11	juu-ichi	21	ni-juu-ichi
2	ni	12	juu-ni	30	san-juu
3	san	13	juu-san	38	san-juu-hachi
4	shi, yon	14	juu-shi (-yon)	40	yon-juu
5	go	15	juu-go	50	go-juu
6	roku	16	juu-roku	60	roku-juu
7	shichi, nana	17	juu-shichi (-nana)	70	nana-juu
8	hachi	18	juu-hachi	80	hachi-juu
9	kyuu, ku	19	juu-kyuu (-ku)	90	kyuu-juu
10	juu	20	ni-juu	99	kyuu-juu-kyuu

1. School grade levels: the counter *-nen-sei* (L. 5)

The counter *-nen-sei* is used when asking about and expressing grade levels in school.

Nan-*nen-sei* desu-ka?	What *grade* are you (in)?
Kookoo ichi-*nen-sei* desu.	I'm a first-*year* high school *student*.
San-*nen-sei* desu-ka?	Is she a third *grader* (third-year student)?
Iie, ni-*nen-sei* desu.	No, she's a second *grader* (second-year student).

NAN-NEN-SEI?			
1	ichi-nen-sei	4	yo-nen-sei
2	ni-nen-sei	5	go-nen-sei
3	san-nen-sei	6	roku-nen-sei

2. Ages: the counter *-sai* (L. 7)

The counter *-sai* is used when asking about and stating a person's age.

Nan-*sai* desu-ka?	How *old* are you?
Juu-roku-*sai* desu.	I'm 16 *years old*.
Sensei-wa yon-juu-san-*sai* desu.	The teacher is 43 *years old*.

NAN-SAI?			
11	juu-is-sai	17	juu-nana-sai
12	juu-ni-sai	18	juu-has-sai
13	juu-san-sai	19	juu-kyuu-sai
14	juu-yon-sai	20	hatachi
15	juu-go-sai	21	ni-juu-is-sai
16	juu-roku-sai	22	ni-juu-ni-sai

3. Clock times: the counters *-ji*, *-ji-han*, and *-pun/fun* (L. 24, 25)

The counter *-ji*, which is usually translated as *o'clock*, is combined with numbers to express the time of day in full hours. The question form is *nan-ji*.

San-*ji* desu.	It's three *o'clock*.
Go-*ji* desu-ka?	Is it five *o'clock*?
Ima juu-ichi-*ji* desu.	It's now 11:00.
Miitingu-wa yo-*ji* desu.	The meeting is at four *o'clock*.

NAN-JI?			
1:00	ichi-ji	7:00	shichi-ji
2:00	ni-ji	8:00	hachi-ji
3:00	san-ji	9:00	ku-ji
4:00	yo-ji	10:00	juu-ji
5:00	go-ji	11:00	juu-ichi-ji
6:00	roku-ji	12:00	juu-ni-ji

By adding *-han*, which means *half*, to any of the times shown on the previous page, you can express times such as four-*thirty* and *half past* eight.

Ima ni-ji-*han* desu.	It's now 2:30.
Deeto-wa yo-ji-*han* desu-ka?	Is your date at four-*thirty*?
Miitingu-wa hachi-ji-*han* desu.	The meeting is at *half past* eight.

The time counter *-pun/fun* is used to express a number of minutes and is used when telling time to the minute. The form of the counter varies, depending on the number with which it is combined.

Ku-ji kyuu-*fun* desu.	It's 9:09.
	It's nine *minutes* past/after nine.
Roku-ji juu-go-*fun* desu-ka?	Is it 6:15?
Ima juu-ji san-juu rop-*pun* desu.	Now it's 10:36.

NAN-PUN?							
1	ip-pun	5	go-fun	9	kyuu-fun	39	san-juu-kyuu-fun
2	ni-fun	6	rop-pun	10	jup-pun	40	yon-jup-pun
3	san-pun	7	nana-fun	14	juu-yon-pun/fun	45	yon-juu-go-fun
4	yon-pun/ yon-fun	8	hap-pun/ hachi-fun	27	ni-juu-nana-fun	58	go-juu-hap-pun/ go-juu-hachi-fun

4. Dates: the counters *-gatsu* and *-nichi* (L. 34)

The names of the months in Japanese consist of the numbers 1-12 combined with the counter *-gatsu*. Notice the forms of 4, 7, and 9 which are used with *-gatsu*. The question form is nan-*gatsu*.

NAN-GATSU?			
January	ichi-gatsu	July	shichi-gatsu
February	ni-gatsu	August	hachi-gatsu
March	san-gatsu	September	ku-gatsu
April	shi-gatsu	October	juu-gatsu
May	go-gatsu	November	juu-ichi-gatsu
June	roku-gatsu	December	juu-ni-gatsu

The counter used for the days of the month is *-nichi*. You will need to memorize the words for the first through the 10th as well as those used for the 14th, 20th, and 24th. All of the other days of the month end with *-nichi*. Notice the forms of 7 and 9 which are used with *-nichi*.

juu-**shichi**-nichi	the 17th
juu-**ku**-nichi	the 19th
ni-juu-**shichi**-nichi	the 27th
ni-juu-**ku**-nichi	the 29th

NAN-NICHI?			
1st	tsuitachi	9th	kokonoka
2nd	futsuka	10th	tooka
3rd	mikka	11th	juu-ichi-nichi
4th	yokka	14th	juu-yokka
5th	itsuka	20th	hatsuka
6th	muika	23rd	ni-juu-san-nichi
7th	nanoka	24th	ni-juu-yokka
8th	yooka	30th	san-juu-nichi

O-tanjoobi-wa nan-*gatsu* desu-ka?	What *month* is your birthday?
Shi-*gatsu* desu.	It's April.
Aa, soo desu-ka? Nan-*nichi* desu-ka?	Oh, really! What *day* (*of the month*)?
Ni-juu-shichi-*nichi* desu.	The 27*th*.
Watashi-no-mo soo desu.	Mine is too!

3

5. Counting people: the counter *-nin* (L. 18)

The counter for people is *-nin*, except in the case of one person (*hitori*) and two people (*futari*). You will need to memorize the forms for 4, 7, and 9.

NAN-NIN?			
1 person	hitori	6 people	roku-nin
2 people	futari	7 people	nana-nin*
3 people	san-nin	8 people	hachi-nin
4 people	yo-nin	9 people	kyuu-nin*
5 people	go-nin	10 people	juu-nin

*You will also hear *shichi-nin* and *ku-nin*.

Go-kazoku-wa nan-*nin* desu-ka?	How many *people* are in your family?
Nana-*nin* desu.	There are seven *people*.
Otooto-ga *hitori* imasu.	I have *one* younger brother.
Kurasu-wa yon-juu-*nin* desu.	There are 40 *people* in the class.

6. *Something*-ga hoshii desu. (L. 38)

This common expression, which is usually translated as *want(s)*, can be used to express what you want or to ask another person about his/her desires. The desired item is followed by the particle *-ga*.

Nani-ga *hoshii* desu-ka?	What do you *want*?
Kuruma-ga *hoshii* desu.	I *want* a car.
Tanjoobi-ni nani-ga *hoshii* desu-ka?	For your birthday what do you *want*?
Yoofuku-to kutsu-ga *hoshii* desu.	I *want* clothes and shoes.

The word *hoshii* is actually an adjective and the desired item is the subject. In Japanese we say *something is desired*. This is why you use the particle *-ga* (NOT *-o*).

HOSHII			
Watashi-wa	rajio-ga	**hoshii**	desu.
(as for me)	(a radio)	(desired)	(is)
TOPIC	SUBJECT	ADJECTIVE	VERB

INTERACTIVE ACTIVITIES

PART 1

❶ Nan-sai desu-ka? Juu-is-sai desu.

Do this activity with a partner. Together choose one of the counters from the box that follows, for example, *-sai*. Then Partner A randomly selects a number from the grid by closing his/her eyes and placing the tip of a pencil on the grid. Partner B asks, *Nan-sai desu-ka?*, and Partner A responds using the correct combination of the selected number and counter. Change roles after each question. Ask and answer five questions with the same counter before choosing a different one. Continue until you have practiced with all of the counters.

EXAMPLES

A and B choose the counter *-sai*
A: (selects 7 from the grid)
B: Nan-sai desu-ka?
A: Nana-sai desu.

A and B choose the counter *-pun/fun*
A: (selects 4 from the grid)
B: Nan-pun desu-ka?
A: Yon-pun desu.

TIP: Think about the meaning of your questions and answers as you do this activity.

-sai	Nan-sai desu-ka?	*How old?*
-ji	Nan-ji desu-ka?	*What time?*
-pun/fun	Nan-pun desu-ka?	*How many minutes?*
-gatsu	Nan-gatsu desu-ka?	*What month?*
-nichi	Nan-nichi desu-ka?	*What day of the month?*
-nin	Nan-nin desu-ka?	*How many people?*

1	4	7	9	11	12	2	8	10	5
6	5	3	10	1	8	4	3	12	6
10	1	9	2	7	5	6	9	11	2
12	2	5	9	4	3	1	12	6	10
4	6	1	7	6	9	9	4	7	3
7	8	3	8	2	9	5	10	1	9
5	10	4	1	3	7	8	2	7	11
8	3	12	5	11	1	10	6	5	4
2	11	7	6	8	4	3	7	2	12
12	4	11	9	12	10	11	8	9	7

Refer to the appropriate charts in the Key Grammar Points section to check your answers

❷ Yomimashoo!

Practice reading the following words with your partner. Partner B covers the *roomaji*. Partner A tells Partner B which words to read. For example, Partner A says, *"San-ban."* Partner B reads さかな correctly as *sakana*. After four words, change roles and continue.

1. うち
2. つぎ
3. さかな
4. えいが
5. なに
6. にく
7. すこし
8. あに
9. おねがい
10. です
11. たのしい
12. きのう
13. くつ
14. あき
15. おかね
16. あした
17. いつ
18. ついたち
19. だいがくせい
20. にがつ

1	ichi-ban	5	go-ban	9	kyuu-ban	14	juu-yon-ban
2	ni-ban	6	roku-ban	10	juu-ban	17	juu-nana-ban
3	san-ban	7	nana-ban	11	juu-ichi-ban	19	juu-kyuu-ban
4	yon-ban	8	hachi-ban	12	juu-ni-ban	20	ni-juu-ban

1. uchi
2. tsugi
3. sakana
4. eiga
5. nani
6. niku
7. sukoshi
8. ani
9. o-negai
10. desu
11. tanoshii
12. kinoo
13. kutsu
14. aki
15. o-kane
16. ashita
17. itsu
18. tsuitachi
19. daigakusei
20. nigatsu

If you have time, take turns with your partner dictating the words above for writing practice.

LEARNING TIP

If you need to review *hiragana*, spend five minutes every day using your flash cards. Say the *hiragana* aloud as you practice. Practice writing them also.

❶ Tanjoobi-ni nani-ga hoshii desu-ka? (Level I)   📄 & ✏️

Do this activity as an entire class. Each student draws a nine-square grid like the one below on a piece of paper. Two students, each with the paper and a pencil or pen, sit at the front of the room. The other students individually complete the grid by copying one word into each square from the list of items. There should be nine different words in the grid. Students with the completed grids take turns asking the students in the front (one at a time):

    Tanjoobi-ni nani-ga hoshii desu-ka?   [What do you want for your birthday?]

The student in the front who was asked responds with one of the items from the list.

    Kuruma-ga hoshii desu.   [I want a car.]

Both students in the front check off the desired item on their lists. The rest of the students check for the item on their grids and cross it off if it appears. The first student to cross off three items in a horizontal, vertical, or diagonal row says, *"Watashi-ga ichi-ban desu."* The winner chooses one other student to join him/her in the front. Draw a nine-square grid on a piece of paper and play the game again.

saifu	kutsu	hon	tokei
terebi	shatsu	tsukue	rajio
fakkusu	o-kane	isu	shiidii
nooto	zubon	manga	sutereo
denwa	gitaa	shashin	kamera
pen	nekutai	akusesarii	keeki

❷ Tanjoobi-ni nani-ga hoshii desu-ka? (Level II)   📄 & ✏️

Follow the same procedure, but add the words below. Draw additional grids as needed.

kakkoii jaketto	kuroi kaban	Doitsu-no kuruma	atarashii konpyuutaa
eigo-no jisho	chairoi booshi	bideo geemu	konsaato-no chiketto

P. 1 電話で 話しましょう

れんしゅう A: Grades and Ages

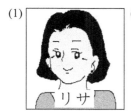

(1) リサ
10th grade
(16 yrs. old)

(2) けんじ
12th grade
(18 yrs. old)

(3) マイク
11th grade
(17 yrs. old)

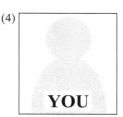

(4) YOU
? th grade
(? yrs. old)

れんしゅう B: Time

(1) 10:00
(2) 4:00

(3) 9:30
(4) 7:30

(5) 3:20
(6) 11:35

(7) 2:18
(8) 6:53

れんしゅう C: Dates and Birthdays

(1) 3/9   (2) 2/14   (3) 9/20   (4) 4/1

(5) 1/10
かな

(6) 10/26
ケント

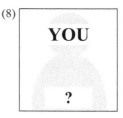

(7) 7/5
アリーシャ

(8) YOU
?

れんしゅう D: How many family members are there?

(1) ティム

(2) キム

(3) みさ

(4) YOU

れんしゅう E: What do you want for your birthday?

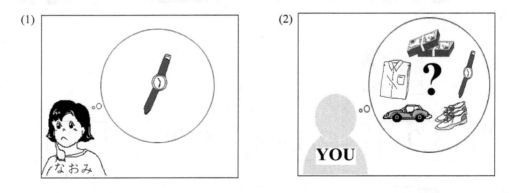

(1) なおみ

(2) YOU

8

PRELIMINARY LESSON 2
Review (Volume 1, Part 2)

This lesson provides you with an opportunity to review the following objectives from Volume 1:

- ☑ Ask about and express likes and dislikes
- ☑ Ask about and state ability
- ☑ Talk about daily, weekly, and monthly activities and schedules
- ☑ Talk about preferences and favorite things
- ☑ Talk about sports, music, and weather
- ☑ Talk about clothing and shopping
- ☑ Read and write the *hiragana*: はひふへほ、まみむめも、やゆよ、らりるれろ、わを、ん

VOCABULARY   たんご

ITSU?			
kyoo	today	sui-yoobi	Wednesday
ashita	tomorrow	moku-yoobi	Thursday
kinoo	yesterday	kin-yoobi	Friday
ima	now	do-yoobi	Saturday
getsu-yoobi	Monday	nichi-yoobi	Sunday
ka-yoobi	Tuesday		

KYOO-NO TENKI-WA DOO DESU-KA?					
hare	clear, sunny, nice	yuki	snow	ii tenki	good weather
ame	rain	kumori	cloudy		
Bosuton-wa yuki desu.		It's snowing in Boston.			

joozu	good at, skilled at
heta	bad at
Kenji-kun-wa uta-ga joozu desu-ka?	Kenji, are you good at singing?
Iie, heta desu.	No, I'm bad at it.

THE NUMBERS 100 - 9,000			
100	hyaku	1,000	sen
200	ni-hyaku	2,000	ni-sen
300	san-byaku	3,000	san-zen
400	yon-hyaku	4,000	yon-sen
500	go-hyaku	5,000	go-sen
600	rop-pyaku	6,000	roku-sen
700	nana-hyaku	7,000	nana-sen
800	hap-pyaku	8,000	has-sen
900	kyuu-hyaku	9,000	kyuu-sen

o-kane	money
takai	expensive
yasui	cheap
kaimasu (kau)	buy
ikura	how much
#-en	# yen (Japanese monetary unit)
#-doru	# dollar(s)

IRO					
kiiro(i)	yellow	shiro(i)	white	murasaki (no)	purple
aka(i)	red	kuro(i)	black	midori (no)	green
ao(i)	blue	chairo(i)	brown	pinku (no)	pink

KEY GRAMMAR POINTS ぶんぽうポイント

This lesson reviews a number of important grammar points from Volume 1. Following each grammar point is the lesson in which it was first presented.

1. The past tense of -*masu* verbs (L. 45, 46)
To form the past tense of verbs ending in -*masu*, change -*masu* to -*mashita*. Verbs ending in -*mashita* can be used with all persons (first, second, and third) and all numbers (singular and plural). The *i* in -*mashita* is a whispered vowel.

Pikunikku-ni *ikimashita*.	We went on a picnic.
Itsu ikimashita-ka?	When did you go?

To form the negative past tense of a verb ending in -*masu*, change -*masu* to -*masen deshita*.

Ueda-san-wa nyuusu-o *mimashita*-ka?	*Did* Mrs. Ueda *see* the news?
Iie, *mimasen deshita*.	No, she *didn't see* it.

THE -*MASU* FORM		
Non-past affirmative	mimasu	see ~ sees ~ will see
Non-past negative	mimasen	don't/doesn't see ~ won't see
Past affirmative	mimashita	saw
Past negative	mimasen deshita	didn't see

2. Dekimasu (L. 55)
This useful verb means *can* (*do something*) or *be able* (*to do something*) and can be used when talking about the ability to play sports, to speak languages, to play musical instruments, or to perform other actions. English translations of *dekimasu* often include *can* plus another verb.

Tenisu-ga *dekimasu*.	I *can play* tennis.
Eigo-ga *dekimasu*.	He *can speak* English.
Dekimasu-ka?	*Can* you *do* it?
Zenzen *dekimasen*.	I *can't do* it at all.

3. X-ga suki desu. (L. 52)
This expression is usually translated as *like*(*s*). The X represents the item which is liked.

Nani-ga *suki desu*-ka?	What *do* you *like*?
Nihongo-ga *suki desu*.	I *like* Japanese.
Aisukuriimu-ga *suki desu*-ka?	*Do* you *like* ice cream?
Hai, *daisuki desu*.	Yes, I *really like* it.
Anmari *suki ja nai desu*.	I *don't like* it very much.
Ongaku-wa nani-ga *suki desu*-ka?	What kind of music *do* you *like*?
Rokku-ga ichiban *suki desu*.	I *like* rock the most.

4. X-ga kirai desu. (L. 52)
Kirai means *is displeasing* and in English is often expressed as *dislike*(*s*) or *hate*(*s*). This is a rather strong expression which you may wish to avoid by substituting a less harsh expression such as *X-wa suki ja nai desu* or *X-wa anmari suki ja nai desu*.

5. The counter *-en* (L. 64)

The *en* (in English *yen*) is the monetary unit of Japan. As a counter, *-en* is combined with numbers to express specific amounts. When you ask for the price of an item, you say, *"Ikura desu-ka?"*

Kono enpitsu-wa *ikura desu-ka?*   *How much is* this pencil?
Kyuu-juu kyuu-*en* desu.   It's 99 *yen*.

-EN			
¥1	ichi-en	¥6	roku-en
¥2	ni-en	¥7	nana-en
¥3	san-en	¥8	hachi-en
¥4	yon-en	¥9	kyuu-en
¥5	go-en	¥10	juu-en

6. The counter *-doru* (L. 64)

The Japanese counter for *dollars* is *-doru*. Use *Ikura desu-ka?* when inquiring about a price. The counter *-doru* combines with the same number forms as shown in the box above.

INTERACTIVE ACTIVITIES

PART 1

❶ **Review of the numbers 100 - 9,000**

Do this activity with a partner. Before you begin, review by yourself the numbers from 100 to 9,000 which are given in a box in the Vocabulary section. Pay close attention to the forms shown in bold type. Then take turns testing each other. Partner A says the えいご, and Partner B says the にほんご. Partner A may say the numbers in any order. Change roles after every five numbers.

❷ **Ikura desu-ka?**   📄 & ✏️

Do this activity with a partner. Partner B closes his/her book and listens to Partner A read each price slowly. Both partners write down the price in numerals. All prices are expressed in *yen* so be sure to write the *yen* symbol before each number (for example, ¥3,985). The handwritten *yen* symbol looks like a handwritten capital Y with an equal sign across it. Check your answers when you have finished. Then switch roles and do the second section. Check your answers.

PARTNER A reads

1. Kyuu-sen nana-hyaku yon-juu go-en
2. Go-sen ni-hyaku san-juu roku-en
3. Yon-sen rop-pyaku ni-juu san-en
4. San-zen yon-hyaku roku-juu kyuu-en
5. Sen san-byaku hachi-juu ni-en

PARTNER B reads

1. Ni-sen hyaku go-juu hachi-en
2. Roku-sen hap-pyaku juu ichi-en
3. Yon-sen go-hyaku nana-juu roku-en
4. San-zen kyuu-hyaku hachi-juu go-en
5. Has-sen ni-hyaku kyuu-juu nana-en

PART 2

❶ **Yomimashoo!**

Practice reading the following words with your partner. Partner B covers the *roomaji*. Partner A tells Partner B which words to read. For example, Partner A says, *"San-ban."* Partner B reads さようなら correctly as *sayoonara*. After five words, change roles and continue.

1. あります	6. まんが	11. ふるい	16. しゃしん
2. がっこう	7. いきました	12. わかります	17. ひらがな
3. さようなら	8. よろしく	13. いくら	18. ちょっと
4. を	9. ひとり	14. なんがつ	19. べんきょう
5. だれ	10. さんじはん	15. じゅぎょう	20. ごきょうだい

11

1. arimasu	6. manga	11. furui	16. shashin
2. gakkoo	7. ikimashita	12. wakarimasu	17. hiragana
3. sayoonara	8. yoroshiku	13. ikura	18. chotto
4. o [particle]	9. hitori	14. nan-gatsu	19. benkyoo
5. dare	10. san-ji-han	15. jugyoo	20. go-kyoodai

If you have time, take turns with your partner dictating the words above for writing practice.

❷ Chigaimasu. Motto takai desu.   📄 & ✎

Form *guruupu* of 3人 (*san-nin*). Player A writes one 4-digit price in **yen** and does not show it to the other players. Player B (on A's left) goes first and guesses what the price is. Player A responds by telling Player B and C whether the actual price is higher (*Motto takai desu.*) or lower (*Motto yasui desu.*) than B's guess. Then Player C guesses. Player A again responds by telling both players whether their next guess needs to be a higher or lower price. Continue taking turns until B or C guesses correctly, thus earning 1 point. Then Player B writes down a price, C guesses first, and the game continues. Continue until you run out of time. The person with the most points wins.

P. 2 電話で 話しましょう

れんしゅう A: How is the weather?

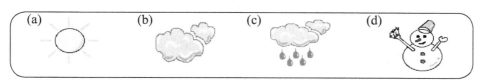

(a)   (b)   (c)   (d)

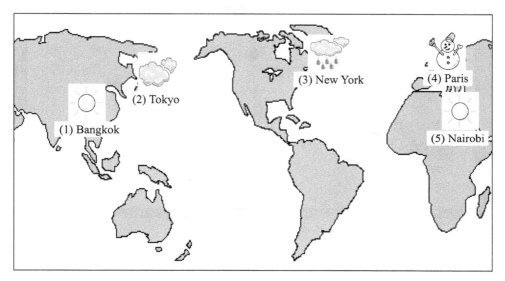

(2) Tokyo
(3) New York
(4) Paris
(1) Bangkok
(5) Nairobi

れんしゅう B: What did they do and when?

しつもん: (a) did what?　　(b) when?　　(c) what time?

(Ex)
ヘンリー　yesterday 6:00~8:30

(1)
ピーター　Saturday 4:00~7:30

(2)
friend's house
バーバラ　Wednesday 5:00

れんしゅう C: What did you do during summer break?

れんしゅう D: よみましょう。

(1) うち　　(2) さかな　　(3) にく

(4) きのう　　(5) おかね　　(6) たのしい

(7) がっこう　　　　(8) おちゃ

(9) としょかん　　　(10) じゅぎょう

LESSON 1
Homestay 1

This lesson provides you with an opportunity to review the following objectives from Volume 1:

- ☑ Greet someone for the first time
- ☑ Introduce yourself
- ☑ Ask for another person's name
- ☑ Greet others at different times of day
- ☑ Apologize to someone
- ☑ Ask about and state grade designation
- ☑ Ask about and state ages
- ☑ Ask about and state school affiliation
- ☑ Ask about and express likes and dislikes
- ☑ Ask about and state ability

VOCABULARY   たんご

Review

Hajimemashite.	How do you do?
Doozo yoroshiku.	Pleased to meet you.
Ohayoo-gozaimasu.	Good morning.
Konnichi-wa.	Hello.
Oyasumi-nasai.	Good night.
Sumimasen.	Excuse me.
Doozo.	Please; Go ahead.
Doomo.	Thanks.
O-namae-wa?	Your name? What is your name?
Nan-sai desu-ka?	How old are you/they (is he/she)?
Nan-nen-sei desu-ka?	What grade are you/they (is he/she) in?
suki	like(s), is/are pleasing
dekimasu (dekiru)	can (do), be able (to do)
zenzen	(not) at all, completely (not)

KEY GRAMMAR POINTS   ぶんぽうポイント

This lesson reviews a number of important grammar points from Volume 1. Following each grammar point is the lesson in which it was first presented.

1. Nan-nen-sei? (L. 5)

The counter *-nen-sei* is used when asking about and expressing grade levels in school.

Chuugaku ni-*nen-sei* desu-ka?	Are you a second-*year* middle school *student*?
Iie, san-*nen-sei* desu.	No, I'm a third-*year student*.

NAN-NEN-SEI?			
1	ichi-nen-sei	4	yo-nen-sei
2	ni-nen-sei	5	go-nen-sei
3	san-nen-sei	6	roku-nen-sei

15

2. Nan-sai? (L. 7)

The counter *-sai* is used when asking about and stating a person's age.

Nan-*sai* desu-ka?	How *old* are you?
Juu-has-*sai* desu.	I'm 18 *years old*.
Chichi-wa yon-juu-san-*sai* desu.	My father is 43 *years old*.

NAN-SAI?			
11	juu-is-sai	17	juu-nana-sai
12	juu-ni-sai	18	juu-has-sai
13	juu-san-sai	19	juu-kyuu-sai
14	juu-yon-sai	20	hatachi
15	juu-go-sai	21	ni-juu-is-sai
16	juu-roku-sai	22	ni-juu-ni-sai

3. X-ga suki desu. (L. 52)

This expression is usually translated as *like(s)*. The X represents the item which is liked.

Kamoku-wa nani-ga *suki desu*-ka?	What school subject *do* you *like*?
Rekishi-ga *suki desu*.	I *like* history.
Yasai-ga *suki desu*-ka?	*Do* you *like* vegetables?
Hai, *daisuki desu*.	Yes, I *really like* them.
Iie, anmari *suki ja nai desu*.	I *don't like* them very much.

4. Dekimasu (L. 55)

This useful verb means *can (do something)* or *be able (to do something)* and can be used when talking about the ability to play sports, to speak languages, to play musical instruments, or to perform other actions. English translations of *dekimasu* often include *can* plus another verb.

Gakki-wa piano-ga sukoshi *dekimasu*.	As for musical instruments, I *can play* the piano a little.
Furansugo-ga *dekimasu*-ka?	*C*an you *speak* French?
Hai, *dekimasu*.	Yes, I can.
Iie, zenzen *dekimasen*.	No, I *can't* speak at all.

YOMIMASHOO!   よみましょう

In the *Yomimashoo!* section of each lesson in Volume 1 the new words, phrases, and expressions appeared in *roomaji* and *kana* to help you develop skill in reading *hiragana* and *katakana*. Beginning with this lesson in Volume 2, the vocabulary will be presented in *kana* and English. Continue to use this section to practice reading on a regular basis.

はじめまして。	How do you do?
どうぞ よろしく。	Pleased to meet you.
おはよう ございます。	Good morning.
すみません。	Excuse me.
どうぞ。	Please; Go ahead.
どうも。	Thanks.
おやすみなさい。	Good night.
おなまえは？	Your name? What is your name?
なんさい ですか。	How old are you/they (is he/she)?
なんねんせい ですか。	What grade are you/they (is he/she) in?
すき	like(s), is/are pleasing
できます・できる	can (do), be able (to do)
ぜんぜん	(not) at all, completely (not)

16

INTERACTIVE ACTIVITIES

PART 1

❶ Hajimemashite.   📄 & ✏️

Do this interview activity as an entire class. Before beginning, each person creates an imaginary identity for himself/herself and writes down the information about the topics in the box below on a piece of paper. Everyone circulates, forming pairs and interviewing each other in turn. Always begin by introducing yourselves. Form pairs four times. For the first two interviews refer to the sample questions and answers as necessary. Look at the needed line(s), and then look at your partner and speak. Do not read aloud from this page. Try to conduct the remaining two interviews while looking only at the topics box.

TOPICS					
namae	#-nen-sei	#-sai	gakkoo	supootsu	ongaku

SAMPLE EXCHANGE

A: Hajimemashite. **A** desu.
B: Hajimemashite. **B** desu.
A: Doozo yoroshiku.
B: Doozo yoroshiku.
A: **B**-san-wa nan-nen-sei desu-ka?
B: **Kookoo ni**-nen-sei desu. **A**-san-wa?
A: **Chuugaku san**-nen-sei desu.
B: **A**-san, nan-sai desu-ka?
A: **Juu-yon**-sai desu. **B**-san-wa?
B: **Juu-nana**-sai desu.
A: Gakkoo-wa doko desu-ka?
B: **Tookyoo Kookoo** desu.
    A-san-no gakkoo-wa?
A: **Jefason Chuugakkoo** desu.
B: **A**-san, supootsu-wa nani-ga dekimasu-ka?
A: **Tenisu**-ga dekimasu. **B**-san-wa?
B: **Bareebooru**-ga dekimasu.
A: Ongaku-wa nani-ga ichiban suki desu-ka?
B: **Jazu**-ga ichiban suki desu. **A**-san-wa?
A: **Rokku**-ga ichiban suki desu.

ADDITIONAL VOCABULARY

SUPOOTSU	
yakyuu	baseball
gorufu	golf
basukettobooru	basketball
futtobooru	football
tenisu	tennis
sakkaa	soccer
bareebooru	volleyball
bokushingu	boxing
resuringu	wrestling
badominton	badminton
booringu	bowling
sofutobooru	softball
sukii	skiing
sukeeto	skating
karate	karate
ONGAKU	
kantorii	country
hebii metaru	heavy metal
kurashikku	classical
rokku	rock
jazu	jazz
rappu	rap
buruusu	blues
and the names of individuals and groups	

❷ **Shitsumon-o shite kudasai.**
Do this activity with a クラスメート. Partner A selects and reads aloud one word from
the chart below. Partner A then asks Partner B a question which includes the target word.
Partner B answers the しつもん truthfully. Take turns asking and answering しつもん
until all of the words in the chart have been selected. Look at the example.

A: O-namae. O-namae-wa? [A has selected the word *o-namae* from the chart.]
B: Ken desu.

-nen-sei	supootsu	suki	gakkoo
dekimasu	tabemono	-sai	ongaku
ichiban	tenisu	kamoku	o-namae

Additional vocabulary you might need is given in the box in the following activity.

PART 2

❶ **Vocabulary review**
Review the following vocabulary with a クラスメート. Partner A says the vocabulary in
えいご and Partner B gives the equivalent in にほんご. Switch roles after every five
words or phrases.

subject	かもく	kamoku	foods	たべもの	tabemono
math	すうがく	suugaku	pizza	ピザ	piza
science	かがく	kagaku	ice cream	アイスクリーム	aisukuriimu
history	れきし	rekishi	cake	ケーキ	keeki
geography	ちり	chiri	hamburger	ハンバーガー	hanbaagaa
P.E.	たいいく	taiiku	salad	サラダ	sarada
art	びじゅつ	bijutsu	spaghetti	スパゲティー	supagetii
English	えいご	eigo	fish	さかな	sakana
Japanese	にほんご	nihongo	meat	にく	niku
Spanish	スペインご	supeingo	vegetables	やさい	yasai
French	フランスご	furansugo	sushi	すし	sushi
German	ドイツご	doitsugo	drinks	のみもの	nomimono
Latin	ラテンご	ratengo	cola	コーラ	koora
sports	スポーツ	supootsu	coffee	コーヒー	koohii
movies	えいが	eiga	iced tea	アイスティー	aisutii
music	おんがく	ongaku	milk	ミルク	miruku
musical instrument	がっき	gakki	juice	ジュース	juusu

can (do) a little	すこし できます	sukoshi dekimasu
can't (do)	できません	dekimasen
can't really (do)	あんまり できません	anmari dekimasen
like, is/are pleasing	すき です	suki desu
don't like, isn't pleasing	すき じゃ ない です	suki ja nai desu
don't really like	あんまり すき じゃ ない です	anmari suki ja nai desu

❷ Tabemono-wa nani-ga ichiban suki desu-ka?

Do this activity with a クラスメート. With eyes closed, Partner A turns this textbook around a couple of times and then touches the page with the eraser end of a pencil. Partner A then asks Partner B a question about the topic closest to the end of the pencil. For each topic there are many different possible questions so it does not matter if the same topic is selected more than once. Partner B answers the しつもん. Take turns selecting and asking questions. Read these three examples aloud with your partner before you begin. The topic is NOMIMONO.

A: Nomimono-wa nani-ga suki desu-ka?
B: Koora-to aisutii-to miruku-ga suki desu.
     OR
A: Koohii-o nomimasu-ka?
B: Iie, nomimasen.
     OR
A: Gakkoo-de nani-o nomimasu-ka?
B: Koora-o nomimasu.

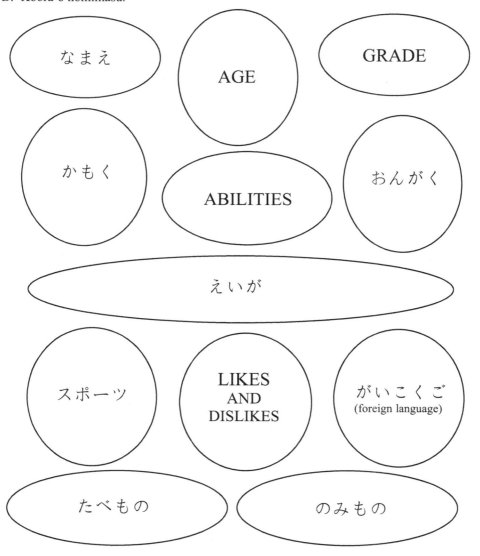

なまえ

AGE

GRADE

かもく

ABILITIES

おんがく

えいが

スポーツ

LIKES AND DISLIKES

がいこくご
(foreign language)

たべもの

のみもの

L.1 電話で話しましょう

れんしゅう A: Interview Sheet

(Ex.)
a) Name:
   Mary Young
b) Age:
   16 yrs.
c) Birthday:
   September 20
d) School:
   West Atlanta HS
e) Grade:
   10th grade

(1)
a) Name:
   _____
b) Age:
   _____
c) Birthday:
   _____
d) School:
   _____
e) Grade:
   _____

YOU

れんしゅう B: What ~ do you like?

(1)
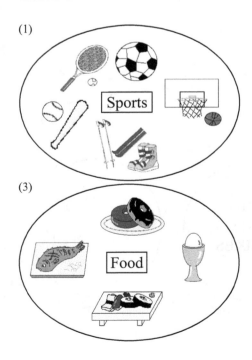
Sports

(2)
Gone with the Storm   E. P.

Mrs. Doubtchild   Movies

Star Battles   Sleepy in Seattle

(3)
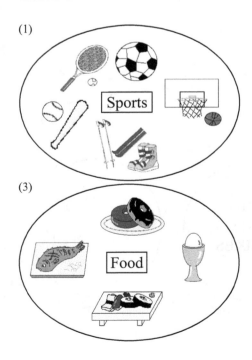
Food

(4)

Subjects

れんしゅう C: How well can you ~?

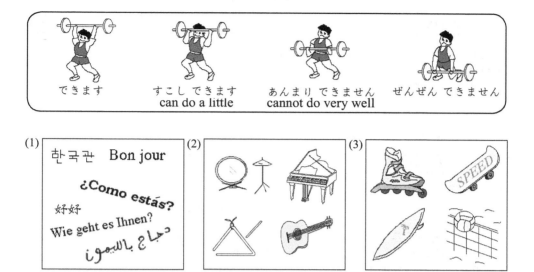

できます　　　すこし できます　　あんまり できません　　ぜんぜん できません
　　　　　　　can do a little　　cannot do very well

(1)
한국관　Bon jour

¿Como estás?

好好

Wie geht es Ihnen?

أهلا وسهلا بكم

(2)

(3)

れんしゅう D: Word Formation

Pick up all *katakana* in the same shape and then create the names of the countries.

(1) △　　(2) ○　　(3) □　　(4) ◎

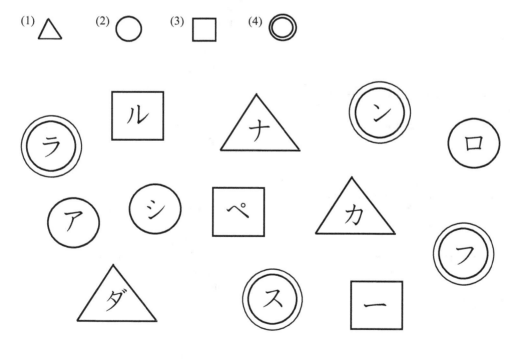

LESSON 2
Homestay 2

This lesson provides you with an opportunity to review the following objectives from Volume 1:

- ☑ Ask for and state calendar dates
- ☑ Tell when your birthday is and ask about others' birthdays
- ☑ Ask and state when holidays and other events occur
- ☑ Ask and tell about leisure-time activities

VOCABULARY   たんご

New

puuru	swiming pool
puuru paatii	pool party
puuru paatii-o shimasu (suru)	have a pool party
pikunikku	picnic
pikunikku-ni ikimasu (iku)	go on a picnic
hoomusutei	homestay

Review

natsu-yasumi	summer vacation
(o)tanjoobi	birthday
#-gatsu	#th month of the year (*a counter*)
#-nichi	#th day of the month (*a counter*)
itsu	when
-kara	from (*a particle*)
-made	to, until (*a particle*)
-ni	in, on, at, during + TIME EXPRESSION (*a particle*)

KEY GRAMMAR POINTS   ぶんぽうポイント

This lesson reviews a number of important grammar points from Volume 1. Following each grammar point is the lesson in which it was first presented.

1. Dates (L. 34)

To state dates in Japanese use the counters *-gatsu* (month) and *-nichi* (day of the month) with the appropriate forms of the numbers 1-31. Remember the forms which are used to express the fourth, seventh, and ninth months: *shi-gatsu* (April), *shichi-gatsu* (July), and *ku-gatsu* (September). You will also want to review the words for the first through the 10th day of the month as well as those used for the 14th, 20th, and 24th.

O-tanjoobi-wa ni-*gatsu* desu-ka?	Is your birthday *February*?
Iie, san-*gatsu* desu.	No, it's *March*.
Paatii-wa nan-*nichi* desu-ka?	What *day* (*of the month*) is the party?
Tsuitachi desu.	It's (on) *the first*.

22

DAYS OF THE MONTH			
1 日	tsuitachi	9 日	kokonoka
2 日	futsuka	10 日	tooka
3 日	mikka	11 日	juu-ichi-nichi
4 日	yokka	14 日	juu-yokka
5 日	itsuka	20 日	hatsuka
6 日	muika	23 日	ni-juu-san-nichi
7 日	nanoka	24 日	ni-juu-yokka
8 日	yooka	30 日	san-juu-nichi

2. ~ kara ~ made (L. 26, 37)

These two particles are frequently used in time expressions to state when activities begin and end. They can be used with days of the month, months, days of the week, clock times, and many other temporal expressions. Their meanings are expressed in English in different ways.

Natsu-yasumi-wa itsu-*kara* deshita-ka?	When did your summer vacation start?
Roku-gatsu tsuitachi-*kara* deshita.	It started June 1. [from June 1]
Itsu-*made* desu-ka?	When is summer vacation over?
Hachi-gatsu ni-juu-san-nichi-*made* desu.	It ends August 23. [until August 23]
Yasumi-wa itsu-*kara* itsu-*made* desu-ka?	When does the break begin and end?
Futsuka-*kara* kokonoka-*made* desu.	It's *from* the second *to* the ninth.
Jugyoo-wa 8-ji-*kara* 9-ji-*made* desu.	The lesson is *from* 8:00 *to* 9:00.
Arubaito-wa 9-gatsu-*kara* desu.	The part-time job starts in September.
Suiyoobi-*made* desu.	It's *until* Wednesday.

3. The time particle -ni (L. 27, 38, 45, 48)

The particle -*ni* can be used with various time expressions and may be translated as *in*, *on*, *at*, or *during*.

Natsu-*ni* puuru-ni ikimasu.	*In* the summer we go to the pool.
Fuyu-yasumi-*ni* Hawai-ni ikimashita.	We went to Hawaii *during* winter break.
Shichi-gatsu-*ni* Amerika-ni kimashita.	She came to America *in* July.
Roku-ji-*ni* okimasu.	She gets up *at* 6:00.
15-nichi-*ni* pikunikku-ni ikimashita.	We went on a picnic *on* the 15th.
Tanjoobi-*ni* paatii-o shimasu.	I'm going to have a party *on* my birthday.

The particle -*ni* is also used with expressions of location and can be translated as *at*, *in*, and *to*. (See L. 40 and 68.) Can you identify which -*ni* are used with a location in the example sentences above?

4. The past tense of -masu verbs (L. 45, 46)

To form the past tense of verbs ending in -*masu*, change -*masu* to -*mashita*. Verbs ending in -*mashita* can be used with all persons (first, second, and third) and all numbers (singular and plural). The *i* in -*mashita* is a whispered vowel.

Shuumatsu, kaimono-o *shimashita*.	I *did* shopping this weekend.
Nani-o *kaimashita*-ka?	What *did* you *buy*?

To form the negative past tense of a verb ending in -*masu*, change -*masu* to -*masen deshita*.

Aoki-san-wa *kimashita*-ka?	*Did* Mr. Aoki *come*?
Iie, *kimasen deshita*.	No, he *didn't*.

プール	swimming pool
プールパーティー	pool party
プールパーティーを します・する	have a pool party
ピクニック	picnic
ピクニックに いきます・いく	go on a picnic
ホームステイ	homestay
なつやすみ	summer vacation
(お)たんじょうび	birthday
#がつ	# th month of the year (*a counter*)
#にち	# th day of the month (*a counter*)
いつ	when
から	from
まで	to, until
に	in, on, at, during + TIME EXPRESSION

INTERACTIVE ACTIVITIES

PART 1

❶ Kotaete kudasai. 🖊

During this activity each student will work as a pair with two different クラスメート to check Assignment #1 from Part 2 of Lesson 1. The goal of the activity is to have two students carefully check your six sentences, mark and discuss with you any errors found, and sign off on your page. Form your first pair and exchange assignments with your partner. Both partners independently check and neatly mark errors for all six sentences. Do not correct errors. Use the editing symbols (see Workbook, Introduction). Return the assignments and go over the first sentence <u>together</u>. Correct your own work. Repeat this procedure for each sentence. Sign off on each other's page. Form new pairs and repeat these steps.

❷ Vocabulary check

Silently review the days of the month in the box in the ぶんぽうポイント section. Then have a クラスメート orally test your knowledge of the words. Your partner says the えいご, and you give the にほんご. Switch and test your partner.

PART 2

❶ O-tanjoobi-wa itsu desu-ka? 📄 & 🖊

In this whole class activity, ask all of your クラスメート one at a time, "*O-tanjoobi-wa itsu desu-ka?*" and record their responses. Before beginning, be sure you can say your own birthday. When you finish, compare answers.

❷ Nani-o shimashita-ka? 📄 & 🖊

Do this activity with a partner. Decide which person is Partner A and which is Partner B. Now use your imagination. You have just returned from a 10-day spring vacation packed with many different activities. In fact, you engaged in a different activity each day from March 1 through March 10. Without showing your クラスメート, select <u>10</u> of the activities listed in the chart on the next page. Next to each activity write the date when you did it (between March 1-10). The dates in the column should be in mixed order. Be sure you are writing your own dates in the correct column.

Take turns asking and answering questions to collect the information you need to complete the chart. When you have completely finished, compare charts and check your work. Your charts should be the same. Read these sample questions and answers aloud with your partner before you begin.

Partner A: B-san-wa tenisu-o shimashita-ka?
Partner B: Iie, shimasen deshita. [Partner B had not selected tennis as one of the 10 activities.]
Partner A: Aa, soo desu-ka. Ja, kaimono-ni ikimashita-ka? [Partner A can ask again.]
Partner B: Hai, ikimashita.
Partner A: Nan-nichi-ni ikimashita-ka? [Since Partner B answered with *Hai*, Partner A now asks for the date.]
Partner B: Mikka-ni ikimashita. A-san-wa karate-o shimashita-ka?
Partner A: Hai, shimashita.
Partner B: Nan-nichi-ni shimashita-ka?
Partner A: Nanoka-ni shimashita.

As you do this activity be sure to use the past tense: *shimashita, ikimashita, yomimashita,* etc.

ACTIVITY	DATE (PARTNER A)	DATE (PARTNER B)
terebi-o mimasu	3 月 日	3 月 日
sakkaa-o shimasu	3 月 日	3 月 日
puuru paatii-o shimasu	3 月 日	3 月 日
kaimono-ni ikimasu	3 月 日	3 月 日
hon-o yomimasu	3 月 日	3 月 日
pikunikku-ni ikimasu	3 月 日	3 月 日
bareebooru-o shimasu	3 月 日	3 月 日
sukii-o shimasu	3 月 日	3 月 日
ongaku-o kikimasu	3 月 日	3 月 日
eiga-ni ikimasu	3 月 日	3 月 日
tenisu-o shimasu	3 月 日	3 月 日
gorufu-o shimasu	3 月 日	3 月 日
karate-o shimasu	3 月 日	3 月 日
doraibu-ni ikimasu	3 月 日	3 月 日

For more practice in reading Japanese, use the chart below:

ACTIVITY	DATE (PARTNER A)	DATE (PARTNER B)
テレビを みます	3 月 日	3 月 日
サッカーを します	3 月 日	3 月 日
プールパーティーを します	3 月 日	3 月 日
かいものに いきます	3 月 日	3 月 日
ほんを よみます	3 月 日	3 月 日
ピクニックに いきます	3 月 日	3 月 日
バレーボールを します	3 月 日	3 月 日
スキーを します	3 月 日	3 月 日
おんがくを ききます	3 月 日	3 月 日
えいがに いきます	3 月 日	3 月 日
テニスを します	3 月 日	3 月 日
ゴルフを します	3 月 日	3 月 日
からてを します	3 月 日	3 月 日
ドライブに いきます	3 月 日	3 月 日

L. 2 電話で 話しましょう

れんしゅう A: Q's and A's about Yumiko's Busy Week

しつもん:
(a) What did Yumiko do?
(b) On what day did she do ~?

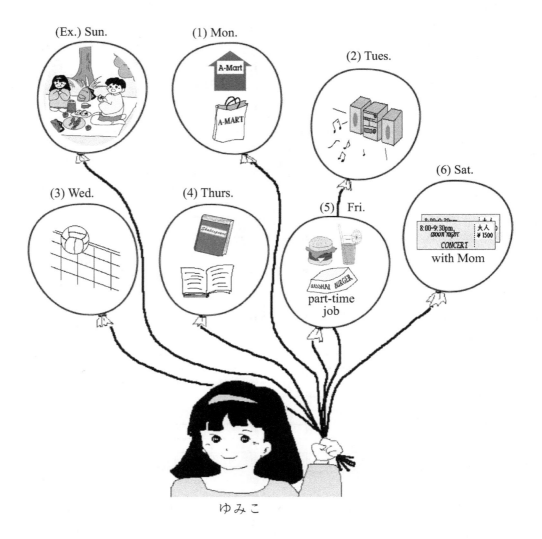

(Ex.) Sun.

(1) Mon.

(2) Tues.

(3) Wed.

(4) Thurs.

(5) Fri.
part-time job

(6) Sat.
8:00-9:30pm
goodn'night
CONCERT
大人 ¥1500
with Mom

ゆみこ

れんしゅう B: Masato's Calendar

APRIL 2006						
日	月	火	水	木	金	土
				1	2	3
4	5	6	7	8	9	10
11 part-time job 8:00~5:00	12	13	14	15	16 English test	17
18	19 Dad's birthday	20	21	22	23	24 classical concert
25 pool party 12:00~6:00	26	27	28	29 basketball game	30	

SPRING BREAK

れんしゅう C: Interview your *sensei*!

birthday?

read newspaper everyday?

did what on weekend?

watched TV yesterday? watched what?

favorite kind of music? good at sports? like shopping?

have a computer? new? old? fast?

LESSON 3
Homestay 3

OBJECTIVES

At the end of this lesson you will be able to:
- ☑ Talk about your town and school
- ☑ Ask others about their town and school

VOCABULARY

New

donna	what kind of

Review

machi	town, city
shizuka (na)	quiet
urusai	noisy, bothersome, loud
kirei (na)	pretty
omoshiroi	interesting
chikai	near, close
kedo	but

COMMUNITY PLACES

pan-ya	bakery	hoteru	hotel
ginkoo	bank	toshokan	library
hon-ya	bookstore	chuugakkoo	middle school
niku-ya	butcher's, meat market	eigakan	movie theater
keeki-ya	cake shop	kooen	park
kamera-ya	camera shop	yuubinkyoku	post office
tokei-ya	clock/watch shop	kutsu-ya	shoe store
fuku-ya	clothing store	chikatetsu	subway
depaato	department store	suupaa	supermarket
shoogakkoo	elementary school	eki	train station
sakana-ya	fish store, fish market	daigaku	university
kookoo	high school	yao-ya	vegetable store

VOCABULARY NOTES

Donna
The word *donna*, which means *what kind of*, can be used directly in front of a noun.

Donna machi desu-ka?	*What kind of* city is it?
Ookii desu. Chotto urusai desu.	It's big. It's a bit noisy.
Donna gakkoo desu-ka?	*What is* your school *like*?
Kirei-na gakkoo desu.	It's a pretty school.
Donna daigaku desu-ka?	*What kind of* college is it?
Chiisai daigaku desu.	It's a small college.

This lesson reviews some important grammar points concerning adjectives. Following each grammar point is the lesson in which it was first presented in Volume 1.

1. *I*-adjectives and *na*-adjectives (L. 57, 61)

Adjectives in Japanese are divided into two groups: *i*-adjectives and *na*-adjectives. Both types of adjectives can precede the nouns they modify or they can be used with the verb *desu*. When a *na*-adjective precedes a noun, you must insert the particle *-na* after the adjective.

Atarashii konpyuutaa-wa *hayai* desu.	The *new* computer is *fast*.
Hayai konpyuutaa-wa *atarashii* desu.	The *fast* computer is *new*.
Kantan-na shitsumon desu.	It's an *easy* question.
Shitsumon-wa *kantan* desu.	The question is *easy*.

2. Negative of adjectives (L. 57, 59)

The negative of *na*-adjectives can be formed with *ja nai*.

Sono shitsumon-wa *kantan ja nai* desu.	That question is *not easy*.
Machi-wa *shizuka ja nai* desu.	The town is *not quiet*.

To form the negative of an *i*-adjective, change the final *i* to *kunai*.

Kono hon-wa *omoshiroi* desu.	This book is *interesting*.
Sono hon-wa *omoshirokunai* desu.	That book is *not interesting*.
Atarashii konpyuutaa-wa *hayai* desu.	The new computer is *fast*.
Furui konpyuutaa-wa *hayakunai* desu.	The old computer is *not fast*.

Can you form the negative of these *i*-adjectives? Check your answers on the last page of this lesson.

1. おおきい	3. ちいさい	5. おもしろい
2. ふるい	4. たのしい	6. うるさい

どんな	what kind of
まち	town, city
しずか (な)	quiet
うるさい	noisy, bothersome, loud
きれい (な)	pretty
おもしろい	interesting
ちかい	near, close
けど	but

Summer greeting cards しょちゅうみまい

Shochuu-mimai (literally, *middle of heat inquiry*) are greeting cards which are sent at the peak of the summer heat around the end of July or beginning of August. The cards are similar in appearance to Japanese New Year's postcards (*nengajoo*) and usually have an attractive design which evokes a sense of coolness. Senders of the cards write an appropriate formalized expression to let others know that they are thinking of them and are concerned as to how they are managing in the hot, humid weather. Japanese send the cards to superiors, clients, relatives, and friends. As noted in earlier lessons in this course, seasonal changes and weather are major points of interest in Japanese daily life.

PART 1

Kirei desu-ka?

With a partner practice forming the negative of *i*-adjectives and *na*-adjectives. Partner A selects any affirmative adjective from the list below (left column) and makes a simple question. Partner B, without looking at the list, responds in the negative using the correct form of the adjective. After every five questions and answers, switch roles and continue. Look at the example.

EXAMPLE

A: *Oishii* desu-ka?
B: Iie, *oishikunai* desu.
A: *Atarashii* desu-ka?
B: Iie, *atarashikunai* desu.
A: *Kantan* desu-ka?
B: Iie, *kantan ja nai* desu.

I- and *NA*-ADJECTIVES		
furui	furukunai	(not) old
ookii	ookikunai	(not) big
chiisai	chiisakunai	(not) small
hayai	hayakunai	(not) fast, early
osoi	osokunai	(not) slow, late
isogashii	isogashikunai	(not) busy
oishii	oishikunai	(not) delicious
tanoshii	tanoshikunai	(not) pleasant, fun
tsumaranai	tsumaranakunai	(not) boring
muzukashii	muzukashikunai	(not) difficult
omoshiroi	omoshirokunai	(not) interesting
urusai	urusakunai	(not) noisy
samui	samukunai	(not) cold
atsui	atsukunai	(not) hot
kawaii	kawaikunai	(not) cute
takai	takakunai	(not) expensive
yasui	yasukunai	(not) cheap
tooi	tookunai	(not) far
chikai	chikakunai	(not) close
ii	yokunai	(not) good
. . . .		
dame	dame ja nai	(not) bad, worthless
kantan	kantan ja nai	(not) easy, simple
suki	suki ja nai	(not) pleasing
joozu	joozu ja nai	(not) skilled
heta	heta ja nai	(not) unskilled
shizuka	shizuka ja nai	(not) quiet
iya	iya ja nai	(not) bad, terrible
kirei	kirei ja nai	(not) pretty
hen	hen ja nai	(not) strange
genki	genki ja nai	(not) healthy

PART 2

Donna machi desu-ka?

Use your imagination in this pair activity. You and your partner are both students who are at a summer Japanese language camp where all of the participants are expected to speak only in Japanese during the two-week session. You and your partner have met just recently and are now asking questions about each other's towns. Before beginning this activity decide what your (imaginary) town is like. (No. 1: choose a name for your town/city. No. 2-6: select one descriptor about your town. No. 7-9: write down a number of the places found in your town.) Do not show your work to your partner. Take turns asking questions and write down your partner's responses. Compare your work when you have completely finished.

1. (name of your town)
2. totemo ookii / ookii / chiisai / totemo chiisai
3. shizuka / urusai
4. kirei / kirei ja nai
5. omoshiroi / omoshirokunai
6. chikai / tooi
7. eigakan (a number of the places)*
8. gakkoo (a number of the places)
9. hoteru (a number of the places)

*hitotsu, futatsu, mittsu, yottsu, itsutsu, muttsu, nanatsu, yattsu, kokonotsu, too

SAMPLE QUESTIONS AND ANSWERS

1. A-san-no machi-no namae-wa nan desu-ka? Winona desu.
2. Ookii desu-ka? Iie, ookikunai desu. Totemo chiisai desu.
3. Shizuka desu-ka? Iie, shizuka ja nai desu. Urusai desu.
4. Kirei desu-ka? Hai, kirei desu.
5. Omoshiroi desu-ka? Iie, anmari omoshirokunai desu.
6. Koko-kara chikai desu-ka? Hai, chikai desu. Basu-de ichi-ji-kan-gurai desu.

7-9. Eigakan-ga (takusan) arimasu-ka? Hai, muttsu arimasu.

If you have time, select different descriptors and repeat the activity.

ANSWER KEY (KEY GRAMMAR POINTS, #2)
1. おおきい → おおきくない 4. たのしい → たのしくない
2. ふるい → ふるくない 5. おもしろい → おもしろくない
3. ちいさい → ちいさくない 6. うるさい → うるさくない

れんしゅう A: Describing Things

(1)
$$\left(3\sqrt{89}\right)^{2}=?$$
easy
difficult
interesting
boring
etc.

(2)
red
black
green
blue
etc.

(3)
really like
like
so-so
etc.

(4)
big
pretty
cool
cute
etc.

(5)
big
small
new
fast
etc.

れんしゅう B: *Katakana* Puzzle

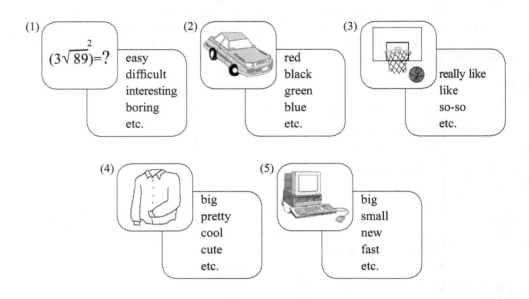

101 ホ	340 イ	600 バ	825 カ
270 テ	403 ニ	1001 ス	560 ト
909 ル	4090 レ	8000 ラ	710 マ
6028 ア	990 ビ	3100 ク	2000 ト

れんしゅう C: Let's talk about Kenji's town!

(1) train station   (2) bus stop   (3) park
(4) movie theater   (5) hotel   (6) library

しつもん：   (a) Is there ~ in Kenji's town?

(b) How many?

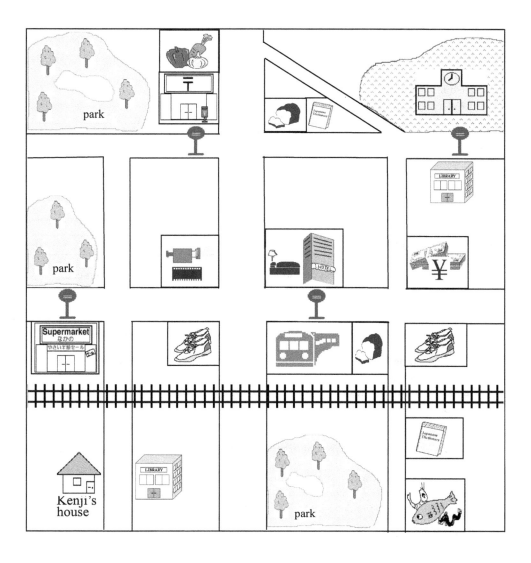

OBJECTIVES　　　　　　　　　　　　　　　　　　　　もくひょう

At the end of this lesson you will be able to:
- ☑ Talk about family and pets

VOCABULARY　　　　　　　　　　　　　　　　　　　　たんご

New

neko	cat
inu	dog
katte-imasu (katte-iru)	keep/have (a pet)
petto	pet

Review

dare	who
shashin	photograph
kawaii	cute

KAZOKU			
kazoku ~ go-kazoku	family	ane ~ oneesan	older sister
kyoodai ~ go-kyoodai	siblings	ani ~ oniisan	older brother
haha ~ okaasan	mother	imooto ~ imooto-san	younger sister
chichi ~ otoosan	father	otooto ~ otootosan	younger brother
Humble forms are given first.			

KEY GRAMMAR POINTS　　　　　　　　　　　ぶんぽうポイント

This lesson reviews two important grammar points from Volume 1. Following each grammar point is the lesson in which it was first presented.

1. The particle *-no* (L. 15)

The particle *-no* can be used to express possession. To express *whose* in Japanese, use *dare-no*.

Kaori-san-*no* baiku desu-ka?	Is it Kaori*'s* motorcycle?
Imooto-*no* inu desu.	It's my younger sister*'s* dog.
Ken-kun-*no* otoosan desu.	It's Ken*'s* father.
Kore-wa *dare-no* neko desu-ka?	*Whose* cat is this?

2. The counter *-nin* (L. 18)

The counter for people is *-nin*, except in the case of *one person* (*hitori*) and *two people* (*futari*).

Go-kazoku-wa yo-*nin* desu-ka?	Are there four *people* in your family?
Iie, go-*nin* desu.	No, five *people*.
Go-kazoku-wa nan-*nin* desu-ka?	How many *people* are in your family?

YOMIMASHOO!　　　　　　　　　　　　　　　　よみましょう

ねこ	cat
いぬ	dog
かっています・かっている	keep/have a pet

34

ペット	pet
ペットをかっていますか。	Do you have any pets?
だれ	who
しゃしん	photograph
かわいい	cute
かぞく、ごかぞく	family
きょうだい、ごきょうだい	siblings
はは、おかあさん	mother
ちち、おとうさん	father
あね、おねえさん	older sister
あに、おにいさん	older brother
いもうと、いもうとさん	younger sister
おとうと、おとうとさん	younger brother

INTERACTIVE ACTIVITIES

PART 1

❶ Vocabulary check
Silently review the vocabulary for Lesson 4, including the words for family members. Then have a クラスメート orally test your knowledge of the Japanese words. Your partner says the えいご, and you give the にほんご. Switch and test your partner.

❷ Go-kazoku-wa nan-nin desu-ka? 📄 & ✎
This activity is done with the entire class. (For large classes, make groups of eight students, and pool the collected information.) Through interviewing your クラスメート one at a time, you will be able to find the answers to the following questions.

1. For how many クラスメート is each of the following statements true?
    a. おねえさんが います。
    b. おにいさんが います。
    c. いもうとさんが います。
    d. おとうとさんが います。
2. だれの ごかぞくが いちばん おおきい ですか。
3. What is the average number of ごきょうだい?

Interview each クラスメート in にほんご and record the number of 人. Use しつもん と こたえ such as these:

Go-kazoku-wa nan-nin desu-ka?	Go-nin desu.
Go-kyoodai-ga imasu-ka?	Hai, imasu. OR Iie, imasen.
(Go-kyoodai-wa) nan-nin imasu-ka?	San-nin imasu.
Oneesan-ga imasu-ka?	Hai, imasu.
Otootosan-ga imasu-ka?	Iie, imasen.

Petto-o katte-imasu-ka? 📄 & ✏

Do this activity as an entire class. Before you begin interviewing クラスメート in pairs to obtain the information on their pets, use your imagination to 'create' your own special pet. Japanese words for pets are given in the box below. First, read the sample questions and answers below and write down your answers about your own pet. After you form a pair, ask your partner all of the questions and record their responses. Switch roles and answer your partner's questions. Form a different pair and repeat. Speak only Japanese.
Dare-no petto-ga ichiban hen desu-ka?

SAMPLE QUESTIONS AND ANSWERS (Use these only to help you get started.)
1. Petto-o katte-imasu-ka?   Hai, *kind of pet*-o katte-imasu.
2. Petto-no namae-wa nan desu-ka?   *Name* desu.
3. Nani-iro desu-ka?   *Color* desu.
4. Ookii desu ka? Chiisai desu-ka?   *Size* desu.
5. Nani-o tabemasu-ka?   *Name of food*-o tabemasu.
6. Nihongo-ga dekimasu-ka?   Hai, (sukoshi) dekimasu. OR
                                               Iie, zenzen dekimasen.

PETTO					
kingyo	goldfish	feretto	ferret	nezumi	mouse
hamusutaa	hamster	usagi	rabbit	inko	parakeet
hebi	snake	kame	turtle	uma	horse
oomu	parrot	iguwana	iguana	ponii	pony
morumotto	guinea pig	kaeru	frog	taranchura-gumo	tarantula

L.4 電話で 話しましょう

れんしゅう A: Does s/he have ~?

しつもん:
(a) Does s/he have a ~? (b) How old? (c) Big/small? (d) Color?

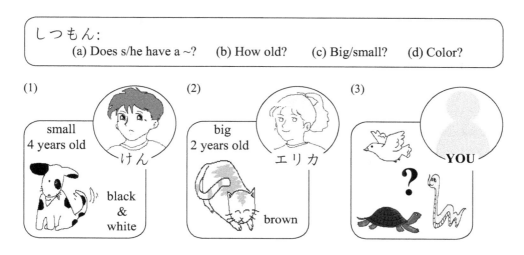

(1) small 4 years old けん black & white

(2) big 2 years old エリカ brown

(3) YOU ?

れんしゅう B: Family Members

(1)

Joe's Family — Father, Mother, Joe, Ken

(2)

Your Family — YOU

How many?

Who?

Name?

How old?

れんしゅう C: Let's converse!

Dialogue:

A: Excuse me, whose <u>pen</u> is this?

B: Well, it's <u>Mr. Tanaka</u>'s.

A: So, is that <u>Mr. Tanaka</u>'s, too?

B: No, that's mine.

A: Is that so? May I use it (for a little while)?

B: Yes, please.

Sample Dialogue:

A: Sumimasen, kore-wa dare-no <u>pen</u> desu-ka?

B: Eeto, <u>Tanaka-san</u>-no desu.

A: Jaa, are-mo <u>Tanaka-san</u>-no desu-ka?

B: Iie, are-wa boku (watashi)-no desu-yo.

A: Soo desu-ka. Chotto, ii desu-ka?

B: Hai, doozo.

れんしゅう D: What's hidden?

Let's find out what's hidden in the following sentences for each category. The number in the parentheses shows how many words are hidden.

Ex.) School subjects (4)

お え い ご が た い い く し ち れ き し だ め に ほ ん ご い き

1) Food (3)

たまごあさかなべつれんにくまり

2) Sports (3)

ケーサッカーダラタスキーネルテニスバッリー

3) Family terms (4)

ちちとかりめろおとうとさんがけにいもうとるはは

LESSON 5
Homestay 5

At the end of this lesson you will be able to:
- ☑ Use the plain form of selected verbs appropriately

This lesson provides you with an opportunity to review the following objectives:
- ☑ Ask for the time
- ☑ Tell time to the hour and half hour
- ☑ Tell time to the minute
- ☑ Tell what time activities take place
- ☑ Tell some of the foods you eat
- ☑ Tell some of the beverages you drink

VOCABULARY   たんご

New
nemui	sleepy
asa-gohan	breakfast
hiru-gohan	lunch
ban-gohan	dinner

Review
mainichi	every day
ima	now
hayai	early
motto hayai	earlier
osoi	late
motto osoi	later
Doo desu-ka?	How is it?
oishii	delicious
gohan	meal
Itadakimasu.	*a polite expression said before eating or drinking*

KEY GRAMMAR POINTS   ぶんぽうポイント

1. Clock times (L. 24, 25, and 27)
This lesson reviews the time counters *-ji, -ji-han,* and *-fun/pun* as well as the particle *-ni* as used in expressions of time. Study these examples and refer to the notes in earlier lessons as needed.

Ima nan-*ji* desu-ka?	What *time* is it now?
San-*ji* desu.	It's three *o'clock*.
Miitingu-wa nan-*ji*-kara desu-ka?	What *time* does the meeting start?
Hachi-*ji-han*-kara desu.	It starts at 8:30.
Nan-*ji*-ni okimasu-ka?	What *time* do you get up?
Mainichi 6-*ji*-ni okimasu.	I get up at 6:00 every day.
Nan-*ji*-ni nemasu-ka?	What *time* does he go to bed?
Juu-*ji*-yon-juu-go-*fun*-ni nemasu.	He goes to bed at 10:45.

2. The plain form of verbs

In Lesson 47 of Volume 1 of this series, you were introduced to the **plain form** of Japanese verbs which is also called the **dictionary form** because verb entries in Japanese dictionaries are given in this form. Beginning with Lesson 47, both the *-masu* and the plain form have been given for all new verbs. You will notice that the plain form, when written in *roomaji*, ends in *-u* or *-ru*. The plain form is sometimes referred to as the **informal form** because it replaces the *-masu* form in conversations between family members and close friends. The *-masu* form, which is also called the **non-past, polite form** (L. 27), is used when speaking with people to whom you wish to show respect because they are older or more important than you or because you do not know them very well. Here are the polite and plain forms of the verbs you have already learned.

POLITE FORM	PLAIN FORM	POLITE FORM	PLAIN FORM
wakarimasu	wakaru	shimasu	suru
chigaimasu	chigau	ikimasu	iku
imasu	iru	kikimasu	kiku
arimasu	aru	yomimasu	yomu
mimasu	miru	kimasu	kuru
okimasu	okiru	kaerimasu	kaeru
nemasu	neru	dekimasu	dekiru
tabemasu	taberu	utaimasu	utau
nomimasu	nomu	kaimasu	kau
narimasu	naru	aruite ikimasu	aruite iku

Notice that when you ask a question using a plain form verb you do not need to say *-ka*. You simply raise your voice to indicate that you are asking a question. The direct object particle *-o* is also often omitted in informal speech. Compare these pairs of sentences.

Nan-ji-ni uchi-ni *kaeru*?	What time are you returning home? [plain]
Nan-ji-ni uchi-ni *kaerimasu*-ka?	What time are you returning home? [polite]
Nani *taberu*?	What are you going to eat? [plain]
Nani-o *tabemasu*-ka?	What are you going to eat? [polite]
Mainichi nan-ji-ni *okiru*?	What time do you get up every day? [plain]
Mainichi nan-ji-ni *okimasu*-ka?	What time do you get up every day? [polite]

YOMIMASHOO!   よみましょう

ねむい	sleepy
あさごはん	breakfast
ひるごはん	lunch
ばんごはん	dinner
まいにち	every day
いま	now
はやい	early
もっと はやい	earlier
おそい	late
もっと おそい	later
どう ですか。	How is it?
おいしい	delicious
ごはん	meal
いただきます。	*a polite expression said before eating or drinking*

INTERACTIVE ACTIVITIES

PART 1

❶ Nan-ji-ni okimasu-ka?　📄 & ✎

Mr. Jones is an incredibly hard-working individual who even on Saturdays packs as much into his schedule as possible. Mr. Jones has already drawn up a detailed schedule for this coming Saturday. Look only at your copy of Mr. Jones's schedule as you exchange information with your partner to complete the schedule by filling in the missing activities and times. For a greater challenge, do not complete the schedule in chronological order.

PARTNER A

ACTIVITY	TIME	ACTIVITY	TIME
okimasu		kooen-ni ikimasu	
asa-gohan-o tabemasu	6:30	basukettobooru-o shimasu	3:30
	7:15		4:45
tenisu-o shimasu	8:00	shinbun-o yomimasu	
kaimono-ni ikimasu	10:15	nyuusu-o mimasu	6:00
	11:30	go-kazoku-to gohan-o tabemasu	7:00
kissaten-ni ikimasu	12:45		8:15
tomodachi-to koohii-o nomimasu	1:00		9:45
	2:00	nemasu	11:00

SAMPLE QUESTIONS

Nan-ji-ni okimasu-ka?
San-ji-ni nani-o shimasu-ka?
Nan-ji-kara tenisu-o shimasu-ka?
Roku-ji-kara nani-o shimasu-ka?

SAMPLE TIMES

9:00	ku-ji
9:15	ku-ji-juu-go-fun
9:30	ku-ji-han
9:45	ku-ji-yon-juu-go-fun

PARTNER B

ACTIVITY	TIME	ACTIVITY	TIME
okimasu	6:00	kooen-ni ikimasu	3:00
	6:30	basukettobooru-o shimasu	
tomodachi-no uchi-ni ikimasu	7:15	uchi-ni kaerimasu	4:45
tenisu-o shimasu		shinbun-o yomimasu	5:15
	10:15	nyuusu-o mimasu	
resutoran-de o-hiru-o tabemasu	11:30		7:00
	12:45	benkyoo-o shimasu	8:15
	1:00	ongaku-o kikimasu	9:45
toshokan-ni ikimasu	2:00		11:00

❷ Ima nan-ji desu-ka?　📄 & ✎

Make a ３人の ちいさい グループ. Without showing the other students, Student A writes a clock time and asks, *"Ima nan-ji desu-ka?"* Students B and C take turns guessing the exact time. After each incorrect guess, Student A gives a hint by saying, *"Chigaimasu. Motto hayai/osoi desu,"* and then repeats the question. All times are a.m. After Student B or C guesses the correct time, Student B writes down a time for Students A and C to guess.

PART 2

❶ Wakaru? Wakarimasu-ka?

Using the completed chart in Assignment #2 from Part 1 of Lesson 9, check your answers with a partner. Then practice giving the plain form equivalent of -*masu* forms and vice versa. Be sure you can say the English equivalents, too.

❷ Orenji juusu nomu?

With a partner practice asking and answering these questions. Use the plain form.

1. Nan-ji-ni okiru?
2. Asa-gohan taberu?
3. Nani taberu?
4. Oishii?
5. Nan-ji-ni gakkoo-ni kuru?
6. Basu-de kuru?
7. Nan-ji-ni uchi-ni kaeru?
8. Uchi-de nani suru?
9. Nan-ji-ni neru?
10. Nihongo benkyoo suru?

L. 5 電話で 話しましょう

れんしゅう A: Meeting and Greeting the New Student

A new student has joined your Japanese II class. Greet him/her, and then introduce yourself. Include three points, such as your: age, grade, birthday, family, likes, etc.

れんしゅう B: Telling Time

(1) (2) (3) (4)

(5) 12:10 (6) 1:56 (7) 8:29 (8) 5:38

れんしゅう C: A Day in the Life of Nickey Mouse

The following is Nickey Mouse's schedule for tomorrow. Group A can only look at Schedule A, and Group B can only look at Schedule B. Ask members of the other group questions and fill in the numbered blanks.

Schedule A

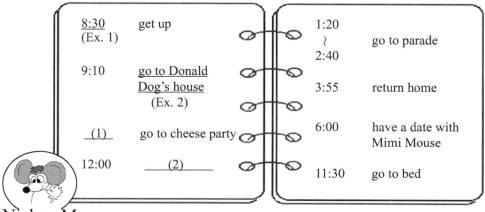

8:30 (Ex. 1)	get up		1:20 ≀ 2:40	go to parade
9:10	go to Donald Dog's house (Ex. 2)		3:55	return home
(1)	go to cheese party		6:00	have a date with Mimi Mouse
12:00	(2)		11:30	go to bed

Nickey Mouse

Schedule B

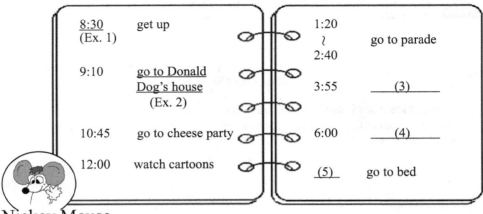

8:30 (Ex. 1) get up
9:10 go to Donald Dog's house (Ex. 2)
10:45 go to cheese party
12:00 watch cartoons

1:20 ~ 2:40 go to parade
3:55 _____ (3)
6:00 _____ (4)
(5)_____ go to bed

Nickey Mouse

れんしゅう D: Let's converse!

Dialogue: (B stayed overnight at A's house.)

A: What do you want for breakfast?
B: What do you have?
A: We have cereal, bagels, and toast.
B: Well then, I'll have toast.
A: O.K. What do you want to drink? We have orange juice and coffee.
B: Um, I'll have coffee.

food and drink selection

| eggs | bananas | rice | fish |
| salad | oranges | ham | bread |

| milk | water | tea |
| grapefruit juice | tomato juice |

Sample Dialogue:

A: Asa-gohan, nani taberu?
B: Nani-ga aru?
A: Shiriaru-to beeguru-to toosuto-ga aru-yo.
B: Uun, jaa, toosuto taberu.
A: Jaa, nani nomu? Orenji juusu-to koohii-ga aru-kedo.
B: Jaa, koohii nomu.*

*formal version

A: Asa-gohan-wa nani-o tabemasu-ka?
B: Nani-ga arimasu-ka?
A: Shiriaru-to beeguru-to toosuto-ga arimasu-yo.
B: Eetto, jaa, toosuto-o tabemasu.
A: Jaa, nani-o nomimasu-ka? Orenji juusu-to koohii-ga arimasu-kedo.
B: Jaa, koohii-o nomimasu.

44

R. 1~5 電話で 話しましょう

れんしゅう A: Doing Something with a Club Member

You recently join a club at school. One of the senior club members invites you to do something. Respond to his/her questions.

れんしゅう B: Fill in the map.

You are trying to find out whether or not the following chain stores are in this town. First, ask if that store is in the town, and if it is, ask how many of them there are. (Since they are chain stores, all bookstores will look the same, all bakeries will look the same, etc.) Then, write down the number of stores in the bracket.

(Ex.) pizza shop [1]   (1) supermarket   [   ]   (2) fish market [   ]
(3) bakery   [   ]   (4) ice cream shop [   ]   (5) bookstore   [   ]

Let's match the stores with their respective buildings.

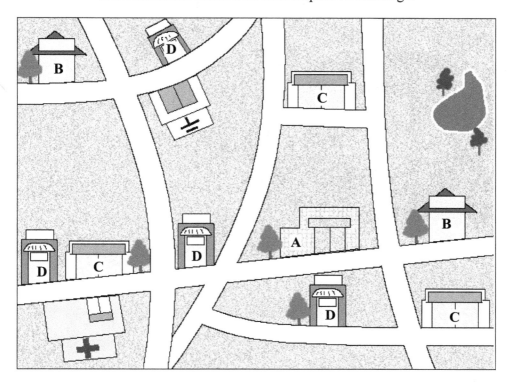

45

いらっしゃいツアー

きょうと
京都

（一泊二日）
¥35,000〜

	スケジュール
10/9 （土）	とうきょう 東京エアポート (7:00 A.M.) ↓ おおさか 大阪エアポート きょうとえき 京都駅 ↓ やさかじんじゃ, ちおいん 八坂神社, 知恩院 ↓ セントラルホテル
10/10 （日）	セントラルホテル ↓ にじょうじょう, きんかくじ 　二条城, 金閣寺 グランドデパート ↓ きょうとえき 京都駅 ↓ とうきょうえき 東京駅　　　(5:00 P.M.)

いらっしゃい観光

LESSON 6
Countries and Languages

OBJECTIVES　　　　　　　　　　　　　　　　　もくひょう

At the end of this lesson you will be able to:

- ☑ Identify some countries of the world
- ☑ Ask and say what language someone speaks
- ☑ Explain the origin and use of *kanji*

VOCABULARY　　　　　　　　　　　　　　　　　たんご

Words

hanashimasu (hanasu)	speak
kuni	country
sekai	world
chizu	map
Igirisu	England
Chuugoku	China

Phrases and expressions

Doko-no chizu desu-ka?	What is this a map of?
Doko-no kuni desu-ka?	What country is this?

Names of selected countries (for your reference)

COUNTRIES							
Tai	Thailand	Kanada	Canada	Itaria	Italy
Betonamu	Vietnam	Mekishiko	Mexico	Suisu	Switzerland
Firipin	Philippines	Koronbia	Colombia	Doitsu	Germany
Indo	India	Burajiru	Brazil	Furansu	France
Taiwan	Taiwan	Aruzenchin	Argentina	Poorando	Poland
Kankoku	Korea	Chiri	Chile	Supein	Spain
Indoneshia	Indonesia	Benezuera	Venezuela	Girisha	Greece
Raosu	Laos	Peruu	Peru	Ejiputo	Egypt
Kanbojia	Cambodia	Suweeden	Sweden	Kenia	Kenya
Oosutoraria	Australia	Roshia	Russia	Morokko	Morocco

KEY GRAMMAR POINTS　　　　　　　　　　ぶんぽうポイント

1. *Language*-o hanashimasu.

The verb *hanashimasu* means *speak* and can be used with the names of languages. The plain form of *hanashimasu* is *hanasu*. The direct object particle *-o* must be used following the name of the language.

Supeingo-o *hanashimasu.*	They speak Spanish.
Roshiago-o *hanashimasu*-ka?	Do they speak Russian?
Eigo-o *hanasu.*	They speak English.

2. Nani-go-o hanashimasu-ka?

To ask what language is spoken by someone, use the question *Nani-go-o hanashimasu-ka?* The word *Nani-go* is replaced by the name of the language in the answer.

Nani-go-o hanashimasu-ka?	What language do they speak?
Doitsugo-o hanashimasu.	They speak German.

47

3. *Place*-de-wa nani-go-o hanashimasu-ka?

To specify a place in your question, begin with the name of the country or other location followed by the particles -*de* and -*wa*. The particle -*de* indicates that action (i.e., speaking) takes place in that location, and the particle -*wa* indicates that the location is the topic of the sentence.

Kanada-*de-wa* nani-go-o hanashimasu-ka?	What language do they speak *in* Canada?
Eigo-to furansugo-o hanashimasu.	They speak English and French.

YOMIMASHOO! よみましょう

はなします・はなす	speak
くに	country
せかい	world
ちず	map
イギリス	England
ちゅうごく	China
どこの ちず ですか。	What is this a map of?
どこの くに ですか。	What country is this?

CULTURE NOTES カルチャーノート

Japanese world map

Most people grow up familiar with world maps that feature their own country in the middle. For example, many maps used in the Western hemisphere show Canada, the U.S., and Latin America in the center. World maps published and used in Japan, however, usually show Japan in the center.

JAPANESE WORLD MAP

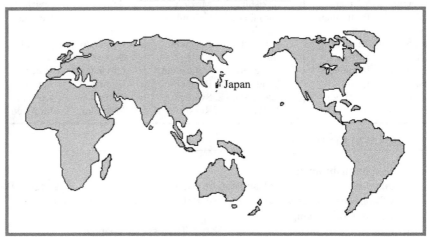

Some maps published in the Western hemisphere do not feature the North and South American continents in the middle. In this case, do the Americas usually appear on the right side of the map (as in the Japanese map above) or on the left side? Why?

KANJI NOTES かんじノート

The origin and use of *kanji*

In the late fifth century A.D. the Japanese began to import and use *kanji* (Chinese characters) to write Japanese. Before that time the Japanese had no writing system. Since

Japanese and Chinese were – and still are – very different languages that are not even related, the Japanese encountered some problems in trying to use the Chinese writing system to represent their own spoken language.

For example, Chinese verbs do not have different endings to show person, number, and tense. Thus, a verb such as 買 (mai) which means *buy* can express all of the following:

I *buy* groceries in Petersville.
She *buys* a new car every year.
They *bought* a new house last week.
My sister *is buying* more than she can afford.
My younger brother *has* already *bought* a new computer.
I *will buy* a new one soon.

Chinese speakers use pronouns (*I, we, she*, etc.) and words such as *yesterday, tomorrow, every day*, and *already* to clarify the meaning of verbs.

Japanese verbs do not have different endings to show person and number, but they do have endings to indicate tense and other grammatical features. When the Japanese borrowed a Chinese character such as 買 with the meaning *buy* to represent in writing their own native word for *buy* (*kau/kaimasu* in contemporary Japanese), they needed some way to represent the various endings. By the ninth century the Japanese had simplified some of the *kanji* to create the *hiragana* syllabary, the symbols of which could be used with borrowed Chinese characters.

A *kanji* always represents the root meaning of a word. Study these examples carefully.

買う。	Kau.
買います。	Kaimasu.
買いました。	Kaimashita.
買いません。	Kaimasen.
買いませんでした。	Kaimasen deshita.
あの人は本を買いました。	Ano hito-wa hon-o kaimashita.

Notice that in the case of both 人 (hito) and 本 (hon) the entire word can be written with *kanji*. These nouns have no endings which require the use of *hiragana*.

Modern Japanese is written with a combination of three systems: *kanji, hiragana*, and *katakana*. The symbols used in the *katakana* syllabary also trace their origin to Chinese characters.

INTERACTIVE ACTIVITIES

PART 1

❶ Vocabulary check
Silently review the vocabulary (words, phrases, and expressions) for Lesson 6. Then have a クラスメート orally test your knowledge of them. Your partner says the えいご, and you give the にほんご. Switch and test your partner.

❷ Doitsu-de-wa nani-go-o hanashimasu-ka?
Use your imagination in this pair activity. Partner A is an *Irasshai* student who always welcomes opportunities to practice speaking Japanese. Partner B is a Japanese-speaking Martian who is visiting Earth for the first time. Before the Martian arrived, he thought that everyone on Earth spoke Japanese because the only Earthling he had ever met on Mars was from Japan. Fortunately, an *Irasshai* student has befriended the Martian. Today the Martian, who is looking at a world map, is asking questions about what languages are spoken in different countries.

Use the following patterns and substitute the names of various countries and languages for the words in **bold** type. Refer to the chart only as long as you need to.

B: **Doitsu**-de-wa nani-go-o hanashimasu-ka?
A: **Doitsugo**-o hanashimasu.
B: **Kanada**-de-wa nani-go-o hanashimasu-ka?
A: **Eigo**-to **furansugo**-o hanashimasu.
B: **Mekishiko**-de-wa nani-go-o hanashimasu-ka?
A: **Supeingo**-o hanashimasu.

KUNI	-GO	KUNI	-GO
Betonamu	betonamugo	Kankoku	kankokugo
Burajiru	porutogarugo	Kenia	suwahirigo
Chiri	supeingo	Koronbia	supeingo
Doitsu	doitsugo	Mekishiko	supeingo
Ejiputo	arabiago	Morokko	arabiago
Firipin	tagarogugo	Oosutoraria	eigo
Furansu	furansugo	Peruu	supeingo
Girisha	girishago	Roshia	roshiago
Indoneshia	indoneshiago	Suisu	doitsugo/furansugo/itariago
Itaria	itariago	Supein	supeingo
Kanada	eigo/furansugo	Tai	taigo

PART 2

❶ **Doko-no kuni desu-ka?**

Play this guessing game with a partner. Sit in such a way that you can both see a world map. If you both brought a map as part of your assignment, you can each look at your own map. Partner A selects a country and writes the name of the country without showing Partner B. Partner A must know what language is spoken in that country. Partner B then asks questions such as those on the next page to determine the country's name. Partner B may guess the name of the country at any time. Partner A records the number of questions Partner B must ask before guessing the correct country. Switch roles and repeat. The person with the lower score is the winner of the round. Play as many rounds as you can. Try to depend less and less on the sample exchange, and remain entirely in Japanese.

> Names of countries are given in the *Tango* section of this lesson.
> Both countries and languages appear in the chart in Interactive Activities Part 1 ❷.

SAMPLE EXCHANGE
A: Sono kuni-de-wa nani-go-o hanashimasu-ka?
B: Supeingo-o hanashimasu.
A: Kuni-wa ookii desu-ka? Chiisai desu-ka?
B: Ookii desu.
A: Amerika-ni chikai desu-ka?
B: Iie, Amerika-kara tooi desu.
A: Burajiru-ni chikai desu-ka?
B: Hai, chikai desu-yo.
A: Koronbia desu-ka?
B: Iie, chigaimasu.
A: Benezuera desu-ka?
B: Hai, soo desu.

MORE COUNTRIES AND LANGUAGES

Noruwee/noruweego [Norway/Norwegian]	Raosu/raosugo [Laos/Laotian]
Sueeden/sueedengo [Sweden/Swedish]	Indo/hinzuu [India/Hindi]
Finrando/finrandogo [Finland/Finnish]	Taiwan/chuugokugo [Taiwan/Chinese]
Oranda/orandago [the Netherlands/Dutch]	Isuraeru/heburaigo [Israel/Hebrew]
Porutogaru/porutogarugo [Portugal/Portuguese]	Toruko/torukogo [Turkey/Turkish]
Oosutoria/doitsugo [Austria/German]	Kanbojia/kanbojiago [Cambodia/Cambodian]
Poorando/poorandogo [Poland/Polish]	Chuugoku/chuugokugo [China/Chinese]

❷ **Yomimashoo!**

With a partner take turns reading the passages below. Partner A looks only at the Japanese text (with the *roomaji* masked) while Partner B looks at the *roomaji* version. Partner B gently prompts Partner A as needed. Switch roles and continue. Consult a world map to check your answers.

PARTNER A READS

この くには アメリカから とおい です。 おおきい です。 ロシアに ちかい です。 この くには モンゴル じゃ ない です。 この くにでは ちゅうごくご を はなします。 どこの くに ですか。

PARTNER B PROMPTS

Kono kuni-wa Amerika-kara tooi desu. Ookii desu. Roshia-ni chikai desu. Kono kuni-wa Mongoru ja nai desu. Kono kuni-de-wa chuugokugo-o hanashimasu. Doko-no kuni desu-ka?

PARTNER B READS

この くにでは スペインごを はなします。 アメリカから とおい です。 でも、 ブラジルと アルゼンチンに ちかい です。 この くには ちいさい です。 パラグアイ じゃ ない です。 どこの くに ですか。

PARTNER A PROMPTS

Kono kuni-de-wa supeingo-o hanashimasu. Amerika-kara tooi desu. Demo, Burajiru-to Aruzenchin-ni chikai desu. Kono kuni-wa chiisai desu. Paraguai ja nai desu. Doko-no kuni desu-ka?

L. 6 電話で 話しましょう

れんしゅう A: What language do you speak?

(1) ピエール — Que mangez-vous le matin?
French

(2) チュー — 我家只有我一个孩子。
Chinese

(3) レベッカ — Wo kann ich diesen Brief einstecken?
German

(4) リサ — English is fun. / РУССКИЙ ЯЗЫК
English and Russian

(5) YOU — ?
?

れんしゅう B: What language do they speak in ~?

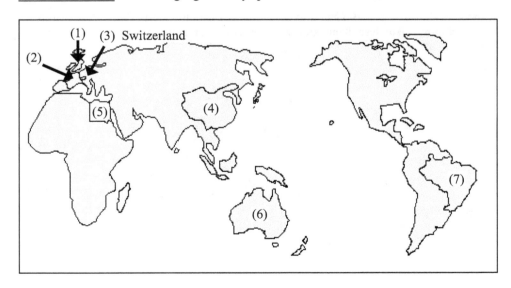

(1) (3) Switzerland (2) (5) (4) (6) (7)

52

<u>れんしゅう C</u>: Fill in the blanks and let's converse!

(1)

A: Shuumatsu, nani-o shimashita-ka?
B: _____ shimashita.

A: _____ ?

B: _____ -to _____ -o kaimashita.
12-gatsu-ni Oosutoraria-ni ikimasu.

A: Eeee! Oosutoraria-wa 12-gatsu-wa
_____ desu-yo.

(2)

A: Tanaka-san, kyoo-wa _____ -ga arimasu-
yo. Kinoo benkyoo-o shimashita-ka?

B: Hai, _____.

A: Hee, sugoi desu-ne!
B: Hai, watashi-wa _____ -ga daisuki-desu.

A: E? Kyoo-no tesuto-wa _____
desu-yo!

<u>れんしゅう D</u>: よみましょう。 こたえましょう。

(1) はじめまして。 マイクです。

(2) おいくつですか。

(3) コンピューターが ありますか。

(4) スポーツは なにが すきですか。

(5) ジャズを ききますか。

(6) あさ、 なんじに おきますか。

(7) バレーボールが できますか。

(8) がっきは なにが できますか。

53

LESSON 7
Locations and Cardinal Directions

OBJECTIVES   もくひょう

At the end of this lesson you will be able to:
- ☑ Ask where someone is from
- ☑ Name six continents
- ☑ Ask about and state locations using cardinal directions
- ☑ Read the *kanji*: 月 and 日

VOCABULARY   たんご

Words

dochira	which, where
kita	north
higashi	east
minami	south
nishi	west

CONTINENTS	
Ajia	Asia
Afurika	Africa
Yooroppa	Europe
Minami Amerika	South America
Kita Amerika	North America
Oosutoraria	Australia

Phrases and expressions

Dochira-kara desu-ka?	Where are you from?

KEY GRAMMAR POINTS   ぶんぽうポイント

1. Dochira-kara desu-ka?

The word *dochira* means *which* (of two choices) or *where*. With the latter meaning, *dochira* is a polite equivalent of the word *doko* and can be used when asking where someone is from.

Dochira-kara desu-ka?	*Where* are you from?
Kanada-kara desu.	I'm from Canada.

2. *Place*-no dochira

This phrase allows you to find out more specifically where someone is from. For example, if you know the name of the country, you can then determine the name of the prefecture, state, or province. A person may sometimes respond with the name of a city.

Nihon-*no dochira*-kara desu-ka?	*Where in* Japan are you from?
Nagano-ken-kara desu.	I'm from Nagano Prefecture.
Tookyoo-kara desu.	I'm from Tokyo.
Amerika-*no dochira*-kara desu-ka?	*Where in* the U.S. are you from?
Sausu Dakota-kara desu.	I'm from South Dakota.
Kanada-*no dochira*-kara desu-ka?	*Where in* Canada are you from?
Otawa-kara desu.	I'm from Ottawa.

3. *Place*-no + cardinal direction
Use this pattern to express relative locations using cardinal directions.

Mekishiko-wa doko-ni arimasu-ka?	Where is Mexico?
Amerika-*no minami*-ni arimasu.	It's *south of* the U.S.
Kanada-wa Amerika-*no kita*-ni arimasu.	Canada is *north of* the U.S.

```
                    RELATIVE LOCATIONS

                        X-no kita

                            ↑

         X-no nishi   ←   X   →   X-no higashi

                            ↓

                      X-no minami
```

YOMIMASHOO! よみましょう

どちら	which, where
きた	north
ひがし	east
みなみ	south
にし	west
アジア	Asia
アフリカ	Africa
ヨーロッパ	Europe
みなみ アメリカ	South America
きた アメリカ	North America
オーストラリア	Australia
どちらから ですか。	Where are you from?
にほんの どちらから ですか。	Where in Japan are you from?
カナダは アメリカの きたに あります。	Canada is north of the U.S.

KANJI NOTES かんじノート

Reading Japanese
As is the case with any language, *reading* means not only to be able to produce the sounds which are represented by the written symbols but also to understand the meaning conveyed by those words. You have already learned the two syllabaries which are used in writing Japanese – *hiragana* and *katakana*. Each *kana* symbol represents a specific syllable with a certain sound value. Each *hiragana* has a *katakana* counterpart which represents the same sound(s).

HIRAGANA	KATAKANA	ROOMAJI
あ	ア	a
え	エ	e
き	キ	ki
と	ト	to
の	ノ	no

Hiragana can be combined to represent entire words such as から、します、and はい. Words borrowed from other languages such as テニス and ハンバーガー are written with *katakana*. Can you read these five Japanese words aloud and tell what they mean in English?

55

Reading *kanji*

In Volume 2 you will learn to read and write some of the most commonly used *kanji* in Japanese. In order to be able to read a *kanji*, you must know how to pronounce it and what it means. The character itself usually does not contain any clues to help you pronounce it correctly. You must memorize the pronunciation of each *kanji* as you learn it. Unlike the *hiragana* and *katakana* symbols, each of which has a specific sound value, a single Chinese character may have more than one way to pronounce it.

Why are there different ways to read the same *kanji*? *Kanji* were imported from different parts of China into different parts of Japan at different times. There were different dialects within both countries. The Japanese used the Chinese characters to represent native Japanese words, but in many cases they also borrowed the Chinese pronunciation of the *kanji*.

In Lesson 19 (Vol. 1) you were introduced to 人, the *kanji* for *hito* (person). This *kanji* can be read as *hito* or as *nin* as in *san-nin* and *roku-nin*. This same *kanji* can also be read as *jin* as in *amerika-jin* and *nihon-jin*. The native Japanese word is *hito* so we refer to this as the **Japanese reading** or ***kun-yomi***. The readings which have been adapted from the original Chinese pronunciations are called the **Chinese readings** or ***on-yomi***. In your *Irasshai* text (as in many other books on the Japanese language), the Chinese reading(s) will be given in upper case whereas the Japanese reading(s) will be presented in lower case. Here is an example:

 NIN, JIN; hito (person)

人	*hito*	person
三人	san-*nin*	three people
六人	roku-*nin*	six people
アメリカ人	amerika-*jin*	American
日本人	nihon-*jin*	Japanese

あの人は日本人ですか。 Ano *hito*-wa nihon-*jin* desu-ka?
三人いますか。 San-*nin* imasu-ka?

Look carefully at the two sentences above and then read these three sentences aloud. What are the English equivalents of these sentences?

1. あの人は日本人ですか。
2. 三人いますか。
3. カナダ人は三人います。

New *kanji*

In this lesson you will learn to read two *kanji* which were first introduced in Lesson 49 (Vol. 1). Be sure that you know the readings of each *kanji* and can tell what the *kanji* means. Readings which are marked by an asterisk are for your reference only; you do not need to learn these at this time. You also do not have to learn any new words which are given in the examples. In Lesson 10 you will learn how to write the *kanji* 月 and 日, using the correct stroke order.

月	GETSU, GATSU; tsuki* (month, moon)		

月曜日	*getsu*-yoobi	Monday
一月	ichi-*gatsu*	January
三月	san-*gatsu*	March
何月	nan-*gatsu*	what month?
月	*tsuki*	moon

何月でしたか。	Nan-*gatsu* deshita-ka?
	(What month was it?)
一月でした。	Ichi-*gatsu* deshita.
	(It was January.)
月曜日に行きました。	*Getsu*-yoobi-ni ikimashita.
	(He went on Monday.)

Many *kanji*, including the ones introduced in this lesson, have been derived from pictures of the things they represent. For many students of Japanese, knowing the origin of a *kanji* can help with both the learning and remembering of it.

日	NICHI, JITSU*; hi* [bi], ~ka (day, sun; *counter for days of the month*)

日	*hi*	sun
日曜日	*nichi*-yoo*bi*	Sunday
火曜日	ka-yoo*bi*	Tuesday
誕生日	tanjoo*bi*	birthday
十一日	juu-ichi-*nichi*	the 11th (day of the month)
二十三日	ni-juu-san-*nichi*	the 23rd
二日	futsu*ka*	the second
三日	mik*ka*	the third
毎日	mai*nichi*	every day

日曜日ですか。	*Nichi*-yoo*bi* desu-ka?
	(Is it Sunday?)
日曜日は十一日ですね。	*Nichi*-yoo*bi*-wa juu-ichi-*nichi* desu-ne.
	(Sunday is the 11th, isn't it?)
エレンさんの誕生日は	Eren-san-no tanjoo*bi*-wa 5-gatsu 27-*nichi* desu.
５月２７日です。	(Ellen's birthday is May 27.)
三日じゃないです。	Mik*ka* ja nai desu.
	(It isn't the third.)

The reading *bi* is given in brackets [bi] because it is a variant of the reading *hi*.

57

INTERACTIVE ACTIVITIES

PART 1

❶ Doko-no kuni desu-ka?

During this activity each student will work as a pair with two different クラスメート to check Assignment #1 from Part 2 of Lesson 6. The goal of the activity is to have two students carefully check your five sentences, mark and discuss with you any errors found, and sign off on your page. Form your first pair and exchange assignments with your partner. Both partners independently check and neatly mark errors for all five sentences. Do not correct errors. Use the editing symbols (see Workbook, Introduction). Return the assignments and go over the first sentence together. Correct your own work. Repeat this procedure for each sentence. Sign off on each other's page. Form new pairs and repeat these steps. After you have finished correcting your work, form pairs with different クラスメート, read each other's descriptions, and see if you can correctly answer the question どこ の くに ですか.

❷ Vocabulary check

Silently review the vocabulary for Lesson 7, including the words for the continents. Then have a クラスメート orally test your knowledge of them. Your partner says the えいご, and you give the にほん ご. Switch and test your partner.

PART 2

❶ Dochira-kara desu-ka?

Do this activity with a クラスメート. In the dialogue below, Partner A is asking where Partner B is from. After finding out the country, Partner A then asks for a more specific location within the country. With your partner, repeat this dialogue three times non-stop, each time substituting new locations. In selecting a country, Partner B must be sure that in the next answer he/she can name a city within that country. Do this activity as quickly as possible, but do not sacrifice accuracy. Switch roles and repeat the activity.

A: Dochira-kara desu-ka?
B: **Nihon**-kara desu.
A: Aa, soo desu-ka? **Nihon**-no dochira-kara desu-ka?
B: **Tookyoo**-kara desu.

❷ Sono kuni-wa doko-ni arimasu-ka?

For this guessing game you will need a copy of a せかい ちず which both you and your partner can see. Partner A writes the name of one of the countries which appeared in Lesson 6 without showing Partner B the くにの なまえ. Partner B tries to find out the name of the country by asking the fewest questions possible. In this activity you may not ask questions about the language spoken in the country, but you may ask questions which include the names of continents or cardinal directions. Partner A must answer each

しつもん truthfully but should try to avoid giving away the answer. Record the number of questions your partner asked. For each round the person with the lower number wins.

SAMPLE EXCHANGE

B: Sono kuni-wa Minami Amerika-ni arimasu-ka?
A: Iie, arimasen.
B: Yooroppa-ni arimasu-ka?
A: Hai, arimasu.
B: Sono kuni-wa Suisu-no minami-ni arimasu-ka?
A: Iie, arimasen.
B: Suisu-no kita-ni arimasu-ka?
A: Hai, arimasu.
B: Doitsu desu-ka?
A: Iie, Doitsu ja nai desu.
B: Doitsu-no kita-ni arimasu-ka?
A: Hai, arimasu.
B: Sueeden desu-ka?
A: Hai, soo desu.

L. 7 電話で 話しましょう

れんしゅう A:　Where are they from?

| メーナ | アリー | ティモ | フェリッペ | リサ |
| (INDIA, Bombay) | (KENYA, Nairobi) | (FINLAND, Helsinki) | (MEXICO, Cancun) | (U.S.A., New York) |

れんしゅう B:　Where is Country X in relation to Country Y?

(1)

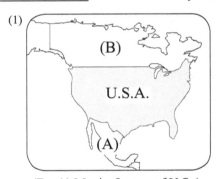

(Ex. A) Mexico? --> ~ of U.S.A.
(Ex. B) Canada? --> ~ of U.S.A.

(2)

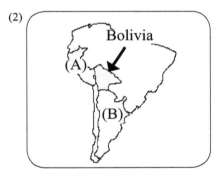

(A) Peru? --> ~ of Bolivia
(B) Argentina?
　　　(Aruzenchin) --> ~ of Bolivia

(3)

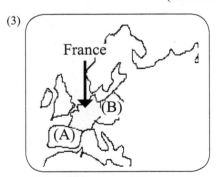

(A) Spain? --> ~ of France
(B) Germany? --> ~ of France

れんしゅう C: Association Game--What country is it?

れんしゅう D: Interview your classmate!

You have recently won a contest prize of $10,000 and took a trip to the country of your dreams. Answer your classmates' questions. USE YOUR IMAGINATION!

Europe   South America   Asia   Africa

can speak the language?

when?

with whom?

went shopping?

did what?

weather?

LESSON 8
Geography

At the end of this lesson you will be able to:
- ☑ Identify certain natural features
- ☑ Identify principal geographic features of Japan
- ☑ Read the *kanji*: 木　本　人　山　川

Words

shima	island
yama	mountain
kawa	river
mizuumi	lake
umi	ocean, sea

Other words and expressions you will hear in this lesson

tsuaa gaido	tour guide
meetoru	meter (unit of measure)

THE FOUR MAIN ISLANDS OF JAPAN		
Hokkaidoo	ほっかいどう	北海道
Honshuu	ほんしゅう	本州
Shikoku	しこく	四国
Kyuushuu	きゅうしゅう	九州

Japan – an island nation 日本
Japan is an archipelago located off the east coast of the Asian mainland. It consists of four main islands and approximately 4,000 smaller ones. Going from northeast to southwest are the islands of Hokkaidoo, Honshuu, Shikoku, and Kyuushuu. From the northern tip of Hokkaidoo to the southernmost point south of Okinawa is approximately 3,000 km (1,850 miles).

Fuji-san 富士山
Approximately 70% of Japan is mountainous. The most famous and the tallest of all mountains in Japan is *Fuji-san* (Mt. Fuji). *San* is the *on-yomi* (reading derived from Chinese) of the *kanji* 山 (mountain). *Fuji-san* is a snow-capped volcano that rises dramatically from close to sea level at its base to 3,776 meters (12,388 feet). Visible from many places in Tokyo when the air is clear, *Fuji-san* has not erupted since 1707. The mountain has figured prominently over the centuries in Japanese literature and art. Still regarded by many Japanese as being sacred, *Fuji-san* is climbed every year by several hundred thousand people.

Biwa-ko 琵琶湖
Biwa-ko is located to the east of the ancient capital city of Kyoto. By far the largest fresh water lake in Japan, *Biwa-ko* covers 268 square miles. *Biwa-ko*'s name is derived from its shape which is similar to that of a *biwa*, a traditional Japanese stringed instrument. The final syllable *-ko* is the *on-yomi* for the *kanji* for *lake*. *Biwa-ko* has long been an important source of water for the surrounding agricultural areas and in recent years has

become a critical source of drinking water for major cities such as Kyoto. Agricultural and industrial pollution of the lake are issues of grave importance to the surrounding area as more and more people become dependent on the lake as a water source.

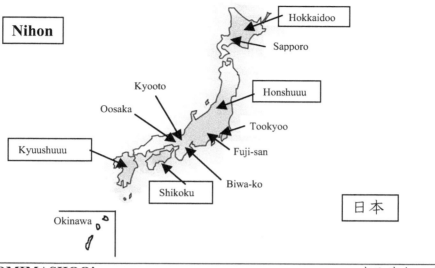

YOMIMASHOO! よみましょう

しま	island
やま (山)	mountain
かわ (川)	river
みずうみ	lake
うみ	ocean, sea
いちばん おおきい しま です。	It's the biggest island.
いちばん きれいな やま です。	It's the most beautiful mountain.
ツアーガイド	tour guide
メートル	meter (unit of measure)

KANJI NOTES かんじノート

In this lesson you will learn to read five *kanji*: 木, 本, 人, 山, and 川. Be sure that you know the readings of each *kanji* and can tell what the *kanji* means. Readings which are marked by an asterisk are for your reference only; you do not need to learn these at this time. You also do not have to learn any new words which are given in the examples. In Lesson 11 you will learn how to write the *kanji* 木, 本, and 人 using the correct stroke order. Information on the correct stroke order for the *kanji* 山 and 川 is given in the Optional Writing Practice section.

> **WRITING *KANJI***
>
> In future lessons you will learn how to write these *kanji* and many more using the correct stroke order. The Writing Practice sections will help you to form the *kanji* correctly from the very beginning so that you continue to develop good writing habits in 日本ご.

MOKU, BOKU*; ki* [gi*] (tree, wood)

| 木曜日 | *moku*-yoobi | Thursday |
| 木 | *ki* | tree |

| 木はありません。 | *Ki*-wa arimasen. | There aren't any trees. |
| 木曜日にしました。 | *Moku*-yoobi-ni shimashita. | She did it on Thursday. |

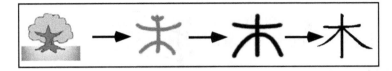

 HON [BON, PON], moto* (book, origin, source; counter *for long, narrow objects*)

本	*hon*	book
日本	Ni*hon*, Nip*pon*	Japan
一本	ip-*pon*	one (pencil, bottle, stick, etc.)
二本	ni-*hon*	two (pencils, bottles, sticks, etc.)
三本	san-*bon*	three (pencils, bottles, sticks, etc.)
山本	Yama*moto*	*family name* [mountain-origin/base]

日本人ですか。	Ni*hon*jin desu-ka?	Is he Japanese?
本がありますか。	*Hon*-ga arimasu-ka?	Are there any books?
一本下さい。	Ip-*pon* kudasai.	Please give me one.
三本下さい。	San-*bon* kudasai.	Please give me three.
日本語の本です。	Ni*hon*go-no *hon* desu.	It's a Japanese language book.

Notice that in the word 日本 (*Nihon*) the *kanji* 日 is pronounced *ni*. What are the more frequent readings for 日?

 NIN, JIN; hito, ~ri (person; *counter for people*)

人	*hito*	person
一人	hito*ri*	one person
二人	futa*ri*	two people
三人	san-*nin*	three people
六人	roku-*nin*	six people
アメリカ人	amerika-*jin*	American
日本人	nihon-*jin*	Japanese
女の人	onna-no *hito*	woman

| あの人は日本人ですか。 | Ano *hito*-wa nihon-*jin* desu-ka? (Is that person Japanese?) |

64

三人いますか。	San-*nin* imasu-ka?	
	(Are there three people?)	
この人の本ですよ。	Kono *hito*-no hon desu-yo.	
	(It's this person's book!)	
女の人が三人います。	Onna-no *hito*-ga san*nin* imasu.	
	(There are three women.)	

Notice that the *hito* in *hitori* is not related to the *hito* meaning *person*. In *hitori* and in *hitotsu* the *hito* means *one*.

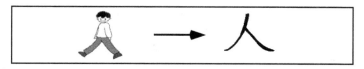

山 **SAN* [ZAN*]; yama** (mountain)

山	*yama*	mountain
富士山	Fuji-*san*	Mt. Fuji

山に行きました。	*Yama*-ni ikimashita.
	(We went to the mountains.)
富士山はきれい	Fuji-*san*-wa kirei desu-ne.
ですね。	(Mt. Fuji is beautiful, isn't it?)

川 **SEN*; kawa [gawa*]** (river)

川	*kawa*	river
川田	*Kawa*ta	*family name* [river-field]
山川	Yama*kawa*	*family name* [mountain-river]
中川	Naka*gawa*	*family name* [middle-river]

日本に川がたくさん	Nihon-ni *kawa*-ga takusan arimasu.
あります。	(There are many rivers in Japan.)
山川さんはいますか。	Yama*kawa*-san-wa imasu-ka?
	(Is Mr. Yamakawa there?)

KANJI IN LESSONS 7 AND 8

月　日　木　本　人　山　川

What do they mean?

INTERACTIVE ACTIVITIES

PART 1

❶ Doko-no kuni desu-ka? ✏

During this activity each student will work as a pair with two different クラスメート to check Assignment #1 from Part 2 of Lesson 7. The goal of the activity is to have two students carefully check your six sentences, mark and discuss with you any errors found, and sign off on your page. Form your first pair and exchange assignments with your partner. Both partners independently check and neatly mark errors for all six sentences. Do not correct errors. Use the editing symbols (see Workbook, Introduction). Return the assignments and go over the first sentence <u>together</u>. Correct your own work. Repeat this procedure for each sentence. Sign off on each other's page. Form new pairs and repeat these steps. After you have finished correcting your work, form pairs with different クラスメート, read each other's descriptions, and see if you can correctly answer the question どこの くに ですか.

❷ Vocabulary check

Silently review the vocabulary for Lesson 8. Then have a クラスメート orally test your knowledge of them. Your partner says the えいご, and you give the にほんご. Switch and test your partner.

PART 2

❶ Yomimashoo! 📄 & ✏

This pair activity provides you with an opportunity to review the five *kanji* which you have learned to read in Lessons 7 and 8. Partner A masks the *roomaji* side and reads the vocabulary in the left column in order. Partner B responds after each with either *Hai, soo desu* or *Iie, chigaimasu. Moo ichido yonde kudasai.* Partner A writes down those which need to be studied. Switch roles and repeat.

かなと かんじ	ローマじ
1. 木よう日	moku-yoobi
2. 本	hon
3. 日本	Nihon, Nippon
4. 日本ご	nihongo
5. 人	hito
6. 3人	san-nin
7. アメリカ人	amerika-jin
8. 日本人	nihon-jin
9. おんなの人	onna-no hito
10. 月よう日	getsu-yoobi
11. 1月	ichi-gatsu
12. 20日	hatsuka
13. なん月	nan-gatsu
14. 日よう日	nichi-yoobi
15. たんじょう日	tanjoobi
16. 14日	juu-yokka
17. 23日	ni-juu-san-nichi
18. 2日	futsuka
19. 3日	mikka

❷ Shima-wa doko-ni arimasu-ka?

Do this activity with a partner. Both クラスメート look at the diagrams below. Take turns selecting one of the diagrams and making a true/false statement about the relative location of the various natural features and the town. Every statement should include a cardinal direction. Your partner will correct any false statements. Study the examples before you begin.

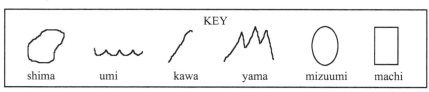

KEY

shima   umi   kawa   yama   mizuumi   machi

EXAMPLES

A: Shima-wa yama-no higashi-ni arimasu.
B: Soo desu-ne.

A: Machi-wa kawa-no kita-ni arimasu.
B: Iie, chigaimasu. Kawa-no minami-ni arimasu.

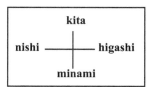

1.

2.

3.

4.

5.

6.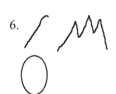

Dialects

The Japanese language includes a number of regional dialects. Some dialects differ from one another based on their verb endings. Sometimes the difference can be much greater, such as the phrase おおきに which means "thank you" in the Kyoto dialect. Dialects are typically named after the region in which they are used. Hence, Osaka dialect is referred to as Osaka-*ben* (大阪弁) and Nagoya dialect is called Nagoya-*ben* (名古屋弁). *Hyoojun-go* (標準語), standard Japanese, is understood by all native speakers – not always the case with the various dialects of Japan. Some people jokingly say that speaking or understanding such-and-such a dialect in Japan is like knowing another foreign language!

れんしゅう A: What did you do over summer break?

> Your telephone teacher wants to know what you did over summer break.
> Answer his/her questions.

れんしゅう B: Natural Features

(1)
(2)

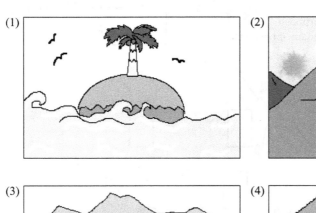

(3)
(4)

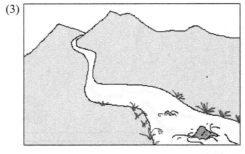

(5)

れんしゅう C: Town Map

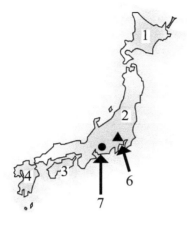

Honshuu　Hokkaidoo
Shikoku　Fuji-san
Kyuushuu　Okinawa
Biwa-ko

れんしゅう D: Jessica's Letter

4月2日 (日よう日)

　きのうは あねのたんじょう日でした。うちで パーティーを
しました。あしたは すうがくのテストが あります。
すうがくは あんまり すきじゃないです。木よう日は 日本ごの
テストが あります。日本ごは おもしろいですけど、ちょっと
むずかしいです。

ジェシカ

しつもん: (Answer in English.)

(1) What date is Jessica's older sister's birthday?

(2) Which day of the week will she have a math test?

(3) What test does she have on Thursday?

(4) What does she think about the Japanese language?

69

LESSON 9
Describing with Superlatives

OBJECTIVES　　　　　　　　　　　　　　　　　もくひょう

At the end of this lesson you will be able to:

☑ Describe people, places, and objects using the superlative
☑ Read the *kanji*: 大 and 小

VOCABULARY　　　　　　　　　　　　　　　　　たんご

Words

nagai	long
takai	high, tall, expensive
ichiban	the most ~ ; the ~est (*with adjectives*)

Other words and expressions you will hear in this lesson

fiito	feet
nan-fiito	how many feet?
mairu	mile
nan-mairu	how many miles?

KEY GRAMMAR POINTS　　　　　　　　　　　ぶんぽうポイント

1. Ichiban + adjective

The word *ichiban*, which literally means *number one*, is used immediately preceding adjectives to form the superlative. In English the superlative is formed with *-est* or *most*.

Ichiban chikai machi desu.	It is *the closest* town.
Kono bideo-wa *ichiban tsumaranai* desu.	This video is *the most boring*.
Ichiban tsumaranai jugyoo deshita.	It was *the most boring* class.
Ichiban nagai kawa-wa nan* desu-ka?	What is *the longest* river?
Antonio-kun-wa *ichiban kakkoii* hito desu.	Antonio is *the coolest* person.

2. *Place/category*-de ichiban + adjective + *noun* desu.

Use this pattern if you want to say that a particular NOUN is the biggest, the longest, the most beautiful, or some other superlative of all of the items or people in a certain place or category. The particle *-de* follows the place or the category. Study these examples carefully.

Sekai-*de* ichiban ookii kuni desu.	It's the biggest country *in* the world.
Nihon-*de* ichiban ookii mizuumi-wa nan* desu-ka?	What is the biggest lake *in* Japan?
Amerika-*de* ichiban nagai kawa-wa Mishishippi-gawa desu-ka?	Is the longest river *in* the U.S. the Mississippi River?

* The word *doko* can be used instead of *nan* in sentences such as these. *Doko* expresses the idea of *which place* or *where*.

YOMIMASHOO!　　　　　　　　　　　　　　　よみましょう

ながい	long
たかい	high, tall, expensive
いちばん	the most ~ ; the ~est (*with adjectives*)
いちばん ちかい	the closest
いちばん つまらない	the most boring
いちばん つまらない じゅぎょう	the most boring class

せかいで いちばん おおきい くに	the biggest country in the world
フィート	feet
なんフィート	how many feet?
マイル	mile
なんマイル	how many miles?

KANJI NOTES かんじノート

In this lesson you will learn to read two *kanji*: 大 and 小. Be sure that you know the readings of each *kanji* and can tell what the *kanji* means. Readings which are marked by an asterisk are for your reference only; you do not need to learn these at this time. You also do not have to learn any new words which are given in the examples. In Lesson 12 you will learn how to write these *kanji* using the correct stroke order.

 DAI, TAI*; oo(kii) (big, large, great)

大きい	*oo*kii	big, large
大学	*dai*gaku	university, college
大好き	*dai*suki	very pleasing, like a lot
大阪	*Oo*saka	*city name* [big slope]

この大学は大きいです。	Kono *dai*gaku-wa *oo*kii desu.
	(This university is big.)
日本の大学ですか。	Nihon-no *dai*gaku desu-ka?
	(Is it a Japanese university?)
それが大好きです。	Sore-ga *dai*suki desu.
	(I really like that one.)
ハンバーガーが大好きです。	Hanbaagaa-ga *dai*suki desu.
	(I like hamburgers a lot.)

Notice that the *kanji* 大 is used for the *oo* part of the word *ookii*. The rest of the word is written with the *hiragana* きい. When *hiragana* are used in this way, they are referred to as *okurigana*.

 SHOO, ko*, o*, chii(sai) (small, little)

小さい	*chii*sai	small, little
小学校	*shoo*gakkoo	elementary school
小屋	*ko*ya	shed
小川	*o*gawa	stream [little river]

小さいバナナですね。	*Chii*sai banana desu-ne.
	(It's a small banana, isn't it?)
小学校はどこですか。	*Shoo*gakkoo-wa doko desu-ka?
	(Where's the elementary school?)
あの家の後ろに小屋が	Ano uchi-no ushiro-ni *ko*ya-ga arimasu.
あります。	(There is a shed behind that house over there.)

71

Notice that the *kanji* 小 is used only for the *chii* part of the word *chiisai*. The rest of the word is written with the *hiragana* さい. What do you call *hiragana* which are used in this way?

INTERACTIVE ACTIVITIES

PART 1

❶ **Adjective review**

Silently review the adjectives below. Then have a クラスメート orally test your knowledge of them. Your partner says the えいご, and you give the 日本ご. Switch and test your partner.

ADJECTIVES			
I-adjectives			
furui	old	ookii	big
chiisai	small	hayai	fast, early
osoi	slow, late	isogashii	busy
oishii	delicious	tanoshii	pleasant, fun
tsumaranai	boring	muzukashii	difficult
omoshiroi	interesting	urusai	noisy
samui	cold	atsui	hot
kawaii	cute	takai	expensive, high
tooi	far	yasui	cheap, inexpensive
chikai	near, close	kakkoii	cool, neat
atarashii	new	nagai	long
Na-adjectives			
dame	bad, worthless	kantan	easy, simple
suki	pleasing	joozu	skilled
heta	unskilled	shizuka	quiet
iya	bad, terrible	kirei	pretty
hen	strange		

❷ **Sono eiga-wa . . . ichiban tsumaranai desu.**

In this pair activity one person begins a sentence, and the other must complete it using a superlative adjective. The sentence must be grammatically correct and make sense. Take turns. Below are some words to get you started, but do not limit yourself to these.

Examples

A: Kono shitsumon-wa . . .　➔　B: Kono shitsumon-wa *ichiban kantan* desu.
A: Tomu-san-no paatii-wa . . .　➔　B: Tomu-san-no paatii-wa *ichiban tanoshii* desu.

shitsumon	inu	hito	hikooki	fuyu	yama
fuku	machi	hon	shatsu	natsu	mizuumi
tenki	ongaku	kuruma	booshi	shima	gakkoo
hanbaagaa	jugyoo	depaato	kutsu	kawa	paatii

❶ Ichiban takai yama-wa nan desu-ka? 📄 & ✏️

Use your imagination in this pair activity. Partner A is an expert on ア の く に, a small country in the equatorial region of Africa whereas Partner B is an authority on カ の く に, an equally small nation in southern Asia. Sharing an interest in superlatives, you are asking each other questions about the two countries to find out what the highest mountain is, the longest river, the oldest city, etc. The names of places (and of many other things as well) in both languages consist of single syllables which means they are all represented in Japanese as single *katakana*.

Before you begin this activity, write down the "correct" answer for each of the 10 sections (*yama, kawa, machi,* etc.) which correspond to the country on which you are an expert. Do not show your partner. Then take turns asking and answering questions using the following pattern. The appropriate adjective (*takai, nagai, furui,* etc.) is given for each section.

    A: **Kanokuni**-de ichiban **takai yama**-wa nan desu-ka?
    B: ____ desu.

Ask about the sections in mixed order so that the same question is not asked twice in a row. Write down the answer which your partner tells you. When you have finished, compare your answers.

NOTE: Refer to your *Katakana* Chart if you are unsure of any of the *katakana*.

		アのくに				カのくに			
yama	takai	1. コ	2. ニ	3. ア	4. ユ	1. ス	2. イ	3. ハ	4. ラ
kawa	nagai	1. タ	2. ウ	3. ヘ	4. リ	1. ケ	2. ル	3. エ	4. ミ
mizuumi	kirei (na)	1. マ	2. レ	3. ト	4. ン	1. テ	2. ロ	3. ワ	4. モ
shima	chiisai	1. ア	2. パ	3. ノ	4. ス	1. ウ	2. ヨ	3. イ	4. コ
machi	furui	1. ナ	2. ヤ	3. ソ	4. ポ	1. カ	2. ピ	3. オ	4. ニ
machi	urusai	1. ラ	2. プ	3. テ	4. ツ	1. ギ	2. ツ	3. メ	4. リ
machi	shizuka (na)	1. イ	2. モ	3. ホ	4. ド	1. ヒ	2. ガ	3. ズ	4. エ
daigaku	ookii	1. フ	2. カ	3. サ	4. メ	1. ク	2. マ	3. レ	4. ア
tabemono	oishii	1. オ	2. ウ	3. ヌ	4. ル	1. ト	2. シ	3. ム	4. ナ
fuku	hen (na)	1. キ	2. ヨ	3. ワ	4. ロ	1. ペ	2. ネ	3. セ	4. マ

❷ Yomimashoo! 📄 & ✏️

This pair activity provides you with an opportunity to review the seven *kanji* which you have learned to read in Lessons 7-9. Partner A masks the *roomaji* side and reads the words in the left column in order. Partner B responds after each with either *Hai, soo desu* or *Iie, chigaimasu. Moo ichido yonde kudasai.* Partner A writes down those which need to be studied. Switch roles and repeat.

かなとかんじ	ローマじ
1. 小さい	chiisai
2. 日本ごの本	nihongo-no hon
3. 2日	futsuka
4. なん月	nan-gatsu
5. 日本	Nihon, Nippon
6. 小がっこう	shoogakkoo
7. 大すき	daisuki
8. 月よう日	getsu-yoobi
9. 3人	san-nin
10. アメリカ人	amerika-jin

かなと かんじ	ローマじ
11. たんじょう日	tanjoobi
12. おんなの人	onna-no hito
13. 大がく	daigaku
14. 木よう日	moku-yoobi
15. 日本人	nihon-jin
16. 日よう日	nichi-yoobi
17. 1月	ichi-gatsu
18. 23日	ni-juu-san-nichi
19. 大きい	ookii

L. 9 電話で 話しましょう

れんしゅう A: Which one is the most ~?

(1)   (a) cheap   (b) new

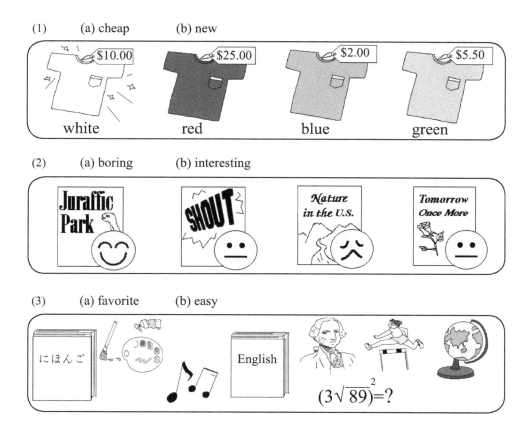

| $10.00 | $25.00 | $2.00 | $5.50 |
| white | red | blue | green |

(2)   (a) boring   (b) interesting

Juraffic Park

SHOUT

Nature in the U.S.

Tomorrow Once More

(3)   (a) favorite   (b) easy

にほんご

English

$(3\sqrt{89})^2 = ?$

れんしゅう B: What is the ~est ~ in ~?

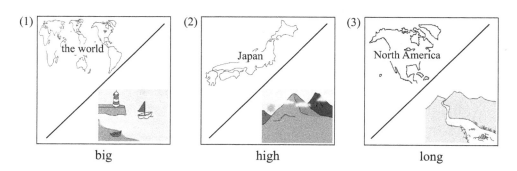

(1) the world — big

(2) Japan — high

(3) North America — long

(4)
South America

long

(5)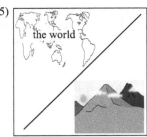
the world

high

(6)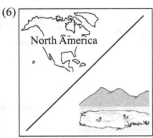
North America

big

れんしゅう C: Where are you from?

(1)

Name:
Savas Kuhl

(a) Country: Turkey *(Toruko)*

(b) City: Istanbul

(c) Location of the country:
East of Greece *(Girisha)*

(d) Languages: Turkish & Chinese

(2)
Name:
Imelda Jagora

(a) Country: Philippines *(Firipin)*

(b) City: Manila

(c) Location of the country:
South of Taiwan

(d) Languages: Tagalog & English

(3)

Name:
José Hernandez

(a) Country: Chile *(Chiri)*

(b) City: Santiago

(c) Location of the country:
West of Argentina *(Aruzenchin)*

(d) Languages: Spanish & French

(4)

Name:
Jastin Mandera

(a) Country: Kenya

(b) City: Nairobi

(c) Location of the country:
North of Tanzania

(d) Languages: English & Swahili

LESSON 10
Telling How Long One Has Done Something

OBJECTIVES　　　　　　　　　　　　　　もくひょう

At the end of this lesson you will be able to:
- ☑ Ask and tell how long one has done something
- ☑ Ask someone to speak slowly
- ☑ Give and receive compliments appropriately
- ☑ Write the *kanji*: 月 and 日

VOCABULARY　　　　　　　　　　　　　　たんご

Words

gaikokugo	foreign language
mada	not yet, still
yukkuri	slowly, leisurely
oshieru (oshiemasu/oshiete)	teach

Phrases and expressions

dore-gurai	how long
atama-ga ii	smart, intelligent
nan-nen-kan	how many years
_____-kan dake	only (a period of time)
Moo ichido yukkuri itte kudasai.	Please say it again slowly.

> Beginning with this lesson, all new verbs in the Vocabulary section will be listed with three important forms: the plain form, the *-masu* form, and the *-te* form.

VOCABULARY NOTES　　　　　　　　　　たんごノート

1. Atama-ga ii

This expression, which literally means *the head is good*, is usually translated in English as *smart*. As in the case of most compliments, the recipient should respond in the negative.

Atama-ga ii desu-ne.	You're smart, aren't you?
Iie, yokunai desu-yo.	No, I'm not smart.

2. Oshiete kudasai.

The verb *oshieru* has a wider range of use than its English counterpart *teach*. In addition to the action performed by teachers, *oshieru* can mean *inform, tell,* or *explain*.

Supeingo-o chotto *oshiete* kudasai.	Please *teach* me a little bit of Spanish.
Denwa bangoo-o *oshiete* kudasai.	Please *tell* me your phone number.

KEY GRAMMAR POINTS　　　　　　　　ぶんぽうポイント

Dore-gurai

If you want to ask *How long?* without specifying hours (*Nan-jikan?*), years (*Nan-nen-kan?*), or some other unit of time, use *dore-gurai*.

Dore-gurai benkyoo-o shimashita-ka?	*How long* did you study?
Dore-gurai arubaito-o shimashita-ka?	*How long* did you work at a part-time job?

がいこくご	foreign language
まだ	not yet, still
ゆっくり	slowly, leisurely
おしえる・おしえます・おしえて	teach
どれぐらい	how long
あたまが いい	smart, intelligent
なんじかんぐらい	about how many hours
なんねんかん	how many years
にねんかん	(a period of) two years
いちねんかん だけ	only one year
なんねんから なんねんまで	from what year to what year
どれぐらい べんきょうを しましたか。	How long did you study?
もう いちど ゆっくり いって ください。	Please say it again slowly.

CULTURE NOTES　　　　　　　　　　　　　　　カルチャーノート

Compliments

As you have already learned in this course, the culturally appropriate Japanese response to a compliment is to deny it. Remember this when you receive a compliment from a Japanese on your excellent command of the Japanese language.

Nihon-jin: Nihongo-ga joozu desu-ne.　　　　Your Japanese is excellent.
Foreigner: Iie, mada heta desu-yo.　　　　　No, it's still poor.

You can also respond with *Iie, mada dame desu*.

KANJI NOTES　　　　　　　　　　　　　　　　　かんじノート

Writing *kanji*

In this lesson you will begin writing *kanji*. As in the case of *hiragana* and *katakana*, each *kanji* has a prescribed stroke order. As you practice writing the *kanji*, it is important that you derive as much benefit as possible from this exercise. Avoid operating in an automatic, mechanical mode. Instead, try to focus on each *kanji*. Say the readings (for which you are responsible) before and after writing each *kanji*. Think about the meaning. Count the strokes as you make them: *ichi, ni, san, shi* . . . You will be pleased with how this strategy helps you learn the *kanji*.

INTERACTIVE ACTIVITIES

PART 1

❶ Kakimashoo!

During this activity each student will work as a pair with two different クラスメート to check Assignment #1 from Part 2 of Lesson 9. The goal of the activity is to have two students carefully check your five sentences, mark and discuss with you any errors found, and sign off on your page. Form your first pair and exchange assignments with your partner. Both partners independently check and neatly mark errors for all five sentences. Do not correct errors. Use the editing symbols (see Workbook, Introduction). Return the assignments and go over the first sentence <u>together</u>. Correct your own work. Repeat this procedure for each sentence. Sign off on each other's page. Form new pairs and repeat these steps.

❷ **Vocabulary check**

Silently review the vocabulary for Lesson 10. Then have a クラスメート orally test your knowledge of them. Your partner says the えいご, and you give the 日本ご. Switch and test your partner.

PART 2

---

❶ **Dialogue**

Practice this dialogue with a partner. Follow the normal procedure for learning the dialogue. Remember to read each line to yourself and then look up and speak to your partner. After you have memorized the dialogue, perform it for another pair.

Two university students have just met each other. Student A is Japanese, and Student B is an American. Student A is impressed with Student B's proficiency in Japanese.

A: Nihongo-ga joozu desu-ne.
B: Iie, mada heta desu-yo.
A: (*earnestly*) Iie, joozu desu-yo. Doko-de benkyoo-o shimashita-ka?
B: Amerika Daigaku-de . . .
A: Aa, Amerika Daigaku-de . . . Dore-gurai benkyoo-o shimashita-ka?
B: Ichi-nen-kan benkyoo-o shimashita.
A: (*surprised*) E? Ichi-nen-kan dake?
B: Hai.

❷ **Yomimashoo!**

Form 3人のグループ. A and B read the dialogue below while C provides any needed assistance. Only student C can look at the *roomaji* version of the dialogue above.

A: 日本ごが じょうず ですね。
B: いいえ、まだ へた ですよ。
A: いいえ、じょうず ですよ。どこで べんきょうを しましたか。
B: アメリカ 大がくで...
A: ああ、アメリカ 大がくで...どれぐらい べんきょうを しましたか。
B: いちねんかん べんきょうを しました。
A: え？いちねんかん だけ？
B: はい。

Now take turns in pairs reading the following sentences. The partner who is reading looks only at the Japanese script. The partner who is prompting may look at the *roomaji* version also.

いちじかん だけ？	Ichi-ji-kan dake?
にほんごが 大すき です。	Nihongo-ga daisuki desu.
どこで べんきょうを しましたか。	Doko-de benkyoo-o shimashita-ka?
いいえ、まだ へた ですよ。	Iie, mada heta desu-yo.
どれぐらい べんきょうを しましたか。	Dore-gurai benkyoo-o shimashita-ka?
日本ごが じょうず ですね。	Nihongo-ga joozu desu-ne.

L.10 電話で 話しましょう

れんしゅう A: How long did you study ~?

(1) Si ganará más, compraria un coche nuevo.

ヘンリー
Spanish / 2 years

(2) Wichtigster Tag des Karnevals in Köln ist der Resenmontag.

グローリア
German / 3 years

(3) 我家只有我一个孩子。

ジェームス
Chinese / 4 years

(4) YOU

한국관
¿Como estás? Bon jour
好好
Wie geht es Ihnen?

?

しつもん:
(a) What language did ~ study?
(b) About how long?

れんしゅう B: Let's converse!

Dialogue:

A and B chat on a park bench.

A: Your <u>Japanese</u> is very good!
B: No, it's still bad.
A: No, it's really good! Where did you study?
B: At <u>Boston University</u>.
A: Wow! For how long?
B: I studied for <u>two years</u>.
A: Wow...that's great!

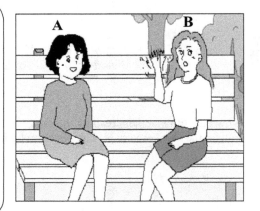

Sample Dialogue:

A: <u>Nihongo</u>-ga joozu desu-ne.
B: Iie, mada heta desu-yo.
A: Soo desu-ka? Joozu desu-yo. Doko-de benkyoo-o shimashita-ka?
B: <u>Bosuton Daigaku</u>-de shimashita.
A: Hee, dore-gurai benkyoo-o shimashita-ka?
B: <u>Ni-nen-kan</u> shimashita.
A: Hee, sugoi desu-ne!

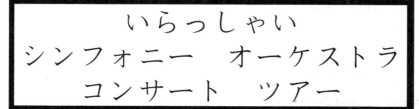

チケット

せき (seat)

S 席: ￥13,000

A 席: ￥8,500

B 席: ￥5,000

ショー
(7:30 ～ 10:00 pm)

★ 1月2日 (火) ～
　　5日 (金):
とうきょう
東京

★ 1月8日 ～ 11日:
なごや
名古屋

★ 2月17日 (土) ～
　　21日 (水):
おおさか
大阪

★ 3月12日 ～ 13日:
ふくおか
福岡

LESSON 11
Current Activities

OBJECTIVES

もくひょう

At the end of this lesson you will be able to:
- ☑ Talk about what someone is doing now
- ☑ Write the *kanji*: 木　本　人

VOCABULARY

たんご

Phrases and expressions

jibun-de　　　　　　　　　　　by oneself, alone, without the help of others

KEY GRAMMAR POINTS

ぶんぽうポイント

1. Learning the *-te* form

Beginning with Lesson 10, all new verbs in the Vocabulary section are listed with three important forms: the plain form, the *-masu* form, and the *-te* form. Some of the best ways to learn to recognize and produce the *-te* forms of different verbs are to listen carefully to your *sensei*, review the Vocabulary sections on a regular basis, and to complete all of the Interactive Activities in your text. Later in your study of 日本ご you may wish to learn the set of rules for making the *-te* form. The *-te* forms for some of the verbs you have learned are given below.

	VERBS IN THE *-TE* FORM*			
	-masu form	plain form	*-te* form	English
-ru Verbs:	mimasu	mi ru ------>	mite	look at, see
	tabemasu	tabe ru ------>	tabete	eat
	okimasu	oki ru ------>	okite	get up
	nemasu	ne ru ------>	nete	go to bed
	oshiemasu	oshie ru ------>	oshiete	teach
-u Verbs:	kakimasu	ka ku ------>	kaite	write
	ikimasu	i ku ------>	itte	go
	kikimasu	ki ku ------>	kiite	listen
	hanashimasu	hana su ------>	hanashite	speak
	nomimasu	no mu ------>	nonde	drink
	kaerimasu	kae ru ------>	kaette	return
	iimasu	i u ------>	itte	say
	kaimasu	ka u ------>	katte	buy
Irregular Verbs:	kimasu	k uru ------>	kite	come
	shimasu	s uru ------>	shite	do

* See Appendix for explanation of rules of the *-te* formation of verbs.

2. Using the *-te* form + *kudasai* to express polite commands

The *-te* **form** is a commonly occurring Japanese verb form which ends in て (*te*) or で (*de*). It can be used in many different patterns in Japanese, including polite commands with *kudasai*.

Namae-o *kaite* kudasai.	Please *write* your name.
Bideo-o *mite* kudasai.	Please *look* at the video.
Shukudai-o *shite* kudasai.	Please *do* your homework.
Moo ichido *itte* kudasai.	Please *say* it again.

Kiite kudasai.   Please *listen*.
Kore-o *yonde* kudasai.   Please *read* this.
In this book you will learn the *-te* form of many different verbs and how to use the *-te*
form in a number of important patterns, including the one introduced in this lesson.

3. Using the *-te* form + *imasu* to express continuous actions

This lesson introduces one important use of the *-te* form. By using the *-te* form with the
verb *imasu* you can express actions which are taking place at the same time you are
speaking. This verb tense is sometimes referred to in English as the **present progressive**
or **present continuous** since it describes actions that are in progress. In English the *-te*
-imasu form is expressed as *am/is/are . . . ing*. Study these examples carefully.

Ima shigoto-o shi*te-imasu*.	I *am* work*ing* now.
Terebi-o mi*te-imasu*.	She *is* watch*ing* television.
Gakusei-wa ima benkyoo-o shi*te-imasu*.	The students *are* study*ing* now.
Ano hito-wa nani-o shi*te-imasu*-ka?	What *is* that person do*ing*?
Ima hon-o yon*de-imasu*.	He *is* read*ing* a book now.

```
      -te-imasu  =  am/is/are . . . ing

  tabete-imasu  =  am/is/are eating
```

YOMIMASHOO!   よみましょう

じぶんで	by oneself, alone, without help
なにごが できますか。	What languages do you speak?
どこで べんきょうを しましたか。	Where did you study?
じぶんで べんきょうを しました。	I studied by myself (with no help).
あの人は なにを していますか。	What is that person doing?
がくせいは いま べんきょうを	The students are studying now.
しています。	

KANJI NOTES   かんじノート

As you practice writing the *kanji* in the Writing Practice section of this lesson, remember
to use the correct stroke order. Say the readings for each *kanji* before and after writing it.
As you are writing each *kanji*, count the strokes as you make them: *ichi, ni, san, shi,
go . . .* These simple strategies will help you to remember more easily how to read and
write the *kanji*.

INTERACTIVE ACTIVITIES

PART 1

❶ Itte kudasai.   📄 & ✏

Silently review the *-te* form of the verbs given in the box in the *Bunpoo Pointo* section of
this lesson. Then have a クラスメート orally test your knowledge of the verbs. Your
partner says the *-masu* form and the plain form. Then you say the *-te* form. Your partner
will tell you whether or not you are correct. After every five or six verbs switch and test
your partner. Write down the verbs you need to study some more. Read this sample
exchange aloud with your partner before you begin.

SAMPLE EXCHANGE

A: Mimasu. Miru.

B: Mite.

A: Hai, soo desu. Tabemasu. Taberu.

B: Tabette.

A: Chotto chigaimasu. Moo ichido doozo. Taberu.

B: Tabete.

A: Hai, soo desu. Okimasu. Okiru.

❷ Nani-o shite imasu-ka?

Form 3人のグループ. Student A mimes one of the verbs given in the box in the *Bunpoo Pointo* section of this lesson while asking *Nani-o shite-imasu-ka?* Students B and C watch without talking. Student A then counts いち、に、さん、し、ご、 and Students B and C say at the same time what they think the answer is (for example, *Yonde-imasu*). Student B goes next, followed by Student C.

PART 2

---

❶ Itte kudasai.

With a partner quickly quiz each other orally on the *-te* form of the verbs given in the box in the *Bunpoo Pointo* section of this lesson. You will need to know these in order to do the following activity.

❷ Tanaka-san-wa nani-o shite-imasu-ka?   📄 & ✏️

In this pair activity you will take turns asking your partner questions to determine what the individuals in the chart are doing right now. Look only at your chart. (Partner B's chart is on the next page.) The beginning of each answer is provided for you. Use the *-te* form + *imasu* of the verb given in the parentheses, and be sure to use the correct particles (*-wa, -o, -to, -ni*). Challenge yourself to use only Japanese during this entire activity. Compare your completed charts to check your accuracy.

SAMPLE EXCHANGE

A: Tanaka-san-**wa** ima nani-o shite-imasu-ka?

B: Yakyuu-**o shite-imasu**.

PARTNER A

DARE?	IMA NANI-O SHITE-IMASU-KA?	
Tanaka-san	Yakyuu-**o shite-imasu**.	(suru)
Watanabe-san		
Kenji-kun	Shukudai	(suru)
Tomoko-chan		
Itoo-sensei	Terebi	(miru)
Amanda-san		
Yamaguchi-san	Tomodachi	(hanasu)
Katsumi-san		
Kurisu-kun	Hanbaagaa	(taberu)
Kawakami-san		
Tanigawa-san		
Yamada-san	Uta	(utau)
Sasaki-sensei	Nihongo	(oshieru)

SAMPLE EXCHANGE

A: Tanaka-san-**wa** ima nani-o shite-imasu-ka?

B: Yakyuu-**o shite-imasu**.

PARTNER B

DARE?	IMA NANI-O SHITE-IMASU-KA?	
Tanaka-san	Yakyuu-**o shite-imasu**.	(suru)
Watanabe-san	Hon	(yomu)
Kenji-kun		
Tomoko-chan	Pan	(taberu)
Itoo-sensei		
Amanda-san	Ongaku	(kiku)
Yamaguchi-san		
Katsumi-san	Kanji	(kaku)
Kurisu-kun		
Kawakami-san	Koohii	(nomu)
Tanigawa-san	Fuku	(kau)
Yamada-san		
Sasaki-sensei		

ふくしゅう: *Te*-form Conjugation

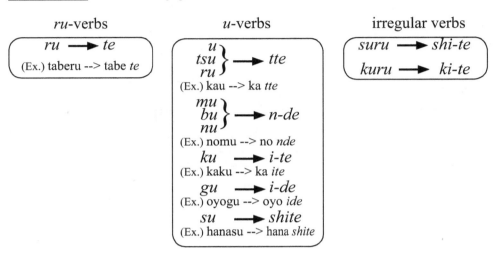

ru-verbs	*u*-verbs	irregular verbs

ru-verbs

ru ⟶ *te*

(Ex.) taberu --> tabe *te*

u-verbs

$\left.\begin{matrix} u \\ tsu \\ ru \end{matrix}\right\}$ ⟶ *tte*

(Ex.) kau --> ka *tte*

$\left.\begin{matrix} mu \\ bu \\ nu \end{matrix}\right\}$ ⟶ *n-de*

(Ex.) nomu --> no *nde*

ku ⟶ *i-te*

(Ex.) kaku --> ka *ite*

gu ⟶ *i-de*

(Ex.) oyogu --> oyo *ide*

su ⟶ *shite*

(Ex.) hanasu --> hana *shite*

irregular verbs

suru ⟶ *shi-te*

kuru ⟶ *ki-te*

れんしゅう A: What are they doing?

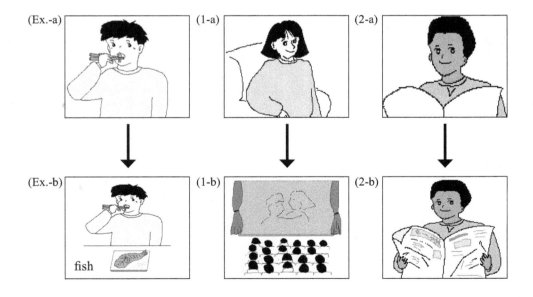

(Ex.-a)　(1-a)　(2-a)

(Ex.-b) fish　(1-b)　(2-b)

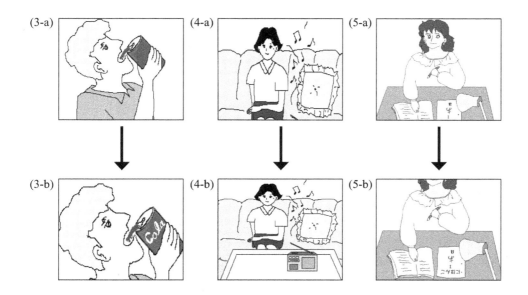

れんしゅう B: What are they doing at this party?

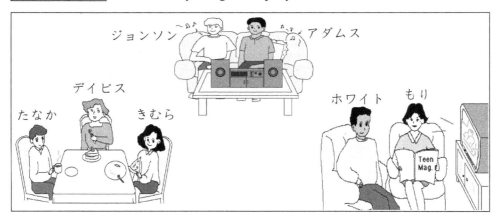

れんしゅう C: Geography Quiz

Game rule: After each question, only the person whom your telephone teacher calls on has the right to answer. If s/he cannot answer the question, a person from the other group gets the right to answer the question. The group that answers the most questions correctly wins.

87

LESSON 12
Talking about What Someone Was Doing

OBJECTIVES   もくひょう

At the end of this lesson you will be able to:
- ☑ Talk about what someone was doing at a certain time
- ☑ Write the *kanji*: 大 and 小

VOCABULARY   たんご

Phrases and expressions

kinoo-no yoru   last night

KEY GRAMMAR POINTS   ぶんぽうポイント

Using the *-te* form + *imashita* to express past continuous actions
This lesson introduces another important use of the *-te* form. By using the *-te* form with
the verb *imashita* (the past tense of *imasu*), you can express actions which were taking
place at some time in the past. This verb tense is sometimes referred to in English as the
past progressive or **past continuous** since it describes actions that were in progress in
the past. The *-te-imashita* form is expressed in English as *was/were . . . ing*. Study these
examples carefully.

Roku-ji-han-ni tabe*te-imashita*.	I *was* eat*ing* at 6:30.
Kinoo 3-ji-ni nani-o shi*te-imashita*-ka?	What *were* you do*ing* at 3:00 yesterday?
Doko-de benkyoo-o shi*te-imashita*-ka?	Where *were* you study*ing*?
Kinoo 10-ji-ni terebi-o mi*te-imashita*.	She *was* watch*ing* TV at 10:00 yesterday.
Shinbun-o yon*de-imashita*.	They *were* read*ing* the newspaper.

> **-te-imashita = was/were . . . ing**
>
> **tabete-imashita = was/were eating**

YOMIMASHOO!   よみましょう

きのうの よる	last night
きのう 3じに なにを していましたか。	What were you doing at 3:00 yesterday?
どこで べんきょうを していましたか。	Where were you studying?
きのう 10じに テレビを みていました。	She was watching TV at 10:00 yesterday.

KANJI NOTES   かんじノート

As you practice writing the *kanji* in the Writing Practice section of this lesson, remember
to use the correct stroke order. Say the readings for each *kanji* before and after writing it.
As you are writing each *kanji*, count the strokes as you make them: *ichi, ni, san, shi,
go . . .* These simple strategies will help you to remember more easily how to read and
write the *kanji*.

INTERACTIVE ACTIVITIES

PART 1

❶ Vocabulary review 📄 & ✏️

Silently review the words and phrases below (from Lessons 7-11). Then have a
クラスメート quiz you orally. Your partner says the えいご, and you give the 日本ご.
Switch and test your partner. Write down those you need to review later on your own.

kita	north
higashi	east
minami	south
nishi	west
Dochira-kara desu-ka?	Where are you from?
Nihon-no dochira-kara desu-ka?	Where in Japan are you from?
Kanada-wa Amerika-no kita-ni arimasu.	Canada is north of the U.S.
shima	island
yama	mountain
kawa	river
mizuumi	lake
umi	ocean, sea
nagai	long
takai	high, tall, expensive
ichiban	the most ~ ; the ~est (*with adjectives*)
ichiban tsumaranai jugyoo	the most boring class
sekai-de ichiban kirei-na kawa	the most beautiful river in the world
gaikokugo	foreign language
dore-gurai	how long?
mada	not yet, still
atama-ga ii	smart
yukkuri	slowly
oshieru (oshiemasu/oshiete)	teach
nan-ji-kan-gurai	about how many hours
nan-nen-kan	how many years
ni-nen-kan	(a period of) two years
nan-nen-kara nan-nen-made	from what year to what year
jibun-de	by oneself, alone, without the help of others

❷ Kinoo 4-ji-ni nani-o shite-imashita-ka?

Do this fluency activity with a クラスメート. Partner A asks the same question (*Kinoo
4-ji-ni nani-o shite-imashita-ka?*) five times in a row, substituting a different clock time
each time. Partner B must quickly respond with a different answer each time. Change
roles and repeat. With your partner read the sample exchange before you begin. Some
ideas for answers are given below, but do not limit yourself to these.

SAMPLE EXCHANGE

A: Kinoo 4-ji-ni nani-o shite-imashita-ka?
B: Shinbun-o yonde-imashita.
A: Kinoo 10-ji-ni nani-o shite-imashita-ka?
B: Tenisu-o shite-imashita.
A: Kinoo 6-ji-ni nani-o shite-imashita-ka?
B: Aisukuriimu-o tabete-imashita.
A: Kinoo 2-ji-ni nani-o shite-imashita-ka?
B: Kooen-de tomodachi-to hanashite-imashita.

NAN-JI-NI?			
1:00	ichi-ji	7:00	shichi-ji
2:00	ni-ji	8:00	hachi-ji
3:00	san-ji	9:00	ku-ji
4:00	yo-ji	10:00	juu-ji
5:00	go-ji	11:00	juu-ichi-ji
6:00	roku-ji	12:00	juu-ni-ji

89

MORE SAMPLE ANSWERS

Chiri-no benkyoo-o shite-imashita.
Depaato-de arubaito-o shite-imashita.
Tomodachi-no uchi-de uta-o utatte-imashita.

Kissaten-de koohii-o nonde-imashita.
Tomodachi-to geemu-o shite-imashita.
Uchi-de shukudai-o shite-imashita.

PART 2

❶ Taberu ~ tabete

Forms pairs. Quickly (a total of five minutes) quiz each other on the *-te* forms of these verbs.

VERBS IN THE *-TE* FORM			
plain form	***-te* form**	**plain form**	***-te* form**
miru	mite	taberu	tabete
kau	katte	neru	nete
oshieru	oshiete	kaku	kaite
kiku	kiite	yomu	yonde
hanasu	hanashite	nomu	nonde
suru	shite	utau	utatte

❷ Daigaku-de nani-o shite-imashita-ka?   📄 & ✏️

Play this game in a 4人のグループ. Two police detectives (Students A and C) are interrogating two suspects (Students B and D) who claim that they could not have robbed the First Federal Union Bank in Doodlesville on Monday evening because they were together in other locations doing various things. The object of the game is for the two suspects to prepare an alibi which is so solid that the police will release them. Follow the procedure below. Vocabulary and sample questions and answers are given after the charts.

PROCEDURE

1. The suspects (B and D) have <u>five</u> minutes to prepare an alibi which covers the three-hour period from 6:00 to 9:00 p.m. They were together the entire time. They were in <u>three</u> different locations doing something different in each place. They used <u>two</u> different means of transportation – one to go to the second location and one to go to the third location. The suspects may use the chart on the next page for planning, but they **may not use this chart or any other notes or materials during the interrogation. They must remember their alibi.**
2. As the suspects are preparing their alibi, the police detectives (A and C) practice the questions they are going to ask the suspects.
3. Detective A questions Suspect B at the same time that Detective C questions Suspect D. The two pairs should sit far enough apart that they cannot hear each other.
4. During the interrogation everyone should speak <u>only Japanese</u>.
5. Each detective records the suspect's responses.
6. The detectives compare the answers they have recorded. If the answers are the same, the suspects are free to leave the station. If the responses are at all different, arrest them!

PLANNING CHART FOR SUSPECTS ~ RECORDING CHART FOR DETECTIVES

NAN-JI-NI?	DOKO-NI/DE?	NANI-O SHITE-IMASHITA-KA?
6:00 - :		
: - :		
: - 9:00		

Means of transportation used: (1)   (2)

SAMPLE COMPLETED CHART

NAN-JI-NI?	DOKO-NI/DE?	NANI-O SHITE-IMASHITA-KA?
6:00 - 7:00	toshokan	shinbun-o yonde-imashita
7:15 - 8:00	kissaten	koohii-o nonde-imashita
8:15 - 9:00	Tomu-san-no uchi	terebi-o mite-imashita

Means of transportation used: (1) basu-de ikimashita   (2) aruite-ikimashita

VOCABULARY

NAN-JI-NI?			
6:00	roku-ji	7:00	shichi-ji
6:15	roku-ji juu-go-fun	8:00	hachi-ji
6:30	roku-ji-han	9:00	ku-ji
6:45	roku-ji yon-juu-go-fun		

DOKO-NI/DE?

resutoran	chuugakkoo	toshokan	uchi
kissaten	hon-ya	taiikukan	___-san-no uchi
daigaku	kooen	depaato	tomodachi-no uchi
gakkoo	eigakan	kutsu-ya	shinseki-no uchi
kookoo			

When you ask where someone <u>was</u>, use the particle -*ni*.
When you ask what someone <u>was doing</u> in a place, use -*de*.

NANI-O SHITE-IMASHITA-KA?

mite-imashita	(miru)	nonde-imashita	(nomu)
tabete-imashita	(taberu)	yonde-imashita	(yomu)
oshiete-imashita	(oshieru)	katte-imashita	(kau)
kaite-imashita	(kaku)	utatte-imashita	(utau)
kiite-imashita	(kiku)	shite-imashita	(suru)
hanashite-imashita	(hanasu)		

SAMPLE QUESTIONS AND ANSWERS (This interrogation goes with the Sample Chart above.)

A: **Roku**-ji-ni doko-ni imashita-ka?
Where were you at **6:00**?

B: **Toshokan**-ni imashita.
I was in the **library**.

A: **Toshokan**-de nani-o shite-imashita-ka?
What were you doing in the **library**?

B: **Shinbun-o yonde**-imashita.
I was **reading the newspaper**.

A: **Roku**-ji **yon-juu-go**-fun-ni doko-ni imashita-ka?
Where were you at **6:45**?

B: Mada **toshokan**-ni imashita.
I was still in the **library**.

A: **Shichi**-ji **juu-go**-fun-ni doko-ni imashita-ka?
Where were you at **7:15**?

B: **Kissaten**-ni imashita.
I was in a **coffee shop**.

A: Nan-de **kissaten**-ni ikimashita-ka?
How did you get to the **coffee shop**?

B: **Basu**-de ikimashita.
I went by **bus**.

A: **Kissaten**-de nani-o shite-imashita-ka?
What were you doing at the **coffee shop**?

B: **Koohii-o nonde**-imashita.
I was **drinking coffee**.

A: **Hachi**-ji-ni doko-ni imashita-ka?
Where were you at **8:00**?

B: Mada **kissaten**-ni imashita.
I was still in the **coffee shop**.

A: **Hachi**-ji **juu-go**-fun-ni doko-ni imashita-ka?
Where were you at **8:15**?

B: **Tomu-san-no uchi**-ni imashita.
I was at **Tom's house**.

A: Nan-de **Tomu-san-no uchi**-ni ikimashita-ka?
How did you get to **Tom's house**?

B: **Aruite-ikimashita**.
I **walked**.

A: **Tomu-san-no uchi**-de nani-o . . . ?
What were you doing . . . ?

L. 12 電話で 話しましょう

れんしゅう A: Competing in a radio quiz show!

You are participating in a radio quiz show now. Answer the host's questions about world geography.

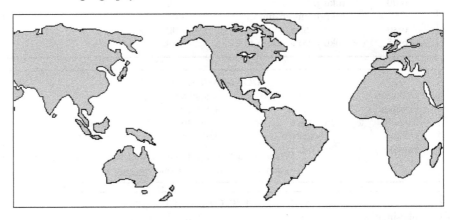

れんしゅう B: Kim's Day Yesterday

しつもん: (a) Where was Kim at?　(b) What was she doing there?

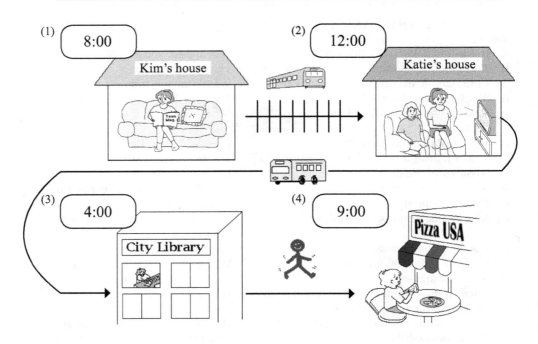

れんしゅう C: What was Kenji's family doing at 9:00 last night?

LESSON 13
Daily School Life

OBJECTIVES   もくひょう

At the end of this lesson you will be able to:
- ☑ Talk about school schedules
- ☑ Talk about daily school life
- ☑ Read the *kanji*: 学 and 校

VOCABULARY   たんご

Words

#-jikan-me	*suffix for class periods*
hajimaru (hajimarimasu/hajimatte)	(something) begins, starts
owaru (owarimasu/owatte)	(something) ends, finishes
kyooshitsu	classroom
taiikukan	gymnasium
shokudoo	cafeteria

Other words and expressions you will hear in this lesson

sooji	cleaning
sooji-o suru (shimasu/shite)	clean (*verb*)

KEY GRAMMAR POINTS   ぶんぽうポイント

#-jikan-me

When combined with numbers, *jikan-me* can be used to designate class periods as in the following examples. The question form is *nan-jikan-me*.

Taiiku-wa *nan-jikan-me* desu-ka?	*What period* is P.E.?
Yo-jikan-me-wa nan-no jugyoo desu-ka?	What class is *fourth period*?
San-jikan-me-wa suugaku desu.	*Third period* is math.
1-jikan-me-wa 9-ji-ni owarimasu.	*First period* ends at 9:00.

NAN-JIKAN-ME DESU-KA?

ichi-jikan-me	first period	go-jikan-me	fifth period
ni-jikan-me	second period	roku-jikan-me	sixth period
san-jikan-me	third period	shichi/nana-jikan-me	seventh period
yo-jikan-me	fourth period	hachi-jikan-me	eighth period

CULTURE NOTES   カルチャーノート

School cleaning 学校のそうじ

In Japan, it is the students' responsibility to keep their school spotless. The task of cleaning individual classrooms, halls, and bathrooms begins in elementary school and continues right through high school. As a result of their efforts, the students tend to be respectful of school property.

YOMIMASHOO!   よみましょう

じかんめ	*suffix for class periods*
はじまる・はじまります・はじまって	begin, start
おわる・おわります・おわって	end, finish
きょうしつ	classroom

94

たいいくかん	gymnasium
しょくどう	cafeteria
かもくは なにが いちばん すき ですか。	What is your favorite subject?
１じかんめは なんの じゅぎょう ですか。	What class is first period?
３じかんめは すうがく です。	Third period is math.
れきしは なんじかんめ ですか。	What period is history?
がっこうは ８じはんに はじまります。	School starts at 8:30.
１じかんめは ９じに おわります。	First period ends at 9:00.
そうじ	cleaning
そうじを する・します・して	clean (*verb*)

KANJI NOTES かんじノート

In this lesson you will learn to read two *kanji*: 学 and 校. Be sure that you know the readings of each *kanji* and can tell what the *kanji* means. Readings which are marked by an asterisk are for your reference only; you do not need to learn these at this time. You also do not have to learn any new words which are given in the examples. In a future lesson you will learn how to write these *kanji* using the correct stroke order.

学 **GAKU** (leaning, science); **mana(bu)*** (learn)

大学	dai*gaku*	university
学校	*gak*koo	school
数学	suu*gaku*	math
学生	*gaku*sei	student
学ぶ	*mana*bu	learn

大学はどこですか。 Dai*gaku*-wa doko desu-ka?
(Where's the university?)

私は大学の数学の Watashi-wa dai*gaku*-no suu*gaku*-no jugyoo-ga daisuki
 授業が大好きでした。 deshita.
(I really liked math class at my university.)

校 **KOO** (school)

学校	gak*koo*	school
小学校	shoogak*koo*	elementary school
中学校	chuugak*koo*	middle school
高校	koo*koo*	high school

学校が三つあります。 Gak*koo*-ga mittsu arimasu.
(There are three schools.)

中学校はあそこに Chuugak*koo*-wa asoko-ni arimasu.
 あります。 (The middle school is over there.)

高校はどこですか。 Koo*koo*-wa doko desu-ka?
(Where's the high school?)

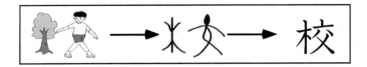

KANJI REVIEW

月　日　木　本　人　山　川　大　小　学　校

How do you read them? What do they mean?

INTERACTIVE ACTIVITIES

PART 1

---

❶ Vocabulary check

Silently review the vocabulary for Lesson 13. Then have a クラスメート orally test your knowledge of them. Your partner says the えいご, and you give the 日本ご. Switch and test your partner.

❷ Rekishi-wa na-jikan-me desu-ka?

In this pair activity take turns with your partner asking and answering various questions about your actual school schedules. Refer to the following patterns to help you get started. Then try to ask and answer questions without looking at the examples.

SAMPLE QUESTIONS AND ANSWERS

1. Roku-jikan-me-wa nan-no jugyoo desu-ka?　　What class is sixth period?
   Suugaku desu.　　　　　　　　　　　　　　It is math.
2. Rekishi-wa nan-jikan-me desu-ka?　　　　What period is history?
   Ichi-jikan-me desu.　　　　　　　　　　　It is first period.
3. Yo-jikan-me-wa nan-ji-ni owarimasu-ka?　　What time does fourth period end?
   10-ji-ni owarimasu.　　　　　　　　　　　It ends at 10:00.
4. Taiiku-wa nan-ji-ni hajimarimasu-ka?　　　What time does P.E. start?
   1-ji-han-ni hajimarimasu.　　　　　　　　It starts at 1:30.
5. Kamoku-wa nani-ga ichiban suki desu-ka?　What is your favorite subject?
   Nihongo-ga ichiban suki desu.　　　　　　I like Japanese the best.

KAMOKU			
suugaku	math	ongaku	music
daisuu	algebra	taiiku	physical education
bibun-sekibun	calculus	kateika	home economics
kika	geometry	bando	band
seibutsu	biology	konpyuutaa	computer
kagaku	chemistry	seijigaku	political science
butsuri	physics	gijutsu	industrial arts
rekishi	history	furansugo	French
chiri	geography	supeingo	Spanish
bijutsu	art	doitsugo	German
rinri	ethics	ratengo	Latin

PART 2

---

❶ San-jikan-me-wa nan-no jugyoo desu-ka?　　　📄 & ✐

In this pair activity take turns asking and answering questions to complete Judy's demanding class schedule below. Look only at your own chart. To make this activity more challenging the class periods are not given in order. You will need to ask three types of questions to obtain the needed information. Refer to the sample questions and answers on the previous page only as long as you need the support. Another question you will need to ask is:

Nan-no jugyoo-ga ___-ji ___-fun/pun-ni hajimarimasu/owarimasu-ka?
What class begins/ends at _____ [time]?

Try to remain in Japanese during this entire activity. Compare your completed charts when you finish. They should be the same.

PARTNER A

NAN-JIKAN-ME?	NAN-NO JUGYOO?	NAN-JI-NI HAJIMARIMASU-KA?	NAN-JI-NI OWARIMASU-KA?
5			12:35
2	nihongo	8:25	9:10
	taiiku		
7	suugaku	1:40	2:25
			8:15
3	kagaku (chemistry)	9:20	10:05
		12:45	
8	doitsugo	2:35	3:20

PARTNER B

NAN-JIKAN-ME?	NAN-NO JUGYOO?	NAN-JI-NI HAJIMARIMASU-KA?	NAN-JI-NI OWARIMASU-KA?
5	rekishi	11:50	12:35
	nihongo		
4	taiiku	10:15	11:15
			2:25
1	eigo	7:30	8:15
		9:20	
6	bijutsu	12:45	1:30
8			3:20

❷ **Yomimashoo!**　　　📄 & ✐

This pair activity provides you with an opportunity to review the nine *kanji* which you have learned to read in Lessons 7-13. Partner A masks the *roomaji* side and reads the vocabulary in the left column in order. Partner B responds after each with either *Hai, soo desu* or *Iie, chigaimasu. Moo ichido yonde kudasai.* Partner A writes down those which need to be studied. Switch roles and repeat.

かなとかんじ	ローマじ	かなとかんじ	ローマじ
1. 小さい	chiisai	12. おとこの人	otoko-no hito
2. 日本ごの本	nihongo-no hon	13. 大学せい	daigakusei
3. 5日	itsuka	14. 木よう日	moku-yoobi
4. なん月	nan-gatsu	15. 日本人	nihon-jin
5. 日本	Nihon, Nippon	16. 日よう日	nichi-yoobi
6. 小学校	shoogakkoo	17. 6月	roku-gatsu
7. 大すき	daisuki	18. 28日	ni-juu-hachi-nichi
8. 月よう日	getsu-yoobi	19. 大きくない	ookikunai
9. 4人	yo-nin	20. 本や	honya
10. カナダ人	kanada-jin	21. なん人	nan-nin
11. たんじょう日	tanjoobi		

L. 13 電話で 話しましょう

れんしゅう A: Class Schedules

8:30	月	火	水	木	金
1	$(3\sqrt{89})^2=?$		♪♪		English
2	こくご *	$(3\sqrt{89})^2=?$	$(3\sqrt{89})^2=?$	Englishı	こくご
3				こくご	
4	Englishı		こくご	$(3\sqrt{89})^2=?$	
5	♪♪	こくご	Englishı		
6		English	/		$(3\sqrt{89})^2=?$

3:30

* こくご literally means "country language," which is Japanese for Japanese students.

ひろし

98

れんしゅう B: Town Map

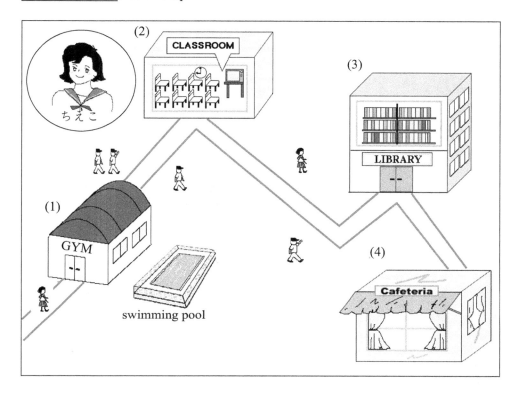

れんしゅう C: よみましょう。こたえましょう。

(1) すう学が すきですか。

(2) 日本ごの じゅぎょうは なんじかんめですか。

(3) 日ようびに べんきょうを しますか。

(4) 学校は なんじに はじまりますか。

(5) 小学校に たいいくかんが ありましたか。

(6) 学校は 大きいですか。小さいですか。

LESSON 14
School Clubs

OBJECTIVES もくひょう

At the end of this lesson you will be able to:
- ☑ Talk about club activities
- ☑ Read the *kanji*: 中 and 高

VOCABULARY たんご

Words

-bu	*suffix for club*
hairu (hairimasu/haitte)	enter, join
haitte-iru	belong to
jikan	time

Phrases and expressions

Nan-no kurabu-ni haitte-imasu-ka?	Which club do you belong to?
____-bu-ni haitte-imasu.	I am in the ____ club.
Ima kurabu-ni haitte-imasen.	I don't belong to a club now.

Other words and expressions you will hear in this lesson

(o)bentoo	boxed lunch
kanji-no jikan	*kanji* time

VOCABULARY NOTES たんごノート

-bu
Meaning *club*, the suffix *-bu* appears in the names of *kurabu* such as the following: *tenisu-bu, juudoo-bu, sakkaa-bu, barebooru-bu*, and *burasu bando-bu* (band).

KEY GRAMMAR POINTS ぶんぽうポイント

1. Using the *-te* form + *imasu* to express continuous actions
In Lesson 11 you learned how to use the *-te* form + *imasu* to express continuous action in the present. These actions are taking place at the same time you are speaking. In English this use of the *-te-imasu* form is usually expressed as *am/is/are . . . ing*.

Ima shigoto-o shi*te-imasu*.	I *am* work*ing* now.
Terebi-o mi*te-imasu*.	She *is* watch*ing* television.

Changing *imasu* to *imashita* enables you to express continuous actions in the past (L.12).

2. Using the *-te* form + *imasu* to express a state or condition
The *-te* form + *imasu* can also be used to express a state or condition which is the result of a previous action. Look at these examples.

Tenisu-bu-ni *haitte-imasu*.	I *belong to* the tennis club (*joined and still belong*).
Kyooshitsu-ni *haitte-imasu*.	She*'s* in the classroom (*entered and is still there*).
Jugyoo-wa *hajimatte-imasu*.	The lesson *is in progress* (*began and is still going on*).
Otooto-wa *okite-imasu*.	My younger brother *is up* (*got up and is still up*).
Sensei-ga *kite-imasu*.	The teacher *is here* (*came and is still here*).

100

How do you know which meaning a verb has?

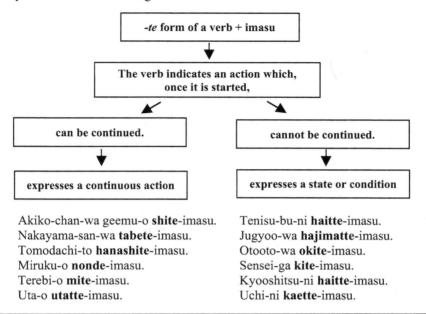

| -te form of a verb + imasu |
| The verb indicates an action which, once it is started, |

can be continued. → expresses a continuous action

cannot be continued. → expresses a state or condition

Akiko-chan-wa geemu-o **shite**-imasu.
Nakayama-san-wa **tabete**-imasu.
Tomodachi-to **hanashite**-imasu.
Miruku-o **nonde**-imasu.
Terebi-o **mite**-imasu.
Uta-o **utatte**-imasu.

Tenisu-bu-ni **haitte**-imasu.
Jugyoo-wa **hajimatte**-imasu.
Otooto-wa **okite**-imasu.
Sensei-ga **kite**-imasu.
Kyooshitsu-ni **haitte**-imasu.
Uchi-ni **kaette**-imasu.

CULTURE NOTES　　　　　　　　　　　カルチャーノート

Japanese boxed lunches お弁当／おべんとう
If you have lived on or visited the West Coast of the U.S. or Hawaii, you probably are
familiar with the word (*o*)*bentoo* (boxed lunches). (*O*)*bentoo* are very popular with
people who want a quick take-out meal that has the appearance and taste of home-cooked
food. In Japanese cities you can find many small shops which specialize in (*o*)*bentoo*.
Many train stations sell (*o*)*bentoo* called *eki-ben* made from local food representative of
that area. You can even purchase them on express and bullet trains.

Although many Japanese students eat the cafeteria lunch, others prefer to bring a meal
from home. Most (*o*)*bentoo* prepared at home are placed in a plastic box called
(*o*)*bentoo-bako*. The inside of the box is often divided into sections with the main section
filled with white steamed rice and the smaller sections containing small servings of meat,
fish, pickled vegetables, fruit, etc. The preparation of (*o*)*bentoo* that are pleasing to the
eye as well as the palate is taken very seriously by Japanese.

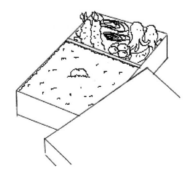

ぶ	*suffix for club*
はいる・はいります・はいって	enter, join
はいっている	belong to
じかん	time
なんの クラブに はいっていますか。	Which club do you belong to?
テニスぶに はいっています。	I am in the tennis club.
いま クラブに はいっていません。	I don't belong to a club now.
おべんとう	boxed lunch
かんじの じかん	*kanji* time

KANJI NOTES　　　　　　　　　　　　　　　　かんじノート

In this lesson you will learn to read two *kanji*: 中 and 高. Be sure that you know the readings of each *kanji* and can tell what the *kanji* means. You do not have to learn any new words which are given in the examples. In a future lesson you will learn how to write these *kanji* using the correct stroke order.

 CHUU; naka (middle, inside, within)

中学校	*chuu*gakkoo	middle school
中	*naka*	the inside
中に	*naka*-ni	inside, inside of
田中	Ta*naka*	*family name* [field-middle]
中川	*Naka*gawa	*family name* [middle-river]
中山	*Naka*yama	*family name* [middle-mountain]

あの人は中山さんです。	Ano hito-wa *Naka*yama-san desu. (He is Mr. Nakayama.)
田中さんは本が大好きですね。	Ta*naka*-san-wa hon-ga daisuki desu-ne. (Mrs. Tanaka, you really like books, don't you?)
中山さんは家の中で大きい犬をかっています。	*Naka*yama-san-wa uchi-no *naka*-de ookii inu-o katte-imasu. (Mr. Nakayama keeps a big dog in his house.)
木曜日に田中さんと中山さんが日本に行きます。	Moku-yoobi-ni Ta*naka*-san-to *Naka*yama-san-ga Nihon-ni ikimasu. (On Thursday Ms. Tanaka and Mr. Nakayama will go to Japan.)
中川さんは小さい大学に行きました。	*Naka*gawa-san-wa chiisai daigaku-ni ikimashita. (Mr. Nakagawa went to a small university.)

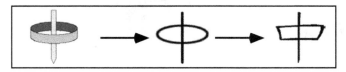

KOO; taka(i) (high, expensive)

高い	*taka*i	high, expensive
高等学校	*koo*toogakkoo	high school*
高橋	*Taka*hashi	*family name* [high-bridge]
高山	*Taka*yama	*family name* [high-mountain]
高田	*Taka*da	*family name* [high-field]

高田さんの家は小さい
です。
*Taka*da-san-no uchi-wa chiisai desu.
(Mr. Takada's house is small.)

あの山は高いです。
Ano yama-wa *taka*i desu.
(That mountain is high.)

日本の大きいメロンは
高いです。
Nihon-no ookii meron-wa *taka*i desu.
(Big melons in Japan are expensive.)

この高校は大きいです。
Kono *koo*koo-wa ookii desu.
(This high school is big.)

*The word *kootoogakkoo* (high school) is commonly shortened to *kookoo* 高校.

Notice that the *kanji* 高 is used only for the *taka* part of the word *takai*. The *i* is written with the *hiragana* い. What do you call *hiragana* which are used this way? For the answer see the *Kanji Nooto* section in Lesson 9.

KANJI REVIEW

月　日　木　本　人　山　川　大　小　学　校　中　高

How do you read them? What do they mean?

INTERACTIVE ACTIVITIES

PART 1

❶ Watashi-no sukejuuru
During this activity each student will work as a pair with two different クラスメート to check Assignment #1 from Part 2 of Lesson 13. The goal of the activity is to have two students carefully check your six sentences, mark and discuss with you any errors found, and sign off on your page. Form your first pair and exchange assignments with your partner. Both partners independently check and neatly mark errors for all six sentences. Do not correct errors. Use the editing symbols (see Workbook, Introduction). Return the assignments and go over the first sentence <u>together</u>. Correct your own work. Repeat this procedure for each sentence. Sign off on each other's page. Form new pairs and repeat these steps.

❷ Vocabulary review
Silently review the vocabulary for both Lesson 13 and 14. Then have a クラスメート orally test your knowledge of them. Your partner says the えいご, and you give the 日本ご. Switch and test your partner.

❶ Dialogue

Practice this dialogue with a partner. Follow the normal procedure for learning the dialogue. Remember to read each line to yourself and then look up and speak to your partner. After you have memorized the dialogue, perform it for another pair.

Two high school students are talking in the gym on club recruitment day.
A: Nan-no kurabu-ni haitte-imasu-ka?
B: Ima kurabu-ni haitte-imasen. A-san-wa?
A: Tenisu-bu-ni haitte-imasu.
B: Aa, soo desu-ka. Tenisu-bu-wa doo desu-ka?
A: Daisuki desu. Totemo tanoshii desu. B-san-mo hairimasen-ka?
B: Soo desu-ne. Demo, heta desu-yo.
A: Daijoobu, daijoobu.
B: Soo desu-ka? Ja, hairimasu!

For a greater challenge while learning the dialogue or for reading practice afterwards, use this:
A: なんの クラブに はいっていますか。
B: いま クラブに はいっていません。＿＿＿＿＿さんは？
A: テニスぶに はいっています。
B: ああ、そう ですか。テニスぶは どう ですか。
A: 大すき です。とても たのしい です。＿＿＿＿＿さんも はいりませんか。
B: そう ですね。でも へた ですよ。
A: 大じょうぶ、大じょうぶ。
B: そう ですか。じゃ、はいります。

Answer the following truthfully about yourself.

> 1. なんの クラブに はいっていますか。　3. なん人 いますか。
> 2. たのしい ですか。

❷ Ima nani-o shite-imasu-ka?

This pair activity will provide you with practice in using the *-te* **form** + *imasu* to express continuous actions (actions which are happening at the same time you are speaking). It will also help you to understand the two uses of the *-te-imasu* form which are discussed in the *Bunpoo Pointo* section of this lesson.

Both partners look at each sentence which expresses a continuous action *or* a state/condition. Partner A asks, *"_____-san/kun/chan-wa ima nani-o shite-imasu-ka?"* If the sentence expresses a continuous action, Partner B replies with that sentence. If the sentence expresses a state or condition, Partner B gives an answer which tells what the person is now doing (imagination). Switch roles for each sentence. Read the sample exchange with your partner before you begin.

SAMPLE EXCHANGE
Kenji-kun-wa yakyuu-o shite-imasu.
A: Kenji-kun-wa ima nani-o shite-imasu-ka?
B: Ima yakyuu-o shite-imasu.

CONTINUOUS ACTION
Kenji is playing baseball now at the same time we are speaking.

Sensei-wa kyooshitsu-ni haitte-imasu.
B: Sensei-wa ima nani-o shite-imasu-ka?
A: Ima oshiete-imasu.

STATE/CONDITION
The teacher is in the classroom as a result of having entered. What is the teacher doing now? She's teaching.

Otooto-wa okite-imasu.

A: Otootosan-wa ima nani-o shite-imasu-ka?

B: Ima asa-gohan-o tabete-imasu.

Tomodachi-wa uta-o utatte-imasu.

B: Tomodachi-wa ima nani-o shite-imasu-ka?

A: Ima uta-o utatte-imasu.

STATE/CONDITION

The younger brother is now up as a result of having gotten out of bed. What is he doing now? He's eating breakfast.

CONTINUOUS ACTION

My friend is singing a song now at the same time we are speaking.

1. Akiko-san-wa **nete**-imasu.   **STATE**
2. Yukari-san-wa terebi-o **mite**-imasu.   **CONTINUOUS ACTION**
3. Taroo-kun-wa tomodachi-to **hanashite**-imasu.   **CONTINUOUS ACTION**
4. Sumisu-san-wa nihongo-bu-ni **haitte**-imasu.   **STATE**
5. Sensei-ga **kite**-imasu.   **STATE**
6. Neko-wa miruku-o **nonde**-imasu.   **CONTINUOUS ACTION**
7. Akiko-chan-wa **okite**-imasu.   **STATE**
8. Masayo-san-wa uta-o **utatte**-imasu.   **CONTINUOUS ACTION**
9. Nakayama-san-wa **tabete**-imasu.   **CONTINUOUS ACTION**
10. Sensei-wa kyooshitsu-ni **haitte**-imasu.   **STATE**

School Clubs

Bukatsudo (部活動) is the term that translates to "school clubs" or "extracurricular activities" in Japan but encompasses much beyond the camaraderie of the soccer team, the flower arranging club, and the English Speaking Society. Japanese take participation in *bukatsudo* as an extremely serious matter. *Bukatsudo* are communities where repetitive practice, cooperative behavior, ritual, routine, group spirit and commitment are emphasized. In *bukatsudo*, students learn the values expected in adult society in terms of the hierarchy of seniors (*senpai* 先輩) and juniors (*koohai* 後輩).

れんしゅう A: International Party

You are at an international party. You meet a Japanese student. Answer his/her questions.

(1)

Name: Kelly Smith
Country: U.S.A.

Grade: 1st year in high school
Language of study: Spanish
Length of study: 2 years

(2)

Name: José Gonzales
Country: Mexico

Grade: 2nd year in high school
Language of study: English
Length of study: 5 years

(3)

Name: María Pérez
Country: Spain

Grade: 3rd year in high school
Language of study: French
Length of study: 1 year

(4)

Name: Kurt Wagner
Country: Germany

Grade: 1st year in high school
Language of study: Chinese
Length of study: 3 years

(5)

Name: Marc White
Country: France

Grade: 2nd year in high school
Language of study: German
Length of study: 4 years

(6)

Name: Su-Yueh Wong
Country: China

Grade: 3rd year in high school
Language of study: English
Length of study: 2 years

れんしゅう B: What club do you belong to?

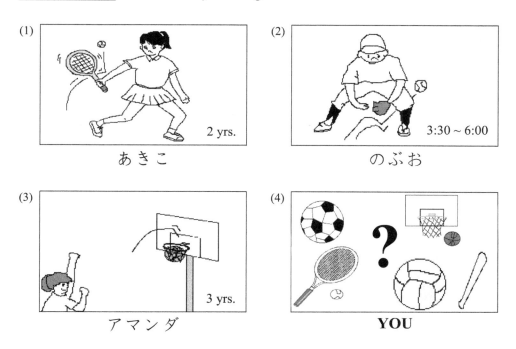

(1) 2 yrs.
あきこ

(2) 3:30 ~ 6:00
のぶお

(3) 3 yrs.
アマンダ

(4) YOU

れんしゅう C: Campus Map

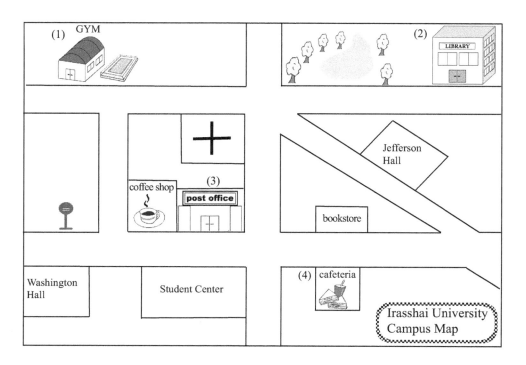

(1) GYM
(2) LIBRARY
Jefferson Hall
coffee shop
(3) post office
bookstore
Washington Hall
Student Center
(4) cafeteria
Irasshai University Campus Map

LESSON 15
Asking for and Giving Permission

At the end of this lesson you will be able to:
- ☑ Ask for and giving permission

This lesson also reviews the reading of the *kanji*: 月 日 木 本 人 山 川 大 小 学 校 中 高

VOCABULARY　　　　　　　　　　　　　　　　たんご

Words

tsukau (tsukaimasu/tsukatte)	use
wasureru (wasuremasu/wasurete)	forget
kyookasho	textbook

KEY GRAMMAR POINTS　　　　　　　　ぶんぽうポイント

-te mo ii desu-ka?

This lesson introduces another common use of the *-te* form of verbs – asking permission. You have already learned one way to ask permission to borrow or use an item (L. 11, Vol. 1).

Sumimasen, hotchikisu, *ii desu-ka?*	Excuse me, *may I use* the stapler?
Keshigomu, *chotto, ii desu-ka?*	*May I borrow* your eraser (*for a little bit)?*

If you want to specify the action you are asking permission to do, use the *-te* form of the verb followed by *-mo ii desu-ka?* Look at these examples.

Sono shashin-o *mite-mo ii desu-ka?*	*May I look at* that photograph?
Kono keeki-o *tabete-mo ii desu-ka?*	*May I eat* this cake?
Kono enpitsu-o *tsukatte-mo ii desu-ka?*	*May I use* this pencil?

When giving permission, you may use *Hai, ii desu-yo* or *Hai, doozo.* Study these two examples.

A: Keshigomu-o tsukatte-mo ii desu-ka?	May I use the eraser?
B: Hai, ii desu-yo.	Yes, you may use it.
A: Doomo arigatoo (gozaimasu).	Thank you very much.
A: Juusu-o nonde-mo ii desu-ka?	May I drink some juice?
B: Hai, doozo.	Go ahead; Please; Here it is.
A: Doomo.	Thanks.

YOMIMASHOO!　　　　　　　　　　　　　よみましょう

つかう・つかいます・つかって	use
わすれる・わすれます・わすれて	forget
きょうかしょ	textbook
しゅくだいを わすれました。	I forgot my homework.
この じしょを つかって ください。	Please use this dictionary.
日本ごの きょうかしょ ですか。	Is it a Japanese language textbook?
その しゃしんを みても いい ですか。	May I look at that photograph?

The importance of review

This lesson provides you with an opportunity to review reading all of the *kanji* you have learned so far. Review is a very important part of learning any new material. For the student who wishes to learn and remember *kanji,* regular and frequent review is essential. As you well know by now, it requires a lot of effort on your part to learn to read and write Japanese. Make sure you protect your investment of time and effort by reviewing *kanji* often. It is far more beneficial to review for shorter periods of time more frequently than to schedule longer periods less often.

LEARNING STRATEGY

Spend five minutes each day reviewing *kanji.* Practice reading and writing them even if you have no specific assignment.

INTERACTIVE ACTIVITIES

PART 1

❶ Vocabulary check

Silently review the vocabulary for Lesson 15 and vocabulary related to classroom supplies. Then have a クラスメート orally test your knowledge of them. Your partner says the えいご, and you give the 日本ご. Switch and test your partner.

❷ Enpitsu-o tsukatte-mo ii desu-ka?

Do this activity with a クラスメート. Partner A points to one of the squares in the grid below. Partner B then asks permission by making a question which uses the target words. Partner A then grants permission and Partner B expresses thanks. Study the example before you begin.

EXAMPLE

B: Keeki-o tabete-mo ii desu-ka?
(A has pointed to *keeki-o taberu*)
A: Hai, ii desu-yo.
B: Doomo.

> The *-te* forms of the verbs below appear on the next page.

keeki-o taberu	kore-o yomu	shashin-o miru
uta-o utau	paatii-ni iku	o-furo-ni hairu
rajio-o kiku	kutsu-o kau	tenisu-bu-ni hairu
sofaa-de neru	yakyuu-o suru	eigo-de hanasu
koko-de oshieru	uchi-ni kaeru	asa juu-ichi-ji-ni okiru
juusu-o nomu	enpitsu-o tsukau	geemu-o suru

❶ Juusu-o nonde-mo ii desu-ka?

Do this activity with a クラスメート. Partner A points to one of the squares in the grid below. Partner B then asks permission by making a question which uses that verb. Make your questions interesting by adding other words. Partner A then grants permission and Partner B expresses thanks. Study the examples before you begin.

EXAMPLES

B: Kono tomato juusu-o nonde-mo ii desu-ka? (A has pointed to *nomu*)
A: Hai, doozo.
B: Doomo.

A: Eigo-de itte-mo ii desu-ka? (B has pointed to *iu*)
B: Hai, doozo.
A: Doomo.

nomu	iku	taberu	hairu
oshieru	kau	yomu	suru
okiru	kaku	kiku	miru
hanasu	tsukau	iu	utau

VERBS IN THE -*TE* FORM

	-*masu* form	plain form		-*te* form	English
-*u* Verbs:	kakimasu	ka ku	------>	kaite	write
	ikimasu	i ku	------>	itte	go
	kikimasu	ki ku	------>	kiite	listen
	hanashimasu	hana su	------>	hanashite	speak
	nomimasu	no mu	------>	nonde	drink
	kaerimasu	kae ru	------>	kaette	return
	iimasu	i u	------>	itte	say
	kaimasu	ka u	------>	katte	buy
	utaimasu	uta u	------>	utatte	sing
	tsukaimasu	tsuka u	------>	tsukatte	use
-*ru* Verbs:	mimasu	mi ru	------>	mite	look at, see
	tabemasu	tabe ru	------>	tabete	eat
	okimasu	oki ru	------>	okite	get up
	nemasu	ne ru	------>	nete	go to bed
	oshiemasu	oshie ru	------>	oshiete	teach
Irregular Verbs:	kimasu	k uru	------>	kite	come
	shimasu	s uru	------>	shite	do

❷ Yomimashoo! 📄 & ✏️

This pair activity provides you with an opportunity to review the *kanji* which you have learned to read. Partner A masks the *roomaji* side and reads the sentences in the left column in order. Partner B responds after each with either *Hai, soo desu* or *Iie, chigaimasu. Moo ichido yonde kudasai.* Partner A writes down those which need to be studied. Switch roles and repeat.

かなと かんじ	ローマじ
1. その 大きい ホテルは 高い ですよ。	1. Sono ookii hoteru-wa takai desu-yo.
2. あの 高校は 小さい ですね。	2. Ano kookoo-wa chiisai desu-ne.
3. 3月25日は 日本の ともだちの たんじょう日 です。	3. San-gatsu ni-juu-go-nichi-wa Nihon-no tomodachi-no tanjoobi desu.
4. あの 人は 日本人 ですか。	4. Ano hito-wa nihon-jin desu-ka?
5. あの 中学校の 中は きれい ですよ。	5. Ano chuugakkoo-no naka-wa kirei desu-yo.

L. 15 電話で 話しましょう

れんしゅう A: What's YOUR alibi?

Tim-*sensei* has been kidnapped! The police suspect that someone at your school is behind the kidnapping. A detective calls to investigate. Answer his/her questions. Use your imagination!

れんしゅう B: May I ~?

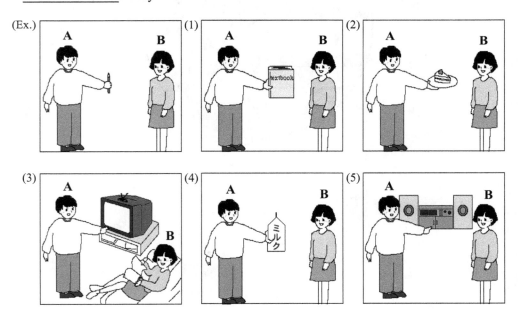

れんしゅう C: Let's converse!

> **Dialogue:**
> A: Everyone, turn in your homework.
> B: <u>Mr. Tanaka</u>, I forgot (to do it).
> A: That's no good, <u>Mr. Suzuki</u>.
> B: I'm sorry.
> A: Well, everyone, please open to page <u>50</u>. Do you know the answer for number <u>1</u>, <u>Mr. Suzuki</u>?
> B: No, I don't. Please teach me.

Sample Dialogue:

A: みなさん、しゅくだいを だしてください。

B: <u>たなか</u>せんせい、わすれました。

A: <u>すずきくん</u>、だめですね。

B: すみません。

A: じゃ、みなさん、きょうかしょの <u>50</u> ページを みてください。じゃ、<u>すずきくん</u>、<u>1</u> ばんが わかりますか。

B: いいえ、わかりません。せんせい、おしえて ください。

Sample Dialogue:

A: Minasan, shukudai-o dashite kudasai.

B: <u>Tanaka</u>-sensei, wasuremashita.

A: <u>Suzuki-kun</u>, dame desu-ne.

B: Sumimasen.

A: Jaa, minasan, kyookasho-no <u>50</u>-peeji-o mite kudasai. Jaa, <u>Suzuki-kun</u>, <u>1</u>-ban-ga wakarimasu-ka?

B: Iie, wakarimasen. Sensei, oshiete kudasai.

れんしゅう A: Dream Land Web Page

http://www.dreamland.travelinfo.com

Dream Land

Population: 1.2 million
Language: Japanese and English
Area: 10,500 mi.²

天気	月	火	水	木	金	土	日
Weather							

Mountains (mi.)	Rivers (mi.)	Islands (mi.²)	Lakes (mi.²)
Mt. Washington 2,578	Blue River 5,976	Cake Island 354	Lake Sushi 156
Mt. Lincoln 1,956	Black River 3,125	Cookie Island 311	Lake Sukiyaki 134
Mt. Kennedy 1,753	Green River 2,997	Candy Island 297	Lake Yakitori 129

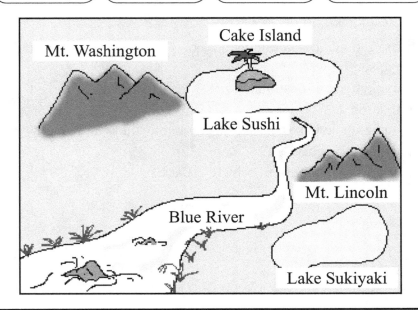

<u>れんしゅう B</u>: What was Mr. Tanaka doing at ~? What time was Mr. Tanaka doing ~?

Two policemen are helping each other fill in the missing information in the last Sunday schedule of the suspect, Mr. Tanaka.

(A)

9:00 a.m.	(2) ?	1:45 p.m.
(1) ?		(3)
3:00 p.m.	(5) ?	(6) 8:00 p.m.
(4)		

(B)

9:00 a.m.	(2) 12:15 p.m.	1:45 p.m.
(1)		(3) ?
3:00 p.m.	(5) 5:15 p.m.	(6) ?
(4) ?		

<u>れんしゅう C</u>: よみましょう。

Let's match the left side and the right side, and form a word!

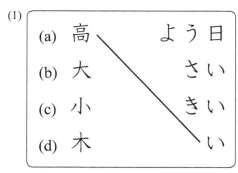

(1)
(a) 高
(b) 大
(c) 小
(d) 木

よう日
さい
きい
い

(2)
(a) 日
(b) 大
(c) 高校
(d) なん

せい
人
学
本

(3)
(a) カナダ
(b) 大
(c) 中
(d) たんじょう

日
学校
すき
人

LESSON 16
More Spatial Relationships

OBJECTIVES　　　　　　　　　　　　　　　もくひょう

At the end of this lesson you will be able to:
- ☑ Ask and state where things are located
- ☑ Comment on housekeeping

This lesson also reviews the writing of the *kanji*: 月 日 木 本 人 大 小

VOCABULARY　　　　　　　　　　　　　　　たんご

Words

ue	top, above, up
shita	under, below, down
kirei	clean, neat
kitanai	dirty, messy
hondana	bookcase
heya	room

Other words and expressions you will hear in this lesson

Oboete-imasu-ka?	Do you remember?
sutereo	stereo
shiidii	CD

VOCABULARY NOTES　　　　　　　　　　　たんごノート

1. Kirei

As you have already learned, *kirei* can mean *attractive* or *pretty*. In this lesson *kirei* is reintroduced with the meaning *clean* or *neat*. *Kirei* is a *na*-adjective.

Kono burausu-wa *kirei* desu-ne.	This blouse is *pretty*, isn't it?
Ichiban *kirei*-na seetaa desu.	It's the most *attractive* sweater.
Oneesan-no heya-wa *kirei* desu.	Her older sister's room is *clean*.
Watashi-no heya-wa *kirei* ja nai desu.	My room is not *neat*.

2. Oboete-imasu-ka?

The verb *oboeru* (*oboemasu/oboete*) means *learn, memorize,* or *remember*. The question *Oboete-imasu-ka?* means *Do you remember?* This is another example of using -*te* form + *imasu* to express a state or condition as discussed in Lesson 14 (Key Grammar Points). As a result of learning or memorizing something, you now remember it.

Tanaka-san-no denwa-bangoo-o *oboete-imasu-ka?*	*Do you remember* Ms. Tanaka's phone number?

KEY GRAMMAR POINTS　　　　　　　　　ぶんぽうポイント

1. Ue ~ shita

This lesson introduces two more common spatial relationship words in Japanese: *ue* and *shita*. *Ue* means *top, above,* or *up*. *Shita* means *under, below,* or *down*. Do you remember *mae* (front), *ushiro* (back/behind), *migi* (right) and *hidari* (left) from Lessons 69 and 70 of Volume 1? *Ue* and *shita* are words that are used in the same patterns that you have already practiced with these words which express location.

Ue-ni arimasu.	It's *above*.
Shita-ni arimasu-ka?	Is it *below*?
Isu-*no shita-ni* arimasu.	It's *under* the chair.

116

Kyookasho-wa hondana-*no ue-ni* arimasu.
Inu-wa teeburu-*no shita-ni* imasu.

The text is *on* (*top of*) the bookcase.
The dog is *under* the table.

X-no *ue*-ni = on (top of) X

X-no *shita*-ni = under X

---

2. Arimasu ~ imasu

When you are asking and telling about the location of inanimate (non-living) things, remember to use the verb *arimasu*. The plain form of *arimasu* is *aru*.

Jisho-wa doko-ni *arimasu*-ka?	Where's the dictionary?
Tsukue-no ue-ni *arimasu*.	It's on the desk.
Kyookasho-wa doko-ni *arimashita*-ka?	Where were the textbooks?
Hondana-no ue-ni *arimashita*.	They were on top of the bookcase.
Manga, doko-ni *aru*?	Where's the comic book?
Isu-no shita-ni *aru*.	It's under the chair.

When you are talking about animate things such as people and animals, be sure to use the verb *imasu*. The plain form of *imasu* is *iru*.

Usagi-wa doko-ni *imasu*-ka?	Where's the rabbit?
Teeburu-no shita-ni *imasu*.	It's under the table.

3. -te mo ii desu-ka? -te mo ii?

In Lesson 15 you learned how to ask permission using the *-te* form of the verb followed by *-te mo ii desu-ka?* This lesson provides additional practice of this useful pattern.

Rajio-o *kiite-mo ii desu-ka?*	*May I listen* to the radio?
Sono shashin-o *mite-mo ii desu-ka?*	*May I look at* that photograph?
Kono keeki-o *tabete-mo ii desu-ka?*	*May I eat* this cake?
Eigo-no jisho, *tsukatte-mo ii?*	*May I use* your English dictionary?

YOMIMASHOO!　　　　　　　　　　　　　　よみましょう

うえ	top, above, up
した	under, below, down
きれい	clean, neat
きたない	dirty, messy
ほんだな	bookcase
へや	room
じしょは どこに ありますか。	Where's the dictionary?
つくえの うえに あります。	It's on the desk.
まんが、どこに ある？	Where's the comic book?
いすの したに ある。	It's under the chair.
この へやは きたない です。	This room is messy.
おねえさんの へやは きれい です。	Her older sister's room is clean.
へやに なにが ありますか。	What do you have in your room?
おぼえていますか。	Do you remember?
ステレオ	stereo

INTERACTIVE ACTIVITIES

PART 1

---

❶ Vocabulary check

Silently review the vocabulary for Lesson 16. Then have a クラスメート orally test your knowledge of them. Your partner says the えいご, and you give the 日本ご. Switch and test your partner.

❷ Dialogue

Practice this dialogue with a partner. Follow the normal procedure for learning the dialogue. Make sure that you understand the meaning of the dialogue before you begin practicing it. Remember to read each line to yourself and then look up and speak to your partner. After you have memorized the dialogue, perform it for another pair. Notice that the verbs in this dialogue are in the plain form.

A and B are best friends. A is at B's house (in B's room) visiting after school. A is always borrowing things from B.

A: Kami, doko-ni aru?
B: Tsukue-no ue-ni aru.
A: Tsukatte-mo ii?
B: Ii-yo.
A: Pen, doko-ni aru?
B: Fudebako-no naka-ni aru.
A: Fudebako nai-yo.
B: Ee, nai? Aa, soko. Kaban-no naka-ni aru.
A: Aa, atta*. Kono heya-wa chotto kitanai-ne. Demo watashi-no heya-wa motto kitanai.

*I got it.

Can you read these words which appear in the dialogue?

きたない	ふでばこ	つくえ	かばん
へや	ちょっと	もっと	つかって

PART 2

---

❶ Manga-wa doko-ni arimasu-ka?   📄 & ✏️

Do this activity with a クラスメート. Use your imagination as you ask and answer questions about the location of various items. Use the vocabulary given in the box below. Partner A begins by asking Partner B where an item is located. Partner B responds, and both partners very quickly draw a simple picture showing the answer. Then Partner B asks a question, and Partner A answers. Continue taking turns asking and answering questions until the time comes. Use the patterns below. Compare your work when you have finished.

QUESTION: CD-wa doko-ni arimasu-ka?
ANSWER: Sutereo-no **migi**-ni arimasu.

As you do this activity, keep firmly in mind that this is <u>not</u> an art exercise but rather an opportunity to practice the spatial relationships which you have learned so far. Your drawings should be very simple and quick. Here are two sample illustrations.

Jisho-wa hondana-no ue-ni arimasu.   Kaban-wa isu-no shita-ni arimasu.

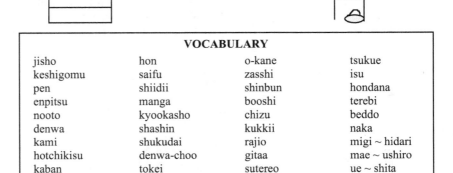

VOCABULARY			
jisho	hon	o-kane	tsukue
keshigomu	saifu	zasshi	isu
pen	shiidii	shinbun	hondana
enpitsu	manga	booshi	terebi
nooto	kyookasho	chizu	beddo
denwa	shashin	kukkii	naka
kami	shukudai	rajio	migi ~ hidari
hotchikisu	denwa-choo	gitaa	mae ~ ushiro
kaban	tokei	sutereo	ue ~ shita

❷ **Kakimashoo!** 📄 & ✏️

Do this activity with a クラスメート. Take turns testing each other on your knowledge of the *kanji* you have learned how to write. Using the pattern below, Partner A tells Partner B which *kanji* to write. The *kanji* may be given in mixed order. Partner B can use blank writing practice sheets or other paper and should <u>not</u> look at this page. Partner B writes only one *kanji* each time. Partner A should look not only at this page but also at Part ❶ of the Writing Practice sections for Lessons 10-12 in the workbook to make sure that Partner B is using the correct stroke order for each *kanji*. Switch roles and repeat.

PARTNER A reads:

1. nichi - - - nichi-yoobi - - - nichi
2. dai - - - daigaku - - - dai
3. nin - - - roku-nin - - - nin
4. chii - - - chiisai - - - chii
5. hon - - - hondana - - - hon
6. getsu - - - getsu-yoobi - - - getsu
7. moku - - - moku-yoobi - - - moku

PARTNER B writes:

1. 日
2. 大
3. 人
4. 小
5. 本
6. 月
7. 木

PARTNER B reads:

1. gatsu - - - ichi-gatsu - - - gatsu
2. hon - - - Nihon - - - hon
3. oo - - - ookii - - - oo
4. jin - - - amerika-jin - - - jin
5. moku - - - moku-yoobi - - - moku
6. nichi - - - mainichi - - - nichi
7. shoo - - - shoogakkoo - - - shoo

PARTNER A writes:

1. 月
2. 本
3. 大
4. 人
5. 木
6. 日
7. 小

If you have time, continue testing each other using different words.

れんしゅう A: Masashi's Room

しつもん: (a) where? (b) is doing what?

Elizabeth (1) (2)

Mom

(3)
Baby sister

You are looking at them from this way.

れんしゅう C: Interview your classmate!

Do you have <u>math</u> class?
- What period is <u>math</u>?
- Is <u>math</u> interesting?

Do you belong to a club?
- What club?
- Do you go to club everyday?

LESSON 17
Sequences of Daily Activities

OBJECTIVES   もくひょう

At the end of this lesson you will be able to:
- ☑ Relate a sequence of daily activities
- ☑ Read the *kanji*: 何

VOCABULARY   たんご

Words

nikki	journal, diary
kaku (kakimasu/kaite)	write

Other words and expressions you will hear in this lesson

Tadaima.	Hello, I'm home!
O-kaeri(nasai).	Welcome home.

VOCABULARY NOTES   たんごノート

Tadaima and o-kaerinasai
These are two expressions which you will frequently hear in Japanese households. *Tadaima* (literally, *just now*) means *Hello, I'm home* or *I'm back* and is said when entering the house. Family members who are already at home respond with *O-kaerinasai* or just *O-kaeri* (based on the verb *kaeru* meaning *return*) which means *Welcome home*.

KEY GRAMMAR POINTS   ぶんぽうポイント

Using the *-te* form to link actions
This lesson introduces yet another important use of the *-te* form – the linking of two or more actions. In English the word *and* can be used to join not only nouns (dogs *and* cats) but also adjectives (big *and* powerful), verbs (sing *and* dance), other parts of speech, and even sentences. In Japanese the particle *-to* is used to join nouns and pronouns only. To express a sequence of actions, you can use the *-te* form of each verb except the last one.

Kookoo-wa nan-ji-ni *hajimatte*, nan-ji-ni *owarimasu*-ka?	What time does high school *start and* what time does it *end*?
Roku-ji-ni uchi-ni *kaette*, gohan-o *tabete*, nyuusu-o *mite*, shinbun-o *yonde*, 10-ji-ni rajio-o *kiite*, 11-ji-ni *nemasu*.	I *return* home at 6:00, *eat* dinner, *watch* the news, *read* the newspaper, *listen* to the radio at 10:00, *and go* to bed at 11:00.

The last verb in the sequence provides such information as tense and level of formality. Study these sentences carefully.

Shukudai-o shite, tesuto-no benkyoo-o shite, *nemasu*.	I *will do* homework, *study* for a test, *and go* to bed. [non-past polite]
Shukudai-o shite, tesuto-no benkyoo-o shite, *neru*.	I *will do* homework, *study* for a test, *and go* to bed. [non-past plain]
Shukudai-o shite, tesuto-no benkyoo-o shite, *nemashita*.	I *did* homework, *studied* for a test, *and went* to bed. [past polite]

You can link any number of verb clauses this way, but the actions must generally be within a fairly short period of time, be in some way related, and be mentioned in the order of occurrence. The subject is the same for all of the verbs in the sequence.

A SEQUENCE OF ACTIONS

-te, . . . -te, . . . -te, . . . -masu/-mashita

YOMIMASHOO!　　　　　　　　　　　　　よみましょう

にっき (日記)	journal, diary
かく・かきます・かいて	write
それから なにを しますか。	Then what do you do?
あさ 6 じに おきて コーヒーを のみます。	I get up at 6:00 and drink coffee.
へやに いって べんきょうを します。	I'm going to my room and study.
ただいま。	Hello, I'm home!
おかえりなさい。	Welcome home.

KANJI NOTES　　　　　　　　　　　　かんじノート

In this lesson you will learn to read the *kanji* 何. Be sure that you know the readings of the *kanji* and can tell what it means. The reading which is marked by an asterisk is for your reference only; you do not need to learn it at this time. In a future lesson you will learn how to write this *kanji* using the correct stroke order.

何　　**KA*; nan, nani** (what, how many; *prefix to form questions*)

何人	nan-nin	how many people
何日	nan-nichi	what day (of the month)
何月	nan-gatsu	what month
何年生	nan-nen-sei	what year student
何時間	nan-ji-kan	how many hours
何マイル	nan-mairu	how many miles

何人いますか。	*Nan*-nin imasu-ka?
	(How many people are there?)
毎日何をしますか。	Mainichi *nani*-o shimasu-ka?
	(What do you do every day?)
何の本ですか。	*Nan*-no hon desu-ka?
	(What kind of book is it?)
今日は何月何日ですか。	Kyoo-wa *nan*-gatsu *nan*-nichi desu-ka?
	(What month and day is it today?)
何曜日ですか。	*Nan*-yoobi desu-ka?
	(What day of the week is it?)

INTERACTIVE ACTIVITIES

PART 1
---

❶ Mimasu ~ miru ~ mite

With a クラスメート take turns quizzing each other on the -*te* form of the following verbs. You say the -*masu* form and the plain form. Then your partner gives the -*te* form. Write down those that need further study.

123

VERBS IN THE -*TE* FORM			
-*masu* form	**Plain form**	**-*te* form**	**English**
mimasu	miru	mite	look at, see
tabemasu	taberu	tabete	eat
okimasu	okiru	okite	get up
oshiemasu	oshieru	oshiete	teach
kakimasu	kaku	kaite	write
kikimasu	kiku	kiite	listen
ikimasu	iku	itte	go
hanashimasu	hanasu	hanashite	speak
nomimasu	nomu	nonde	drink
yomimasu	yomu	yonde	read
kaerimasu	kaeru	kaette	return
iimasu	iu	itte	say
kaimasu	kau	katte	buy
utaimasu	utau	utatte	sing
shimasu	suru	shite	do
tsukaimasu	tsukau	tsukatte	use
hairimasu	hairu	haitte	enter, join
wasuremasu	wasureru	wasurete	forget

❷ **Kinoo 6-ji-ni okite, . . .**

Do this activity in 4人のグループ. The first person begins by saying *Kinoo 6-ji-ni okite*. The second person repeats what the first person says and adds the next activity in the sequence of yesterday's activities. The third person repeats in order what the first and second people say and adds the third activity. Continue adding activities in this way, each time repeating all that has been said before and using the -*te* form. Try to go around the circle at least twice. The final activity is *nemashita*.

PART 2

❶ **Kakimashoo!** 🖉

During this activity each student will work as a pair with two different クラスメート to check Assignment #2 from Part 1 of this lesson. The goal of the activity is to have two students carefully check the entry in your *nikki*, mark and discuss with you any errors found, and sign off on your page. Form your first pair and exchange assignments with your partner. Both partners independently check and neatly mark errors for the entire entry. Use the same editing symbols as usual.

> **Are these included?**
> ● The date written in *kanji*
> ● One sentence about the weather
> ● One sentence with at least five activities
>   All but the last verb in the sequence of activities are in the -*te* form.
>   The final verb in the sequence ends in -*mashita*.

❷ **Kinoo 7-ji-ni okite, . . .** 📄 & 🖉

Do this activity with a クラスメート. Partner A begins by saying *Kinoo 7-ji-ni okite*. Partner B then adds the next activity in the sequence of yesterday's activities (without repeating what Partner A has said). Continue taking turns with each person adding another activity until you run out of ideas. The final activity is *nemashita*. Repeat the activity if you have time. Record the number of activities you and your partner (together) were able to relate in each round.

L. 17 電話で 話しましょう

<u>れんしゅう A</u>: A Visit to Your School

A Japanese Board of Education official is visiting your school and 10 other high schools to research education in the U.S. Answer his/her questions.

<u>れんしゅう B</u>: Mariko's Day Today

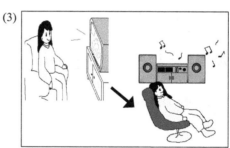

れんしゅう C: Let's converse!

Dialogue:

A: <u>Masako</u>, what are you
   going to do tomorrow?
B: I am going to <u>play tennis</u>.
A: That's good. Who will you
   <u>play</u> with?
B: I'll <u>play</u> with <u>Jeff</u>. What are
   you going to do, <u>Lisa</u>?
A: I am going to <u>go shopping
   and watch a movie</u>.

Suggested activities

watch TV
go to a restaurant
study
play tennis
go to a concert
read a book

Sample Dialogue:

A: まさこさん、 あした なにを
   しますか。
B: テニスを します。
A: いいですね。 だれと しますか。
B: ジェフくんと します。 リサさん
   は なにを しますか。
A: わたしは かいものに いって、 えいがを みます。

Sample Dialogue:

A: <u>Masako-san</u>, ashita nani-o shimasu-ka?
B: <u>Tenisu-o shimasu</u>.
A: Ii desu-ne. Dare-to <u>shimasu</u>-ka?
B: <u>Jefu-kun</u>-to <u>shimasu</u>. Risa-san-wa nani-o shimasu-ka?
A: Watashi-wa <u>kaimono-ni itte, eiga-o mimasu</u>. *

---

* informal version:

A: <u>Masako</u>, ashita nani suru?
B: <u>Tenisu suru</u>.
A: Ii-ne. Dare-to?
B: <u>Jefu</u>-to. <u>Risa</u>-wa nani suru?
A: Watashi-wa <u>kaimono-ni itte, eiga miru</u>.

LESSON 18
Weekend Activities

OBJECTIVES   もくひょう

At the end of this lesson you will be able to:
- ☑ Relate a sequence of weekend activities
- ☑ Read the *kanji*: 今 and 私

VOCABULARY   たんご

Words

au (aimasu/atte)	meet, see
nani-mo	nothing, anything
dare-mo	no one, nobody
nani-ka	something
dare-ka	someone, somebody

Phrases and expressions

____-ni au	meet/see (someone)

Other words and expressions you will hear in this lesson

Itte-kimasu.	Good-bye. (said when leaving home)
Itterasshai.	Good-bye. (said to person leaving home)
kantorii kurabu	country club
hito-tachi	people

VOCABULARY NOTES   たんごノート

Itte-kimasu and itterasshai

These two expressions are both used when a family member is leaving home. *Itte-kimasu*, which is said by the person who is leaving, literally means *I'm going and coming*. It is formed from the *-te* form of the verb *iku* (go) and the *-masu* form of the verb *kuru* (come). *Itterasshai*, which literally means *go and come* and which is said by the family member(s) remaining at home, could be translated as *We'll look forward to your return* or *We'll see you when you get back*. This set expression is formed with the *-te* form of *iku* and *irasshai* (an honorific form of *kuru*). When *itte* and *irasshai* are combined, the resulting form is *itterasshai*.

	LEAVING HOME	RETURNING HOME
PERSON COMING/GOING	Itte-kimasu.	Tadaima.
PERSON AT HOME	Itterasshai.	O-kaeri(nasai).

KEY GRAMMAR POINTS   ぶんぽうポイント

1. The use of particles

Particles in Japanese can sometimes be translated as prepositions in English. In these cases they are easy to learn and remember. Some examples of these include the following.

Hachi-ji-*ni* gakkoo-*ni* ikimasu.	*At* 8:00 I will go *to* school.
Bosuton-*kara* kimashita.	He came *from* Boston.
Tomodachi-*to* hanashite-imasu.	She's talking *with* her friend.

In some cases the particle does not have an equivalent in English.

Terebi-*o* mite-imashita. We were watching television.
Shuumatsu-*wa* tanoshii desu-ka? Are weekends pleasant?
Tenisu-*ga* dekimasu. He can play tennis.

Sometimes from the English speaker's point of view, the particle used with a certain Japanese verb does not seem to be the logical choice. In these cases it is important to memorize which particle is used with a particular verb. Here is an example from this lesson.

Booifurendo-*ni* aimashita. She met her boyfriend.

***Someone*-ni au (aimasu/atte)**

2. Nani-mo, dare-mo, nani-ka, dare-ka

This lesson introduces four indefinite pronouns some of which you are already familiar with from previous lessons. Study the chart and examples carefully.

	-ka	-mo
dare	**dare-ka** (someone, somebody)	**dare-mo*** (no one, nobody, anyone, anybody)
nani	**nani-ka** (something)	**nani-mo*** (nothing, anything)

*used with a negative verb

Dare-ka oboete-imasu-ka? Does *someone* remember?
Nani-ka nomimashita-ka? Did you drink *something*?
Nani-mo shimasen deshita. I didn't do *anything*.
Dare-mo wakarimasen. *No one* understands.

Notice that the particles -*ga*, -*wa*, and -*o* are not used with pronouns ending in -*ka* or -*mo*.

YOMIMASHOO! よみましょう

あう・あいます・あって	meet, see
何も	nothing, anything
だれも	no one, nobody
何か	something
だれか	someone, somebody
ともだちに あいます	meet/see a friend
きょうは 何も しません でした。	I didn't do anything today.
いってきます。	Good-bye. (said when leaving home)
いってらっしゃい。	Good-bye. (said to person leaving home)
カントリー クラブ	country club
人たち	people

KANJI NOTES かんじノート

In this lesson you will learn to read two *kanji*: 今 and 私. Be sure that you know the readings of each *kanji* and can tell what the *kanji* means. Readings which are marked by an asterisk are for your reference only; you do not need to learn these at this time. You also do not have to learn any new words which are given in the examples. The correct stroke order for these *kanji* will be given in a future lesson.

今　**KON, KIN*; ima** (now, the present)

今	*ima*	now
今から	*ima*-kara	from now (on)
今まで	*ima*-made	until now
今日	kyoo	today, this day
今日は	*kon*nichi-wa	hello
今月	*kon*getsu	this month
今週	*kon*shuu	this week

今何をしていますか。	*Ima* nani-o shite-imasu-ka? (What is he doing now?)
先生、今日は。	Sensei, *kon*nichi-wa. (Hello, teacher.)
今日は何月何日ですか。	Kyoo-wa nan-gatsu nan-nichi desu-ka? What month and day is it today?)
今から１０時まで ここにいます。	*Ima*-kara 10-ji-made koko-ni imasu. (I'll be here from now until 10:00.)

私　**SHI*; watashi, watakushi* (I, privacy)**

私	watashi	I
私の	watashi-no	my, mine
私に	watashi-ni	to me, me (*indirect object*)
私を	watashi-o	me (*direct object*)
私と	watashi-to	with me

私の大学は大きいです。	*Watashi*-no daigaku-wa ookii desu. (My university is big.)
私に聞いて下さい。	*Watashi*-ni kiite kudasai. (Please ask me.)
私は日本語の本を 買いました。	*Watashi*-wa nihongo-no hon-o kaimashita. (I bought a Japanese language book.)

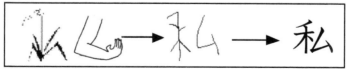

***KANJI* REVIEW**

月　日　木　本　人　山　川　大　小　学　校　中　高　何
今　私　　　　　How do you read them? What do they mean?

PART 1

❶ Vocabulary check

Silently review the vocabulary for Lesson 18. Then have a クラスメート orally test your knowledge of them. Your partner says the えいご and you give the 日本ご. Switch and test your partner.

❷ Shuumatsu-ni nani-o shimasu-ka?

Do this activity in 3人のグループ. Student A mimes two activities which might take place on a weekend and asks *Watashi-wa shuumatsu-ni nani-o shimasu-ka?* Student B begins the answer by telling the first activity and using a *-te* form verb. Student C completes the sentence by telling the second activity and using a *-masu* form verb. Student B mimes next and then Student C. Study the example carefully before you begin.

A: (mimes reading a newspaper and listening to music)
B: Shinbun-o **yonde**, . . .
C: . . . ongaku-o **kikimasu**.
A: Hai, soo desu.

If B and/or C give an incorrect answer, A responds with *Iie, chigaimasu. Moo ichido yoku mite kudasai.* A then mimes the same activities again, and B and C try to provide a correct answer.

PART 2

❶ Doyoobi-wa 7-ji-ni okite, . . .   📄 & ✏️

Do this activity with a クラスメート. Partner A begins by saying *Doyoobi-wa 7-ji-ni okite.* Partner B then adds the next activity in the sequence of Saturday's activities (without repeating what Partner A has said). Continue taking turns with each person adding another activity until you run out of ideas. The final activity is *nemashita.* Repeat the activity if you have time. Record the number of activities you and your partner (together) were able to relate in each round.

❷ Yomimashoo!   📄 & ✏️

This pair activity provides you with an opportunity to review the *kanji* which you have learned to read. Partner A masks the *roomaji* side and reads the vocabulary in the left column in order. Partner B responds after each with either *Hai, soo desu* or *Iie, chigaimasu. Moo ichido yonde kudasai.* Partner A writes down those which need to be studied. Switch roles and repeat.

かなと かんじ	ローマじ
1. 何日	1. nan-nichi
2. 私	2. watashi
3. 今	3. ima
4. 私の大学	4. watashi-no daigaku
5. 日本人	5. nihon-jin
6. 何月	6. nan-gatsu
7. 小さい高校	7. chiisai kookoo
8. 今日は	8. konnichi-wa
9. 大きいホテル	9. ookii hoteru

かな と かんじ	ローマじ
10. 何人	10. nan-nin
11. ３月２５日	11. san-gatsu ni-juu-go-nichi
12. 木よう日	12. moku-yoobi
13. 中学校の中	13. chuugakkoo-no naka
14. 何	14. nan, nani
15. 月よう日	15. getsu-yoobi
16. 日本のともだち	16. Nihon-no tomodachi
17. 高い山	17. takai yama
18. 小学校の本	18. shoogakkoo-no hon
19. ながい川	19. nagai kawa
20. 今日	20. kyoo

れんしゅう A: Something/Nothing; Somebody/Nobody

れんしゅう B: And what did YOU do yesterday?

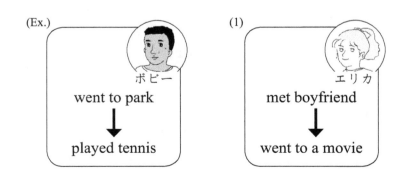

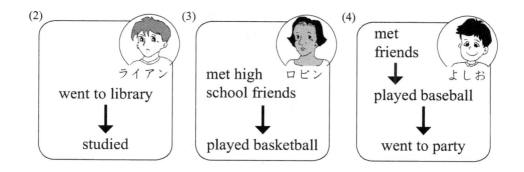

(2) ライアン
went to library
↓
studied

(3) ロビン
met high school friends
↓
played basketball

(4) よしお
met friends
↓
played baseball
↓
went to party

れんしゅう C: Julia's Diary

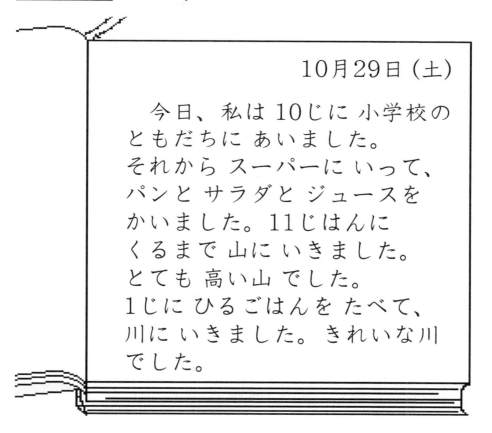

10月29日（土）

　今日、私は 10じに 小学校の
ともだちに あいました。
それから スーパーに いって、
パンと サラダと ジュースを
かいました。11じはんに
くるまで 山に いきました。
とても 高い山 でした。
1じに ひるごはんを たべて、
川に いきました。きれいな川
でした。

しつもん: (Answer in English.)

(1) Who did Julia see on this day?

(2) What time did they meet?

(3) What did they buy at the supermarket?

(4) How did they go to the mountains?

(5) Where did they go after lunch?

LESSON 19
Hobbies and Interests

OBJECTIVES
もくひょう

At the end of this lesson you will be able to:
- ☑ Ask and tell about hobbies and interests
- ☑ Write the *kanji*: 何 and 今

VOCABULARY
たんご

Words

shumi	hobby, pastime, interest
ryokoo	travel, trip
ryoori	cooking
atsumeru (atsumemasu/atsumete)	collect
e	picture

Phrases and expressions

ryokoo(-o) suru (shimasu/shite)	travel (verb)
ryoori(-o) suru (shimasu/shite)	cook (verb)
e-o kaku (kakimasu/kaite)	draw a picture
Shumi-wa nan desu-ka?	What are your hobbies?

Other words and expressions you will hear in this lesson

nuigurumi	stuffed animal
hiku (hikimasu/hiite)	play (stringed and keyboard instruments)
fuku (fukimasu/fuite)	play (wind instruments)
tataku (tatakimasu/tataite)	play (percussion instruments)

VOCABULARY NOTES
たんごノート

1. Kaku (kakimasu/kaite)
In Japanese the words for *write* and *draw* are pronounced the same although they are written with different *kanji*. All writing in Japan was originally done with a brush and ink so the *kanji* were actually "drawn."

2. Hiku ~ fuku ~ tataku
Although in English the verb *play* can be used with any musical instrument, in Japanese you use different verbs with different types of instruments. *Hiku* is used with stringed and keyboard instruments, *fuku* with wind instruments, and *tataku* with percussion instruments.

Mainichi gitaa-o *hikimasu*.	He *plays* guitar every day.
Tomodachi-to kurarinetto-o *fukimasu*.	She *plays* clarinet with her friend.
Gakkoo-de doramu-o *tataku*.	They *play* drums at school.

KEY GRAMMAR POINTS
ぶんぽうポイント

Changing verbs into nouns
In English we can change a verb into a noun (a gerund) by adding the ending *-ing*. Compare these sentences.

I *watch* movies.	[*Watch* is a verb; it expresses the action in the sentence.]
I like *watching* movies.	[*Watching* is a noun; *watching movies* is the object of the verb *like*.]

134

I *swim* often. [*Swim* is a verb; it expresses the action in the sentence.]
Swimming is fun. [*Swimming* is a noun; *swimming* is the subject of the sentence.]

We cannot use a verb as a subject or an object of a sentence. We must change it into a noun. In Japanese also we must generally change verbs into noun phrases if we wish to use them as subjects or objects. One way to do this (for example, when telling what your *shumi* are) is to use the **plain form of the verb + koto**. Study these examples.

Mainichi hon-o *yomimasu*. I read books every day. [*Yomimasu* is a verb.]
hon-o *yomu-koto* reading books [*Yomu-koto* is a noun phrase.]
Shumi-wa hon-o *yomu-koto* desu. My hobby is reading books. [*Yomu-koto* is a noun phrase which can be used as a noun.]

Eiga-o *mimasu*. I watch movies. [*Mimasu* is a verb.]
eiga-o *miru-koto* watching movies [*Miru-koto* is a noun phrase.]
Shumi-wa eiga-o *miru-koto* desu. My hobby is watching movies. [*Miru-koto* is a noun phrase which can be used as a noun.]

> **PLAIN FORM OF THE VERB + KOTO = VERB + ING (A NOUN)**
>
> **hon-o *yomu-koto* = *reading* books**
> **eiga-o *miru-koto* = *watching* movies**

YOMIMASHOO! よみましょう

しゅみ	hobby, pastime, interest
りょこう	travel, trip
りょうり	cooking, cuisine
あつめる・あつめます・あつめて	collect
え	picture
りょこう (を) する・します・して	travel (verb)
りょうり (を) する・します・して	cook (verb)
えを かく・かきます・かいて	draw a picture
しゅみは なん ですか。	What are your hobbies?
みかさんの しゅみは りょうり です。	Mika's hobby is cooking.
はやしさんの しゅみは なん ですか。	What are Mr. Hayashi's hobbies?
しゅみは なにも ありません。	He doesn't have any hobbies.
ぬいぐるみ	stuffed animal
ひく・ひきます・ひいて	play (stringed and keyboard instruments)
ふく・ふきます・ふいて	play (wind instruments)
たたく・たたきます・たたいて	play (percussion instruments)

CULTURE NOTES カルチャーノート

Shumi

Japanese enjoy pursuing a wide range of hobbies and interests, many of which are familiar to you. The word *shumi* is often translated into English as *hobby*, but it actually has a much broader meaning. Which of the *shumi* on the next page would be referred to as *hobbies* in English? For more information on the word *shumi* and the importance of *shumi* in Japanese culture, read the カルチャーノート in Lesson 20.

135

SHUMI

ryoori	supootsu-o miru-koto
ryokoo	supootsu-o suru-koto
konpyuutaa	yakyuu(-o suru-koto)
kaimono	basukettobooru(-o suru-koto)
doraibu	bareebooru(-o suru-koto)
engei (gardening)	gorufu(-o suru-koto)
hon-o yomu-koto	suiei
konsaato-ni iku-koto	tsuri(-ni iku-koto) (fishing)
terebi-o miru-koto	hantingu(-o suru-koto) (hunting)
e-o kaku-koto	yoga(-o suru-koto)
eiga-o miru-koto	ongaku-o kiku-koto
tomodachi-to asobu-koto (playing with friends)	uta-o utau-koto
bideo-geemu-o suru-koto (playing video games)	piano(-o hiku-koto)
toranpu-o suru-koto (playing cards)	baiorin(-o hiku-koto)
shashin-o toru-koto (taking photos)	kurarinetto(-o fuku-koto) (playing clarinet)
kitte-o atsumeru-koto (collecting stamps)	furuuto(-o fuku-koto) (playing flute)
amimono-o suru-koto (knitting)	karaoke (singing to recorded accompaniment)
shugei (handicrafts)	maajan (mah-jong, a Chinese game)
bonsai (miniaturized trees/shrubs)	pachinko (Japanese pinball)
sadoo (tea ceremony)	go (a Japanese board game)
ikebana (flower arrangement)	taberu-koto
shodoo (brush calligraphy)	neru-koto

INTERACTIVE ACTIVITIES

PART 1

❶ **Vocabulary check**

Silently review the vocabulary for Lesson 19. Then have a クラスメート orally test your knowledge of them. Your partner says the えいご, and you give the 日本ご. Switch and test your partner.

❷ **Shumi-wa nan desu-ka?** 📄 & 🖊

Do this interview activity as an entire class. If there are more than 16 students in your class, form groups of eight to 10. Everyone stands up and finds a partner. Partner A asks about Partner B's interests, and then Partner B asks about Partner A's interests. Each person records the answer the partner gives. As soon as a pair has finished, each person then finds a new partner to interview. Try to interview everyone. Refer to the chart above as needed.

    A: Shumi-wa nan desu-ka?
    B: **Ryokoo**-to **e-o kaku-koto**-to **suiei** desu.

PART 2

Kawaguchi-san-no shumi-wa nan desu-ka? 📄 & 🖊

Do this activity with a クラスメート. Look only at your chart. By taking turns asking and answering questions, find out the name, age, and interest(s) of each individual. Refer to the sample questions and answers as needed. Challenge yourself to speak only Japanese during this activity. When you have finished, compare your charts.

PARTNER A

O-NAMAE	NAN-SAI?	SHUMI
Kawaguchi-san	52	hon-o yomu-koto-to yoga-o suru-koto
Hayashi-san	16	ryoori-to konpyuutaa
	27	
		e-o kaku-koto
Mika-san	17	eiga-o miru-koto
Yamakawa-san	20	tomodachi-to asobu-koto
		terebi-geemu-o suru-koto
Watanabe-sensei	61	ryokoo-to yakyuu-o suru-koto
Fujimoto-san		ongaku-o kiku-koto
Mikawa-kun		basukettobooru-o suru-koto
Satake-san		
Miwako-chan	7	piano-o hiku-koto
Ueda-sensei		
Ikeda-san	38	

SAMPLE QUESTIONS AND ANSWERS

1. To find out the **hobby**: **Kawaguchi-san**-no shumi-wa nan desu-ka?
   Hon-o yomu-koto-to **yoga-o suru-koto** desu.

2. To find out the **person**: **Terebi-o miru-koto**-wa dare-no shumi desu-ka?
   Saitoo-san-no shumi desu.

   Dare-ga **23**-sai desu-ka?
   Takeda-sensei desu.

3. To find out the **age**: **Mimura-kun**-wa nan-sai desu-ka?
   18-sai desu.

NAN-SAI?					
1	is-sai	6	roku-sai	20	hatachi
2	ni-sai	7	nana-sai	30	san-jus-sai
3	san-sai	8	hassai	45	yon-juu-go-sai
4	yon-sai	9	kyuu-sai		
5	go-sai	10	jus-sai		

PARTNER B

O-NAMAE	NAN-SAI?	SHUMI
Kawaguchi-san	52	hon-o yomu-koto-to yoga-o suru-koto
Hayashi-san		
Itoo-san	27	konsaato-ni iku-koto
Yukari-chan	10	e-o kaku-koto
		eiga-o miru-koto
	20	
Kenji-kun	15	terebi-geemu-o suru-koto
Watanabe-sensei		
Fujimoto-san	19	
Mikawa-kun	18	
Satake-san	24	supootsu-o miru-koto
		piano-o hiku-koto
Ueda-sensei	30	kaimono-to suiei
Ikeda-san		terebi-geemu-o suru-koto

L. 19 電話で 話しましょう

れんしゅう A: What is your hobby?

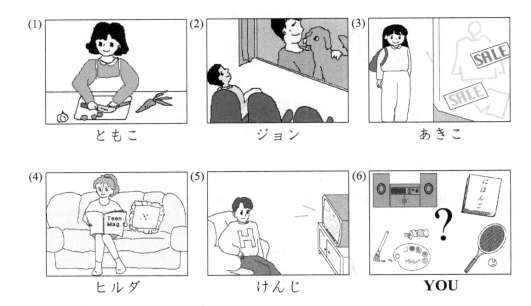

(1) ともこ
(2) ジョン
(3) あきこ
(4) ヒルダ
(5) けんじ
(6) **YOU**

れんしゅう B: Let's find out about their hobbies!

(1)
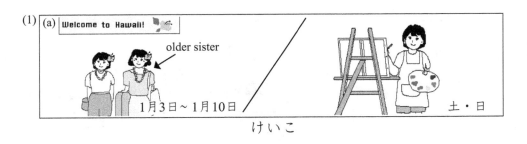

(a) Welcome to Hawaii!
older sister
1月3日～1月10日
土・日
けいこ

(2)
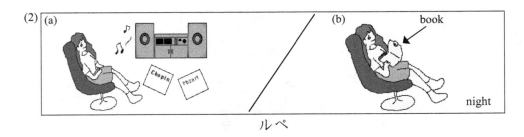

(a) Chopin Mozart
(b) book
night
ルペ

(3)

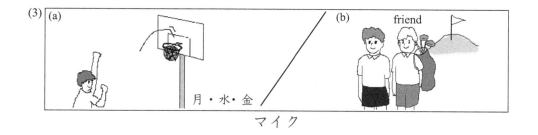

月・水・金

マイク

れんしゅう C: At the Table

139

LESSON 20
Writing to a Pen Pal

OBJECTIVES もくひょう

At the end of this lesson you will be able to:
- ☑ Talk about more hobbies and interests
- ☑ Introduce yourself to a pen pal
- ☑ Read the *kanji*: 火 水 金 土

VOCABULARY たんご

Words

tegami	letter
kitte	postage stamp
-ni	to (a person)
yoku	often
pen-paru	pen pal

VOCABULARY NOTES たんごノート

Yoku

In this lesson the word *yoku* is used with the meaning *often*. *Yoku* can also mean *well* as in *Yoku dekimashita.*

Yoku ryoori-o shimasu-ka?	Do you cook *often*?
Tomodachi-ni *yoku* tegami-o kakimasu.	I *often* write letters to my friends.

KEY GRAMMAR POINTS ぶんぽうポイント

-ni

You have already learned how to use the particle *-ni* with time expressions and with locations. In English *-ni* is usually expressed as *at, on, in,* or *to*. Review the following examples from earlier lessons. For more information and examples, refer to Lessons 27, 38, and 40 (Vol. 1).

Nan-ji-*ni*? San-ji-*ni*.	*At* what time? *At* three o'clock.
Nan-nichi-*ni*? Tsuitachi-*ni*.	*On* what day of the month? *On* the first.
Nan-gatsu-*ni*? Ku-gatsu-*ni*.	*In* what month? *In* September.
Fuyu-*ni*.	*In* winter.
O-shoogatsu-*ni*.	*On/at* New Year's.
Kanada-*ni* ikimashita.	He went *to* Canada.
Ashita daigaku-*ni* ikimasu.	Tomorrow she will go *to* the university.
Tsukue-no ue-*ni* arimasu.	It's *on* the desk.

This lesson introduces the use of the particle *-ni* with people to express *to someone*. In English the person may appear as an indirect object without the word *to*.

Tomodachi-*ni* tegami-o kakimashita.	I wrote a letter *to* my friend.
	I wrote my friend a letter.
Dare-*ni* tegami-o kakimasu-ka?	*To* whom do you write letters?

YOMIMASHOO! よみましょう

てがみ	letter
きって	postage stamp

140

に	to (a person)
よく	often
ペンパル	pen pal
ははに てがみを かきました。	I wrote my mother a letter.
だれに てがみを かいていますか。	Who(m) are you writing a letter to?
ペンパルが いますか。	Do you have a pen pal?

CULTURE NOTES　　　　　　　　カルチャーノート

Shumi 趣味

The word *shumi* is usually translated into English as *hobby*. The actual meaning of *shumi* is broader in scope than *hobby*. It refers to those activities which are of particular interest to a person. *Shumi* can include the kinds of activities which people in the West often identify as hobbies, such as stamp collecting, gardening, cooking, travel, and movies. It can also refer to other activities which people enjoy during leisure time.

For Japanese women, shopping, visiting friends, watching TV, and reading are among the most popular *shumi*. For Japanese men, watching TV, fishing, sleeping, and listening to music rank very high as *shumi*. Some of these may seem like strange hobbies to many of us, but if you remember that *shumi* refers to those activities which have special appeal for people, all of these activities make perfect sense. If you rarely get more than four or five hours of sleep a night, as many Japanese secondary students and businessmen do, you can easily see why sleeping during their free time might be particularly appealing to them.

Shumi are an expression of an individual's interests and thus help define a person. For that reason, Japanese will frequently inquire about your *shumi* soon after meeting you for the first time. Even if you think you do not have any *shumi*, it is a good idea to have at least one in mind so that you can easily respond when asked, "*Shumi-wa nan desu-ka*?" If you think of *shumi* as those things you enjoy doing, you will suddenly find that you may have many *shumi*. If you respond by saying, "*Shumi-wa nani-mo arimasen*," Japanese may think that you are an extraordinarily boring person.

KANJI NOTES　　　　　　　　かんじノート

In this lesson you will learn to read four *kanji*: 火 水 金 土. Be sure that you know the readings of each *kanji* and can tell what the *kanji* means. Readings which are marked by an asterisk are for your reference only; you do not need to learn these at this time. You also do not have to learn any new words which are given in the examples. In a future lesson you will learn how to write these *kanji* using the correct stroke order.

 KA; hi* [bi]* (fire)

火曜日	*ka*yoobi	Tuesday
火事	*ka*ji	fire
花火	hana*bi*	fireworks ["flower-fire"]
火星	*Ka*sei	Mars ["fire-star"]

火曜日に本を買いました。	*Ka*yoobi-ni hon-o kaimashita.
	(On Tuesday I bought books.)
きれいな花火を見ました。	Kirei-na hana*bi*-o mimashita.
	(I saw beautiful fireworks.)

水	**SUI; mizu** (water)	
水	*mizu*	water
水曜日	*sui*yoobi	Wednesday
水星	*Sui*sei	Mercury ["water-star"]
水色	*mizu*-iro	light blue

水曜日に来ました。
*Sui*yoobi-ni kimashita.
(She came on Wednesday.)

お水をお願いします。
O-*mizu*-o o-negai-shimasu.
(Water, please.)

この水色のシャツが
大好きです。
Kono *mizu*-iro-no shatsu-ga daisuki desu.
(I really like this light blue shirt.)

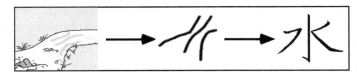

金	**KIN; KON*** (gold); **kane** (money)	
お金	o-*kane*	money
金曜日	*kin*yoobi	Friday
金星	*Kin*sei	Venus ["gold-star"]

お金がたくさんあります。
O-*kane*-ga takusan arimasu.
(They have a lot of money.)

金曜日に何をしましたか。
*Kin*yoobi-ni nani-o shimashita-ka?
(What did you do on Friday?)

土	**DO, TO*; tsuchi*** (earth, soil)	
土曜日	*do*yoobi	Saturday
土	*tsuchi*	earth, soil
土星	*Do*sei	Saturn ["earth-star"]

今日は土曜日ですね。
Kyoo-wa *do*yoobi desu-ne.
(Today's Saturday, isn't it?)

ここの土はいいですね。
Koko-no *tsuchi*-wa ii desu-ne.
(The soil here is good, isn't it?)

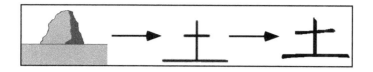

KANJI REVIEW

月	日	木	本	人	山	川	大	小	学
校	中	高	何	今	私	火	水	金	土

How do you read them? What do they mean?

INTERACTIVE ACTIVITIES

PART 1

❶ Vocabulary check

Silently review the vocabulary for Lesson 20 and vocabulary related to days and dates. Then have a クラスメート orally test your knowledge of them. Your partner says the えいご, and you give the 日本ご. Switch and test your partner.

❷ Nan-nen-sei desu-ka?

Do this interview activity with a クラスメート. Take turns asking each other questions to elicit information which would be included in a self-introduction. You may ask questions in any order about the following topics.

Name	School subjects	Likes and dislikes
Age	Favorite subject	Friends
Birthday	Your family	Daily schedule
Grade	Your pets	Daily activities
School name	Your hobbies and interests	Weekend activities
Clubs you belong to	What you can and cannot do	Vacations

Here are some sample questions to help you get started, but do not limit yourself to these.

O-namae-wa?
Nan-sai desu-ka?
O-tanjoobi-wa nan-gatsu nan-nichi desu-ka?
Nan-nen-sei desu-ka?
Gakkoo-wa doko desu-ka?
Nan-no kurabu-ni haitte-imasu-ka?
Suugaku-wa nan-yoobi desu-ka?
Kamoku-wa nani-ga ichiban suki desu-ka?
Go-kazoku-wa nan-nin imasu-ka?
Petto-o katte-imasu-ka?
Nan-no petto-o katte-imasu-ka?

Petto-no namae-wa nan desu-ka?
Shumi-wa nan desu-ka?
Supootsu-ga dekimasu-ka?
Furansugo-ga dekimasu-ka?
Gakki-ga dekimasu-ka?
Eiga-ga suki desu-ka?
Nihonjin-no tomodachi-ga imasu-ka?
Nan-ji-ni gakkoo-ni kimasu-ka?
Mainichi shinbun-o yomimasu-ka?
Shuumatsu-ni nani-o shimasu-ka?
Fuyu-yasumi-ni nani-o shimasu-ka?

PART 2

❶ Hajimemashite. Kurisu Sumisu desu.

Do this activity with a クラスメート. Partner A gives an oral self-introduction of four minutes, including as much information as possible. The information should be similar to that which would be written in a letter to a pen pal. Partner A may not use any notes or materials. Partner B listens carefully without interrupting and without taking any notes. After Partner A has finished speaking, Partner B must make five true statements about Partner A. The statements should contain information which Partner B learned by listening to the self-introduction (not name, age, grade, name of school, etc.). Switch roles and repeat.

❷ **Yomimashoo!**　📄 & ✎

This pair activity provides you with an opportunity to review the *kanji* which you have learned to read. Partner A masks the *roomaji* side and reads the vocabulary in the left column in order. Partner B responds after each with either *Hai, soo desu* or *Iie, chigaimasu. Moo ichido yonde kudasai.* Partner A writes those which need to be studied. Switch roles and repeat.

かな と かんじ	ローマじ
1. 何の本	1. nan-no hon
2. 火よう日	2. ka-yoobi
3. お金	3. o-kane
4. 今	4. ima
5. 何人	5. nan-nin
6. 水	6. mizu
7. 土よう日	7. do-yoobi
8. 何月何日	8. nan-gatsu nan-nichi
9. 水よう日	9. sui-yoobi
10. 今日	10. kyoo
11. 何よう日	11. nan-yoobi
12. 今日は	12. konnichi-wa, kyoo-wa
13. 金よう日	13. kin-yoobi

L.20 電話で 話しましょう

<u>れんしゅう</u> A: What's in this room?

Answer the questions based on the picture below.

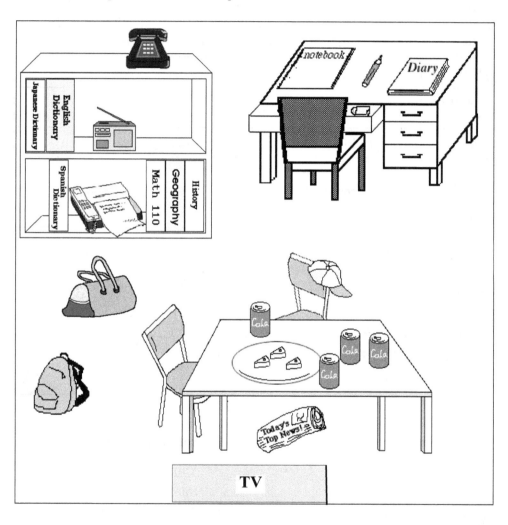

145

れんしゅう B: Find out about these three people.

Name	Kelly Smith	Brian Miller	Emily Davis
Grade	1st year in high school	(1) 3rd year in high school	2nd year in high school
Club	volleyball	(2) basketball	tennis
Hobby	travelling	drawing	(4) cooking
Favorite Subject	geography	art	(5) English
Pet	dog (white)	(3) ✕	cat (brown)

れんしゅう C: Let's converse!

Dialogue:

A: <u>Ms. Yamakawa</u>, what are you doing?
B: Well, I'm writing a letter to my pen pal.
A: Oh, where is your pen pal?
B: She is in <u>Tokyo</u>.
A: Do you write to her often?
B: Yes, I do.

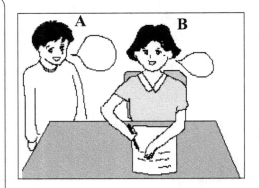

Sample Dialogue:

A: <u>山川さん</u>、何を していますか。
B: ペンパルに てがみを かいています。
A: へえ、ペンパルは どこに いますか。
B: <u>とうきょう</u>に います。
A: よく てがみを かきますか。
B: はい、 かきます。

Sample Dialogue:

A: <u>Yamakawa-san</u>, nani-o shite-imasu-ka?
B: Pen-paru-ni tegami-o kaite-imasu.
A: Hee, pen-paru-wa doko-ni imasu-ka?
B: <u>Tookyoo</u>-ni imasu.
A: Yoku tegami-o kakimasu-ka?
B: Hai, kakimasu.

REVIEW LESSON 1
(Volume 1, Lessons 50~57)

OBJECTIVES   もくひょう

This lesson provides you with an opportunity to review the following objectives from Volume 1, Lessons 50 through 57:

- ☑ Tell what day of the week subjects are scheduled and when classes begin and end
- ☑ Comment on school subjects
- ☑ Ask about and express likes and dislikes
- ☑ State what you like and what another person likes best
- ☑ Invite someone to do something, and accept or decline invitations
- ☑ Ask about and state preferences
- ☑ Ask about and state ability
- ☑ Give and respond to compliments
- ☑ Comment on music
- ☑ State the uses of *katakana*
- ☑ Read and write *katakana*

VOCABULARY   たんご

Sports-Related Words:
supootsu [sports]
yakyuu [baseball]
futtobooru [football]
tenisu [tennis]
bareebooru [volleyball]
sakkaa [soccer]
suiei [swimming]
basukettobooru [basketball]
chiimu [team]
sumoo [sumo (wrestling)]
karate [karate]
juudoo [judo]
kendoo [kendo (Japanese fencing)]
Taiiku-no hi [Sports Day]

School Subjects:
kamoku [(school) subject, course]
suugaku [mathematics, math]
rekishi [history]
chiri [geography]
kagaku [science]
furansugo [French (language)]
doitsugo [German (language)]
supeingo [Spanish (language)]
taiiku [physical education]
bijutsu [art]

Verbs:
dekimasu (dekiru)
[can (do), be able (to do)]
utaimasu (utau) [to sing]

Music-Related Words:
piano [piano]   baiorin [violin]
doramu [drums]   gitaa [guitar]
furuuto [flute]   gakki [musical instrument]
uta [song]

Adjectives:
-i **Adjectives:**
muzukashii [difficult, hard]
urusai [noisy, bothersome]
omoshiroi [interesting, enjoyable]

-na **Adjectives:**
kantan (na) [easy, simple]
suki (na) [like, is pleasing]
daisuki (na) [like very much, is very pleasing]
kirai (na) [dislike, hate, is displeasing]
joozu (na) [good at, skilled at]
heta (na) [bad at]
shizuka (na) [quiet]
daijoobu (na) [O.K., all right, no problem]

Adverbs:
tokidoki [sometimes]
ichiban [number one, the best, the most]
zenzen [(not) at all, completely (not)]
anmari [not very much]
sukoshi [a little]

Conjunctions:
demo [but, however]

147

> **Phrases and Expressions:**
> __-wa nan-yoobi desu-ka? [What day is _ (scheduled)?]
> __-no benkyoo-o shimasu [will study / study / studies _]
> Nani-ga suki desu-ka? [What do you like?]
> __-ga suki desu. [I like _.]
> __-wa suki ja nai desu. [I don't like _.]
> Anmari suki ja nai desu. [I don't like it very much; I really don't like it.]
> __-wa nani-ga suki desu-ka? [What _ do you like?]
> Dare-ga ichiban suki desu-ka? [Who(m) do you like best?]
> Ganbatte. (pronounced *gambatte*) [Do your best!; Try hard!; Go, go!]
> Omedetoo gozaimasu. [Congratulations.]
> Issho-ni __mashoo. [Let's _ together.]

VOCABULARY NOTES   たんごノート

Joozu ~ heta (L. 55)
Joozu means *good at* or *skilled at* whereas *heta* means *bad at* or *not skilled at*. In Japanese a person would generally not use the word *joozu* when speaking about himself/herself since this could be considered boasting or bragging which would be impolite.

Ueda-san-wa doitsugo-ga joozu desu.	Mrs. Ueda is good at German.
Uta-ga joozu desu-ne.	You're good at singing, aren't you?
Iie, heta desu-yo.	No, I'm bad at it.

KEY GRAMMAR POINTS   ぶんぽうポイント

The number in parentheses after each grammar point is the lesson in which it was first presented.

1. Telling the day on which events are scheduled (L. 50)
By adding a topic followed by the topic particle *-wa*, you can ask and state on which day events, including classes, are scheduled.

A: Eigo-no jugyoo-*wa* nan-yoobi desu-ka?	What day is English class?
B: Ka-yoobi-to moku-yoobi desu.	(English class is) on Tuesday(s) and Thursday(s).

2. (*Person*-wa) X-ga suki/daisuki/kirai desu.
(*Person*-wa) X-wa anmari suki ja nai desu. (L. 52)
Suki desu is usually translated as *like(s)*. The X represents the item which is liked. *Daisuki* means *is very pleasing* and is often translated in English as *like(s) very much*. *Daisuki* and *suki* are both adjectives in Japanese and are used in the same way.

Nani-ga *suki* desu-ka?	What do you *like*?
Piza-ga *daisuki* desu.	I *like* pizza *very much*.

Kirai means *is displeasing* and in English is often expressed as *dislike(s)* or *hate(s)*. This is a rather strong expression which you may wish to avoid by substituting a less harsh expression such as *X-wa anmari suki ja nai desu*, means which *X is not really pleasing*, and is often translated as *do(es)n't really like X*.

Sushi-wa anmari *suki ja nai* desu.	I *do not* really *like* sushi.

If you want to tell not only which thing is pleasing or displeasing but also the person who feels that way about it, include the person followed by the topic particle *-wa*.

Mari-san-*wa* tomato juusu-ga kirai desu.	Mari dislikes tomato juice.

3. *Category*-wa X-ga (ichiban) suki/kirai desu. (L. 53)

By adding the word *ichiban,* you can express the idea of liking X the best of all of a set of items or people. If the context (the set of all possible items or people) has not been established, you can ask this way:

Supootsu-wa nani-ga *ichiban* suki desu-ka?	What sports do you like the *best/most*? [The context is *all sports*.]

When the context is already established, you can answer this way:

Suiei-ga *ichiban* suki desu.	I like swimming the *best/most*. [of all sports]

4. ~masen-ka? ~mashoo (L. 54)

You can use the verb ending *-masen-ka?* to invite people to do various activities. The ending *-mashoo* has the meaning of *Let's* and suggests a course of action. You can use this form when you want to accept an invitation.

A: Kyoo yakyuu-o shi*masen-ka?*	*Would you like to* play baseball today?
B: Soo desu-ne . . . Ja, *shimashoo!*	Hmm . . . O.K., *let's play!*

5. *Category*-wa nani-o ~masu-ka? (L. 54)

You can state a category first and then ask what another person's preference is within that category. You can use a similar pattern when the category or context is established first.

A: *Supootsu-wa* nani-o shimasu-ka?	What *sports* do you play?
B: *Ongaku-wa* nani-o kikimasu-ka?	What *music* do you listen to?

6. X-ga dekimasu ~ X-wa dekimasen (L. 55)

Remember that the particles *-ga* and *-wa* are both used with the verb *dekimasu,* and which is used depends on whether the verb is affirmative or negative.

A: Supootsu-wa nani-*ga* dekimasu-ka?	What sport(s) can you play?
B: Bareebooru-*ga* sukoshi dekimasu.	I can play volleyball a little.
A: Futtobooru-*mo* dekimasu-ka?*	Can you play football also?
B: Iie, futtobooru-*wa* zenzen dekimasen.	No, I can't play football at all.

*The particle *-mo* (also) replaces *-ga*.

7. Kedo ~ demo (L. 56)

Although the words *kedo* and *demo* can both be expressed in English as *but*, they differ in how they are used. The word *kedo* appears within a single sentence where it serves to connect two parts of the sentence.

Sakkaa-ga suki desu *kedo*, anmari joozu ja nai desu.	I like soccer, *but* I'm not very good at it.
Sakkaa-ga suki desu. *Demo*, anmari joozu ja nai desu.	I like soccer. *But*, I'm not very good at it.

8. Sorekara ~ -to (L. 56)

The word *sorekara*, which can also mean *then*, is used to connect sentences, whereas the particle *-to* is used to connect nouns only.

Kinoo 8-ji-made hon-o yomimashita. *Sorekara*, geemu-o shimashita.	Yesterday I read a book until 8:00. *Then*, I played a game.
Shuumatsu, shukudai-*to* geemu-o shimashita.	I did homework *and* played games on the weekend.

9. *I*-adjectives and *Na*-adjectives (L. 57)

Remember *i*-adjectives, which end in *i* in *roomaji* and in い in *hiragana*, can precede the noun that they modify or can be used alone with *desu*. Like *i*-adjectives, *na*-adjectives can precede the nouns they modify or can be used with the verb *desu/deshita*. When they precede a noun, you must insert the particle *-na* after the adjective.

Kantan-na tesuto deshita.	It was an *easy* test.

These same *na*-adjectives do not require -*na* when they are used with *desu*.

    Tesuto-wa *kantan* deshita.   The test was *easy*.

You can form the negative of *na*-adjectives with *ja nai*.

    Sono shitsumon-wa *kantan ja nai* desu.   That question is *not easy*.

10. Particles

Particle	L. #	Note(s)	Sample Sentence
が **ga**	52 55 56	Used with *suki desu, kirai desu, dekimasu, joozu desu, heta desu* to indicate that which is liked /pleasing or disliked /displeasing and that which one is able to do and skilled/ not skilled at	テニスがすきです。 (I like tennis.) ピアノがすこしできます。 (I can play the piano a little.) たなかさんはすいえいがとてもじょうずです。 (Ms. Tanaka is very good at swimming.)
は **wa**	52 55 56	Used with *suki ja nai desu, dekimasen, joozu ja nai desu* to replace *ga* above in negative sentences	テニスはすきじゃないです。 (I do not like tennis.) ピアノはぜんぜんできません。 (I cannot play the piano at all.) すいえいはじょうずじゃないです。 (I am not good at swimming.)
	53 54 56	Used as a topic marker to indicate a category of things	がっきはなにができますか。 (As for musical instruments, what can you play?)

CULTURE NOTES   カルチャーノート

1. Declining an invitation (L. 54)
The word *chotto* can be used to soften refusals, as well as when politely declining an invitation. The speaker's voice trails off after *chotto* . . .

    A: Yakyuu-o shimasen-ka?   Would you like to play baseball?
    B: Yakyuu desu-ka?   Baseball? Baseball's a *little* . . .
        Yakyuu-wa *chotto* . . .

2. Japanese traditional sports (L. 55)
Traditional Japanese sports such as judo, kendo, karate are usually referred to in English as *martial arts*. These sports are, indeed, art forms whose every movement is carefully choreographed much like an intricate dance form. They operate on a distinctly different premise from Western tests of strength. Speed, agility, and an understanding of the basic laws of movement are the determining factors as to who might win in competition. As with all sports and arts in Japan, mental discipline as well as a certain degree of ritual and formality are integral parts of the training.

a. Juudoo 柔道 （じゅうどう）
The word *juudoo* is written with two *kanji*: 柔道. The first *kanji* 柔 (*juu*) means *soft* while the second *kanji* 道 (*doo*) means *way* or *path*. By carefully borrowing the strength of one's opponent, a person can quickly defeat someone of far greater physical strength and size. Since judo is largely defensive in nature, competitors are not allowed to use weapons or moves that might injure the opponent. The sport is usually performed in large open rooms on surfaces covered with very thick *tatami* (rice straw) mats. The color of the belt indicates a person's rank.

b. Karate 空手 （からて）
The word *karate* is written with two *kanji* 空手. The first *kanji* 空 (*kara*) means *empty* while the second one 手 (*te*) means *hand*. Like judo, karate does not allow the use of weapons. Karate differs from judo in that while judo relies on specific throws and holds to defeat an opponent, while in karate one must rely on the use of hands, feet, elbows, and knees to defeat one's opponent. As in judo, the color of the belt indicates a person's rank as well in karate.

c. Kendoo 剣道 （けんどう）

Kendo is believed to have originated in Japan. It is written with two kanji 剣道, meaning *sword* and *way* or *path*. The second *kanji* is the same as the second *kanji* as in *juudoo*. Traditionally in Japan, the sword has been imbued with an almost spiritual power. Those who were allowed to carry swords (the samurai/warrior class) never let their swords out of their care. The art of sword-making stretches back at least 1,500-2,000 years.

d. Sumoo 相撲 （すもう）

The sport of sumo wrestling, which is a national sport of tremendous popularity in Japan, has grown out of a tradition that stretches back at least 1,000 years. The origins of the sport are religious in nature with the earliest recorded wrestling matches having taken place on the grounds of Shinto shrines. *Sumoo* is written with the *kanji* 相撲, meaning *mutual* and *slap* or *hit*. The sumo wrestler who succeeds in forcing his opponent out of the circle or in pushing him to the ground so that a body part other than the soles of his feet is touching the ground wins the bout.

3. Compliments (L. 56)

While many Americans readily accept compliments and praise from others, adult Japanese do their best to deny compliments even though they may be inwardly pleased. The following is a typical compliment paid to a foreigner who then responds in a culturally appropriate manner.

Nihon-jin (Japanese person):   Nihongo-ga o-joozu desu-ne.
Gaikoku-jin (Foreigner):   Iie, mada heta desu kedo...

4. Karaoke (L. 56)

Literally empty orchestra, *karaoke* became a popular form of entertainment in Japan in the late 1970's. Karaoke enables people to sing their favorite songs to a professional-sounding orchestral accompaniment.

5. Japanese traditional musical instruments (L. 57)

a. Koto 琴 （こと）

The *koto* is a 13-stringed instrument which is approximately six feet long and one foot wide. The *koto* is placed flat on the floor (on *tatami* mats) before the musician who is seated in traditional *seiza* style with legs folded beneath the body.

b. Shamisen 三味線 （しゃみせん）

The *shamisen* is a three-stringed instrument originally imported from China in the late 16th century. The *shamisen* is held much like a banjo and is played with a large paddle-like plectrum. The three *kanji* used to write the word *shamisen* literally mean *three-flavor-string*.

c. Shakuhachi 尺八 （しゃくはち）

The *shakuhachi* is a five-hole bamboo flute whose name is derived from its length expressed in traditional Japanese units of measurement. The flute is one *shaku* (approximately one foot) and eight-*sun* (approximately one tenth of a *shaku*) in length.

d. Taiko 太鼓 （たいこ）

A *taiko* is a very large cylindrical drum which is generally placed on its side on a wooden stand or suspended from a wooden frame.

Like the *hiragana* syllabary, the *katakana* syllabary consists of 46 basic sounds. *Katakana*, however, tend to be more angular in form with fewer curved strokes.

ン	ワ	ラ	ヤ	マ	ハ	ナ	タ	サ	カ	ア
n	wa	ra	ya	ma	ha	na	ta	sa	ka	a
	リ			ミ	ヒ	ニ	チ	シ	キ	イ
	ri			mi	hi	ni	chi	shi	ki	i
	ル	ユ	ム	フ	ヌ	ツ	ス	ク	ウ	
	ru	yu	mu	fu	nu	tsu	su	ku	u	
	レ		メ	ヘ	ネ	テ	セ	ケ	エ	
	re		me	he	ne	te	se	ke	e	
ヲ	ロ	ヨ	モ	ホ	ノ	ト	ソ	コ	オ	
(w)o	ro	yo	mo	ho	no	to	so	ko	o	

The line beginning with *ka* from the basic chart is
　カ キ ク ケ コ (ka, ki, ku, ke, ko)
By adding two little marks called *dakuten* you can create five new *hiragana*.
　ガ ギ グ ゲ ゴ (ga, gi, gu, ge, go)
In the same way, you can create three additional lines beginning with *za*, *da*, and *ba*.
　ザ ジ ズ ゼ ゾ (za, ji, zu, ze, zo)
　ダ ヂ ヅ デ ド (da, ji, zu, de, do) Remember that ジ and ズ are used for ヂ
　　　　　　　　　　　　　　and ヅ respectively.
　バ ビ ブ ベ ボ (ba, bi, bu, be, bo)
By adding a small circle called a *handakuten*, the *pa* line is formed from the *ha* line.
　パ ピ プ ペ ポ (pa, pi, pu, pe, po)

Double consonants
When the *katakana* ツ (*tsu*) appears in a word and is about half the size of the other *katakana* it is a marker for a double consonant sound. Whenever you see the small ツ, it doubles the following consonant sound, as in クッキー (*kukkii*).

Long vowels in *katakana*
Each long vowel in *katakana* is written with the symbol for the single vowel followed by a horizontal line. Each long vowel requires twice the length of time to produce it as does its single counterpart.
　アー is twice as long as　ア
　イー　　　"　　　　　イ
Here is an example of *gairaigo* which has long vowels in it.
　コンピューター　　　　　　　　　konpy**uutaa**
When Japanese is written vertically, the long mark is written vertically below the vowel.

Uses of *katakana*
Katakana is generally used to represent foreign words (*gairaigo*), foreign names such as *Sumisu* (Smith), and onomatopoetic words (*giseigo*) such as *wan-wan* for *bow-wow*. They are also widely used in advertising to write words which would otherwise be written in *hiragana*. Messages in telegrams are also written in *katakana*.

Examples of words written in *katakana*

You have already learned in this course a large number of *gairaigo* which are commonly used in everyday Japanese. All of these borrowed words are written in *katakana*. Do you remember the examples given in the chart?

GAIRAIGO			
Objects		**Places**	
konpyuutaa	コンピューター	Amerika	アメリカ
fakkusu	ファックス	Kariforunia	カリフォルニア
supuun	スプーン	Furansu	フランス
terebi	テレビ	Supein	スペイン
bideo	ビデオ	resutoran	レストラン
Activities		**People**	
tenisu	テニス	kurasumeeto	クラスメート
arubaito	アルバイト	Sumisu	スミス
paatii	パーティー	Amanda	アマンダ
Food		**Other**	
hanbaagaa	ハンバーガー	zero	ゼロ
keeki	ケーキ	doru	ドル
piza	ピザ	tesuto	テスト
supagetii	スパゲティー	guruupu	グループ

INTERACTIVE ACTIVITIES

PART 1

❶ Pair work – Information gap   📄 & ✏

This is Maiko's weekly morning schedule. Both Partners A and B have only half of her schedule. Divide into groups of A and B. Ask members of the other group questions and complete her schedule. Partner A will find the information for (1) through (4) and Partner B will find the information for (5) through (8).

Questions:
1. *Subject name*-は なんようび ですか。
2. *Subject name*-は なんじから なんじまで ですか。

MAIKO-SAN-NO JUGYOO: chiri, eigo, kagaku, ongaku, rekishi, supeingo, suugaku, taiiku
FOR REFERENCE: Telling time (L. 24); Days of the week (L. 48); Kanji for the days (L. 49)

PARTNER A

Find out what days of the week and the time her (1) math, (2) music, (3) English and (4) science classes are scheduled.

	月	火	水	木	金
8:00 – 8:50		スペインご		スペインご	スペインご
9:00 – 9:50	ちり		ちり		
10:00 – 10:50			たいいく		たいいく
11:00 – 11:50	れきし		れきし		れきし

153

Questions:
1. *Subject name*-は なんようび ですか。
2. *Subject name*-は なんじから なんじまで ですか。

MAIKO-SAN-NO JUGYOO: chiri, eigo, kagaku, ongaku, rekishi, supeingo, suugaku, taiiku
FOR REFERENCE: Telling time (L. 24); Days of the week (L. 48); Kanji for the days (L. 49)

PARTNER B
Find what days of the week and the time her (5) geography, (6) Spanish, (7) history and
(8) P.E. classes are scheduled.

	月	火	水	木	金
8:00 – 8:50	おんがく		おんがく		
9:00 – 9:50		かがく		かがく	かがく
10:00 – 10:50	えいご	えいご		えいご	
11:00 – 11:50		すうがく		すうがく	

❷ Presentation   📄 & ✏️
Using the guideline below, write out a report of the information obtained from the
activity above, and give a presentation on Maiko's schedule to the class. Check your
work with the answer key on the next page.

まいこさんは _____と_____と_____と_____と
_____と_____と_____と_____の じゅぎょうが あり
ます。_____の じゅぎょうは_____ようびと _____ようび
(と _____ようび) です。_____の じゅぎょうは _____から
_____まで です。

PART 2

❶ Gairaigo   📄 & ✏️
Work in pairs. For 1~4, Partner A reads the *gairaigo* and Partner B matches pictures.
Then, switch roles for 5~8. Write down your answers and check them with the answer
key on the next page.

1. バスケットボール
2. コンピューター
3. ドラム
4. スパゲティー

5. アイスクリーム
6. サンドイッチ
7. ギター
8. オレンジジュース

a.   b.   c.   d.

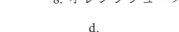

e.   f.   g.   h.

❷ Interview your classmates 📄 & ✏️

Using the following category in the boxes, interview your classmates to find out what they like the best and are good at. As you interview your classmates, take notes of their responses.

Questions:
1. Category-は なにが （いちばん） すき ですか。
2. Category-は なにが できますか。

QUESTION 1			
のみもの	えいが	かもく	おんがく

QUESTION 2	
スポーツ	がっき

❸ Writing practice 📄 & ✏️

Based on the information that you have obtained from the interview, write a summary of what your classmates like and are good at. Refer to the answer key when you are done.

ANSWERS (INTERACTIVE ACTIVITIES):
PART 1❷
まいこさんは おんがくと スペインごと ちりと かがくと えいごと たいいくと れきしと すうがくの じゅぎょうが あります。れきしの じゅぎょうは げつ／月ようびと すい／水ようびと （きん／金ようび） です。(Sample Answer) れきしの じゅぎょうは じゅういちじから じゅういちじ ごじゅっぷんまで です。 * This answer may vary.
PART 2 ❶
1. (a) 2. (c) 3. (f) 4. (g) 5. (h) 6. (b) 7. (e) 8. (d)
PART 2 ❸
Examples: ジョンくんは おんがくは ロックが すきです。スポーツは サッカーが できます。セーラさんは のみものは こうちゃが すきです。がっきは ピアノが すこし できます。ヨンヘさんは かもくは にほんごの じゅぎょうが いちばん すきです。えいがは SFが すきです。

RL. 1 電話で 話しましょう

れんしゅう A: Invitation to an Activity

You want to do something with your Japanese classmate this weekend.
Invite him or her to do something with you.

れんしゅう B: What can you do?

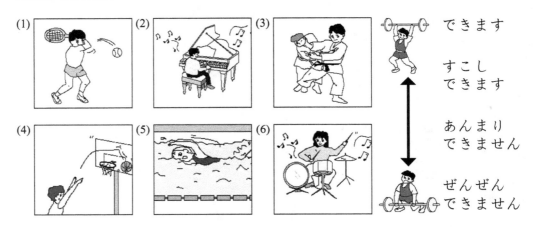

(1) (2) (3)

できます

すこし
できます

あんまり
できません

(4) (5) (6)

ぜんぜん
できません

れんしゅう C: What do you like best?

(1)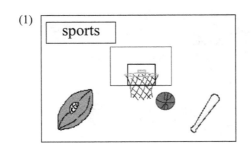

sports

(2)

subjects

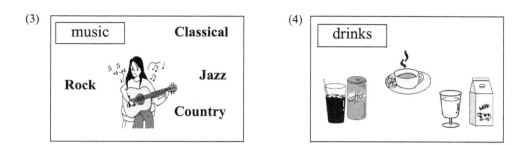

(3) music | Classical | Rock | Jazz | Country

(4) drinks

<u>れんしゅう D</u>: S/he is good at ~ but bad at ~.

(Ex.) しょうこ — good at / not good at

(1) ゆうじ — like / don't like

(2) ゆみ — Spanish able to speak / German not able to speak

<u>れんしゅう E</u>: Particle Review

Write the appropriate particles in *hiragana* in the boxes.

(1) エリカさん ☐ バスケットボール ☐ とてもじょうず
です。

(2) スポーツ ☐ なに ☐ いちばんおもしろいですか。

(3) スペインご ☐ ぜんぜんできません。

(4) ピザ ☐ だいすきです。でも、スパゲティー ☐
あんまりすきじゃないです。

157

REVIEW LESSON 2
(Volume 1, Lessons 58~66)

OBJECTIVES
もくひょう

This lesson provides you with an opportunity to review the following objectives from Volume 1, Lessons 58 through 66:

- ☑ Talk about the weather and temperature
- ☑ Identify common items of clothing
- ☑ Comment on clothing and accessories
- ☑ Describe objects in terms of color
- ☑ Ask and state the price of objects
- ☑ Count from 100 through 9,999
- ☑ Count objects using the general counters *hitotsu ~ too*
- ☑ Ask for and state the quantity of things
- ☑ Read and write *katakana*

VOCABULARY
たんご

Weather-Related and Seasonal Words:

(o)tenki [weather]	ame [rain]
hare [clear, sunny]	kumori [cloudy]
yuki [snow]	iya (na) [bad, terrible]
atsui [hot]	samui [cold]
#-do [degrees]	atatakai [warm]
suzushii [cool]	-mitai [seems~, looks~]
tsuyu [rainy season]	taifuu [typhoon]
tsukimi [moon viewing]	hanami [cherry-blossom viewing]

Phrases and Expressions – Weather:

Ii tenki desu. [It's nice weather.]
Iya-na tenki desu. [It's bad weather.]
_____-no tenki-wa doo desu-ka? [How's the weather in _____?]
_____-wa #-do desu. [It's # degrees in _____.]
_____-wa nan-do desu-ka? [What's the temperature in _____?]
Ame-mitai desu. [It looks like rain.]

Shopping-Related Words:

kaimasu [buy]	takai [expensive]
ikura [how much]	yasui [cheap]
hyaku [hundred]	takusan [many, much]
sen [thousand]	depaato [department store]
#-en [# yen]	(o)mise [store]
#-doru [# dollars]	ikutsu [how many things]
#-sento [# cents]	

People-Related Words:

otoko-no-hito [man]   onna-no-hito [woman]

Clothing-Related Words:

kawaii [cute]	kirei (na) [pretty]
hen (na) [strange]	kakkoii [cool, neat]
booshi [hat]	fuku [clothes]
kutsushita [socks]	zubon [pants]

Colors:

iro [color]	kiiro(i) [yellow]
murasaki [purple]	shiro(i) [white]
chairo(i) [brown]	

Nani-iro desu-ka? [What color is it?]

Phrases and Expressions – Clothing and Shopping:

_____-wa doo desu-ka? [How about _____?]
Dono fuku-ni shimashoo-ka? [Which clothes should I wear?]
Kore-ni shimashoo. [Let's get this.]
_____-wa ikura desu-ka? [How much is/are _____?]
motto (adj.) [more (adj.)]
Ikutsu arimasu-ka? [How many are there?]
Kudasai. [Please give me.]
_____-o kudasai. [Please give me _____.]
_____-o #-to _____-o # kudasai. [Please give me # _____s and # _____s.]

The number in parentheses after each grammar point is the lesson in which it was first presented.

1. -do (L. 59)

The counter *do* is used to express degrees. Notice the forms for 4, 7, and 9 degrees.

DEGREES			
ichi-do	1 degree	nana-do	7 degrees
ni-do	2 degrees	hachi-do	8 degrees
san-do	3 degrees	kyuu-do	9 degree
yon-do	4 degrees	juu-do	10 degree
go-do	5 degrees	juu-ni-do	12 degree
roku-do	6 degrees	ni-juu-san-do	23 degrees

Atoranta-wa nan-*do* desu-ka?　　　What's the *temperature* in Atlanta?
San-juu-nana-*do* desu.　　　　　　It's 37 *degrees* (in Atlanta).

2. Forming the negative of *i*-adjectives (L. 59)

To form the negative of an *i*-adjective, change the final *i* to *kunai*.

THE NEGATIVE FORMS OF *I*-ADJECTIVES		
furui	furu**kunai**	(not) old
ookii	ooki**kunai**	(not) big
chiisai	chiisa**kunai**	(not) small
hayai	haya**kunai**	(not) fast, early
osoi	oso**kunai**	(not) slow, late
isogashii	isogashi**kunai**	(not) busy
tsumaranai	tsumarana**kunai**	(not) boring
omoshiroi	omoshiro**kunai**	(not) interesting
samui	samu**kunai**	(not) cold
atsui	atsu**kunai**	(not) hot
Irregular ii	yo**kunai**	(not) good

3. Adjective/noun + -mitai (L. 60)

By adding *-mitai* to the end of an adjective or noun you can express the idea of *it looks like ~* or *it seems ~*. If you tell someone something which appears to be true (such as tomorrow's weather), but you are not absolutely sure, then you use *-mitai*.

Ame-*mitai* desu.　　　　　　　　　It *looks like* it will rain.
Atsui-*mitai* desu.　　　　　　　　　It *looks like* it will be hot.
Suzushikunai-*mitai* desu.　　　　　It *looks like* it won't be cool.
Ashita-wa ii tenki-*mitai* desu.　　　It *looks like* good weather tomorrow.

4. *Na*-adjectives (L. 61)

The Japanese language has borrowed several adjectives from English and treats them as *na*-adjectives. Since they are borrowed, they are written in *katakana*. Two of these adjectives are included in the list on the next page.

		NA-ADJECTIVES		
kantan	かんたん	easy, simple	kantan-na shitsumon
suki	すき	pleasing	suki-na tabemono
shizuka	しずか	quiet	shizuka-na hito
iya	いや	bad, terrible	iya-na tenki
kirei	きれい	pretty	kirei-na burausu
hen	へん	strange	hen-na fuku
hansamu	ハンサム	handsome	hansamu-na-hito
romanchikku	ロマンチック	romantic	romanchikku-na resutoran

5. Colors (L. 63)

In English, a color word, such as *red* or *blue*, can be either a noun or an adjective. The same is true for some color words in Japanese, however, there are some color words in Japanese that are always nouns. Two examples are *midori* (green) and *murasaki* (purple). When they modify or describe other nouns, the particle *-no* must be used between the two nouns.

Murasaki-ga suki desu.	I like *purple*.
Midori-no seetaa-ga hoshii desu.	I want a *green* sweater.

Some Japanese color words, such as *kiiroi*, *shiroi*, and *aoi* end in *i*. These adjectives can be changed into nouns by dropping the final *i*.

Ao-ga suki desu.	I like *blue*.
Kiiro-no burausu-o kaimashita.	I bought a *yellow* blouse.

6. The Numbers (100 ~ 9,000) (L. 64)

THE NUMBERS 100 ~ 9,000			
100	hyaku	1,000	sen
200	ni-hyaku	2,000	ni-sen
300	san-byaku	3,000	san-zen
400	yon-hyaku	4,000	yon-sen
500	go-hyaku	5,000	go-sen
600	rop-pyaku	6,000	roku-sen
700	nana-hyaku	7,000	nana-sen
800	hap-pyaku	8,000	has-sen
900	kyuu-hyaku	9,000	kyuu-sen

7. #-en, #-doru, #-sento (L. 64, 65)

The monetary unit of Japan is *en* (in English, yen), and as a counter is combined with numbers to express specific amounts. Remember, prices can be written in two ways: using the kanji for *-en* (円), as in 300円, or the yen symbol, ¥300.

-EN			
¥1	ichi-en	¥6	roku-en
¥2	ni-en	¥7	nana-en
¥3	san-en	¥8	hachi-en
¥4	yo(n)-en	¥9	kyuu-en
¥5	go-en	¥10	juu-en

The Japanese counter for *dollars* is *-doru*. This counter combines with the same number forms as shown in the preceding box. The counter for *cents* is *-sento*. Use this counter combined with a number to express prices in cents. Note the pronunciation changes for 1, 8, and 10 cents in the box below.

-SENTO			
1 cent	is-sento	6 cents	roku-sento
2 cents	ni-sento	7 cents	nana-sento
3 cents	san-sento	8 cents	has-sento
4 cents	yon-sento	9 cents	kyuu-sento
5 cents	go-sento	10 cents	jus-sento

8. #-nen (L. 65)

The counter *-nen*, means *year* and is used with the calendar year to express a date. The question form is *Nan-nen?*

-NEN			
1	ichi-nen	6	roku-nen
2	ni-nen	7	nana-nen
3	san-nen	8	hachi-nen
4	yo-nen	9	kyuu-nen
5	go-nen	10	juu-nen

Ni-sen-roku-*nen* desu.	It's (the year) 2006.
Tookyoo Orinpikku-wa nan-*nen* deshita-ka?	What year were the Tokyo Olympics?
Sen kyuu-hyaku roku-juu-yo-*nen* deshita.	They were (in) 1964.

9. General Counters (*hitotsu ~ too*) (L. 66)

Do you remember the set of general counter words when the item being counted does not call for a specific counter? You can also make yourself understood by using these general counters to count things (not people) which do not have specific counters.

IKUTSU?			
1 thing	hitotsu	6 things	muttsu
2 things	futatsu	7 things	nanatsu
3 things	mittsu	8 things	yattsu
4 things	yottsu	9 things	kokonotsu
5 things	itsutsu	10 things	too

Remember that particles are not used with the counters when the item is not mentioned. When both the item and the counter are used, then the appropriate particle follows the name of the item.

Tomato-ga arimasu.	There is a tomato. / There are tomatoes.
Itsutsu arimasu.	There are *five*.
Chiizubaagaa-o kudasai.	Please give me a cheeseburger.
Mittsu kudasai.	Please give me *three*.

NOUN	-ga	COUNTER	arimasu.
NOUN	-o	COUNTER	tabemasu/kudasai.

You can use the particle *-to* (and) to express the quantity of two or more things.

Hanbaagaa-o futatsu-*to* koora-o hitotsu kudasai.	Please give me two hamburgers *and* one cola.

10. Verb + kudasai (L. 66)

When used with verbs to ask someone to do something, *kudasai* means *please*. These verbs must be in what is called the -*te* form.

    Kore-o *mite kudasai.*   *Please look* at this.
    Nihongo-de *itte kudasai.*   *Please say* it in Japanese.

KATAKANA

Small *katakana* ャ、 ュ、 ョ (ya, yu, yo)

Remember, as in the case of small *hiragana* や、 ゆ、 ょ (L. 24), small *katakana* ャ、 ュ、 ョ can combine with any preceding *katakana* ending with the vowel *i* to represent additional sounds. When combined, the smaller ャ、 ュ、 ョ are written about half as high as the other *katakana*, and these combinations represent a single syllable rather than two distinct syllables.

KATAKANA WITH SMALL ャ、 ュ、 ョ					
キャ kya	シャ sha	チャ cha	ヒャ hya	ピャ pya	リャ rya
キュ kyu	シュ shu	チュ chu	ヒュ hyu	ピュ pyu	リュ ryu
キョ kyo	ショ sho	チョ cho	ヒョ hyo	ピョ pyo	リョ ryo
ギャ gya	ジャ ja	ニャ nya	ビャ bya	ミャ mya	
ギュ gyu	ジュ ju	ニュ nyu	ビュ byu	ミュ myu	
ギョ gyo	ジョ jo	ニョ nyo	ビョ byo	ミョ myo	

CULTURE NOTES   カルチャーノート

1. Greetings:
a. Ii tenki desu-ne. (L.58)
Japanese often comment on the weather as a way of starting a conversation.

b. O-genki desu-ka? (L. 63)
Roughly translating to "How are you?," this is used only when you have not seen people recently enough to know how their health is.

c. O-hisashiburi desu(-ne). (L. 63)
This greeting ("It's been a long time.") is used after a long absence.

d. Irasshaimase. (L. 63)
It is more formal than "*Irasshai*" and is often used by clerks to welcome customers into their store.

2. Celsius – Fahrenheit (L. 59)
Japan, which uses the metric system, measures temperature according to the Celsius scale. To convert a Celsius temperature to Fahrenheit, multiply it by 9, divide by 5, and add 32. Conversely, to convert a Fahrenheit temperature to Celsius, subtract 32, multiply by 5, and divide by 9.

3. Seasonal events (L. 60)
Japan has four distinct seasons with major annual events closely associated with them. *Hanami* (cherry blossom viewing) is from late March to early April. *Taifuu* (typhoons) hit in late August through September. *Tsukimi* (moon viewing) is the harvest moon activity held in the fall. There are many festivals associated with winter in Japan, the most famous of which is the Sapporo Snow Festival on the northern island of Hokkaido.

4. Japanese money (L. 64)

Japanese yen has six denominations of coins (1, 5, 10, 50, 100, and 500) and four denominations of bills (1,000, 2,000, 5,000, and 10,000).

5. Japanese department stores (L. 65)

Often seven stories or higher, department stores in Japan are different from those in the U.S. in many ways: the basement or lower level is a combination of supermarket and individual food counters, the top floor holds restaurants, and during the summer, the roofs serve as beer gardens for adults and amusement parks for children. The high quality of customer service in Japanese department stores is very obvious. Still employed in some of the most exclusive department stores in Japan are "elevator girls", whose job is to announce the categories of items available on each floor, and transport customers to their desired floors by operating the elevator.

INTERACTIVE ACTIVITIES

PART 1

❶ Conversation practice

Practice conversing with a partner, as in the sample dialog below. You can also make up an imaginary trip.

Ex.

Place: Kyoto
Today's weather: clear
Temperature: 54°

Tomorrow's weather: rain

(1)

Place: Washington D.C.
Today's weather: rain
Temperature: 37°

Tomorrow's weather: snow

(2)

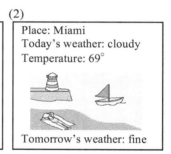

Place: Miami
Today's weather: cloudy
Temperature: 69°

Tomorrow's weather: fine

EX. SAMPLE DIALOGUE

A: きょう どこに いきますか。
B: <u>きょうとに</u> いきます。
A: <u>きょうとの</u> てんきは どうですか。
B: <u>はれ</u> です。
A: なんど ですか。
B: <u>５４ど</u> です。
A: あしたの てんきは どう ですか。
B: <u>あめみたい</u> です。

❷ Presentation – Report of the weather in various locations 📄 & ✐

Using the guideline below, write out a report of your Conversation practice in ❶ using any one of the cards. Add a comment on what you will do there. Then give a presentation to the class.

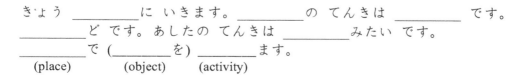

きょう ＿＿＿＿に いきます。＿＿＿＿の てんきは ＿＿＿＿ です。
＿＿＿＿ど です。あしたの てんきは ＿＿＿＿みたい です。
＿＿＿＿で (＿＿＿を) ＿＿＿ます。
  (place)   (object)   (activity)

❸ Conversation practice
In pairs, dress up a Tim-*sensei* doll with various colors of different clothing items. Take turns asking each other questions about the clothes you will choose to dress Tim-*sensei* in, as in the sample dialogue below.

SAMPLE DIALOGUE
A: なにいろの ジャケットに しましょうか。

B: くろい ジャケットに しましょう。

PART 2

❶ Shopping spree 📄 & ✏️
Partner A and Partner B went to the mall together. They decided to go off separately to different stores. They found some clothes that they liked but were not sure if they should buy them. They took pictures of the items with their cell phones and sent them to each other, asking for the other's opinion of them. Use the charts below to make up a mini-dialogue of their discussion of the items, as in the model dialogue below the charts.

Partner A:

Item:	(A's photo)	(B's photo)	(A's photo)	(B's photo)	(A's photo)
Price:	¥8,800		¥7,600		¥3,500

MODEL DIALOGUE
A: この (A's item) は どう ですか。

B: _____ です。いくら ですか。

A: _____ えん です。

B: (Write down the price s/he tells you.) Check your answer by looking at each other's chart after the activity.

164

Partner B:

Item:	(A's photo)	(B's photo)	(A's photo)	(B's photo)	(A's photo)
Price:		¥900		¥4,100	

MODEL DIALOGUE

B: この (B's item) は どう ですか。

A: _____ です。いくら ですか。

B: _____ えん です。

A: (Write down the price s/he tells you.) Check your answer by looking at each other's chart after the activity.

❷ **Information gap**: _____ が _____ あります。 📄 & ✏

Divide into groups of A and B. Pair up with a partner in the other group, and ask each other questions to find out how many **hamburgers**, **slices of cake, bags, hats, watches/clocks** and **lemons** are in each other's room. Cover your partner's picture and look only at your picture. Use the sentence pattern [Item] が いくつ ありますか。 S/he will respond [Number of item] あります。 Write down the answers and check them by looking at each other's picture after the activity.

A's Room

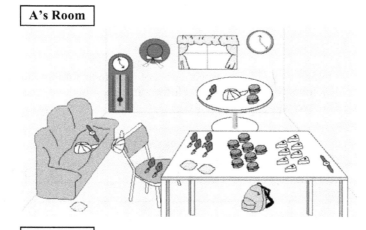

B's Room

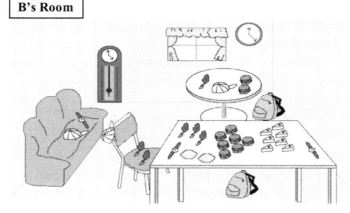

165

RL. 2　電話で　話しましょう

れんしゅう A:　World Weather Report

(1) シャンハイ 　　11 °C	(3) ダブリン 　　-5 °C	(5) ホノルル 　　90 °F	(7) ローマ 　　13 °C
(2) シアトル 　　39 °F	(4) きょうと 　　-4 °C	(6) マイアミ 　　82 °F	(8) シドニー 　　20 °C

れんしゅう B:　John's and Mariko's Shopping Lists

Two groups, looking only at their respective set of lists, must find missing information on either John's or Mariko's list. Partners in each group will start out by asking <u>what</u> John and Mariko bought. (ジョンくん／まりこさんはなにをかいましたか。)

SET A　　　**John's list**

	ITEM	QUANTITY	COST
✓	hamburgers	4	$8.00
✓	colas	5	$7.25
✓	doughnuts	6	$3.60
✓	tomatoes	7	$10.90

Mariko's list

	ITEM	QUANTITY	COST
✓	a. _____	3	e. ¥_____
✓	b. _____	1	¥950
✓	bags	c. _____	¥2,600
✓	oranges	d. _____	f. ¥_____

Questions: (1) [to ask about QUANTITY] _____をいくつかいましたか。

(2) [to ask about COST of an item] _____はいくらでしたか。

SET B **John's list**

	ITEM	QUANTITY	COST
✓	g. _____	4	k. $ _____
✓	h. _____	5	$7.25
✓	doughnuts	i. _____	l. $ _____
✓	tomatoes	j. _____	$10.90

Mariko's list

	ITEM	QUANTITY	COST
✓	erasers	3	¥150
✓	hats	1	¥950
✓	bags	2	¥2,600
✓	oranges	10	¥700

Questions: (1) [to ask about QUANTITY] _____ をいくつかいましたか。
(2) [to ask about COST of an item] _____ はいくらでしたか。

れんしゅう C: Which ~ is ~'s?

You threw a party at your house and now it is time for everyone to leave.
Ask each of your guests which shoes, hat, and jacket is theirs.

(1)

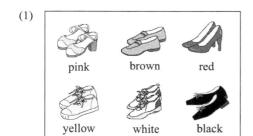

pink   brown   red

yellow   white   black

(2)

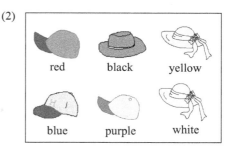

red   black   yellow

blue   purple   white

(3)

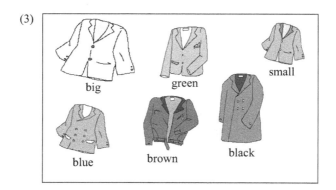

big   green   small

blue   brown   black

167

REVIEW LESSON 3
(Volume 1, Lessons 67~73)

OBJECTIVES　　　　　　　　　　　　　　　　　　もくひょう

This lesson provides you with an opportunity to review the following objectives from
Volume 1, Lessons 67 through 73:

- ☑ Ask and state the existence/location of places in the community
- ☑ Ask about and describe spatial relationships
- ☑ Ask and state how to get to a place
- ☑ Identify some means of transportation
- ☑ Ask and state how long it takes to get to a place
- ☑ Read and write *katakana*

VOCABULARY　　　　　　　　　　　　　　　　　　たんご

Community-Related Words:
machi [town, city]
-ya [*a suffix indicating a specialty store*]
kutsu-ya [shoe store]
niku-ya [butcher's, meat market]
pan-ya [fish store, fish market]
hon-ya [bookstore]
yao-ya [vegetable store, vegetable stand]
kooen [park]
eigakan [movie theater]
hoteru [hotel]
eki [train station]
basu-tei [bus stop]
toshokan [library]
ginkoo [bank]
yuubinkyoku [post office]
posuto [mail box]
biru [building]
kooban [local police station]
o-mawarisan [police officer, policeman]

Distance-Related Words and Phrases:
tooi [far]
chikai [near, close]
(Place 1)-kara (place 2)-made tooi/chikai desu-ka?
[Is it far/near from (place 1) to (place 2)?]
-gurai [about, approximately]
#-jikan [hours (duration of time)]
#-mairu [mile]
Nan-mairu desu-ka? [How many miles is it?]
(Transportation)-de nan-jikan/pun gurai desu-ka?
[About how many hours/minutes is it by (transportation)?]

Transportation-Related Words and Phrases:
baiku [motorcycle]　　　　　jitensha [bicycle]
densha [train]　　　　　　　basu [bus]
takushii [taxi]　　　　　　　hikooki [airplane]
aruite [on foot]　　　　　　chikatetsu [subway]
aruite ikimasu/iku [go on foot]
Nan-de (place)-ni ikimasu-ka? [How will you go to
(place)?]

Spatial Relationship Words:
mae [front]　　　　naka [in, inside]　　　　migi [right]
ushiro [back, behind]　　soto [outside]　　　　hidari [left]

KEY GRAMMAR POINTS　　　　　　　　　　ぶんぽうポイント

The number in parentheses after each grammar point is the lesson in which it was first
presented.

1. *Location*-ni *something*-ga arimasu. (L. 68)
In this lesson you review how to use *arimasu/arimasen* with a location. Use the particle
-*ni* after the location. Look at these examples.

Kono machi-*ni* kissaten-ga *arimasu*-ka?　　*Are there* coffee shops *in* this town?
Usually the particle -*wa* is used with *arimasen*.

Kono machi-*ni* ookii hon-ya-*wa arimasen*.　*There aren't* any large bookstores *in* this
　　　　　　　　　　　　　　　　　　　　town.

168

2. Spatial relationships (L. 69, 70, and 71)

This lesson reviews six common spatial relationship words in Japanese: *mae, ushiro, migi, hidari, naka,* and *soto*. These words, which are all nouns, can be used with particles to describe the location of people and things. The verb *arimasu* is used to talk about the existence of non-living things whereas the verb *imasu* is used for people and animals. Study the following examples of patterns and sentences describing the location of X in reference to Y:

X-**wa** Y-*no migi-ni* arimasu/imasu.	X is (located) *to the right of* Y.
X-**wa** Y-*no hidari-ni* arimasu/imasu.	X is (located) *to the left of* Y.
X-**wa** Y-*no mae-ni* arimasu/imasu.	X is (located) *in front of* Y.
X-**wa** Y-*no ushiro-ni* arimasu/imasu.	X is (located*) behind* Y.
X-**wa** Y-*no naka-ni* arimasu/imasu.	X is (located) *in* Y.
X-**wa** Y-*no soto-ni* arimasu/imasu.	X is (located) *outside* Y.
Hon-**wa** kaban-*no naka-ni* arimasu.	The book is (located) *in* the bag.
Ani-**wa** watashi-*no ushiro-ni* imasu.	My older brother is (located) *behind* me.

> **QUESTION:** X-**wa** *doko-ni* arimasu/imasu-ka?
> **ANSWER:** (Object/Person)-*no LOCATION WORD-ni* arimasu/imasu.
> *(migi, hidari, mae, ushiro)*

Compare the above sentences with the following, which ask WHO/WHAT is at a specific location:

> **QUESTION:** Y(Object/Person)-*no LOCATION WORD-ni* **nani/dare-ga** arimasu/imasu-ka?
> *(migi, hidari, mae, ushiro)*
> **ANSWER:** (Object/Person)-**ga** arimasu/imasu.

Isu-*no hidari-ni* **nani-ga** arimasu-ka?	What is (there) *to the left of* the chair?
(Isu-*no hidari-ni*) kaban-**ga** arimasu.	(To the left of the chair) there is a bag.
Miki-san-*no ushiro-ni* **dare-ga** imasu-ka?	Who is (there) *behind* Miki?
(Miki-san-*no ushiro-ni*) Ken-kun-**ga** imasu.	(*Behind* Miki) there is Ken.

Note: If the location comes at the beginning of the sentence, the particle for the subject is changed from *-wa* to *-ga*.

Y-*no migi-ni* X-**ga** arimasu/imasu.	*To the right of* Y, there is X.
Y-*no hidari-ni* X-**ga** arimasu/imasu.	*To the left of* Y, there is X.
Y-*no mae-ni* X-**ga** arimasu/imasu.	*In front of* Y, there is X.
Y-*no ushiro-ni* X-**ga** arimasu/imasu.	*Behind* Y, there is X.
Hon-ya-*no mae-ni* basu-tei-**ga** arimasu.	*In front of* the bookstore (there) is a bus sto
Biru-*no soto-ni* Mari-san-**ga** imasu.	*Outside* the building (there) is Mari.

3. Aruite ikimasu. (L. 71)

Literally meaning *walking go*, this verbal expression is composed of the *-te* form of the verb *aruku/arukimasu* (walk) and the verb *ikimasu* (go). The **-te form** was introduced in Lesson 66. In English *aruite ikimasu* is often translated as *go on foot* and is similar in meaning to the phrases above which indicate means of transportation. The verb *ikimasu* can be changed to a negative or past form. Notice that the particle *-de* is not used with *aruite ikimasu*.

Gakkoo-made *aruite ikimashita*.	I *went* to school *on foot*.
Aruite ikimasu-ka?	*Are* you *going to go on foot?*

4. Counter Words: *-pun/fun*, *-jikan*, and *-mairu* (L. 72)

As you learned in Lesson 25, the counter *-pun/fun* is used to count the number of minutes. The question form is *nan-pun*.

NAN-PUN?			
ip-pun	1 minute	rop-pun	6 minutes
ni-fun	2 minutes	nana-fun	7 minutes
san-pun	3 minutes	hap-pun	8 minutes
yon-pun	4 minutes	kyuu-fun	9 minutes
go-fun	5 minutes	jup-pun	10 minutes

The counter *-jikan* is used to count a number of hours. It combines with the same number forms which are used with the counter *-ji* (Vol. 1, L. 24) except that 7 hours can be either *shichi-jikan* or *nana-jikan*. The corresponding question form is *nan-jikan*.

NAN-JIKAN?			
ichi-jikan	1 hour	roku-jikan	6 hours
ni-jikan	2 hours	shichi-jikan	7 hours
san-jikan	3 hours	hachi-jikan	8 hours
yo-jikan	4 hours	ku-jikan	9 hours
go-jikan	5 hours	juu-jikan	10 hours

The counter for miles is *-mairu*. The question form is *nan-mairu*. Note that the Japanese measure distances in kilometers (*kiro*), not in *mairu* (1 mile = 1.6 kilometers).

NAN-MAIRU?			
ichi-mairu	1 mile	roku-mairu	6 miles
ni-mairu	2 miles	nana- mairu	7 miles
san-mairu	3 miles	hachi-mairu	8 miles
yon-mairu	4 miles	kyuu-mairu	9 miles
go-mairu	5 miles	juu-mairu	10 miles

Uchi-kara aruite *jup-pun* desu.	It's *10 minutes* on foot from home.
San-juu-mairu-gurai desu.	It's about *30 miles*.

5. Particles

Particle	L. #	Note(s)	Sample sentence
で de	67	preceded by a place noun; indicates the occurrence of an action	このおみせでかいました。(I bought it **at** this shop.)
	71	preceded by a means of transportation; is usually translated in English as *by*.	くるまでいきます。(I will go **by** car.)
が ga は wa	68	*Ga* is used with *arimasu* and preceded by the subject of sentence to talk about the existence of inanimate things. Usually the particle *wa* is used with *arimasen*.	ちいさいデパートがあります。おおきいデパートはありません。(There is a small department store. There aren't any large department stores.)
に ni	68	preceded by some place (somewhere) and followed by existence verbs such as *imasu* and *arimasu*	いま、きょうとにいます。(I am **in** Kyoto right now.)

170

1. Specialty shops (L. 67)

Although Japanese do shop at *suupaa* (supermarkets) and in large *depaato* (department stores), they still like to shop at small specialty shops. Because buying fresh food is very important for the Japanese, the majority of housewives still shop daily at the specialty shops.

2. O-miyage (souvenir gifts) おみやげ (L. 67)

It is customary to buy おみやげ for family, classmates, business colleagues, and others whenever one goes on a trip. There are two aspects to おみやげ giving that are important. First, you must select something that is representative of the area you have visited. Typical おみやげ from trips within Japan include gifts such as regional foods and sweets, bottled beverages, handicrafts, items from temples and shrines, and key chains. Second, you must buy the same item for everyone who is a member of the group for which you are buying おみやげ.

3. Getting around in Japan (L. 68)

Japan has an excellent rail and bus system which offers commuters, shoppers, students, and travelers a convenient and relatively inexpensive alternative to the car. Trains and *chikatetsu* 地下鉄 (subways) are clean, fast, conveniently scheduled, and almost always on time. Tokyo's subways and surface train lines, however, are extremely crowded during morning and evening rush hour. Bus lines link urban, suburban, and rural areas and offer service to communities which are not on a rail line. Communities have developed around *eki* えき (train stations). Department stores, theaters, banks, and major travel agencies are clustered around train stations. The えき is also where people often agree to meet one another for social purposes.

4. Some *kanji* commonly seen in a Japanese community (L. 68)

Knowledge of a few basic *kanji* such as those for *entrance* 入口 (*iriguchi*), *exit* 出口 (*deguchi*), *north* 北 (*kita*), *south* 南 (*minami*), *east* 東 (*higashi*), and *west* 西 (*nishi*) can help considerably. Two other survival *kanji* are those you often see on restroom doors: 男 (*otoko*) *men* and 女 (*onna*) *women*.

5. Postal symbol and mailboxes (L. 70)

Wherever you see the symbol 〒 written in red on a white background you know that you have found a *yuubinkyoku* (post office). This postal symbol is also used in addresses (including those on envelopes and business cards) just before the zip code. *Posuto* (mailboxes) are rectangular in shape and red.

6. Japanese police (L. 70)

Rather than patrolling the streets in police cruisers, many policemen (おまわりさん) work out of small police stations known as こうばん which are often located near train stations, busy entertainment areas, and residential districts. One of the most common tasks of an おまわりさん is responding to pedestrians' requests for directions. Another common task of an おまわりさん is helping people with their lost property.

WRITING JAPANESE

Katakana **combinations with small** ア, イ, ウ, エ, **and** オ

These special combinations are used to represent foreign sounds which did not originally occur in Japanese. These sounds were introduced with がいらいご, most of which came from English. Some of the more common combinations are given with examples on the next page.

SPECIAL *KATAKANA* COMBINATIONS				
ウィ	wi	ウィスコンシン	Wisukonshin	Wisconsin
シェ	she	ミルクシェーキ	mirukusheeki	milk shake
チェ	che	チェス	chesu	chess
ティ	ti	アイスティー	aisutii	iced tea
ファ	fa	ファッション	fasshon	fashion
フォ	fo	フォーク	fooku	fork
ジェ	je	ジェシカ	Jeshika	Jessica
ディ	di	キャンディー	kyandii	candy

For the above combinations which do not begin with ウ, you add the consonant sound of the first *katakana* to the vowel sound of the second *katakana*.

ティ	te	+	i	=	ti
ファ	fu	+	a	=	fa
シェ	shi	+	e	=	she

INTERACTIVE ACTIVITIES

PART 1

❶ **Shopping list**   📄 & ✏

Work in pairs. First, Partner A asks Partner B by saying, # ばんは なんの おみせ (shop) ですか. Partner B answers, [type of store] です. If it is correct, both partners write down the answers on line. Take turns repeating the question and answering until both partners have the answers through number 6. Then, looking at the *katakana* words in the box, Partner A asks Partner B, (a) は なん ですか. Partner B answers, ベーグル です. Partner A, then asks, ベーグルは どこに ありますか. Partner B answers, [type of store] です. If it is correct, both partners write down the letter in the appropriate parentheses. Take turns asking questions and answering them through (l). Check your answers with the answer key at the end of this lesson.

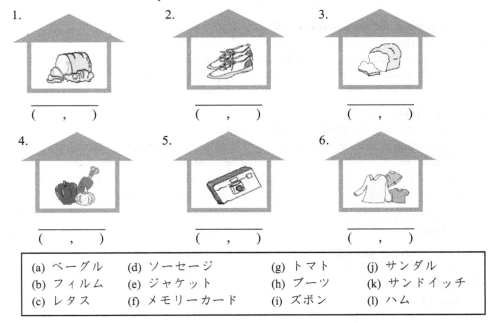

(a) ベーグル	(d) ソーセージ	(g) トマト	(j) サンダル
(b) フィルム	(e) ジャケット	(h) ブーツ	(k) サンドイッチ
(c) レタス	(f) メモリーカード	(i) ズボン	(l) ハム

172

❷ Building a business street　📄 & ✏️

A. Work in pairs. You (A) and your partner (B) create a model business street by following descriptions. Partner A reads the first sentence and Partner B who is standing in the street places one of the stores/buildings in the right spot. Take turns to read instructions sentence by sentence. Check your answers with the answer key at the end of this lesson.

えきの まえに バスていが あります。
こうばんの みぎに ほんやが あります。
さかなやの ひだりに にくやが あります。
さかなやの みぎに やおやが あります。
こうばんの まえに パンやが あります。
パンやの ひだりに きっさてんが あります。
やおやの まえに レストランが あります。
ホテルの まえに ポストが あります。

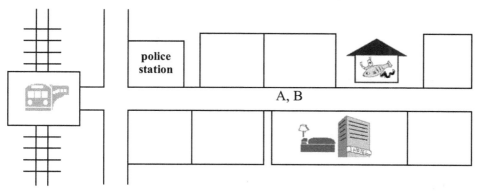

B. Partner A reads the first question and Partner B answers the question by filling in the blank with a spatial relationship word. Then, switch roles and repeat the question and answer. Check your answers with the answer key at the end of this lesson.

1. レストランは どこに ありますか。　ホテルの＿＿＿＿＿に あります。
2. きっさてんは どこに ありますか。　ほんやの＿＿＿＿＿に あります。
3. さかなやは どこに ありますか。　にくやの＿＿＿＿＿に あります。
4. こうばんは どこに ありますか。　パンやの＿＿＿＿＿に あります。
5. ポストは どこに ありますか。　ホテルの＿＿＿＿＿に あります。

PART 2

Shopping survey　📄 & ✏️

A. Interview your partner about his/her shopping preferences. First, write down the questions and check your work with the answer key at the end of this lesson. Then, ask the questions and write down your partner's responses.

1. name of town?
2. any supermarkets?
   (If yes) how many?
   go to which most often?
   how far from home?
   how get there?
   how long it takes?

3. any malls?
   (If yes) how many?
   go to which most often?
   how far from home?
   how get there?
   how long it takes?

173

B. Now write a summary of your interview using the model script below. A sample script is given below.

---

1. name of the interviewee のまち

2. スーパー (number): names of the supermarkets

   name of the interviewee は よく name of his/her favorite supermarket に

   いきます。 name of the interviewee の うちから the name of the supermarket

   まで number マイルぐらい です。 type of transportation で length of time

   ぐらい です。

3. モール (number): name(s) of the shopping mall(s)

   name of the interviewee は よく name of his/her favorite shopping mall に

   いきます。 name of the interviewee の うちから the name of the shopping mall

   まで number マイルぐらい です。 type of transportation で length of time

   ぐらい です。

ANSWERS (INTERACTIVE ACTIVITIES):
PART 1 ❶
1. にくや (d, l) 3. パンや (a, k) 5. カメラや (b, f)
2. くつや (h, j) 4. やおや (c, g) 6. ふくや (e, i)
PART 1 ❷
A. in front of the station: bus stop
   first row from left to right: bookstore, meat shop, vegetable store
   second row from left to right: bakery, coffee shop, restaurant
   in front of the hotel: mailbox
B. 1. ひだり 2. まえ 3. みぎ 4. まえ 5. まえ
PART 2
A. 1. うちは どの まちに ありますか。
   2. スーパーが ありますか。いくつ ありますか。どの スーパーに よく いきますか。
      うちから スーパーまで なんマイルぐらい ですか。なんで いきますか。
      〜で どれぐらい ですか。
   3. モールが ありますか。いくつ ありますか。どの モールに よく いきますか。
      うちから モールまで なんマイルぐらい ですか。なんで いきますか。
      〜で どれぐらい ですか。
B. (Sample script)
1. キースくんの まち
2. スーパー (3): ウィンマート、ジェネラルフーズ、フードキング
   キースくんは よく フードキングに いきます。キースくんの うちから フードキング
   まで 0.5マイルぐらい です。じてんしゃで 5ふんぐらい です。
3. モール (2): ノースリバー、ノースマウント
   キースくんは よく ノースリバーモールに いきます。キースくんの うちから ノース
   リバーモールまで 6マイルぐらい です。でんしゃで 3ぷんぐらい です。

れんしゅう A: Building a Shopping Mall

Your company is building a shopping mall. Your group is in the process of deciding the location of the stores in the mall. Look at the list of stores and decide with your group where to put these retailers.

Apparel:
  G. Crew
  New Navy
Bookstore:
  Grand Books
Camera Shop:
  Coyote Camera

Clock Store:
  Around the Clock
Computer Store:
  PC City
Department Stores:
  Richer's
  JC Nickels

Food and Drinks:
  Cookie Monger
  Tea Factory
Luggage Store:
  Bags to Go
Shoe Store:
  Walkers

Richer's			PC City			JC Nickels
	Tea Factory			Cookie Monger		

れんしゅう B: Let's converse!

Dialogue:
A: Is there a <u>bank</u> in this town?
B: Yes, there is.
A: Is it near here?
B: <u>Yes, it is</u>. It takes <u>five minutes on foot</u>.
A: Where is the <u>bank</u>?
B: It is <u>in front of</u> the <u>train station</u>.

Sample Dialogue:
A: このまちに<u>ぎんこう</u>があ
   りますか。
B: はい、ありますよ。
A: ここから<u>ちかい</u>ですか。
B: <u>はい、ちかいです</u>。<u>あるい</u>
   <u>て</u><u>5ふん</u>ぐらいですよ。
A: <u>ぎんこう</u>はどこにありま
   すか。
B: <u>えきのまえ</u>にありますよ。

Sample Dialogue:
A: Kono machi-ni <u>ginkoo</u>-ga
   arimasu-ka?
B: Hai, arimasu-yo.
A: Koko-kara chikai desu-ka?
B: <u>Hai, chikai desu</u>. <u>Aruite</u> <u>go-fun</u>-
   gurai desu-yo.
A: <u>Ginkoo</u>-wa doko-ni arimasu-ka?
B: <u>Eki</u>-no <u>mae</u>-ni arimasu-yo.

175

れんしゅう C: Whose family is it?

You will hear the description of one of the following family pictures. Select the picture that is being described.

(a)  (b)  (c)

れんしゅう D: よみましょう。

Read the following passage and answer the questions in English. Then, create your own passage changing the underlined parts.

　　わたしのまちは スプリングフィールドと いいます。
スプリングフィールドは ウィスコンシンに あります。
マディソンから くるまで １じかんはん ぐらいです。
スプリングフィールドは あんまり おおきくないです。
ファーストフードのレストランが ４つあります。
イタリアのレストランとインドのレストランも あります。
わたしは かぞくと よく メキシコのレストランに いきます。
うちから ちかいです。 そのレストランのたべものは
エンチラーダとタコサラダが すきです。

しつもん: (Answer in English.)

(1) What is the name of the town?
(2) In which state is the town?
(3) What is the name of the nearest major city to the town?
(4) How far is the major city from the town?
(5) What kinds of restaurants are there in the town?
(6) Which restaurant does the author often go to with her family?
(7) What are her favorite dishes at that restaurant?

REVIEW LESSON 4
(Volume 2, Lessons 6~15)

OBJECTIVES　　　　　　　　　　　　　　　　　もくひょう

This lesson provides you with an opportunity to review the following objectives from Volume 2, Lessons 6 through 15:

- ☑ Identify some countries in the world; name six continents
- ☑ Ask and say what language someone speaks; ask where someone is from
- ☑ Ask about and state locations using cardinal directions
- ☑ Identify certain natural features; Identify principal geographic features of Japan
- ☑ Ask and tell how long someone has done something
- ☑ Give and receive compliments appropriately
- ☑ Talk about what someone is doing now and was doing at a certain time
- ☑ Talk about school schedules, daily school life, club activities
- ☑ Ask for and give permission
- ☑ Explain the origin and use of *kanji*
- ☑ Read and write the *kanji*: 月、日、木、本、人、大、小
- ☑ Read the *kanji*: 学、校、中、高、山、川

VOCABULARY　　　　　　　　　　　　　　　　　　たんご

Geography-Related Words and Phrases:
kuni [country]
sekai [world]
chizu [map]
Chuugoku [China]　　Igirisu [England]
dochira [which, where]
kita [north]　　　　higashi [east]
minami [south]　　　nishi [west]
shima [island]　　　yama [mountain]
kawa [river]　　　　mizuumi [lake]
umi [sea, ocean]
nagai [long]　　　　takai [tall, high]
ichiban __ [the most ___, the ___est]
Doko-no kuni desu-ka? [What country is this?]
Dochira-kara desu-ka? [Where are you from?]

School Schedule and Activity-Related Words and Phrases:
kyooshitsu [classroom]　shokudoo [cafeteria]
taiikukan [gymnasium]　kyookasho [textbook]
-bu [*suffix for club*]
jikan [time]
#-jikan-me [*suffix for class periods*]

Phrases and Expressions – Doing ~ for ~ length of time
atama-ga ii [smart, intelligent]
gaikokugo [foreign language]
Nani-go-ga dekimasu-ka?
[What languages do you speak?]
nan-ji-kan-gurai? [about how many hours?]
nan-nen-kan? [how many years?]
jibun-de [by oneself, alone, without the help of others]
Dore-gurai ~mashita-ka?
[How long did you ~?]
ichi-nen-kan-dake [only one year]
yukkuri [slowly]
Moo ichido yukkuri itte kudasai.
[Please say it again slowly.]
Mada heta desu-yo. [I'm still poor at it.]

Verbs:
hanasu [speak]　　　　oshieru [teach]
hairu [enter, join]　　tsukau [use]
haitte-iru [belong to]　wasureru [forget]
hajimaru [(something) begins]
owaru [(something) ends, finishes]

VOCABULARY NOTES　　　　　　　　　　　　　たんごノート

The number in parentheses after each grammar point is the lesson in which it was first presented.

Oshiete kudasai. (L. 10)
The verb *oshieru* in Japanese includes the meanings of *inform*, *tell*, or *explain* as well as to *teach*.

Denwa bangoo-o *oshiete* kudasai.　　　Please *tell* me your phone number.
Furansugo-o chotto *oshiete* kudasai.　　Please *teach* me a little bit of French.

177

The number in parentheses after each grammar point is the lesson in which it was first presented.

1. Speaking languages (L. 6)
a. *Language*-o hanashimasu (hanasu)
The verb *hanashimasu* (*hanasu*) means *speak* and can be used with the names of languages. The direct object particle *-o* must be used following the name of the language.

Supeingo-*o hanashimasu*-ka?	Do you *speak* Spanish?
Eigo-*o hanasu.*	They *speak* English.
Nani-go-*o hanashimasu*-ka?	What language do they *speak*?

b. *Place*-de-wa nani-go-o hanashimasu-ka?
To specify a place in your question, begin with the name of the country or other location followed by the particles *-de* and *-wa*.

Kanada-de-wa nani-go-o hanashimasu-ka?	What language do they speak *in Canada*?

2. Where are you from? (L. 7)
a. Dochira-kara desu-ka?
The word *dochira* means *which* (of two choices) or *where*. With the latter meaning, *dochira* is a polite equivalent of the word *doko* and can be used when asking where someone is from.

Dochira-kara desu-ka?	*Where are you from?*
Kanada-kara desu.	I'm from Canada.

b. *Place*-no dochira
This phrase allows you to find out more specifically where someone is from, such as what city within a state, or state or province within a country.

Nihon-*no dochira*-kara desu-ka?	*Where in* Japan are you from?
Nagano-ken-kara desu.	I'm from Nagano Prefecture.
Amerika-*no dochira*-kara desu-ka?	*Where in* the U.S. are you from?
Sausu Dakota-kara desu.	I'm from South Dakota.

3. *Place*-no + cardinal direction (L. 7)
Use this pattern to express relative locations using cardinal directions.

Mekishiko-wa doko-ni arimasu-ka?	Where is Mexico?
Amerika-*no minami*-ni arimasu	It's *south of* the U.S.
Kanada-wa Amerika-*no kita*-ni arimasu.	Canada is *north of* the U.S.

4. Superlatives (L. 9)
a. Ichiban + adjective
The word *ichiban,* which literally means *number one,* is used immediately preceding adjectives to form the superlative. In English the superlative is formed with *-est* or *most*.

Ichiban chikai machi desu.	It's *the closest* town.
Ichiban nagai kawa-wa nan desu-ka?	What is *the longest* river?

b. *Place/category*-de ichiban + adjective + *noun* desu.
This pattern is used when you want to say that a particular NOUN is the biggest, the longest, the most beautiful, or some other superlative of all of the items or people in a certain place or category. The particle *-de* follows the place or the category.

Sekai-*de* ichiban ookii kuni desu.	It is the biggest country *in* the world.
Amerika-*de* ichiban nagai kawa-wa Mishishippi-gawa desu-ka?	Is the longest river *in* the U.S. the Mississippi River?

5. Dore-gurai (L. 10)
Use *dore-gurai* if you want to ask *how long* without specifying hours (*nan-jikan*), years (*nan-nen-kan*), or some other unit of time.

Dore-gurai benkyoo-o shimashita-ka?   *How long* did you study?

6. The *-te* form of verbs (L. 11)

The *-te* form of verbs, sometimes ending in *-de*, can be used in many different patterns, including polite commands with *kudasai*.

Kono kanji-o *kaite* kudasai.   Please *write* this kanji.
Shukudai-o *shite* kudasai.   Please *do* your homework.
Kiite kudasai.   Please *listen*.

<table>
<tr><th colspan="5" align="center">VERBS IN THE -TE FORM</th></tr>
<tr><th></th><th>-masu form</th><th>plain form</th><th>-te form</th><th>English</th></tr>
<tr><td>-ru Verbs:</td><td>mimasu</td><td>mi r̶u̶ →</td><td>mite</td><td>look at, see</td></tr>
<tr><td></td><td>tabemasu</td><td>tabe r̶u̶ →</td><td>tabete</td><td>eat</td></tr>
<tr><td></td><td>okimasu</td><td>oki r̶u̶ →</td><td>okite</td><td>get up</td></tr>
<tr><td></td><td>nemasu</td><td>ne r̶u̶ →</td><td>nete</td><td>go to bed</td></tr>
<tr><td></td><td>oshiemasu</td><td>oshie r̶u̶ →</td><td>oshiete</td><td>teach</td></tr>
<tr><td>-u Verbs:</td><td>kakimasu</td><td>ka k̶u̶ →</td><td>kaite</td><td>write</td></tr>
<tr><td></td><td>ikimasu</td><td>i k̶u̶ →</td><td>itte</td><td>go</td></tr>
<tr><td></td><td>kikimasu</td><td>ki k̶u̶ →</td><td>kiite</td><td>listen</td></tr>
<tr><td></td><td>hanashimasu</td><td>hana s̶u̶ →</td><td>hanashite</td><td>speak</td></tr>
<tr><td></td><td>nomimasu</td><td>no m̶u̶ →</td><td>nonde</td><td>drink</td></tr>
<tr><td></td><td>kaerimasu</td><td>kae r̶u̶ →</td><td>kaette</td><td>return</td></tr>
<tr><td></td><td>iimasu</td><td>i u̶ →</td><td>itte</td><td>say</td></tr>
<tr><td></td><td>kaimasu</td><td>ka u̶ →</td><td>katte</td><td>buy</td></tr>
<tr><td>Irregular Verbs:</td><td>kimasu</td><td>k u̶r̶u̶ →</td><td>kite</td><td>come</td></tr>
<tr><td></td><td>shimasu</td><td>s u̶r̶u̶ →</td><td>shite</td><td>do</td></tr>
</table>

a. Using the *-te* form + *imasu* to express continuous actions (L. 11)

By using the *-te* form with the verb *imasu*, you can express actions which are taking place at the same time you are speaking. This verb tense is sometimes referred to as the **present progressive** or **present continuous** since it describes actions that are in progress. In English, the *-te imasu* form is expressed as *am/is/are ...ing*.

Ima shigoto-o shi*te imasu*.   I *am* work*ing* now.
Ano hito-wa nani-o mi*te-imasu*-ka?   What *is* that person look*ing* at?

b. Using the *-te* form + *imashita* to express past continuous actions (L. 12)

By using the *-te* form with the verb *imashita*, you can express actions which were taking place at some time in the past. This verb tense is sometimes referred to as the **past progressive** or **past continuous** since it describes actions that were in progress in the past. In English, the *-te imashita* form is expressed as *was/were ...ing*.

Kinoo 3-ji-ni nani-o shi*te- imashita*-ka?   What *were* you do*ing* at 3:00 yesterday?
Shinbun-o yon*de-imashita*.   I *was* read*ing* the paper.

c. Using the *-te* form + *imasu* to express a state or condition (L. 14)

The *-te* form + *imasu* is also used to express a state or condition which is the result of a previous action.

Tenisu-bu-ni hai*tte-imasu*.   I *belong* to the tennis club *(joined and still belong)*.

Jugyoo-wa hajima*tte-imasu*.   The lesson *is in progress (began and is still going on)*.

Sensei-ga ki*te-imasu*.   The teacher *is here (came and is still here)*.

d. Using the *-te* form + *mo ii desu-ka?* to ask for permission (L. 15)

By adding *mo ii desu-ka?* to the *-te* form, you can formulate sentences that ask for permission. Similarly, a statement with a verb in its *-te* form + *mo ii desu*, you can say that it is permissible to do something.

Jisho-o tsuka*tte-mo ii desu-ka*?　　　*May I* use the dictionary?
Pen-de kai*te-mo ii desu-yo*.　　　*You may* write in pen.

7. #-jikan-me (L. 13)

When combined with numbers, *jikan-me* can be used to designate class periods as in the following examples. The question form is *nan-jikan-me*.

　　Taiiku-wa *nan-jikan-me* desu-ka?　　　*What period* is P.E.?
　　San-jikan-me-wa suugaku desu.　　　*Third period* is math.

NAN-JIKAN-ME DESU-KA?			
ichi-jikan-me	1st period	go-jikan-me	5th period
ni-jikan-me	2nd period	roku-jikan-me	6th period
san-jikan-me	3rd period	shichi/nana-jikan-me	7th period
yo-jikan-me	4th period	hachi-jikan-me	8th period

8. Particles

Particle	L. #	Note(s)	Sample sentence
では dewa	6	*De* indicates that the action takes place in that location, and *wa* indicates that the location is the topic of the sentence.	カナダ**では**フランスごとえいごをはなします。(In Canada, they speak French and English.)
の から no kara	7	*No* indicates the modification of the noun that follows it by the noun that precedes it. *Kara* indicates a given place from someone originates. Used in (place)-*no dochira kara desu-ka*?	日本**の**どちら**から**ですか。(Where in Japan are you from?) スミスさんはジョージア**の**アセンズ**から**です。(Ms. Smith is from Athens, Georgia.)
で de	9	indicates a place or category, used in (place/category)-*de* + adjective + noun *desu*	ロシアはせかい**で**いちばんおおきいくにです。(Russia is the largest country in the world.)
に ni	14	indicates an organization a person belongs to, used in (organization)-*ni haitte-iru*.	サッカーぶ**に**はいっています。(I belong to the soccer club.)

KANJI NOTES　　　　　　　　　　　　　　　かんじノート

Kanji	L. #	Pronunciation(s)	Meaning	Examples
月	7	GETSU, GATSU; tsuki*	month, moon	月曜日 (*getsu*-yoobi: Monday); 何月 (nan-*gatsu*: what month?)
日	7	NICHI, JITSU*; hi*, [bi], ~ka	day, sun; *counter for days of the month*	日曜日 (*nichi*-yoobi: Sunday); 十三日 (juu-san-*nichi*: the 13th); 二日 (futsu-*ka*: the 2nd)
木	8	MOKU, BOKU*; ki* [gi*]	tree, wood	木曜日 (*moku*-yoobi: Thursday)
本	8	HON [PON, BON]; moto*	book, origin, *counter for long, narrow objects*	本 (*hon*: book); 日本 (ni*hon*: Japan)
人	8	NIN, JIN; hito, ~ri	person, *counter for people*	人 (*hito*: person); 二人 (futa-*ri*: two people); 日本人 (nihon-*jin*: Japanese)
山	8	SAN* [ZAN*]; yama	mountain	山 (*yama*: mountain); 富士山 (*Fuji-san*: Mt. Fuji)

Kanji	L. #	Pronunciation(s)	Meaning	Examples
川	8	SEN*; kawa [gawa*]	river	川 (*kawa*: river); 山川 (Yama*kawa*: *family name*)
大	9	DAI, TAI*; oo(kii)	big, large, great	大きい (*ookii*: big, large); 大学 (*dai*gaku: university, college)
小	9	SHOO; ko*, o*, chii(sai)	small, little	小さい (*chii*sai: small, little); 小学校 (*shoo*gakkoo: elementary school)
学	13	GAKU; mana(bu) *	learning, science, learn	学校 (*gakkoo*: school)
校	13	KOO	school	学校 (gak*koo*: school)
中	14	CHUU; naka	middle, inside, within	中学校 (*chuu*gakkoo); 田中 (Ta*naka*: family name)
高	14	KOO; taka(i)	high, expensive	高校 (*kookoo*: high school); 高い (*taka*i: high, expensive)

* For reference only.

CULTURE NOTES　　　　　　　　　カルチャーノート

1. Japanese world map (L. 6)
World maps published and used in Japan usually show Japan in the center as opposed to maps used in the Western hemisphere which show Canada, the U.S., and Latin America in the center.

2. The origins and use of *kanji* (L. 6)
Japan had no writing system until the late fifth century, when they began importing and using *kanji* (Chinese characters) to write Japanese. Since Japanese and Chinese were – and still are – very different languages that are not even related, the Japanese encountered some problems in trying to use the Chinese writing system to represent their own spoken language. By the ninth century, the Japanese had simplified some of the *kanji* to create the *hiragana* syllabary, and used these symbols with the *kanji*, which represented the root meaning of a word, as endings to indicate tense and other grammatical features.

3. Japan – an island nation (L. 8)
Japan is an archipelago located off the east coast of the Asian mainland. It consists of four main islands and approximately 4,000 smaller ones. From the northeast to the southwest are the islands of Hokkaidoo, Honshuu, Kyuushuu, and Shikoku. It is approximately 3,000 km (1,850 miles) from the northern most tip of Hokkaidoo to the southernmost point of Okinawa.

4. Fuji-san (L. 8)
In Japan, which is about 70% mountainous, the tallest and most famous of all mountains is *Fuji-san*, or Mt. Fuji. (*San* is the *on-yomi*, or Chinese reading of the *kanji* 山, meaning *mountain*.) It is a snow-capped volcano standing up to 3,776 meters (12,388 feet), which has not erupted since 1707. It is regarded by many Japanese as sacred, and is climbed by several hundred people every year.

5. Biwa-ko (L. 8)
The largest fresh water lake in Japan, covering 268 square miles, *Biwa-ko* is located to the east of Kyoto. (The final syllable *-ko* is the *on-yomi* for the *kanji* for lake.) Its name is derived from its shape, which is similar to that of the *biwa*, a traditional Japanese stringed instrument. It is the source of water for the surrounding agricultural areas as well as drinking water for major cities such as Kyoto.

6. Compliments (L. 10)
The culturally appropriate response to a compliment is to deny it. If you are complimented on your excellent command of Japanese, it would be appropriate to

respond with *Iie, mada heta desu-yo.* ("No, it's still poor.") or *Iie, mada dame desu.* ("No, it's still bad.")

7. School cleaning (L. 13)
In Japan, it is the students' responsibility to keep the classrooms, halls and bathrooms in their school spotless. The task begins in elementary school and continues through high school. As a result of their efforts, students tend to be respectful of school property.

8. Japanese boxed lunches (L. 14)
Called *o-bento*, these boxed lunches can be purchased in readily-found *o-bento* shops or are prepared at home. Many students bring them from home in plastic boxes called *o-bento bako*, which are divided into sections. The main section is filled with white steamed rice and the smaller sections contain small servings of meat, fish, pickled vegetables, fruit, etc.

INTERACTIVE ACTIVITIES

PART 1

❶ **Yes-No question guessing game**
In pairs, choose a country in the world with the help of a world map. Each partner must guess which country his/her partner chose by asking only questions that can be answer by "yes" or "no". The questions must use cardinal directions or ask about size (ie., "Is it big /small?") Quickly try to guess your partner's country as in the sample dialogue.

SAMPLE DIALOGUE

A: その くには ヨーロッパに ありますか。

B: はい、あります。

A: おおきい くに ですか。

B: いいえ、おおきい くに じゃ ない です。

A: ドイツに ちかい ですか。

B: はい、ちかい です。

A: ドイツの にしに ありますか。

B: いいえ、ありません。

A: イタリアの きたに ありますか。

B: はい、あります。

A: オーストリア ですか。

B: いいえ、ちがいます。

A: スイス ですか。

B: はい、スイス です。

❷ **Saturday errands** 📄 & ✏️
Partner A and Partner B are getting ready for up-coming trips. They each spent the whole day Saturday running errands. At the end of the day, they touch base to see where they were and what they were doing at various times of the day. Looking only at your chart, ask your partner questions to find out the missing information. Take notes of your partner's responses and check them by looking at each other's chart when you finish the activity. When answering questions about the activity, be sure to change the given verb to the *-te* form + *imashita*.

182

Partner A looks at:

Partner A's activities

Place	Time	Activities
デパート	10:30	かばんのかいものをする
きっさてん	1:00	コーヒーをのむ
ともだちのうち	4:00	はなす
レストラン	7:00	すしをたべる

Partner B's activities

Place	Time	Activities
A.	11:00	くつのかいものをする
本や	12:00	B.
デパート	C.	D.
E.	5:30	サンドイッチをたべる

Questions to find out:
(a) place: #じに **どこ**に いましたか。
(b) time: **なんじ**に (place) に いましたか。
(c) activity: (place) で／(time) に **なに**を していましたか。

Partner B looks at:

Partner B's activities

Place	Time	Activities
くつや	11:00	くつのかいものをする
本や	12:00	ガイドブックをよむ
デパート	3:00	ジャケットのかいものをする
レストラン	5:30	サンドイッチをたべる

Partner A's activities

Place	Time	Activities
デパート	10:30	F.
きっさてん	G.	コーヒーをのむ
H.	4:00	I.
レストラン	J	すしをたべる

PART 2

❶ Conversation practice

With a partner, ask questions about his/her class schedule today, as in the sample
dialogue below.

SAMPLE DIALOGUE

A: きょう、 なんの じゅぎょうが ありますか。

B: <u>日本ごと すうがくと びじゅつと えいご</u>が あります。

A: <u>1</u>じかんめは なん ですか。

B: <u>えいご</u> です。

A: <u>すうがく</u>は なんじかんめ ですか。

B: <u>5</u>じかんめ です。

A: <u>5</u>じかんめは なんじに おわりますか。

B: <u>3じはん</u>に おわります。

❷ May I…?

In pairs, complete the following statements asking permission. Your partner will either
grant you permission or refuse permission as in the example. Check your answers with
the answer key on the next page.

Ex. えんぴつを ＿＿＿＿＿。 →
    A:　えんぴつを <u>つかっても いい ですか</u>。
    B:　はい、いい ですよ／どうぞ／つかっても いい ですよ。or
       ああ、えんぴつは ちょっと....。

1. クッキーを ＿＿＿＿＿＿＿＿＿。
2. ミルクを ＿＿＿＿＿＿＿＿＿＿。
3. うたを ＿＿＿＿＿＿＿＿＿＿＿。
4. テレビを ＿＿＿＿＿＿＿＿＿＿。

5. おんがくを ＿＿＿＿＿＿＿＿＿。
6. てがみを ＿＿＿＿＿＿＿＿＿＿。
7. その本を ＿＿＿＿＿＿＿＿＿＿。
8. うちに ＿＿＿＿＿＿＿＿＿＿＿。

ANSWERS (INTERACTIVE ACTIVITIES):
PART 2 ❷
1. クッキーを <u>たべても いいですか</u>。
2. ミルクを <u>のんでも いいですか</u>。
3. うたを <u>うたっても いいですか</u>。
4. テレビを <u>みても いいですか</u>。

5. おんがくを <u>きいても いいですか</u>。
6. てがみを <u>かいて／よんで／みても いいですか</u>。
7. その本を <u>みて／よんでも いいですか</u>。
8. うちに <u>かえっても いいですか</u>。

RL. 4　電話で　話しましょう

れんしゅう A: しゅうまつ

> しつもん: (a) しゅうまつ　なにを　しましたか。
> 　　　　 (b) どれぐらい〜ましたか。

			(a) activity	(b) time
1.		さやか	played tennis	3:00-5:00
2.		ジェフ	studied history	8:30-10:00
3.		アンナ	taught piano	1:00-2:00
4.		りゅうじ	played computer games	4:30-5:00

れんしゅう B: なにを　していましたか。

Your friend called you. S/he wants to know what you were doing when s/he called.

You were:

(1) listening to music

(2) reading a magazine

(3) watching TV

(4) drinking coffee

(5) writing in your diary

(6) talking to your sister

Read the following excerpt of a letter from your pen pal and answer the questions below.

こうべは 大さかの にしに あります。こうべの にしに 山が あります。大きい 川は ありませんけど、うみが あります。わたしの いちばんすきな まちはさんのみやです。さんのみやの えきの ちかくにおもしろい おみせが たくさん あります。おいしいレストランも たくさん あります。こうべに あそびにきてください。

しつもん: (Answer in English.)

(1) Where is Kobe located?
(2) What do you find to the west of Kobe?
(3) What is the name of the place in Kobe that your pen pal likes the most?
(4) What is there in that place?

れんしゅう D: よみましょう。こたえましょう。

Write the appropriate particles in *hiragana* in the boxes and answer the questions.

(1) なんのクラブ ☐ はいっていますか。

(2) アメリカ ☐ 一ばん高い山 ☐ なんですか。

(3) メキシコは アメリカ ☐ みなみ ☐ ありますか。
きた ☐ ありますか。

(4) ベルギー ☐ ☐ なにご ☐ はなしますか。

REVIEW LESSON 5
(Volume 2, Lessons 16~20)

OBJECTIVES

This lesson provides you with an opportunity to review the following objectives from Volume 2, Lessons 16 through 20:

- ☑ Ask and state where things are located
- ☑ Comment on housekeeping
- ☑ Relate a sequence of daily and weekend activities
- ☑ Ask and tell about hobbies and interests
- ☑ Introduce yourself to a pen pal
- ☑ Read the *kanji*: 火、水、金、土、私
- ☑ Read and write the *kanji*: 何、今

VOCABULARY たんご

Hobbies and Interests-Related Words and Phrases:

shumi [hobby]	nikki [diary]
ryokoo [travel, trip]	ryoori [cooking]
e [picture, drawing]	tegami [letter]
kitte [postage stamp]	pen paru [pen pal]

e-o kaku (kakimasu) [draw a picture]
nikki-o kaku (kakimasu) [write in a diary/journal]
atsumeru (atsumemasu) [collect]
au (aimasu) [meet (someone)]
hiku (hikimasu)
[play (stringed and keyboard instruments)]
fuku (fukimasu) [play (wind instruments)]
tataku (tatakimasu) [play (percussion instruments)]
Shumi-wa nan desu-ka? [What are your hobbies?]
yoku [often]

Phrases and Expressions:
Tadaima. [I'm home.]
O-kaeri(nasai). [Welcome home.]
Itte-kimasu. [I'm leaving.]
Itterasshai.
[We'll see you when you get back.]
Oboete-imasu-ka? [Do you remember?]

Indefinite Pronouns:

nani-ka [something]	dare-ka [someone]
nani-mo [nothing]	dare-mo [no one]

Adjectives:
kirei (na) [clean, neat; pretty]
kitanai [dirty, messy]

Location-Related Words:

ue [top, above, up]	shita [under, below, down]	hondana [bookcase]	heya [room]

KEY GRAMMAR POINTS ぶんぽうポイント

The number in parentheses after each grammar point is the lesson in which it was first presented.

1. Ue ~ shita (L. 16)
Ue (above, on), shita (below, under), mae, ushiro, migi, and *hidari (front, behind, right, and left* respectively) are words that express location, such as

Isu-no *shita-ni* arimasu.	It's *under* the chair.
Kyookasho-wa hondana-no *ue-ni* arimasu.	The textbook is *on* the bookcase.

2. Aru (Arimasu) ~ Iru (Imasu) (L. 16)
Remember that *arimasu* is used to ask and tell about the location of inanimate things, and *imasu* is used with animate things. The plain forms of these verbs are *aru* and *iru* respectively, and are used as casual speech with family members and close friends.

Manga, doko-ni *aru*?	Where*'s* the comic book?
Teeburu-no shita-ni *aru*-yo.	It*'s* under the table.
Mari-chan-wa doko-ni *iru*?	Where *is* Mari?

3. Using the *-te* form to link actions (L. 17)

As you have learned, this pattern expresses a sequence of actions. You can link any number of verbs this way, but the actions must generally be within a fairly short period of time, be in some way related, and be mentioned in order of occurrence. The subject is the same for all of the verbs in the sequence. If more than one verb is used, they are all put in the *-te* form except for the last one.

Ban-gohan-o *tabete*, tesuto-no benkyoo-o *shite*, nemashita.	I *ate* dinner, *studied* for the test, and *went* to bed.

4. The use of particles (L. 18)

Particles in Japanese can sometimes be translated as prepositions in English.

Hachi-ji-*ni* gakkoo-*ni* ikimashita.	I went *to* school *at* 8:00.

In some cases the particle does not even have an English equivalent.

Tenisu-*ga* dekimasu.	He can play tennis.
Terebi-*o* mite-imashita.	We were watching TV.

5. Nani-mo, dare-mo, nani-ka, dare-ka (L. 18)

The four indefinite pronouns *dare-ka, dare-mo, nani-ka, nani-mo* do not take the particles *-ga, -wa,* or *-o.*

Dare-ka oboete-imasu-ka?	Does *anyone* remember?
Nani-ka nomimashita-ka?	Did you drink *something*?
Nani-mo shimasen deshita.	I didn't do *anything*.
Dare-mo wakarimasen.	*No one* understands.

6. Changing verbs into nouns (L. 19)

In Japanese, as in English, we must generally change verbs into noun phrases if we wish to use them as subjects or objects. One way to do this is by using **the plain form of the verb + koto**.

Shumi-wa hon-o *yomu-koto* desu.	My hobby is *reading* books.
Shumi-wa eiga-o *miru-koto* desu.	My hobby is *watching* movies.

7. Particles

Particle	L. #	Note(s)	Sample sentence
に ni	18	indicates a person one meets, used in (person)-*ni au*	6 じにボーイフレンドにあいました。(She met her boyfriend at 6:00.)
	20	indicates the indirect object (and addressee) of a sentence whom something is directed toward	ともだちにてがみをかきました。(I wrote a letter **to** a friend.)
	20	indicates time/locations when/where an action occurs, translated as *at, on, in,* or *to*	なんじにいきますか。(**At** what time are you going?) とうきょうにいきますか。(Are you going **to** Tokyo?)

KANJI NOTES   かんじノート

Kanji	L. #	Pronunciation(s)	Meaning	Examples
何	17	KA*; nan, nani	what, how many; *prefix to form questions*	何人 (*nan-nin*: how many people?); 何をしましたか。(*Nani-o shimashita-ka?*: What did you do?)

Kanji	L. #	Pronunciation(s)	Meaning	Examples
私	18	SHI*; watashi, watakushi*	I; privacy	私 (*watashi:* I, me); 私の (*watashi*-no: mine)
今	18	KON, KIN*; ima	now, the present	今 (*ima:* now); 今日 (*kyoo:* today); 今日は。(*Konnichi-wa.:* Hello.)
火	20	KA; hi*, [bi] *	fire	火曜日 (*ka*-yoobi: Tuesday); 火鉢 (*hi*-bachi: charcoal grill); 花火 (hana-*bi:* fireworks)
水	20	SUI; mizu	water	水曜日 (*sui*-yoobi: Wednesday); 水 (*mizu:* water)
金	20	KIN, KON*; kane	gold, money	金曜日 (*kin*-yoobi: Friday); お金 (o-*kane:* money)
土	20	DO, TO*; tsuchi*	earth, soil	土曜日 (*do*-yoobi: Saturday); 土 (*tsuchi:* earth, soil)

* For reference only.

CULTURE NOTES　　　　　　　　　　カルチャーノート

Shumi (L. 19, 20)

Translated as *hobby* in English, *shumi* actually has a broader scope in that it can also refer to activities which people enjoy doing during leisure time. Thus, shopping, visiting friends, and watching TV are all considered *shumi*, and very popular ones in Japan. They are an expression of an individual's interests and thus help define a person. For that reason, Japanese will frequently inquire about your *shumi* soon after meeting your for the first time, and if you say, "*Shumi-wa nani-mo arimasen,*" they may think that you are an extremely boring person.

INTERACTIVE ACTIVITIES

PART 1

❶ Conversation practice

Practice conversing with a partner, as in the sample dialogue below. Be creative in your choice of activities.

EX. SAMPLE DIALOGUE

A: まりさん、こんしゅうまつ 何を しますか。
B: こうえんに いって、テニスを します。
A: いい ですね。だれと しますか。
B: あねと します。アリサさんは？
A: わたしは デパートに いって、かばんを かいます。

Try it also in plain, casual speech:

A: まり、こんしゅうまつ 何 する？
B: こうえん いって、テニス する。
A: いいね。だれと？
B: あねと。アリサは？
A: わたしは デパート いって、かばん かう。

189

❷ Locating items in a room – Information gap　📄 & ✏️

Choose any three items and place them in the room, either above or below, to the right or left of the furniture already in there (i.e., the desk, bed, and bookcase). Work with a partner, who has done the same task. Asking Yes-No questions only, find out where s/he placed the items s/he chose, and duplicate his/her drawing. Start with the generic question: 〜さんの へやに (item) が あります／いますか。 If the response is "yes", ask (item) は つくえの (location word) に あります／いますか。 Compare illustrations after all items have been located.

> Items:
> phone, dictionary, bag, dog, cat

Your room

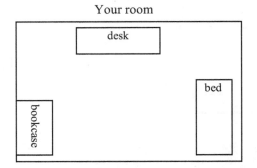

Your partner's room

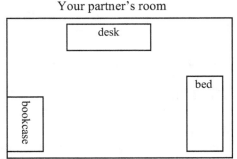

PART 2

❶ Interview your partner　📄 & ✏️

Work with a partner. First, write your own personal information about the topics in the box below in Japanese. Then interview your partner about the topics and write down his/her responses.

> **TOPICS**
> age　　birthday　　favorite subject　　abilities　　hobbies　　daily activities
> weekend activities　　any topic you like (ex. likes/dislikes, family, etc.)

❷ Presentation

Give a presentation to the class, telling them about the information you learned about your partner.

SAMPLE PRESENTATION

〜さんは ＃さい です。おたんじょう日は 〜月〜日 です。
いちばん すきな かもくは 〜です。〜が できます。
しゅみは 〜 (こと) と 〜 (こと) です。
しゅうまつは よく 〜て、〜ます。
まいにち 〜じに おきて、〜じに がっこうに いきます。
ごかぞくは ＃人 です。

RL. 5 電話で 話しましょう

れんしゅう A: にちようび

(1)

としお

Sunday
9:00
10:00
11:00
12:00   went to the park
1:00   played soccer
2:00
3:00   went home
4:00   did homework
5:00
6:00
7:00
8:00

(2)

ノエル

Sunday
9:00
10:00
11:00   cooked
12:00
1:00
2:00
3:00   went to a party
4:00
5:00   played game
6:00
7:00
8:00

(3)

ゆき

Sunday
9:00
10:00
11:00
12:00
1:00
2:00   went to school gym
3:00
4:00   played volleyball
5:00
6:00   went home
7:00   studied math
8:00

(4)

ジョン

Sunday
9:00
10:00   went to the lake
11:00
12:00   went on a picnic
1:00
2:00   went swimming
3:00
4:00
5:00
6:00
7:00
8:00

(5)

マット

Sunday
9:00
10:00
11:00
12:00
1:00
2:00
3:00   met friends
4:00   watched a
5:00   Japanese film
6:00
7:00   ate at a restaurant
8:00

(6)

YOU

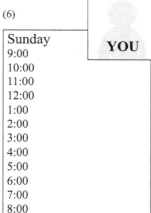

Sunday
9:00
10:00
11:00
12:00
1:00
2:00
3:00
4:00
5:00
6:00
7:00
8:00

れんしゅう B: よみましょう。こたえましょう。

Write the appropriate particles in *hiragana* in the boxes and answer the questions.

(1) あさ、何 ☐ のみましたか。 (Did you drink anything this morning?)

(2) しゅうまつ、ともだち ☐ あいましたか。

(3) ピアノ ☐ できますか。

(4) 何じ ☐ 学校 ☐ きますか。

191

れんしゅう C: ペンパルからのてがみ

Read the following excerpt of a letter from your pen pal and answer the
questions below.

私のしゅみは テニスです。よく、土よう日に あねとテニスをします。でも、今日は あめです。テニスは できませんでした。今日は 何もしませんでした。ジェーンさんのしゅみは 何ですか。また、てがみをかいてください。

しつもん: (Answer in English.)

(1) When does your pen pal play tennis?
(2) With whom does s/he play tennis?
(3) What is the weather like today in her/his town?
(4) What did s/he do today?

れんしゅう D: Interview your classmates!

LESSON 21
Writing a Letter to a Friend

OBJECTIVES
もくひょう

At the end of this lesson you will be able to:
- ☑ Talk more about weather
- ☑ Write a short letter to a friend
- ☑ Read the *kanji*: 天　元　気

VOCABULARY
たんご

Words

kasa	umbrella
kaze	wind
tsuyoi	strong
mado	window
akeru (akemasu/akete)	open (something)
shimeru (shimemasu/shimete)	close (something)

Other words and expressions you will hear in this lesson

reinkooto	raincoat
sakura	cherry blossoms
e	to

VOCABULARY NOTES
たんごノート

1. Akeru ~ shimeru
The verbs *akeru* and *shimeru*, which mean *open* and *close* respectively, must be used with a direct object. In Japanese the particle *-o* follows a direct object. Verbs which require a direct object are called **transitive verbs**.

Mado-*o akete*-mo ii desu-ka?	May I *open* the window?
Mado-*o shimemashita.*	I *closed* the window.
Doa-*o shimete*-mo ii desu-ka?	May I *close* the door?

2. The particle *-e*
The particle *-e*, which is usually translated as *to*, is written as へ but is pronounced without the *h*-sound. This particle is commonly used with the verbs *iku*, *kuru*, and *kaeru* which indicate movement in a certain direction. As you have learned, the particle *-ni* can also be used to mean *to*. You will also see the particle へ at the beginning of letters.

Ashita Tookyoo-*e* ikimasu.	Tomorrow I'm going *to* Tokyo.
Oneesan-mo paatii-*e* kimasu-ka?	Is your sister also coming *to* the party?
Mariko-san-*e*	*To* Mariko [in a letter]

CULTURE NOTES
カルチャーノート

Seasonal references in letters
You learned in Lesson 58 (Vol. 1) that Japanese often make comments about the weather when greeting each other. It is also a common practice to include a seasonal reference near the very beginning of a letter. The writer may choose from a number of rather set expressions for each of the four seasons. A typical one for spring might be *Zuibun haru-rashiku natte kimashita* (随分春らしくなってきました), which means *It has become very spring-like.*

Rather than attempting to be original by creating your own seasonal references in Japanese, you would be wise to buy a book with a list of all of the acceptable expressions along with other rules of letter writing. In this way you will not run the risk of insulting someone unintentionally or being misunderstood. As with many aspects of Japanese culture, doing things the "correct" way is extremely important.

Four seasons in Japan
The video section of this lesson includes a beautiful culture segment featuring the four seasons in Japan and common activities and events associated with each season. For more information on the four seasons, reread the Culture Notes in Lesson 60 (Vol. 1).

YOMIMASHOO!　　　　　　　　　　　　　　　　よみましょう

かさ	umbrella
かぜ	wind
つよい	strong
まど	window
あける・あけます・あけて	open (something)
しめる・しめます・しめて	close (something)
よくない	not good
今日の 天気は どう ですか。	How's the weather today?
ミシガンの 天気は いい ですか。	Is Michigan's weather nice?
フロリダの なつは どう ですか。	How are Florida's summers?
ここは かぜが つよい ですね。	The wind is strong here, isn't it?
どれに しましょうか。	Which should I choose?
レインコート	raincoat
さくら	cherry blossoms
へ	to

KANJI NOTES　　　　　　　　　　　　　　　　かんじノート

In this lesson you will learn to read three *kanji*: 天, 元 and 気. Be sure that you know the readings of each *kanji* and can tell what the *kanji* means. Readings which are marked by an asterisk are for your reference only; you do not need to learn these at this time. You also do not have to learn any new words which are given in the examples. The correct stroke order for these *kanji* is given in the Optional Writing Practice section.

 TEN; ame*, ama* (sky, heaven)

天気	*ten*ki	weather
天井	*ten*joo	ceiling
天の川	*Ama*-no gawa	Milky Way

今日の天気はどうですか。	Kyoo-no *ten*ki-wa doo desu-ka?	How's the weather today?
火曜日の天気は雨でした。	Ka-yoobi-no *ten*ki-wa ame deshita.	Tuesday's weather was rain.

194

３月の天気はどう ですか。	San-gatsu-no *ten*ki-wa doo desu-ka?	How's the weather in in March?

元 **GEN, GAN*; moto*** (beginning, foundation)

元気	*gen*ki	good health

お元気ですか。	O-*gen*ki desu-ka?	How are you?
元気じゃないです。	*Gen*ki ja nai desu.	I'm not well.

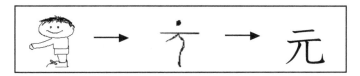

気 **KI, KE*** (spirit, energy)

天気	ten*ki*	weather
元気	gen*ki*	good health
病気	byoo*ki*	sickness, illness

今日の天気はどう ですか。	Kyoo-no ten*ki*-wa doo desu-ka?	How's the weather today?
お元気ですか。	O-gen*ki* desu-ka?	How are you?
今病気です。	Ima byoo*ki* desu.	He's sick now.

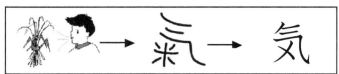

KANJI REVIEW

月　日　木　本　人　山　川　大　小　学　校　中

高　何　今　私　火　水　金　土　天　元　気

How do you read them? What do they mean?

PART 1

❶ Kakimashoo!   🖊

During this activity each student will work as a pair with two different クラスメート to check Assignment #1 from Part 2 of Lesson 20. The goal of the activity is to have two students carefully check the sentences in your letter to a Japanese pen pal, mark and discuss with you any errors found, and sign off on your page. Form your first pair and exchange assignments with your partner. Both partners independently check and neatly mark errors for the entire assignment. Use the same editing symbols as usual.

❷ Vocabulary check

Silently review the vocabulary for Lesson 21. Then have a クラスメート orally test your knowledge of them. Your partner says the えいご and you give the 日本ご. Switch and test your partner.

PART 2

❶ Yomimashoo!

With a クラスメート take turns reading the following てがみ and checking each other's accuracy. Partner A looks only at the letter. Partner B looks at the ローマじ equivalent on the right. If Partner A makes a mistake, Partner B says, "*Moo ichido yonde kudasai,*" and then provides additional help if needed. Change partners and repeat the activity.

READING WARM-UP
Read these words aloud before you read the letter.

ジェフ (Jefu)	日本 (Nihon)	とても (totemo)	ともだち (tomodachi)
へ (e)	今 (ima)	きれい (kirei)	山 (yama)
元気 (genki)	はる (haru)	今日 (kyoo)	ピクニック (pikunikku)
私 (watashi)	さくら (sakura)	天気 (tenki)	また (mata)

PARTNER A	PARTNER B
4月3日 土よう日　 はれ ジェフくんへ ジェフくん、 お元気ですか。 私は元気です。 日本は今、 はるです。 さくらが とても きれいです。 今日は いい 天気 でした。 私は ともだちと 山に いって、 ピクニックを しました。 ジェフくん、 また てがみを かいて ください。 さようなら。 　　　　　　　　　　 ゆきえ	Shi-gatsu Mikka Doyoobi Hare Jefu-kun-e Jefu-kun, o-genki desu-ka? Watashi-wa genki desu. Nihon-wa ima, haru desu. Sakura-ga totemo kirei desu. Kyoo-wa ii tenki deshita. Watashi-wa tomodachi-to yama-ni itte, pikunikku-o shimashita. Jefu-kun, mata tegami-o kaite kudasai. Sayoonara. 　　　　　　　　　　 Yukie

❷ Let's ask and answer!

After you and your partner have both read the letter in the previous activity, take turns asking each other the following しつもん. You may ask them **in any order**. Partner A asks one question which Partner B answers without looking at the answer given below. Partner B may, however, refer back to the letters. Then Partner B asks a question.

QUESTIONS

1. Nan-gatsu nan-nichi-no tegami desu-ka?

2. Dare-ga kono tegami-o kakimashita-ka?

3. Yukie-san-wa dare-ni kono tegami-o kakimashita-ka?

4. Nihon-wa ima fuyu desu-ka?

5. Nani-ga totemo kirei desu-ka?

6. Tenki-wa doo deshita-ka?

7. Yukie-san-wa doko-ni ikimashita-ka?

8. Yukie-san-wa dare-to yama-ni ikimashita-ka?

9. Yukie-san-wa yama-de nani-o shimashita-ka?

ANSWERS

1. Shigatsu mikka-no (tegami) desu.
2. Yukie-san-ga kakimashita.
3. Jefu-kun-ni kakimashita.
4. Iie, haru desu.
5. Sakura-ga totemo kirei desu.

6. Ii tenki deshita.
7. Yama-ni ikimashita.
8. Tomodachi-to ikimashita.
9. Pikunikku-o shimashita.

L. 21 電話で 話しましょう

れんしゅう A: Today's Weather

まち	天気	きおん	かぜ
Miami	☀	86 °F	light
Denver	(1) ☁	74 °F	strong
Boston	☂	(2) 59 °F	light
San Francisco	(3) ☀	80 °F	✕
Chicago	☁	(4) 63 °F	strong

れんしゅう B: May I ...?

(Ex.)

(1)

(2)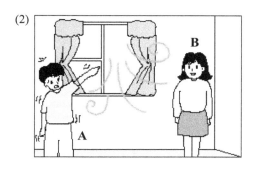

(3)

(4)

(5)

<u>れんしゅう C</u>: A Letter to a Friend

10 月 15 日 （金）

ともみさんへ

　お元気ですか。私は元気です。日本は今、あきです。*こうようが きれいです。しゅうまつ、天気が よかったです。ともだちと 山にいって、ハイキングを しました。ともみさんはしゅうまつ、何を しましたか。また てがみを ください。さようなら。

れいこ

*こうよう: red leaves

しつもん: (Answer in English.)

(1) What season is it in Japan now?

(2) When did Reiko go to the mountains?

(3) What did she do in the mountains?

LESSON 22
Seasons and Activities

OBJECTIVES　　　　　　　　　　　　　　　　　　もくひょう

At the end of this lesson you will be able to:
- ☑ Talk about seasons
- ☑ Talk about the weather and activities for last week, this week, and next week
- ☑ Write the *kanji*: 火 and 水

VOCABULARY　　　　　　　　　　　　　　　　　　　たんご

Words

kisetsu	season
senshuu	last week*
konshuu	this week*
raishuu	next week*

Other words and expressions you will hear in this lesson

hoka-no	another
hoka-no gakusei	another student
Samui kisetsu-ni narimashita-ne?	It's getting pretty cold, isn't it?

*These time words **do not** take the particle *-ni*.

KEY GRAMMAR POINTS　　　　　　　　　　　ぶんぽうポイント

Past tense of *i*-adjectives
In Japanese *i*-adjectives have a past tense form just as verbs do. To form the past tense of *i*-adjectives, drop the final *-i* (い), and add *-katta* (かった). Study these examples.

Ryokoo-wa *tanoshikatta* desu.	The trip was pleasant.
Ryoori-wa *oishikatta* desu.	The food was delicious.
Hoteru-wa *takakatta* desu-ka?	Was the hotel expensive?
Sono hon-wa *omoshirokatta* desu.	That book was interesting.
Kono zasshi-wa *yasukatta* desu.	This magazine was cheap.

The plain past form of *i*-adjectives is made the same way, but you simply drop the *desu*.

Ryokoo-wa *tanoshikatta*.	The trip was pleasant.
Ryoori-wa *oishikatta*?	Was the food delicious?
Shikago-wa *samukatta*.	Chicago was cold.

The plain past form of *na*-adjectives is made by simply changing *desu* to *deshita*.

Kissaten-wa *shizuka deshita*.	The coffee shop was quiet.
Otooto-san-wa *genki deshita*.	His younger brother was healthy.
Dame deshita.	It was no good.

YOMIMASHOO!　　　　　　　　　　　　　　　　よみましょう

きせつ	season
せんしゅう	last week
こんしゅう (今しゅう)	this week
らいしゅう	next week
どの きせつが いちばん すき ですか。	Which season do you like the best?

さむい きせつに なりましたね。	It's getting pretty cold, isn't it?
なつに 何を しますか。	What do you do in the summer?
ふゆが あんまり すき じゃ ない です。	I don't really like winter.
らいしゅうの 天気は どう ですか。	How is next week's weather?
こんしゅう どこに いきますか。	Where are you going this week?
せんしゅうの 月よう日に きました。	He came last Monday.
ほかの	another
ほかの 学生	another student

INTERACTIVE ACTIVITIES

PART 1

❶ **Tegami-o kakimashoo!**

During this activity each student will work as a pair with two different クラスメート to check Assignment #1 from Part 2 of Lesson 21. The goal of the activity is to have two students carefully check the sentences in your letter to a Japanese friend, mark and discuss with you any errors found, and sign off on your page. Form your first pair and exchange assignments with your partner. Both partners independently check and neatly mark errors for the entire assignment. Use the same editing symbols as usual.

❷ **Dialogue**

With a クラスメート memorize the dialogue following the normal procedure. Make sure that you understand the meaning of the dialogue before you begin practicing.

Spring vacation begins next week. A is asking about B's plans for the vacation.
A: Raishuu-kara haru-yasumi-ga hajimarimasu-ne.
B: Aa, soo desu-ne. (*happily*)
A: B-san-wa doko-ka-ni ikimasu-ka?
B: Hai, kazoku-to ryokoo-ni ikimasu.
A: Ryokoo desu-ka? Ii desu-ne. Doko-ni ikimasu-ka?
B: Hawai-ni ikimasu.
A: Aa, Hawai desu-ka? Watashi-mo fuyu-yasumi-ni Hawai-ni ikimashita-yo.
B: E? Soo desu-ka? Doo deshita-ka?
A: Totemo tanoshikatta desu-yo.

For a greater challenge, use this version of the dialogue.
A: らいしゅうから はるやすみが はじまりますね。
B: ああ、そう ですね。(*happily*)
A: Bさんは どこかに いきますか。
B: はい、かぞくと りょこうに いきます。
A: りょこう ですか。いい ですね。どこに いきますか。
B: ハワイに いきます。
A: ああ、ハワイ ですか。私も ふゆやすみに ハワイに いきましたよ。
B: え？そう ですか。どう でしたか。
A: とても たのしかった ですよ。

❶ Haru-yasumi-wa itsu-kara hajimarimasu-ka?

With a different partner from before, review the dialogue which you practiced in Part 1. Then take turns asking and answering questions about the dialogue. You may refer back to the dialogue if needed. Place the tip of a pencil on the dot in the center of the circle below with one end of a paper clip around the pencil tip. Use this as a spinner to select a number on the wheel. Look at the example before you begin.

D: C-san-no ban desu. [ban = turn]
C: Hai. (*spins a 3*)
D: (*reads question number 3*) B-san-wa doko-ka-ni ikimasu-ka?
C: (*answers the question*) Hai, ryokoo-ni ikimasu.
    D-san-no ban desu.

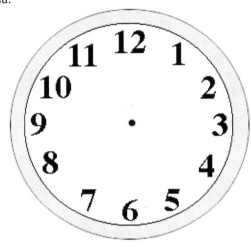

QUESTIONS
1. Haru-yasumi-wa itsu-kara hajimarimasu-ka?
2. Haru-yasumi-wa konshuu-kara hajimarimasu-ka?
3. B-san-wa doko-ka-ni ikimasu-ka?
4. B-san-wa dare-to ryokoo-ni ikimasu-ka?
5. B-san-wa doko-ni ikimasu-ka?
6. B-san-wa dare-to Hawai-ni ikimasu-ka?
7. B-san-wa itsu Hawai-ni ikimasu-ka?
8. A-san-wa itsu Hawai-ni ikimashita-ka?
9. Dare-ga haru-yasumi-ni Hawai-ni ikimasu-ka?
10. Dare-ga fuyu-yasumi-ni Hawai-ni ikimashita-ka?
11. A-san-no ryokoo-wa doo deshita-ka?
12. A-san-wa fuyu-yasumi-ni Hawai-ni ikimashita-ka?

❷ Konshuu nani-o shimasu-ka?

Do this interview activity as an entire class. Form pairs. Each person asks and answers at least two questions about weather and activities for last week, this week, and/or next week. Feel free to use your imagination when answering. Change pairs as soon as you have finished your mini-conversation. Try to speak with as many different クラスメート as you can. Here are some sample questions and answers to help you get started.

Q: Senshuu nani-o shimashita-ka?
A: Ryooko-ni ikimashita.
Q: Doko-ni ikimashita-ka?
A: Mekishiko-ni ikimashita.

Q: Mekishiko-de nani-o shimashita-ka?
A: Mainichi umi-ni itte, saafin*-o shite, bareebooru-o shimashita.
Q: Tenki-wa doo deshita-ka?
A: Mainichi hare deshita. Atsukatta desu.   *surfing

ACTIVITIES

Q: **Senshuu** nani-o shimashita-ka?
A: Kuruma-o kaimashita.
Q: Doko-de kaimashita-ka?
A: Suupaa Kaa-de kaimashita.
Q: Takakatta desu-ka?
A: Iie, totemo yasukatta desu.

Q: **Konshuu** nani-o shimasu-ka?
A: Benkyoo-o shimasu.
Q: Doko-de shimasu-ka?
A: Toshokan-de shimasu.
Q: Dare-to shimasu-ka?
A: Tomodachi-to shimasu.
Q: Nan-yoobi-ni shimasu-ka?
A: Mainichi shimasu.

Q: **Raishuu** nani-o shimasu-ka?
A: Ryokoo-ni ikimasu.
Q: Doko-ni ikimasu-ka?
A: Kanada-ni ikimasu.
Q: Dare-to ikimasu-ka?
A: Haha-to ikimasu.

WEATHER

Q: **Senshuu**-no tenki-wa doo deshita-ka?
A: Yuki deshita.
   Hare deshita
   Ii tenki deshita.
   Kaze-ga tsuyokatta desu.

Q: **Kyoo**-no tenki-wa doo desu-ka?
A: Ii tenki desu.
   Iya-na tenki desu.
   Anmari yokunai desu.
   Ame/yuki desu.
   Hare/kumori desu.
   Kaze-ga tsuyoi desu.
Q: Nan-do desu-ka?
A: 66-do desu.

Q: **Raishuu**-no tenki-wa doo desu-ka?
A: Raishuu-wa ii-mitai desu.
   Ame-mitai desu.
   Getsu-yoobi-to ka-yoobi-wa yuki-
     mitai desu kedo, sui-yoobi-kara
     hare-mitai desu.

L. 22 電話で 話しましょう

れんしゅう A: How was ~? It was [*i*-adjective].

(1) hot

(2) Welcome to Hawaii! fun

(3) Bob's old

(4) $280.00 expensive

(5) Adventure of Cutting Grass boring

(6) 山川 big

れんしゅう B: Kazumi's Schedule

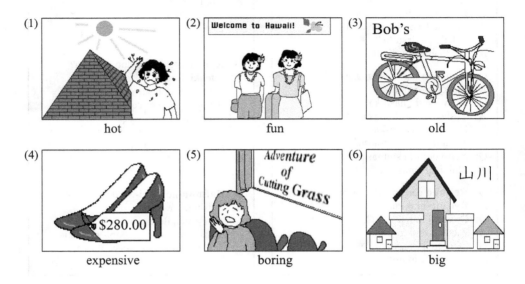

	Last week	This week	Next week
日	went shopping	(2)	(4)
月	watched a movie		
火	(1) drew a picture	**today** go to the library	(5) study French
水			
木		(3) play volleyball	

れんしゅう C: What does Tadashi do in the spring/summer/fall/winter?

しつもん： (a) do what? (b) with whom?

(1) はる — Friend

(2) なつ — Family

ただし — My favorite season!

(3) あき — Older brother

(4) ふゆ — Friend

LESSON 23
Talking about a Trip

At the end of this lesson you will be able to:
- ☑ Talk about a trip you took
- ☑ Talk about how the weather was
- ☑ Write the *kanji*: 金 and 土

VOCABULARY   たんご

Other words and expressions you will hear in this lesson

shashin-o toru (torimasu/totte)	take a photograph
saafin	surfing
saafin-o suru (shimasu/shite)	surf, go surfing
kin-yoobi-no kin	the *kin* in *kin-yoobi**

*Because different *kanji* may sometimes have an identical reading, Japanese will often identify a specific *kanji* by giving a word in which it occurs. For example, the *kin* intended may be *kin-yoobi-no kin* (金), not *saikin-no kin* (近). The *kanji* 金, and 近 each have a reading which is *kin*.

KEY GRAMMAR POINTS   ぶんぽうポイント

Past negative of *i*-adjectives

To make the past negative form of *i*-adjectives, drop the final *-i* (い) and add *-ku-nakatta* (く なかった). Study these examples.

Hoteru-wa *takaku-nakatta* desu.	The hotel wasn't expensive.
Saafin-wa *muzukashiku-nakatta* desu.	Surfing wasn't difficult.
Tenki-wa *yoku-nakatta* desu.	The weather wasn't good.

I-ADJECTIVES		
	Affirmative	**Negative**
Non-past	samu**i** desu	samu**ku-nai** desu
Past	samu**katta** desu	samu**ku-nakatta** desu

The negative past of *na*-adjectives is formed by simply adding *ja nakatta* (じゃ なかった).

Sono machi-wa *shizuka ja nakatta* desu.	That town *wasn't quiet*.
Ano hito-wa anmari *joozu ja nakatta* desu.	That person *wasn't* very *good*.

NA-ADJECTIVES		
	Affirmative	**Negative**
Non-past	kantan desu	kantan **ja nai** desu
Past	kantan deshita	kantan **ja nakatta** desu

You make the plain form of negative past adjectives the same way, but do not say *desu*.

Hoteru-wa *takaku-nakatta*.	The hotel wasn't expensive.
Sono machi-wa *shizuka ja nakatta*.	That town wasn't quiet.

しゅうまつに りょこうに いきました。	I went on a trip this weekend.
どこに いきましたか。	Where did you go?
フロリダに いきました。	I went to Florida.
りょこうの しゃしんが ありますか。	Do you have photos of your trip?
はい、たくさん あります。	Yes, I have a lot.
天気は どう でしたか。	How was the weather?
よかった です。	It was good.
しゃしんを とる・とります・とって	take a photograph
サーフィンを する・します・して	surf, go surfing
金よう日の 金	the *kin* in *kin-yoobi*

INTERACTIVE ACTIVITIES

PART 1

❶ Dialogue

With a クラスメート memorize the dialogue following the normal procedure. Make sure that you understand the meaning of the dialogue before you begin practicing. After you have learned the dialogue, perform for another pair.

A is looking at photos from B's recent trip and is asking questions.
A: Ryokoo-wa doo deshita-ka?
B: **Tanoshikatta** desu.
A: Hoteru-wa **takakatta** desu-ka?
B: Iie, **takaku-nakatta** desu. Totemo **yasukatta** desu.
A: Resutoran-mo **yasukatta** desu-ka?
B: Iie, **yasuku-nakatta** desu.
A: Machi-wa **omoshirokatta** desu-ka?
B: Iie, **omoshiroku-nakatta** desu.
A: Aa, saafin-o shimashita-ka?
B: Hai, shimashita-yo.
A: **Muzukashikatta** desu-ka?
B: Iie, zenzen **muzukashiku-nakatta** desu.

❷ Omoshirokatta desu-ka? Iie, omoshiroku-nakatta desu.

With a partner practice the past affirmative and negative forms of *i*-adjectives. Only Partner A looks at the adjectives given in the box on the next page and asks a simple question with one of the past affirmative adjectives. Partner B responds in the negative to every question. After every four questions, change roles. Look at the example.

A: **Chiisakatta** desu-ka? [past tense affirmative]   Was it small?
B: Iie, **chiisaku-nakatta** desu. [past tense negative]   No, it wasn't small.

I-ADJECTIVES		
Non-past Affirmative	samui desu	omoshiroi desu
Non-past Negative	samuku-nai desu	omoshiroku-nai desu
Past Affirmative	yasukatta desu	omoshirokatta desu
Past Negative	yasuku-nakatta desu	omoshiroku-nakatta desu

I-ADJECTIVES

1. furui	old	furukatta	furuku-nakatta
2. chiisai	small	chiisakatta	chiisaku-nakatta
3. osoi	slow, late	osokatta	osoku-nakatta
4. oishii	delicious	oishikatta	oishiku-nakatta
5. samui	cold	samukatta	samuku-nakatta
6. nemui	sleepy	nemukatta	nemuku-nakatta
7. nagai	long	nagakatta	nagaku-nakatta
8. tsuyoi	strong	tsuyokatta	tsuyoku-nakatta
9. takai	high, tall, expensive	takakatta	takaku-nakatta
10. ookii	big	ookikatta	ookiku-nakatta
11. hayai	fast, early	hayakatta	hayaku-nakatta
12. isogashii	busy	isogashikatta	isogashiku-nakatta
13. tanoshii	pleasant, fun	tanoshikatta	tanoshiku-nakatta
14. atsui	hot	atsukatta	atsuku-nakatta
15. chikai	close	chikakatta	chikaku-nakatta
16. kitanai	dirty, messy	kitanakatta	kitanaku-nakatta
17. urusai	noisy	urusakatta	urusaku-nakatta
18. ii (yoi)	good	yokatta	yoku-nakatta
19. tsumaranai	boring	tsumaranakatta	tsumaranaku-nakatta
20. omoshiroi	interesting	omoshirokatta	omoshiroku-nakatta
21. muzukashii	difficult	muzukashikatta	muzukashiku-nakatta

PART 2

❶ Hayakatta desu-ka? 📄 & ✏

Do this activity with a クラスメート. Partner A, without Partner B looking, selects one thing, place, or event from the list, write it down, and then chooses up to three past tense adjectives which describe it and again write them down. Partner A tells Partner B how many adjectives have been chosen. Partner B must then guess the adjectives first before guessing the selected item. After Partner B has successfully guessed both the adjectives and the item, change roles and repeat. Read the example aloud with your partner before you begin. In the example Partner A has selected two adjectives.

B: **Hayakatta** desu-ka?
A: Iie, **hayaku-nakatta** desu.
B: **Furukatta** desu-ka?
A: Hai, **furukatta** desu.
B: **Yasukatta** desu-ka?
A: Iie, **yasuku-nakatta** desu.
B: **Takakatta** desu-ka?
A: Hai, **takakatta** desu.
B: Resutoran-ga **takakatta** desu-ka?
A: Iie, **takaku-nakatta** desu.
B: Hoteru-ga **takakatta** desu-ka?
A: Hai, **takakatta** desu.

THINGS, PLACES, AND EVENTS		
hoteru	keeki	eiga
resutoran	shukudai	kaze
paatii	fuyu	ongaku
tokei	heya	machi
kuruma	yama	hikooki
tesuto	konpyuutaa	inu
ryoori	hon	kawa
natsu	ryokoo	jugyoo

Be sure to use the correct past tense forms of the adjectives.

ADJECTIVES			
muzukashii	tanoshii	atsui	nagai
oishii	samui	urusai	kitanai
hayai	chiisai	ookii	tsumaranai
takai	omoshiroi	furui	tsuyoi

❷ Finish my sentence!

Do this activity with a クラスメート. Place the tip of a pencil on the dot in the center of the circle below with one end of a paper clip around the pencil tip. Use this as a spinner to select a number on the wheel. Partner A then begins a sentence using the selected noun following the pattern below, but stops with -*wa*. Partner B must complete the sentence with an appropriate adjective in the past affirmative or past negative form. Continue taking turns.

PATTERN: NOUN-wa PAST ADJECTIVE (AFFIRMATIVE OR NEGATIVE) desu.

EXAMPLES: Hoteru-wa . . . kirei desu.
Kono hoteru-wa . . . yokatta desu.
Ano furui hoteru-wa . . . yasukatta desu.
Watashi-no daisuki-na hoteru-wa . . . takaku-nakatta desu.

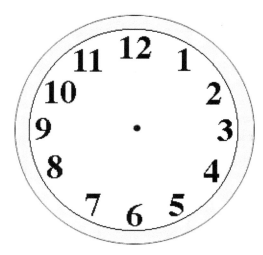

1. ホテル
2. コンピューター
3. ケーキ
4. シャツ
5. パーティー
6. バス
7. えいが
8. おんがく
9. 本
10. 山
11. 川
12. 大学

209

L. 23 電話で 話しましょう

れんしゅう A: Last Sunday's Schedule

One of the following is your schedule for last Sunday. Answer your teacher's questions.

(1)
8:00	got up and drank orange juice
10:00	went to a movie
3:00	went home and watched TV

(2)
10:45	watched the news
12:00	ate a sandwich and read a magazine
5:30	went to the department store and bought a shirt

(3)
7:30	got up and ate eggs
11:45	went to the supermarket and bought milk
6:00	played basketball

(4)
9:15	went to the library and studied
1:00	went to Kaori's house
10:30	watched TV and went to bed

(5)
11:30	went to the park and played tennis
2:00	ate lunch at a restaurant
8:00	read a book and drank coffee

(6)
8:30	got up and drank coffee
1:30	went to a friend's house and studied
5:00	watched a movie

れんしゅう B: How was ~? It was [*na*-adjective].

(1)
さとこ
skillful

(2)
山川
healthy

(3)
bad

(4)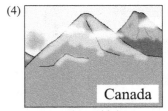
Canada
beautiful

(5)
quiet

(6)
やまだ
unskillful

れんしゅう C: Was it [*i*-adjective]? No, it wasn't [*i*-adjective].

(1) delicious?

(2) cold?

(3) Bob busy?

(4) new?

(5) expensive?

(6) good?

れんしゅう D: *Kanji* Puzzle

15 何	29 月	72 中	156 小
48 日	37 人	481 学	56 高
60 本	732 大	1008 校	19 木
2500 山	83 金	64 川	358 土

R. 16~23 電話で 話しましょう

れんしゅう A: Dream Trip Come True

しつもん:
(a) went where?
(b) weather?
(c) hot? cold?
(d) how was it?

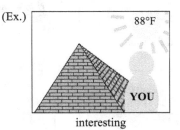

(Ex.) 88°F
YOU
interesting

(1)
90°F
YOU
good

(2)
32°F
YOU
fun

(3)
94°F
YOU
clean

れんしゅう B: Reading an Illustrative Passage

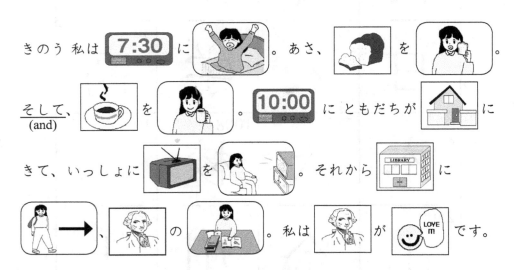

きのう 私は [7:30] に ____。 あさ、____ を ____。 そして、(and) ____ を ____。 [10:00] に ともだちが ____ に きて、いっしょに ____ を ____。 それから ____ に ____ → ____ の ____。 私は ____ が ____ です。

(1) さとし
hobby: _____

(2) キム
hobby: _____

(3) ジャック
hobby: _____

(4) モイーシャ
hobby: _____

(5) でんわの せんせい
hobby: _____

LESSON 24
Telephoning

OBJECTIVES   もくひょう

At the end of this lesson you will be able to:

- ☑ Ask for someone on the telephone
- ☑ Leave a message on an answering machine
- ☑ Read common Japanese family names written with the *kanji*:

川 山 中 本 高 田

VOCABULARY   たんご

Words

rusu	out, away, not in
goro	around, about + TIME

Phrases and expressions

ato-de	later
Person's name-wa irasshaimasu-ka?	Is *person's name* there? (used on the telephone)
Nan-ji-ni o-kaeri desu-ka?	What time will he/she return?

Other words and expressions you will hear in this lesson

rusuban denwa	answering machine
naga denwa	long telephone call

VOCABULARY NOTES   たんごノート

This lesson provides you with an opportunity to review what you have already learned about making telephone calls in Japanese and to learn how to leave a message for someone. By the end of this lesson you will be able to use a lot of useful telephone language including that given below.

TELEPHONE LANGUAGE

denwa	telephone, telephone call
naga denwa	a long telephone call
denwa-choo	telephone directory
denwa-bangoo	telephone number
denwa shimasu	make a telephone call, telephone
tomodachi-ni denwa shimasu	call a friend
moshi-moshi	hello
-no	*particle used to separate parts of a phone number* (525-7362 = go-ni-go-*no* nana-san-roku-ni)
rusu desu	am/is/are not at home
rusu deshita	was/were not at home
rusuban denwa	answering machine
A, sumimasen, machigaemashita.	Oh, I'm sorry. I've got the wrong number.
Mata machigaemashita.	I've made a mistake again.
Nakayama-san desu-ka?	Is this the Nakayama residence?
Tanaka desu kedo . . .	This is Tanaka . . .
Irasshai-no Timu Kukku desu kedo . . .	This is Tim Cook from *Irasshai* . . .

214

Eriko-san-wa irasshaimasu-ka?	Is Eriko in?
Chotto matte kudasai.	Just a moment, please.
Watashi-ni denwa-o shite kudasai.	Please call me.
Shitsurei shimasu.	Good-bye. (sorry to bother you)
Nan-ji-ni okaeri desu-ka?	What time will he/she be home?
Roku-ji-goro kaerimasu.	He/she will be back about 6:00.
Ja, mata ato-de denwa shimasu.	Well, I'll call again later.
Honda-san-no denwa-bangoo-o oshiete kudasai.	Please tell me Ms. Honda's phone number.

RUSUBAN DENWA-NO MESSEEJI

Suzuki desu. Ima, rusu-ni shite-orimasu*.	This is Suzuki. I'm not at home now.
O-namae-to messeeji-o o-negai-shimasu.	Please (leave) your name and message.

Shite-orimasu is a humble equivalent of *shite-imasu*.

KEY GRAMMAR POINTS   ぶんぽうポイント

1. Irasshaimasu

The verb *irasshaimasu*, which is the honorific form of *iru/imasu*, is used when asking if a person is present.

Ueda-san-wa *irasshaimasu*-ka?	Is Mrs. Ueda there?
Sumisu-san-wa *irasshaimasu*-ka?	Is Mr. Smith in?

2. -goro

The suffix *-goro*, which means *around* or *about*, is used with a specific point in time such as clock times.

Watashi-wa asa roku-ji-*goro* okimasu.	I get up *around* 6:00 in the morning.
Yo-ji-*goro* kimasu.	He is coming at *about* 4:00.
Itsu-*goro* ikimasu-ka?	*About* when are you going?
Nan-ji-*goro* kaerimasu-ka?	*Around* what time are you going home?

YOMIMASHOO!   よみましょう

るす	out, away, not in
ごろ	around, about + TIME
あとで	later
中山さんは いらっしゃいますか。	Is Mr. Nakayama there?
何じに おかえり ですか。	What time will he/she return?
るすばん でんわ	answering machine
なが でんわ	long telephone call

CULTURE NOTES   カルチャーノート

Important Japanese telephone numbers

In Japan there are some special telephone numbers for summoning help in emergencies and for accessing information on time and weather. For life and death matters there are 110 (pronounced *hyaku-too-ban*) for police and 119 (*hyaku-juu-kyuu-ban*) for fire or ambulance. The number 117 (*ichi-ichi-nana-ban*) can be dialed for time and 177 (*ichi-nana-nana-ban*) for weather. The suffix *-ban* means *number*. This same word element occurs in *denwa-bangoo*.

In this lesson you will learn to read some common Japanese family names which are written with the *kanji* 川, 中, 本, 高 and 田. The *kanji* 田 was first introduced for recognition in Lesson 6. Be sure that you know the reading *ta* [*da*] for 田 and can tell what the *kanji* means. The reading which is marked by an asterisk is for your reference only; you do not need to learn it at this time. You also do not have to learn any new words which are given in the examples. The correct stroke order for this *kanji* is given in the Optional Writing Practice section.

| 田 | **DEN*; ta [da]** (rice field, paddy) |

田中	*Ta*naka	Tanaka
川田	Kawa*da*, Kawa*ta*	Kawada, Kawata
中田	Naka*ta*, Naka*da*	Nakata, Nakada
田植え	*ta*ue	rice planting

田中さんは何月何日に
きますか。
中田さんと川田さんが
いますか。

*Ta*naka-san-wa nan-gatsu nan-nichi-ni kimasu-ka?
(What month and day is Mr. Tanaka coming?)
Naka*ta*-san-to Kawa*da*-san-ga imasu-ka?
(Are Mrs. Nakata and Mrs. Kawada there?)

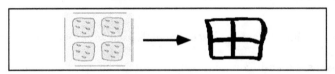

***KANJI* REVIEW**
月　日　木　本　人　山　川　大　小　学　校　中
高　何　今　私　火　水　金　土　天　元　気　田
How do you read them? What do they mean?

Japanese family names

In both English and Japanese, many common family names trace their origin to words for various features of the landscape. In English one finds names such as Woods, Fields, Brooks, Meadows, Rivers, Bridges, and Ford along with their many variants. Such names developed from descriptions of where individuals and their families lived. "John by the woods" or "John in the woods" became John Woods. Many Japanese names were derived in a similar manner. You can already read many of these which include the *kanji* 川, 山, 中, 本, 高 and 田.

JAPANESE FAMILY NAMES			
川田	Kawada, Kawata	本田	Honda
山川	Yamakawa	山本	Yamamoto*
山田	Yamada	中山	Nakayama
田中	Tanaka	山中	Yamanaka
中田	Nakata, Nakada	中川	Nakagawa
高田	Takada	高山	Takayama
*When the *kanji* 本 appears in a name, it is usually pronounced *moto*.			

INTERACTIVE ACTIVITIES

PART 1

❶ Telephone vocabulary review

Silently review the following vocabulary which are associated with telephoning. Then have a クラスメート orally test your knowledge of them. Your partner says the えいご, and you give the 日本ご. Switch and test your partner.

denwa	telephone, telephone call
denwa-bangoo	telephone number
denwa shimasu	make a telephone call, telephone
tomodachi-ni denwa shimasu	call a friend
Watashi-ni denwa-o shite kudasai.	Please call me.
moshi-moshi	hello
rusu desu	am/is/are not at home
A, sumimasen, machigaemashita.	Oh, I'm sorry. I've got the wrong number.
Nakayama-san desu-ka?	Is this the Nakayama residence?
Tanaka desu kedo . . .	This is Tanaka . . .
Irasshai-no Timu Kukku desu kedo . . .	This is Tim Cook from *Irasshai* . . .
Eriko-san-wa irasshaimasu-ka?	Is Eriko in?
Chotto matte kudasai.	Just a moment, please.
Shitsurei shimasu.	Good-bye. (sorry to bother you)
Nan-ji-ni okaeri desu-ka?	What time will he/she be home?
Roku-ji-goro kaerimasu.	He/she will be back about 6:00.
Ja, mata ato-de denwa shimasu.	Well, I'll call again later.

❷ Yomimashoo!

Practice reading the following with a クラスメート. Partner A looks only at the left column. Partner B looks only at the right column. If Partner A makes a mistake, Partner B says, "*Chotto chigaimasu. Moo ichido yonde kudasai.*" After Partner A has finished reading, change roles and repeat.

PARTNER A	PARTNER B
1. 中川さんの でんわばんごう です。	1. Nakagawa-san-no denwa-bangoo desu.
2. 高山 ですけど。	2. Takayama desu kedo . . .
3. 山中さん ですか。	3. Yamanaka-san desu-ka?
4. 川田さんは いらっしゃいますか。	4. Kawada-san-wa irasshaimasu-ka?
5. 田中さんは 何じに おかえり ですか。	5. Tanaka-san-wa nan-ji-ni o-kaeri desu-ka?

PART 2

❶ Dialogue

With a クラスメート memorize the dialogue following the normal procedure. Make sure that you understand the meaning of the dialogue before you begin practicing. After you have learned the dialogue, perform for some other pairs.

Kenji telephones the Tanaka residence and wants to speak with Eriko who happens to be out. Kenji and Eriko are both students at *Tookyoo-Daigaku*.

Kenji: (makes the phone call)
Tanaka: Moshi-moshi?
Kenji: Aa, Tanaka-san desu-ka?
Tanaka: Hai, soo desu.

Kenji: Aa, Tookyoo-Daigaku-no Nakayama desu kedo . . . Eriko-san-wa irasshaimasu-ka?

Tanaka: Ima rusu desu kedo . . .

Kenji: Aa, soo desu-ka? Nan-ji-ni o-kaeri desu-ka?

Tanaka: Roku-ji-goro kaerimasu.

Kenji: Aa, soo desu-ka? Ja, mata ato-de denwa shimasu.

Tanaka: Hai, wakarimashita.

Kenji: Shitsurei shimasu.

❷ Rusuban denwa-no messeeji   📄 & ✏️

You are calling Japanese friends to invite them to join you for some activity tomorrow. With a クラスメート decide on and write the message which you will leave on the るすばん でんわ of those ともだち who are not home. Include enough information that your friends will want to join you and will respond to your request to call you back. Share your messages with other pairs.

L. 24 電話で 話しましょう

れんしゅう A: Student Life Survey

The interviewer wants to know about student life. Answer his/her questions.

れんしゅう B: Telephone Conversations

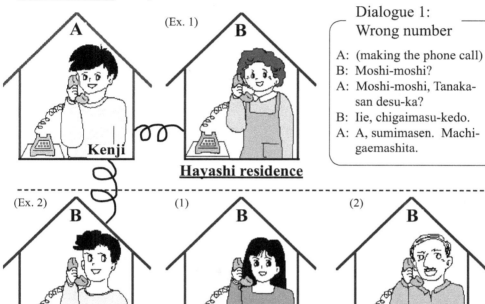

(Ex. 1)

A Kenji

B Hayashi residence

Dialogue 1: Wrong number

A: (making the phone call)
B: Moshi-moshi?
A: Moshi-moshi, Tanaka-san desu-ka?
B: Iie, chigaimasu-kedo.
A: A, sumimasen. Machi-gaemashita.

(Ex. 2) **B** Tanaka residence
Ask for: Kyooko
(will return at 6:00)

(1) **B** Mori residence
Ask for: Takashi
(will return at 3:30)

(2) **B** Smith residence
Ask for: Greg
(will return at 8:30)

Dialogue 2: The person is not home.

A: (making the phone call)
B: Moshi-moshi?
A: Moshi-moshi, <u>Tanaka-san</u> desu-ka?
B: Hai, soo desu.
A: <u>ABC-kookoo</u>-no <u>Kenji</u> desu-kedo, <u>Kyooko-san</u>-wa irasshaimasu-ka?
B: Ima rusu desu-kedo....
A: Aa, soo desu-ka. Nan-ji-ni o-kaeri desu-ka?
B: <u>Roku-ji</u>-goro kaerimasu.
A: Soo desu-ka. Jaa, mata ato-de denwa shimasu.
B: Hai, wakarimashita.
A: Shitsurei shimasu.

<u>れんしゅう C</u>: Weather Forecast

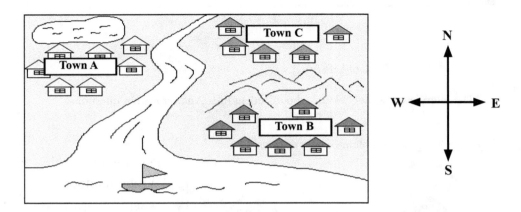

あしたの天気

まち	天気	きおん	かぜ
A	○	63°F	(3) strong
B	(1) ☁	78°F	strong
C	(2) 🌧	55°F	light

<u>れんしゅう D</u>: Japanese Family Names

(1) 山川   (2) 田中   (3) 高山

(4) 本田   (5) 中川

LESSON 25
Expressing Wants

OBJECTIVES　　　　　　　　　　　　　　　　もくひょう

At the end of this lesson you will be able to:
- ☑ Talk about what you did this year
- ☑ Talk about what you want to do next year

In this lesson you will also have an opportunity to review reading all of the *kanji* which have been introduced so far.

VOCABULARY　　　　　　　　　　　　　　　　たんご

Words

sengetsu	last month*
kongetsu	this month*
raigetsu	next month*
kyonen	last year*
kotoshi	this year*
rainen	next year*

Other words and expressions you will hear in this lesson

kyanpu-o suru (shimasu/shite)	go camping

*These time words **do not** take the particle *-ni*.

KEY GRAMMAR POINTS　　　　　　　　　ぶんぽうポイント

1. -tai

To express the idea of *want to do something*, replace the *-masu* ending of a verb with *-tai desu*. Generally, you can only use this form to talk about what you yourself want to do and to ask others what they want to do. It is best to avoid statements about what others (he, she, they) want to do since from the Japanese point of view this is a bit presumptuous to think that you would know what someone else wants.

Nani-o *shitai desu*-ka?	What do you *want to do*?
Umi-ni *ikitai desu*.	I *want to go* to the beach.

The informal (plain) form does not use *desu*.

Yama-ni *ikitai*?	Do you *want to go* to the mountains?
Yasai-o takusan *tabetai*.	I *want to eat* lots of vegetables.

The *-tai* form is actually an adjectival form so you can form the negative, the past affirmative, and the past negative the same way that you do for *i*-adjectives.

	-TAI	
Ikimasu --->	Iki-**tai desu.**	I **want to** go.
	Iki-**taku nai desu.**	I **do not want to** go.
	Iki-**takatta desu.**	I **wanted to** go.
	ki-**taku-nakatta desu.**	I **did not want to** go.

Both the particle *-o* and the particle *-ga* can occur with the *-tai* form. There is little difference in meaning.

Eiga-*o* mitai desu.	I want to see a movie.
Eiga-*ga* mitai desu.	I want to see a movie.

221

2. Kon/sen/rai-getsu-no + day of the month

To express a specific date in this month, last month, or next month, use the appropriate word *kongetsu, sengetsu,* or *raigetsu* followed by the particle *-no* and then the day of the month.

kongetsu-no 30-nichi(-ni)	(on) the 30th *of this month*
sengetsu-no 12-nichi(-ni)	(on) the 12th *of last month*
raigetsu-no tsuitachi(-ni)	(on) the first *of next month*

3. Kotoshi/kyonen/rainen-no + a period of time

To identify a period of time (such as *April, summer*, or *vacation*) as being in this year, last year, or next year, use the appropriate word *kotoshi, kyonen,* or *rainen* followed by the particle *-no* and then the period of time.

kotoshi-no shi-gatsu	*this* April
kyonen-no natsu	*last* summer
rainen-no fuyu-yasumi	*next year's* winter vacation

These constructions can, in turn, be used to modify other words.

kyonen-no natsu-no ryokoo	*last* summer's trip

YOMIMASHOO! よみましょう

せん月 (せんげつ)	last month
今月 (こんげつ)	this month
らい月 (らいげつ)	next month
きょねん	last year
ことし	this year
らいねん	next year
今月の３０日に	on the 30th of this month
らいしゅうの 月よう日に	next Monday
せん月の１２日に	on the 12th of last month
きょねんの なつの りょこう	last summer's trip
ことしの４月	this April
らいねんの りょこう	next year's trip
何を したい ですか。	What do you want to do?
うみに いきたい です。	I want to go to the beach.
キャンプを する・します・して	go camping

	LAST	THIS	NEXT
WEEK	せんしゅう	こんしゅう	らいしゅう
MONTH	せんげつ	こんげつ	らいげつ
YEAR	きょねん	ことし	らいねん

INTERACTIVE ACTIVITIES

PART 1

❶ Rusuban denwa-no messeeji ✎

During this activity each student will work as a pair with two different クラスメート to check Assignment #1 from Part 2 of Lesson 24. The goal of the activity is to have two students carefully check the sentences in your telephone message, mark and discuss with you any errors found, and sign off on your page. Form your first pair and exchange assignments with your partner. Both partners independently check and neatly mark errors for the entire assignment. Use the same editing symbols as usual.

❷ **Vocabulary check**

Silently review the vocabulary for Lesson 25 and all the action verbs you have learned so far. Then have a クラスメート orally test your knowledge of them. Your partner says the えいご, and you give the 日本ご. Switch and test your partner.

PART 2

❶ **San-ban-wa raigetsu-no tooka desu.**　📄 & ✏️

Do this activity with a partner. Look only at your own grid. Partner A thinks of a date in this month, last month, or next month and writes it in one of the cells in the grid. The cells can be used in any order. Partner A then tells Partner B what to write and where to write it. Change roles after every date. When you finish, compare your work and check it for accuracy.

If the actual current month is December, for example, and your partner says "*San-ban-wa raigetsu-no tooka desu,*" you will write 1月10日 in the third cell.

OBOETE-IMASU-KA?					
ichi-ban	roku-ban	ichi-gatsu	shichi-gatsu	tsuitachi	nanoka
ni-ban	nana-ban	ni-gatsu	hachi-gatsu	futsuka	yooka
san-ban	hachi-ban	san-gatsu	ku-gatsu	mikka	kokonoka
yon-ban	kyuu-ban	shi-gatsu	juu-gatsu	yokka	tooka
go-ban		go-gatsu	juu-ichi-gatsu	itsuka	juu-ichi-nichi
		roku-gatsu	juu-ni-gatsu	muika	hatsuka (20th)

1	2	3
4	5	6
7	8	9

❷ **Yasumi-ni nani-o shitai desu-ka?**　📄 & ✏️

Do this interview activity as an entire class. Form pairs and ask each other the question *Yasumi-ni nani-o shitai desu-ka?* Write down your partner's name and answer. Then quickly form another pair and repeat. Try to interview as many クラスメート as possible. Use your imagination when answering. Try to give a different answer to each person who interviews you.

Example:　Yasumi-ni nani-o shitai desu-ka?
　　　　　Yama-ni itte pikunikku-o shitai desu.

223

L. 25 電話 で 話しましょう

れんしゅう A: Where did/will Mary go last/this/next year?

Last year	This year	Next year
(1) Welcome to Hawaii! friend / 4 月	(3) / 5 月	(5) Irasshai University / 9 月
(2) winter break	(4) summer break	

れんしゅう B: Toshio's Schedule

Group A can only look at Schedule A, and Group B can only look at Schedule B. Ask the other group questions and fill in the lettered blanks.

Schedule A

	Last month		This month			Next month
(Ex.1) 25	went to a rock concert	(b) 1	?		8	
(Ex.2) 26	played baseball	2			(c) 9	?
(a) 27	?	3	TODAY		10	go to the lake
28	wrote a letter to pen pal	4	go to a relative's house		11	

224

Schedule B

	Last month		This month			Next month
(Ex.1) 25	went to a rock concert	1	saw a movie		8	
(Ex.2) 26	played baseball	2			9	see a German friend
27	bought a new watch	3	TODAY		(f) 10	?
(d) 28	?	(e) 4	?		11	

れんしゅう C: What do you want to do next year?

(1)

(2)

(3)

(4)

(5)

(6)

　　　　　　　　　　　　　もくひょう

At the end of this lesson you will be able to:

☑ Talk about adult and child admission prices

☑ Express what you do not want to do

In this lesson you will also have an opportunity to review writing all of the *kanji* which have been introduced so far.

VOCABULARY　　　　　　　　　　　　　　　たんご

Words

doobutsu	animal
doobutsuen	zoo
otona	adult
kodomo	child

Phrases and expressions

Onaka-ga sukimashita/suita.	I am hungry.
Otona/kodomo-wa ikura desu-ka?	How much is it for adults/children?

Other words and expressions you will hear in this lesson

shinseki-no ko	a relative's child

VOCABULARY NOTES　　　　　　　　　　　たんごノート

In this lesson you will hear the names of a number of common zoo animals. These as well as others are given in the box below for your reference.

		DOOBUTSUEN-NO DOOBUTSU			
raion	ライオン	lion	panda	パンダ	panda
tora	とら	tiger	kuma	くま	bear
hyoo	ひょう	leopard	kangaruu	カンガルー	kangaroo
gorira	ゴリラ	gorilla	kirin	きりん	giraffe
saru	さる	monkey	kaba	かば	hippopotamus
koara	コアラ	koala	zoo	ぞう	elephant
rama	ラマ	llama	shimauma	しまうま	zebra
rakuda	らくだ	camel	sai	さい	rhinoceros
azarashi	あざらし	seal	kame	かめ	turtle

KEY GRAMMAR POINTS　　　　　　　　　ぶんぽうポイント

1. -takunai desu

As you learned in Lesson 25, you can express the idea of *want to do something* by replacing the verb ending *-masu* with *-tai desu*. The *-tai* form is actually an *i*-adjective. To form the negative, drop the final *i* and add *-kunai* just as you do for other *i*-adjectives. Look at these examples.

Kono hon-wa omoshiro*i* desu.	This book is interesting.
Yomita*i* desu.	I want to read it.
Sono hon-wa omoshiro*kunai* desu.	That book is not interesting.
Yomita*kunai* desu.	I do not want to read it.

2. -tai desu

This form in Japanese, which is usually expressed in English as *want to*, often includes an element of hope. *Nihon-ni ikitai desu* means *I want to go to Japan* and is the speaker's desire and hope. The *-tai* form is not used for making invitations although in English one might say *want* as in *Do you want some coffee?* For invitations use the form you have already learned.

Koohii-o nomimasen-ka?
Won't you drink some coffee?
Would you like some coffee?
Do you want some coffee?

YOMIMASHOO!	よみましょう

どうぶつ	animal
どうぶつえん	zoo
おとな	adult
こども	child
おなかが すきました・すいた。	I am hungry.
パンダは どこの くにの どうぶつ ですか。	What country is the panda from?
ライオンと コアラは どうぶつえんに います。	Lions and koalas are in the zoo.
いぬは どうぶつえんに いません。	Dogs are not in zoos.
どうぶつは 何が いちばん すき ですか。	What animal do you like best?
大人は 一人 1,000えん です。	Adults are 1,000 yen each.
こどもは いくら ですか。	How much is it for children?
したい ですか。したくない ですか。	Do you want to do it or not?
しんせきのこ	a relative's child

CULTURE NOTES	カルチャーノート

Admission prices for adults and children

In Japan, as in many countries, there is often a difference in entrance fees and public transportation fares for adults and children. Most signs and tickets use the *kanji* 大人 (literally, big person) for adults and 小人 (literally, small person) for children. When buying adults' and children's tickets, a person usually says the words *otona* and *kodomo*. Even though you may not have been able to read 大人 and 小人 with the correct pronunciation when you first saw them, you were no doubt able to understand what they mean. You can easily see the value of knowing even a few basic *kanji*.

SAMPLE ADULT AND CHILD ADMISSION PRICES	
大人	¥3,000
小人	¥1,500

INTERACTIVE ACTIVITIES

PART 1

❶ **Yomimashoo!**

Form 三人のグループ. Compare your work for Assignment #1 in Part 2 of Lesson 25. If you have written your answers in *roomaji* only, at this time write them in *hiragana* also.

❷ **Nomitai desu-ka?**

Do this activity with a partner. Place the tip of a pencil on the dot in the center of the circle on the next page with one end of a paper clip around the pencil tip. Use this as a spinner to select a number on the wheel. Partner A spins first and makes a question using the *-tai* form of the selected verb. Partner B always responds with the negative and then

227

the affirmative form of the same verb. Your answers do not have to be true. Look at the example before you begin.

    B: A-san-no ban desu. [ban = turn]
    A: Hai. (*spins a 3*) B-san-wa, puruun* juusu-o **nomitai** desu-ka?   *prune
    B: Iie, **nomitakunai** desu. Orenji juusu-ga **nomitai** desu.
    A: B-san-no ban desu.

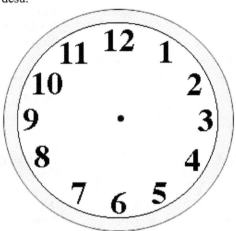

1. ikimasu	4. yomimasu	7. shimasu	10. kikimasu
2. mimasu	5. tabemasu	8. kakimasu	11. tsukaimasu
3. nomimasu	6. kaimasu	9. kaerimasu	12. aimasu

PART 2

---

❶ Otona-wa ikura desu-ka?   📄 & ✏

Do this activity with a partner. Look only at your own chart. Take turns asking and answering questions to determine the adult and child admission prices at the various places listed in the left-hand column. Look at the sample question and answer before you begin. After you have completed the charts, compare your answers.

    A: Wandaa-paaku-wa otona-wa ikura desu-ka?
    B: Otona-wa ¥3,000-en desu.

THOUSANDS / HUNDREDS					
sen	yon-sen	nana-sen	hyaku	yon-hyaku	nana-hyaku
ni-sen	go-sen	has-sen	ni-hyaku	go-hyaku	hap-pyaku
san-zen	roku-sen	kyuu-sen	san-byaku	rop-pyaku	kyuu-hyaku

PARTNER A

どこ	おとな	こども
Wandaarando	¥6,000	
Suupaa-paaku		¥5,000
doobutsuen	¥1,000	
puuru		¥1,200
Supootsu-rama	¥8,000	
Suupaa-mini-gorufu	¥5,500	
Tekisasu-baabekyuu		¥2,300

PARTNER B

どこ	おとな	こども
Wandaarando		¥3,000
Suupaa-paaku	¥7,000	
doobutsuen		¥600
puuru	¥2,800	
Supootsu-rama		¥4,500
Suupaa-mini-gorufu		¥3,000
Tekisasu-baabekyuu	¥4,000	

❷ Vocabulary check

Silently review the vocabulary for Lesson 26. Then have a クラスメート orally test your knowledge of them. Your partner says the えいご, and you give the 日本ご. Switch and test your partner.

L. 26 電話で 話しましょう

<u>れんしゅう A</u>: Travel Agency Assistance

You are working at a travel agency. Suggest one of the cities in the chart to your telephone teacher. Then answer his/her questions.

まち	ばしょ	天気	かぜ	きおん
San Diego	south of Los Angeles	☀	strong	75°F
Boston	north of New York	🌧	light	62°F
Detroit	east of Chicago	☁	strong	64°F
Houston	west of New Orleans	☁	light	80°F
Miami	south of Orlando	☀	strong	83°F
Seattle	north of Portland	🌧	light	71°F

<u>れんしゅう B</u>: Do you want to ~? No, I don't.

(Ex)

(1)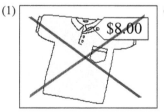

(2)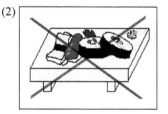

(3)

(4)

(5)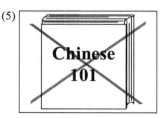

れんしゅう C: Take me out to the zoo/ball game

(1)
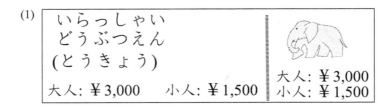

いらっしゃい
どうぶつえん
(とうきょう)

大人: ¥3,000   小人: ¥1,500

大人: ¥3,000
小人: ¥1,500

(2)
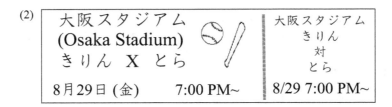

大阪スタジアム
(Osaka Stadium)
きりん X とら

8月29日 (金)   7:00 PM~

大阪スタジアム
きりん
対
とら

8/29 7:00 PM~

れんしゅう D: Irasshai Zoo

LESSON 27
Sporting Events

OBJECTIVES
もくひょう

At the end of this lesson you will be able to:
- ☑ Ask and state who won and lost a sporting event
- ☑ Ask and state the score of a sporting event
- ☑ Read the *kanji*: 見 and 行

VOCABULARY
たんご

Words
shiai	sporting match, game
renshuu	practice (noun)
katsu (kachimasu/katte)	win
makeru (makemasu/makete)	lose
yowai	weak
sukoa	score
# tai #	# to # (a score)

Phrases and expressions
renshuu(-o) suru (shimasu/shite)	practice (verb)
____-no renshuu-o suru (shimasu/shite)	practice ____
Doko/dare-ga kachimashita-ka?	Who won?
Sukoa-wa doo deshita-ka?	What was the score?

Other words and expressions you will hear in this lesson
zannen	too bad
takkyuu	ping pong/table tennis

VOCABULARY NOTES
たんごノート

1. Shiai
The word *shiai* (a competitive sporting event) may be expressed in English in various ways.

sakkaa-no *shiai*	soccer *game*
booringu-no *shiai*	bowling *tournament*
tenisu-no *shiai*	tennis *match*, tennis *game*

2. Renshuu
Japanese has borrowed an enormous number of words from Chinese. As in the case of many other nouns of Chinese origin, the Japanese noun *renshuu* (*practice*) can be used with forms of *suru* (*do, make*) to function as a verb. These combinations are usually expressed in English as verbs.

Renshuu-wa owari desu.	*Practice* is over. [noun]
Renshuu(-o) shimashoo!	Let's *practice*! [verb]
Mainichi takkyuu-no *renshuu*-o shimasu.	Every day I *practice* ping pong. [verb]

3. Zannen
Zannen, which is commonly translated as *too bad*, is a common way to express disappointment.

231

しあい	sporting match, game
サッカーの しあい	soccer game
テニスの しあい	tennis match
れんしゅう	practice (noun)
れんしゅう する・します・して	practice (verb)
すいえいの れんしゅうを する	practice swimming
今 やきゅうの れんしゅうを しています。	They're practicing baseball now.
いつ じゅうどうの れんしゅうを しますか。	When do you practice judo?
かつ・かちます・かって	win
どこ (だれ) が かちましたか。	Who won?
まける・まけます・まけて	lose
よわい	weak
スコア	score
スコアは どう でしたか。	What was the score?
# たい #	# to # (a score)
9 たい 0 でした。	It was 9 to 0.
ざんねん	too bad
たっきゅう	ping pong

KANJI NOTES　　　　　　　　　　　　　かんじノート

In this lesson you will learn to read two *kanji*: 見 and 行. Be sure that you know the readings of each *kanji* and can tell what the *kanji* means. Readings which are marked by an asterisk are for your reference only; you do not need to learn these at this time. You also do not have to learn any new words which are given in the examples. In Lesson 28 you will learn how to write these *kanji* using the correct stroke order.

見　　**KEN*; mi(ru)** (see, look at, watch)

見る	*mi*ru	see, look at, watch
見ます	*mi*masu	see, look at, watch
見せる	*mi*seru	show
月見	tsuki*mi*	moon-viewing
見本	*mi*hon	sample, viewing copy
見物	*ken*butsu	sightseeing
見学	*ken*gaku	study by observation

私はテレビを見ました。　Watashi-wa terebi-o *mi*mashita.
　　　　　　　　　　　(I watched television.)

何を見ていますか。　　Nani-o *mi*te-imasu-ka?
　　　　　　　　　　　(What are you looking at?)

この本を見て下さい。　Kono hon-o *mi*te kudasai.
　　　　　　　　　　　(Please look at this book.)

日本のお金を見せて　　Nihon-no o-kane-o *mi*sete kudasai.
　下さい。　　　　　　(Please show me the Japanese money.)

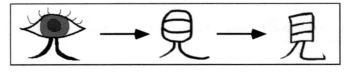

232

行	**KOO*, GYOO*; i(ku)** (go), **yu(ki)*** (bound for)	

行く	*i*ku	go
行きます	*i*kimasu	go
急行	kyuu*koo*	express (train)
東京行きの電車	Tookyoo-*yuki*-no densha	a train bound for Tokyo

学校に行きますか。 　　Gakkoo-ni *i*kimasu-ka?
　　　　　　　　　　　　(Are you going to the school?)

田中さんは急行で東京に 　Tanaka-san-kyuu*koo*-de Tookyoo-ni *i*kimashita.
行きました。 　　　　　　(Mr. Tanaka went to Tokyo by express train.)

The *kanji* 行 was derived from a picture of crossroads.

NOTE

Notice that the *kanji* introduced in this lesson (見 and 行) must both be
accompanied by *hiragana* in order to write forms such as **miru, mimasu,
mimashita, mite, iku, ikimasu, ikimashita,** and **ikimasen.** The *ku/ki* of the verb
iku/ikimasu is written in *hiragana* – not just the verb endings. What do you
call *hiragana* which are used in this way? See Lesson 9 for the answer.

KANJI REVIEW

今	私	火	月	行	天	日	木	本	金	元	土	気
田	見	小	学	高	何	水	川	大	校	中	人	山

How do you read them? What do they mean?

INTERACTIVE ACTIVITIES

PART 1

❶ **Kakimashoo!** ✎
Form 三人のグループ. Check your answers for Assignment #3 in Part 2 of Lesson 26.

❷ **Kyuu-juu-san tai hachi-juu-roku deshita.** 📄 & ✎
Do this activity with a クラスメート. Without showing each other, Partner A and
Partner B each write down five different final バスケットボールのスコア. All of the
scores are between 30 and 100. Take turns asking and answering the following question
to determine what the scores are. Compare your answers when you have finished. Read
the example aloud with your partner before you begin. Refer to SUKOA-WA DOO
DESHITA-KA? on the next page for scores in Japanese.

A: Sukoa-wa doo deshita-ka? 　　　　　　What was the score?
B: Kyuu-juu-san *tai* hachi-juu-roku deshita. 　It was 93 to 86.

A: Sukoa-wa doo deshita-ka? 　　　　　　What was the score?
B: Roku-juu-nana *tai* go-juu-yon deshita. 　It was 67 to 54.

233

SUKOA-WA DOO DESHITA-KA?

For 4, 7, and 9, use *yon*, *nana*, and *kyuu*. Notice the special forms
for some of the numbers when preceding *tai*.

0-2	zero *tai* ni	7-1	nana *tai* ichi
1-0	ichi *tai* zero OR **it**-*tai* zero	8-5	hachi *tai* go OR **hat**-*tai* go
2-4	ni *tai* yon	9-0	kyuu *tai* zero
3-7	san *tai* nana	10-6	**jut**-*tai* roku
4-1	yon *tai* ichi	21-10	ni-juu-ichi *tai* (OR **it**-*tai*) juu
5-3	go *tai* san	58-21	go-juu-hachi *tai* (OR **hat**-*tai*) ni-juu-ichi
6-9	roku *tai* kyuu	70-88	nana-**jut**-*tai* hachi-juu-hachi

PART 2

❶ Yomimashoo! 📄 & 🖊

This pair activity provides you with an opportunity to review the *kanji* which you have
learned to read. Partner A masks the *roomaji* side and reads the vocabulary in the left
column in order. Partner B responds after each with either *Hai, soo desu* or *Iie,
chigaimasu. Moo ichido yonde kudasai.* Partner A writes down those which need to be
studied. Switch roles and repeat.

かなと かんじ	ローマじ
1. 何の本	1. nan-no hon
2. 火よう日	2. ka-yoobi
3. お金	3. o-kane
4. 今	4. ima
5. 天気	5. tenki
6. 水	6. mizu
7. 私	7. watashi
8. 何月何日	8. nan-gatsu nan-nichi
9. 水よう日	9. sui-yoobi
10. 今日	10. kyoo
11. 何よう日	11. nan-yoobi
12. 今日は	12. konnichi-wa
13. 元気	13. genki
14. 小さい小学校	14. chiisai shoogakkoo
15. 見ます	15. mimasu
16. 今月	16. kongetsu
17. 金よう日	17. kin-yoobi
18. 何人	18. nan-nin
19. 行きました	19. ikimashita
20. 土よう日	20. do-yoobi

❷ Raionzu-ga kachimashita-ka? Makemashita-ka? 📄 & 🖊

Do this activity with a クラスメート. Before beginning, Partner A and B fill in the
missing information for the baseball teams each is familiar with (shown as A or B in the
chart). Decide whether the team in the left-hand column won (*kachimashita*) or lost
(*makemashita*), and write the appropriate word in the correct column. Also write the final
score using only single digits from zero to nine.

Chiimu-no namae	A/B	Kachimashita / Makemashita	Sukoa
Raionzu	A		tai
Gorirazu	B		tai
Pandazu	A		tai
Kangaruuzu	B		tai

Chiimu-no namae	A/B	Kachimashita / Makemashita	Sukoa
Tora (Tigers)	A		tai
Saru (Monkeys)	B		tai
Ramazu (Llamas)	A		tai
Zoo (Elephants)	B		tai
Kirin (Giraffes)	A		tai

Using the following dialogue, take turns getting the missing information you need to complete the chart.

B: Kinoo-no yakyuu-no shiai-wa Raionzu-ga kachimashita-ka? Makemashita-ka?
A: Kachimashita. [A says *kachimashita* because that is what A had already recorded on the chart.]
B: Sukoa-wa doo deshita-ka?
A: Kyuu tai zero deshita. [A says the score recorded on the chart.]

After you have finished, check your accuracy by comparing charts.

NOTE

Refer to the *Sukoa-wa doo deshita-ka?* box in Part 1 of the Interactive Activities if you are unsure of the correct form of the numbers to use with *tai*.

Animal Proverbs

The Japanese language is rich in proverbs and famous ancient sayings. The Japanese tend also to have an affinity to animals, and as such, it is not surprising to see proverbs related to animals. Here are a few of the more famous ones: *Neko ni koban* (猫に小判) – a gold coin to a cat, suggesting that you should not waste your time, energy or resources on someone who is incapable of appreciating them. *Isseki ni-choo* (一石二鳥) – [to kill] two birds with one stone. There is also the popular *Saru mo ki kara ochiru* (猿も木から落ちる) – even monkeys fall from trees, implying that nobody's perfect, everyone makes mistakes.

L. 27 電話で 話しましょう

れんしゅう A: Scoreboards

しつもん:
(a) What kind of game is it?
(b) Who won?
(c) What was the score?

(Ex)
Snakes   Cats

5   ⚽   **0**

(1)
Cheetahs   Tigers

3   ⚾   **2**

(2)
Crows   Bees

100 🏀 **16**

(3)
Eagles   Jaguars

15 🏐 **9**

(4)
Bluebirds   Redbirds

21 🏉 **0**

れんしゅう B: Finding Out about Club Activities

(1)
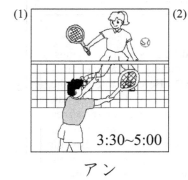
3:30~5:00

アン

(2)

4:00~6:30

キース

(3)

3:00~7:30

しんじ

	A	B	Calling for	Wrong #	Out	Return Time
(Ex.)	Caller	Yokoyama	Yooko Suzuki	✓	——	——
(1)	Caller	Yamakawa	Satoshi Yamakawa	——	✓	About 3:00
(2)	Caller	Tanaka	Akiko Tanaka	——	✓	About 4:30
(3)	Caller	Takayama	Tetsuya Takayama	——	✓	About 9:00

Sample
Dialogue 1: Wrong number

A: (making the phone call)

B: Moshi-moshi?

A: Moshi-moshi, Suzuki-san desu-ka?

B: Iie, chigaimasu-kedo.

A: A, sumimasen. Machigaemashita.

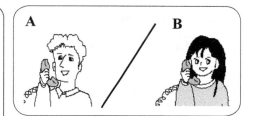

Sample
Dialogue 2: The person is not home.

A: (making the phone call)

B: Moshi-moshi?

A: Moshi-moshi, Yamakawa-san desu-ka?

B: Hai, soo desu.

A: ABC-kookoo-no Kenji desu-kedo, Satoshi-kun-wa irasshaimasu-ka?

B: Ima rusu desu-kedo....

A: Aa, soo desu-ka. Nan-ji-ni o-kaeri desu-ka?

B: San-ji-goro kaerimasu.

A: Soo desu-ka. Jaa, mata ato-de denwa shimasu.

B: Hai, wakarimashita.

A: Shitsurei shimasu.

LESSON 28
Leisure Time

OBJECTIVES
もくひょう

At the end of this lesson you will be able to:
- ☑ Ask friends what they want to do in their spare time
- ☑ Write the *kanji*: 見 and 行

VOCABULARY
たんご

Words

hima	free time
asobu (asobimasu/asonde)	play, have fun
watashi-tachi	we

Phrases and expressions

asobi-ni iku (ikimasu/itte)	go to play, go to have fun

VOCABULARY NOTES
たんごノート

Asobu

The Japanese verb *asobu* (*asobimasu/asonde*) can be translated in English as *play*, but it has many other meanings as well and can refer to leisure time activities for people of all ages. *Asobu* can also mean *have fun, have a good time, amuse oneself, get together for fun,* or *loaf around.* If you want to invite a friend to have some fun, just say *Asobi-ni ikimashoo.*

KEY GRAMMAR POINTS
ぶんぽうポイント

1. Watashi-tachi

Watashi-tachi, which is the plural form of *watashi* (I), means *we*. As in the case of *watashi*, the use of different particles with *watashi-tachi* results in different meanings.

Watashi-tachi-*wa* kooen-ni ikimasu.	we [topic]
Watashi-tachi-*ga* ichiban desu.	we [subject]
Watashi-tachi-*no* kuruma desu.	our [possessive pronoun]
Watashi-tachi-*o* mimashita.	us [direct object]
Watashi-tachi-*ni* tegami-o kakimashita.	us [indirect object]

The plural suffix *-tachi* may also be used with some other nouns referring to people, including some you have already learned: *sensei-tachi* (teachers), *gakusei-tachi* (students), *hito-tachi* (people), and *kodomo-tachi* (children).

2. Non-past negative of plain form verbs

This lesson introduces the negative equivalents of non-past plain form verbs such as *suru*, *taberu*, and *nomu*. Remember that non-past verbs can express present or future actions.

Tenisu *shinai.*	I don't/won't play tennis.
Banana *tabenai.*	She doesn't eat bananas.
Puruun juusu *nomanai.*	He doesn't drink prune juice.
O-kane *nai.*	I don't have any money.
Ryokoo-ni *ikanai.*	We aren't going on a trip.
Nikki *kakanai.*	I will not write in my journal.
Sono hon *yomanai.*	I won't read that book.

The chart on the next page summarizes the affirmative and negative forms of both *-masu* and plain form verbs you have learned in this course.

238

THE NON-PAST OF -*MASU* AND PLAIN FORM VERBS

-*MASU* Affirmative	Negative	PLAIN Affirmative	Negative	ENGLISH
-*u* Verbs:				
arimasu	arimasen	aru	nai	exist, be [inanimate]
aimasu	aimasen	au	awanai	meet, see
chigaimasu	chigaimasen	chigau	chigawanai	be different
hairimasu	hairimasen	hairu	hairanai	enter, join
hajimarimasu	hajimarimasen	hajimaru	hajimaranai	(something) begins
hanashimasu	hanashimasen	hanasu	hanasanai	speak
ikimasu	ikimasen	iku	ikanai	go
iimasu	iimasen	iu	iwanai	say
kaerimasu	kaerimasen	kaeru	kaeranai	return
kakimasu	kakimasen	kaku	kakanai	write
kachimasu	kachimasen	katsu	katanai	win
kaimasu	kaimasen	kau	kawanai	buy
kikimasu	kikimasen	kiku	kikanai	listen
narimasu	narimasen	naru	naranai	become
nomimasu	nomimasen	nomu	nomanai	drink
owarimasu	owarimasen	owaru	owaranai	(something) ends
tsukaimasu	tsukaimasen	tsukau	tsukawanai	use
utaimasu	utaimasen	utau	utawanai	sing
wakarimasu	wakarimasen	wakaru	wakaranai	understand
yomimasu	yomimasen	yomu	yomanai	read
-*ru* Verbs:				
akemasu	akemasen	akeru	akenai	open (something)
atsumemasu	atsumemasen	atsumeru	atsumenai	collect
imasu	imasen	iru	inai	exist, be [animate]
makemasu	makemasen	makeru	makenai	lose
mimasu	mimasen	miru	minai	look at, see
nemasu	nemasen	neru	nenai	go to bed/sleep
okimasu	okimasen	okiru	okinai	get up
oshiemasu	oshiemasen	oshieru	oshienai	teach
shimemasu	shimemasen	shimeru	shimenai	close (something)
tabemasu	tabemasen	taberu	tabenai	eat
wasuremasu	wasuremasen	wasureru	wasurenai	forget
Irregular Verbs:				
kimasu	kimasen	kuru	konai	come
shimasu	shimasen	suru	shinai	do

At this point in your study of Japanese, you may find it easier to learn the non-past negative of the plain form by listening carefully to your *bideo-no sensei* and *denwa-no sensei-tachi* and by reviewing the verbs above on a regular basis until the forms seem "natural" to you. If you prefer to begin learning the rules for forming the non-past negative and other verb forms, please refer to the Appendix.

YOMIMASHOO!　　　　　　　　　　　　よみましょう

ひま	free time
あした ひま ですか。	Are you free tomorrow?
あそぶ・あそびます・あそんで	play, have fun
あそびに 行きます	go to play, go to have fun
あの 二人は あそびに 行きます。	Those two are going to go have fun.
私たち	we
今日 いそがしくない です。	Today I am not busy.
どこかに 行きましょう。	Let's go somewhere.

239

---

❶ Kakimashoo! ✐

During this activity each student will work as a pair with two different クラスメート to check Assignment #1 from Part 2 of Lesson 27. Have two students carefully check your completed sentences, mark and discuss with you any errors found, and sign off on your page.

❷ Dialogue

With a クラスメート practice the dialogue until you can perform it smoothly. You do not have to memorize the dialogue, and you may refer to this page. In the dialogue, A would like to go out and have some fun with B. A suggests a number of different activities.

A: Konshuu-no do-yoobi-wa hima desu-ka?

B: Konshuu-no do-yoobi? (thinks) Eeto . . . Gomen-nasai. Hima ja nai desu. Shinseki-no uchi-ni asobi-ni ikimasu.

A: Aa, soo desu-ka? Ja, raishuu-no do-yoobi-wa hima desu-ka?

B: Raishuu-no do-yoobi? (thinks) Mada wakarimasen kedo . . .

A: Eeto . . . (takes out two tickets) Konsaato-no chiketto-ga arimasu kedo . . . Issho-ni ikimasen-ka?

B: (looks at tickets) Beetooben shinfonii desu-ka? (not interested) Gomen-nasai. Kurasshiku-wa kikimasen.

A: E? Kikimasen-ka? (shocked) Aa, soo desu-ka. (thinks) Ja, eiga-wa? (takes out two tickets) Supiido Faibu-wa omoshiroi desu-yo.

B: (looks at tickets) Supiido Faibu? Gomen-nasai. Akushon eiga-wa mimasen.

A: E? Mimasen? Aa, soo desu-ka. (thinks) Ja, oishii keeki-ya-ga arimasu kedo . . . Issho-ni ikimasen-ka?

B: Keeki-ya? (shakes head) Ikimasen. Keeki-wa suki ja nai desu.

A: (shocked) Aa, soo desu-ka.

B: (feels sorry for A) Ja, doraibu-wa?

A: (happily) E? Doraibu? Ikimasu, ikimasu.

B: (stands up) Ja, raishuu-no do-yoobi desu-ne. (smiles and leaves)

A: (waves) Ja, mata. (looks very happy) Doraibu! A! (puts hand on forehead) Kuruma-ga nai . . .

---

❶ Yomimashoo!

In Part 1 of the Interactive Activities you practiced a dialogue which is written below in 日本ご. With a クラスメート practice reading the dialogue until you can do so fluently.

A: 今しゅうの 土よう日は ひま ですか。

B: 今しゅうの 土よう日？ (thinks) ええと、 ごめんなさい。 ひま じゃない です。 しんせきの うちに あそびに 行きます。

A: ああ、 そう ですか。 じゃ、 らいしゅうの 土よう日は ひま ですか。

B: らいしゅうの 土よう日？ (thinks) まだ わかりません けど。

A: ええと (takes out two tickets) コンサートの チケットが あります けど。 いっしょに 行きませんか。

B: (looks at tickets) ベートーベン シンフォニー ですか。 (not interested)
ごめんなさい。 クラシックは ききません。

A: ええ？ ききませんか。 (shocked) ああ、そう ですか。 (thinks) じゃ、
えいがは？ (takes out two tickets) スピード ファイブは おもしろい
ですよ。

B: (looks at tickets) スピード ファイブ？ ごめんなさい。 アクション
えいがは 見ません。

A: え？ 見ません？ ああ、そう ですか。 (thinks) じゃ、おいしい
ケーキやが ありますけど。 いっしょに 行きませんか。

B: ケーキや？ (shakes head) 行きません。 ケーキは すき じゃ ない です。

A: (shocked) ああ、そう ですか。

B: (feels sorry for A) じゃ、ドライブは？

A: (happily) え？ ドライブ？ 行きます、行きます。

B: (stands up) じゃ、らいしゅうの 土よう日 ですね。 (smiles and leaves)

A: (waves) じゃ、また。 (looks very happy) ドライブ！ あ！ (puts hand on
forehead) くるまが ない。

❷ Iku? Iie, ikanai.

With a partner practice the non-past negative of some common plain form verbs. Take
turns with your partner asking and answering questions using the plain form of the verbs
in the grid below. Keep all of your questions very simple (the verb only) as if they are
part of a conversation where the context is clear to both of you. Refer back to the chart in
the *Bunpoo Pointo* section of this lesson as needed.

EXAMPLE

A: (chooses *ikimasu*) Iku?
B: Uun, ikanai.

TIP
Think about the meaning of what you are saying. This will help you learn the new forms.

arimasu	yomimasu	kakimasu	ikimasu
mimasu	tabemasu	imasu	wakarimasu
shimasu	kikimasu	hanashimasu	kaimasu

If you have time, make your own grid using verbs from the grid above as well as verbs
from the chart in the *Bunpoo Pointo* section, and do the activity again.

L. 28 電話で 話しましょう

れんしゅう A: Making a Phone Call

You are calling one of the following residences, and asking for the person indicated on the chart.

If s/he's not home:
Ask what time s/he'll return, OR say you'll call back later.

	(1)	(2)	(3)	(4)	(5)	(6)
Residence:	Tanaka	Yamada	Nishikawa	Suzuki	Kimura	Itoo
You wish to speak to:	Yuuko	Kazuo	Taroo	Sachiko	Maki	Takashi

れんしゅう B: Do you ~? No, I don't.

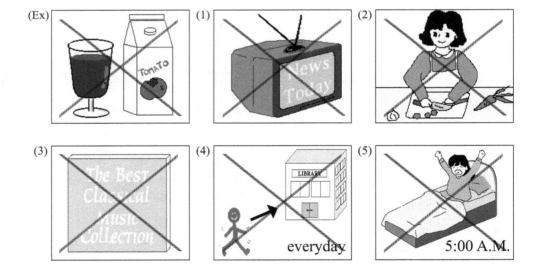

(Ex)　(1)　(2)

(3)　(4) everyday　(5) 5:00 A.M.

れんしゅう C: Let's converse!

Dialogue:
A: Are you free <u>this Saturday</u>?
B: Yeah, I am.
A: Then, will you go somewhere (to have fun)?
B: Sounds good. To where?
A: How about <u>Disneyland</u>?
B: O.K.

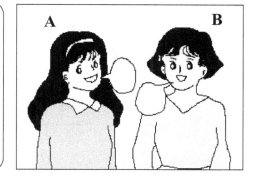

Sample Dialogue:

A: <u>今しゅうの土よう日</u>、ひま？
B: うん、ひま。
A: じゃ、あそびに行かない？
B: いいね。どこ 行く？
A: <u>ディズニーランド</u>はどう？
B: いいよ。

Sample Dialogue:

A: <u>Konshuu-no do-yoobi</u>, hima?
B: Un, hima.
A: Jaa, asobi-ni ikanai?
B: Ii-ne. Doko iku?
A: <u>Dizuniirando</u>-wa doo?
B: Ii-yo. *

*formal version
A: <u>Konshuu-no do-yoobi</u>, hima desu-ka?
B: Hai, hima desu-yo.
A: Jaa, asobi-ni ikimasen-ka?
B: Ii desu-ne. Doko-ni ikimashoo-ka?
A: <u>Dizuniirando</u>-wa doo desu-ka?
B: Ii desu-yo.

れんしゅう D: よみましょう。

Let's match left side and right side, and create a word!

(1)
(a) 大 　 る
(b) 金 　 校
(c) 高 　 人
(d) 見 　 よう日

(2)
(a) 行 　 気
(b) 小学 　 月
(c) 元 　 く
(d) 何 　 校

LESSON 29
Having a Party

OBJECTIVES もくひょう

At the end of this lesson you will be able to:
- ☑ Invite someone to your house
- ☑ Talk about preparations for a party
- ☑ Read the *kanji*: 来 and 年

VOCABULARY たんご

Words

tsukuru (tsukurimasu/tsukutte)	make

Phrases and expressions

asobi-ni kuru (kimasu/kite)	come over (and have fun)
Mata asobi-ni kite kudasai-ne.	Please come again soon.

Other words and expressions you will hear in this lesson

anata	you
kanojo	she
kare	he

CULTURE NOTES カルチャーノート

Personal Pronouns

As you have already learned in this course, Japanese prefer to avoid the use of personal pronouns, particularly those in the second and third person (you, your, he, his, him, she, her, they, their, them). In most cases it is clear from the context about whom or to whom the individual is speaking. Since native speakers of English and many other languages frequently use personal pronouns, they often want to use them in Japanese in much the same way they do in their first language.

The word *anata* (you) is a perfect example. Learners of Japanese often misuse and overuse this word because they are directly translating from their own language. While Japanese are somewhat used to "foreign Japanese," they can find the use of this word extremely rude and offensive.

When it is not clear from the context of a sentence which person is being referred to, Japanese will usually say the person's name with a title suffix (*-san, -kun, -chan*). If you follow this strategy, you can avoid a common mistake that foreigners make in Japanese, and your Japanese will sound much better.

YOMIMASHOO! よみましょう

つくる・つくります・つくって	make
ケーキを つくります	I will make a cake.
だれが 何を つくりますか。	Who is making what?
あそびに 来る・来ます・来て	come over (and have fun)
私の うちに あそびに 来ませんか。	Do you want to come over to my house?
また あそびに 来て くださいね。	Please come again soon.
今日の よる うちで パーティーを します。	I'm having a party at my house this evening.

244

パーティーは 6 じから 9 じまで です。	The party is from 6:00 to 9:00.
大人は 7人 来ます。	Seven adults are coming.
あなた	you
かのじょ	she
かれ	he

KANJI NOTES　　　　　　　　　　　　　　かんじノート

In this lesson you will learn to read two *kanji*: 来 and 年. Be sure that you know the readings of each *kanji* and can tell what the *kanji* means. Readings which are marked by an asterisk are for your reference only; you do not need to learn these at this time. You also do not have to learn any new words which are given in the examples. The correct stroke order for 来 is given in the Optional Writing Practice section. You will learn the correct stroke order for 年 in a future lesson.

RAI; ku(ru), ki(masu) (come)

来る	*ku*ru	come
来ます	*ki*masu	come
来年	*rai*nen	next year
来月	*rai*getsu	next month
来週	*rai*shuu	next week

今日友達が来ました。	Kyoo tomodachi-ga *ki*mashita.
	(My friend came today.)
何人来ますか。	Nan-nin *ki*masu-ka?
	(How many people are coming?)
来月は何月ですか。	*Rai*getsu-wa nan-gatsu desu-ka?
	(What month is next month?)
来週の火曜日に山に	*Rai*shuu-no ka-yoobi-ni yama-ni ikitai desu.
行きたいです。	(I want to go to the mountains next Tuesday.)

The *kanji* 来 is derived from a picture of a stalk of wheat. Wheat is not native to China, and in ancient times it "came" into China from other lands.

年　**NEN; toshi** (year)

来年	rai*nen*	next year
今年	ko*toshi*	this year
何年	nan-*nen*	how many years, which year
一年生	ichi-*nen*-sei	first-year student, first grade
何年間	nan-*nen*-kan	how many years (a period)
お年寄り	o-*toshi*yori	old person

私は来年高校一年生に	Watashi-wa rai*nen* kookoo ichi-*nen*-sei-ni narimasu.
なります。	(Next year I'll be a first-year student in high school.)

245

三年生が二人来ます。　　San-*nen*-sei-ga futari kimasu.
　　　　　　　　　　　　(Two third graders are coming.)
今年がもうすぐ終わる。　Ko*toshi*-ga moo sugu owaru.
　　　　　　　　　　　　(This year will be ending soon.)
来年日本から友達が　　　Rai*nen* Nihon-kara tomodachi-ga kimasu.
　来ます。　　　　　　　(Next year a friend is coming from Japan.)

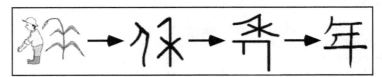

The *kanji* 年 is derived from a picture of a stalk of rice and a farmer sowing seeds.
Throughout Asia, the planting of rice occurs every *year*.

KANJI REVIEW													
今	私	火	月	行	天	日	木	本	来	金	元	土	気
年	田	見	小	学	高	何	水	川	大	校	中	人	山

How do you read them? What do they mean?

INTERACTIVE ACTIVITIES

PART 1

❶ Dialogue

With a クラスメート memorize the dialogue following the normal procedure. Make sure
that you understand the meaning of the dialogue before you begin practicing. Harumi and
Kazuko are both female names. If you wish to substitute other female names or male
names, you may select them from the box below or use others that you know. After you
have memorized the dialogue, perform it for another pair.

Nakagawa-san is inviting Takayama-san to a party at Nakagawa-san's house.
N: (dials phone)
T: (answers phone) Moshi-moshi?
N: Moshi-moshi. Takayama-san desu-ka?
T: Hai, soo desu.
N: Nakagawa desu kedo. **Harumi**-san-wa irasshaimasu-ka?
T: A, **Kazuko**-san? Watashi desu kedo.
N: A, konnichi-wa. **Harumi**-san, kyoo-no yoru isogashii desu-ka?
T: Kyoo-no yoru desu-ka? Hima desu kedo.
N: A, yokatta. Watashi-no uchi-ni asobi-ni kimasen-ka? Paatii-o shimasu. Honda-san-mo
　　Yamamoto-san-mo Tanaka-san-mo kimasu-yo.
T: (excited) Aa, soo desu-ka. Ikitai desu. Nan-ji-kara desu-ka?
N: Shichi-ji-kara desu.

JAPANESE GIVEN NAMES					
Female			**Male**		
Atsuko	Kaori	Naomi	Daiki	Kenta	Shoota
Ayaka	Katsumi	Rie	Goroo	Masahide	Takumi
Haruka	Makiko	Saori	Haruyuki	Masakazu	Taroo
Harumi	Masako	Yui	Kenji	Naoki	Yuuta

❷ **Vocabulary check**

Silently review the vocabulary for Lesson 29 and any vocabulary related to having a party. Then have a クラスメート orally test your knowledge of them. Your partner says the えいご, and you give the 日本ご. Switch and test your partner.

PART 2

---

❶ Yomimashoo!

With a クラスメート read the dialogue below which you memorized in the last class. Choose appropriate given names in the blanks before you begin. You may choose ones from the box on the previous page or use others. Partner B may look at the *roomaji* version as well as the *kana* version and check if Partner A reads the dialogue correctly. Partner A can only look at the *kana* version. Switch and repeat.

中川: (dials phone)

高山: (answers phone) もしもし。

中川: もしもし。高山さん ですか。

高山: はい、そう です。

中川: 中川 です けど。＿＿＿＿＿さんは いらっしゃいますか。

高山: あ、＿＿＿＿＿さん？ 私 です けど。

中川: あ、今日は。＿＿＿＿＿さん、今日の よる いそがしい ですか。

高山: 今日の よる ですか。ひま です けど。

中川: あ、よかった。私の うちに あそびに 来ませんか。パーティーを
　　　します。本田さんも 山本さんも 田中さんも 来ますよ。

高山: (excited) ああ、そう ですか。行きたい です。何じから ですか。

中川: 7じから です。

ROOMAJI VERSION
N: (dials phone)
T: (answers phone) Moshi-moshi?
N: Moshi-moshi. Takayama-san desu-ka?
T: Hai, soo desu.
N: Nakagawa desu kedo. ＿＿＿＿＿-san-wa irasshaimasu-ka?
T: A, ＿＿＿＿＿-san? Watashi desu kedo.
N: A, konnichi-wa. ＿＿＿＿＿-san, kyoo-no yoru isogashii desu-ka?
T: Kyoo-no yoru desu-ka? Hima desu kedo.
N: A, yokatta. Watashi-no uchi-ni asobi-ni kimasen-ka? Paatii-o shimasu. Honda-san-mo
　　Yamamoto-san-mo Tanaka-san-mo kimasu-yo.
T: (excited) Aa, soo desu-ka. Ikitai desu. Nan-ji-kara desu-ka?
N: Shichi-ji-kara desu.

❷ Dare-ga nani-o tsukurimasu-ka?　　📄 & ✏

Do this activity with a クラスメート. Take turns asking and answering questions to find out WHO (DARE) will make WHAT (NANI) for the party. Look only at your own chart. Before you begin, read the sample questions and answers aloud with your partner. After you finish, compare your charts to check your accuracy. For a greater challenge, use the charts in Japanese.

SAMPLE QUESTIONS AND ANSWERS

To find out WHO (DARE): **Dare**-ga keeki-o tsukurimasu-ka?
Ueda-san-ga tsukurimasu.

To find out WHAT (NANI): Yamaguchi-san-wa **nani**-o tsukurimasu-ka?
Kukkii-o tsukurimasu.

PARTNER A

DARE	NANI
Takayama	
Yamakawa	sarada
Tanaka	furaido chikin
	furuutsu panchi
Yamamoto	
Honda	keeki
Kawata	yasai sutikku
Yamada	aisutii
Nakayama	
Takada	remoneedo
	aisu koohii
Nakata	

PARTNER B

DARE	NANI
Takayama	kukkii
Yamakawa	
Tanaka	
Nakagawa	furuutsu panchi
Yamamoto	sandoitchi
	keeki
Kawata	
Yamada	
Nakayama	appuru pai
	remoneedo
Yamanaka	aisu koohii
Nakata	hanbaagaa

SAMPLE QUESTIONS AND ANSWERS

To find out だれ:　だれが ケーキを つくりますか。
うえださんが つくります。

To find out 何:　山口さんは 何を つくりますか。　　山口 = Yamaguchi
クッキーを つくります。

PARTNER A

だれ	なに
高山	
山川	サラダ
田中	フライドチキン
	フルーツパンチ
山本	
本田	ケーキ
川田	やさいスティック
山田	アイスティー
中山	
高田	レモネード
	アイスコーヒー
中田	

PARTNER B

だれ	なに
高山	クッキー
山川	
田中	
中川	フルーツパンチ
山本	サンドイッチ
	ケーキ
川田	
山田	
中山	アップルパイ
	レモネード
山中	アイスコーヒー
中田	ハンバーガー

L. 29 電話で 話しましょう

れんしゅう A: Sporting Events

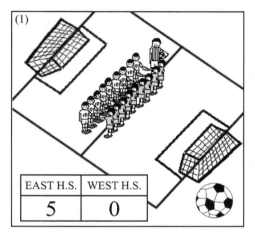

(1)

EAST H.S.	WEST H.S.
5	0

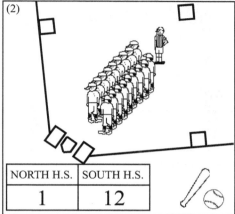

(2)

NORTH H.S.	SOUTH H.S.
1	12

れんしゅう B: International Student Party Preparations

These are lists of food and activity preparations for an International Student Party. Group A can only look at List A, and Group B can only look at List B. Ask members of the other group questions and fill in the lettered blanks.

List A

Food	Activities
(Ex.1) Russo .... bread	Yee .... sing a song
Kawaguchi .... (1)	(Ex.3) draw pictures Jackson .... (portraits)
(Ex.2) Lopez .... salad	Copperfield .... magic tricks
Patel .... curry	Suzuki .... (3)
(2) .... sandwiches	Lewis .... tell jokes
Duncan .... cake	

249

List B

Food	Activities
(Ex.1) Russo .... bread	Yee .... (6)
Kawaguchi .... sushi	(Ex.3) draw pictures Jackson .... (portraits)
(Ex.2) Lopez .... salad	Copperfield .... magic tricks
(4) .... curry	Suzuki .... karate
Miller .... sandwiches	Lewis .... tell jokes
Duncan .... (5)	

れんしゅう C: Let's converse!

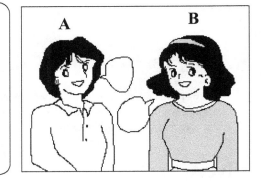

Dialogue:

A: <u>Ms. Yamada</u>, I'm having a party <u>this Saturday</u>. Won't you come?

B: That sounds great! Shall I make something?

A: Oh, yeah. Would you make <u>a salad</u> then?

B: O.K. What time is the party from?

A: It's from <u>8:00</u>.

Sample Dialogue:

A: <u>山田さん</u>、<u>今しゅうの土よう日</u>に
　　パーティーをしますけど、あそびに来ませんか。

B: いいですね。何かつくりましょうか。

A: そうですね。じゃ、<u>サラダ</u>をおねがいします。

B: はい、わかりました。パーティーは何じからですか。

A: <u>8じ</u>からです。

Sample Dialogue:

A: <u>Yamada-san,</u> <u>konshuu-no do-yoobi</u>-ni paatii-o shimasu-kedo, asobi-ni kimasen-ka?

B: Ii desu-ne. Nani-ka tsukurimashoo-ka?

A: Soo desu-ne. Jaa, <u>sarada</u>-o o-negai-shimasu.

B: Hai, wakarimashita. Paatii-wa nan-ji-kara desu-ka?

A: <u>8-ji</u>-kara desu.

LESSON 30
Review

At the end of this lesson you will be able to:

☑ Read the *kanji*: 一　二　三　四　五　六

VOCABULARY   たんご

Words and expressions you will hear in this lesson

fukushuu	review (noun)
fukushuu(-o) suru (shimasu/shite)	review (verb)
yume	dream (noun)
Yume-ga takusan arimasu-ne.	You have a lot of dreams, don't you?
wasuremono	item forgotten, left behind

VOCABULARY NOTES   たんごノート

1. Wasuremono

The word *mono* means *thing* (*tangible item*) and is frequently combined with the verb stem to create a noun which is related in meaning. You will encounter other words which are formed this same way. What do these words mean? Check your answers by looking at the last page of this lesson.

1. tabemono
2. nomimono
3. wasuremono
4. kaimono
5. kimono (kiru = wear)
6. norimono (noru = ride)

2. NOUN of Chinese origin (+ suru)

In Lesson 27 you learned how many nouns of Chinese origin, such as *renshuu* (practice), can be used with the verb *suru*. In this lesson you will hear another such noun – *fukushuu* (review). Here are the other such nouns you have learned in this course.

NOUNS OF CHINESE ORIGIN WHICH CAN BE USED WITH *SURU*			
benkyoo	study	ryoori	cooking
fukushuu	review	shitsurei	rudeness, impoliteness
renshuu	practice	sooji	cleaning
ryokoo	trip		

KEY GRAMMAR POINTS   ぶんぽうポイント

This lesson provides you with an opportunity to review some important grammatical points, including the *-tai* (want to) form of verbs (L. 25) and the plain form in both the affirmative and the negative (L. 28). Refer back to the given lessons for explanations and examples.

YOMIMASHOO!   よみましょう

きょ年は 何を しましたか。	What did you do last year?
きょ年の なつの りょこうは たのしかった。	Last summer's trip was fun.
せかい りょこうを したい です。	I want to travel around the world.
ふくしゅう	review (noun)
ふくしゅう する・します・して	review (verb)
ゆめ	dream (noun)
ゆめが たくさん ありますね。	You have a lot of dreams, don't you?
わすれもの	item forgotten, left behind

In this lesson you will learn to read the *kanji* for the numbers 1 through 6: 一, 二, 三, 四, 五 and 六. Be sure that you know the readings of each *kanji* and can tell what the *kanji* means. Information on the correct stroke order for these *kanji* is given in the Optional Writing Practice section.

NOTE: Japanese today use both *kanji* and Arabic numerals (1, 2, 3 . . .). Arabic numerals are commonly used for telephone numbers, lists of items, and in schedules. All math calculations are performed with Arabic numerals. In counting people and things both systems are used. The *kanji* for the numbers one through 10 are among the first *kanji* that Japanese first graders are expected to learn.

   ICHI; hito(tsu) (one)

一月	*ichi*-gatsu	January
一つ	*hito*tsu	one (thing)
一人	*hito*ri	one person
一分	*ip*-pun	one minute
一日	tsuitachi	first (day of the month)

一月一日に日本人の　　*Ichi*-gatsu tsuitachi-ni nihon-jin-no tomodachi-ga *hito*ri
友達が一人家に　　　　　uchi-ni kimashita.
来ました。　　　　　　　(On January 1 a Japanese friend came to my house.)

   NI; futa(tsu) (two)

二年生	*ni*-nen-sei	second-year student
二年間	*ni*-nen-kan	(a period of) two years
二つ	*futa*tsu	two (things)
二人	*futa*ri	two people
二日	*futsu*ka	second (day of the month)

二年間大学で日本語の　　*Ni*-nen-kan daigaku-de nihongo-no benkyoo-o shimashita.
勉強をしました。　　　　(I studied Japanese at the university for two years.)
中学二年生が二人　　　　Chuugaku *ni*-nen-sei-ga *futa*ri paatii-ni kimashita.
パーティーに来ました。　(Two second-year middle school students came to the
　　　　　　　　　　　　　party.)

三   **SAN; mit(tsu)** (three)

三十	*san*-juu	30
三年生	*san*-nen-sei	third-year student
三人	*san*-nin	three people
三つ	*mit*tsu	three (things)
三日	*mik*ka	third (day of the month)

あの小学校では三年生　　Ano shoogakkoo-de-wa *san*-nen-sei-kara nihongo-no
から日本語の勉強を　　　benkyoo-o shite-imasu.
しています。　　　　　　(At that elementary school, they study Japanese from the
　　　　　　　　　　　　　third grade.)

四 | **SHI; yon, yo, yot(tsu) (four)**

四月	*shi*-gatsu	April
四才	*yon*-sai	four years old
四時間目	*yo*-jikan-me	fourth period (class)
四年生	*yo*-nen-sei	fourth-year student
四つ	*yot*tsu	four (things)

私は来年大学四年生 Watashi-wa rainen daigaku *yo*-nen-sei-ni narimasu.
になります。 (I will be a senior at the university next year.)
四時間目は三時四十分 *Yo*-jikan-me-wa san-ji *yon*-jup-pun-made desu.
までです。 (Fourth period goes to 3:40.)

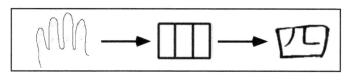

五 | **GO; itsu(tsu) (five)**

五月	*go*-gatsu	May
五年生	*go*-nen-sei	fifth-grade student
五人	*go*-nin	five people
五つ	*itsu*tsu	five (things)
五日	*itsu*ka	fifth (day of the month)

五月五日に親戚の家に *Go*-gatsu *itsu*ka-ni shinseki-no uchi-ni ikimasu.
行きます。 (On May 5, I'm going to my relative's house)
大人五人と小人四人 Otona *go*-nin-to kodomo yo-nin o-negai-shimasu.
お願いします。 (Five adults and four children, please. [making reservation at
  a restaurant])

 | **ROKU; mut(tsu) (six)**

六人	*roku*-nin	six people
六才	*roku*-sai	six years old
六分	*rop*-pun	six minutes
六つ	*mut*tsu	six (things)
六日	*mui*ka	sixth (day of the month)

今日、弟は六才に Kyoo otooto-wa *roku*-sai-ni narimashita.
なりました。 (Today my younger brother became six.)
六月六日の六時十六分の *Roku*-gatsu *mui*ka-no *roku*-ji juu-*rop*-pun-no Shinkansen-
新幹線で大阪に de Oosaka-ni ikimasu.
行きます。 (On June 6 I am going to Osaka on the 6:16 Shinkansen*.)

  *the "Bullet Train"

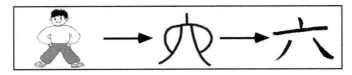

Some historians believe that the *kanji* 六 represents the six major parts of the body: two arms, two legs, the head, and the trunk.

INTERACTIVE ACTIVITIES

PART 1

❶ Shitsumon-ni kotaete kudasai.
During this activity each student will work as a pair with two different クラスメート to check Assignment #1 from Part 2 of Lesson 29. The goal of the activity is to have two students carefully check your five answers, mark and discuss with you any errors found, and sign off on your page. Form your first pair and exchange assignments with your partner. Both partners independently check and neatly mark errors for all five sentences. Do not correct errors. Use the same editing symbols as usual. If you think that the entire answer is incorrect (based on the dialogue), put a question mark in front of the sentence. Check the sentence after your partner has answered it again.

❷ Omedetoo-gozaimasu! (Congratulations!)
Use your imagination as you do this activity with a クラスメート. Take turns asking and answering questions. The *Irasshai* Prize Patrol has just presented you with a check for one million dollars! The television reporters are now interviewing you to find out what you want to do with all of your money. Each reporter (Partner A) will ask you (Partner B) what you want to do and then, in response to your answer, will ask you one more question.

  A: Nani-o shitai desu-ka?
  B: Hawai-ni ikitai desu.
  A: Hawai-de nani-o shitai desu-ka?
  B: Umi-ni itte, saafin-o shitai desu.

  A: Nani-o shitai desu-ka?
  B: Atarashii kuruma-o kaitai desu.
  A: Donna kuruma-o kaitai desu-ka?
  B: *Make of car*-o kaitai desu.

PART 2

❶ Iku? Ikanai.
With a partner practice the non-past negative of some common plain form verbs. Place the tip of a pencil on the dot in the center of the circle with one end of a paper clip around the pencil tip. Use this as a spinner to select a number on the wheel. Take turns with your partner asking and answering questions using the plain form of the verbs given below. Keep all of your questions very simple (the verb only) as if they are part of a conversation where the context is clear to both of you. Refer back to the chart in the *Bunpoo Pointo* section of Lesson 28 to check your answers. Look at the example before you begin.

  A: B-san-no ban desu. [ban = turn]
  B: Hai. (*spins a 2*)
  A: Iku?
  B: Ikanai. A-san-no ban desu.

VERBS

1. miru	4. taberu	7. wasureru	10. kiku
2. iku	5. yomu	8. suru	11. [Choose any verb below]
3. nomu	6. kuru	9. wakaru	12. [Choose any verb below]

aru	hairu	akeru	hanasu	kaeru
kaku	okiru	oshieru	atsumeru	neru
iru	hajimaru	shimeru	tsukau	iu
kau	naru	makeru	owaru	uta

❷ **Yomimashoo!** 📄 & ✏️

This pair activity provides you with an opportunity to review the *kanji* which you have learned to read in this lesson. Partner A masks the *roomaji* side and reads the vocabulary in the left column in order. Partner B responds after each with either *Hai, soo desu* or *Iie, chigaimasu. Moo ichido yonde kudasai.* Partner A writes down those which need to be studied. Switch roles and repeat.

かなとかんじ	ローマじ	かなとかんじ	ローマじ
1. 三じ	1. san-ji	12. 五人	12. go-nin
2. 五えん	2. go-en	13. 一年せい	13. ichi-nen-sei
3. 二人	3. futari	14. 三さい	14. san-sai
4. 一つ	4. hitotsu	15. 一月	15. ichi-gatsu
5. 四月	5. shi-gatsu	16. 六ばん	16. roku-ban
6. 三日	6. mikka	17. 一日	17. tsuitachi
7. 五日	7. itsuka	18. 四つ	18. yottsu
8. 四じかん	8. yo-jikan	19. 二ドル	19. ni-doru
9. 二月	9. ni-gatsu	20. 三つ	20. mittsu
10. 二つ	10. futatsu	21. 六年せい	21. roku-nen-sei
11. 四分	11. yon-pun		

ANSWERS (VOCABULARY NOTES):
1. things eaten = food 2. things drunk = beverage 3. things forgotten, left behind 4. things bought = purchase 5. things worn = kimono (traditionally worn clothing) 6. things ridden = vehicle

L. 30　電話で 話しましょう

れんしゅう A:　What's your fortune?

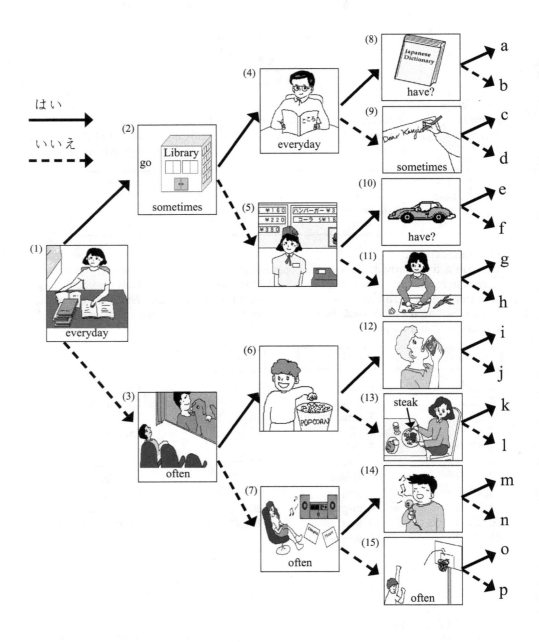

Your fortune is:

a. You are most likely to succeed.
b. You are a walking dictionary.
c. You will have many friends.
d. You are a great speaker.
e. You are popular with everyone.
f. You will save lots of money.
g. You will become a famous chef.
h. You will marry a great chef.
i. You will own your own movie theater.

j. You are health conscious.
k. You are a meat lover.
l. You are a vegetarian.
m. You will be a great singer.
n. You will be a famous composer.
o. You will be an Olympic gold medalist.
p. You will be a great writer of fortune cookie fortunes.

れんしゅう B: Your dream come true!

(1) You just won a million dollars.

(2) You just graduated from high school.

れんしゅう C: Interview your classmate!

(3) worked a part-time job last month?

(4) cook today?

(5) go/went to a lake this month?

(2) saw a movie last week?

(6) play sports next week?

(1) took a trip last year?

(7) [Ask any question you like.]

257

LESSON 31
Review

OBJECTIVES もくひょう

At the end of this lesson you will be able to:
- ☑ Read the *kanji*: 七　八　九　十

VOCABULARY たんご

Words

onaji	same

Phrases and expressions

Onaji desu-ka?	Are they the same?
Onaji ja nai desu.	They are not the same.
Naka-ni nani-ga haitte-imasu-ka?	What is in (the bag)?

KEY GRAMMAR POINTS ぶんぽうポイント

This lesson provides you with an opportunity to review some important grammar points. Refer back to the given lessons for explanations and examples.

1. Ichiban + ADJECTIVE	Lesson 9
2. The -te-imasu form	Lessons 11, 14
3. The -te-mo ii form	Lesson 15
4. The -te form used for a sequence of actions	Lesson 17
5. Changing verbs into nouns with suru-koto	Lesson 19
6. Spatial relationship words	Lessons 69 (Vol. 1), 16

YOMIMASHOO! よみましょう

おなじ	same
おなじ ですか。	Are they the same?
おなじ じゃ ない です。	They are not the same.
どちらから ですか。	Where are you from?
アラスカから です。	I'm from Alaska.
何ごを はなしますか。	What language do they speak?
せかいで 一ばん ながい 川 です。	It is the longest river in the world.
ラジオを きいて 本を よみます。	I'll listen to the radio and then read a book.
この 本を よんでも いい ですか。	May I read this book?
まだ コーヒーを のんでいますか。	Is he still drinking coffee?
いいえ、 のんでいません。	No, he's not.
何を していますか。	What is he doing?
テレビを 見ています。	He's watching television.
私は しゅみが たくさん あります。	I have a lot of hobbies.
しゅみは やきゅうを 見る ことと えを かくことと りょうり です。	(My) hobbies are watching baseball, drawing pictures, and cooking.
ざっしは つくえの したに あります。	The magazines are under the desk.
あかい かばんの 中に 何が はいって いますか。	What's in the red bag?

In this lesson you will learn to read the *kanji* for the numbers 7 through 10: 七, 八, 九 and 十. Be sure that you know the readings of each *kanji* and can tell what the *kanji* means. Information on the correct stroke order for these *kanji* is given in the Optional Writing Practice section.

SHICHI; nana(tsu) (seven)

七月	*shichi*-gatsu	July
七時	*shichi*-ji	seven o'clock
七人	*nana*-nin	seven people
七才	*nana*-sai	seven years old
七日	*nano*ka	seventh (day of the month)

七月七日に七才に なりました。	*Shichi*-gatsu *nano*ka-ni *nana*-sai-ni narimashita. (He became seven on July 7th.)
アラスカからアリゾナ まで車で七日間です。	Arasuka-kara Arizona-made kuruma-de nanoka-kan desu. (From Alaska to Arizona it's seven days by car.)

Historians are uncertain as to the origin of this *kanji*. It is easy to remember, however, because it resembles a European seven turned upside down.

HACHI; yat(tsu) (eight)

八月	*hachi*-gatsu	August
八円	*hachi*-en	eight yen
八人	*hachi*-nin	eight people
八つ	*yat*tsu	eight (things)
八日	*yoo*ka	eighth (day of the month)

私の学校は八時から です。	Watashi-no gakkoo-wa hachi-ji kara desu. (My school starts at 8:00.)
八月八日は火曜日 ですか。	*Hachi*-gatsu *yoo*ka-wa kayoobi desu-ka? (Is August 8th a Tuesday?)

This *kanji* is derived from two curved lines which symbolize division.

九 **KU; KYUU; kokono(tsu)** (nine)

九月	*ku*-gatsu	September
九時	*ku*-ji	nine o'clock
九分	*kyuu*-fun	nine minutes
九つ	*kokono*tsu	nine (things)
九日	*kokono*ka	ninth (day of the month)

九時に九段下駅で
大学の友達に会います。

Ku-ji-ni *Ku*danshita eki-de daigaku-no tomodachi-ni aimasu.
(At 9:00 I will be meeting my university friends at Kudanshita train station.)

ハンバーガーを九つ
買います。

Hanbaagaa-o *kokono*tsu kaimasu.
(We'll buy nine hamburgers.)

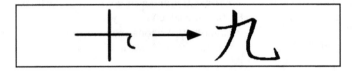

This *kanji* resembles the *kanji* for *ten*, but part of the horizontal stroke drops away. Think of this as indicating one less than ten – *nine*.

十 **JUU; too** (ten)

十円	*juu*-en	10 yen
十人	*juu*-nin	10 people
五十二	go-*juu*-ni	52
二十歳	hatachi	20 years old
十日	*too*ka	10th (day of the month)

今日は十度です。

Kyoo-wa *juu*-do desu.
(It's 10 degrees today.)

その日本語の本は十九
ドルです。

Sono nihongo-no hon-wa *juu*-kyuu-doru desu.
(That Japanese book is 19 dollars.)

INTERACTIVE ACTIVITIES

PART 1

❶ Ichiban

Do this activity with a クラスメート. Take turns with your partner asking and answering questions about the things in the grid on the next page. Do not choose the same word twice. Partner B uses the superlative form of an appropriate adjective in the answer. Use the pattern given in the example. Refer to the Adjective Chart in Part 1 of the Interactive Activities of Lesson 9 as needed. Other adjectives you have learned include *kitanai* (dirty, messy), *tsuyoi* (strong), and *yowai* (weak).

EXAMPLE

A: (chooses *machi*) Donna **machi** desu-ka?　[What kind of city is it?]

B: Sekai-de ichiban **urusai machi** desu.　　[It's the noisiest city in the world.]

yama	jugyoo	daigaku	mizuumi
fuku	kuruma	kawa	sensei
hoteru	eiga	konpyuutaa	tabemono
heya	chiimu	machi	doobutsuen

❷ Mimasu ~ miru ~ mite 　　📄 & 🖊

With a クラスメート take turns quizzing each other on the *-te* form of the following verbs. You say the *-masu* form and the plain form. Then your partner gives the *-te* form. Write down those that need further study.

VERBS IN THE *-TE* FORM

-masu form	Plain form	*-te* form	English
mimasu	miru	mite	look at, see
tabemasu	taberu	tabete	eat
okimasu	okiru	okite	get up
oshiemasu	oshieru	oshiete	teach
nemasu	neru	nete	sleep, go to bed
atsumemasu	atsumeru	atsumete	collect
akemasu	akeru	akete	open (something)
shimemasu	shimeru	shimete	close (something)
makemasu	makeru	makete	lose
hanashimasu	hanasu	hanashite	speak
shimasu	suru	shite	do
kimasu	kuru	kite	come
wasuremasu	wasureru	wasurete	forget
nomimasu	nomu	nonde	drink
yomimasu	yomu	yonde	read
asobimasu	asobu	asonde	play, have fun
aimasu	au	atte	meet, see
iimasu	iu	itte	say
kaimasu	kau	katte	buy
utaimasu	utau	utatte	sing
tsukaimasu	tsukau	tsukatte	use
ikimasu	iku	itte	go
kaerimasu	kaeru	kaette	return
tsukurimasu	tsukuru	tsukutte	make
hairimasu	hairu	haitte	enter, join
kachimasu	katsu	katte	win
kakimasu	kaku	kaite	write
kikimasu	kiku	kiite	listen

❸ Nani-o shite-imasu-ka?

Form 3人のグループ. Student A mimes one of the verbs given in the box above while asking *Nani-o shite-imasu-ka?* Students B and C watch without talking. Student A then counts いち、に、さん、し、ご、 and Students B and C say at the same time what they think the answer is (for example, *Yonde-imasu*). Student B goes next, followed by Student C.

❶ **Kinoo 6-ji-ni okite, . . .**

Do this activity in ４人のグループ. The first person begins by saying *Kinoo 6-ji-ni okite*. The second person repeats what the first person says and adds the next activity in the sequence of yesterday's activities. The third person repeats in order what the first and second people say and adds the third activity. Continue adding activities in this way, each time repeating all that has been said before and using the *-te* form. Try to go around the circle at least twice. The final activity is *nemashita*.

❷ **Yomimashoo!**　　　📄 & ✐

This pair activity provides you with an opportunity to review the *kanji* which you have learned to read. Partner A masks the *roomaji* side and reads the vocabulary in the left column in order. Partner B responds after each with either *Hai, soo desu* or *Iie, chigaimasu. Moo ichido yonde kudasai*. Partner A writes down those which need to be studied. Switch roles and repeat.

かな と かんじ	ローマじ
1. 八	1. hachi
2. 五えん	2. go-en
3. 十人	3. juu-nin
4. 一つ	4. hitotsu
5. 四月三日	5. shi-gatsu mikka
6. お金	6. o-kane
7. 元気	7. genki
8. 来年	8. rainen
9. 日本の大学	9. nihon-no daigaku
10. 天気	10. tenki
11. 小学校	11. shoogakkoo
12. 九	12. ku, kyuu
13. 一年せい	13. ichi-nen-sei
14. 行く	14. iku
15. 一月七日	15. ichi-gatsu nanoka
16. 六年	16. roku-nen
17. 今日	17. kyoo
18. 四つ	18. yottsu
19. 見ました	19. mimashita
20. 三つ	20. mittsu
21. 高校	21. kookoo
22. 私	22. watashi
23. お水	23. o-mizu
24. 何月何日	24. nan-gatsu nan-nichi

❸ **Kono machi-ni hon-ya-ga arimasu-ka?**　　　📄 & ✐

Do this activity with a partner. The maps on the next page are for two different towns with only some of the places identified. Without showing each other, each partner labels all of the places which have not been identified. Select place names from the box. Make sure you have only one of each place on the map (i.e., two places cannot have the same label). Take turns asking each other questions to complete your partner's map. (Choose places from the box right below your partner's map.) The winner is the first person to finish labeling the other person's map correctly. Practice reading aloud the sample exchange (which is not based on the following maps) before you begin.

PARTNER A'S MAP (A creates this map; B asks questions about it.)

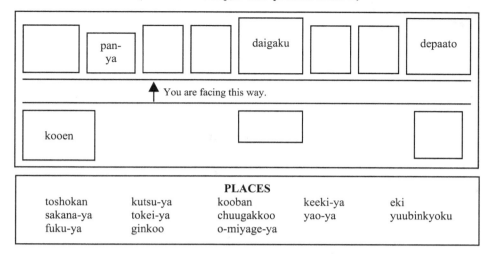

| | pan-ya | | | daigaku | | | depaato |

↑ You are facing this way.

| kooen | | | |

PLACES

toshokan	kutsu-ya	kooban	keeki-ya	eki
sakana-ya	tokei-ya	chuugakkoo	yao-ya	yuubinkyoku
fuku-ya	ginkoo	o-miyage-ya		

SAMPLE EXCHANGE

A: Kono machi-ni hon-ya-ga arimasu-ka? [A is looking at B's map in A's text.]

B: Hai, arimasu. [A now knows there is a *hon-ya* and can ask for its location.]

A: Hon-ya-wa doko-ni arimasu-ka?

B: Depaato-no hidari-ni arimasu. [A writes *hon-ya* on the building to the left of the department store.]

B: Kono machi-ni yaoya-ga arimasu-ka? [B is looking at A's map in B's text.]

A: Yaoya-wa arimasen. [B's turn now ends since A did not respond affirmatively.]

PARTNER B'S MAP (B creates this map; A asks questions about it.)

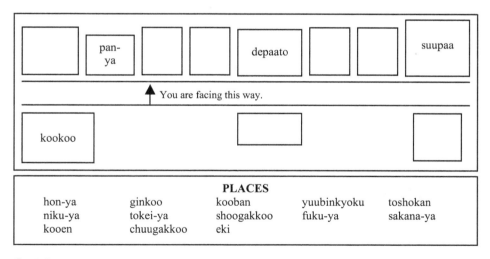

| | pan-ya | | | depaato | | | suupaa |

↑ You are facing this way.

| kookoo | | | |

PLACES

hon-ya	ginkoo	kooban	yuubinkyoku	toshokan
niku-ya	tokei-ya	shoogakkoo	fuku-ya	sakana-ya
kooen	chuugakkoo	eki		

❹ Hai, soo desu.

Form new pairs. Both partners look at one of the completed maps from the previous activity. Take turns making true or false statements about the map. Your partner must as quickly as possible respond with *Hai, soo desu* or *Iie, chigaimasu*. Use statements such as the following:

Hon-ya-wa eki-no hidari-ni arimasu.   The bookstore is to the left of the station.

Pan-ya-no migi-ni kooen-ga arimasu.   To the right of the bakery (there) is a park.

L. 31 電話で 話しましょう

れんしゅう A: Irasshai Town

(1) hotels	(2) parks	(3) libraries
(a) how many?	(a) how many?	(a) how many?
(b) the smallest?	(b) the biggest?	(b) the oldest?
(c) location?	(c) location?	(c) location?

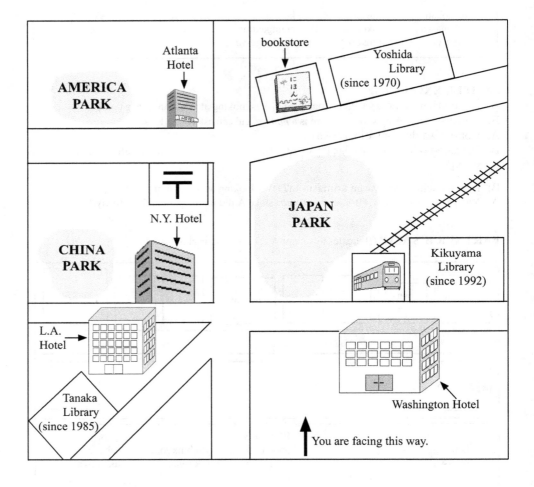

れんしゅう B: Are they the same?

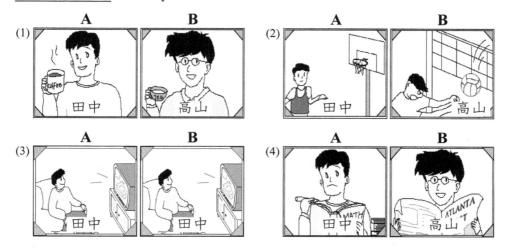

れんしゅう C: かんじをよみましょう。

(1) 四　　　　　　　　　　(2) 六

(3) 九　　　　　　　　　　(4) 一、八

(5) 七、二　　　　　　　　(6) 五、三、十

(7) 六、四、五　　　　　　(8) 九、一、一

れんしゅう D: Derek's Essay

　　　　　　　　　　　　　　デリック・ホワイト

　きょ年の九月に、日本に行きました。日本の高校
で、れきしと日本ごのべんきょうをしました。火よう
日と木よう日に、バレーボールのれんしゅうをして、
しゅうまつに、プールに行きました。

　来年の七月に、日本のともだちがアメリカに来ま
す。ディズニーランドにいっしょに行きたいです。

しつもん: (Answer in English.)

(1) When did the writer go to Japan?
(2) What did he do on weekends while he was in Japan?
(3) What does he want to do during the summer?

R. 24~31 電話で 話しましょう

れんしゅう A: Asking for Permission

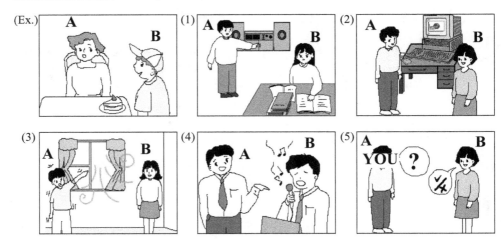

れんしゅう B: Getting to Know about Others

Name	Hometown	Foreign Language		Hobby
Steve	Atlanta	French	3 yrs.	tennis and swimming
Gina	(1) Dallas	(2) German	(3) 1 yr.	(4) drawing pictures
You	(5) ?	(6) ?	(7) ?	(8) ?

266

LESSON 32
Reviewing Counting and Prices

OBJECTIVES   目標

At the end of this lesson you will be able to:
- ☑ Talk about one of two items
- ☑ Express what you do not want to do

In this lesson you will also have an opportunity to review reading the following *kanji*:

見　行　来　年　一　二　三　四　五　六　七　八　九　十

VOCABULARY   単語

Words

dotchi	which one (of two)
kotchi	this one
sotchi	that one
atchi	that one over there

Phrases and expressions

zenbu-de	altogether, in all

Other words and expressions you will hear in this lesson

katarogu	catalogue
meron	melon
retasu	lettuce
gureepufuruutsu	grapefruit

KEY GRAMMAR POINTS   文法ポイント

1. Kotchi - sotchi - atchi - dotchi
In this course you have already learned about three sets of *ko-so-a-do* words:
    kore, sore, are, dore
    kono, sono, ano, dono
    koko, soko, asoko, doko
This lesson introduces you to another set of high-frequency *ko-so-a-do* words: *kotchi, sotchi, atchi,* and *dotchi*. A common meaning of *dotchi* is *which one (of two)*.

Dotchi desu-ka?	*Which one* is it?
Kotchi desu.	It's *this one*.

2. Dotchi-ga *ADJECTIVE* desu-ka?
Since *dotchi* is used only when asking about one of two things, an adjective used with *dotchi* is often translated in English as a comparative form (cheap**er**, fast**er**, **more** beautiful, **more** delicious, etc.).

Dotchi-ga *yasui* desu-ka?	Which one is *cheaper*?
Kotchi-ga *yasui* desu-yo.	This one is *cheaper*!
Dotchi-ga *oishii* desu-ka?	Which one is *more delicious*?
Sotchi-ga *oishii* desu.	That one is *more delicious*.

3. Dore-ga ichiban *ADJECTIVE* desu-ka? (Review)
If there are three or more choices and you want to ask *which one*, use *dore*.

Dore-ga ichiban omoshiroi desu-ka?	*Which one* is the most interesting?
Kore-ga ichiban omoshiroi desu.	*This one* is the most interesting.

268

4. General counters: *hitotsu ~ too* (Review)

In addition to the new grammar points explained above, this lesson reviews the general counters *hitotsu ~ too* which were introduced in Lesson 66 (Vol. 1). This set of counters is used when the item being counted does not call for a specific counter. *Hitotsu, futatsu, mittsu*, etc., are very useful words to learn since they are used to count many things which do not belong to a specific classification. These general counters can also be used by learners of Japanese to count things (not people) which do have specific counters. You may not always be correct, but Japanese will understand you. You will be able to express quantities of things in Japanese until you learn the specific counters. The question form which corresponds to the general counters is the word *ikutsu*.

IKUTSU?			
1 thing	hitotsu	6 things	muttsu
2 things	futatsu	7 things	nanatsu
3 things	mittsu	8 things	yattsu
4 things	yottsu	9 things	kokonotsu
5 things	itsutsu	10 things	too

In the following examples, notice how particles are not used with the counters when the item is not mentioned. If both the item and the counter are used, then the appropriate particle follows the name of the item.

Orenji-ga arimasu.	There are (some) oranges.
Itsutsu arimasu.	There are *five*.
Orenji-ga *itsutsu* arimasu.	There are *five* oranges.
Meron-o kaimashita.	I bought (some) melons.
Mittsu kaimashita.	I bought *three*.
Meron-o *mittsu* kaimashita.	I bought *three* melons.
Ikutsu arimashita-ka?	How many were there?
Nanatsu arimashita.	There were *seven*.
Gureepufuruutsu-ga *nanatsu* arimashita.	There were *seven* grapefruits.

NOUN -ga	COUNTER	**arimasu.**
NOUN -o	COUNTER	**tabemasu/kaimasu/kudasai, etc.**

You can use the particle *-to* (and) to express the quantity of two or more things.

Meron-ga yottsu-*to* orenji-ga futatsu arimasu.	There are four melons *and* two oranges.

5. Numbers up to 999 (Review)

This lesson also reviews the numbers up to 999. Review the following chart carefully, and then check your knowledge of the numbers by masking the words and saying the numbers. Uncover each word after you have said the number.

TENS AND HUNDREDS			
10	juu	100	hyaku
20	ni-juu	200	ni-hyaku
30	san-juu	300	**san-byaku**
40	**yon**-juu	400	yon-hyaku
50	go-juu	500	go-hyaku
60	roku-juu	600	**rop-pyaku**
70	**nana**-juu	700	nana-hyaku
80	hachi-juu	800	**hap-pyaku**
90	**kyuu**-juu	900	kyuu-hyaku

どっち	which one (of two)
どっちに しましょうか。	Which should I get?
どっちが やすい ですか。	Which one is cheap(er)?
こっち	this one
そっち	that one
あっち	that one over there
ぜんぶで	altogether, in all
ぜんぶで いくら ですか。	How much is it in all?
ぜんぶで ９６０えん です。	Altogether it's 960 yen.
コーヒーは いくら ですか。	How much is the coffee?
いくつ かいましたか。	How many did you buy?
六つ かいました。	I bought six.
カタログ	catalogue
メロン	melon
レタス	lettuce
グレープフルーツ	grapefruit

SECTION HEADINGS IN JAPANESE

Have you noticed something new about your *Irasshai* text? The section headings are in both English and Japanese including *kanji*. As you read and study the Notes for each lesson, read the section headings aloud, too.

Objectives	Mokuhyoo	目標
Vocabulary	Tango	単語
Vocabulary Notes	Tango Nooto	単語ノート
Key Grammar Points	Bunpoo Pointo	文法ポイント
Let's Read	Yomimashoo!	読みましょう
Culture Notes	Karuchaa Nooto	カルチャーノート
Kanji Notes	Kanji Nooto	漢字ノート

INTERACTIVE ACTIVITIES

PART 1

❶ Hitotsu, futatsu, mittsu . . .

Silently review the general counters in the *IKUTSU?* box in the 文法ポイント section. Then have a クラスメート orally test your knowledge of the counters **in mixed order**. Partner A says the 日本ご, and Partner B gives the えいご. Switch roles and repeat. Then Partner A says the えいご, and Partner B gives the 日本ご. Switch roles and repeat.

❷ Ikutsu arimasu-ka?　　📄 & ✏

You and your partner work in a Japanese hamburger shop which specializes in preparing picnic lunches-to-go for families and small groups. The maximum number of hamburgers which can be packed in one "hamburger box" is 10. You have been very busy today taking orders, cooking the burgers, and packing the picnic lunches. Unfortunately, 10 identical "hamburger boxes" (with differing numbers of hamburgers) have become mixed up. You and your partner are checking the number of *hanbaagaa* in each box so that it can be labeled correctly. Partner B checks the boxes and tells Partner A the correct number to write on the top of each box. Each time Partner B answers, he/she should say a different number (using imagination).

Partner A: Ikutsu arimasu-ka?

Partner B: (looking in the box) Nanatsu arimasu. [B tells the number so A can write it on the box top.]

Partner A: Nanatsu . . . Hai, tsugi-no-wa? [A writes the number.]

Partner B: Mittsu arimasu.

PARTNER A writes

Now switch roles and repeat the activity.

PARTNER B writes

PART 2

---

❶ Dotchi-ga furui desu-ka?　　　　📄 & ✏️

Do this activity with a クラスメート. If you have not already prepared the materials as part of your last assignment, please do that now. Each partner prepares a set of nine "cards."

1. Fold a sheet of plain white paper to form nine boxes.
2. Cut or tear the sheet on the creases to form nine "cards."
3. Fold each of the nine cards in half crosswise so that it will stand up (looking like a pup tent) on a flat surface.
4. On one side of each folded card write the word (in *hiragana* or *roomaji*) or make a simple line drawing for items in the box below. If you and your partner are creating the cards at the same time, choose a total of six different items (three different ones for each person). Put each item on three cards.

Now you are ready for the activity. Sit facing your partner. Partner B selects two identical cards from the 18 cards which both partners have made. Partner B puts the two cards in two different locations: close to A, close to B, or not close to A or B. Partner A begins by asking Partner B a question using this pattern with an appropriate adjective:

Dotchi-ga <u>ADJECTIVE</u> desu-ka?

Read this sample exchange aloud with your partner. Be sure to gesture to the item as you mention it. Partner B has selected two cards each with a picture of a car. One card is near A; the other card is not close to A or B.

A: Dotchi-ga furui desu-ka? [A chooses an adjective which can refer to cars.]

B: Sotchi desu. [Using imagination, B speaks and gestures to the card placed near A.]

A: A, kotchi desu-ka? [A asks for confirmation.]

B: Hai, soo desu.

ITEMS:	tokei	terebi	shiidii	kukkii	konpyuutaa
	hon	denwa	manga	keeki	kuruma
ADJECTIVES:	atarashii	takai	hayai	ii	omoshiroi
	furui	yasui	shizuka	oishii	kirei

When you are ready for a greater challenge, instead of always selecting two identical cards, choose three cards at times. Place them near A, near B, and not near A or B. Ask **Dore-ga _____ desu-ka?** You and your partner will use **kore, sore,** and **are** in your exchange. *Ganbatte!*

271

❷ Zenbu-de ikura desu-ka?   📄 & ✎

Do this activity with a クラスメート. Take turns reading the math problems to each other. Look only at your part. Both partners solve the problem and then compare answers. If the answers are the same, continue with the next problem. If the answers are different, do the problem together to determine the correct answer.

PARTNER A reads

1. Orenji-wa hitotsu 120-en desu. Orenji-o kokonotsu kaimasu. Meron-wa hitotsu 210-en desu. Meron-o muttsu kaimasu. Zenbu-de ikura desu-ka?

3. Meron-wa hitotsu 340-en desu. Meron-o yottsu kaimasu. Gureepufuruutsu-wa hitotsu 190-en desu. Gureepufuruutsu-o futatsu kaimasu. Zenbu-de ikura desu-ka?

5. Gureepufuruutsu-wa hitotsu 400-en desu. Gureepufuruutsu-o mittsu kaimasu. Orenji-wa hitotsu 150-en desu. Orenji-o futatsu kaimasu. Zenbu-de ikura desu-ka?

7. グレープフルーツは 一つ ２００えん です。グレープフルーツを 四つ かいます。メロンは 一つ ４２０えん です。メロンを 二つ かいます。 ぜんぶで いくら ですか。

PARTNER B reads

2. Gureepufuruutsu-wa hitotsu 210-en desu. Gureepufuruutsu-o mittsu kaimasu. Meron-wa hitotsu 480-en desu. Meron-o itsutsu kaimasu. Zenbu-de ikura desu-ka?

4. Orenji-wa hitotsu 170-en desu. Orenji-o nanatsu kaimasu. Meron-wa hitotsu 290-en desu. Meron-o futatsu kaimasu. Zenbu-de ikura desu-ka?

6. Meron-wa hitotsu 560-en desu. Meron-o mittsu kaimasu. Gureepufuruutsu-wa hitotsu 330-en desu. Gureepufuruutsu-o futatsu kaimasu. Zenbu-de ikura desu-ka?

8. オレンジは 一つ １５０えん です。オレンジを 六つ かいます。 メロンは 一つ ２８０えん です。メロンを 一つ かいます。ぜんぶで いくら ですか。

If you have time, make up your own problems for your partner using the same pattern as above. Include prices of three digits with the final digit being 0. Do not use prices above 990 yen.

L. 32 電話で 話しましょう

れんしゅう A: Your Wonderful Winter Break

You just came back to school after winter break. Use your imagination and brag about your BIG trip.

れんしゅう B: Which one is more ~?

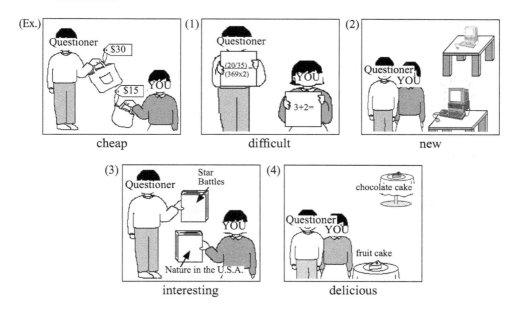

(Ex.)
Questioner
$30
YOU
$15

cheap

(1)
Questioner
(20/35)
(369x2)
YOU
3+2=

difficult

(2)
Questioner
YOU

new

(3)
Questioner
Star Battles
YOU
Nature in the U.S.A.

interesting

(4)
chocolate cake
Questioner
YOU
fruit cake

delicious

れんしゅう C: How much is it altogether?

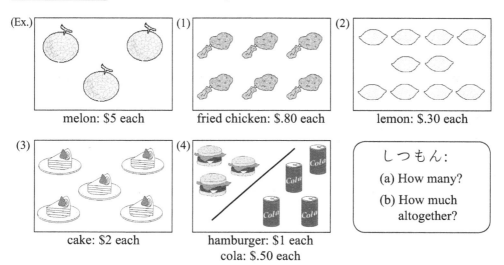

(Ex.)
melon: $5 each

(1)
fried chicken: $.80 each

(2)
lemon: $.30 each

(3)
cake: $2 each

(4)
hamburger: $1 each
cola: $.50 each

しつもん:

(a) How many?

(b) How much altogether?

れんしゅう D: Let's converse!

Dialogue:

A: Welcome!

B: Excuse me. Please give me <u>two melons</u> and <u>three</u> tomatoes.

A: Um, we have <u>big melons</u> and <u>small ones</u>. Which would you like?

B: Ah, please give me the <u>big</u> ones.

A: That will be <u>3,500 yen</u> altogether. Thank you very much.

Sample Dialogue:

A: いらっしゃいませ。

B: すみません。<u>メロン</u>を<u>二つ</u>と <u>トマト</u>を<u>三つ</u>ください。

A: えっと、<u>大きいメロン</u>と<u>小さいメロン</u>がありますけど、 どっちがいいですか。

B: じゃ、<u>大きいメロン</u>をください。

A: ぜんぶで <u>3,500えん</u>です。 ありがとうございました。

Sample Dialogue:

A: Irasshaimase.

B: Sumimasen. <u>Meron</u>-o <u>futatsu</u>-to <u>tomato</u>-o <u>mittsu</u> kudasai.

A: Etto, <u>ookii meron</u>-to <u>chiisai meron</u>-ga arimasu-kedo, dotchi-ga ii desu-ka?

B: Jaa, <u>ookii meron</u>-o kudasai.

A: Zenbu-de <u>3,500-en</u> desu. Arigatoo gozaimashita.

Suggested items

ケーキ　ベーグル (bagel)　ドーナッツ

LESSON 33
Nearby Locations

OBJECTIVES 目標

At the end of this lesson you will be able to:
- ☑ Ask and state the location of nearby places
- ☑ Count thin, flat objects using the counter *-mai*

In this lesson you will also have an opportunity to review writing all of the *kanji* which have been introduced so far.

VOCABULARY 単語

Words

-mai	*counter for thin, flat objects*
chikaku	vicinity
tonari	(the place) next to, adjoining

Phrases and expressions

kono chikaku-ni	around here, in this vicinity

Other words and expressions you will hear in this lesson

suuji	number

VOCABULARY NOTES 単語ノート

Tonari

The word *tonari*, which is a noun in Japanese, means (*the place*) *next to* or *adjoining*. In English it is usually translated as *next to* or *next door to*. The word *tonari* frequently occurs with the particle *-ni* and the verb *arimasu* as in the examples below.

Ginkoo-wa hoteru-no *tonari-ni* arimasu.	There's a bank *next to* the hotel.
Toshokan-wa doko-ni arimasu-ka?	Where's the library?
Yuubinkyoku-no *tonari-ni* arimasu.	It's *next door to* the post office.

The word *tonari* can be used in the same way as *mae, ushiro, migi, hidari,* and other spatial relationship words.

KEY GRAMMAR POINTS 文法ポイント

1. -mai

This lesson introduces the counter *-mai* which is used to count thin, flat objects such as sheets of paper, stamps, CD's, hamburger patties, photographs, tickets, T-shirts, and cookies. The question form is *nan-mai*. The counter *-mai* appears in the same patterns as the general counters *hitotsu ~ too*. Notice that the particle is used only if the item is specified.

Kami-wa *nan-mai* arimasu-ka?	*How many* sheets of paper are there?
Ni-mai arimasu.	There are *two*.
Kitte-o *go-mai* kudasai.	Please give me *five* stamps.

NAN-MAI?					
1	ichi-mai	5	go-mai	9	kyuu-mai
2	ni-mai	6	roku-mai	10	juu-mai
3	san-mai	7	nana-mai	11	juu-ichi-mai
4	yon-mai	8	hachi-mai	12	juu-ni-mai

275

2. Kono chikaku-ni ___-ga arimasu.

The noun *chikaku* means *vicinity*. The phrase *kono chikaku-ni* may be translated in many ways.

Kono *chikaku-ni* ginkoo-ga arimasu-ka?

Is there a bank *in this vicinity*?
Is there a bank *near here*?
Is there a bank *around here*?
Is there a bank *close by*?

CULTURE NOTES	カルチャーノート

Addressing an envelope Japanese style

Many of us grow up thinking that there is only one correct way of doing things. Take for example the very simple task of addressing an envelope. Although Japanese do use envelopes similar to the ones you are used to with the flap on the long side, the traditional Japanese envelope has the flap on the end. Since Japanese is traditionally written from top to bottom and right to left, the end is actually the top! Look at the sample illustrations below. Notice the seven boxes for the postal code at the top of the envelope. Each locale has a seven-digit *yuubinbangoo* written as three digits, dash, four digits, for example, 123-4567. The stamp is placed in the upper left corner of the envelope.

The address is written directly below the *yuubinbangoo* boxes vertically from right to left. Whereas we are used to writing the person's name first followed by the street number, street name, city, state or province, Japanese use the opposite order. They begin by writing the prefecture name followed by the city, the district within the city, the block number within the district, and the house number within the block. The person's name comes at the very end of the sequence and is written approximately along the center vertical line in larger characters so that it stands out. The person's surname comes first followed by the given name. The person's title comes at the very end. Most letters are addressed using the universal honorific title of 様 (*sama*).

The sender's name and address are written on the back of the envelope on the lower left-hand side. Japanese envelopes even include boxes for the sender's zip code just so there is no possibility of any confusion or oversight regarding this important tracking information.

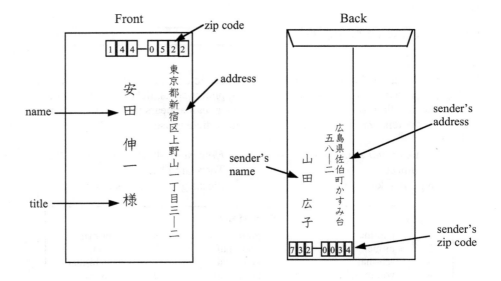

まい	counter for thin, flat objects
きっては 何まい ありますか。	How many stamps are there?
７０えん きってを 四まい ください。	Please give me four ¥70 stamps.
ちかく	vicinity
となり	(the place) next to, adjoining
この ちかくに としょかんが ありますか。	Is there a library near here?
としょかんは この ちかくに ありません。	There isn't a library near here.
この ちかくに ぎんこうが ありますか。	Is there a bank around here?
ゆうびんきょくの となりに あります。	There's one next to the post office.
えきは ここから とおい です。	The station is far from here.
アメリカまで おねがいします。	I'd like to send this to the U.S.
中に 何が はいっていますか。	What's inside?
ようふくと ビデオゲームが はいって います。	Some clothes and a video game are inside.
すうじ	number

INTERACTIVE ACTIVITIES

PART 1

❶ **Roku-mai kaimashita-ka?** 📄 & ✏

The object of this pair guessing game is to find the correct answers by asking the fewest questions. Each question is worth one point. The winner is the partner with the lower score. Partner A begins by thinking of a specific number of a certain thin, flat object (imagination) that he/she bought yesterday and writes it down as the example below either in *roomaji* or *kana*. Partner A does not show Partner B the sentence. Partner B then asks yes-no questions to determine what item Partner A bought and how many of that item were bought. Change roles and repeat the activity. Read the example aloud before you begin.

EXAMPLE: Kinoo CD-o san-mai kaimashita. [Partner A writes down the sentence.]
きのう CD を ３まい かいました。

B: Kami-o kaimashita-ka? [Partner B begins asking yes-no questions to determine the object.]
A: Iie, kami-wa kaimasen deshita.
B: Kukkii-o kaimashita-ka?
A: Iie, kukkii-wa kaimasen deshita.
B: CD-o kaimashita-ka?
A: Hai, kaimashita.
B: Roku-mai kaimashita-ka? [Partner B begins asking yes-no questions to determine the number of CD's.]
A: Iie.
B: Ichi-mai kaimashita-ka?
A: Iie.
B: San-mai kaimashita-ka?
A: Hai, san-mai kaimashita. [Partner B asked a total of six questions so Partner B's score is six.]

NAN-MAI?			
かみ	kami [paper]	チケット	chiketto [ticket]
きって	kitte [stamp]	クッキー	kukkii [cookie]
CD	shiidii [CD]	したじき	shitajiki [underlay for writing]
Tシャツ	tiishatsu [T-shirt]	ポスター	posutaa [poster]

❷ Kaimono-ni ikimashita-ka?   📄 & ✏️

This pair activity provides an opportunity to ask and answer questions about an imaginary shopping trip. With your partner try to keep the conversation going for at least four minutes with no significant pauses. Imagine that Partner A has completed a successful shopping trip during which he/she bought a number of different items, including one which in Japanese is counted with the counter *-mai*. Partner B asks questions such as the ones given below but is not limited to these. As Partner B listens to Partner A's answers, he/she will think of additional questions to ask. Change partners and repeat the activity several times. Before you start, answer the questions about your shopping trip in the box below and write them down.

SOME POSSIBLE QUESTIONS

    Nan-yoobi-ni ikimashita-ka?
    Dare-to ikimashita-ka?
    Nani-o kaimashita-ka?
    _____-wa ikura deshita-ka?
    Nan-mai kaimashita-ka?
    Dore-ga ichiban takakatta-desu-ka? [which of three or more items]
    Zenbu-de ikura deshita-ka?
    _____-wa nani-iro desu-ka?
    _____-wa ookii/chiisai/hayai/kirei/etc. desu-ka?
    _____-wa doko-de kaimashita-ka?

> 　　　　　私は かいもの に 行きました。
> 1. 何よう日？
> 2. だれと？
> 3. 何を かいましたか。(4 items)　いくら？　どこで？
> 4. ぜんぶで いくら？

PART 2

---

❶ Dialogue   📄 & ✏️

With a クラスメート memorize the dialogue following the normal procedure. Make sure that you understand the meaning of the dialogue before you begin practicing. For props you will need a piece of paper and a pen/pencil. After you have memorized the dialogue, perform for another pair or for the class.

A and B work in the same office. A is a new employee and is not familiar with the area around the office building. A needs to go to the post office during lunch and asks B for directions.

A: Sumimasen, kono chikaku-ni yuubinkyoku-ga arimasu-ka?
B: (thinks) Ee, arimasu-yo. Ginkoo-no tonari-ni arimasu.
A: (confused) Ginkoo-no tonari desu-ka? Ginkoo-wa doko desu-ka?
B: (gets a piece of paper and pen/pencil) Ja, chizu-o kakimashoo.
A: Aa, sumimasen. (watches B draw the map)
B: (drawing) Eeto . . . Ima koko desu. Koko-ga eki de*, koko-ga ginkoo desu.
A: (nodding) Aa, soo desu-ka?
B: (finishes the map by drawing the 〒 symbol on the post office) Yuubinkyoku-wa ginkoo-no tonari-ni arimasu.
A: (understands and nods) Aa, wakarimashita. Doomo. (takes map)

The linking (-te*) form of *desu* is *de*.

If you prefer, use the following dialogue for more practice reading Japanese.

278

A: すみません。 この ちかくに ゆうびんきょくが ありますか。

B: (thinks) ええ、 ありますよ。 ぎんこうの となりに あります。

A: (confused) ぎんこうの となり ですか。 ぎんこうは どこ ですか。

B: (gets a piece of paper and pen/pencil) じゃ、 ちずを かきましょう。

A: ああ、 すみません。 (watches B draw the map)

B: (drawing) ええと、 今 ここです。 ここが えきで、 ここが ぎんこう
です。

A: (nodding) ああ、 そう ですか。

B: (finishes the map by drawing the 〒 symbol on the post office) ゆうびんきょくは
ぎんこうの となりに あります。

A: (understands and nods) ああ、 わかりました。 どうも。 (takes map)

❷ **Kono chikaku-ni yuubinkyoku-ga arimasu-ka?**

Do this activity with a クラスメート. Both partners should prepare their own "maps" at
the same time without showing the other person. Select and write the names of six places
in the inner circle (= CHIKAKU). Then write the names of the six remaining places in
the outer circle (= TOOI). Partner A goes first. By asking Partner B questions, determine
as quickly as possible which six places are nearby and which six are far away. Record the
information by writing each place name in either the inner or outer circle. Compare your
answers when you have finished.

SAMPLE EXCHANGE
A: Kono chikaku-ni *yuubinkyoku*-ga arimasu-ka?
B: Ee, arimasu-yo. Asoko desu. (pointing) [B writes *yuubinkyoku* in the inner circle.]
A: Kono chikaku-ni *niku-ya*-ga arimasu-ka?
B: Iie, *niku-ya*-wa kono chikaku-ni arimasen-yo. *Niku-ya*-wa koko-kara tooi desu.
[B writes *niku-ya* in the outer circle.]

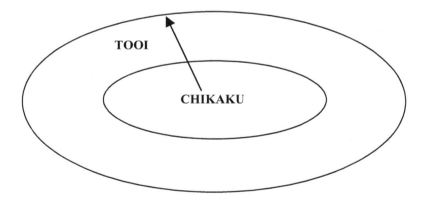

PLACES			
kutsu-ya	hoteru	pan-ya	yuubinkyoku
hon-ya	ginkoo	depaato	kamera-ya
suupaa	niku-ya	tokei-ya	toshokan

279

L. 33 電話で 話しましょう

れんしゅう A: Is there a ~ near here?

(1) fish market   (2) post office   (3) mailbox   (4) bank
(5) bakery   (6) supermarket   (7) shoe store   (8) meat shop

> しつもん: (a) Is there a ~ near here?   (b) Where is it?

JAPAN PARK	bookstore		Supermarket Irasshai University
(fish)		high school	department store
	AMERICA PARK	+	elementary school
library			
	(bread)		CHINA PARK (bread) (shoes)
¥ Irasshai Hotel	(train)		(post office)

280

れんしゅう B: How many ~ are there?

(1)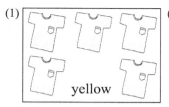
yellow

(2)

(3)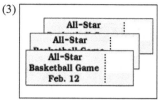

(4)

(5)

れんしゅう C: Catalog Order

Dialogue:

A: What's that?

B: It's a JT Penny's catalog.

A: Are you going to buy something?

B: Yes, I want these <u>sweaters</u>.

A: <u>How many</u> are you going to buy?

B: <u>Two</u>.

A: What color do you want?

B: I want a <u>red</u> one and a <u>black</u> one.

Sample Dialogue:

A: それは何ですか。

B: JT Penny のカタログです。

A: へえ、何かかいますか。

B: はい、この<u>セーター</u>がほしいです。

A: <u>何まい</u>かいますか。

B: <u>二まい</u>かいます。

A: へえ、何いろのがほしいですか。

B: <u>あかいの</u>と<u>くろいの</u>がほしいです。

Sample Dialogue:

A: Sore-wa nan desu-ka?

B: JT Penny-no katarogu desu.

A: Hee, nani-ka kaimasu-ka?

B: Hai, kono <u>seetaa</u>-ga hoshii desu.

A: <u>Nan-mai</u> kaimasu-ka?

B: <u>Ni-mai</u> kaimasu.

A: Hee, nani-iro-no-ga hoshii desu-ka?

B: <u>Akai</u>-no-to <u>kuroi</u>-no-ga hoshii desu.

LESSON 34
More Spatial Relationships

OBJECTIVES   目標

At the end of this lesson you will be able to:

☑   Ask and state the numeric order of objects
☑   Write the *kanji*: 学 and 校

VOCABULARY   単語

Words
    #-ban-me   the #th (numeric order)

Phrases and expressions
    Ichiban ue-no ____ desu.   It's the ____ on the very top.
    Sorekara?   Anything else?

Other words and expressions you will hear in this lesson
    600-en-no o-kaeshi desu.   600 yen is your change.
    pekopeko   very hungry
    poteto chippu   potato chips

KEY GRAMMAR POINTS   文法ポイント

1. #-ban-me

Since the beginning of *Irasshai* you have been using *ichi-ban, ni-ban, san-ban*, etc. In
this lesson you will learn how, by adding the suffix *-me* (cf. *jikan-me*), you can create
ordinal numbers to express the numeric order of objects. Study these examples carefully.

    Nan-ban-me desu-ka?   *Which number* is it (in the series)?
    Roku-ban-me desu.   It's the *sixth* one (in a line or series).

The *n* in *ban-me* is pronounced like an *m*.

NAN-BAN-ME?			
ichi-ban-me	first	roku-ban-me	sixth
ni-ban-me	second	nana-ban-me	seventh
san-ban-me	third	hachi-ban-me	eighth
yon-ban-me	fourth	kyuu-ban-me	ninth
go-ban-me	fifth	juu-ban-me	tenth

2. Migi-kara #-ban-me desu.

You can express a range of spatial relationships by using the ordinal numbers such as
ichi-ban-me, ni-ban-me, and *san-ban-me* with words such as *migi, hidari, ue, shita, mae,*
and *ushiro*. Study these examples carefully.

    Shita-kara san-ban-me desu.   It's *the third one from the bottom.*
    Hidari-kara go-ban-me-no doonattsu-o   Please give me two of the doughnuts
      futatsu kudasai.   that are *fifth from the left.*
    Ue-kara ni-ban-me-no doonattsu-o   Please give me four of the doughnuts
      yottsu kudasai.   that are *second from the top.*

282

一ばんめ	the first
二ばんめ です。	It's the second one.
みぎから 三ばんめ です。	It's the third one from the right.
うえから 五ばんめの ドーナッツを 二つ ください。	Please give me two of the doughnuts that are fifth from the top.
一ばん うえの ドーナッツ です。	It's the doughnut on the very top.
一ばん ひだり ですか。	Is it on the far left?
あの ピンクの ドーナッツを ください。	Please give me that pink doughnut.
それから？	Anything else?
６００えんの おかえし です。	¥600 is your change.
おなかが すきました・すいた	I am hungry.
ぺこぺこ	very hungry
ポテトチップ	potato chips

Japanese vending machines *Nihon-no jidoo hanbaiki* (日本の自動販売機)
For Westerners visiting Japan for the first time, Japan appears to be the land of vending machines. Everywhere you look there are clusters of vending machines selling everything under the sun. Japanese value convenience and want to have their needs met wherever they are. Vending machines are the perfect answer to a busy consumer's dream.

These colorful, high-tech machines, which almost always operate flawlessly, can be found in predictable places such as train stations and along busy streets. They can also be found, however, in some unexpected places such as along a walking path between rice fields or in residential areas.

As for the types of consumer products available from Japanese vending machines, there are the expected products such as hot and cold beverages, snacks, and cigarettes. There is also a range of items that one might not commonly associate with vending machines. These include things such as clothing, flowers, ready-to-eat noodles, cooked rice, and magazines.

INTERACTIVE ACTIVITIES

PART 1

❶ **Vocabulary review**
Silently review the following vocabulary. Then have a クラスメート orally test your knowledge of them. Your partner says the えいご, and you give the 日本ご. Switch and test your partner.

1. まえ	front	11. 中	in, inside
2. まえから	from the front	12. うえから	from the top
3. うしろ	back, behind	13. ひだりに	to/on the left
4. した	bottom	14. うしろから	from the back
5. みぎ	right	15. 一ばん ひだり	the far left
6. ひだり	left	16. 一ばん みぎ	the far right
7. みぎに	to/on the right	17. 一ばん うえ	the very top
8. ひだりから	from the left	18. 一ばん した	the very bottom
9. したから	from the bottom	19. みぎから	from the right
10. うえ	the top	20. うしろに	in the back

❷ **Migi-kara ni-ban-me-no doonattsu-o mittsu kudasai.** 📄 & ✏️

Do this activity with a クラスメート. Partner A works as a salesperson in a doughnut shop. Partner B is buying <u>30 doughnuts</u> and has decided on <u>six kinds</u> of doughnuts shown below in the rack behind the salesperson. They are not labeled so Partner B must tell the salesperson which ones <u>and</u> how many of each. Partner B buys different numbers of the different kinds (but not more than nine of any one kind). Read the sample exchange with your partner before you begin. Both partners record the requested number of doughnuts.

A: O-kimari desu-ka?
B: Migi-kara ni-ban-me-no doonattsu-o mittsu kudasai.
A: Ni-ban-me-no doonattsu desu-ka?
B: Hai, sore desu.
A: Sorekara?

GENERAL COUNTERS	
hitotsu	muttsu
futatsu	nanatsu
mittsu	yattsu
yottsu	kokonotsu
itsutsu	too

								3	

Compare your answers when you have finished. Change roles and repeat the activity.

PART 2

❶ **Kakimashoo!** ✏️

With a partner check each other's work for Assignment #3 of Part 1.

❷ **Migi-kara ni-ban-me-no doonattsu-o mittsu kudasai.** 📄 & ✏️

Repeat Activity ❷ of Part 1. Try adding some of the following phrases and sentences. Use your imagination.

1. 一ばん ひだり　　　　　　　　the far left
2. 一ばん みぎ　　　　　　　　　the far right
3. 一ばん みぎの ドーナッツ　　　the doughnut(s) on the far right
4. 一ばん ひだりの ドーナッツ　　the doughnut(s) on the far left
5. 何の ドーナッツ ですか。　　　What kind of doughnut is it?
6. オレンジの ドーナッツ　　　　the orange doughnut
7. レモンの ドーナッツ　　　　　the lemon doughnut
8. ピンクの ドーナッツ　　　　　the pink doughnut
9. チョコレートの ドーナッツ　　the chocolate doughnut
10. クリームの ドーナッツ　　　　the cream doughnut

L. 34 電話で 話しましょう

れんしゅう A: Which ones are the ~ cookies?

(Ex.) oatmeal (1) chocolate (2) cinnamon (3) chocolate chip (4) sugar (5) peanut butter

chocolate chip	oatmeal	sugar	peanut butter	chocolate	cinnamon

れんしゅう B: Buying Sushi

You are in Japan at a fast-food sushi shop. You want to buy some sushi, but you cannot read the kanji on the labels. Tell the salesperson which ones you want.

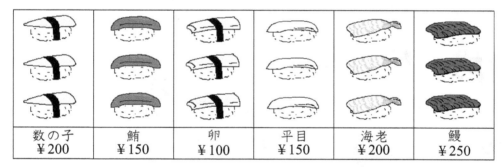

数の子 ¥200	鮪 ¥150	卵 ¥100	平目 ¥150	海老 ¥200	鰻 ¥250

Dialogue:

A: Welcome! What would you like?
B: Please give me the <u>second</u> sushi <u>from the right.</u>
A: How many?
B: <u>Three</u>, please.
A: OK, that'll be <u>600</u> yen altogether.

Sample Dialogue:

A: いらっしゃいませ。おきまりですか。
B: みぎから二ばんめのすしをください。
A: いくつですか。
B: 三つ、おねがいします。
A: はい、ぜんぶで600えんです。

Sample Dialogue:

A: Irasshaimase. O-kimari desu-ka?
B: <u>Migi-kara ni-ban-me</u>-no sushi-o kudasai.
A: Ikutsu desu-ka?
B: <u>Mittsu</u>, o-negai-shimasu.
A: Hai, zenbu-de <u>600</u>-en desu.

れんしゅう B: Who is your friend?

This is a scene at a party. Decide which person your friend is. Then, giving the three hints below, describe your friend, and let your classmates figure out which person it is.

Hints: (1) male/female; (2) S/he is ~ing; and (3) His/her sweater is [color].

LESSON 35
Numbers up to 100,000

OBJECTIVES　　　　　　　　　　　　　　　　　　　　目標

At the end of this lesson you will be able to:
- ☑ Use the numbers up to 100,000
- ☑ Write the *kanji*: 中 and 高

VOCABULARY　　　　　　　　　　　　　　　　　　　単語

Words

-man	10,000
miseru (misemasu/misete)	show
morau (moraimasu/moratte)	receive, get

Phrases and expressions

_____-kara moraimashita.	I got it from _____.

Other words and expressions you will hear in this lesson

iyaringu	earring(s)
toosutaa	toaster

KEY GRAMMAR POINTS　　　　　　　　　　文法ポイント

1. -man

You have already learned how to express tens (*juu*), hundreds (*hyaku*), and thousands (*sen*) in Japanese. In this lesson you will learn how to say the numbers from 10,000 through 100,000. For speakers of English, numbers in this range are expressed as thousands. For the Japanese, however, the highest unit in these numbers is 10,000 or *man*. You will find it easy to read these larger numbers if you count in four digits from the right and mentally insert a comma. Then begin reading the number from the left and when you get to the mental comma, say *man*. Read these numbers aloud.

10,000	→	think:	1,0000	→	read as: ichi-man
12,000	→	think:	1,2000	→	read as: ichi-man ni-sen
15,000	→	think:	1,5000	→	read as: ichi-man go-sen
18,300	→	think:	1,8300	→	read as: ichi-man has-sen san-byaku
27,400	→	think:	2,7400	→	read as: ni-man nana-sen yon-hyaku
59,130	→	think:	5,9130	→	read as: go-man kyuu-sen hyaku san-juu
80,006	→	think:	8,0006	→	read as: hachi-man roku
99,011	→	think:	9,0011	→	read as: kyuu-man juu-ichi
103,205	→	think:	10,3205	→	read as: juu-man san-zen ni-hyaku go

TEN THOUSANDS (MAN)			
10,000	ichi-man	60,000	roku-man
20,000	ni-man	70,000	nana-man
30,000	san-man	80,000	hachi-man
40,000	yon-man	90,000	kyuu-man
50,000	go-man	100,000	juu-man

2. #-nen-mae

As you have learned, *mae* means *front* and can be used in describing locations.

Ginkoo-no *mae*-ni posuto-ga arimasu.　　There's a mailbox in *front* of the bank.

Mae-kara san-ban-me desu.　　It's the third one from the *front*.

287

Mae can also be used in time expressions.

    Go-nen-mae-ni kore-o moraimashita.   I received this *five years ago.*
    Ni-nen-mae-no tanjoobi-ni moraimashita.   I got it for my birthday *two years ago.*

3. PLAIN FORM OF VERB + -n desu

In the video lesson, you are introduced to verb constructions consisting of the plain form of the verb plus *-n desu*. As you continue your study of Japanese, you will learn how to use this common form. Look at these examples. The information in brackets is the context for the sentences with *-n desu.*

Nani-o *kau-n desu*-ka?   [I see you're buying something.] What are you buying?
Doko-ka, *iku-n desu*-ka?   [I see you're packing.] Are you going somewhere?
Tabenai-n desu-ka?   [I see you didn't order any food.] Aren't you eating?

The plain form of the verb plus *-n desu*, which is just as formal as the *-masu* form, is used by Japanese when they already "see" the situation, but need to fill in some missing information. Can you tell the *-masu* form counterparts to these *-n desu* forms?

-N DESU		
1. kau-n desu	5. katsu-n desu	9. konai-n desu
2. ikanai-n desu	6. suru-n desu	10. miru-n desu
3. yomu-n desu	7. neru-n desu	11. okiru-n desu
4. taberu-n desu	8. utawanai-n desu	12. kaku-n desu

Check your own answers by finding the verbs in Lesson 28 in the box in the *Bunpoo Pointo* section.

YOMIMASHOO!   読みましょう

まん	10,000
見せる・見せます・見せて	show
一ばん みぎの ネックレスを 見せて ください。	Please show me the necklace on the far right.
もらう・もらいます・もらって	receive, get
たんじょう日に ネクタイを もらいました。	I got a necktie on my birthday.
ははから もらいました。	I got it from my mother.
五年まえに	five years ago
きょ年の たんじょう日に	on my birthday last year
イヤリング	earring(s)
トースター	toaster

CULTURE NOTES   カルチャーノート

O-chuugen and *o-seibo* お中元とお歳暮

The giving of gifts is a significant aspect of Japanese culture, and the Japanese take it very seriously. There are two major gift-giving seasons in Japan; *o-chuugen* in July or August (depending on where one lives in Japan) and *o-seibo* in December.

It is customary to send gifts during these two seasons to people who you are indebted to such as important customers, business partners, bosses, relatives, and friends. Popular items for *o-chuugen* and *o-seibo* are gourmet food, beer, coffee, detergent and soap sets or gift certificates. Gift prices range from $30 to $300, and the importance of the recipient is usually reflected in the price of the gift. Department stores reserve special areas or even whole floors to display hundreds of different gift items, and they are arranged by price so customers can easily find a gift within their price range. Department stores also have extra staff members at these times of the year to assist customers choose appropriate gifts. After the gifts are chosen, they are neatly wrapped and delivered.

INTERACTIVE ACTIVITIES

PART 1

❶ San-juu-man   📄 & ✏️

With a クラスメート practice reading, listening to, and writing five- and six-digit numbers in 日本ご. Before beginning, write down different numbers without showing your partner. Now Partner A reads a number, and Partner B writes it. Check for accuracy, and then change roles and repeat.

❷ Yomimashoo!

In this pair reading activity, Partner A looks only at the Japanese side. Partner B looks at both columns while Partner A reads each line. Partner B responds with *Hai, yoku dekimashita* or with *Chotto chigaimasu. Moo ichido yonde kudasai.* After Partner A has read all of the lines, change roles and repeat.

一年	ichi-nen
一年まえに	ichi-nen-mae-ni
五年まえに 行きました。	Go-nen-mae-ni ikimashita.
五年まえに この えいがを 見ました。	Go-nen-mae-ni kono eiga-o mimashita.
八年まえに この本を よみました。	Hachi-nen-mae-ni kono hon-o yomimashita.
八年まえに この本を かいました。	Hachi-nen-mae-ni kono hon-o kaimashita.
十年まえに その本を かいました。	Juu-nen-mae-ni sono hon-o kaimashita.
十年まえに その小さい本を かいました。	Juu-nen-mae-ni sono chiisai hon-o kaimashita.

PART 2

❶ Ueda-san-wa doyoobi-ni Itoo-san-kara neko-o moraimashita.   📄 & ✏️

In this pair activity take turns asking and answering questions to exchange the information you and your partner need to complete your charts. Look only at your own chart. After you have finished, compare the charts.

SAMPLE QUESTIONS AND ANSWERS

Ueda-san-wa **nani-o** moraimashita-ka?   **Neko-o** moraimashita.
Ueda-san-wa **dare-kara** neko-o moraimashita-ka?   **Itoo-san-kara** moraimashita.
Ueda-san-wa **itsu** neko-o moraimashita-ka?   **Doyoobi-ni** moraimashita.

PARTNER A

DARE?	ITSU?	DARE-KARA?	NANI?
Tanaka-san		Honda-san	
Nakagawa-san			
Yamamoto-san	tanjoobi	Yamada-san	bideo-geemu
Kawata-san			o-kane
Nakayama-san	natsu-yasumi		jitensha
Honda-san			
Yamakawa-san	moku-yoobi	Tanaka-san	CD
Takada-san		otoosan	
Yamada-san	shichi-gatsu	Yamakawa-san	

SAMPLE QUESTIONS AND ANSWERS

Ueda-san-wa **nani-o** moraimashita-ka?   **Neko-o** moraimashita.

Ueda-san-wa **dare-kara** neko-o moraimashita-ka?   **Itoo-san-kara** moraimashita.

Ueda-san-wa **itsu** neko-o moraimashita-ka?   **Doyoobi-ni** moraimashita.

PARTNER B

DARE?	ITSU?	DARE-KARA?	NANI?
Tanaka-san	senshuu		nekkuresu
Nakagawa-san	getsu-yoobi	Nakayama-san	keeki
Yamamoto-san			
Kawata-san	suiyoobi	Takada-san	
Nakayama-san		Yamamoto-san	
Honda-san	shi-gatsu	Nakagawa-san	neko
Yamakawa-san			
Takada-san	O-shoogatsu		otoshidama
Yamada-san			inu

❷ **Chigaimasu. Motto ookii desu.**   📄 & ✏️

Play this number guessing game with a クラスメート. Partner A writes down a five- or six-digit number (the last two digits are zeros) and does <u>not show</u> Partner B. Partner B then tries to guess what the number is. After each guess, Partner A gives Partner B a hint by responding with *Chigaimasu. Motto ookii/chiisai desu.* Change roles and repeat.

THE NUMBERS 100 ~ 9,000			
100	hyaku	1,000	sen
200	ni-hyaku	2,000	ni-sen
300	**san-byaku**	3,000	**san-zen**
400	yon-hyaku	4,000	yon-sen
500	go-hyaku	5,000	go-sen
600	**rop-pyaku**	6,000	roku-sen
700	nana-hyaku	7,000	nana-sen
800	**hap-pyaku**	8,000	has-**sen**
900	kyuu-hyaku	9,000	kyuu-sen

Refer to the TEN THOUSANDS box in the 文法ポイント section of this lesson if you need any of the forms with -*man*.

L. 35 電話で 話しましょう

れんしゅう A: Numbers

(1) 12,000　　(2) 54,300　　(3) 78,200　　(4) 36,950

(5) 49,860　　(6) 95,120　　(7) 23,497　　(8) 67,518

れんしゅう B: What did they receive from each other?

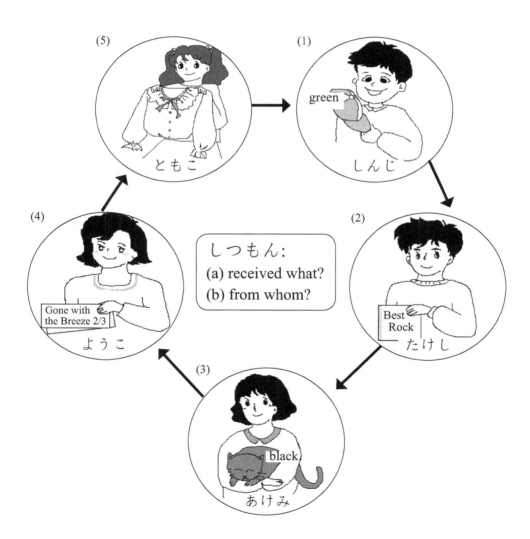

しつもん:
(a) received what?
(b) from whom?

れんしゅう C: John's Memories

(1) John's family — 13 yrs. ago

(2) 8 yrs. ago

(3) Father / Made a bookshelf — 4 yrs. ago

(4) Burger Shop — 3 yrs. ago

(5) Japanese car — 1 yr. ago

れんしゅう D: How many ~?

Ask how many of the following are in this room.
(1) (pieces of) paper   (2) chairs   (3) cookies   (4) people

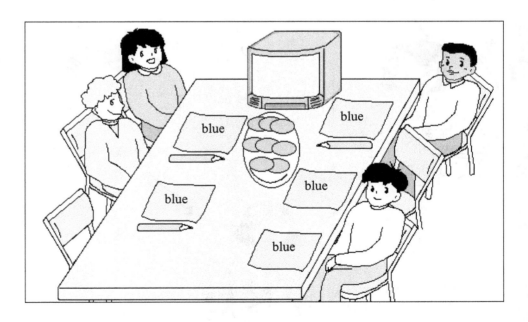

LESSON 36
Expressing Needs

OBJECTIVES   目標

At the end of this lesson you will be able to:

- ☑ Count long, cylindrical objects using the counter *-hon*
- ☑ Express needs
- ☑ Write the *kanji*: 年

VOCABULARY   単語

Words

iru (irimasu)	need (verb)
kudamono	fruit
kudamono-ya	fruit store
#-hon, #-bon, #-pon	*counter for long, cylindrical objects*

Phrases and expressions

hoka-ni	anything else

Other words and expressions you will hear in this lesson

mayoneezu	mayonnaise
masshuruumu	mushroom(s)
ninjin	carrot

KEY GRAMMAR POINTS   文法ポイント

1. #-hon, #-bon, #-pon 本

This lesson introduces the counter *-hon* (and its variants *-bon* and *-pon*) which is used to count long, cylindrical objects such as pencils, pens, bottles, carrots, bananas, trees, poles, arms, and legs. The question form is *nan-bon*. The counter *-hon* appears in the same patterns as the general counters *hitotsu ~ too*. Notice that the particle is used only if the item is specified.

Banana-o *ni-hon* kudasai.	Please give me *two* bananas.
Ni-hon kudasai.	Please give me *two* (long, cylindrical objects).
Enpitsu-ga *rop-pon* arimasu.	There are *six* pencils.
Rop-pon arimasu.	There are *six* (long, cylindrical objects).
Zenbu-de ninjin-o *juu-ip-pon* kaimashita.	I bought *11* carrots in all.
Pen-o *nan-bon* kaimasu-ka?	*How many* pens should we buy?

NAN-BON?							
1	ip-pon	4	yon-hon	7	nana-hon	10	jup-pon
2	ni-hon	5	go-hon	8	hap-pon	11	juu-ip-pon
3	san-bon	6	rop-pon	9	kyuu-hon	12	juu-ni-hon

2. Iru (irimasu)

The verb *iru* (*irimasu*) is usually expressed in English as *need* or *be necessary*. Study the following examples.

Hamu-ga *irimasu*.	I *need* (some) ham.
Sakana-mo *irimasu*-ka?	Do we *need* fish, too?
Iie, *irimasen*.	No, I *don't* (*need* them).
Hoka-ni nani-ga *irimasu*-ka?	What else do we *need?*

293

Pan-ga *irimasu*-ne. We *need* bread, don't we?

The plain form of both *irimasu* (need) and *imasu* (be, be located) is *iru*.

いる・いります	need (verb)
ハムが いります。	I need (some) ham.
さかなも いりますか。	Do we need fish, too?
ほかに 何が いりますか。	What else do we need?
いくつ いりますか。	How many do we need?
くだもの	fruit
くだものや	fruit store
本 (ほん、ぼん、ぽん)	*counter for long, cylindrical objects*
ぜんぶで にんじんを 十一本	I bought 11 carrots in all.
かいました。	
スパゲティーと サラダと デザートを	I'll make spaghetti, salad, and
つくります。	dessert.
日本人は おみやげに くだものを	Japanese people buy fruit as gifts.
かいます。	
マヨネーズ	mayonnaise
マッシュルーム	mushroom(s)
にんじん	carrot

CULTURE NOTES カルチャーノート

Fruit as a gift

Gift giving is an extremely important aspect of Japanese culture. There are many formal and informal occasions on which Japanese are expected to give gifts. For example, it is generally considered polite to take a gift when visiting another person's home. On such an occasion one might take confections or fruit as a gift.

Fruits selected for gifts are of exceptionally high quality and are generally quite expensive. While fruit in Japan is generally more expensive than what one would buy in the U.S., the fruits that are intended as gifts are shockingly expensive for first-time visitors to Japan. Melons, for example, might cost anywhere from $20 to $100 each. A box with a dozen strawberries might cost around $35. These are obviously not intended to be casually bought and eaten at home. To the well-trained eye of a sophisticated Japanese shopper, these fruits are very different from the average melon or strawberries. These have been raised, selected, and packaged with perfection as the goal. The shape of each of the strawberries, for example, is completely regular. The color of the strawberries and the way they are arranged in the box is absolutely perfect. There is not even the slightest evidence of a bruise on the fruit. As you can see, there is a very good reason why certain fruits in Japan are sold at high prices. Japanese consumers are willing to pay a very high price when they are assured that the product is of the highest quality.

INTERACTIVE ACTIVITIES

PART 1

❶ Rop-pon kaimashita-ka? 📄 & ✏️

The object of this pair guessing game is to find the correct answers by asking the fewest questions. Each question is worth one point. The winner is the partner with the lower score. Partner A begins by thinking of a specific number of a certain long, cylindrical object (imagination) that he/she bought yesterday and writes it down as the example below either in *roomaji* or *kana*. Partner A does not show Partner B the sentence. Partner B then asks yes-no questions to determine what item Partner A bought and how many of that item were bought. Change roles and repeat the activity. Read the example with your partner before you begin.

EXAMPLE: Kinoo banana-o san-bon kaimashita. [Partner A writes down the sentence.]
きのう バナナ を３本 かいました。

B: Pen-o kaimashita-ka? [Partner B begins asking yes-no questions to determine the object.]
A: Iie, pen-wa kaimasen deshita.
B: Enpitsu-o kaimashita-ka?
A: Iie, enpitsu-wa kaimasen deshita.
B: Banana-o kaimashita-ka?
A: Hai, kaimashita.
B: Rop-pon kaimashita-ka? [Partner B begins asking yes-no questions to determine the number of bananas.]
A: Iie.
B: Ip-pon kaimashita-ka?
A: Iie.
B: San-bon kaimashita-ka?
A: Hai, san-bon kaimashita. [Partner B asked a total of six questions so Partner B's score is six.]

NAN-BON?					
えんぴつ	enpitsu	バナナ	banana	ネクタイ	nekutai
ペン	pen	にんじん	ninjin	ズボン	zubon

❷ Ikutsu? Nan-bon? Nan-mai? Nan-nin?

With a partner review the general counters (*hitotsu ~ too*) as well as the counters -*hon*, -*mai*, and -*nin*. Partner A places a pencil on one of the four sets of counters given in the first row in the box on the next page. Partner B covers the box. Partner B places the tip of a pencil on the dot in the center of the circle with one end of a paper clip around the pencil tip. Using this as a spinner, Partner B spins once to select a number on the wheel. Partner A then asks a question using the selected counter, and Partner B responds using the number on the spinner plus the correct form of the counter. If the answer is incorrect, Partner A supplies the correct form. Change roles and continue. Read the example aloud with your partner before you begin.

A: B-san-no ban desu. [ban = turn]
B: Hai. (*spins a 3*)
A: (*asks a question with the selected counter*) Paatii-ni *nan-nin* imashita-ka?
B: (*answers the question using the number on the spinner*) *San-nin* imashita. A-san-no ban desu.

	Ikutsu?	Nan-bon?	Nan-mai?	Nan-nin?
1	hitotsu	ip-pon	ichi-mai	hitori
2	futatsu	ni-hon	ni-mai	futari
3	mittsu	san-bon	san-mai	san-nin
4	yottsu	yon-hon	yon-mai	yo-nin
5	itsutsu	go-hon	go-mai	go-nin
6	muttsu	rop-pon	roku-mai	roku-nin
7	nanatsu	nana-hon	nana-mai	shichi/nana-nin
8	yattsu	hap-pon	hachi-mai	hachi-nin
9	kokonotsu	kyuu-hon	kyuu-mai	kyuu-nin
10	too	jup-pon	juu-mai	juu-nin
11	juu-ichi	juu-ip-pon	juu-ichi-mai	juu-ichi-nin
12	juu-ni	juu-ni-hon	juu-ni-mai	juu-ni-nin

PART 2

❶ Ninjin-ga irimasu-ka?　　　📄 & ✏

Use your imagination as you do this activity with a クラスメート. By asking questions, each partner identifies which food items are needed for the other's secret recipe for a very unusual dish. Before beginning the questioning, each partner selects the <u>six</u> needed foods from the たべもの box and writes them down. Then Partner A asks Partner B questions until all of the foods have been identified and written down. Check for accuracy. Then change roles and repeat. Read the sample exchange aloud before you begin.

SAMPLE EXCHANGE

A: Ninjin-ga irimasu-ka?
B: Iie, irimasen.
A: Meron-ga irimasu-ka?
B: Hai, irimasu. [A writes down *meron*.]
A: Sakana-mo irimasu-ka?
B: Iie, irimasen.
A: Banana-ga irimasu-ka?
B: Iie, irimasen.
A: Orenji-ga irimasu-ka?
B: Hai, irimasu. [A writes down *orenji*.]
A: Remon-mo irimasu-ka?
B: Hai, irimasu. [A writes down *remon*.]
A: Tomato-mo irimasu-ka?

たべもの			
banana	バナナ	retasu	レタス
meron	メロン	ninjin	にんじん
ichigo*	いちご	tomato	トマト
ringo**	りんご	sakana	さかな
orenji	オレンジ	hamu	ハム
papaiya	パパイヤ	gohan	ごはん
remon	レモン	miruku	ミルク
jamu	ジャム		
mayoneezu	マヨネーズ		
masutaado***	マスタード		
gureepufuruutsu	グレープフルーツ		
masshuruumu	マッシュルーム		

*strawberry　**apple　***mustard

❷ Kaimono-ni ikimashita-ka?　　　📄 & ✏

This pair activity provides an opportunity to ask and answer questions about an imaginary shopping trip. With your partner try to keep the conversation going for at least four minutes with no significant pauses. Imagine that Partner A has completed a successful shopping trip during which he/she bought at least two of two different items (one of which in Japanese is counted with the counter -*mai* and the other which is counted with the counter -*hon*). Partner B asks questions such as the ones given below but is not limited to these. As Partner B listens to Partner A's answers, he/she will think of additional questions to ask. Change partners and repeat the activity several times. Before you start, answer the questions about your shopping trip in the box below and write them down.

SOME POSSIBLE QUESTIONS

Nan-yoobi-ni ikimashita-ka?
Dare-to ikimashita-ka?
Nani-o kaimashita-ka?
Nan-mai/-bon kaimashita-ka?
_____-wa ikura deshita-ka?
_____-wa doko-de kaimashita-ka?
Zenbu-de ikura deshita-ka?

私は かいものに 行きました。
1. 何よう日？
2. だれと？
3. 何を かいましたか。(2 items)
　　何まい・何本？ いくら？ どこで？
4. ぜんぶで いくら？

Meibutsu (名物)

Meibutsu are local foods or crafts for which particular regions in Japan are famous. Hokkaido's *meibutsu* include white chocolate, milk and other dairy products. In Nagasaki, Kyushu, Nagasaki *chanpon* (長崎ちゃんぽん), a hearty noodle dish with many vegetables, is popular. Rice and rice wine (お酒) are specialties on the Japan Sea side of Japan (which include Fukui and Toyama prefectures), thanks to the cold winters and the cold water that is an essential ingredient to these products. Likewise, the town of Wajima, in Ishikawa prefecture, is best known for its high quality, beautiful and long-lasting lacquerware. Japanese people are avid travelers, domestic and otherwise, and buying *meibutsu* as souvenirs (おみやげ) for friends and relatives is a must.

L. 36 電話で 話しましょう

れんしゅう A: Where is ~?

Your friend has just moved into town and is still learning his/her way around.
Answer his/her questions.

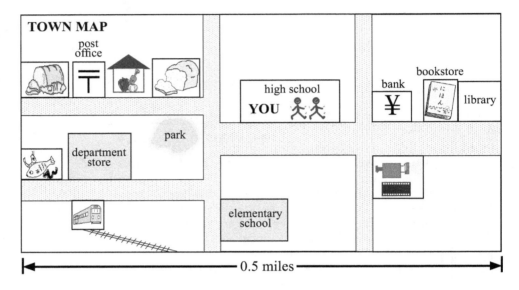

れんしゅう B: How many did you buy?

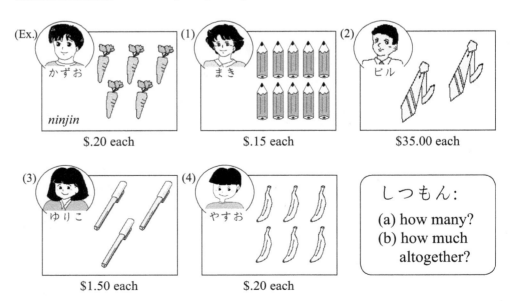

(Ex.) かずお
ninjin
$.20 each

(1) まき
$.15 each

(2) ビル
$35.00 each

(3) ゆりこ
$1.50 each

(4) やすお
$.20 each

しつもん:
(a) how many?
(b) how much altogether?

れんしゅう C: What do you need?

LIST 1: pizza, salad, sandwich   LIST 2: Alaska, Hawaii, Russia

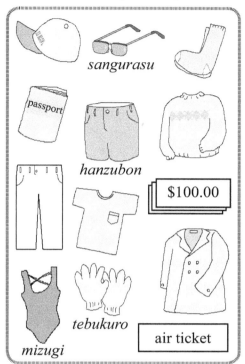

retasu

ninjin

tamanegi

masshuruumu

sooseeji

peparoni

piiman

sangurasu

hanzubon

$100.00

mizugi

tebukuro

air ticket

れんしゅう D: What's missing?

Fill in the missing *kanji* with the most appropriate *kanji* (a)~(f) given below.

(Ex.) お [金]
　　　 [金] よう日

(1) ☐ 学 校
　　 ☐ さ い

(2) 何 ☐
　　 来 ☐
　　 三 ☐ せ い

(3) フ ラ ン ス ☐
　　 お と こ の ☐
　　 一 ☐

(4) 火 よ う ☐
　　 今 ☐
　　 ☐ 本

(5) ☐ 学
　　 ☐ き い
　　 ☐ 人

(a) 日　(b) 人　(c) 木　(d) 年　(e) 小　(f) 大

299

LESSON 37
Asking for and Giving Reasons

OBJECTIVES 目標

At the end of this lesson you will be able to:
- ☑ Ask for and give a reason
- ☑ Read the *kanji*: 上 and 下

VOCABULARY 単語

Words

dooshite	why
kara	because

Phrases and expressions

Dooshite desu-ka?	Why?

Other words and expressions you will hear in this lesson

gareeji seeru	garage sale

KEY GRAMMAR POINTS 文法ポイント

1. Dooshite

The word *dooshite*, which means *why* in English, is placed at the beginning of the question you want to ask and the particle *-ka* comes at the end. Look at these examples.

Dooshite Nihon-ni ikimasu-*ka*?	*Why* are you going to Japan?
Dooshite furui kuruma-o kaimasu-*ka*?	*Why* are you buying an old car?
Dooshite kimasen-*ka*?	*Why* aren't you coming?

2. Plain form + kara (desu)

When responding to a *why* question in English, you often answer with the word *because* followed by the reason rather than including the information in the question.

Why aren't you coming?	→	Because I'm too busy.
Why are you tired?	→	Because I went to bed late.
Why are you studying Japanese?	→	Because I'm going to Japan.

This is common in Japanese also. To answer questions with *dooshite*, you can use the plain form of a verb, an *i*-adjective, or *desu* followed by *kara* or *kara desu*. The plain form of *desu* is *da*.

KARA

Verbs

Dooshite kimasen-ka?	*Why* aren't you coming?
Shukudai-o *suru-kara* (kimasen).	(I'm not coming) *Because I'm going to do* my homework.
Dooshite ikimasen-ka?	*Why* aren't you going?
Kaimono-o *shitai-kara* (ikimasen).	(I'm not going) *Because I want to do* shopping.
Dooshite eigo-no benkyoo-o shite-imasu-ka?	*Why* are you studying English?
Igirisu-ni *iku-kara* (benkyoo-o shite-imasu).	(I'm studying) *Because I'm going* to England.

I-adjectives

Ueda-san-wa *dooshite* kimasen-ka?	*Why* isn't Mrs. Ueda coming?
Isogashii-kara (kimasen).	(She's not coming) *Because she's busy.*

Dooshite sono eiga-o mitaku-nai desu-ka?	*Why* don't you want to see that movie?
Furui-kara (mitaku-nai desu).	(I don't want to see it) *Because it's* old.
Dooshite nana-hon kaimashita-ka?	*Why* did you buy seven?
Totemo *yasukatta-kara* (kaimashita).	(I bought seven) *Because they were* so cheap.

Desu

Dooshite asoko-ni ikimashita-ka?	*Why* did you go there?
Ookii depaato *da-kara* (ikimashita).	(I went there) *Because it's* a big department store.
Dooshite Furorida-ni ikitai desu-ka?	*Why* do you want to go to Florida?
Umi-ga suki* *da-kara* (ikitai desu). [* na-adjective]	(I want to go) *Because* I like the ocean.

This *kara* means *because* and is different from the *kara* which means *from* as in *Kanada-kara kimashita.*

If you are not answering a question and want to tell why you did something, you can make a longer sentence with the plain form + *kara* (do not use *desu*) in the first part of the sentence. Remember that the first part is the "because" part of the sentence.

> **. . . kara, . . .**
>
> **Nihon-ni iku-*kara*, nihongo-no benkyoo-o shimasu.**
> *Because* I'm going to Japan, I will study Japanese.
>
> **Totemo yasukatta-*kara*, nana-hon kaimashita.**
> *Because* (they) were very cheap, I bought seven.

3. -n desu(-ka)

You were introduced to the sentence ending *-n desu(-ka)* in Lesson 35. Very common in spoken Japanese, it is used to convey the sense that both the speaker and listener share information that is of mutual interest. Depending on the tone of voice, it can be used to communicate interest, surprise, disbelief, or shock. Often there is the implication that an explanation is requested or required. When used at the end of a statement, it is emphatic and is similar to "as you can see" or "the fact of the matter is." *Iku-n desu* and *Ikimasu* are of the same level of politeness. *-n desu(-ka)* immediately follows a verb or adjective in the plain form.

> Iku-n desu-ka?   Ikanai-n desu-ka?   Isogashii-n desu-ka?

You are not expected to use this form in speaking at this point. It is presented so that you will be aware of its existence and the frequency of its use among native speakers of Japanese.

YOMIMASHOO!   読みましょう

どうして	why
から	because
行かないん ですか。どうして ですか。	You're not going? Why?
かいものを したいから。	Because I want to go shopping.
上田さんは どうして 来ませんか。	Why isn't Mrs. Ueda coming?
いそがしいから、来ません。	She's not coming because she's busy.
ともだちは どうして 来ませんか。	Why isn't your friend coming?
しゅくだいを するから、来ません。	She's not coming because she's going to do her homework.
どうして 七本 かいましたか。	Why did you buy seven?
とても やすかったから、かいました。	I bought them because they were so cheap.
ガレージセール	garage sale

In this lesson you will learn to read two *kanji*: 上 and 下. Be sure that you know the readings of each *kanji* and can tell what the *kanji* means. Readings which are marked by an asterisk are for your reference only; you do not need to learn these at this time. You also do not have to learn any new words which are given in the examples. The correct stroke order for these *kanji* is given in the Optional Writing Practice section.

上   **JOO*; ue** (top, up, above, over), **kami*** (upper), **a(geru)*** (raise), **a(garu)*** (rise)

上	*ue*	top
上から	*ue*-kara	from the top, from above
上田	*Ueda*	*family name* [upper-field]
川上	Kawa*kami*	*family name* [upstream]
以上	i*joo*	more than

本はベッドの上にある。	Hon-wa beddo-no *ue*-ni aru.
[plain form]	(The book is on the bed.)
上から五ばんめの本を 見せてください。	*Ue*-kara go-ban-me-no hon-o misete kudasai. (Please show me the fifth book from the top.)
今日上田さんが 来ました。	Kyoo *Ueda*-san-ga kimashita. (Mrs. Ueda came today.)

The *kanji* 上 was derived from a symbolic representation of the concept "above."

下   **KA*, GE*; shita** (bottom, down, under), **shimo*** (lower), **sa(geru)*** (hang lower), **sa(garu)*** (hang down), **kuda(saru)** (give me)

下	*shita*	bottom, down, under
下から	*shita*-kara	from the bottom
山下	Yama*shita*	*family name* [mountain-bottom]
地下鉄	chi*ka*tetsu	subway
下さい	*kuda*sai	please (give me)
川下	kawa*shimo*	downstream

本の下にあります。	Hon-no *shita*-ni arimasu. (It is under the book.)
下から二ばんめの本を 見せて下さい。	*Shita*-kara ni-ban-me-no hon-o misete *kuda*sai. (Please show me the second book from the bottom.)
地下鉄で行きました。	Chi*ka*tetsu-de ikimashita. (She went by subway.)
私の大学に来て下さい。	Watashi-no daigaku-ni kite *kuda*sai. (Please come to my university.)

The *kanji* 下 was derived from a symbolic representation of the concept "below."

INTERACTIVE ACTIVITIES

PART 1

❶ Dialogue

With a partner practice the following dialogue following the usual procedure. If Partner A is not female, change *nekutai* to *pen* and *booifurendo* to *gaarufurendo* in the dialogue. Make sure you understand the meaning of each line before you begin. After you have memorized the dialogue, perform it for another pair.

Both A and B have been out shopping alone. Each is carrying a shopping bag. The two friends meet by chance in the train station.

A: Aa, B-san! Konnichi-wa.
B: A-san, konnichi-wa.
A: (Looking at B's bag) Takusan kaimashita-ne? (Pointing at the bag)
    Sore-wa nan-desu-ka?
B: T-shatsu desu. T-shatsu-o roku-mai kaimashita.
A: Roku-mai? Dooshite desu-ka?
B: Totemo yasukatta-kara.
A: Aa . . .
B: A-san-wa nani-o kaimashita-ka?
A: (Opening the bag) Nekutai-o san-bon kaimashita.
B: Nekutai? San-bon? Dooshite desu-ka?
A: Booifurendo-ga ashita-kara atarashii shigoto-o suru-kara . . . Kore-wa purezento desu.
B: Aa, soo desu-ka?

Use this version of the dialogue for greater reading practice.

A: ああ、Bさん。こんにちは。
B: Aさん、こんにちは。
A: (Looking at B's bag) たくさん かいましたね。 (Pointing at one bag)
    それは 何 ですか。
B: Tシャツ です。Tシャツを 六まい かいました。
A: 六まい? どうして ですか。
B: とても やすかった から。
A: ああ。
B: Aさんは 何を かいましたか。
A: (Opening the bag) ネクタイを 三本 かいました。
B: ネクタイ? 三本? どうして ですか。
A: ボーイフレンド が あしたから あたらしい しごとを するから。
    これは プレゼント です。
B: ああ、そう ですか。

❷ Reviewing the plain form of verbs 📄 & ✎

To answer questions with *dooshite*, you can use the plain form of a verb, adjective or *desu* (*da*) followed by *kara*. With a partner review the plain form of the following verbs and write down the ones which need to be studied. When you have finished, switch roles and repeat.

PLAIN FORM OF SOME COMMON VERBS

-masu form	Plain form	English
-*u* Verbs		
hanashimasu	hanasu	speak
wasuremasu	wasureru	forget
nomimasu	nomu	drink
yomimasu	yomu	read
asobimasu	asobu	play, have fun
aimasu	au	meet, see
kaimasu	kau	buy
utaimasu	utau	sing
tsukaimasu	tsukau	use
moraimasu	morau	receive, get
ikimasu	iku	go
kaerimasu	kaeru	return
tsukurimasu	tsukuru	make
hairimasu	hairu	enter, join
kakimasu	kaku	write
kikimasu	kiku	listen
irimasu	iru	need
-*ru* Verbs		
mimasu	miru	look at, see
tabemasu	taberu	eat
okimasu	okiru	get up
oshiemasu	oshieru	teach
nemasu	neru	sleep, go to bed
misemasu	miseru	show
Irregular Verbs		
kimasu	kuru	come
shimasu	suru	do

PART 2

---

❶ Reviewing the past form of adjectives

Spend a total of five minutes drilling each other on the past tense of selected adjectives from the chart on the next page. Take turns giving your partner an adjective from the first column and having him/her give you the correct past form. For a greater challenge, respond with both the affirmative and negative past forms. Both of these plain verb forms can be used with *kara*.

When responding to a *dooshite* question, you may use the plain form of an adjective followed by *kara*. The adjective may be in the past or non-past form.

Dooshite nana-hon kaimasu-ka?	Why are you buying seven?
Totemo *yasui-kara* (kaimasu).	(I'm buying them) *Because* they *are* so *cheap*.
Dooshite nana-hon kaimashita-ka?	Why did you buy seven?
Totemo *yasukatta-kara* (kaimashita).	(I bought them) *Because* they *were* so *cheap*.

Do you remember how to form the past of *i*-adjectives? Simply drop the final *-i* (い) and add *-katta* (かった). Add *desu* if you want the adjective to be on the same level of politeness as the *-masu* form of verbs. See Lesson 22 for more information and examples.

hay*ai* → hay*akatta*   isogash*ii* → isogash*ikatta*

		I-ADJECTIVES		
Non-Past Affirmative	**Non-Past Negative**	**Past Affirmative**	**Past Negative**	**English**
1. furui	furuku-nai	furukatta	furuku-nakatta	old
2. chiisai	chiisaku-nai	chiisakatta	chiisaku-nakatta	small
3. osoi	osoku-nai	osokatta	osoku-nakatta	slow, late
4. oishii	oishiku-nai	oishikatta	oishiku-nakatta	delicious
5. samui	samuku-nai	samukatta	samuku-nakatta	cold
6. nemui	nemuku-nai	nemukatta	nemuku-nakatta	sleepy
7. nagai	nagaku-nai	nagakatta	nagaku-nakatta	long
8. tsuyoi	tsuyoku-nai	tsuyokatta	tsuyoku-nakatta	strong
9. yowai	yowaku-nai	yowakatta	yowaku-nakatta	weak
10. ookii	ookiku-nai	ookikatta	ookiku-nakatta	big
11. hayai	hayaku-nai	hayakatta	hayaku-nakatta	early, fast
12. isogashii	isogashiku-nai	isogashikatta	isogashiku-nakatta	busy
13. tanoshii	tanoshiku-nai	tanoshikatta	tanoshiku-nakatta	pleasant, fun
14. atsui	atsuku-nai	atsukatta	atsuku-nakatta	hot
15. chikai	chikaku-nai	chikakatta	chikaku-nakatta	close
16. kitanai	kitanaku-nai	kitanakatta	kitanaku-nakatta	dirty, messy
17. urusai	urusaku-nai	urusakatta	urusaku-nakatta	noisy
18. ii (yoi)	yoku-nai	yokatta	yoku-nakatta	good
19. tsumaranai	tsumaranaku-nai	tsumaranakatta	tsumaranaku-nakatta	boring
20. omoshiroi	omoshiroku-nai	omoshirokatta	omoshiroku-nakatta	interesting
21. muzukashii	muzukashiku-nai	muzukashikatta	muzukashiku-nakatta	difficult
22. takai	takaku-nai	takakatta	takaku-nakatta	high, tall, expensive

❷ **Dooshite kimasen-ka?**

As you and a クラスメート do this activity together, use your imagination to respond to *dooshite* questions. Each answer should be an appropriate response to the question and should include one of the following:

plain form of adjective + kara (+ verb)   OR   plain form of verb + kara (+ verb)
      (non-past or past)   (non-past)

Ask your partner why a certain person did <u>or</u> does <u>or</u> is going to do a certain thing.* Read the sample exchange aloud before you begin.

A: Tanaka-san-wa dooshite furansugo-no-benkyoo-o shite-imasu-ka?
B: Furansu-ni *iku-kara* (benkyoo-o shite-imasu).

B: Yamakawa-san-wa dooshite paatii-ni kimasen-ka?
A: *Isogashii-kara* (kimasen).

A: Ueda-san-wa dooshite nekutai-o go-hon kaimashita-ka?
B: Totemo *yasukatta-kara* (kaimashita).

B: *Your partner's name*-san-wa dooshite Oosaka-ni ikimasu-ka?
A: Kaimono-o *shitai-kara* (ikimasu).

SOME NAMES	
川田	山川
山田	田中
中田	高田
本田	中山
山中	中川
高山	上田

*Since you have not yet learned the past tense of plain form verbs, use an appropriate non-past verb or a past adjective instead.

Could you read all of the names in the box titled SOME NAMES? Here they are in *roomaji*.

川田	Kawada, Kawata	山中	Yamanaka	高田	Takada
山田	Yamada	高山	Takayama	中山	Nakayama
中田	Nakata, Nakada	山川	Yamakawa	中川	Nakagawa
本田	Honda	田中	Tanaka	上田	Ueda

L. 37 電話で 話しましょう

れんしゅう A: Jason's Bad Week

しつもん:
(a) What did he do on ~day?
(b) How was ~?

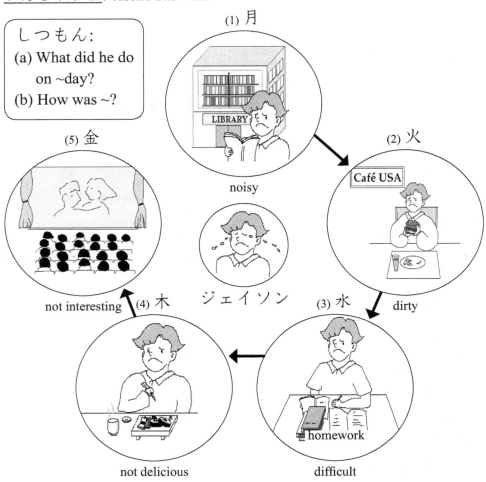

(1) 月
noisy

(2) 火
dirty

(3) 水
homework
difficult

(4) 木
not delicious

(5) 金
not interesting

ジェイソン

れんしゅう B: Why?

(1) Friday's Party Attendance List
   date: 3/17   time: 2:00 p.m. ~

name	will attend	reason
けんた	✓	——
さとし	✗	part-time job
りょうこ	✓	——
ひとみ	✗	math test

(2) Students' Language Study Survey

name	language	reason
クリス	Spanish	will go to Spain next year
たかこ	Chinese	has a Chinese friend
ラリー	Japanese	It's fun!

れんしゅう C: Fill in the blanks and let's converse!

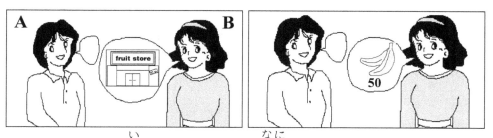

A: きのうどこに行きましたか。
い

B: _____

A: 何をかいましたか。
なに

B: _____ を _____ かいました。

A: _____ 50本かいましたか。
ぽん

B: _____ から、かいました。

れんしゅう D: Buying a Watch

You want to buy a watch for a member of your family. Ask the clerk to show
you a watch. Specify which one. Then, ask the price.

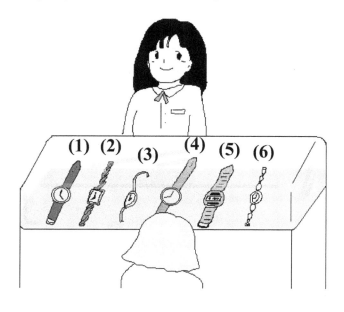

LESSON 38
Locating Items in a Department Store

OBJECTIVES

目標

At the end of this lesson you will be able to:

- ☑ Ask and tell on what floor something can be found
- ☑ Talk about whether or not you have done something yet
- ☑ Read the *kanji*: 円

VOCABULARY

単語

Words

moo	already, yet
mada	not yet, still
#-kai, #-gai	#th floor
chika	basement

Phrases and expressions

Mada desu.	Not yet.

Other words and expressions you will hear in this lesson

suniikaa	sneakers

VOCABULARY NOTES

単語ノート

Moo and mada

When the adverb *moo* is used with an affirmative verb, it means *already* or *yet*. The adverb *mada* expresses the opposite concept and is usually expressed in English as *not yet*. Study these examples.

Moo purezento-o kaimashita-ka?	Have you *already* bought a present?
Hai, *moo* kaimashita.	Yes, I've *already* bought one.
Iie, *mada* desu.	No, *not yet.*
Moo shukudai-o shimashita-ka?	Have you done your homework *yet*?
Hai, *moo* shimashita.	Yes, I've *already* finished it.
Iie, *mada* desu.	No, *not yet.*

KEY GRAMMAR POINTS

文法ポイント

1. #-kai (#-gai)

This lesson introduces the counter *-kai* which is used to count floors in buildings. The question form is *nan-kai*.

Handobaggu-wa *nan-kai* desu-ka?	*What floor* are the handbags on?
Ni-kai desu.	The *second floor.*
Go-kai-ni nani-ga arimasu-ka?	What's on the *fifth* floor?
Terebi-ga arimasu.	The TVs (are).

NAN-KAI?			
ik-kai	1st floor	nana-kai	7th floor
ni-kai	2nd floor	hachi-kai*	8th floor
san-kai*	3rd floor	kyuu-kai	9th floor
yon-kai	4th floor	juk-kai*	10th floor
go-kai	5th floor	juu-ik-kai	11th floor
rok-kai	6th floor	juu-ni-kai	12th floor
*You may also encounter these alternate forms: *san-gai, hak-kai,* and *jik-kai.*			

2. Plain past form

To form the past tense of plain form verbs, simply replace the -te (-de) of te-form verbs with -ta (-da).

(mimasu)   mite   →   mita (saw)   (yomimasu) yonde → yonda (read)
(tabemasu) tabete →   tabeta (ate)

PLAIN PAST VERBS

-*masu* form	Plain form	-*te* form	Plain past	English
-*u* Verbs				
hanashimasu	hanasu	hanashite	hanashita	speak
wasuremasu	wasureru	wasurete	wasureta	forget
nomimasu	nomu	nonde	nonda	drink
yomimasu	yomu	yonde	yonda	read
asobimasu	asobu	asonde	asonda	play, have fun
aimasu	au	atte	atta	meet, see
iimasu	iu	itte	itta	say
kaimasu	kau	katte	katta	buy
utaimasu	utau	utatte	utatta	sing
tsukaimasu	tsukau	tsukatte	tsukatta	use
moraimasu	morau	moratte	moratta	receive, get
ikimasu	iku	itte	itta	go
kaerimasu	kaeru	kaette	kaetta	return
tsukurimasu	tsukuru	tsukutte	tsukutta	make
hairimasu	hairu	haitte	haitta	enter, join
kachimasu	katsu	katte	katta	win
kakimasu	kaku	kaite	kaita	write
kikimasu	kiku	kiite	kiita	listen
irimasu	iru	itte	itta	need
-*ru* Verbs				
mimasu	miru	mite	mita	look at, see
tabemasu	taberu	tabete	tabeta	eat
okimasu	okiru	okite	okita	get up
oshiemasu	oshieru	oshiete	oshieta	teach
nemasu	neru	nete	neta	sleep, go to bed
misemasu	miseru	misete	miseta	show
atsumemasu	atsumemeru	atsumete	atsumeta	collect
akemasu	akeru	akete	aketa	open (something)
shimemasu	shimeru	shimete	shimeta	close (something)
makemasu	makeru	makete	maketa	lose
Irregular Verbs				
kimasu	kuru	kite	kita	come
shimasu	suru	shite	shita	do

YOMIMASHOO!   読みましょう

もう	already, yet
まだ	not yet, still
かい、がい	floor
ちか (地下)	basement
もうすぐ まりさんの たんじょう日 です。	Mari's birthday is coming soon.
もう プレゼントを かいましたか。	Have you bought a present already?
まだ です。	Not yet.
バッグは 何かい ですか。	What floor are the handbags on?
三かい です。	The third floor.
一かいに 何が ありますか。	What's on the first floor?
くつが あります。	The shoes (are).
スニーカー	sneakers

309

In this lesson you will learn to read the *kanji* 円. Be sure that you know the reading of the *kanji* and can tell what the *kanji* means. You do not have to learn any new words which are given in the examples. In Lesson 39 you will learn how to write this *kanji* using the correct stroke order.

  EN (yen, circle)

円	*en*	yen (Japanese monetary unit)
一円	ichi-*en*	one yen
五円	go-*en*	five yen
十円	juu-*en*	10 yen

ペンは九十九円です。 Pen-wa kyuu-juu-kyuu-*en* desu.   The pen is 99 yen.
全部で千二百円です。 Zenbu-de sen ni-hyaku-*en* desu.   It's 1,200 yen altogether.

The *kanji* for *en* is one of the few characters developed in Japan. It is derived from a picture of a bank teller's window through which money was passed.

KANJI REVIEW

私	六	月	行	天	九	日	木	四	本	七	人	山	十
田	一	小	学	高	何	三	水	川	校	火	五	下	金
来	上	二	見	今	大	中	年	円	八	気	元	土	

How do you read them? What do they mean?

INTERACTIVE ACTIVITIES

PART 1

---

❶ Dooshite kimasen-ka?

During this activity each student will work as a pair with two different クラスメート to check Assignment #1 from Part 2 of Lesson 37. The goal of the activity is to have two students carefully check your five sentences, mark and discuss with you any errors found, and sign off on your page. Form your first pair and exchange assignments with your partner. Both partners independently check and neatly mark errors for the entire assignment. Use the same editing symbols as usual. Check for the following:

● The meaning of the answer is appropriate for the question.
● Each answer includes one of the following: plain form of adjective (non-past or past) + *kara*
                    OR plain form of verb (non-past) + *kara*

310

❷ Moo shatsu-o ni-mai kaimashita-ka? 📄 & ✏️

Use your imagination as you do this activity with a クラスメート. You and your partner are friends who are both intent on doing as much as possible each day. At the beginning of each day you tell each other what you hope to accomplish that day and then at lunch time you talk on the phone to check on each other's progress. Take turns asking and answering questions (using the -*masu* form) to determine which tasks your partner has completed. Before you begin, choose the tasks you have already accomplished (four or five) and write down its number. Whenever your partner indicates a task has been completed, write down its number also. When you have finished, compare your work to check your accuracy. Look at the examples.

A: Moo shatsu-o ni-mai kaimashita-ka? → B: Iie, mada desu.
B: Moo zasshi-o yomimashita-ka? → A: Hai, moo yomimashita. [B writes down "1".]

PARTNER A
1. zasshi-o yomu
2. Tanaka-san-ni denwa-o suru
3. keeki-o tsukuru
4. nyuusu-o miru
5. Ueda-san-to hanasu
6. doitsugo-no benkyoo-o suru
7. Bitamin-Pawaa-o nomu
8. rajio-o kiku
9. yuubinkyoku-ni iku

PARTNER B
1. shatsu-o ni-mai kau
2. sensei-ni au
3. jisho-o kau
4. atarashii konpyuutaa-o tsukau
5. depaato-ni iku
6. tegami-o kaku
7. shinbun-o yomu
8. inu-to asobu
9. piano-no renshuu-o suru

PART 2

❶ Rok-kai desu-ka?

Play this guessing game with a クラスメート. Partner A thinks of a specific floor in a 12-floor building and writes the floor number. Partner B asks as many questions as needed to guess the correct floor. After each incorrect guess, Partner A gives a hint, telling Partner B whether the floor is above or below the floor guessed. Each question is worth one point. The player with the lower score is the winner. Read the example aloud before you begin.

A: Nan-kai desu-ka? [A has selected a specific floor and has written down the number.]
B: Rok-kai desu-ka?
A: Chigaimasu. Motto ue desu.
B: Juu-ik-kai desu-ka?
A: Chigaimasu. Motto shita desu.
B: Kyuu-kai desu-ka?
A: Hai, soo desu. [B asked three questions so B has three points.]

❷ Go-kai-ni nani-ga arimasu-ka? 📄 & ✏️

Do this activity with a クラスメート. Take turns asking and answering questions such as the ones below to determine which items are on which floors of a 12-floor department store. Look only at your own chart. The items you need to locate are given next to your chart. Read these sample questions and answers aloud before you begin.

SAMPLE QUESTIONS AND ANSWERS

Baggu-wa nan-kai desu-ka? → **Juu-ni**-kai desu.
Ik-kai-ni nani-ga arimasu-ka? → **Jitensha**-ga arimasu.

PARTNER A

NAN-KAI?	NANI-GA ARIMASU-KA?
12	geemu
11	wafuku (Japanese clothes)
10	
9	kodomo-fuku
8	hon
7	shinshi-fuku (men's clothes)
6	
5	
4	tokei
3	futon (bedding)
2	
1	kaban suutsu-keesu baggu

Find out on which floor these items can be found:

zasshi   nooto
rajio   kamera
kutsu   pen
terebi
fujin-fuku (women's clothes)
supootsu-yoohin (sporting goods)

PARTNER B

NAN-KAI?	NANI-GA ARIMASU-KA?
12	supootsu-yoohin (sporting goods)
11	
10	nooto pen
9	
8	zasshi
7	
6	fujin-fuku (women's clothes)
5	kutsu
4	kamera
3	
2	rajio terebi
1	

Find out on which floor these items can be found:

suutsu-keesu   hon
baggu   tokei
kodomo-fuku   geemu
wafuku (Japanese clothes)
futon (bedding)
shinshi-fuku (men's clothes)

❸ **Yomimashoo!**

Mask the *roomaji* and read the following for your partner who will check your accuracy. Change roles and repeat. All of the words are from the activity above.

かな	ローマじ

1. ざっし
2. くつ
3. こどもふく
4. ほん
5. とけい
6. ふとん
7. かばん
8. ラジオ
9. カメラ
10. ペン
11. テレビ
12. バッグ
13. ゲーム
14. スポーツ
15. ノート
16. スーツケース

1. zasshi
2. kutsu
3. kodomo-fuku
4. hon
5. tokei
6. futon
7. kaban
8. rajio
9. kamera
10. pen
11. terebi
12. baggu
13. geemu
14. supootsu
15. nooto
16. suutsu-keesu

L. 38 電話で 話しましょう

れんしゅう A: Buying a Camera

You are shopping for a camera. Ask the clerk to show you a camera. Specify which one by its location, then ask the price. If it is not a price you want to pay, ask to see another one. (Your budget is ¥20,000.)

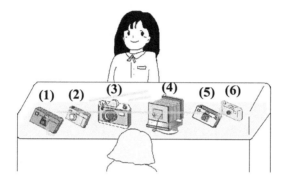

れんしゅう B: Shopping at the Department Store

You are trying to find out what floor the following items are on. Group A can only look at Diagram A, and Group B can only look at Diagram B. Ask members of the other group questions and write down the items on your diagram.

Diagram A

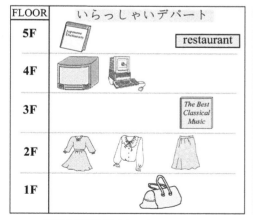

Items you need to find

(Ex.) CD
(1) shoes
(2) telephone
(3) men's clothes

Diagram B

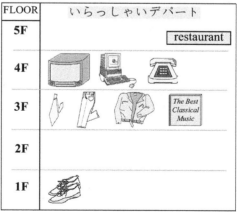

Items you need to find

(Ex.) CD
(1) books
(2) bags
(3) women's clothes

313

れんしゅう C: Have you ~ already?

スーザン

Things to do today				
(1) ☐ write a letter			(4) ✓ watch the news	
(2) ✓ do homework			(5) ☐ buy a watch	
(3) ☐ go to the post office				

れんしゅう D: Let's converse!

Dialogue:

A: Have you <u>eaten lunch</u>, <u>Mayumi</u>?
B: No, not yet.
A: Do you want to <u>eat</u> together now?
B: O.K. Where do you want to go?
A: How about <u>Pizza U.S.A.</u>?
B: That sounds good!

┌─ Suggested activities ─┐

see [movie title] *(mita)*
buy a present *(katta)*
do homework *(shita)*
eat dinner *(tabeta)*

Sample Dialogue:

A: ねえ、<u>まゆみ</u>、もう <u>ひるごはん たべた</u>?
B: ううん、まだ。
A: じゃ、今から いっしょに <u>たべる</u>?
B: いいよ。どこに 行く?
A: <u>Pizza U.S.A.</u> は どう?
B: いいよ。

Sample Dialogue:

A: Nee, <u>Mayumi</u>, moo <u>hiru-gohan tabeta</u>?
B: Uun, mada.
A: Jaa, ima-kara issho-ni <u>taberu</u>?
B: Ii-yo. Doko-ni iku?
A: <u>Pizza U.S.A.</u>-wa doo?
B: Ii-yo.

LESSON 39
Past Experiences

OBJECTIVES   目標

At the end of this lesson you will be able to:
- ☑ Ask and tell if someone has ever done something
- ☑ Write the *kanji*: 円

VOCABULARY   単語

Words

amai	sweet (taste)
karai	spicy, hot, salty
tsumetai	cold (to the touch)

VOCABULARY NOTES   単語ノート

Tsumetai

The adjective *tsumetai* means *cold* to the touch. The word *samui*, on the other hand, is used to describe air temperatures and weather conditions.

KEY GRAMMAR POINTS   文法ポイント

Past plain verb + -koto-ga arimasu

This useful phrase can be used to ask and talk about past experiences – what one has or has not experienced. It is formed with a past plain verb and the phrase *-koto-ga arimasu* or *-koto-ga arimasen*. These structures are equivalent to other *-masu* forms in terms of level of politeness. Study these examples. Notice that in the English equivalents the word *ever* often appears in the question.

Mangoo-o *tabeta-koto-ga arimasu*-ka?	*Have* you *ever eaten* a mango?
Hai, *arimasu.*	Yes, I *have.*
Iie, *arimasen.*	No, I *haven't.*
Guwaba juusu-o *nonda-koto-ga arimasu*-ka?	*Have* you *ever drunk* guava juice?
Tai-ryoori-no resutoran-ni *itta-koto-ga arimasu.*	I*'ve been* to a Thai restaurant.
Daigaku-de eigo-o *oshieta-koto-ga arimasu.*	I*'ve taught* English at the university.
Tenisu-o *shita-koto-ga arimasen.*	I *have never played* tennis.
Tomu-san-wa mada Oosaka-ni *itta-koto-ga arimasen.*	Tom *hasn't been/gone* to Osaka yet.
Mita-koto-ga arimasen-ka?	*Haven't* you *ever seen* it?
Kore-o *tsukatta-koto-ga arimasen*-ka?	*Haven't* you *ever used* this?

> **Past plain verb + -koto-ga arimasu-ka? = Have you ever + verb?**

YOMIMASHOO!   読みましょう

あまい	sweet (taste)
からい	spicy, hot, salty
つめたい	cold (to the touch)
マンゴーを たべた ことが ありますか。	Have you ever eaten a mango?
いいえ、ありません。	No, I haven't.
はい、あります。	Yes, I have.

315

どう でしたか。	How was it?
あまかった です。	It was sweet.
その レストランに 行った ことが あります。	I've been/gone to that restaurant.
見た ことが ありませんか。	Haven't you ever seen it?

INTERACTIVE ACTIVITIES

PART 1

❶ Vocabulary review 📄 & ✏️

Silently review the following vocabulary which are from Lessons 32 through 39. Then have a クラスメート orally test your knowledge of them. Your partner says the えいご and you give the 日本ご. Switch and test your partner. Write down those which need further study.

1.	zenbu-de	ぜんぶで	altogether, in all
2.	dotchi	どっち	which one (of two)
3.	kotchi	こっち	this one (of two)
4.	-mai	まい	*counter for thin, flat objects*
5.	tonari	となり	(the place) next to, adjoining
6.	chikaku	ちかく	vicinity
7.	nan-ban-me	何ばんめ	which number (in a series)
8.	ichi-man	一まん	10,000
9.	miseru (misemasu)	見せる	show
10.	morau (moraimasu)	もらう	receive, get
11.	iru (irimasu)	いる	need
12.	kudamono	くだもの	fruit
13.	kudamono-ya	くだものや	fruit store, fruit stand
14.	-hon, -bon, -pon	本	*counter for long, cylindrical object*
15.	dooshite	どうして	why
16.	kara	から	because
17.	moo	もう	already, yet
18.	mada	まだ	not yet
19.	-kai, -gai	かい、がい	*counter for floors in a building*
20.	amai	あまい	sweet (taste)
21.	karai	からい	spicy, hot, salty
22.	tsumetai	つめたい	cold (to the touch)

❷ Mangoo-o tabeta-koto-ga arimasu-ka? 📄 & ✏️

Do this interview activity as an entire class (if you have a small class) or in groups of four or six people. Look at the chart on the next page. Write the names of your クラスメート. Then form pairs. Each partner may ask and answer only one question before changing partners. The questions may be asked in any order. Answer all questions truthfully. Continue until you have interviewed everyone and have recorded all of the responses (はい or いいえ). Read this sample exchange aloud with your first partner.

    A: B-san-wa mangoo-o tabeta-koto-ga arimasu-ka?
    B: Hai, arimasu.

    B: A-san-wa gorufu-o shita-koto-ga arimasu-ka?
    A: Iie, arimasen.

クラスメートの なまえを かいて ください。 →					
この しつもんを して ください。↓					
Mangoo-o tabeta-koto-ga arimasu-ka?					
Guwaba juusu-o nonda-koto-ga arimasu-ka?					
Umi-ni itta-koto-ga arimasu-ka?					
(Name of a movie)-o mita-koto-ga arimasu-ka?					
(Name of a song)-o kiita-koto-ga arimasu-ka?					
Gorufu-o shita-koto-ga arimasu-ka?					
Tai-ryoori-no resutoran-ni itta-koto-ga arimasu-ka? [Thai]					
Keeki-o tsukutta-koto-ga arimasu-ka?					

PART 2

❶ Moraimasu ~ morau ~ moratta

With a partner review the plain past of the verbs in the box in the 文法ポイント section of Lesson 38. You say the *-masu* form of the verb and the plain form. Then your partner will say the plain past form. Give your partner feedback on each response: *Hai, soo desu* or *Chotto chigaimasu.* Change roles after every five or six verbs. You may ask about the verbs in any order.

❷ Nihon-ryoori-o tabeta-koto-ga arimasu-ka?   📄 & ✏️

Do this interview activity as an entire class (if you have a small class) or in groups of four or six people. Write the names of your クラスメート. Then form pairs. Each partner may ask and answer only one question before changing partners. The questions may be asked in any order. Answer all questions truthfully. Continue until you have interviewed everyone and have recorded all of the responses (はい or いいえ). Read this sample exchange aloud with your first partner.

A: B-san-wa nihon-ryoori-o tabe**ta-koto-ga arimasu-ka**?
B: Hai, arimasu.

B: A-san-wa tenisu-o shi**ta-koto-ga arimasu-ka**?
A: Iie, arimasen.

> Be sure to change all verbs into the **plain past form** + *koto-ga arimasu-ka?* as in the examples above. Refer to the box (plain past verb forms) in the 文法ポイント section of Lesson 38 as needed.

クラスメートの なまえを かいて ください。 →					
この しつもんを して ください。↓					
nihon-ryoori-o taberu					
guwaba juusu-o nomu					
Nyuu-Yooku-ni iku					
kitte-o atsumeru					
o-tanjoobi-ni o-kane-o morau					
kuruma-o kau					
inu-to asobu					
(name of a movie)-o miru					
(name of a song)-o kiku					
(name of a sport)-o suru					
kurabu-ni hairu					
nihonjin-to hanasu					
betonamu [Vietnamese]-ryoori-no resutoran-ni iku					
kukkii-o tsukuru					

317

L. 39　電話で　話しましょう

れんしゅう A: Have you ever ~?

(1) YOU

(2) YOU Shakespeare

(3) YOU イエスタデー

(4) YOU →

(5) YOU

(6) YOU famous person

れんしゅう B: Have you ever ~? How was it?

(Ex.) cold まこと

(1) mangos sweet キム

(2) Indian cuisine *(Indo ryoori)* hot (spicy) アンディー

(3) いろは　こうえん Iroha Park dirty サム

(4) Japanese Movie good リサ

しつもん:
(a) Have you ever ~?
(b) How was it?

れんしゅう C: What do you need, and how many do you need?

Your Japanese friend is going shopping. Tell him/her what you need, and specify the quantity.

(1)
School supplies order form
for the new semester

		Qty
☐	pencils	____
☐	red pens	____
☐	blue pens	____
☐	staplers	____
☐	erasers	____

Office Mix

(2)
Grocery order form
(for salad)

		Qty
☐	carrots (ninjin)	____
☐	tomatoes	____
☐	mushrooms (masshuruumu)	____
☐	cucumbers (kyuuri)	____
☐	lettuce	____

CROGER

(3)
Department store order form

		Qty
☐	sweaters	____
☐	neckties	____
☐	T-shirts	____
☐	skirts	____
☐	wallets	____

Maci's

319

LESSON 40
Review

OBJECTIVES   目標

At the end of this lesson you will be able to:
- ☑ Read the *kanji*: 百 and 千

This lesson reviews the key vocabulary and grammar points from Lessons 32 through 39.

VOCABULARY   単語

Other words and expressions you will hear in this lesson

Barentain-dee	Valentine's Day
romanchikku	romantic

CULTURE NOTES   カルチャーノート

Valentine's Day (Barentain-dee) バレンタインデー
The Japanese imported the custom of Valentine's Day many years ago. This particular custom has since become distinctively Japanese. Valentine's Day in the West is generally an opportunity for men to express their affection for the special women in their lives such as girlfriends, wives, and mothers. One of the most common gifts, of course, is chocolate.

In the Japanese version of Valentine's Day, things are reversed although the gift of choice remains chocolate. Rather than receiving chocolate from their male admirers, young women give chocolate and other gifts such as neckties to the young men they find attractive. Valentine's Day allows women the opportunity to express their true feelings to that special person. Many women also give chocolate to their male bosses, co-workers, and male friends to show gratitude for the kindness they receive. This type of chocolate is called *giri-choko* (obligatory chocolate). From mid-January until Valentine's Day, department stores throughout the country dedicate a large amount of space to display chocolate.

To return the favor, men are expected to give gifts to the women on March 14, a month after Valentine's Day. It is called "White Day." The return gifts used to be white marshmallows which represented "White" Day. However, nowadays, the gifts can be anything from cookies to accessories.

YOMIMASHOO!   読みましょう

何か もらいましたか。	Did you get anything?
何を もらいましたか。	What did you get?
チョコレートを 二つ もらいました。	I got two boxes of chocolate.
カードを 四まい もらいました。	I got four cards.
日本の おとこのこは おんなのこから チョコレートを もらいます。	Boys in Japan get chocolate from girls.
バレンタインデー	Valentine's Day
バレンタインデーに 何も もらったことがありません。	I have never received anything for Valentine's Day.
ロマンチック	romantic

In this lesson you will learn to read two *kanji*: 百 and 千. Be sure that you know the readings of each *kanji* and can tell what the *kanji* means. The reading which is marked by an asterisk is for your reference only; you do not need to learn it at this time. The correct stroke order for these *kanji* is given in the Optional Writing Practice section.

百 **HYAKU [BYAKU, PYAKU]** (hundred)

二百	ni-*hyaku*	200
三百	san-*byaku*	300
六百	rop-*pyaku*	600
八百	hap-*pyaku*	800

百円もらいました。	*Hyaku*-en moraimashita.	I received 100 yen.
三百人いました。	San-*byaku*-nin imashita.	There were 300 people.
紙が二百枚いります。	Kami-ga ni-*hyaku*-mai irimasu.	I need 200 sheets of paper.
六百ドルでした。	Rop-*pyaku*-doru deshita.	It was 600 dollars.

The *kanji* 百 was derived from the *kanji* for *one* 一 and the *kanji* for *white* 白 (from a grain of rice which is white). One bag of white rice weighs *100* Chinese pounds.

  SEN [ZEN], chi* (thousand)

三千	san-*zen*	3,000
四千	yon-*sen*	4,000
七千	nana-*sen*	7,000
九千	kyuu-*sen*	9,000

八千円もらいました。	Has-*sen*-en moraimashita.	I received 8,000 yen.
三千人いました。	San-*zen*-nin imashita.	There were 3,000 people.
車は九千ドルでした。	Kuruma-wa kyuu-*sen*-doru deshita.	The car was $9,000.

The *kanji* 千 was derived from the *kanji* for *person* 人 and the *kanji* for *ten* 十. Ten people weigh *1,000* Chinese pounds.

KANJI REVIEW

私	六	月	行	天	九	日	木	四	本	七	人	山	十	田
一	小	学	高	何	三	水	川	千	校	火	五	下	金	百
来	上	二	見	今	大	中	円	年	八	気	元	土		

How do you read them? What do they mean?

PART 1

❶ Kaimasu ~ kau ~ katta

With a partner review the plain past of the verbs in the box in the 文法ポイント section of Lesson 38. You say the *-masu* form of the verb and the plain form. Then your partner will say the plain past form. Give your partner feedback on each response: *Hai, soo desu* or *Chotto chigaimasu*. Change roles after every five or six verbs. You may ask about the verbs in any order.

❷ Guwaba juusu-o nonda-koto-ga arimasu-ka?   📄 & 🖊

Do this interview activity as an entire class (if you have a small class) or in groups of four or six people. Write the names of your クラスメート. Then form pairs. Each partner may ask and answer only one question before changing partners. The questions may be asked in any order. Answer all questions truthfully. Continue until you have interviewed everyone and have recorded all of the responses (はい or いいえ). Read this sample exchange aloud with your first partner.

    A: B-san-wa guwaba juusu-o non**da-koto-ga arimasu-ka**?
    B: Hai, arimasu.

    B: A-san-wa gorufu-o shi**ta-koto-ga arimasu-ka**?
    A: Iie, arimasen.

> Be sure to change all verbs into the **plain past form** + *koto-ga arimasu-ka?* as in the examples above.

Before you begin, change these verbs into the plain past and then compare your answers with those of your partner.

1. miru	4. iku	7. asobu	10. atsumeru
2. taberu	5. morau	8. kau	11. hairu
3. suru	6. hanasu	9. tsukuru	12. kiku

クラスメートの なまえを かいて ください。 ➜ しつもんを つくって、クラスメートに きいて ください。 ⬇						
chokoreeto-o morau						
furansu-jin-to hanasu						
Washinton (D.C.)-ni iku						
kitte-o atsumeru						
nihon-ryoori-o taberu						
jitensha-o kau						
kooen-de asobu						
(name of a movie)-o miru						
(name of a song)-o kiku						
(name of a sport)-o suru						
kurabu-ni hairu						
guwaba juusu-o nomu						
kyanpu-o suru [go camping]						
aisu kuriimu-o tsukuru						

322

❶ Nyuu-yooku-ni itta-koto-ga arimasu.   📄 & 🖊

As part of your last assignment, you wrote six sentences about past experiences you have had using the pattern: . . . plain past verb + *koto-ga arimasu*. Three of the sentences are true, and three of them are false. Form pairs. Partner A and Partner B both look at Partner A's sentences. Partner A reads each sentence, Partner B suggests any needed corrections, and then Partner B guesses whether the sentence is true or false. After you have completed all of Partner A's sentences, follow the same procedure with Partner B's sentences.

❷ Yomimashoo!   📄 & 🖊

This pair activity provides you with an opportunity to review the *kanji* for numbers. Partner A masks the *roomaji* side and reads the numbers and sentences in the left column in order. Partner B responds after each with either *Hai, soo desu* or *Iie, chigaimasu. Moo ichido yonde kudasai.* Partner A writes down those which need to be studied. Switch roles and repeat.

かな と かんじ	ローマじ
1. 百	1. hyaku
2. 千	2. sen
3. 五百	3. go-hyaku
4. 三百	4. san-byaku
5. 二千	5. ni-sen
6. 四千六百	6. yon-sen rop-pyaku
7. 三千九百円	7. san-zen kyuu-hyaku-en
8. 九千二百十円	8. kyuu-sen ni-hyaku juu-en
9. 八千四百五十七円	9. has-sen yon-hyaku go-juu-nana-en
10. 六千七百八十円	10. roku-sen nana-hyaku hachi-juu-en
11. 千百五十一円	11. sen hyaku go-juu-ichi-en
12. 七千八百四十二円	12. nana-sen hap-pyaku yon-juu-ni-en
13. ぜんぶで八千三百円です。	13. Zenbu-de has-sen san-byaku-en desu.
14. ぜんぶで四千九百円です。	14. Zenbu-de yon-sen kyuu-hyaku-en desu.
15. ぜんぶで六千二百円ですか。	15. Zenbu-de roku-sen ni-hyaku-en desu-ka?

❸ Dooshite kimasen-ka?

With a クラスメート redo Activity ❷ from Part 2 of Lesson 37. Use your imagination to respond to *dooshite* questions. Each answer should be an appropriate response to the question and should include one of the following:

> plain form of adjective + *kara*   OR   plain form of verb + *kara*
> (non-past or past)   (non-past or past)

Ask your partner why a certain person did <u>or</u> does <u>or</u> is going to do a certain thing. Refer to Lesson 37 for examples and possible names to use. Since you have now learned the past plain form of verbs, you may wish to give some answers using these.

L. 40 電話で 話しましょう

れんしゅう A: What do we need for the party?

You are having a party tomorrow, and a friend of yours is going shopping for you. Tell him/her at least 3 different items that you need, and how many of each you need.

Sample Items

koppu

kamizara

れんしゅう B: Which one do you want? Why?

You won a prize! Choose one of the two items.

しつもん:
(a) Which one do you want?
(b) Why?

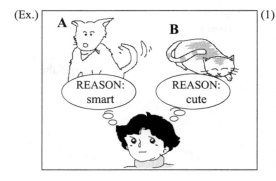

(Ex.)
A   B
REASON: smart
REASON: cute

(1)
A   B
REASON: cute
REASON: cool

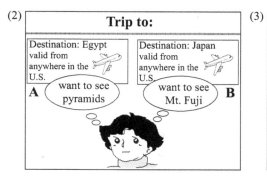

(2)

Trip to:

Destination: Egypt valid from anywhere in the U.S.	Destination: Japan valid from anywhere in the U.S.
A want to see pyramids	want to see Mt. Fuji **B**

(3)

Dinner certificate

Japanese restaurant **A**	Mexican restaurant **B**
want to eat sushi	want to eat tacos (*takosu*)

れんしゅう C: よみましょう。

Read the words and guess how much they would cost in Japan.

(1) けしゴム   (a) 百円ぐらい

(2) ファションざっし   (b) 三千五百円ぐらい

(3) バースデーケーキ   (c) 五百円ぐらい

(4) ジーンズ   (d) 七千円ぐらい

れんしゅう D: Interview your classmate!

R. 32~40 電話で 話しましょう

れんしゅう A: What did Keith receive?

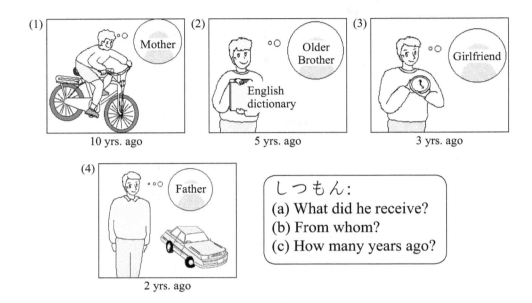

(1) Mother — 10 yrs. ago

(2) Older Brother / English dictionary — 5 yrs. ago

(3) Girlfriend — 3 yrs. ago

(4) Father — 2 yrs. ago

しつもん:
(a) What did he receive?
(b) From whom?
(c) How many years ago?

れんしゅう B: Talking about Past Experiences

Talk about what you have done in the past. Include your impressions of how it was, and any additional information.

(Ex. 1)   Trip

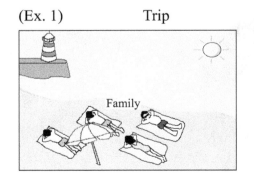

Family

(Ex. 2)   Foreign movies

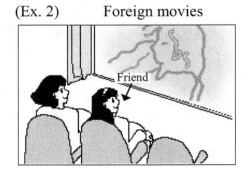

Friend

れんしゅう C: Ordering Food

You are at a fast-food Japanese restaurant and want to try something different.
First, order your food, specifying its location on the menu (e.g., the 2nd from the
top, etc.). After ordering, ask the price.

メニュー

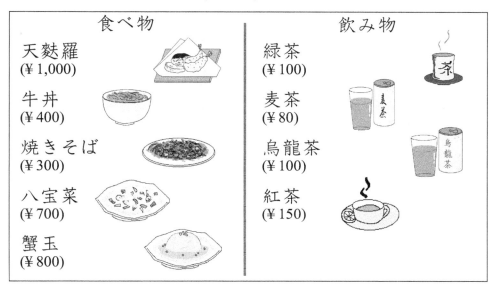

食べ物

天麩羅
(¥1,000)

牛丼
(¥400)

焼きそば
(¥300)

八宝菜
(¥700)

蟹玉
(¥800)

飲み物

緑茶
(¥100)

麦茶
(¥80)

烏龍茶
(¥100)

紅茶
(¥150)

れんしゅう D: よみましょう。こたえましょう。

(1) 土よう日に 何をしましたか。

(2) 日本のアニメを 見たことがありますか。

(3) 大学に 行きたいですか。

(4) きょ年のたんじょう日に 何をもらいましたか。

(5) 今、つくえの上に 何がありますか。

(6) せかいで一ばん高い山は 何ですか。

LESSON 41
Parts of the Body

OBJECTIVES 目標

At the end of this lesson you will be able to:
- ☑ Name some parts of the body
- ☑ Read the *kanji*: 万

VOCABULARY 単語

Words

me	eye
hana	nose
kuchi	mouth
mimi	ear
te	hand, arm
ashi	foot, leg

ADDITIONAL BODY PARTS

atama	head	hiji	elbow
kao	face	hiza	knee
kubi	neck	ashi-kubi	ankle
mune	chest	te-kubi	wrist
senaka	back	yubi	finger
kata	shoulder	ashi-no-yubi	toe
onaka	stomach	karada	body

These words are provided for your reference only.

Other words and expressions you will hear in this lesson

akachan	baby

VOCABULARY NOTES 単語ノート

1. *Te* 手 and *ashi* 足

In Japanese, as in many other languages, a single word (*te*) can refer to both the hands and arms and another (*ashi*) to both the legs and feet. The context will generally clarify which body part is being talked about.

2. Karate 空手

The word *karate*, which refers to a form of Japanese martial arts, is composed of the words *kara* (empty) and *te* (hand). A person who is skilled in karate can stop an attacker by using only his bare (empty) hands, elbows, knees, and feet as weapons.

CULTURE NOTES カルチャーノート

Common expressions related to body parts

Japanese, like many other languages, has numerous expressions which are based on different parts of the body. One expression that you already know is *atama-ga ii* (literally, the head is good) which has the figurative meaning of *be smart*. Here are some other expressions with their literal and figurative meanings.

EXPRESSIONS WITH BODY PARTS

Expression	Literal meaning	Figurative meaning
me-ga ii	good eyes	be observant
mimi-ga tooi	distant ears	hard of hearing
kuchi-ga katai	hard mouth	able to keep a secret
hana-ga takai	high nose	proud
kao-ga hiroi	wide face	be widely known
hara-ga tatsu	belly stands	be angry
koshi-ga omoi	heavy hips	be slow to act
atama-ga katai	hard head	be stubborn

Can you think of any expressions in English or in other languages which include the following?

1. leg   2. hand   3. nose   4. arm

YOMIMASHOO!   読みましょう

め	eye	て	hand, arm
はな	nose	あし	foot, leg
くち	mouth	からて	karate
みみ	ear	あかちゃん	baby

ADDITIONAL BODY PARTS					
あたま	head	かた	shoulder	てくび	wrist
かお	face	おなか	stomach	ゆび	finger
くび	neck	ひじ	elbow	あしのゆび	toe
むね	chest	ひざ	knee	からだ	body
せなか	back	あしくび	ankle		

KANJI NOTES   漢字ノート

In this lesson you will learn to read the *kanji* 万. Be sure that you know the reading for the *kanji* and can tell what the *kanji* means. The reading which is marked by an asterisk is for your reference only; you do not need to learn this. You also do not have to learn any new words which are given in the examples. The correct stroke order for this *kanji* is given in the Optional Writing Practice section.

万   **MAN** (ten thousand), **BAN***

四万	yon-*man*	40,000
十万	juu-*man*	100,000
万年筆	*man*nenhitsu	fountain pen [10,000-year brush]
万歳	*banzai*	hurray!

三万二千五百円です。   San-*man* ni-sen go-hyaku-en desu.
(It is 32,500 yen.)

万年筆が六本あります。   *Man*nenhitsu-ga rop-pon arimasu.
(There are six fountain pens.)

The *kanji* 万 is based on an ancient Hindu and Buddhist symbol of good luck called a *manji*.

INTERACTIVE ACTIVITIES

PART 1

❶ Dooshite ikimasen-ka?

In pairs, check the answers to Assignment #1 in Part 2 of Lesson 40.

❷ Migi desu-ka?

Play this guessing game with a クラスメート. Partner A, without showing Partner B, writes the name of one of the six body parts listed in the 単語 section of this lesson. Partner B then asks the question "_____ *desu-ka?*" to determine the selected part. Each question is worth one point. Then change roles and repeat. The player with the lower score is the winner of the round. As you play additional rounds, try to avoid looking at the vocabulary list. Read this sample exchange aloud before you begin.

A: (writes down *kuchi*)
B: Mimi desu-ka?
A: Iie, chigaimasu.
B: Ashi desu-ka?
A: Iie, chigaimasu.
B: Kuchi desu-ka?
A: Hai, soo desu. [Partner B asked three questions and now has a score of three.]

❸ Hana desu.

Play this familiar game with a クラスメート. The object is to fool your partner into doing and saying what you are doing and saying even though your words do not match your actions. Use only those body parts listed in the box. The game must be played very quickly. After about every five or six statements, change roles and continue. Do not worry about keeping score. Just enjoy the game. Study this sample exchange before you begin.

A: Hana desu. [A is pointing to his own nose.]
B: Hana desu. [B quickly repeats while pointing to her own nose.]
A: Kuchi desu. [A is pointing to his own mouth.]
B: Kuchi desu. [B quickly repeats while pointing to her own mouth.]
A: Ashi desu. [A is pointing to his own arm which is not correct.]
B: [B says and does nothing because A's words and actions do not match.]
A: Mimi desu. [A is pointing to his own eye which is not correct.]
B: Mimi desu. [B quickly repeats while pointing to her own eye. B has been fooled!]

me	mimi
hana	te
kuchi	ashi

PART 2

❶ Yomimashoo!

This pair activity provides you with an opportunity to review the *kanji* for numbers. Partner A masks the *roomaji* side and reads the prices in the left column in order. Partner

330

B responds after each with either *Hai, soo desu* or *Iie, chigaimasu. Moo ichido yonde kudasai.* Partner A writes down those which need to be studied. Switch roles and repeat.

漢字

1. 七万一千六百円
2. 八万四千九百円
3. 九万三千六百円
4. 二万六千三百円
5. 五万二千百円
6. 十万六千七百円
7. 一万七千八百円
8. 三万九千二百円
9. 六万五千四百円
10. 四万八千三百円

ローマ字

1. nana-man is-sen rop-pyaku-en
2. hachi-man yon-sen kyuu-hyaku-en
3. kyuu-man san-zen rop-pyaku-en
4. ni-man roku-sen san-byaku-en
5. go-man ni-sen hyaku-en
6. juu-man roku-sen nana-hyaku-en
7. ichi-man nana-sen hap-pyaku-en
8. san-man kyuu-sen ni-hyaku-en
9. roku-man go-sen yon-hyaku-en
10. yon-man has-sen san-byaku-en

❷ **Kao-o kakimashoo*! (Let's draw a face!)**

In this activity Partner A begins by drawing (without Partner B seeing) a face with ears, eyes, nose, and/or mouth. It is the face of an alien so the features may be a bit unusual in terms of both number and location. For example, there may be one eye, two noses, one ear, and no mouth. Partner A must explain to Partner B in 日本ご (of course!) how to draw the same face. Partner B may ask as many questions in 日本ご as needed to complete the task. Partner A needs to watch Partner B closely as Partner B draws but may not point to Partner B's drawing at any time. When you have finished, compare the two drawings. Do the two faces have the same number of features, and are the features in approximately the same location? Change roles and repeat.

*In Japanese *kakimashoo* can mean *let's write* or *let's draw*. The *kanji* are different.

USEFUL WORDS		USEFUL EXPRESSIONS	
mimi	ear	Hana-ga futatsu arimasu.	There are two noses.
me	eye	Mimi-ga arimasu-ka?	Are there any ears?
hana	nose	Ikutsu arimasu-ka?	How many are there?
kuchi	mouth	Mittsu arimasu.	There are three.
hitotsu	one	Kuchi-o kaite kudasai.	Please draw a mouth.
futatsu	two	Soko ja nai desu.	Not there.
mittsu	three	Motto shita desu.	It's lower (farther down).
motto	more, -er	Motto ue desu.	It's higher (farther up).
shita	down	Motto migi desu.	It's farther to the right.
ue	up	Motto hidari desu.	It's farther to the left.
migi	right	Hana-no migi desu.	It's to the right of the nose.
hidari	left	Kuchi-no hidari desu.	It's to the left of the mouth.
chiisai	small	Me-wa hana-no shita desu.	The eye is below the nose.
ookii	large	Ii desu-ka? Hai, ii desu.	Is this good? Yes, that's good.
sukoshi	a little	Motto ookii/chiisai desu.	It's bigger/smaller.
owari	the end	Moo sukoshi ue/shita desu.	It's a little farther up/down.

L. 41 電話で 話しましょう

れんしゅう A: Body Parts

(1)
(2)
(3)
(4)
(5)
(6)

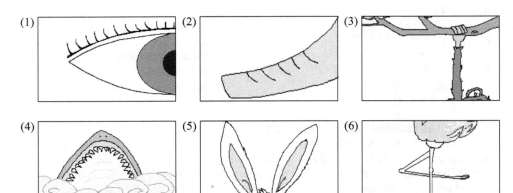

Word Bank

chiitaa

washi

zoo

kirin

kaba

pengin

saru

Draw a picture of the alien based on the description. (kao=face)

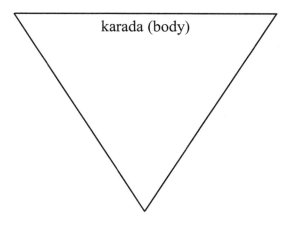

karada (body)

れんしゅう C: Where is ~?

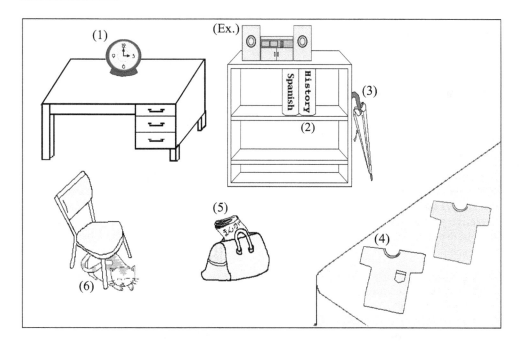

333

LESSON 42
Asking about and Describing Health Conditions

OBJECTIVES   目標

At the end of this lesson you will be able to:
- ☑ Ask what is wrong with someone
- ☑ Describe physical conditions
- ☑ Read the *kanji*: 口　目　耳

VOCABULARY   単語

Words

ha	tooth, teeth
nodo	throat

Phrases and expressions

Doo shita-n desu-ka?	What's wrong? What's happened?
____-ga itai-n desu.	My ____ hurts; I have a ____-ache.
O-daiji-ni.	Get well soon; Take care of yourself. (*said to a sick or injured person*)
Kyoo, o-yasumi shite-mo ii desu-ka?	May I take today off?
Daijoobu desu-ka?	Are you O.K.?

Other words and expressions you will hear in this lesson

Itai!	Ouch!
migi-te	right hand
hidari-te	left hand

CULTURE NOTES   カルチャーノート

Japanese medicine

Being very practical when it comes to health matters, Japanese rely on both Eastern health practices, which trace their origins to ancient China, and the very best of Western medicine. Both Western and Chinese remedies are advertised in the media and sold in drugstores in Japan. In the West in recent years the medical community has shown increasing interest in Eastern medicine. Many patients are already benefiting from a combination of Eastern and Western medical practices.

Western and Eastern medicine operate on fundamentally different principles. Western medicine continues to view the human body as an assemblage of interrelated mechanical systems. If one system or part of a system fails, one attempts to treat or replace the defective part, much the way one would repair a car or other machine. Heart, kidney, and liver transplants along with hip and knee replacements are examples of this type of approach.

Eastern medicine views *ki* (*chi*)* – the vital life force or energy – as the critical element which determines an individual's health. If the flow of *ki* is blocked, predictable health problems will result. Acupuncture and acupressure are two means of balancing the flow of *ki*. Acupuncture uses needles which are inserted at specific locations in the body to treat a wide range of ailments by controlling the flow of *ki*. If properly performed by a trained physician, acupuncture is a painless procedure. Physicians who use acupressure apply pressure to key places on a patient's body with their fingers to treat various ailments.

*Pronounced *ki* in Japanese and *chi* in Chinese, the *kanji* 気 is used to represent this vital life force. This is, of course, the same 気 as in 天気 (weather) and 元気 (good health).

は	tooth, teeth
のど	throat
どう したん ですか。	What's wrong? What's happened?
あたまが いたいん です。	My head hurts; I have a headache.
おだいじに。（お大事に。）	Get well soon; Take care of yourself.
今日、おやすみ しても いい ですか。	May I take today off?
だいじょうぶ ですか。（大丈夫ですか。）	Are you O.K.?
いたい！	Ouch!
みぎて	right hand
ひだりて	left hand

KANJI NOTES 漢字ノート

In this lesson you will learn to read three *kanji*: 口, 目 and 耳. Be sure that you know the readings of each *kanji* and can tell what the *kanji* means. Readings which are marked by an asterisk are for your reference only; you do not need to learn these at this time. You also do not have to learn any new words which are given in the examples. The correct stroke order for these *kanji* is given in the Optional Writing Practice section.

口 **KOO*, KU*; kuchi [guchi]** (mouth, opening)

口	*kuchi*	mouth
入口	iri*guchi*	entrance
出口	de*guchi*	exit
川口	Kawa*guchi*	*family name* [river-mouth]
山口	Yama*guchi*	*family name* [mountain-mouth]
窓口	mado*guchi*	window [ex: ticket window]
人口	jin*koo*	population

今日、川口さんが来ました。	Kyoo, Kawa*guchi*-san-ga kimashita. (Today Mr. Kawaguchi came.)
日本の人口は何人ぐらいですか。	Nihon-no jin*koo*-wa nan-nin-gurai desu-ka? (What is Japan's population?)
入口の前にポストがあります。	Iri*guchi*-no mae-ni posuto-ga arimasu. (In front of the entrance (there) is a mailbox.)
来年、山口さんは高校に行きます。	Rainen, Yama*guchi*-san-wa kookoo-ni ikimasu. (Next year Ms. Yamaguchi will go to high school.)

目 **MOKU*; me** (eye; *ordinal suffix*)

目	*me*	eye
台風の目	taifuu-no *me*	eye of the typhoon
目標	*moku*hyoo	objective, mark, target
二時間目	ni-jikan-*me*	second period (class)
三番目	san-ban-*me*	the third (one)

目が痛いんです。	*Me*-ga itai-n desu.
	(My eye hurts.)
今日の二時間目は	Kyoo-no ni-jikan-*me*-wa nihongo desu-ka?
日本語ですか。	(Is second period today Japanese?)
右から三番目の本は	Migi-kara san-ban-*me*-no hon-wa nan-no hon desu-ka?
何の本ですか。	(What kind of book is the third one from the right?)

耳　**JI*; mimi** (ear)

耳	*mimi*	ear
耳が遠い	*mimi*-ga tooi	hard of hearing [distant ears]

耳が痛いんです。	*Mimi*-ga itai-n desu.
	(I have an earache.)
私の犬の耳は小さい	Watashi-no inu-no *mimi*-wa chiisai desu.
です。	(My dog's ears are small.)
私の父は少し耳が遠い	Watashi-no chichi-wa sukoshi *mimi*-ga tooi desu.
です。	(My father is a little hard of hearing.)

INTERACTIVE ACTIVITIES

PART 1

❶ Yomimashoo!　📖 & ✏️

This pair activity provides you with an opportunity to review many of the *kanji* which you have learned to read. Partner A masks the *roomaji* side and reads the vocabulary in the left column in order. Partner B responds after each with either *Hai, soo desu* or *Iie, chigaimasu. Moo ichido yonde kudasai.* Partner A writes down those which need to be studied. Switch roles and repeat.

漢字	ローマ字	漢字	ローマ字
1. 上	1. ue	13. 一年せい	13. ichi-nen-sei
2. 五円	2. go-en	14. 行く	14. iku
3. 十人	3. juu-nin	15. 一月七日	15. ichi-gatsu nanoka
4. 一つ	4. hitotsu	16. 六年	16. roku-nen
5. 四月三日	5. shi-gatsu mikka	17. 今日	17. kyoo
6. お金	6. o-kane	18. 四つ	18. yottsu
7. 元気	7. genki	19. 見ました	19. mimashita
8. 来年	8. rainen	20. 三つ	20. mittsu
9. 日本の大学	9. Nihon-no daigaku	21. 高校	21. kookoo
10. 天気	10. tenki	22. 私	22. watashi
11. 小学校	11. shoogakkoo	23. お水	23. o-mizu
12. 下	12. shita	24. 何月何日	24. nan-gatsu nan-nichi

336

Now try these prices:

25. 一万八千四百五十七円   25. ichi-man has-sen yon-hyaku go-juu-nana-en
26. 六千七百八十円   26. roku-sen nana-hyaku hachi-juu-en
27. 千百五十一円   27. sen hyaku go-juu-ichi-en
28. 十万七千八百四十二円   28. juu-man nana-sen hap-pyaku yon-juu-ni-en

❷ Dialogue

With a partner, practice the following dialogue following the usual procedure. Make sure you understand the meaning of the dialogue before you begin.

A Japanese woman (Yamashita-san 山下さん) is calling in sick to work although she is in perfect health. She is looking forward to a relaxing day at home. Her co-worker (Tanaka-san 田中さん) answers the telephone.

山下: (happily dials the phone)
田中: (picks up phone) Hai, Tanaka desu.
山下: Moshi-moshi? Tanaka-san? Ohayoo gozaimasu. Yamashita desu.
田中: (surprised) A, Yamashita-san? Ima, doko desu-ka?
山下: Ima, uchi desu. Eeto . . . sumimasen-kedo, kyoo, shigoto, o-yasumi shite-mo ii desu-ka?
田中: (worried) E? Doo shita-n desu-ka?
山下: Eeto . . . (suddenly appears to be in great pain) ha-ga itai-n desu.
田中: (concerned) Aa, soo desu-ka? Ja, o-daiji-ni.
山下: (still looking terrible) Doomo, sumimasen. (bows) Shitsurei shimasu. (hangs up and smiles)

For a greater challenge, use the Japanese equivalent of the dialogue.

山下: (happily dials the phone)
田中: (picks up phone) はい、田中です。
山下: もしもし？ 田中さん？ おはよう ございます。 山下です。
田中: (surprised) あ、山下さん？ 今、どこ ですか。
山下: 今、うち です。 ええと、 すみませんけど、 今日、 しごと、 おやすみ しても いい ですか。
田中: (worried) え？ どうしたん ですか。
山下: ええと、 (suddenly appears to be in great pain) は が いたいん です。
田中: (concerned) ああ、 そう ですか。 じゃ、 お大じに。
山下: (still looking terrible) どうも、 すみません。 (bows) しつれい します。 (hangs up and smiles)

> As you practice the dialogue, remember:
> 1. Read the line silently to yourself.
> 2. Look up and say the line (in this case, as if speaking on the phone).
> 3. If you forget part of the line, stop speaking, reread the forgotten part silently, look up, and continue speaking.
> 4. Try to avoid reading and speaking at the same time.

PART 2

---

❶ Kanji review

With a partner, check your answers to Assignment #2 of Part 1. Keep in mind that there may be many correct answers. Refer to the 漢字ノート sections of Lessons 7 through 41 as needed.

❷ Dialogue

With a different partner, review the dialogue (Activity ❷ of Part 1). Change the reason for missing work by substituting a different part of the body. After you have memorized the dialogue and can deliver it with the appropriate gestures and facial expressions, perform it for the class.

BODY PARTS					
head	あたま	atama	foot, leg	あし	ashi
eye	め (目)	me	shoulder	かた	kata
nose	はな	hana	elbow	ひじ	hiji
ear	みみ (耳)	mimi	knee	ひざ	hiza
neck	くび	kubi	ankle	あしくび	ashi-kubi
chest	むね	mune	wrist	てくび	te-kubi
back	せなか	senaka	finger	ゆび	yubi
stomach	おなか	onaka	toe	あしのゆび	ashi-no-yubi
hand, arm	て	te			

L. 42 電話で 話しましょう

れんしゅう A: School Celebrity

You are an exchange student at a Japanese high school. The school newspaper wants to interview you. Answer the reporter's questions.

れんしゅう B: What's wrong?

(Ex.)

(1)

(2)

(3)

(4)

<u>れんしゅう</u> C: Let's converse!

Dialogue:
A: (Dials the phone.)
B: Hello. This is <u>Tanaka</u>.
A: Hello. This is <u>Yamakawa</u>.
   May I take today off?
B: What's wrong?
A: I have a <u>head</u>ache.
B: Oh, really? Please take care of
   yourself.
A: Thank you. Good-bye.

Sample Dialogue:

A: (Dials the phone.)
B: もしもし。<u>田中</u>です。
A: もしもし。<u>山川</u>ですけ
   ど、今日おやすみしても
   いいですか。
B: どうしたんですか。
A: <u>あたま</u>がいたいんです。
B: あ、そうですか。じゃ、
   お大じに。
A: すみません。しつれいします。

Sample Dialogue:
A: (Dials the phone.)
B: Moshi-moshi? <u>Tanaka</u> desu.
A: Moshi-moshi? <u>Yamakawa</u> desu-
   kedo, kyoo o-yasumi shite-mo ii
   desu-ka?
B: Doo shita-n desu-ka?
A: <u>Atama</u>-ga itai-n desu.
B: A, soo desu-ka. Jaa, o-daiji-ni.
A: Sumimasen. Shitsurei shimasu.

<u>れんしゅう</u> D: Reading an Illustrative Passage

私の学校は からです。 と $(3\sqrt{89})^2 = ?$ と のじゅぎょうがあります。 が です。 は 月よう日と水よう日の です。

私は ぶに はいっています。まい日、 から まで れんしゅうをします。 は とても

 です。

340

れんしゅう B: The Irasshai Alien (Sample Illustration)

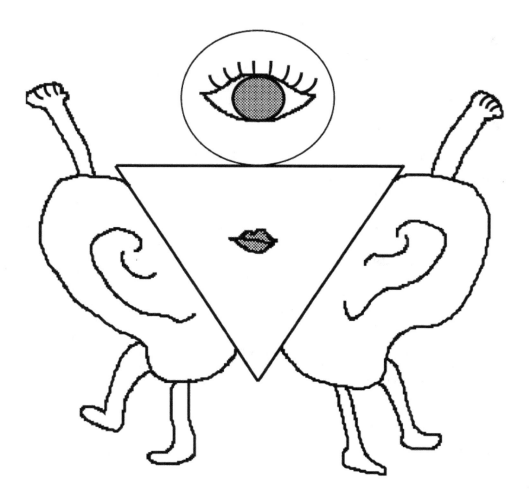

LESSON 43
Asking about and Describing Health Conditions

OBJECTIVES
目標

At the end of this lesson you will be able to:
- ☑ Describe more physical conditions

VOCABULARY
単語

Words

byooki	sick, ill
byooin	hospital, doctor's office
kaze	cold
netsu	fever

Phrases and expressions

Kaze na-n desu.	I have a cold.
Netsu-ga aru-n desu.	I have a fever.

Other words and expressions you will hear in this lesson

Deeto-wa kyanseru.	(My) date was canceled.
Ki-o tsukete kudasai.	Take care; Be careful.

CULTURE NOTES
カルチャーノート

Giving flowers to a sick person

In Japan, as in other countries, visiting friends and relatives who are hospitalized is considered the right thing to do. Japanese recognize the importance of letting friends, colleagues, and loved ones know that they are thinking of them and are praying for their speedy recovery. Visiting those who are sick or who have been injured is called *o-mimai* おみまい in Japanese. Taking flowers to cheer someone up is always a good idea, but it is important to select a culturally appropriate floral gift. Chrysanthemums and potted plants should be avoided. Chrysanthemums are often associated with funerals and, for obvious reasons, would be a poor choice. Potted plants have roots that are well established which might convey to the patient the idea that he may have to remain in the hospital permanently. Cut flowers other than chrysanthemums are therefore the most appropriate choice.

YOMIMASHOO!
読みましょう

びょうき (病気)	sick, ill
びょういん	hospital, doctor's office
かぜ	cold
ねつ	fever
かぜ なん です。	I have a cold.
ねつが あるん です。	I have a fever.
あの人は 元気 じゃ ない です。	That person isn't well.
もう びょういんに 行きましたか。	Did she already go to the hospital?
デートは キャンセル。	(My) date was canceled.
気を つけて ください。	Take care; Be careful.

LEARNING TIP

Practice reading the words and sentences in the 読みましょう sections on a regular basis. Even a few minutes a day will help you to develop your reading skills.

---

❶ **Vocabulary review** 📄 & ✏️

Silently review the following which are from Lessons 41 through 43. Then have a
クラスメート orally test you on them. Your partner says the えいご, and you give the
日本ご. Switch and test your partner. Writes down those which need further study.

1. me	目	eye
2. hana	はな	nose
3. kuchi	口	mouth
4. mimi	耳	ear
5. te	て	hand, arm
6. ashi	あし	foot, leg
7. atama	あたま	head
8. onaka	おなか	stomach
9. ha	は	tooth, teeth
10. nodo	のど	throat
11. byooki	びょうき	sick, ill
12. byooin	びょういん	hospital, doctor's office
13. kaze	かぜ	cold
14. netsu	ねつ	fever
15. Doo shita-n desu-ka?		What's wrong? What's happened?
16. Atama-ga itai-n desu.		My head hurts; I have a headache.
17. O-daiji-ni.		Get well soon; Take care of yourself.
		(*said to a sick or injured person*)
18. Daijoobu desu-ka?		Are you O.K.?
19. Kaze na-n desu.		I have a cold.
20. Netsu-ga aru-n desu.		I have a fever.
21. Ano hito-wa genki ja nai desu.		That person isn't well.
22. Moo byooin-ni ikimashita-ka?		Did she already go to the hospital?

❷ **Mimi-ga itai-n desu-ka?** 📄 & ✏️

Play this guessing game with a クラスメート. Partner A, without showing Partner B,
writes down one of the ailments listed in the box below. Partner B then asks yes-no
questions to determine the ailment. Each question is worth one point. Then change roles
and repeat. The player with the lower score is the winner of the round. As you play
additional rounds, try to avoid looking at the vocabulary list. Read this sample exchange
aloud before you begin.

A: (writes down *Nodo-ga itai-n desu.*)
B: Kaze na-n desu-ka?
A: Iie, chigaimasu.
B: Netsu-ga aru-n desu-ka?
A: Iie, chigaimasu.
B: Me-ga itai-n desu-ka?
A: Iie, chigaimasu.
B: Nodo-ga itai-n desu-ka?
A: Hai, soo desu. [Partner B asked four questions and now has a score of four.]

> **AILMENTS**
> _____ -ga itai-n desu
> (atama, me, hana, mimi, onaka,
> te, ashi, ha, nodo)
> Kaze na-n desu.
> Netsu-ga aru-n desu.

❶ Kakimashoo! 🖊

During this activity work with a クラスメート to check the answers for Assignment #3 from Part 1 of this lesson. Have your partner carefully check your assignment, mark and discuss with you any errors found, and sign off on the work.

❷ Tanaka-san-wa doo shita-n desu-ka? 📄 & 🖊

In this pair activity take turns asking and answering questions to exchange the information you and your partner need to complete your charts. Look only at your own chart. After you have finished, compare the charts.

PARTNER A

NAME	AGE	MEDICAL PROBLEM
	55	
Ueda-san		
Nomura-kun	10	te
Michiko-chan		kaze
Watanabe-san	68	mimi
Fujimoto-san	79	
Yamakawa-san		
Morita-sensei	36	
	91	senaka (back)
Noda-san	87	atama

NAN-SAI?	
1	is-sai
2	ni-sai
3	san-sai
4	yon-sai
5	go-sai
6	roku-sai
7	nana-sai
8	has-sai
9	kyuu-sai
10	jus-sai

SAMPLE QUESTIONS AND ANSWERS

To find out the name (if you know the age):   Dare-ga 27-sai desu-ka?
Suzuki-san desu.

To find out the age (if you know the name):   Saitoo-san-wa nan-sai desu-ka?
83-sai desu.

To find out the problem (if you know the name):   Itoo-san-wa doo shita-n desu-ka?
Onaka-ga itai-n desu.

NOTE
Some of the information which you need you will not be able to request directly. You and your partner will need to collaborate in order to successfully complete both charts.

Taguchi-san-wa doo shita-n desu-ka?
Kaze na-n desu.

Mori-san-wa doo shita-n desu-ka?
Netsu-ga aru-n desu.

PARTNER B

NAME	AGE	MEDICAL PROBLEM
Tanaka-san	55	nodo
Ueda-san	24	ashi
Nomura-kun		
Michiko-chan	2	
	68	
Fujimoto-san		me
Yamakawa-san	43	netsu
	36	onaka
Nakamura-sensei	91	
Noda-san		

NAN-SAI?	
1	is-sai
2	ni-sai
3	san-sai
4	yon-sai
5	go-sai
6	roku-sai
7	nana-sai
8	has-sai
9	kyuu-sai
10	jus-sai

L. 43 電話で 話しましょう

れんしゅう A: Let's converse!

Dialogue:

A: <u>Ms. Honda</u>, are you alright?

B: Well, I <u>have a little fever</u>.

A: Have you gone to the hospital (doctor's) yet?

B: No, not yet, but I'm going around <u>2:00</u>.

A: Oh, really. Well, take care of yourself!

Sample Dialogue:

A: <u>本田さん</u>、大じょうぶですか。

B: ちょっと <u>ねつが あるんです</u>。

A: もう びょういんに 行きましたか。

B: いいえ、まだですけど、<u>二じ</u>ご
ろ行きます。

A: そうですか。お大じに。

Sample Dialogue:

A: <u>Honda-san</u>, daijoobu desu-ka?

B: Chotto <u>netsu-ga aru-n desu</u>.

A: Moo byooin-ni ikimashita-ka?

B: Iie, mada desu-kedo, <u>ni-ji</u>-goro ikimasu.

A: Soo desu-ka. O-daiji-ni.

れんしゅう B: Irasshai Hospital Medical Charts

You are trying to find missing information on your Irasshai Hospital Medical Chart. Group A can only look at Chart A, and Group B can only look at Chart B. Ask members of the other group questions and write down the answers on your chart.

Chart A

名前	とし	Medical Problem
やました 山下	(Ex. 1) 56 yrs.	(Ex. 2) fever
たなか 田中	42 yrs.	(1)
やまぐち 山口	(2)	cold
うえだ 上田	38 yrs.	(3)
ほんだ 本田	19 yrs.	earache
たかやま 高山	24 yrs.	headache

345

Chart B

名前	とし	Medical Problem
やました 山下	(Ex. 1) 56 yrs.	(Ex. 2) fever
たなか 田中	42 yrs.	sore throat
やまぐち 山口	71 yrs.	cold
うえだ 上田	(4)	toothache
ほんだ 本田	19 yrs.	(5)
たかやま 高山	24 yrs.	(6)

れんしゅう C: Interview your classmate!

346

LESSON 44
Taking Medicine

OBJECTIVES 目標

At the end of this lesson you will be able to:
- ☑ Ask and tell when to take different medicines
- ☑ Read the *kanji*: 名 and 前

VOCABULARY 単語

Words
isha	doctor
kusuri	medicine
nomu (nomimasu/nonde)	take (medicine)

Phrases and expressions
mae-ni	before
ato-de	after
Nan-no kusuri desu-ka?	What kind of medicine is it?
____-no kusuri desu.	It is medicine for your ____.

VOCABULARY NOTES 単語ノート

1. Isha いしゃ (医者)
The word *isha* is used to refer only to medical doctors. The polite equivalent *o-isha-san* may be used when talking about a doctor.

2. Nomu のむ (飲む)
The verb *nomu/nomimasu* (drink) is used in the Japanese equivalent of the expression *take medicine*. Even if the medicine is a pill, the verb *nomu* is used. Look at these examples.

Itsu kono kusuri-o *nomimasu*-ka?	When do I *take* this medicine?
Yoru-no hachi-ji-ni *nonde* kudasai.	Please *take* it at 8:00 p.m.
Asupirin-o *nomimashita*-ka?	Did you *take* aspirin?

KEY GRAMMAR POINTS 文法ポイント

1. *Event*-no mae-ni の前に
In Lesson 69 (Vol. 1) you learned how to express spatial relationships with the noun *mae*.

watashi-no *mae*-ni	in *front* of me
kamera-ya-no *mae*-ni	in *front* of the camera store

This lesson re-introduces *mae* in the time expression -*no mae-ni* which in English is usually expressed as *before*. Look at these examples.

Gohan-*no mae-ni* kusuri-o nonde kudasai.	Please take the medicine *before* meals.
Miitingu-*no mae-ni* bideo-o mimashita.	I watched the video *before* the meeting.
Tesuto-*no mae-ni* benkyoo-o shimashita.	I studied *before* the test.

2. *Event*-no ato-de の後で
The opposite of -*no mae-ni* is -*no ato-de* which is usually expressed in English as *after*. Read these examples aloud.

Asa-gohan-*no ato-de* nonde kudasai.	Please take it *after* breakfast.
Miitingu-*no ato-de* uchi-ni kaerimasu.	I'll go home *after* the meeting.
Paatii-*no ato-de* nemashita.	I went to sleep *after* the party.

```
EVENT X -no mae-ni  =  before EVENT X

EVENT Y -no ato-de  =  after EVENT Y
```

いしゃ	doctor
くすり	medicine
のむ・のみます・のんで	take (medicine)
前に	before
あとで	after
口を あけて ください。	Please open your mouth.
何の くすり ですか。	What kind of medicine is it?
これは のどの くすりです。	This is medicine for the throat.
いつ この くすりを のみますか。	When do I take this medicine?
よるの 八じに のんで ください。	Please take it at 8:00 p.m.
あさごはんの あとで のんで ください。	Please take it after breakfast.
ごはんの 前に くすりを のんで ください。	Please take the medicine before meals.

できますか。

Can you unscramble these 単語, all of which appear in the 読みましょう section above? Then write the meaning in えいご. Check your answers with your クラスメート.

1. すりく　　　　　　3. まのすみ　　　　　5. でとあ
2. さごはあん　　　　4. いだくさ　　　　　6. しゃい

KANJI NOTES 　　　　　　　　　　　　　漢字ノート

In this lesson you will learn to read two *kanji*: 名 and 前. Be sure that you know the readings of each *kanji* and can tell what the *kanji* means. Readings which are marked by an asterisk are for your reference only; you do not need to learn these at this time. You also do not have to learn any new words which are given in the examples. The correct stroke order for these *kanji* is given in the Optional Writing Practice section.

名　　**MEI*; MYOO*** (name, fame), **na** (name)

名前	*na*mae	name
有名	yuu*mei*	famous, well-known
名人	*mei*jin	expert
名刺	*mei*shi	name card
名字	*myoo*ji	surname, family name

あの人の名前は何 　　　Ano hito-no *na*mae-wa nan desu-ka?
ですか。　　　　　　　(What is that person's name?)

The *kanji* 名 was derived from two *kanji*: 夕 (evening) and 口 (mouth). In the darkness of the evening, a guard asks what a person's name is.

前	**ZEN***; **mae** (before, front)		

前	*mae*	before, front
前に	*mae*-ni	in front
前から	*mae*-kara	from the front
前の	*mae*-no	previous, front
午前	go*zen*	morning, a.m.
前田	*Mae*da	*family name* [front-field]

ご飯の前に薬を飲んで
ください。

Gohan-no *mae*-ni kusuri-o nonde kudasai.
(Take the medicine before meals.)

前から三番目の車は
私のです。

Mae-kara san-ban-me-no kuruma-wa watashi-no desu.
(The third car from the front is mine.)

The *kanji* 前 was derived from pictures of a ram's horns, the moon, and a sword. Horns are in front of a ram, the moon comes before the sun, and a warrior holds his sword in front of him.

KANJI REVIEW														
行	天	九	日	木	四	気	本	七	人	山	十	何	三	水
田	一	小	学	高	川	前	千	校	火	五	下	金	百	来
上	名	二	見	今	万	大	中	円	年	八	元	土	口	目
耳	私	六	月	名	How do you read them? What do they mean?									

INTERACTIVE ACTIVITIES

PART 1

❶ **Kyoo-no nikki (Today's journal entry)**
During this activity each student will work as a pair with two different クラスメート to check Assignment #1 from Part 2 of Lesson 43. Have two students carefully check your imaginary journal entry (making sure that you followed the directions), mark and discuss with you any errors found, and sign off on your assignment.

❷ **Dialogue**
With a partner, practice the dialogue following the usual procedure. Make sure you understand the meaning of each line before you begin. After you have memorized the dialogue, perform it for another pair. Person B, who has a sore throat, goes to see the doctor (A).

A: Kyoo-wa doo shita-n desu-ka?
B: (touches throat and looks pained) Asa-kara nodo-ga itai-n desu.
A: Nodo desu-ne. (picks up a tongue depressor) Ja, kuchi-o akete kudasai.
B: (opens mouth)
A: (examining throat) Akai desu-ne. (takes medicine from a cabinet) Kore-wa nodo-no kusuri desu. Kore-o nonde kudasai.

349

B: Hai. Itsu nomimasu-ka?
A: Gohan-no ato-de nonde kudasai.
B: Gohan-no ato desu-ne. Wakarimashita.
A: O-daiji-ni.
B: Doomo arigatoo gozaimashita.

Use this version of the dialogue for greater reading practice.

A: 今日は どう したん ですか。
B: (touches throat and looks pained) あさから のどが いたいん です。
A: のど ですね。 (picks up a tongue depressor) じゃ、口を あけて ください。
B: (opens mouth)
A: (examining throat) あかい ですね。 (takes medicine from a cabinet) これは のどの くすり です。 これを のんで ください。
B: はい。 いつ のみますか。
A: ごはんの あとで のんで ください。
B: ごはんの あと ですね。 わかりました。
A: お大じに。
B: どうも ありがとう ございました。

PART 2

❶ Time line ✎
During this activity you will work as a pair with two different クラスメート to check Assignment #2 from Part 1 of this lesson. Have two students carefully check your completed sentences, mark and discuss with you any errors found, and sign off on your assignment.

❷ Yon-ban-me-no kusuri-wa itsu nomimasu-ka?   📄 & ✎
Do this activity with a クラスメート. Below is a picture of Ikeda-san's pill box with each of the eight compartments clearly numbered. Each day Ikeda-san takes one of each of the pills at a time specified by the doctor. Ikeda-san has unfortunately misplaced the slip of paper with the information about when to take the different *kusuri*. Ikeda-san (Partner A) calls the doctor's assistant (Partner B) to ask for the needed information (in mixed order!). Partner B should use his/her imagination and answer the questions while both of you writing down the information. When you have finished, compare the recorded information. Then change roles and repeat. Look at the example.

A: **Hachi**-ban-me-no kusuri-wa itsu nomimasu-ka?
B: **Ban-gohan-no ato-de** nonde kudasai.
A: Hai, wakarimashita. Sorekara, **ni**-ban-me-no kusuri-wa itsu nomimasu-ka?

pill box
1
2
3
4
5
6
7
8

> Asa/Hiru/Ban-gohan-no mae-ni/ato-de
>
> Asa/Yoru-no 7-ji-ni

れんしゅう A: Taking Medicine

pharmacist　　patient

At the Clinic

しつもん:
(a) What kind of medicine?
(b) When to take it?

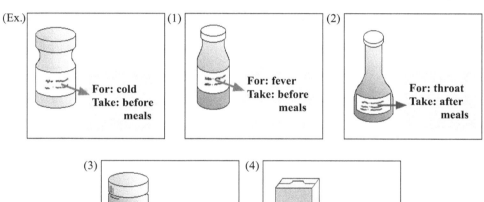

(Ex.)
For: cold
Take: before
　　meals

(1)
For: fever
Take: before
　　meals

(2)
For: throat
Take: after
　　meals

(3)
For: stomach
Take: before
　　meals

(4)
For: ear
Take: after
　　meals

れんしゅう B: What do you do before ~ / after ~?

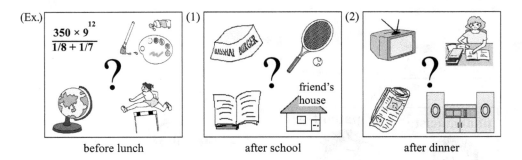

(Ex.) before lunch　　(1) after school　　(2) after dinner

れんしゅう C: Which one doesn't belong?

(1)
(a) 目
(b) 耳
(c) 木
(d) 口

(2)
(a) きって
(b) いしゃ
(c) 学せい
(d) せんせい

(3)
(a) くもり
(b) あめ
(c) はれ
(d) あに

(4)
(a) フランス
(b) ブラジル
(c) ブラウス
(d) シンガポール

(5)
(a) 大学
(b) 名前
(c) 高校
(d) 中学校

LESSON 45
Describing People (Personality)

OBJECTIVES　　　　　　　　　　　　　　　　　　　目標

At the end of this lesson you will be able to:
- ☑ Describe people in terms of personality
- ☑ Read the *kanji*: オ

VOCABULARY　　　　　　　　　　　　　　　　　　　単語

Words

kibishii	strict
yasashii	warm, kind, lenient
akarui	cheerful
majime (na)	serious

MORE WORDS FOR DESCRIBING PEOPLE

genki (na)	energetic	shizuka (na)	quiet
okashii	funny	nigiyaka (na)	lively
shoojiki (na)	honest	shinsetsu (na)	kind
omoshiroi	interesting		

The new words are provided for your reference only.

KEY GRAMMAR POINTS　　　　　　　　　　　　文法ポイント

Linking adjectives (*-te* form)

In English the word *and* can be used to join nouns (dogs *and* cats), adjectives (big *and* powerful), verbs (sing *and* dance), other parts of speech, and even sentences. In Japanese the particle *-to* is used to join nouns and pronouns only.

Ringo-*to* banana-o kaimashita.	I bought apples and bananas.
Itoo-san-*to* Suzuki-san-ni aimashita.	I met Ms. Itoh and Ms.Suzuki.

In Lesson 17 you learned how to link actions by using the *-te* form of the verb.

Hachi-ji-ni uchi-ni *kaette*, gohan-o *tabete*, nyuusu-o *mite*, 11-ji-ni *nemasu*.	I *return* home at 8:00, *eat* dinner, *watch* the news, *and go to bed* at 11:00.
Shukudai-o *shite*, tesuto-no benkyoo-o *shite*, *nemashita*.	I *did* homework, *studied* for a test, *and went to bed*.

In this lesson you will learn how to link adjectives by using their *-te* form. The *-te* form of *i*-adjectives can be formed by dropping the final *i* and adding *-ku-te*. The *-te* form of *na*-adjectives is formed with *-de* (do not use *-na*). Read these examples aloud.

Kibishi*ku-te* majime desu.	She's strict and serious.
Shizuka-*de* majime-na hito desu.	He's a quiet, serious person.
Chiisa*ku-te* hayai kuruma-ga hoshii desu.	I want a small, fast car.

-*TE* FORM OF ADJECTIVES

I-adjectives: change -*i* to -*ku-te*　　　Na-adjectives: add -*de*

YOMIMASHOO!　　　　　　　　　　　　　　　読みましょう

きびしい	strict
やさしい	warm, kind, lenient
あかるい	cheerful
まじめ (な)	serious

353

山川せんせいは どう ですか。	How's Mr. Yamakawa?
きびしい ですよ。	He's strict.
あの せんせいは やさしくて おもしろい です。	That teacher is kind and interesting.
上田せんせいは どんな せんせい ですか。	What kind of teacher is Mrs. Ueda?
きびしくて つまらない です。	She's strict and boring.
しずかで やさしい です。	She's quiet and kind.
田中せんせいの じゅぎょうは ながくて つまらないです。	Mr. Tanaka's classes are long and boring.

KANJI NOTES   漢字ノート

In this lesson you will learn to read the *kanji* オ. Be sure that you know the reading of the *kanji* and can tell what it means. You do not have to learn any new words which are given in the examples. You will learn how to write this *kanji* correctly in Lesson 46.

オ   **SAI** (talent; *suffix for counting age*)

一オ	is-*sai*	one year old
四オ	yon-*sai*	four years old
七オ	nana-*sai*	seven years old
八オ	has-*sai*	eight years old
九オ	kyuu-*sai*	nine years old
十オ	jus-*sai*	10 years old
十六オ	juu-roku-*sai*	16 years old
天オ	ten*sai*	genius

中山さんは 何オですか。	Nakayama-san-wa nan-*sai* desu-ka?	How old is Mr. Nakayama?

オ → 才

The *kanji* オ was derived from a picture of a pruned tree. A tree needs to be pruned at certain stages in its growth.

KANJI REVIEW

行 天 九 日 木 四 気 本 七 人 山 十 何 三 水
田 一 小 学 高 川 前 千 校 火 五 下 金 百 来
上 名 二 見 今 万 大 中 円 年 八 元 土 口 オ
耳 私 六 月 名 目   How do you read them? What do they mean?

INTERACTIVE ACTIVITIES

PART 1

❶ Dekimasu-ka?

In pairs or 三人のグループ check your answers for Assignment #1 from Part 2 of Lesson 44. Compare not only the words which do not belong but also the reason you gave for excluding each one.

❷ Ano sensei-wa yasashiku-te omoshiroi desu.

Do this activity with a クラスメート. Partner A masks the right side of the page (B) and looks only at the left side of the page (A). Partner B looks at both sides. Partner A reads each sentence, substituting the correct *-te* form of the adjective in parentheses. Partner B checks the accuracy of each sentence and responds with either *Hai, soo desu.* OR *Chotto chigaimasu. Moo ichido yonde kudasai.* After Partner A has read a sentence correctly, both partners decide how it would be expressed in English. When you finish, change roles and repeat the activity.

A	B
1. Ano sensei-wa (yasashii) omoshiroi desu.	1. yasashiku-te
2. Ueda-san-wa (akarui) yasashii desu.	2. akaruku-te
3. Tanaka-sensei-no jugyoo-wa (nagai) tsumaranai desu.	3. nagaku-te
4. Taroo-kun-wa (shizuka) majime desu.	4. shizuka-de
5. Atarashii uchi-wa (ookii) kirei desu.	5. ookiku-te
6. Nakamura-sensei-wa (majime) kibishii desu.	6. majime-de
7. Sono eiga-wa (takai) tsumaranai desu.	7. takaku-te
8. Watashi-no konpyuutaa-wa (furui) osoi desu.	8. furuku-te
9. Kono tesuto-wa (muzukashii) nagai desu.	9. muzukashiku-te
10. Sono hanbaagaa-wa (yasui) oishii desu.	10. yasuku-te

PART 2

❶ Kakimashoo! 🖉

With a クラスメート check your answers for Assignment #2 from Part 1. Sign off on your partner's assignment when you have finished. If you or your partner added any words to create more interesting sentences, then your answers may be different. Be sure to check the following:

> ● *kana* and *kanji*
> ● borrowed words are written in *katakana*
> ● necessary particles such as は and の have been added
> ● title suffixes such as さん, せんせい, and くん have been added to names
> ● the first adjective is in the *-te* form (see the 文法ポイント section of this lesson)

❷ Donna sensei desu-ka? 📄 & 🖉

Do this activity with a クラスメート. Both Partner A and B independently complete their lines in the chart by writing two adjectives in the right column. Look only at your own chart. For each line choose two different adjectives from the ADJECTIVES box on. Be sure that the adjectives you choose to describe one person would be used together, for example, *akarui* (cheerful) and *yasashii* (kind). Link each pair of adjectives two different ways as shown in the example. After each partner has completed the three lines in the chart, begin the questioning. Follow the pattern shown in the sample exchange.

SAMPLE EXCHANGE

B: Yamada-sensei-wa kibishii desu-ka?
A: Iie, chigaimasu.

> Be sure to add *-sensei* to each teacher's name.

B: Yamada-sensei-wa akarui desu-ka?
A: Hai, akarui desu. [B writes *akarui* in the *-te* form since it is the first of two linked adjectives.]
B: Yamada-sensei-wa yasashii desu-ka? [*Yasashii* is a good guess since B knows already that Yamada-sensei is *akarui*.]
A: Iie, chigaimasu.
B: Yamada-sensei-wa genki desu-ka?
A: Hai, genki desu. [B writes *genki* after *akaruku-te*]
B: Ja, Yamada-sensei-wa akaruku-te genki desu-ka?
A: Hai, akaruku-te genki desu. [Now A will ask about Suzuki-sensei.]

355

	O-NAMAE	DONNA SENSEI DESU-KA?
A	Yamada	akaruku-te genki OR genki-de akarui
B	Suzuki	
A	Mori	
B	Watanabe	
A	Maetani	
B	Takeda	
A	Hayashi	

ADJECTIVES

kibishii
yasashii
shizuka (na)
akarui
majime (na)
omoshiroi
tsumaranai
genki (na)

L. 45　電話で 話しましょう

れんしゅう A: Describing People and Things

(Ex.) 田中

kind, interesting

(1) 山下せんせい

serious, strict

(2)

cheerful, fun

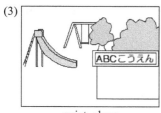

(3) ABCこうえん

quiet, clean

(4) *mangoo*

sweet, delicious

(5) Adventure of Cutting Grass

long, boring

れんしゅう B: Let's converse!

Dialogue:

A: <u>Makoto</u>, what class do you have next?

B: Um, I have <u>English</u>.

A: Who is your <u>English</u> teacher?

B: <u>Ms. Yamada</u>.

A: Really? How is she?

B: She's <u>kind and serious</u>.

A　　　　　　　　B

— Personality characteristics —
きびしい　　あかるい
おもしろい　元気 (energetic)
しずか

Sample Dialogue:

A: <u>まことくん</u>、今から 何のじゅぎょうがありますか。

B: ええと、<u>えいご</u>があります。

A: <u>えいご</u>のせんせいは だれですか。

B: <u>山田</u>せんせいです。

A: へえ、<u>山田</u>せんせいはどうですか。

B: <u>やさしくて、まじめ</u>です。

Sample Dialogue:

A: <u>Makoto-kun</u>, ima-kara nan-no jugyoo-ga arimasu-ka?

B: Eeto, <u>eigo</u>-ga arimasu.

A: <u>Eigo</u>-no sensei-wa dare desu-ka?

B: <u>Yamada</u>-sensei desu.

A: Hee, <u>Yamada</u>-sensei-wa doo desu-ka?

B: <u>Yasashiku-te, majime</u> desu.

れんしゅう C: What's wrong?

You are talking with your Japanese host mother. Tell her what's wrong. Be sure to ask when to take the medicine she recommends.

	(Ex.)	(1)	(2)	(3)
Medical problem:	stomachache	fever	cold	headache
From when:	this morning	last night	last Sunday	yesterday
Take:	before dinner	before meals	after meals	after breakfast

LESSON 46
Describing People (Physical Characteristics)

OBJECTIVES 目標

At the end of this lesson you will be able to:
- ☑ Describe people in terms of physical characteristics
- ☑ Write the *kanji*: 才

VOCABULARY 単語

Words

kami	hair
mijikai	short (opposite of long)
kinpatsu	blond hair, blond
se	height
hikui	low

Phrases and expressions

se-ga takai	tall (person's height)
se-ga hikui	short (person's height)

Other words and expressions you will hear in this lesson

ki-ga nagai	patient
ki-ga mijikai	impatient
senchi	centimeter

KEY GRAMMAR POINTS 文法ポイント

NOUN-ga *ADJECTIVE* desu.

In this lesson there are many examples of this common sentence pattern. Notice that the subject is followed by the subject particle -*ga*. Look at these examples.

Kami-ga nagai desu.	His hair is long.
Se-ga takai desu-ka?	Is she tall?
Ki-ga nagai desu.	She's patient.
Ki-ga mijikai desu.	He's impatient.

YOMIMASHOO! 読みましょう

かみ	hair
みじかい	short (opposite of long)
きんぱつ (金髪)	blond hair, blond
せ	height
ひくい	low
せが 高い	tall (person's height)
せが ひくい	short (person's height)
まさこさんは かみが ながい ですか。	Does Masako have long hair?
ケンくんの かみは 何いろ ですか。	What color is Ken's hair?
きんぱつ です。	It's blond.
私の かみは くろくて ながい です。	My hair is black and long.
だれが 一ばん せが 高い ですか。	Who is the tallest?

359

どっちが せが 高い ですか。	Which is taller?
サムくんは 六フィート です。	Sam is six feet tall.
金ぱつで、せが あんまり 高くない です。	She has blond hair, and she's not very tall.
気が ながい	patient
気が みじかい	impatient
センチ	centimeter

INTERACTIVE ACTIVITIES

PART 1

❶ Kakimashoo! 🖊
During this activity each student will work as a pair with two different クラスメート to check Assignment #1 from Part 2 of Lesson 45. Have two students carefully check your description of an imaginary teacher (making sure that you followed the directions), mark and discuss with you any errors found, and sign off on your assignment.

❷ Kami-ga kuroi desu-ka? 📄 & 🖊
Do this activity with a クラスメート. Partner A, without showing Partner B, writes down the name of one of the six people shown in the chart. Partner B then spins once (using a paper clip), gets a number which corresponds to a personal characteristic (hair color, hair length, etc.), and asks one yes-no question to find out that information about the person Partner A has selected. Partner A must answer all questions truthfully. Partner B continues spinning and asking yes-no questions until he/she has enough information to correctly identify the person Partner A has chosen. Each spin is worth one point. If Partner B spins the same number more than once (and has already asked that question), the spin still counts as one point. Change roles. The player with the lower score is the winner of the round. Read the sample questions and answers aloud before you begin.

SAMPLE QUESTIONS AND ANSWERS
1. Kami-ga kuroi desu-ka?
    Iie, chigaimasu.
2. Kami-ga nagai desu-ka?
    Hai, soo desu.
3. Se-ga takai desu-ka?
    Iie, chigaimasu.
4. Shizuka-de tsumaranai desu-ka?
    Hai, soo desu.

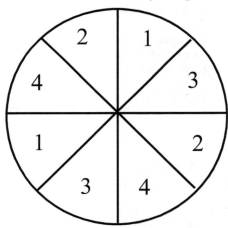

	1. hair color	2. hair length	3. height	4. personality
Takeda	kuroi	mijikai	se-ga takai	akaruku-te yasashii
Fujita	chairoi	nagai	se-ga takai	akaruku-te yasashii
Arai	kuroi	nagai	se-ga takai	majime-de kibishii
Mori	chairoi	nagai	se-ga hikui	shizuka-de tsumaranai
Ueda	chairoi	mijikai	se-ga hikui	shizuka-de tsumaranai
Itoo	kuroi	mijikai	se-ga hikui	majime-de kibishii

360

❶ Kami-ga kuroi desu-ka?   📄 & ✏️

Repeat Activity ❷ (Part 1). Try to avoid looking at the sample questions and answers.

❷ Dare desu-ka?   📄 & ✏️

Do this activity with a クラスメート. Use the chart on the previous page. Each partner selects one person from the chart (without telling the other partner) and writes a description of that person as in the TWO EXAMPLES. You may write in *roomaji*. Then Partner A reads the description to Partner B who listens carefully while looking at the chart and then responds. Change roles.

TWO EXAMPLES

(*Name of person*-san): Kono hito-wa kami-ga chairoku-te nagai desu. Se-ga hikui desu. Akaruku-te yasashii desu. Dare desu-ka? [This is not an actual person in the chart.]

(*Name of person*-san): Kono hito-wa kami-ga kuroku-te mijikai desu. Se-ga takai desu. Shizuka-de tsumaranai desu. Dare desu-ka? [This is not an actual person in the chart.]

For a greater challenge, have your partner listen to the entire description without looking at the chart and then refer to the chart before answering. Also try giving the description smoothly without writing it first. がんばって。

L. 46 電話で 話しましょう

<u>れんしゅう A</u>: A Visit to the Doctor's

You are at a doctor's office. Answer the doctor's questions. After s/he gives you your medicine, ask him/her when you should take it.

	(1)	(2)	(3)	(4)	(5)	(6)
Medical problem	headache	fever	cold	stomach-ache	sore throat	sore leg

<u>れんしゅう B</u>: Describing Physical Characteristics

(1)

(2)
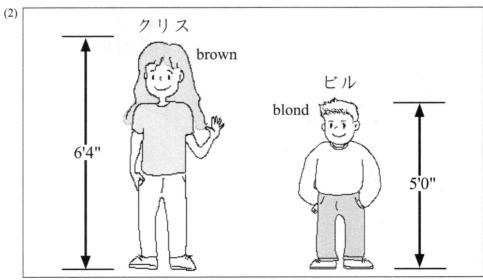

れんしゅう C: Let's talk about your family!

Describe them according to their hair (color/length) and height.

LESSON 47
Describing People (Clothing)

OBJECTIVES
目標

At the end of this lesson you will be able to:
- ☑ Describe people in terms of clothing
- ☑ Read the *kanji*: 先 and 生

VOCABULARY
単語

Words

megane	glasses

Phrases and expressions

megane-o shite-iru (shite-imasu)	wear glasses
se-ga hikui hito	a short person

Other words and expressions you will hear in this lesson

doroboo	thief

KEY GRAMMAR POINTS
文法ポイント

Article of clothing-no *person*
You have already learned how to describe people, places, and things by placing
i-adjectives (such as *omoshiroi* and *kawaii*) and *na*-adjectives (such as *shizuka* and *hen*)
in front of them.

omoshiroi hito	an *interesting* person
kawaii akachan	a *cute* baby
shizuka-na kodomo	a *quiet* child
hen-na otoko-no-hito	a *strange* man

People (as well as other nouns) can also be modified by nouns. The describing noun is
followed by the particle -*no*.

rekishi-no sensei	a *history* teacher
nihon-jin-no tomodachi	a *Japan*ese friend
Kumiko-san-no booifurendo	*Kumiko*'s boyfriend
shinseki-no ko	a *relative*'s child
Tookyoo-Daigaku-no Tanaka-san	Mr. Tanaka of *Tokyo University*

In this lesson you will learn how to describe people in terms of the clothing they are
wearing. The clothing (which is a noun) can be used with the particle -*no* to describe the
person. Study the English equivalents carefully.

booshi-no hito	the person with the *hat*
chairoi booshi-no hito	the person in the *brown hat*
kuroi zubon-no kodomo	the child in the *black pants*
shiroi seetaa-no sensei	the teacher in the *white sweater*
akai shatsu-no otoko-no-hito	the man in the *red shirt*
aoi wanpiisu-no onna-no-hito	the woman in the *blue dress*
hen-na kooto-no otoko-no-hito	the man in the *strange coat*
megane-no otoko-no-ko	the boy with *glasses*

364

めがね	glasses
めがねを している・しています	wear glasses
めがねの人	the person with glasses
あかい シャツの おとこの人	the man in the red shirt
ぼうしの おんなの人	the woman with the hat
どんな人 でしたか。	What did the person look like?
せが ひくい人 でした。	It was a short person.
どろぼう	thief

KANJI NOTES 漢字ノート

In this lesson you will learn to read two *kanji*: 先 and 生. Be sure that you know the readings of each *kanji* and can tell what the *kanji* means. Readings which are marked by an asterisk are for your reference only; you do not need to learn these at this time. You also do not have to learn any new words which are given in the examples. You will learn to write these *kanji* in Lesson 48.

先 **SEN; saki*** (previous, ahead)

先生	*sen*sei	teacher
先週	*sen*shuu	last week
先月	*sen*getsu	last month
先日	*sen*jitsu	the other day
先払い	*saki*barai	advance payment

私の先生はとても 厳しいです。	Watashi-no *sen*sei-wa totemo kibishii desu. (My teacher is very strict.)
山口さんは先週の 金曜日、日本に 帰りました。	Yamaguchi-san-wa *sen*shuu-no kin-yoobi, Nihon-ni kaerimashita. (Mrs. Yamaguchi returned to Japan on Friday last week.)
先日はどうもありがとう ございました。	*Sen*jitsu-wa doomo arigatoo gozaimashita. (Thank you very much for (what you did) the other day.)

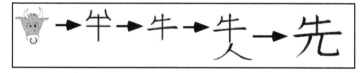

The *kanji* 先 was derived from a picture of a farmer leading a cow. The picture of the cow was simplified and the farmer was represented by the kanji for person 人.

生 **SEI, SHOO*, JOO*** (birth, life); **u(mareru)** (be born), **i(kiru)*** (live), **nama*** (raw)

先生	sen*sei*	teacher
大学生	daigaku*sei*	university student
高校生	kookoo*sei*	high school student
中学生	chuugaku*sei*	middle school student
小学生	shoogaku*sei*	elementary school student
生まれる	*u*mareru	be born
誕生日	tan*joo*bi	birthday

今年の日本語の先生は
だれですか。

どこで生まれましたか。

お誕生日はいつですか。

Kotoshi-no nihongo-no sen*sei*-wa dare desu-ka?
(Who is the Japanese language teacher this year?)
Doko-de *u*maremashita-ka?
(Where were you born?)

O-tan*joo*bi-wa itsu desu-ka?
(When is your birthday?)

The *kanji* 生 was derived from a picture of life springing from the ground in the form of a plant.

KANJI REVIEW

上	名	二	見	今	万	大	中	円	年	八	元	土	口	前
日	木	四	気	本	七	人	山	十	何	三	水	名	目	才
田	一	小	学	高	川	千	校	火	五	下	金	百	来	耳
先	私	六	生	月	行	天	九							

How do you read them? What do they mean?

INTERACTIVE ACTIVITIES

PART 1

❶ **Vocabulary review** 📄 & ✏️

Silently review the following which are from Lessons 46 and 47. Words for colors and clothing as well as some past tense adjectives have also been included. Then have a クラスメート orally test you on them. Your partner says the えいご, and you give the 日本ご. Switch and test your partner. Write down those which need further study.

1.	kami	hair
2.	mijikai	short (opposite of long)
3.	mijikai kami	short hair
4.	Kami-ga mijikai desu.	(Her) hair is short.
5.	kinpatsu	blond hair, blond
6.	Kinpatsu desu.	He's blond.
7.	nagai	long
8.	kuroi	black
9.	chairoi	brown
10.	nagaku-te chairoi	long and brown
11.	nagaku-te chairoi kami	long, brown hair
12.	mijikaku-te kuroi	short and black
13.	Kami-ga mijikaku-te kuroi desu.	(His) hair is short and black.
14.	Kami-ga mijikaku-te kurokatta desu.	(His) hair was short and black.
15.	Kami-ga nagaku-te kinpatsu desu.	(Her) hair is long and blond.
16.	Kami-ga nagaku-te kinpatsu deshita.	(Her) hair was long and blond.
17.	se-ga takai	tall (person's height)
18.	se-ga hikui	short (person's height)
19.	megane	glasses

20. megane-no hito	the person with glasses
21. akai shatsu-no otoko-no-hito	the man in the red shirt
22. aoi booshi-no onna-no-hito	the woman with the blue hat
23. shiroi zubon-no kodomo	the child with the white pants
24. pinku-no wanpiisu-no onna-no-ko	the girl in the pink dress
25. midori-no seetaa-no hito	the person in the green sweater

❷ Dialogue

With a partner practice the dialogue following the usual procedure. Make sure you understand the meaning of each line before you begin. As you practice the dialogue, use gestures and facial expressions. After you have memorized the dialogue, perform it for another pair. Change roles and learn the other part.

A thief has just run from a grocery store with a choice bunch of bananas, leaving behind on the floor dozens of less desirable fruit. A policemen (A) is interviewing the store clerk (B) who witnessed the event.

B: (looking in dismay at the bananas, sees the policeman approaching) A, o-mawari-san! (gestures to come) Kotchi desu!
A: Doo shita-n desu-ka?
B: (upset) Doroboo desu! Mite kudasai. (points to the bananas)
A: (shakes head) Aa. Doroboo-o mimashita-ka?
B: Hai, mimashita.
A: (pulls out pad and pen, starts taking notes) Donna hito deshita-ka?
B: Se-ga hikui otoko deshita. (shows approximate height with hand)
A: (writing) Se-ga hikui otoko . . .
B: Sorekara, kami-ga chairoku-te mijikakatta desu.
A: (writing) Kami-ga chairoku-te mijikakatta-n desu-ne.
B: (nodding) Hai.
A: Nan-sai-gurai deshita-ka?
B: (thinks hard) Eeto . . . Kyuu-juu-go-sai-gurai deshita.
A: (looks surprised)

Use this version of the dialogue for greater reading practice.

B: (looking in dismay at the bananas, sees the policeman approaching)
　あ、おまわりさん！(gestures to come) こっち です。
A: どう したん ですか。
B: (upset) どろぼう です。見て ください。(points to the bananas)
A: (shakes head) ああ。どろほうを 見ましたか。
B: はい、見ました。
A: (pulls out pad and pen, starts taking notes) どんな人 でしたか。
B: せが ひくい おとこ でした。(shows approximate height with hand)
A: (writing) せが ひくい おとこ...
B: それから、かみが ちゃいろくて みじかかった です。
A: (writing) かみが ちゃいろくて みじかかったん ですね。
B: (nodding) はい。
A: 何才ぐらい でしたか。
B: (thinks hard) ええと、九十五才ぐらい でした。
A: (looks surprised)

❶ Changing the dialogue

During this activity each student will work as a pair with a クラスメート to check Assignment #2 from Part 1 of this lesson. Have your partner carefully check your version of the dialogue (making sure that you followed the directions), mark and discuss with you any errors found, and sign off on your assignment. Then read both of the "new" dialogues with your partner.

❷ Kuroi wanpiisu-no hito-wa dare desu-ka?

Play this memory game with a クラスメート. Sit facing each other. Partner A looks quickly at each of the other people in the class (if you have a large class, limit the number of people Partner A looks at to five to eight), making a mental note of their clothing and accessories. Partner A, with eyes now closed, tries to answer Partner B's questions. If Partner A cannot remember who is wearing a particular item, then he/she may ask questions to determine the person's identity. After Partner A has identified the person, change roles. Read the sample exchange aloud before you begin.

SAMPLE EXCHANGE
A: (looks at the target people and then closes eyes)
B: Kuroi wanpiisu-no hito-wa dare desu-ka? [looking at Mei-Po who is wearing a black dress today]
A: Mei-Po-san desu-ka?
B: Hai, soo desu. [Partner A has guessed correctly on the first try. The partners change roles.]
B: (looks at the target people and then closes eyes)
A: Aoi shatsu-no hito-wa dare desu-ka? [looking at Tina who is wearing a blue shirt today]
B: Antonio-kun desu-ka?
A: Iie, chigaimasu. [Partner B has not guessed correctly and may now ask questions to help identify the person]
B: Otoko-no-hito desu-ka? Onna-no-hito desu-ka?
A: Onna-no-hito desu.
B: Se-ga takai desu-ka?
A: Iie, anmari takaku-nai desu.
B: Kami-wa nani-iro desu-ka?
A: Kinpatsu desu.
B: A! Wakarimashita! Tina-san desu-ne.
A: Hai, soo desu.

CLOTHING	
burausu	sukaato
shatsu	wanpiisu
T-shatsu	jaketto
seetaa	nekkuresu
jiinzu, jiipan	booshi
shootopantsu	

COLORS				
kiiro(i)	ao(i)	murasaki (no)	murasaki-**no** shatsu	aka-**to** midori-**no** sukaato
shiro(i)	chairo(i)	midori (no)	midori-**no** jiipan	chairo-**to** kuro-**no** seetaa
aka(i)	kuro(i)	pinku (no)	pinku-**no** wanpiisu	kiiro-**to** aka-**no** T-shatsu
			midori-**to** pinku-**no** jaketto	ao-**to** chairo-**no** booshi

Many color words have both an adjective (with -*i*) and a noun form. When you use two colors to describe something, use the noun forms linked by the particle -*to*. After the second color, use the particle -*no*. The colors *murasaki, midori*, and *pinku* are always nouns.

L. 47　電話で　話しましょう

れんしゅう A: Which person is s/he?

Describe using the distinguishing characteristics.

(Ex.)

blond

red

たなか
田中

やまだ
山田

かわぐち
川口

ミラー

やまかわ
山川

れんしゅう B: Let's converse!

Dialogue:

A: Who's that guy in the blue shirt?

B: Oh, that's Mark.

A: Is he a friend of yours?

B: Yeah.

A: What kind of person is he?

B: He's kind and smart.

A: Oh.

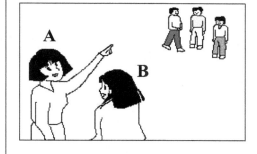

A

B

Sample Dialogue:

A: あのあおいシャッツの人は
　　だれですか。

B: ああ、マークくんです。

A: ともだちですか。

B: はい、そうです。

A: どんな人ですか。

B: やさしくて、あたまがいい
　　人ですよ。

A: そうですか。

Personality characteristics

しずか
おもしろい
元気 (energetic)
あかるい
しょうじき (honest)

Sample Dialogue:

A: Ano <u>aoi shatsu-no</u> hito-wa dare desu-ka?

B: Aa, <u>Maaku-kun</u> desu.

A: Tomodachi desu-ka?

B: Hai, soo desu.

A: Donna hito desu-ka?

B: <u>Yasashiku-te</u>, <u>atama-ga ii</u> hito desu-yo.

A: Soo desu-ka.

*informal version:

A: あの<u>あおいシャッツの</u>人、だれ？

B: ああ、<u>マーク</u>。

A: ともだち？

B: うん、そう。

A: どんな人？

B: <u>やさしくて</u>、<u>あたまがいい</u>人。

A: ふうん。

れんしゅう C: Guessing Game: Who is it?

This is a scene at a train station waiting room. Listen to the hints and try to figure out which person is being described.

LESSON 48
Knowing People and Things

OBJECTIVES 目標

At the end of this lesson you will be able to:
- ☑ Ask if someone knows someone/something
- ☑ Write the *kanji*: 先 and 生

VOCABULARY 単語

Words

| shitte-iru (shitte-imasu) | know(s) |

Phrases and expressions

| Shirimasen. | I don't know. |
| Zenzen oboete-imasen. | I can't remember at all. |

VOCABULARY NOTES 単語ノート

1. Shitte-imasu しっています (知っています)

Shitte-imasu means *know(s)* or *have/has knowledge of something or someone*. To express the equivalent of *don't know*, the Japanese say *shirimasen*. Look at these examples.

Watashi-no sensei-o *shitte-imasu*-ka?	Do you *know* my teacher?
Iie, *shirimasen*.	No, I *don't know* (her/him).
Kono hito-no namae-o *shitte-imasu*-ka?	Do you *know* this person's name?
Hai, *shitte-imasu*.	Yes, I *know* (it).

The verb *shiru/shirimasu* means to *come to know* so if you have already reached the point of knowing something, you use the *-te-imasu* form (*shitte-imasu*) to express that state or condition. To review this grammar point, refer to Lesson 14. The plain form equivalents of *shitte-imasu* and *shirimasen* are *shitte-iru* and *shiranai*, respectively.

2. Shitte-imasu ~ wakarimasu しっています〜わかります (分かります)

It is important to understand the difference between these two verbs. Whereas *shitte-imasu* means *know(s)* or *have/has knowledge of something or someone*, *wakarimasu* implies that you understand or recognize something or someone. English equivalents of *wakarimasu* include words such as *understand, recognize, be clear, can tell, be evident, figure out,* and *see*.

Wakarimasu-ka?	Do you *understand*? Do you *see*?
	Do you *get it*? *Is* it *clear*? *Can* you *tell*?
Hai, *wakarimasu*.	Yes, I *understand*, etc.
Sumimasen kedo, *wakarimasen*.	I'm sorry, but I *don't understand*.
Kimasu-ka? Mada *wakarimasen*.	Will he come? It's *not clear* yet.
Taroo-kun-ga *wakarimasu*-ka?	Do you *recognize* Taro?

YOMIMASHOO! 読みましょう

しっています	know(s)
しりません。	I don't know.
ぜんぜん おぼえていません。	I can't remember at all.
あの人を おぼえていません でした。	I couldn't remember who that person was.
あの人に あったことが ありますか。	Have you ever met that person?

371

私の先生を しっていますか。   Do you know my teacher?

この人の 名前を しっていますか。   Do you know this person's name?

あったことが ありますけど、   I've met her, but I've forgotten her name.

名前を わすれました。

INTERACTIVE ACTIVITIES

PART 1

❶ Yomimashoo! 🖊

Work with two different クラスメート in pairs to check your answers for Assignment #1 from Part 2 of Lesson 47. For each *kanji* there is only <u>one</u> correct reading since it occurs within a context. Sign off on each partner's assignment when you have finished.

❷ Describing people 📄 & 🖊

Silently review the following which are from Lessons 45-47. Words for colors and clothing have also been included. Then have a クラスメート orally test you on them. Your partner says the えいご and you give the 日本ご. Switch and test your partner. Write down those which need further study.

1. yasashiku-te omoshiroi	kind and interesting
2. kibishiku-te tsumaranai	strict and boring
3. shizuka-de yasashii	quiet and kind
4. genki-de akarui	energetic and cheerful
5. se-ga takai	tall (person's height)
6. se-ga hikui	short (person's height)
7. se-ga hikui hito	a short person
8. se-ga anmari takaku-nai	not very tall
9. Kami-ga mijikai desu.	(Her) hair is short.
10. Kinpatsu desu.	He's blond.
11. nagaku-te chairoi kami	long, brown hair
12. mijikaku-te kuroi kami	short, black hair
13. Kami-ga mijikaku-te akai desu.	(His) hair is short and red.
14. kinpatsu-de nagai	blond and long
15. Kami-ga nagaku-te kinpatsu desu.	(Her) hair is long and blond.
16. megane-no hito	the person with glasses
17. akai shatsu-no otoko-no-hito	the man in the red shirt
18. kiiroi booshi-no onna-no-hito	the woman with the yellow hat
19. shiroi zubon-no kodomo	the child with the white pants
20. pinku-no wanpiisu-no onna-no-ko	the girl in the pink dress
21. midori-no seetaa-no hito	the person in the green sweater
22. dono hito	which person
23. donna hito	what kind of person

PART 2

❶ Dialogue

With a partner practice the dialogue following the usual procedure. Make sure you understand the meaning of each line before you begin. As you practice the dialogue, use gestures and facial expressions. After you have memorized the dialogue, perform it for another pair. Change roles and learn the other part.

Two friends, Yamaguchi-san (山口さん) and Nakagawa-san (中川さん), are at a reception with about 30 people in attendance. Yamaguchi-san keeps looking at a woman (Takada-san 高田さん) across the room whose name does not come to mind.

山口： (looking at Takada-san) Nakagawa-san, ano hito-o shitte-imasu-ka?
中川： (looks in same direction) Dono hito desu-ka?
山口： (gestures with head, unobtrusively) Ano aoi wanpiisu-no hito desu.
中川： (sees two women in the same color dress) Megane-no hito desu-ka?
山口： Iie, shiroi baggu-no hito desu.
中川： Aa, ano hito desu-ka?
山口： (still looking, nods) Ee. Shitte-imasu-ka?
中川： (shaking head) Iie, shirimasen kedo, Yamaguchi-san-wa? Shitte-imasu-ka?
山口： (looking uncertain) Atta-koto-ga arimasu kedo, namae-o wasuremashita.

Use this version of the dialogue for greater reading practice.

山口： (looking at Takada-san) 中川さん、 あの人を しっていますか。
中川： (looks in same direction) どの人 ですか。
山口： (gestures with head, unobtrusively) あの あおい ワンピースの人 です。
中川： (sees two women in the same color dress) めがねの人 ですか。
山口： いいえ、 しろい バッグの人 です。
中川： ああ、 あの人 ですか。
山口： (still looking, nods) ええ。 しっていますか。
中川： (shaking head) いいえ、 しりません けど、 山口さんは？
　　　 しっていますか。
山口： (looking uncertain) あったことが ありますけど、 名前を わすれました。

❷ Ano hito-o shitte-imasu-ka?

Change partners. Imagine that you are both attending a reception where you each know about half of the people present. Modify the dialogue you have just learned by substituting new descriptive words and phrases for those shown in **bold** in the dialogue that follows. You can describe Takada-san, who can be a man or a woman, in terms of height, hair color, hair length, clothing, or a combination of these. In some versions of the dialogue (as in the original), Nakagawa-san doesn't know Takada-san. In other versions, Nakagawa-san does know Takada-san in which case you can extend the dialogue as shown in the example.

山口： (looking at Takada-san) Nakagawa-san, ano hito-o shitte-imasu-ka?
中川： (looks in same direction) Dono hito desu-ka?
山口： (gestures with head, unobtrusively) **Ano aoi wanpiisu**-no hito desu.
中川： (sees two people who fit that description) **Megane-no hito desu-ka?**
山口： Iie, **shiroi baggu-no hito desu.**
中川： Aa, ano hito desu-ka?

373

Shirimasen

中川 : (shaking head) Iie, shirimasen
kedo, Yamaguchi-san-wa?
Shitte-imasu-ka?

山口 : (looking uncertain) Atta-koto-ga
arimasu kedo, namae-o
wasuremashita.

Shitte-imasu

中川 : (nods) Hai, yoku shitte-imasu.
Takada-san desu. **Kookoo-no**
sensei desu.

山口 : Donna hito desu-ka?

中川 : **Shizuka-de yasashii** hito desu.

SAMPLE DESCRIPTIVE WORDS AND PHRASES

1. *Color + clothing*-no hito [Lesson 47]
    chairoi suutsu-no hito
2. *Accessory*-no hito [Lesson 47]
    kirei-na nekkurasu-no hito
3. Se-ga takai/hikui desu-ka? [Lesson 46]
4. Kami-ga nagai/mijikai desu-ka? [Lesson 46]
5. Kami-ga *color + length* desu-ka? [Lesson 46]
    Kami-ga kuroku-te nagai desu-ka?
    Kinpatsu-de mijikai desu-ka?
6. *Personality adjective(s)* desu. [Lesson 45]
    Kibishiku-te tsumaranai hito desu.
    Genki-de akarui hito desu.

CLOTHES/ACCESSORIES	
wanpiisu	dress
burausu	blouse
sukaato	skirt
seetaa	sweater
suutsu	suit
waishatsu	dress shirt
zubon	pants
nekutai	necktie
booshi	hat
megane	glasses
nekkuresu	necklace
baggu	handbag/purse
kaban	briefcase/bag

L. 48 電話で 話しましょう

<u>れんしゅう A</u>: Do you know ~?

(1)
person

(2)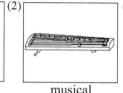
musical
instrument

(3)
movie

(4)
person

(5)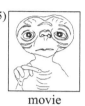
movie

<u>れんしゅう B</u>: Let's converse!

(Ex.) blue 6'8"
(1) blond 4'9"
(2) brown
(3) red

Sample Dialogue:

A: 田中さん、あの人をしっていますか。

B: どの人ですか。

A: あのせが高い人です。

B: あおいセーターの人ですか。

A: はい。しっていますか。

B: あったことがありますけど、名前をわすれました。

Dialogue:

A: <u>Mr. Tanaka</u>, do you know that person?

B: Which person?

A: That <u>tall</u> person.

B: The person <u>in the blue sweater</u>?

A: Yes. Do you know him?

B: I have met him, but I forgot his name.

Sample Dialogue:

A: <u>Tanaka-san</u>, ano hito-o shitte-imasu-ka?

B: Dono hito desu-ka?

A: Ano <u>se-ga takai</u> hito desu.

B: <u>Aoi seetaa-no</u> hito desu-ka?

A: Hai. Shitte-imasu-ka?

B: Atta-koto-ga arimasu-kedo, namae-o wasuremashita.

れんしゅう C: What kind of person is ~?

(1)

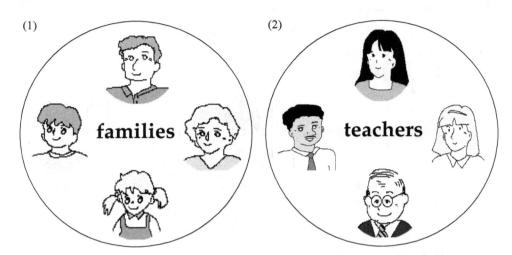

しつもん: What kind of person is [family member]?

(2)

しつもん: What kind of person is [teacher's name]?

(3)

しつもん: What kind of person is [best friend]?

R. 41~48 電話で 話しましょう

れんしゅう A: Let's converse!

 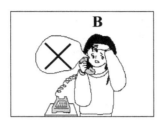 

┌────── Activities ──────┐
party	concert	movie
basketball	soccer	baseball
going to a restaurant		picnic

┌────── Medical problems ──────┐
fever	cold
sore leg	stomachache
earache	toothache

れんしゅう B: Let's find your ideal partner!

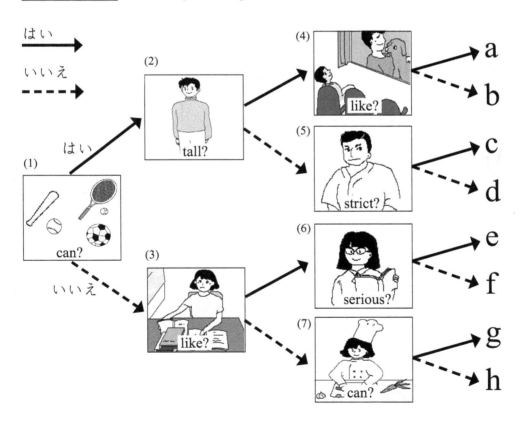

377

Your ideal partner:

a. may be an Oscar-winning movie star.
b. may be a super-model.
c. may be a martial arts Olympic gold medalist.
d. may be a famous TV aerobics instructor.
e. may be a world-renown researcher.
f. may be the world's funniest stand-up comedian.
g. may be a best-selling cookbook writer.
h. may be an international restaurant critic.

れんしゅう C: Irasshai Game!

Choose a question from one of the categories. Listen to the hints and guess what is being described. (If you don't know the answer in Japanese, you may answer in English.)

Famous People	Fruit	Animals
100	100	100
200	200	200
300	300	300

LESSON 49
Life Events (Birth and Marriage)

OBJECTIVES   目標

At the end of this lesson you will be able to:

- ☑ Ask and state if someone is married
- ☑ Ask and state when and where someone was born
- ☑ Read the *kanji*: 父 and 母

VOCABULARY   単語

Words

kekkon	marriage
kekkon suru (shimasu/shite)	get married, marry
akachan	baby
umareru (umaremasu/umarete)	be born
#-ka-getsu	# month(s)
nan-ka-getsu	how many months

Other words and expressions you will hear in this lesson

o-miai	arranged meeting (see Culture Notes)

VOCABULARY NOTES   単語ノート

Akachan あかちゃん (赤ちゃん)

Akachan, the Japanese word for *baby*, is composed of *aka* and *chan*. *Aka* means *red* and *chan* is the suffix used with the names of small children. Many Japanese view their babies as having pinkish or reddish faces.

KEY GRAMMAR POINTS   文法ポイント

1. #-ka-getsu か月

This lesson introduces *-ka-getsu*, the counter for number of months. When the numbers *ichi, ni, san*, etc., are combined with *-ka-getsu*, some of them change form. Pay close attention to the italicized ones in the chart below. The corresponding question form is *nan-ka-getsu*.

Akachan-wa *nan-ka-getsu* desu-ka?	*How many months* (old) is the baby?
Ni-ka-getsu desu.	It's *two months* (old).
Nan-ka-getsu Nihon-ni imashita-ka?	*How many months* were you in Japan?
Nana-ka-getsu Nihon-ni imashita.	I was in Japan *seven months*.

NAN-KA-GETSU?			
ik-ka-getsu	1 month	nana-ka-getsu	7 months
ni-ka-getsu	2 months	*hak*-ka-getsu	8 months
san-ka-getsu	3 months	kyuu-ka-getsu	9 months
yon-ka-getsu	4 months	*juk*-ka-getsu	10 months
go-ka-getsu	5 months	juu-*ik*-ka-getsu	11 months
rok-ka-getsu	6 months	juu-ni-ka-getsu	12 months

2. Kekkon shite-imasu けっこん しています

Kekkon suru means to *get married*. To express the state or condition which results from this action, use the *-te-imasu* form of the verb: *kekkon shite-imasu* (am/is/are married). Look at these examples.

379

Ashita kekkon shimasu.	He will get married tomorrow.
Kinoo kekkon shimashita.	He got married yesterday.
Ima kekkon shite-imasu.	Now he is married.
Kekkon shite-imasu-ka?	Are you married?
Hai, kekkon shite-imasu.	Yes, I'm married.
Iie, kekkon shite-imasen.	No, I'm not married.
Iie, mada desu.	No, not yet.

3. *Time expression*-ni に (Review)

The particle *-ni* can be used with time expressions such as years, months, dates, days, seasons, and clock times. In English *-ni* is usually expressed as *in, on,* or *at.*

1997-nen-*ni* umaremashita.	She was born *in* 1997.
Juu-gatsu-*ni* umaremashita.	He was born *in* October.
Shi-gatsu muika-*ni* umaremashita.	I was born *on* April 6.
Senshuu-no sui-yoobi-*ni* umaremashita.	She was born *on* Wednesday last week.
Fuyu-*ni* umaremashita-ka?	Were they born *in* the winter?
Boku-wa yoru-no 8-ji-*ni* umaremashita.	I was born *at* 8:00 in the evening.

4. *Place*-de で (Review)

In Lesson 47 (Vol. 1), you learned that when the particle *-de* follows a place noun such as *Tookyoo, uchi,* or *byooin,* it indicates the occurrence of an action in that place. When *-de* marks the location of an action, it is usually expressed in English as *at* or *in.*

Doko-*de* umaremashita-ka?	Where were you born?
Kariforunia-*de* umaremashita.	I was born *in* California.
Uchi-*de* umaremashita.	I was born *at* home.
Doko-*de* kekkon shimashita-ka?	Where did you get married?
Atoranta-*de* kekkon shimashita.	We got married *in* Atlanta.
Kyookai-*de* kekkon shimashita.	We got married *at* a church.

YOMIMASHOO! 読みましょう

けっこん	marriage
けっこん する・します	get married, marry
あかちゃん	baby
生まれる・生まれます・生まれて	be born
三か月	three months
何か月	how many months
５月１０日にけっこん します。	He will get married on May 10.
とうきょうでけっこん します。	He will get married in Tokyo.
何年前にけっこん しましたか。	How many years ago did she marry?
一年前にけっこん しました。	She got married one year ago.
高山さんはけっこん していますか。	Is Mr. Takayama married?
おねえさんは こどもさんが いますか。	Does your sister have any children?
私は４月２６日に 生まれました。	I was born on April 26.
どこで 生まれましたか。	Where were you born?
おみあい (お見合い)	arranged meeting

LEARNING TIP

Practice reading the words and sentences in the 読みましょう sections on a regular basis. Even a few minutes a day will help you to develop your reading skills. Read the Japanese line aloud several times, taking note of the English equivalent. Then mask the right side with a piece of paper, read the Japanese aloud, and say the English equivalent. Move the paper down one line at a time to check your accuracy.

O-miai おみあい (お見合い)

O-miai refers to an arranged meeting which can lead to an arranged marriage. It is important to understand that an arranged marriage does not mean a forced marriage. It is very rare that a young person is forced into a marriage against his or her will.

The percentage of *o-miai kekkon* has been in steady decline since the end of World War II. By the mid-1970's half of new marriages were *ren-ai kekkon* (love marriages) and half were *o-miai kekkon* (arranged marriages). By the mid-1980's the percentage of *o-miai kekkon* had dropped to about one third. At the end of the 20th century only about 12% of all new marriages were *o-miai kekkon*.

When a young person is of marriageable age, the parents compile a marriage résumé for their son or daughter which includes a formal portrait photo. The parents then engage the services of a trusted family friend or business colleague who, in assuming the extremely important role of go-between, is willing to search for an eligible and suitable marriage partner. The parents provide the go-between with specific guidelines as to the type of person they desire. The go-between then brings marriage résumés and photos for the parents and son or daughter to examine. When they find an individual who appears to be a possible match, an *o-miai* is set up. These meetings, which are often rather formal affairs, usually occur in hotel lobbies. Often both sets of parents as well as the go-between are present at the first meeting. If the two young people wish to meet again, they go out on a series of dates until they make a final decision whether or not to marry.

The traditional custom of *o-miai kekkon* has many benefits. It is an excellent means of finding spouses for those whose social circles may be quite limited. *O-miai kekkon* also assures that a couple with compatible social backgrounds and interests is brought together. It takes into consideration the fact that a marriage is not just the union of two people but also of two families. Statistics indicate that arranged marriages are less likely to end in divorce than love marriages.

KANJI NOTES　　　　　　　　　　　　　　　　漢字ノート

In this lesson you will learn to read two *kanji*: 父 and 母. Be sure that you know the readings of each *kanji* and can tell what the *kanji* means. The readings which are marked by an asterisk are for your reference only; you do not need to learn them at this time. You also do not have to learn any new words which are given in the examples.

| 父 | **FU*; chichi, too** (father) |

父	*chichi*	father [humble]
父母	*fubo*	parents
祖父	*sofu*	grandfather [humble]
お父さん	*otoosan*	father [honorific]
父の日	*Chichi*-no hi	Father's Day

私の父は四十五オです。	Watashi-no *chichi*-wa yon-juu-go-sai desu. (My father is 45 years old.)
今日川口さんのお父さんが学校に来ました。	Kyoo Kawaguchi-san-no *otoo*san-ga gakkoo-ni kimashita. (Ms. Kawaguchi's father came to school today.)
父の日にお父さんと何をしますか。	*Chichi*-no hi-ni *otoo*san-to nani-o shimasu-ka? (What are you going to do with your father on Father's Day?)

The *kanji* 父 was derived from a picture of an arm holding a stone hatchet and came to represent a father or an old man. You will perhaps find it easier to remember this *kanji* if you visualize a father wearing suspenders which form an "X."

 BO*; haha, kaa (mother)

母	*haha*	mother [humble]
お母さん	*okaa*san	mother [honorific]
母国	*bokoku*	mother country
母国語	*bokokugo*	mother tongue
祖母	*sobo*	grandmother [humble]
母の日	*Haha*-no hi	Mother's Day

私の母から電話が
ありましたか。

Watashi-no *haha*-kara denwa-ga arimashita-ka?
(Was there a telephone call from my mother?)

お母さんは何時頃
お帰りですか。

Okaasan-wa nan-ji-goro o-kaeri desu-ka?
(About what time will your mother (be) return(ing)?)

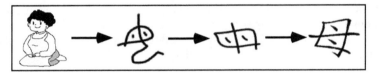

The *kanji* 母 was derived from a picture of a mother sitting on her legs.

KANJI REVIEW

上	名	二	見	今	万	大	中	円	年	八	元	土	口	前
日	木	四	気	本	七	人	山	十	何	三	水	九	目	才
田	一	小	学	高	川	千	校	火	五	下	金	百	来	耳
母	先	私	六	生	父	月	行	天						

How do you read them? What do they mean?

INTERACTIVE ACTIVITIES

PART 1

❶ Akachan-wa go-ka-getsu desu-ka?　　　📄 & ✐

Play this guessing game with a クラスメート. Partner A, without showing Partner B, writes down the age of the (imaginary) baby. The baby is between one and 11 months old. Partner B then asks the question *"Akachan-wa ___-ka-getsu desu-ka?"* to determine the age. Each question is worth one point. Then change roles and repeat. The player with the lower score is the winner of the round. The number forms which occur with *-ka-getsu* are given in the 文法ポイント section of this lesson. As you play additional rounds, try to avoid referring to this. Read the sample exchange aloud before you begin.

A: (writes down *hak-ka-getsu*)
B: Akachan-wa go-ka-getsu desu-ka?
A: Iie, chigaimasu.
B: Akachan-wa san-ka-getsu desu-ka?
A: Iie, chigaimasu.
B: Akachan-wa hak-ka-getsu desu-ka?
A: Hai, soo desu. [Partner B asked three questions and now has a score of three.]

❷ Doko-de umaremashita-ka? 📄 & ✏️

Do this interview activity as an entire class. Form pairs. Interview each other to find out where (city, state, or country) and when your partner was born and write them down. Refer to the sample questions and answers as needed. When you have finished, find a new partner to interview.

SAMPLE QUESTIONS AND ANSWERS

Doko-de umaremashita-ka?	Honoruru-de umaremashita.
Itsu umaremashita-ka?	1987-nen* 6-gatsu 11-nichi-ni umaremashita.
	(*sen kyuu-hyaku hachi-juu-nana-nen)

DAYS OF THE MONTH			
1 日	tsuitachi	9 日	kokonoka
2 日	futsuka	10 日	tooka
3 日	mikka	11 日	juu-ichi-nichi
4 日	yokka	14 日	juu-yokka
5 日	itsuka	20 日	hatsuka
6 日	muika	24 日	ni-juu-yokka
7 日	nanoka	25 日	ni-juu-go-nichi
8 日	yooka	30 日	san-juu-nichi

PART 2

---

❶ Kakimashoo! ✏️

During this activity each student will work as a pair with two different クラスメート to check Assignment #2 from Part 1 of this lesson. The goal of the activity is to have two students carefully check the sentences in your journal entry, mark and discuss with you any errors found, and sign off on your page. Form your first pair and exchange assignments with your partner. Both partners independently check and neatly mark errors for the entire assignment. Use the same editing symbols as usual.

❷ Maetani-san-wa doko-de umaremashita-ka? 📄 & ✏️

In this pair activity take turns asking and answering questions to exchange the information you and your partner need to complete your charts. Look only at your own chart. If you cannot answer your partner's question (because you do not have enough information), respond with *Mada wakarimasen*. After you have finished, compare the charts. Looking at the "Maetani" line on your own chart, read the sample questions and answers aloud with your partner before you begin.

PARTNER A

NAMAE	DOKO-DE UMAREMASHITA-KA?	KEKKON SHITE-IMASU (IMASEN)	NAN-NEN-MAE-NI	KODOMO-SAN-GA IMASU (IMASEN)
Maetani	Sapporo	hai	24	3
Yamaguchi		iie		0
	Tookyoo		2	1
Watanabe	Kyooto			
Yoneda				
	Kagoshima			0
Fujita	Oosaka			
Honda	Koobe	hai	13	4
Matsumoto	Hiroshima	hai	36	
Mizutani		hai	47	
	Morioka	iie		0

SAMPLE QUESTIONS AND ANSWERS

Maetani-san-wa . . .
. . . doko-de umaremashita-ka?   **Sapporo**-de umaremashita.
. . . kekkon shite-imasu-ka?   **Hai**, kekkon shite-**imasu**.
. . . nan-nen-mae-ni kekkon shimashita-ka?   **24**-nen-mae-ni kekkon shimashita.
. . . kodomo-san-ga imasu-ka?   **Hai, 3**-nin **imasu**.

Dare-ga
. . . **Sapporo**-de umaremashita-ka?   **Maetani**-san desu.
. . . **24**-nen-mae-ni kekkon shimashita-ka? **Maetani**-san desu.

COUNTING PEOPLE			
hitori	1 person	yo-nin	4 people
futari	2 people	go-nin	5 people
san-nin	3 people	roku-nin	6 people

PARTNER B

NAMAE	DOKO-DE UMAREMASHITA-KA?	KEKKON SHITE-IMASU (IMASEN)	NAN-NEN-MAE-NI	KODOMO-SAN-GA IMASU (IMASEN)
Maetani	Sapporo	hai	24	3
Yamaguchi	Yokohama			
Nakamura		hai	2	
	Kyooto	hai	6	2
Yoneda	Wakayama	hai	5	2
Murakami	Kagoshima	hai	9	
Fujita		iie		0
Honda				
	Hiroshima			5
	Sendai		47	6
Suzuki	Morioka			

L. 49 電話で 話しましょう

<u>れんしゅう A</u>: Family Survey

Someone from the census bureau is calling you to collect information for a family survey. Answer his/her questions.

<u>れんしゅう B</u>: Personal History

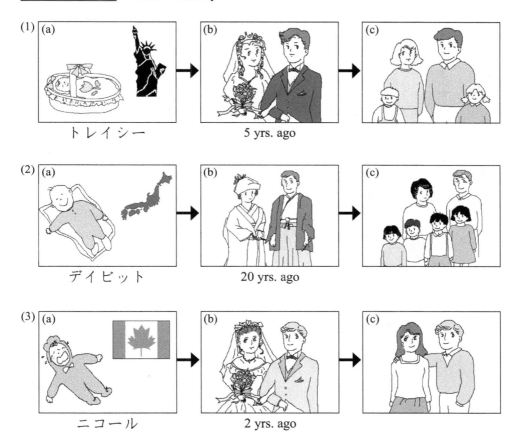

(1)
(a) トレイシー
(b) 5 yrs. ago
(c)

(2)
(a) デイビット
(b) 20 yrs. ago
(c)

(3)
(a) ニコール
(b) 2 yrs. ago
(c)

れんしゅう C: Let's talk about your family!

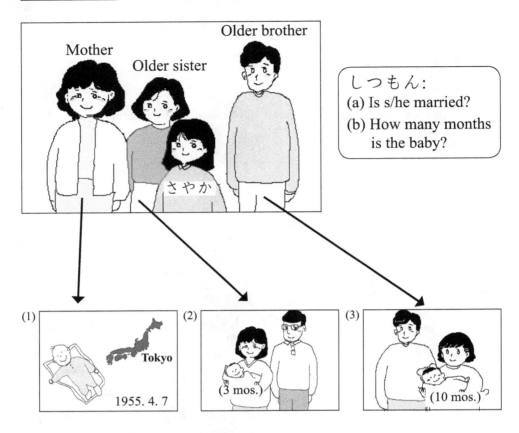

しつもん:
(a) Is s/he married?
(b) How many months is the baby?

(1) Tokyo 1955. 4. 7

(2) (3 mos.)

(3) (10 mos.)

LESSON 50
Where People Live

OBJECTIVES   目標

At the end of this lesson you will be able to:
- ☑ Ask and state where someone lives
- ☑ Read the *kanji*: 子

VOCABULARY   単語

Words

sunde-iru (sunde-imasu)	live(s)

Phrases and expressions

____-no toki	when ____, at the time when ____
____-ni sunde-iru (sunde-imasu)	live(s) in ____

KEY GRAMMAR POINTS   文法ポイント

1. *Place*-ni sunde-imasu. に すんでいます (住んでいます)

To ask or tell where someone lives, use the name of the place followed by -*ni sunde-imasu(-ka?)*. *Sunde-imasu* is the -*te-imasu* form of the verb *sumu*. Read these examples aloud.

Doko-ni *sunde-imasu*-ka?	Where do you *live*?
Ima, Washinton-ni *sunde-imasu*.	Now I *live* in Washington.
Atoranta-ni *sunde-imasen*.	She *doesn't live* in Atlanta.

You can also use this useful expression to talk about the past.

Sengetsu-made Oosaka-ni *sunde-imashita*.	Until last month I *lived* in Osaka.
Dore-gurai Mekishiko-ni *sunde-imashita*-ka?	How long *did* you *live* in Mexico?
San-ka-getsu Mekishiko-ni *sunde-imashita*.	I *lived* in Mexico for three months.

2. ____-no toki の とき (の時)

The word *toki* by itself means *time*, but when it is modified by another noun followed by the particle -*no*, it means *when* or *at the time when*. Look at these examples.

kodomo-*no toki*	*when* (I, you, etc., was/were) a child
daigakusei-*no toki*	*at the time when* she was a college student
nana-sai-*no toki*	*when* I was seven years old

CULTURE NOTES   カルチャーノート

Choosing a name for a child in Japan

Selecting a name for a newborn child is an extremely important decision in any country. In Japan, the decision can be especially complicated because of the nature of the writing system and certain cultural considerations.

In addition to the sound of the name, the *kanji* that are selected to represent the name in written form are a very important consideration. Because there are so many *kanji* that have the same sound value, a single name can be written using many different *kanji*. The selection of the *kanji* is important because the *kanji* give meaning to the name. When selecting the *kanji* for their child's name, parents often think of specific qualities or characteristics that they would like their child to have.

Another important consideration when selecting *kanji* is the number of strokes needed to write each *kanji*. Some people believe that the combined number of strokes for the family and the given names can influence the course of a person's life. Many people refer to books when they choose a name for their child to make sure that their new-born baby has a lucky name. They may even seek the advice of an expert when selecting a name for their child.

SOME JAPANESE GIVEN NAMES AND THEIR MEANINGS						
Female				**Male**		
Ayaka	彩花	colorful - flower		Daiki	大樹	great - tree
	彩夏	colorful - summer			大輝	great - shining
	綾香	design - fragrant			大貴	great - valuable
Keiko	敬子	respect - child		Takumi	匠	artisan
	慶子	celebrate - child			巧	skilled
	啓子	open - child			拓海	pioneer - ocean
Megumi	恵	blessing		Kenta	健太	healthy - thick
	恵美	blessing - beauty			賢太	wise - thick

YOMIMASHOO!   読みましょう

父は、今、ジョージアに すんでいます。	My father lives in Georgia now.
どこに すんでいますか。	Where do you live?
どこで 生まれましたか。	Where were you born?
シカゴで 生まれました けど、今、	I was born in Chicago, but now I
ボストンに すんでいます。	live in Boston.
今、とうきょうに すんでいます。でも、	I live in Tokyo now. However,
先月まで 大さかに すんでいました。	until last month I lived in Osaka.
あかちゃんの とき	when (I, you, etc., was/were) a baby
子どもの とき	when I was a child
高校生の とき	when I was a high school student
十五オの とき	when I was 15 years old
三十四オから 五十六オまで	from age 34 to age 56
二年かん	(a period of) two years
どれぐらい 日本に すんでいましたか。	How long did you live in Japan?
三か月 日本に すんでいました。	I lived in Japan for three months.

KANJI NOTES   漢字ノート

In this lesson you will learn to read the *kanji* 子. Be sure that you know the reading for the *kanji* and can tell what the *kanji* means. The readings which are marked by an asterisk are for your reference only; you do not need to learn these. You also do not have to learn any new words which are given in the examples. The correct stroke order for this *kanji* is given in the Optional Writing Practice section.

子   **SHI*, SU*; ko [go] (child)**

子供	*ko*domo	child
原子	gen*shi*	atom
様子	yoo*su*	appearance
電子	den*shi*	electron
扇子	sen*su*	fan
子	*ko*	child
お子さん	o*ko*san	child [honorific]

子供は何人いますか。　　*Ko*domo-wa nan-nin imasu-ka?
　　　　　　　　　　　　(How many children are there?)

お子さんは五才ですね。　*O*kosan-wa go-sai desu-ne.
　　　　　　　　　　　　(Your child is five, isn't he?)

The *kanji* 子 is derived from a picture of a small child.

KANJI REVIEW

上	名	二	見	今	万	大	中	円	年	八	元	土	口	前
耳	母	日	木	四	気	本	七	人	山	十	何	三	水	目
才	私	六	子	田	一	小	学	高	川	千	校	火	五	下
金	百	来	先	生	父	月	行	天	九					

How do you read them? What do they mean?

INTERACTIVE ACTIVITIES

PART 1

❶ Maeda-san-wa kodomo-no toki doko-ni sunde-imashita-ka?
In this pair activity take turns asking and answering questions to exchange the information you and your partner need to complete your charts. Look only at your own chart. If you cannot answer your partner's question (because you do not have enough information), respond with *Mada wakarimasen.* After you have finished, compare the charts. Looking at the "Maeda" line on your own chart, read the sample questions and answers aloud with your partner before you begin.

SAMPLE QUESTIONS AND ANSWERS
Maeda-san-wa . . .
..   doko-de umaremashita-ka?   **Sapporo**-de umaremashita.
..   kodomo-no toki doko-ni sunde-imashita-ka?   **Tookyoo**-ni sunde-imashita.
..   ima doko-ni sunde-imasu-ka?   **Yokohama**-ni sunde-imasu.
..   dore-gurai **Yokohama**-ni sunde-imasu-ka?   **10-nen-kan** sunde-imasu.

Dare-ga . . .
..   **Sapporo**-de umaremashita-ka?   **Maeda**-san desu.
..   kodomo-no toki **Tookyoo**-ni sunde-imashita-ka?   **Maeda**-san desu.
..   ima **Yokohama**-ni sunde-imasu-ka?   **Maeda**-san desu.

389

PARTNER A

NAME	BIRTH PLACE	LIVED AS CHILD	LIVES NOW	HOW LONG
Maeda	Sapporo	Tookyoo	Yokohama	10-nen-kan
Yamakawa		Yokohama		41-nen-kan
	Tookyoo			73-nen-kan
Watanabe		Okayama		3-ka-getsu
		Wakayama		2-ka-getsu
			Nagasaki	18-nen-kan
Itoo	Oosaka	Oosaka	Tookyoo	
Honda	Koobe		Kyooto	
Matsumoto	Hiroshima		Oosaka	
Mizutani	Sendai	Sapporo	Yokohama	
Noguchi	Morioka	Kawasaki	Koobe	

PARTNER B

NAME	BIRTH PLACE	LIVED AS CHILD	LIVES NOW	HOW LONG
Maeda	Sapporo	Tookyoo	Yokohama	10-nen-kan
Yamakawa	Yokohama		Tookyoo	
Nakamura	Tookyoo	Tookyoo	Tookyoo	
Watanabe	Kyooto		Oosaka	
Tanaka	Wakayama	Wakayama	Oosaka	
Murakami	Kagoshima	Nagasaki	Nagasaki	
		Oosaka		25-nen-kan
Honda		Koobe		8-ka-getsu
Matsumoto		Hiroshima		9-ka-getsu
	Sendai			34-nen-kan
			Koobe	6-nen-kan

❷ **Vocabulary review** 📄 & ✏

Silently review the following which are from Lessons 48 through 50. Then have a
クラスメート orally test you on them. Your partner says the えいご, and you give the
日本ご. Switch and test your partner. Write down those which need further study.

1. Shitte-imasu.	I know.	
2. Shirimasen.	I don't know.	
3. Zenzen oboete-imasen.	I can't remember at all.	
4. kekkon	marriage	
5. Kekkon shite-imasu.	I am married.	
6. Raigetsu kekkon shimasu.	I will get married next month.	
7. Nan-nen-mae-ni kekkon shimashita-ka?	How many years ago did you marry?	
8. akachan	baby	
9. nan-ka-getsu	how many months	
10. ik-ka-getsu	1 month	
11. yon-ka-getsu	4 months	
12. juk-ka-getsu	10 months	
13. Doko-de umaremashita-ka?	Where were you born?	
14. Doko-ni sunde-imasu-ka?	Where do you live?	
15. Tookyoo-ni sunde-imasu.	I live in Tokyo.	
16. kodomo-no toki	when I was a child	
17. shoogakusei-no toki	when I was an elementary school student	
18. 15-sai-no toki	when I was 15	

❶ Nakamura-san-wa Tookyoo-de umaremashita.

Do this activity with a クラスメート. Looking at the completed chart in Activity ❶ (Part 1) of this lesson, take turns making true-false statements about the people in the chart. Look at the chart and read the sample exchange aloud with your partner before you begin.

SAMPLE EXCHANGE

A: Nakamura-san-wa Tookyoo-de umaremashita.
B: Hai, soo desu.

B: Murakami-san-wa kodomo-no toki Okayama-ni sunde-imashita.
A: Iie, chigaimasu. Nagasaki-ni sunde-imashita.

❷ Intabyuu

Do this interview activity as an entire class. Form pairs and interview each other asking about the topics in the box below. Refer to the sample questions and answers as needed. When you have finished, find a new partner to interview.

SAMPLE QUESTIONS AND ANSWERS

Doko-de umaremashita-ka?   **Kanada**-de umaremashita.
Shoogakusei-no toki doko-ni sunde-imashita-ka?   **Otawa**-ni sunde-imashita.

TOPICS	
birth place (city, state or county)	**place lived during elementary school** (if more than one place, say *place name* と *place name*)

L. 50 電話で 話しましょう

れんしゅう A: Tim's Friends Around the World

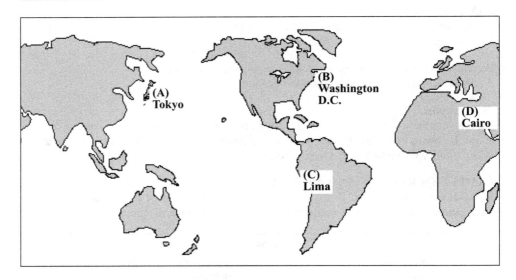

		まゆみ	フリオ	アリー	モイーシャ
(1)	Place of residence	A	C	D	B
(2)	Married	Yes	No	No	Yes
(3)	Language	Japanese, Chinese	Spanish, French	Arabic, Italian	English, Spanish

れんしゅう B: When I was a child...

(1)
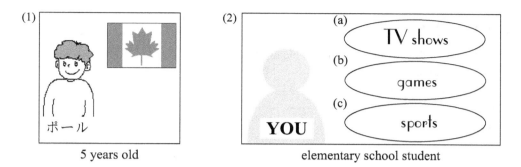
ポール

5 years old

(2)
(a) TV shows
(b) games
(c) sports
YOU

elementary school student

れんしゅう C: Tim's Life in a Nutshell

しつもん: (a) how long? (b) doing what?

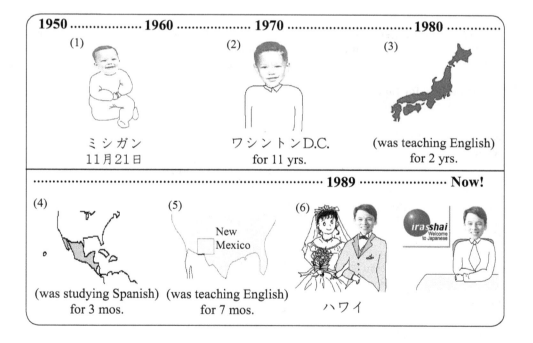

1950 .... 1960 .... 1970 .... 1980 ....

(1) ミシガン
11月21日

(2) ワシントンD.C.
for 11 yrs.

(3) (was teaching English)
for 2 yrs.

.... 1989 .... Now!

(4) (was studying Spanish)
for 3 mos.

(5) New Mexico
(was teaching English)
for 7 mos.

(6) ハワイ

irasshai
Welcome
to Japanese

393

LESSON 51
Relatives

OBJECTIVES 目標

At the end of this lesson you will be able to:
- ☑ Talk about relatives

VOCABULARY 単語

Words

obaasan	grandmother
ojiisan	grandfather

Phrases and expressions

hitori-de	alone, by oneself

Other words and expressions you will hear in this lesson

obasan	aunt
ojisan	uncle
itoko	cousin

VOCABULARY NOTES 単語ノート

1. Ojiisan ~ ojisan おじいさん ~ おじさん
These two words differ in pronunciation by the length of the second vowel. Be careful to make this distinction since it is critical to meaning. Listen carefully to your *terebi-no sensei*. *Obaasan* and *obasan* are also distinguished by the length of the second vowel.

2. Vocabulary for family members and relatives
In Lessons 15 and 16 (Vol. 1) you learned the vocabulary for members of the immediate family. Those words, in addition to others which you may use in activities and assignments in this lesson, are given below. Both the humble and honorific forms are included.

FAMILY MEMBERS AND RELATIVES

Humble	Honorific	Japanese	English
kazoku	go-kazoku	（ご）かぞく	family
haha	okaasan	母・お母さん	mother
chichi	otoosan	父・お父さん	father
ryooshin	go-ryooshin	（ご）りょうしん	parents
ane	oneesan	あね・おねえさん	older sister
ani	oniisan	あに・おにいさん	older brother
imooto	imooto-san	いもうと（さん）	younger sister
otooto	otooto-san	おとうと（さん）	younger brother
kyoodai	go-kyoodai	（ご）きょうだい	siblings
musume	musume-san	むすめ（さん）	daughter
musuko	musuko-san	むすこ（さん）	son
kodomo	kodomo-san	こども（さん）	child
sobo	obaasan	そぼ・おばあさん	grandmother
sofu	ojiisan	そふ・おじいさん	grandfather
mago	o-mago-san	（お）まご（さん）	grandchild
oi	oigo-san	おい（ごさん）	nephew
mei	meigo-san	めい（ごさん）	niece

394

Humble	Honorific	Japanese	English
shujin	go-shujin	（ご）しゅじん	husband
kanai	okusan	かない・おくさん	wife
oba	obasan	おば（さん）	aunt
oji	ojisan	おじ（さん）	uncle
itoko	itoko-san	いとこ（さん）	cousin
shinseki	go-shinseki	（ご）しんせき	relatives

YOMIMASHOO!　　　　　　　　　　　　　読みましょう

おばあさん	grandmother
おじいさん	grandfather
一人で	alone, by oneself
私は しんせきが たくさん います。	I have a lot of relatives.
ごかぞくと いっしょに すんでいますか。	Do you live with your family?
ゆきさんは だれと すんでいますか。	With whom does Yuki live?
私は 一人で すんでいます。	I live by myself.
おじいさんの いもうとさん です。	It's your grandfather's younger sister.
４０年前に アメリカ人と けっこんして、アメリカに 行きました。	She married an American 40 years ago and went to America.
田中さんは おばあさんが います。私は もう いません。	She has a grandmother. I don't have one any more.
おじさんと おばさんが 何人 いますか。	How many aunts and uncles do you have?
おばさん	aunt
おじさん	uncle
いとこ	cousin

できますか。

Can you unscramble these 単語, all of which appear in the 読みましょう section above? Then write the meaning in えいご. Check your answers with your クラスメート.

1. きんせし　　　　3. さんばおあ　　　　5. いさじんお
2. ぞかくご　　　　4. いせんま　　　　　6. こっんけ

CULTURE NOTES　　　　　　　　　　　カルチャーノート

Traditional Japanese Calendar

The traditional Japanese calendar is based on a 12-year cycle. Each year is named after a different animal. Each animal gives the year it is associated with a distinctive quality or qualities. As with so many other aspects of traditional Japanese culture, the calendar also traces its origins to China.

The 12 animals associated with the 12 years of each cycle are the rat, ox, tiger, rabbit, dragon, snake, horse, sheep, monkey, rooster, dog, and wild boar. Not only do these animals give specific characteristics to the years with which they are associated, but these same characteristics are believed to be present in people born in these years. Thus, someone born in the Year of the Tiger (1938, 1950, 1962, 1974, 1986, 1998, 2010) is thought to be aggressive, brave, honest, and sensitive. All of the animals, including those that may seem somewhat less appealing, have many positive characteristics.

In addition to understanding another aspect of Japanese culture, knowledge of the traditional Japanese calendar is helpful in figuring out another person's age when it might not be polite to ask directly, *"O-ikutsu desu-ka?"* or *"Nan-sai desu-ka?"* All you have to do is ask, *"Nani-doshi desu-ka?"* or *"What year are you?"* Since you probably will not have the entire list of animals and their corresponding years committed to memory, you can just make a mental note of the animal year and refer to the handy chart below when you get back home. Have fun!

何年 (なにどし) ですか。							
rat (nezumi)	1936	1948	1960	1972	1984	1996	2008
ox (ushi)	1937	1949	1961	1973	1985	1997	2009
tiger (tora)	1938	1950	1962	1974	1986	1998	2010
rabbit (usagi)	1939	1951	1963	1975	1987	1999	2011
dragon (tatsu)	1940	1952	1964	1976	1988	2000	2012
snake (hebi)	1941	1953	1965	1977	1989	2001	2013
horse (uma)	1942	1954	1966	1978	1990	2002	2014
sheep (hitsuji)	1943	1955	1967	1979	1991	2003	2015
monkey (saru)	1944	1956	1968	1980	1992	2004	2016
rooster (tori)	1945	1957	1969	1981	1993	2005	2017
dog (inu)	1946	1958	1970	1982	1994	2006	2018
wild boar (inoshishi)	1947	1959	1971	1983	1995	2007	2019

INTERACTIVE ACTIVITIES

PART 1

❶ **Yomimashoo!**   📄 & ✏️

This pair activity provides you with an opportunity to review *kanji* you have learned in this course. Partner A masks the *roomaji* side and reads the phrases and sentences in the left column in order. Partner B responds after each with either *Hai, soo desu* or *Iie, chigaimasu. Moo ichido yonde kudasai.* Partner A writes down those which need to be studied. Switch roles and repeat.

かなと漢字	ローマ字
1. 何月何日 ですか。	1. Nan-gatsu nan-nichi desu-ka?
2. 今年、何才に なりますか。	2. Kotoshi, nan-sai-ni narimasu-ka?
3. 今、高校何年生 ですか。	3. Ima, kookoo nan-nen-sei desu-ka?
4. 大学の 日本語の 先生 でした。	4. Daigaku-no nihongo-no sensei deshita.
5. 中学校の中	5. chuugakkoo-no naka
6. その 小さい本は 高い ですね。	6. Sono chiisai hon-wa takai desu-ne.
7. 父と母は 今日、学校に 行きます。	7. Chichi-to haha-wa kyoo, gakkoo-ni ikimasu.
8. 上田さんと 山下さんが 来ました。	8. Ueda-san-to Yamashita-san-ga kimashita.
9. 川口さんは 元気じゃない です。	9. Kawaguchi-san-wa genki ja nai desu.
10. お名前は？	10. O-namae-wa?
11. 口と目と耳	11. kuchi-to me-to mimi
12. 木よう日の 天気	12. moku-yoobi-no tenki
13. 私は 先しゅう それを 見ました。	13. Watashi-wa senshuu sore-o mimashita.
14. 六千五百九十円	14. roku-sen go-hyaku kyuu-juu-en
15. 七千八百四十二円	15. nana-sen hap-pyaku yon-juu-ni-en
16. 三万九千二百円	16. san-man kyuu-sen ni-hyaku-en

❷ Takeshi-san-wa dare-to kekkon shite-imasu-ka? 📄 & ✏️

Do this activity with a クラスメート. Look only at your own family tree. By asking and answering questions, exchange information with your partner to complete the three-generation Tanaka family tree. Find out the name and age of each person. If your partner responds with *Mada wakarimasen*, try asking a different question or giving your partner some information (in Japanese, of course!). Individuals shown at the end of horizontal lines are a married couple. Individuals at the end of vertical lines are children of the couple above them in the tree. Write the age of each person in the parentheses below the person's name. The names of all of the people who appear in the family tree are given in the box. Read the sample questions and answers (with names which do not appear in the tree) aloud with your partner before you begin. When you have finished, compare your completed charts.

PARTNER A

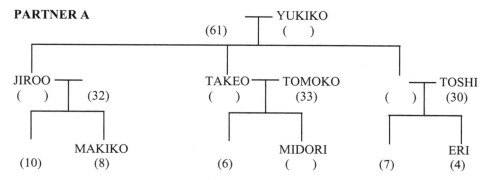

SAMPLE QUESTIONS AND ANSWERS

Takeshi-san-wa dare-to kekkon shite-imasu-ka?   Masayo-san-to kekkon shite-imasu.
Tetsuya-san-no okaasan-wa dare desu-ka?   Naomi-san desu.
Naomi-san-wa imooto-san-ga imasu-ka?   Iie, imasen.
Suzuko-san-wa nan-sai desu-ka?   45-sai desu.
Dare-ga 32-sai desu-ka?   Mada wakarimasen.

THE TANAKA FAMILY				
Males			**Females**	
Hirofumi	Toshi		Akiko	Mayumi	Rie
Kenji	Yukio		Yukiko	Midori	Eri
Jiroo	Takeo		Makiko	Tomoko	

PARTNER B

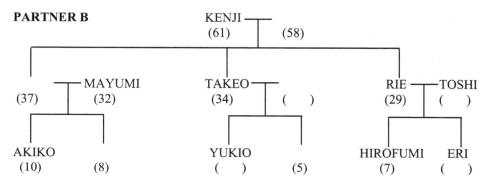

❸ Takeo-san-wa Mayumi-san-to kekkon shite-imasu.

If you have time after you have finished and compared your Tanaka family tree charts, take turns making true-false statements about the family tree (names, ages, relationships, number of children/sisters/brothers/cousins, etc.). Use a variety of sentence patterns.

❶ Kikimashoo!

Do this activity with a クラスメート. Using the sentences which you wrote for Assignment #2 from Part 1 and the Tanaka family tree in Activity #2 from Part 1, take turns reading one sentence at a time to your partner. Your partner will listen carefully to the sentence, look at the family tree, and respond with either *Hai, soo desu* or *Iie, chigaimasu*. If the sentence is false, the listener must provide the correct information. Read the sample exchange aloud with your partner before you begin.

A: Tomoko-san-wa Kenji-san-to kekkon shite-imasu.
B: Iie, chigaimasu. Tomoko-san-wa Takeo-san-to kekkon shite-imasu.
A: Aa, soo desu-ne.

B: Yukio-san-no okaasan-wa 33-sai desu.
A: Hai, soo desu.

❷ Kakimashoo!

Now have your partner carefully check your written sentences, mark and discuss with you any errors found, and sign off on your assignment.

❸ Obaasan-ga imasu-ka?

Do this interview activity with a partner. Before you begin, write down the information about the topics in the box below, starting with the name of one of your grandmothers, grandfathers, aunts, or uncles who is still living. You may create an imaginary relative if you prefer. If you do not know your relative's birth place or some other information, you can make it up.

Before your partner begins to interview you, tell your partner which relative you have selected (*obaasan, ojiisan*, etc.). Your partner's first question will be based on this information so that your first answer will be *Hai, imasu*. Sample questions are provided as a reference, but please do not limit yourself to these.

The interviewer should listen carefully to all of the responses without taking notes. At the end of the interview, the interviewer tells three facts about the partner's relative.

SAMPLE QUESTIONS

Obaasan/Ojiisan-ga imasu-ka?
Ojisan/Obasan-ga imasu-ka?
O-namae-wa nan desu-ka?
Nan-sai desu-ka?
Otoosan-no okaasan desu-ka?
Okaasan-no imooto-san desu-ka?
Doko-de umaremashita-ka?
O-tanjoobi-wa nan-gatsu nan-nichi desu-ka?
Kodomo-no toki doko-ni sunde-imashita-ka?
Kookoosei-no toki doko-ni sunde-imashita-ka?
Daigakusei-no toki doko-ni sunde-imashita-ka?
Ima doko-ni sunde-imasu-ka?
Kekkon shite-imasu-ka?
Itsu kekkon shimashita-ka?
Kodomo-san-ga imasu-ka?
Nan-nin imasu-ka?
Obaasan-wa donna hito desu-ka?

TOPICS

- name
- age
- relationship to your mother/father
- birth place
- birthday
- where lived as a child
- other places lived
- where lives now
- (if aunt/uncle) married? when? how many children?
- description (height, hair color, eye color, personality)

NEED HELP?			
birth place	49*	height	46
birthday	49	hair color	46
residence	50	glasses	47
-no toki	50	personality	45
marriage	49	relatives	51
*lesson number			

L. 51 電話で 話しましょう

れんしゅう A: Completing the Family Tree

Find out where the following people are in the family tree below. Ask your A.I. teacher questions and fill in the blanks.

(Ex.1) ただし	(Ex.2) けんじ	(1) すずこ	(2) すすむ
(3) くみこ	(4) さだお	(5) じゅんこ	

しつもん: (a) Is s/he married? — YES → (b) Who is s/he married to?

NO → (c) Who is his/her mother/father?

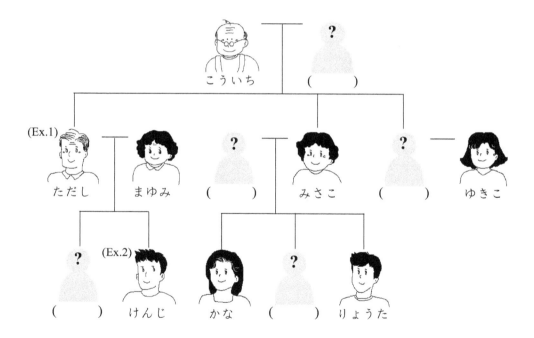

れんしゅう B: Makoto's Adventure

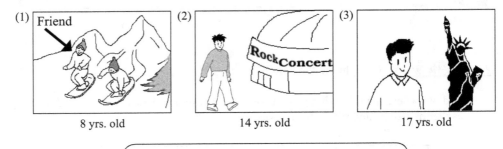

(1) Friend　8 yrs. old
(2) RockConcert　14 yrs. old
(3) 17 yrs. old

しつもん：　(a) What did Makoto do?
　　　　　　(b) With whom?
　　　　　　(c) When?

れんしゅう C: Emily's Essay

きょ年のなつやすみ

エミリー・モア

　私は きょ年、日本でホームステイをしました。私
の日本のかぞくは 三人です。お父さんは とてもやさ
しい人です。高校の先生です。お母さんは あかるく
て元気な人です。りょうりがとてもじょうずです。
おねえさんは 大学四年生です。二十一才です。
来年、おねえさんは アメリカにあそびに来ます。

しつもん：(Answer in English.)

(1) Who is in Emily's host family?

(2) What does Emily's host father do?

(3) What kind of person is Emily's host mother?

(4) Who is coming to America and when?

LESSON 52
Occupations

OBJECTIVES　　　　　　　　　　　　　　　　　　　　　目標

At the end of this lesson you will be able to:
- ☑ Talk about occupation

VOCABULARY　　　　　　　　　　　　　　　　　　　　　単語

Words

kaisha	company
sarariiman	white collar worker
hataraku (hatarakimasu/hataraite)	work

Phrases and expressions

O-shigoto-wa nan desu-ka?	What kind of job do you have?

Other words and expressions you will hear in this lesson

taihen (na)	terrible, difficult, awful

VOCABULARY NOTES　　　　　　　　　　　　　　　単語ノート

1. Sarariiman サラリーマン

The word *sarariiman*, which is derived from the English *salaried man*, refers to male white-collar workers.

2. Hataraku はたらく (働く)

The verb *hataraku/hatarakimasu*, which means *work*, is used to express future action. It is also used to describe in general terms where people work. The *-te-imasu* form is used to describe where a particular person works. The *-te-imasu* form can also be used to express *am/is/are working*.

Ashita 3-ji-kara 7-ji-made *hatarakimasu*.	I *will work* from 3:00 to 7:00 tomorrow.
Isha-wa byooin-de *hatarakimasu*.	Doctors *work* in hospitals.
Mori-san-wa kaisha-de *hataraite-imasu*.	Ms. Mori *works* at a company.
Ima, *hataraite-imasu*.	She *is working* now.

3. Vocabulary for occupations

In this course you have already learned some words for different occupations. Those words, in addition to others which you may use in activities and assignments, are given below.

OCCUPATIONS

accountant	kaikeishi	driver, chauffeur	untenshu
actor, actress	haiyuu, joyuu	engineer	enjinia
administrative assistant	hisho	eye doctor	me-isha
		farmer	noofu
architect	kenchikuka	fisherman	ryooshi
bank employee	ginkooin	flight attendant	furaito atendanto
broker	burookaa	journalist	jaanarisuto
carpenter	daiku	lawyer	bengoshi
dentist	ha-isha	missionary	senkyooshi
designer	dezainaa	musician	ongakuka
diplomat	gaikookan	nurse	kangoshi/naasu
doctor	isha	office worker	jimuin

painter, artist	gaka	serviceman (armed forces)	gunjin
pastor, minister	bokushi		
pilot	pairotto	shop clerk	ten'in*
policeman	keikan	singer	kashu
politician/statesman	seijika	teacher	sensei/kyooshi
professor	kyooju	waiter	ueetaa
salesman	seerusuman	waitress	ueetoresu
		writer	sakka

*The apostrophe in this word indicates that the Japanese word is てんいん, not てにん.

YOMIMASHOO!　　　　　　　　　　　　　　　　読みましょう

かいしゃ	company
サラリーマン	white collar worker
はたらく・はたらきます・はたらいて	work
今日、9じから8じまで はたらきます。	I'm going to work from 9:00 to 8:00 today.
来しゅうから あたらしい しごとが はじまります。	My new job is starting next week.
おしごとは 何ですか。	What kind of job do you have?
ぎんこうで はたらいています。	I work at a bank.
どこで はたらいていますか。	Where does he work?
びょういんで はたらいています。	He works at a hospital.
しごとは たいへん ですね。	Work is hard, isn't it?
私の今日の スケジュール	my schedule for today
高校の ときの ともだち	a friend from high school (days)
たいへん (大変)	terrible, difficult

できますか。

Can you unscramble these 単語, all of which appear in the 読みましょう section above? Then write the meaning in えいご. Check your answers with your クラスメート.

1. いあしらた	3. リマサーラン	5. こうぎん
2. しゃいか	4. らはくた	6. いへんた

INTERACTIVE ACTIVITIES

PART 1

❶ Yomimashoo!　✎

During this activity each student will work with a クラスメート to check Assignment #1 from Part 2 of Lesson 51. Have your partner carefully check your completed sentences, mark and discuss with you any errors found.

❷ Obaasan-wa doko-de hataraite-imasu-ka?　📄 & ✎

In this pair activity take turns asking and answering questions to exchange the information you and your partner need to complete your charts on the next page. Look only at your own chart. Each chart, when completed, will show Masayo's relatives, their occupations, their places of work, and their work hours tomorrow. After you have finished, compare the charts. Before you begin, read these sample questions and answers aloud with your partner.

PARTNER A

DARE	SHIGOTO	DOKO-DE HATARAITE-IMASU-KA?	NAN-JI-KARA NAN-JI-MADE?
otooto-san	keikan [policeman]	Ueno-no kooban [police box]	5:00 - 3:30
ojiisan	gaka [artist]		
oneesan		Higashiyama-Byooin	
ojisan			8:00 - 7:00
imooto-san	ginkooin [bank employee]	Yonwa-Ginkoo	8:30 - 2:30
obaasan		Ikeda-Byooin	6:00 - 3:00
otoosan	kyooju [professor]		8:30 - 5:30
oniisan	ten'in [store clerk]	Mitsuba-Keeki-ya	
okaasan	jimuin [office worker]	Minami-Kookoo	
obasan			7:30 - 4:30
itoko-san		Rooma-Resutoran	

SAMPLE QUESTIONS AND ANSWERS

Otooto-san-no o-shigoto-wa nan desu-ka?   Keikan desu.

Otooto-san-wa doko-de hataraite-imasu-ka?   Ueno-no kooban-de hataraite-imasu*.

Otooto-san-wa ashita, nan-ji-kara nan-ji-made   5-ji-kara 3-ji han-made hatarakimasu**.
  hatarakimasu-ka?

Hataraite-imasu is used to describe where a particular person (for example, the *otooto-san*) works.

**Hatarakimasu* is used to express future action (in this case, tomorrow).

PARTNER B

DARE	SHIGOTO	DOKO-DE HATARAITE-IMASU-KA?	NAN-JI-KARA NAN-JI-MADE?
otooto-san	keikan [policeman]	Ueno-no kooban [police box]	5:00 - 3:30
ojiisan		uchi	10:00 - 4:00
oneesan	isha		1:00 - 10:00
ojisan	sarariiman	Amerika-no kaisha	
imooto-san			
obaasan	kangofu [nurse]		
otoosan		Irasshai-Daigaku	
oniisan			9:00 - 6:00
okaasan			8:00- 5:00
obasan	sensei	Kita-Chuugakkoo	
itoko-san	ueetaa		3:00 - 11:00

PART 2

❶ Kakimashoo! 🖉

During this activity each student will work as a pair with two different クラスメート to check Assignment #2 from Part 1. The goal of the activity is to have two students carefully check the sentences in your description, mark and discuss with you any errors found, and sign off on your assignment. Form your first pair and exchange assignments with your partner. Both partners independently check and neatly mark errors for the entire assignment.

❷ Watashi-wa dare desu-ka? 📄 & 🖉

Do this guessing activity with a クラスメート. In the Yamaguchi family, whose three-generational tree is shown below, everyone is engaged in one of five occupations. Both partners look at the tree. Partner A chooses one person (male or female) whose identity he/she assumes and writes it down without showing Partner B. Partner B must ask as few questions as possible to determine who Partner A is. The question *Person's name desu-*

ka? is not allowed. You must identify the person by asking about the occupation and relationships. After the identity has been correctly guessed, change roles and repeat. Play as many rounds as you can. Read the sample exchange aloud with your partner before you begin.

A: (chooses Toshi and write down the name)
B: O-shigoto-wa nan desu-ka?
A: Isha desu.
B: Mayumi-san-no go-shujin desu-ka?
A: Iie, chigaimasu.
B: Eri-san-no otoosan desu-ka?
A: Hai, soo desu. [Partner B has 3 points.]

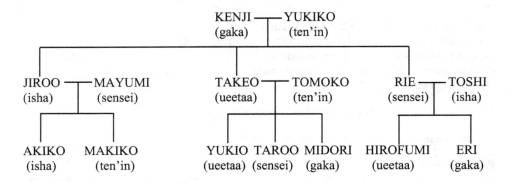

KENJI ——— YUKIKO
(gaka)   (ten'in)

JIROO ——— MAYUMI   TAKEO ——— TOMOKO   RIE ——— TOSHI
(isha)   (sensei)   (ueetaa)   (ten'in)   (sensei)   (isha)

AKIKO   MAKIKO   YUKIO TAROO MIDORI   HIROFUMI   ERI
(isha)   (ten'in)   (ueetaa) (sensei) (gaka)   (ueetaa)   (gaka)

Kaishain (会社員) vs. *Koomuin* (公務員)

Japanese workers typically identify themselves as either *kaishain* (company employees) or *koomuin* (government employees). Therefore, when asked about their jobs, they would refer to either of these terms when they don't want to get into the specifics of their job titles or roles.

L. 52 電話で 話しましょう

れんしゅう A: Masayo's Family Information Sheet

	(1) father	(2) mother	(3) grandfather	(4) grandmother
(a) Occupation	journalist *(jaanarisuto)*	secretary *(hisho)*	doctor	cooking teacher
(b) Where?	Japan Newspaper	SONIE	Irasshai Hospital	home

れんしゅう B: Ryoota's Father's Daily Schedule

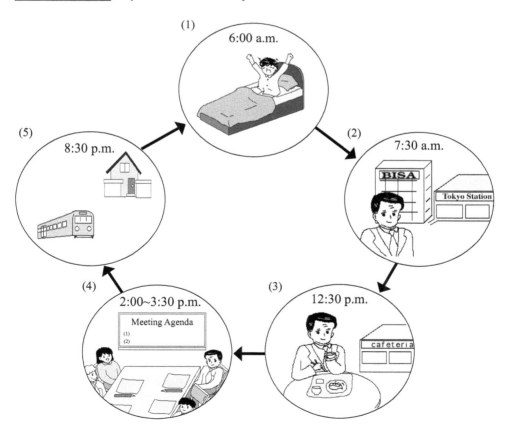

れんしゅう C: Exchange Applicants' Information Sheet

(1)
(a) Name: Andy Jones
(b) Age: 20 yrs. old
(c) Birthday: March 9th
(d) Birthplace: Chicago
(e) Current Address: Boston, MA
(f) Marital Status : (single) married

(2)
(a) Name: Jill Campbell
(b) Age: 25 yrs. old
(c) Birthday: April 29th
(d) Birthplace: Dallas
(e) Current Address: Portland, OR
(f) Marital Status : single (married)

(3)
(a) Name: _____
(b) Age: _____
(c) Birthday: _____
(d) Birthplace: _____
(e) Current Address: _____
(f) Marital Status : single married

YOU

LESSON 53
Getting a Job

OBJECTIVES   目標

At the end of this lesson you will be able to:

- ☑ Talk about getting a job
- ☑ Read the *kanji*: 言 and 話

VOCABULARY   単語

Words

juusho	address
unten	driving (noun)
unten suru (shimasu/shite)	drive

Phrases and expressions

Ichi-jikan ikura?	How much money per hour?
ichi-jikan *amount*	*amount* per hour
Kuruma-no unten-ga dekimasu.	I can drive (a car).

Other words and expressions you will hear in this lesson

rirekisho	résumé

CULTURE NOTES   カルチャーノート

1. Japanese résumés (rirekisho) りれきしょ (履歴書)

Rirekisho are a standard part of Japanese culture along with name cards (*meishi* 名刺). They serve to both identify and define an individual. A person's affiliations (school, family, work, and other professional organizations) are regarded as essential to understanding who a person is.

A *rirekisho* is a standard pre-printed form which everyone uses. A completed *rirekisho* includes information such as name, age, current educational status, address, telephone number, school history, licenses and certificates, hobbies and interests, and family information.

Rirekisho are essential for seeking any kind of employment including a part-time summer job as a high school student. Résumés are even used in the case of *o-miai* (meetings which may lead to arranged marriages).

2. Owning and driving a car in Japan

Japanese auto manufacturers are among the top producers of cars in the world. Names such as Toyota, Honda, Nissan, Mazda, and Suzuki are as well-known in North America as are Ford, Chrysler, and General Motors. With so many cars being manufactured in Japan, one might think that every family must have at least two cars and that driving in Japan should be no more complicated or demanding than in other countries that have achieved a similar level of economic development.

The truth is that, while there are a lot of cars in Japan, most Japanese choose to own no more than one car. The major reason for this is the sheer expense and complexity of car ownership in Japan. Just obtaining a driver's license can be a somewhat daunting undertaking. One cannot apply for a driver's license until the age of 18. Most Japanese attend driving school although the tuition is quite expensive. The standard 60-hour course costs about $3,000. On completion of the course, one must pass a written exam and four separate driving tests.

Once having obtained a license, the person then faces the maze of requirements and long list of expenses associated with buying and owning a car. There is a national law in Japan which requires that people must have written proof of permanent off-road parking before they can even buy a car. Since only a relatively small percentage of Japanese can afford the luxury of their own private garage or even a private driveway beside their house, most people have to make other arrangements. This often means renting a parking place by the month. This can add a couple thousand dollars each year to the cost of owning a car.

In addition to paying for permanent off-road parking, there are other expenses. Major expenses include *shaken* (inspection for registration), which is usually around $1,200 for two years, *zeikin* (national tax), which usually runs about $400 a year, and *hoken* (insurance). Actual operating expenses such as gasoline and tolls can also add considerably to one's budget. While driving in North America can often be a very trying experience, particularly during rush hour in large urban areas, Japan, with its twisting, narrow roadways, can present an even more frustrating experience.

It is no wonder that many Japanese prefer to use the nation's rapid transit system. It is clean, safe, efficient, almost always on time, and relatively inexpensive. For the foreigner traveling to Japan for the first time, it is not a good idea to rent a car at Narita International Airport in Narita or Kansai International Airport near Osaka and drive off into the sunset. Definitely take the train!

YOMIMASHOO!	読みましょう

じゅうしょ	address
うんてん	driving (noun)
うんてんする・します・して	drive
一じかん いくら？	How much money per hour?
一じかん ９ドル です。	It's nine dollars per hour.
アルバイトを しますか。	Will you have a part-time job?
デパートの アルバイト	a part-time job at a department store
しごとは 何よう日 ですか。	What days is the job?
何じから 何じまで ですか。	What are the hours?
レストランの しごとを したい ですか。	Do you want the restaurant job?
どんな しごとを したい ですか。	What kind of work do you want?
どうして したい ですか。	Why do you want it?
どうして したくない ですか。	Why don't you want it?
とおいから、 しません。	I'm not going to do it because it's (too) far.
くるまの うんてんが できます。	I can drive (a car).
りれきしょ	résumé

KANJI NOTES	漢字ノート

In this lesson you will learn to read two *kanji*: 言 and 話. Be sure that you know the readings of each *kanji* and can tell what the *kanji* means. The readings which are marked by an asterisk are for your reference only; you do not need to learn them at this time. You also do not have to learn any new words which are given in the examples. The correct stroke order for these *kanji* is given in the Optional Writing Practice section.

言　**GEN*, GON*** (speech, statement); **koto*** (word, speech, expression), **i(u)** (say)

言います	*ii*masu	say
言葉	*koto*ba	word, language
言語	*gen*go	language
方言	hoo*gen*	dialect

408

今年は日本に行かないと 言いました。	Kotoshi-wa Nihon-ni ikanai-to *i*imashita. (He said that he is not going to Japan this year.)
これは日本語で何と 言いますか。	Kore-wa nihongo-de nan-to *i*imasu-ka? (What do you call this in Japanese?)
もっと大きい声で 言ってください。	Motto ookii koe-de *i*tte kudasai. (Please say it in a louder voice.)

The *kanji* 言 was derived from the *kanji* 口 (mouth) with the lines being spoken shown above it.

話 **WA; hanashi* (story), hana(su) (speak)**

話します	*hana*shimasu	speak
話	*hana*shi	story
話中	*hana*shichuu	while talking; the line is busy
電話	den*wa*	telephone
会話	kai*wa*	conversation

お父さんはだれと話して いますか。	Otoosan-wa dare-to *hana*shite-imasu-ka? (Who is Father talking to?)
今、田中さんの電話は 話し中です。	Ima, Tanaka-san-no den*wa*-wa *hana*shichuu desu. (Mr. Tanaka's phone is busy now.)
英会話の授業は何時から 何時までですか。	Eikai*wa*-no jugyoo-wa nan-ji-kara nan-ji-made desu-ka? (What time does the English conversation class begin and end?)

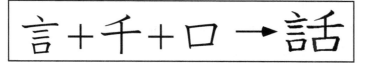

The *kanji* 話 was created by combining the *kanji* 言, 口, and 千. When you *speak*, you *say* a *thousand* words from your *mouth*.

KANJI REVIEW

上	名	二	見	今	万	大	中	円	年	八	元	土	口	前
日	木	四	気	本	七	人	山	十	何	三	水	話	目	才
田	一	小	学	高	川	千	校	火	五	下	金	百	来	言
耳	母	先	私	六	生	父	月	行	天	九				

How do you read them? What do they mean?

INTERACTIVE ACTIVITIES

PART 1

❶ Kakimashoo! ✐

During this activity work with a クラスメート to check the answers for Assignment #2 from Part 2 of Lesson 52. Have your partner carefully check your assignment, mark and discuss with you any errors found, and sign off on the work.

❷ Dialogue

With a partner, practice the dialogue following the usual procedure. Make sure you understand the meaning of each line before you begin. As you practice the dialogue, use gestures and facial expressions. After you have memorized the dialogue, perform it for another pair. If you have time, change roles and learn the other part.

Yamaguchi-san (山口さん) is a student who is interviewing for a summer job at Aisu-kuriimu-rando. (If 山口さん is male, change the name Tetsuko to Tetsuya.) Nakagawa-san (中川さん), the interviewer, is looking at Yamaguchi-san's résumé and is asking questions.

中川: (looking at résumé) Namae-wa . . . Yamaguchi Tetsuko-san desu-ne. (looks up)

山口: (nods earnestly, trying to make a good impression) Hai, soo desu.

中川: (scanning résumé) Eeto . . . 19-sai de . . . (looks up) daigakusei desu-ne.

山口: (nods, answers energetically) Hai.

中川: (looking at résumé) Juusho-wa . . . (surprised) Ee? Tookyoo-to*? Shinjuku-ku**? (looks up) Tooi desu-ne. Daijoobu desu-ka?

山口: (nods) Ee, daijoobu desu.

中川: Soo desu-ka? Sorekara . . . (looks at résumé and is a bit surprised) A, shumi-wa yakyuu-o miru-koto desu-ka? (looks up)

山口: Hai.

中川: (looking at résumé) A, Furansu-go-ga dekimasu-ka? (looks up)

山口: (nods, modestly) Hai, sukoshi.

中川: Sorekara . . . (looks at résumé) A, kuruma-no unten-mo dekimasu-ne. (looks up)

山口: Hai.

中川: (nods, then looks intently at 山口さん) Yamaguchi-san-wa dooshite kono kaisha-de hatarakitai-n desu-ka?

山口: (smiles and answers quickly, excitedly) Aisu-kuriimu-o takusan tabetai-kara desu. (realizes what he/she said, suddenly embarrassed)

*-to = metropolitan area   **-ku = ward (section of a city)

For greater reading practice, use the Japanese equivalent of the dialogue below.

中川: (looking at résumé) 名前は... 山口てつ子さん です ね。(looks up)

山口: (nods earnestly, trying to make a good impression) はい、そう です。

中川: (scanning résumé) ええと、 １９才で (looks up) 大学生 です ね。

山口: (nods, answers energetically) はい。

中川: (looking at résumé) じゅうしょは？ (surprised) ええ？ とうきょうと？ しんじゅくく？ (looks up) とおい ですね。大じょうぶ ですか。

山口: (nods) ええ、大じょうぶ です。

中川: そう です か。 それから、 (looks at résumé and is a bit surprised) あ、 しゅみは やきゅうを 見る こと ですか。(looks up)

山口: はい。

中川: (looking at résumé) あ、 フランスごが できますか。(looks up)

山口: (nods, modestly) はい、 すこし。

中川: (looks at résumé) あ、 くるまの うんてんも できますね。(looks up)

山口: はい。

中川: (nods, then looks intently at 山口さん) 山口さんは どうして この かいしゃで はたらきたいん ですか。

山口: (smiles and answers quickly, excitedly) アイスクリームを たくさん たべたいから です。 (realizes what he/she said, suddenly embarrassed)

❶ **Creating your own dialogue**

Do this activity with a クラスメート. Using the dialogue you learned in Part 1, **orally** fill in the spaces below with information from your partner's résumé (Assignment #2 in Part 1) as you conduct the job interview. Add more questions, answers, and comments. Change roles.

> Before you begin the dialogue, tell your partner what job you are interviewing for so that you can both play your roles appropriately.

A: **Namae**-wa . . . _____-san desu-ne.
B: Hai, soo desu.
A: Eeto . . . _____-**sai** de . . . _____ **sei** desu-ne.
B: Hai.
A: **Juusho**-wa . . . Ee? _____? _____? Tooi desu-ne. Daijoobu desu-ka?
B: Ee, daijoobu desu.
A: Soo desu-ka? Sorekara . . . A, **shumi**-wa _____ desu-ka?
B: Hai.
A: A, _____-**go**-ga dekimasu-ka?
B: Hai, sukoshi.
A: Sorekara . . . A, _____-**mo dekimasu**-ne.
B: Hai.
A: _____-san-wa dooshite koko-de hatarakitai-n desu-ka?
B: _____-kara desu.

❷ **Arubaito-o shite-imasu-ka?** 📄 & ✒

Use your imagination as you do this activity with a クラスメート. You and your friend are having a conversation about your new part-time jobs which you just started. In your conversation, include questions and answers about the following:

- whether you have a part-time job (you do!)
- what kind of part-time job you have
- where you work
- what days you work
- what hours you work
- how much you make an hour
- whether you like the job
- why you like or do not like the job

> **NOTE**
> Make some notes about your imaginary part-time job <u>before</u> you begin your conversation. Make your conversation as realistic as possible. Avoid using an "interview" approach where one person asks all the questions and the other only answers.

SAMPLE QUESTIONS AND ANSWERS

Arubaito-o shite-imasu-ka?
Hai, roku-gatsu futsuka-kara shite-imasu.

Nan-no arubaito-o shite-imasu-ka?
Depaato-no arubaito-o shite-imasu.

Doko-de hataraite-imasu-ka?
Biggu-disukaunto-shoppu-de hataraite-imasu.

Arubaito-wa nan-yoobi desu-ka?
Ka-yoobi-kara do-yoobi-made desu. Nichi-yoobi-to getsu-yoobi-wa yasumi desu.

Nan-ji-kara nan-ji-made desu-ka?
8-ji-kara 5-ji-made desu.

Ichi-jikan ikura desu-ka?
10-doru desu.

Arubaito-ga suki desu-ka?
Daisuki/Suki desu.
Suki/Anmari suki ja nai desu.

Dooshite arubaito-ga suki desu-ka?
Omoshiroi-kara, suki desu.
Tanoshii-kara, suki desu.
O-kane-ga ii-kara, suki desu.

Dooshite arubaito-ga suki ja nai desu-ka?
O-kane-ga yoku-nai-kara, anmari suki ja nai desu. [Because the money is not good, . . .]
Tsumaranai-kara, suki ja nai desu.
Jikan*-ga nagai-kara, suki ja nai desu. *hours
Taihen da-kara, suki ja nai desu.
Yoru-mo arubaito-ga aru-kara, suki ja nai desu.

L. 53 電話で 話しましょう

れんしゅう A: Visiting Your Boyfriend/Girlfriend

You are visiting your boyfriend/girlfriend's house for the first time. Answer his/her overly-protective parent's questions.

れんしゅう B: Job Advertisement

(1)
a) Sales clerk *(ten'in)*

b) Mon., Wed., & Sat.

c) 10:00 A.M. - 5:00 P.M.

d) $ 6.00 / hr.

e) Papaya Republic
666-2459

(2)
a) Office worker *(jimuin)*

b) Mon. ~ Fri.

c) 8:30 A.M. - 5:00 P.M.

d) $ 10.00 / hr.

e) Irasshai
685-2811

(Command of Japanese required)

(3)
a) Lifeguard *(raifu gaado)*

b) Fri., Sat., & Sun.

c) 1:00 P.M. - 6:00 P.M.

d) $ 12.00 / hr.

e) Aloha Beach
333-oahu

(CPR certificate required)

名前 やまだ　はなこ	山田　花子	男・女	山田
せいねんがっぴ 生年月日	1989 年 8 月 20 日		
じゅうしょ 住所	とうきょうと　うえだし 東京都　上田市　2 - 6 - 4		
でんわばんごう 電話番号	(03) 3456 - 7890		

年	月	学歴・職歴
2001	4	上田市立前川中学校　入学
2004	3	上田市立前川中学校　卒業
2004	4	東京都立本田高校　入学
2007	3	東京都立本田高校　卒業
2007	4	私立名水大学　入学

年	月	免許・資格　(Licenses, Certificates, and Qualifications)
2007	8	うんてんめんきょ 運転免許　取得

しゅみ 趣味	しゃしん　りょこう 写真、旅行	健康 状態	良好
スポーツ	テニス		
かもく 科目	えいご 英語		

413

LESSON 54
After Graduation

OBJECTIVES

At the end of this lesson you will be able to:
- ☑ Talk about plans for after graduation
- ☑ Read the *kanji*: 国 and 語

VOCABULARY 単語

Words

sotsugyoo	graduation
sotsugyoo suru (shimasu/shite)	graduate
-go	after/in + LENGTH OF TIME
	LENGTH OF TIME + later
tabun	maybe, perhaps, probably

Phrases and expressions

sono ato	after that
_____-o sotsugyoo suru	graduate from _____

Other words and expressions you will hear in this lesson

sotsugyoo shiki	graduation ceremony

KEY GRAMMAR POINTS 文法ポイント

The suffix -go in time expressions ご（後）

When affixed to expressions of length of time, the suffix -go indicates the length of time after some event. In English -go can be expressed as *in, after,* or *later*, depending on the context of the sentence. The suffix -go is written with the same *kanji* as the word *ato*.

Ima, daigaku ni-nen-sei desu.	Now I'm a college sophomore.
Ni-nen-*go*-ni sotsugyoo shimasu.	I'll graduate *in* two years. [two years from now]
2004-nen-ni daigaku-sei-ni narimashita.	In 2004 she became a college student.
Yo-nen-*go*-ni sotsugyoo shimashita.	She graduated four years *later*.
Kanada-ni ikitai desu. Sorekara,	I want to go to Canada. Then, *after* two
ni-nen-*go*-ni Amerika-ni ikitai desu.	years, I want to go to the U.S.

ni-nen-*go*-ni	→	*in* two years/*after* two years/ two years *later*

YOMIMASHOO! 読みましょう

そつぎょう	graduation
そつぎょうする・します・して	graduate
その あと	after that
二年ご	after two years
三年ご	in three years
五年ご	five years later
たぶん	maybe, perhaps, probably
来年、そつぎょう します。	I will graduate next year.
今年、そつぎょう しますか。	Will she graduate this year?

414

えりさんは 二年ごに そつぎょう します。		Eri will graduate in two years.
十六年前に そつぎょう しました。		I graduated 16 years ago.
いつ 大学を そつぎょう しますか。		When will she graduate from college?
そのあと、何を しますか。		What are you going to do after that?
おんがくの 先生に なりたいです。		I want to become a music teacher.
そつぎょうしき		graduation ceremony

KANJI NOTES 漢字ノート

In this lesson you will learn to read two *kanji*: 国 and 語. Be sure that you know the readings of each *kanji* and can tell what the *kanji* means. The readings which are marked by an asterisk are for your reference only; you do not need to learn them at this time. You also do not have to learn any new words which are given in the examples. The correct stroke order for these *kanji* is given in the Optional Writing Practice section.

国 **KOKU [GOKU]; kuni [guni]** (country)

国	*kuni*	country
中国	Chuu*goku*	China
中国語	chuu*goku*go	Chinese (language)
四国	Shi*koku*	Shikoku [Japanese island]
外国人	gai*koku*jin	foreigner
天国	ten*goku*	heaven

中国はとても大きい国です。	Chuu*goku*-wa totemo ookii *kuni* desu. (China is a very large country.)
どこの国の人ですか。	Doko-no *kuni*-no hito desu-ka? (What country is that person from?)
外国に行ったことがありますか。	Gai*koku*-ni itta-koto-ga arimasu-ka? (Have you ever been to a foreign country?)

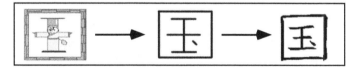

The *kanji* 国 was derived from a picture of a jewel with a border around it.

語 **GO** (word, speech); **katari [gatari]*** (narration), **kata(ru)*** (tell, speak)

外国語	gaikoku*go*	foreign language
日本語	nihon*go*	Japanese (language)
英語	ei*go*	English (language)
何語	nani-*go*	what language
語学	*go*gaku	language study

中国語ができますか。	Chuugoku*go*-ga dekimasu-ka? (Can you speak Chinese?)
中山さんは語学の勉強が大好きだと言っていました。	Nakayama-san-wa *go*gaku-no benkyoo-ga daisuki da-to itte-imashita. (Mr. Nakayama was saying that he really likes his language study.)
中田さんは何語ができますか。	Nakada-san-wa nani-*go*-ga dekimasu-ka? (What languages can Mr. Nakada speak?)

415

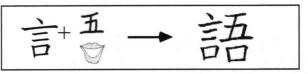

The *kanji* 語 was created by combining three *kanji*: 言, 五, and 口. *Five* different *mouths* are *saying* things in different *languages*.

						KANJI REVIEW								
上	名	二	見	今	万	大	中	円	年	八	元	土	口	前
山	耳	母	日	木	四	気	本	七	人	国	十	何	三	水
六	目	才	天	九	来	田	一	小	学	高	川	千	校	火
五	下	金	百	語	父	話	月	行	生	言	先	私		

How do you read them? What do they mean?

INTERACTIVE ACTIVITIES

PART 1

❶ **Yomimashoo!** ✎

During this activity each student will work with a クラスメート to check Assignment #1 from Part 2 of Lesson 53. Have your partner carefully check your answers, mark and discuss with you any errors found, and sign off on your assignment.

❷ **Itsu daigaku-o sotsugyoo shimasu-ka?** 📄 & ✎

In this pair activity take turns asking and answering questions to exchange the information you and your partner need to complete your charts below and on the next page. Look only at your own chart. If you cannot answer your partner's question (because you do not have enough information), respond with *Mada wakarimasen*. After you have finished, compare the charts. Read the sample questions and answers aloud with your partner before you begin.

SAMPLE QUESTIONS AND ANSWERS

Watanabe-san-wa itsu sotsugyoo shimasu-ka?　　**2-nen-go-ni** sotsugyoo shimasu.
Sono ato, nani-o shimasu-ka?*　　　　　　　　　**Me-isha**-ni narimasu.
Doko-de hatarakimasu-ka?　　　　　　　　　　**Daigaku byooin**-de hatarakimasu.
Dare-ga **daigaku byooin**-de hatarakimasu-ka?　**Watanabe**-san desu.

* In order to ask this question, you must have just asked the preceding question since *sono ato* means *after that*.

PARTNER A

NAMAE	SOTSUGYOO	SONO ATO	DOKO-DE HATARAKIMASU-KA?
Watanabe	2-nen-go	me-isha [eye doctor]	daigaku byooin
Fujimoto			Amerika-no kaisha
Mori	3-nen-go		
Takada		ginkooin	Yonwa Ginkoo
Yamaguchi		isha	supootsu sentaa
Saitoo	2-nen-go		
Ikeda	3-nen-go	kangofu	
Nishihara	4-nen-go		uchi
Noyama	3-nen-go	isha	machi-no byooin
		suugaku-no sensei	kookoo

PARTNER B

NAMAE	SOTSUGYOO	SONO ATO	DOKO-DE HATARAKIMASU-KA?
Watanabe	2-nen-go	me-isha [eye doctor]	daigaku byooin
Fujimoto	kotoshi	sarariiman	
Mori		ongaku-no sensei	chuugakkoo
Takada	kotoshi		
Yamaguchi	rainen		
Saitoo		kekkon shimasu	hatarakimasen
Ikeda			otoosan-no byooin
Nishihara	4-nen-go	gaka	
			machi-no byooin
Matsumoto	rainen	suugaku-no sensei	

SAMPLE QUESTIONS AND ANSWERS

Watanabe-san-wa itsu sotsugyoo shimasu-ka?   **2-nen-go-ni** sotsugyoo shimasu.

Sono ato, nani-o shimasu-ka?*   **Me-isha**-ni narimasu.

Doko-de hatarakimasu-ka?   **Daigaku byooin**-de hatarakimasu.

Dare-ga **daigaku byooin**-de hatarakimasu-ka?   **Watanabe**-san desu.

* In order to ask this question, you must have just asked the preceding question since *sono ato* means *after that*.

PART 2

❶ Kakimashoo! 🖊

During this activity each student will work as a pair with two different クラスメート to check Assignment #3 from Part 1. The goal of the activity is to have two students carefully check the sentences in your description, mark and discuss with you any errors found, and sign off on your assignment. Form your first pair and exchange assignments with your partner. Both partners independently check and neatly mark errors for the entire assignment.

❷ Intabyuu 📄 & 🖊

Do this interview activity as an entire class. Imagine that you are now a university student. Decide your own personal (imaginary) information about the topics in the box below and write them down. Then form pairs and interview each other. Refer to the sample questions and answers as needed. When you have finished, find a new partner to interview.

SAMPLE QUESTIONS AND ANSWERS

O-namae-wa?   **Sumisu** desu.

Ima, nan-nen-sei desu-ka?   **Ichi**-nen-sei desu.

Itsu daigaku-o sotsugyoo shimasu-ka?   **San-nen-go-ni** sotsugyoo shimasu.

Sono ato, nani-o shitai desu-ka?   **Sensei**-ni naritai desu.

   Hoteru-no shigoto-o shitai desu.

Doko-de hatarakitai desu-ka?   **Chuugakkoo**-de hatarakitai desu.

If you have a large class, form groups of about eight students each.

TOPICS

- which class you are in (*ichi-nen-sei*, etc.)
- when you will graduate (*kotoshi, rainen, ni-nen-go*, etc.)
- what (kind of work) you want to do after that
- where you want to work

L. 54 電話で 話しましょう

<u>れんしゅう A</u>: When are you going to graduate?

> しつもん: (a) When will s/he graduate from ~?
> (b) What is s/he going to do after that?

(1) Atlanta High School — ドーン — in 2 yrs. → Irasshai College

(2) ABC International High School — ケン — in 3 yrs. →

(3) Peach Star University — アリシア — in 2 yrs. →

<u>れんしゅう B</u>: Let's converse!

Dialogue: (Mike is talking with his teacher from his high school.)

A: <u>Mike</u>, when are you going to graduate?
B: I'm going to graduate <u>in 2 years</u>.
A: What are you going to do after that?
B: Maybe <u>I'll become a teacher</u>.
A: Oh. Good luck!

— Suggested plans —
go to ~ にいく *(~ni iku)*
work at ~ ではたらく *(~de hataraku)*
become ~ になる *(~ni naru)*

Sample Dialogue:

A: <u>マイクくん</u>は いつ そつぎょう？

B: <u>二年ごに</u> そつぎょうします。

A: そのあと、何する？

B: たぶん、<u>先生になります</u>。

A: そう。がんばって。

Sample Dialogue:

A: <u>Maiku-kun</u>-wa itsu sotsugyoo?

B: <u>Ni-nen-go-ni</u> sotsugyoo shimasu.

A: Sono ato, nani suru?

B: Tabun, <u>sensei-ni narimasu</u>.

A: Soo. Ganbatte.

れんしゅう C: What does Daniel want to be?

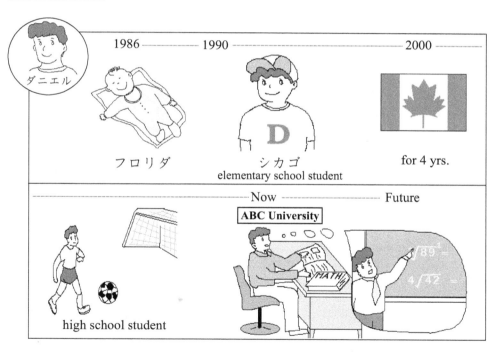

419

LESSON 55
Dreams for the Future

OBJECTIVES　　　　　　　　　　　　　　　　　　目標

At the end of this lesson you will be able to:
- ☑ Talk about dreams for the future
- ☑ Read the *kanji*: 読

VOCABULARY　　　　　　　　　　　　　　　　　　単語

Words

shoorai	future
yuumei (na)	famous
sumimasu	will live

Other words and expressions you will hear in this lesson

Shoorai-no yume-wa nan desu-ka?	What are your dreams for the future?

VOCABULARY NOTES　　　　　　　　　　　　　単語ノート

1. Yuumei ゆうめい (有名)

Yuumei, which is expressed in English as *famous*, literally means *have a name*. As a *na*-adjective, *yuumei* appears in the same forms as other *na*-adjectives such as *kantan*, *shizuka, genki,* and *hen.*

Yuumei-na hito-ni aimashita.	I met a *famous* person.
Ano hito-wa *yuumei* desu.	That person is *famous*.
Omoshiroku-te *yuumei*-na hito desu.	She is an interesting and *famous* person.
Omoshiroku-te *yuumei* desu.	It is (an) interesting and *famous* (place).
Yuumei deshita.	He was *famous*.
Yuumei-ni narimasu.	She will be(come) *famous*.

2. Sumimasu すみます (住みます)

You have already learned to use the *-te-imasu* form of the verb *sumu* to express *live(s)* or *am/is/are living*. The form *sumimasu* is used to talk about where someone *will live* in the future. *Sumitai* is used to talk about where you *want to live*.

Doko-ni *sunde-imasu*-ka?	Where do you *live*?
Eki-no chikaku-ni *sunde-imasu*.	I *live* near the train station.
Ima, apaato-ni *sunde-imasu*.	He *is living* in an apartment now.
Rainen-kara Mekishiko-ni *sumimasu*.	Beginning next year I *will live* in Mexico.
Shoorai Hawai-ni *sumitai* desu.	I *want to live* in Hawaii in the future.

KEY GRAMMAR POINTS　　　　　　　　　　　文法ポイント

Narimasu なります

Narimasu is usually translated in English as *become* or *be*. The particle *-ni* follows nouns and *na*-adjectives which occur with *narimasu*.

Nani-*ni naritai* desu-ka?	What do you want to be(come)?
Pianisuto-*ni naritai* desu.	I want to be(come) a pianist.
Isha-*ni naritaku-nai* desu.	I do not want to be(come) a doctor.
Sensei-*ni naritakatta* desu.	I wanted to be(come) a teacher.
Yuumei-*ni naritai* desu.	I want to be(come) famous.
Yuumei-*ni narimashita*.	She became famous.

しょうらい (将来)	future
ゆうめい (有名)	famous
すみます	will live
やさしくて あたまが いい人と	I want to marry a kind, intelligent
けっこん したい です。	person.
子どもが 二人 ほしい です。	I want two children.
私は けっこん したくない です。	I don't want to get married.
私は はたらきたくない です。	I don't want to work.
しょう来 何に なりたい ですか。	What do you want to be in the future?
ゆう名な ピアニストに なりたい です。	I want to be a famous pianist.
私は 子どもの とき、いしゃに なりたか	When I was a child, I wanted to become
った です。でも、先生に なりました。	a doctor. But I became a teacher.
しょう来 ゆうめいに なりたい ですか。	In the future do you want to be famous?
どうして 先生に なりたい ですか。	Why do you want to be a teacher?
しょう来、ハワイに すみたい です。	In the future I want to live in Hawaii.
しょう来の ゆめは 何ですか。	What are your future dreams?

できますか。

Can you unscramble these vocabulary, all of which appear in the 読みましょう section above? Then write the meaning in えい語. Check your answers with your クラスメート.

1. いよらうし	3. めいうゆ	5. りっかたたな
2. たないり	4. すすみま	6. ならきくはたいた

In this lesson you will learn to read the *kanji* 読. Be sure that you know the reading and meaning of the *kanji*. The readings which are marked by an asterisk are for your reference only; you do not need to learn them at this time. You also do not have to learn any new words which are given in the examples. The correct stroke order for this *kanji* is given in the Optional Writing Practice section.

読 **DOKU*, TOKU*; yo(mu)** (read)

読みます	*yo*mimasu	read
読みました	*yo*mimashita	read [past tense]
読書	*doku*sho	reading [the activity]
読本	*toku*hon	reader [a book]

日本語の本を読むのが	Nihongo-no hon-o *yomu*-no-ga suki desu.
好きです。	(I like reading Japanese books.)
先月とても面白い本を	Sengetsu totemo omoshiroi hon-o *yomimashita*.
読みました。	(Last month I read a very interesting book.)
今、中国語の本を	Ima, chuugokugo-no hon-o *yonde-imasu*.
読んでいます。	(He is reading a Chinese book now.)

INTERACTIVE ACTIVITIES

PART 1

❶ Yomimashoo!

During this activity each student will work with a クラスメート to check Assignment #1 from Part 2 of Lesson 54. Have your partner carefully check your answers, mark and discuss with you any errors found.

❷ Kodomo-no toki nani-ni naritakatta desu-ka?

In this interview activity, Partner A selects one individual from the chart below and assumes that person's identity. Partner B then asks Partner A questions to determine his/her identity. Partner A looks at the chart during the interview. Partner B may <u>not</u> look at the chart and must remember Partner A's responses. After the interview, Partner B looks at the chart and tells Partner A who he/she is. Continue taking turns, striving each time for greater accuracy and fluency. Read the sample questions and answers aloud with your partner before you begin.

SAMPLE QUESTIONS AND ANSWERS

Kodomo-no toki nani-ni naritakatta desu-ka?   **Isha**-ni naritakatta desu.
Shoorai nani-ni naritai desu-ka?   **Pianisuto**-ni naritai desu.
Kekkon shitai desu-ka?   **Hai**, shitai desu/**Iie**, shitaku-nai desu.
Kodomo-ga hoshii desu-ka?   **Hai**, **futari** hoshii desu/Iie, hoshiku-nai desu.

Shoorai doko-ni sumitai desu-ka?   **Arabama**-ni sumitai desu.

NAMAE	NARITAKATTA	NARITAI	KEKKON	KODOMO	SUMITAI
Murakami	haisha	sensei	hai	2	Kororado
Buraun	sensei	isha	hai	3	Montana
Sumisu	isha	sensei	iie	0	Aiowa
Miyamoto	haisha	isha	hai	3	Montana
Joonzu	sensei	isha	hai	1	Montana
Romero	haisha	sensei	hai	2	Kariforunia
Fujita	isha	sensei	iie	0	Aidaho
Kuroda	sensei	haisha	hai	2	Kariforunia

PART 2

❶ Kakimashoo!

During this activity each student will work as a pair with two different クラスメート to check Assignment #2 from Part 1. The goal of the activity is to have two students carefully check the sentences in your description, mark and discuss with you any errors found, and sign off on your assignment. Form your first pair and exchange assignments with your partner. Both partners independently check and neatly mark errors for the entire assignment.

❷ Shoorai nani-ni naritai desu-ka?

In this interview activity, find out what dreams your クラスメート have for the future. Ask the questions given in the box below. Answer all questions truthfully. Sample answers are given in Activity ❷ in Part 1. Do this activity as an entire class. If you have a large class, form groups of about six students.

QUESTIONS

- Kodomo-no toki nani-ni naritakatta desu-ka?
- Shoorai nani-ni naritai desu-ka?
- Kekkon shitai desu-ka?
- Kodomo-ga hoshii desu-ka?
- Shoorai doko-ni sumitai desu-ka?

れんしゅう A: What **do** you want to become in the future?
What **did** you want to become?

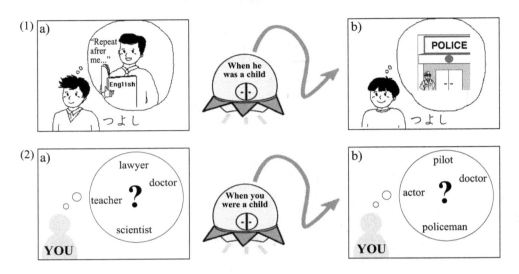

(1) a) つよし   When he was a child   b) POLICE つよし

(2) a) lawyer doctor teacher **?** scientist YOU   When you were a child   b) pilot doctor actor **?** policeman YOU

れんしゅう B: Your Future Plans

	けっこん	子ども	すみたい
ホワイト	○	2	Vancouver
山下	✕	0	New York
You	(1) **?**	(2) **?**	(3) **?**

れんしゅう C: What did Tim say?

We asked Tim-*sensei* what he thought was the <u>most famous</u> ~ in the U.S.
Guess what his answers were!

irasshai Welcome to Japanese	Car	University	*irasshai* Welcome to Japanese
Movie	Book	Drink	City
irasshai Welcome to Japanese	Mountain	Cartoon Character	*irasshai* Welcome to Japanese

LESSON 56
Review

OBJECTIVES 目標

At the end of this lesson you will be able to:

☑ Read the *kanji*: 書

VOCABULARY REVIEW 単語のふくしゅう

shoorai	future
yuumei (na)	famous
sumimasu	will live
sunde-iru (sunde-imasu)	live(s)
sensei-ni naru (narimasu/natte)	will become a teacher
sotsugyoo suru (shimasu/shite)	graduate
sono ato	after that
-go	after/in + LENGTH OF TIME
	LENGTH OF TIME + later
tabun	maybe, perhaps, probably
juusho	address
unten	driving (noun)
Ichi-jikan ikura desu-ka?	How much money per hour?
ichi-jikan #-doru	# dollars per hour
kaisha	company
hataraku (hatarakimasu/hataraite)	work
hitori-de	alone, by oneself
_____-no toki	when _____, at the time when _____
kekkon suru (shimasu)	get married, marry
kekkon shite-iru (shite-imasu)	be married
akachan	baby
umareru (umaremasu/umarete)	be born
#-ka-getsu	# month(s)
nan-ka-getsu	how many months

CULTURE NOTES カルチャーノート

Religion in Japan

If one defines religion as an organized spiritual practice that is based on written texts which clearly define a belief system that governs people's daily lives and includes regular attendance at group-worship services, then today's Japan cannot be regarded as a highly religious society. Most Japanese claim not to have any strong religious beliefs, and few attend religious services on a regular basis. The majority of Japanese, however, would identify themselves as both Buddhist and Shintoist.

Buddhism traces its origins back to India and China and was first brought to Japan beginning around 600 A.D. *O-tera* (Buddhist temples) can be found all over Japan. *Shinto*, which dates back to prehistoric times in Japan, is native to the country. *Jinja* (Shinto shrines) can be readily identified by the distinctive *torii* at the entrance. *Shinto*, which literally means *way of the gods*, acknowledges the existence of thousands of gods. The most powerful of these is Amaterasu, the sun-goddess from whom the Japanese Imperial Family was believed to be directly descended. Traditionally, the gods were believed to govern all the forces of nature and to be present in all of creation. Even mountains, rocks, and trees were thought to have divinity.

The importance of these two religions in contemporary Japan lies in how they govern certain major life events. *Shinto* is usually associated with birth, youth, successfully passing school entrance exams, and marriage. It is also at *Shinto* shrines throughout Japan that *matsuri* (festivals) are celebrated marking special seasonal events such as rice planting and harvesting according to the traditional agricultural calendar. Buddhism, on the other hand, is most often associated in Japan with death. While Japanese are usually married in a *Shinto* ceremony, their funerals and the recurring observances of the passing of family members over a number of years are handled according to Buddhist practice.

A SHINTO TORII

YOMIMASHOO! 読みましょう

しょうらい (将来)	future
ゆうめい (有名)	famous
すみます	will live
日本に すんでいる・すんでいます	live(s) in Japam
先生に なる・なります・なって	will become a teacher
そつぎょう する・します・して	graduate
そのあと	after that
二年ご	after two years
三年ご	in three years
五年ご	five years later
たぶん	maybe, perhaps, probably
じゅうしょ	address
うんてん	driving (noun)
一じかん いくら ですか。	How much money per hour?
一じかん 9ドル	nine dollars per hour
かいしゃ	company
はたらく・はたらきます・はたらいて	work
一人で	alone, by oneself
小学生の とき	when I was an elementary student
けっこん する・します	get married, marry
けっこん している・しています	be married
あかちゃん	baby
生まれる・生まれます・生まれて	be born
三か月	three months
何か月	how many months

LEARNING TIP

Test yourself on the 読みましょう section above. Mask the right side with a piece of paper, read the 日本語 aloud, and say the English equivalent. Move the paper down one line at a time to check your accuracy. Write down those which you need to review. After you have studied them, have a クラスメート test your knowledge.

In this lesson you will learn to read the *kanji* 書. Be sure that you know how to read the *kanji* and can tell what it means. The reading which is marked by an asterisk is for your reference only; you do not need to learn it at this time. You also do not have to learn any new words which are given in the examples. The correct stroke order for this *kanji* is given in the Optional Writing Practice section.

SHO*; ka(ku) (write)

書きます	*ka*kimasu	write
辞書	ji*sho*	dictionary
教科書	kyooka*sho*	textbook
図書館	to*sho*kan	library
履歴書	rireki*sho*	résumé
書道	*sho*doo	calligraphy

お名前を書いてください。   O-namae-o *ka*ite kudasai.
                        (Please write your name.)

日本の履歴書を見た   Nihon-no rireki*sho*-o mita-koto-ga arimasu-ka?
　ことがありますか。   (Have you ever seen a Japanese résumé?)
今、何を書いて   Ima, nani-o *ka*ite-imasu-ka?
　いますか。   (What are you writing now?)

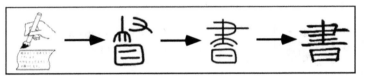

KANJI REVIEW														
上	名	二	見	今	万	大	中	円	年	八	元	土	口	前
目	才	六	日	木	四	気	本	七	人	国	十	何	三	水
子	金	百	語	月	行	田	一	小	学	高	川	私	千	校
火	五	下	天	九	来	書	生	言	父	読	山	耳	母	先
話														

How do you read them? What do they mean?

INTERACTIVE ACTIVITIES

PART 1

❶ Kakimashoo!

During this activity each student will work as a pair with two different クラスメート to check Assignment #1 from Part 2 of Lesson 55. The goal of the activity is to have two students carefully check the sentences in your description, mark and discuss with you any errors found, and sign off on your assignment. Form your first pair and exchange assignments with your partner. Both partners independently check and neatly mark errors for the entire assignment.

❷ Fukushuu-o shimashoo! (Let's review!)

With a クラスメート take turns asking and answering the questions on this page, all of which are drawn from Lessons 49-55. Answer all questions truthfully. Do not limit yourself to these sample questions and answers.

O-namae-wa?	Sumisu desu.
Doko-de umaremashita-ka?	Honoruru-de umaremashita.
Itsu umaremashita-ka?	1987*-nen 6-gatsu 11-nichi-ni umaremashita. [*sen kyuu-hyaku hachi-juu-nana-nen]
Kodomo-no toki doko-ni sunde-imashita-ka?	Tookyoo-ni sunde-imashita.
Shoogakusei-no toki doko-ni sunde-imashita-ka?	Otawa-ni sunde-imashita.
Ima, doko-ni sunde-imasu-ka?	Yokohama-ni sunde-imasu.
Dore-gurai Yokohama-ni sunde-imasu-ka?	10-nen-kan Yokohama-ni sunde-imasu.
Go-kazoku-to issho-ni sunde-imasu-ka?	Hai, haha-to imooto-to sunde-imasu.
Kookoosei desu-ka? Daigakusei desu-ka?	Kookoosei desu.
Ima, nan-nen-sei desu-ka?	Ichi-nen-sei desu.
Itsu kookoo-o sotsugyoo shimasu-ka?	Ni-nen-go-ni sotsugyoo shimasu.
Sono ato, nani-o shimasu-ka?	Daigaku-ni ikimasu.

For the following section, if you do not have a part-time job, imagine that you do!

Arubaito-o shite-imasu-ka?	Hai, shite-imasu.
Donna arubaito-o shite-imasu-ka?	Depaato-no arubaito-o shite-imasu.
Doko-de hataraite-imasu-ka?	Biggu-Disukaunto-Shoppu-de hataraite-imasu.
Arubaito-wa nan-yoobi desu-ka?	Ka-yoobi-kara do-yoobi-made desu. Nichi-yoobi-to getsu-yoobi-wa yasumi desu.
Nan-ji-kara nan-ji-made desu-ka?	8-ji-kara 5-ji-made desu.
Ichi-jikan ikura desu-ka?	10-doru desu.
Arubaito-ga suki desu-ka?	Hai, daisuki/Suki desu.
	Iie, suki/anmari suki ja nai desu.
Dooshite arubaito-ga suki desu-ka?	Omoshiroi-kara, suki desu.
	Tanoshii-kara, suki desu.
	O-kane-ga ii-kara, suki desu.
Dooshite arubaito-ga kirai desu-ka?	O-kane-ga yoku-nai-kara, kirai desu.
	Tsumaranai-kara, kirai desu.
	Jikan*-ga nagai-kara, kirai desu. *hours
	Taihen da-kara, kirai desu.
	Yoru-mo shigoto-ga aru-kara, kirai desu.
Kodomo-no toki nani-ni naritakatta desu-ka?	Isha-ni naritakatta desu.
Shoorai nani-ni naritai desu-ka?	Pianisuto-ni naritai desu.
Shoorai yuumei-ni naritai desu-ka?	Hai, naritai desu.
Kekkon shitai desu-ka?	Hai, shitai desu.
	Iie, shitaku-nai desu.
Kodomo-ga hoshii desu-ka?	Hai, futari hoshii desu.
	Iie, hoshiku-nai desu.
Shoorai doko-ni sumitai desu-ka?	Arabama-ni sumitai desu.

❶ Kakimashoo!

During this activity each student will work as a pair with two different クラスメート to check Assignment #2 from Part 1. The goal of the activity is to have two students carefully check the sentences in your description, mark and discuss with you any errors found, and sign off on your assignment. Form your first pair and exchange assignments with your partner. Both partners independently check and neatly mark errors for the entire assignment.

❷ Fukushuu-o shimashoo! (Let's review!)

With a different partner, continue practicing the questions and answers from Activity ❷ of Part 1. Without looking at your text, ask your partner five questions. You may assume an imaginary identity when you answer the questions, but all of your answers must be compatible. Then change roles. If you need additional practice with a specific topic, you may wish to redo an appropriate activity in an earlier lesson.

れんしゅう A: Talking about Your Family

(1) El Paso

(2) St. Louis

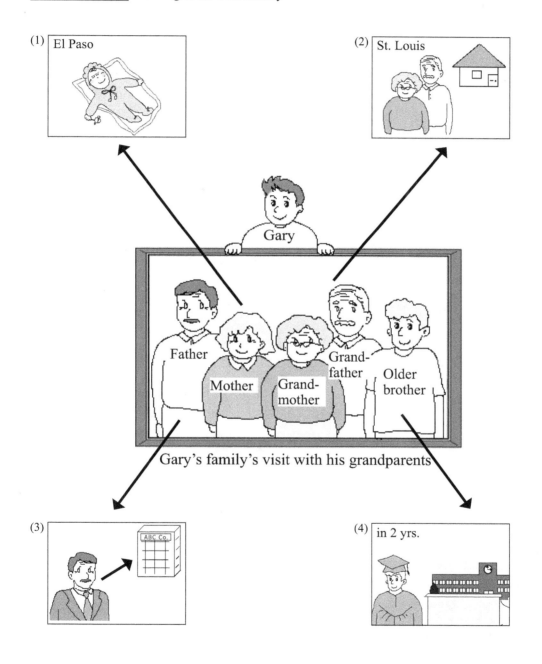

Gary

Father
Mother
Grand-mother
Grand-father
Older brother

Gary's family's visit with his grandparents

(3) ABC Co.

(4) in 2 yrs.

Read the following sets of words and choose the most closely related word from those listed below.

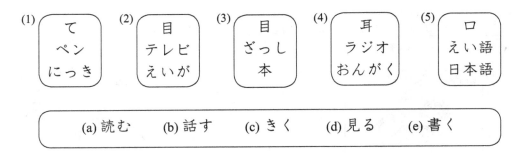

(1)
て
ペン
にっき

(2)
目
テレビ
えいが

(3)
目
ざっし
本

(4)
耳
ラジオ
おんがく

(5)
口
えい語
日本語

(a) 読む　　(b) 話す　　(c) きく　　(d) 見る　　(e) 書く

れんしゅう C: Let's interview your classmates!

(2) Want to marry in the future?

(3)
(a) Want to live abroad?
(b) Where?

(4) What do you want to be in the future?

(1)
(a) Want kids in the future?
(b) How many?

(5) What did you want to be when you were a kid?

れんしゅう A: Natalie's Childhood

(1)

ninjin

food

(2)

Nicky
Mouse

cartoon

(3)

Colorado

trip

れんしゅう B: Find the best job for these people!

(1)
(a) Name:
Jackie Chen

(b) Hobby: travel
(c) Favorite subjects:
Spanish and French
(d) Character: kind and
cheerful
Others: 20/20 vision

(2)
(a) Name:
David Malden

(b) Hobby: judo
(c) Favorite subject:
physical education
(d) Character: strict and
serious
Others: excellent
driving record

cooking
teacher

gaka

(3)
(a) Name:
Martha Hall

(b) Hobby: going to
restaurants
(c) Favorite subject:
home economics
(*kateika*)
(d) Character: cheerful
and fun
Others: creative

(4)
(a) Name:
Mike Steward

(b) Hobby: golf
(c) Favorite subject:
biology (*seibutsu*)
(d) Character: serious
and kind
Others: perfect health

furaito atendanto

433

れんしゅう C: Let's talk about your future!

	ルーシー	チャーリー	YOU
(1) graduate when?	in 2 yrs.	in 3yrs.	?
(2) plans after graduation?	go to college	work at a bakery	?
(3) want to get married?	no	yes	?
(4) want children?	no	1	?
(5) want to live where?	Paris	Nashville	?

LESSON 57
Length of Events

OBJECTIVES　　　　　　　　　　　　　　　　　　目標

At the end of this lesson you will be able to:
- ☑ Ask about and state the length of events
- ☑ Read the *kanji*: 聞 and 間

VOCABULARY　　　　　　　　　　　　　　　　　単語

Words

#-shuu-kan	# week(s), a period of # weeks
ichi-nichi	(for) one day, all day

Other words and expressions you will hear in this lesson

hanemuun	honeymoon
tsuaa	tour
gaikoku	foreign country
gaido-bukku	guidebook

KEY GRAMMAR POINTS　　　　　　　　　　　文法ポイント

1. #-shuu-kan しゅうかん (週間)

This lesson introduces *-shuu-kan*, the counter for weeks. This *-shuu*, which means *week*, is the same as in the words *senshuu, konshuu, raishuu,* and *shuumatsu* (weekend).

Natsu-yasumi-wa *is-shuu-kan* desu.	Summer vacation is *one week*.
Yon-shuu-kan-no ryokoo	a *four-week* trip
Hawai-ni *ni-shuu-kan* imashita.	We were in Hawaii for *two weeks*.

NAN-SHUU-KAN?			
1	is-shuu-kan	6	roku-shuu-kan
2	ni-shuu-kan	7	nana-shuu-kan
3	san-shuu-kan	8	has-shuu-kan
4	yon-shuu-kan	9	kyuu-shuu-kan
5	go-shuu-kan	10	jus(jis)-shuu-kan

2. -kan かん (間)

The counter *-kan*, which means *period* or *duration*, is used to count units of time such as minutes, hours, days, weeks, months, and years. You **must** use *-kan* when talking about hours and weeks. Its use is optional with minutes, days, months, and years. The chart on the next page summarizes the forms with *-kan* for the units of time you have learned in this course.

Study these examples.

Fuyu-yasumi-wa *ni-shuu-kan* desu.	Winter vacation is *two weeks*.
San-shuu-kan-no ryokoo-o shimashita.	I took a *three-week* trip.
Muika-kan-no Kyooto ryokoo deshita.	It was a *six-day* trip to Kyoto.
Bosuton-kara Maiami-made kuruma-de *nan-ji-kan*-gurai desu-ka?	About *how many hours* is it by car from Boston to Miami?
Nihon-ni *go-nen-kan* sunde-imashita.	I lived in Japan for *five years*.
Oosutoraria-de *yon-ka-getsu-kan* hatarakimashita.	She worked in Australia for *four months*.
Satomi-san-wa *juu-go-fun-kan* utaimashita.	Satomi sang for *15 minutes*.

435

	Minutes	**Hours**	**Days**
	nan-pun(-kan)	nan-ji-kan	nan-nichi(-kan)
1	ip-pun(-kan)	ichi-ji-kan	ichinichi*
2	ni-fun(-kan)	ni-ji-kan	futsuka(-kan)
3	san-pun(-kan)	san-ji-kan	mikka(-kan)
4	yon-pun(-kan)	yo-ji-kan	yokka(-kan)
5	go-fun(-kan)	go-ji-kan	itsuka(-kan)
6	rop-pun(-kan)	roku-ji-kan	muika(-kan)
7	nana-fun(-kan)	nana-ji-kan	nanoka(-kan)
8	hap-pun(-kan)	hachi-ji-kan	yooka(-kan)
9	kyuu-fun(-kan)	ku-ji-kan	kokonoka(-kan)
10	jup-pun(-kan)	juu-ji-kan	tooka(-kan)
11	juu-ip-pun(-kan)	juu-ichi-ji-kan	juu-ichi-nichi(-kan)
14	juu-yon-pun(-kan)	juu-yo-ji-kan	juu-yokka(-kan)
20	ni-jup-pun(-kan)	ni-juu-ji-kan	hatsuka(-kan)

	Weeks	**Months**	**Years**
	nan-shuu-kan	nan-ka-getsu(-kan)	nan-nen(-kan)
1	is-shuu-kan	ik-ka-getsu(-kan)	ichi-nen(-kan)
2	ni-shuu-kan	ni-ka-getsu(-kan)	ni-nen(-kan)
3	san-shuu-kan	san-ka-getsu(-kan)	san-nen(-kan)
4	yon-shuu-kan	yon-ka-getsu(-kan)	yo-nen(-kan)
5	go-shuu-kan	go-ka-getsu(-kan)	go-nen(-kan)
6	roku-shuu-kan	rok-ka-getsu(-kan)	roku-nen(-kan)
7	nana-shuu-kan	nana-ka-getsu(-kan)	nana-nen(-kan)
8	has-shuu-kan	hak-ka-getsu(-kan)	hachi-nen(-kan)
9	kyuu-shuu-kan	kyuu-ka-getsu(-kan)	kyuu-nen(-kan)
10	jus-shuu-kan	juk-ka-getsu(-kan)	juu-nen(-kan)
11	juu-is-shuu-kan	juu-ik-ka-getsu(-kan)	juu-ichi-nen(-kan)
14	juu-yon-shuu-kan	juu-yon-ka-getsu(-kan)	juu-yo-nen(-kan)
20	ni-jus-shuu-kan	ni-juk-ka-getsu(-kan)	ni-juu-nen(-kan)

*-*kan* is not used with *ichinichi* but may be used with all of the other days.

YOMIMASHOO! 読みましょう

三しゅう間	(a period of) three weeks
一日	(for) one day, all day
なつやすみは 一しゅう間 です。	Summer vacation is one week.
二しゅう間の りょこう	a two-week trip
がい国に 行きたい です。	I want to go to a foreign country.
六日間の きょうと りょこう	a six-day trip to Kyoto
ハワイに どれぐれい いましたか。	How long were you in Hawaii?
それは どんな ツアー ですか。	What kind of tour is that?
どうぶつえんで 一日 あそびました。	We had fun at the zoo all day.
ハネムーン	honeymoon
ツアー	tour
がい国	foreign country
ガイドブック	guidebook

KANJI NOTES 漢字ノート

In this lesson you will learn to read two *kanji*: 聞 and 間. Be sure that you know the readings of each *kanji* and can tell what the *kanji* means. The readings which are marked by an asterisk are for your reference only; you do not need to learn them at this time. You also do not have to learn any new words which are given in the examples. The correct stroke order for these *kanji* is given in the Optional Writing Practice section.

聞

BUN*; ki(ku) (hear, listen to, ask), **ki(koeru)*** (be heard)

聞きます	*ki*kimasu	hear, listen to, ask
聞いた	*ki*ita	heard [plain past]
新聞	shin*bun*	newspaper [new-hear]
見聞	ken*bun*	information, experience

明日、英語の先生に
聞いてください。 — Ashita, eigo-no sensei-ni *ki*ite kudasai.
(Please ask the English teacher tomorrow.)

今日の新聞をもう
読みましたか。 — Kyoo-no shin*bun*-o moo yomimashita-ka?
(Did you already read today's newspaper?)

今日のニュースを
ラジオで聞きましたか。 — Kyoo-no nyuusu-o rajio-de *ki*kimashita-ka?
(Did you hear today's news on the radio?)

The *kanji* 聞 was derived from a picture of an *ear* at a *gate* as if someone were *listening* in on someone else's conversation.

間

KAN, KEN*; aida* (interval, space), **ma*** (interval, room, time)

時間	ji*kan*	time
何時間	nan-ji-*kan*	how many hours
三日間	mikka-*kan*	(a period of) three days
二週間	ni-shuu-*kan*	(a period of) two weeks
七か月間	nana-kagetsu-*kan*	(a period of) seven months
五年間	go-nen-*kan*	(a period of) five years
間	*aida*	interval, space

私はアメリカに三年間
いました。 — Watashi-wa Amerika-ni san-nen-*kan* imashita.
(I was in the U.S. for three years.)

中山さんと上田さんは
二週間の旅行をしました。 — Nakayama-san-to Ueda-san-wa ni-shuu-*kan*-no ryokoo-o
shimashita.
(Mr. Nakayama and Mr. Ueda took a two-week trip.)

東京から京都まで電車で
何時間ぐらいですか。 — Tookyoo-kara Kyooto-made densha-de nan-ji*kan*-gurai
desu-ka? (About how many hours is it from Tokyo to
Kyoto by train?)

The *kanji* 間 was created from the *kanji* 門 (gate) and 日 (sun). The *sun* shines through the same *space* in the *gate* for the same *interval* every day.

437

```
┌─────────────────────────────────────────────────────────────────────┐
│                         KANJI REVIEW                                  │
│  上  名  二  見  今  万  大  中  円  年  八  元  土  口  前           │
│  目  才  六  言  話  日  木  四  気  本  七  人  国  十  何           │
│  三  水  子  金  百  語  月  行  田  一  小  学  高  川  千           │
│  校  火  五  下  天  九  来  書  生  父  私  読  山  間  耳           │
│  母  聞  先            How do you read them? What do they mean?       │
└─────────────────────────────────────────────────────────────────────┘
```

INTERACTIVE ACTIVITIES

PART 1

❶ Ni-shuu-kan-no ryokoo desu-ka?   📄 & ✏

Play this guessing game with a クラスメート. Partner A, without showing Partner B, writes the length of his/her trip in weeks (one to 10 weeks). Partner B then asks the question "____ -shuu-kan-no ryokoo desu-ka?" to determine the correct length. Each question is worth one point. Then change roles and repeat. The player with the lower score is the winner of the round. Refer to the box in the 文法ポイント section of this lesson as needed. Read this sample exchange aloud before you begin.

A: (writes down *yon-shuu-kan*)
B: Roku-shuu-kan-no ryokoo desu-ka?
A: Iie, motto mijikai desu.
B: Ni-shuu-kan-no ryokoo desu-ka?
A: Iie, motto nagai desu.
B: Yon-shuu-kan-no ryokoo desu-ka?
A: Hai, soo desu. [Partner B asked three questions and now has a score of three.]

❷ Yamaguchi-san-no shigoto-wa nan desu-ka?   📄 & ✏

In this pair activity take turns asking and answering questions to exchange the information you and your partner need to complete your charts on the next page. Look only at your own chart. After you have finished, compare the charts. Before you begin, read the sample questions and answers aloud.

SAMPLE QUESTIONS AND ANSWERS

Yamaguchi-san-no o-shigoto-wa nan desu-ka?	**Pairotto** desu.
Yamaguchi-san-wa doko-ni ikimashita-ka?	**Hawai**-ni ikimashita.
Yamaguchi-san-wa Hawai-ni dore-gurai imashita-ka?	**Is-shuu-kan** imashita.
Yamaguchi-san-wa nani-o shimashita-ka?	**Umi-de asobimashita.**
Dare-ga **pairotto** desu-ka?	**Yamaguchi**-san desu.
Dare-ga **Hawai**-ni ikimashita-ka?	**Yamaguchi**-san desu.
Dare-ga **umi-de asobimashita**-ka?	**Yamaguchi**-san desu.

PARTNER A

NAMAE	SHIGOTO	DOKO-NI	DORE-GURAI	NANI-O SHIMASHITA
Yamaguchi	pairotto	Hawai	is-shuu-kan	umi-de asobimashita
Ueda	sensei		san-ka-getsu-kan	doitsugo-no benkyoo-o shimashita
		Amerika		e-o kakimashita
Maetani	hisho	Kanada	yo-nen-kan	
Nishikawa	pianisuto			
	ha-isha			daigaku-de oshiemashita
Miura	haiyuu	Igirisu	san-shuu-kan	
Nomura		Furansu	ni-ka-getsu-kan	resutoran-de hatarakimashita

Vocabulary: gaka (painter, artist), haiyuu (actor), hisho (secretary), Kankoku (Korea),
Igirisu (England)

PARTNER B

NAMAE	SHIGOTO	DOKO-NI	DORE-GURAI	NANI-O SHIMASHITA
Yamaguchi	pairotto	Hawai	is-shuu-kan	umi-de asobimashita
Ueda		Doitsu		
Itoo	gaka	Amerika	go-shuu-kan	
	hisho			kaisha-de hatarakimashita
Nishikawa		Kankoku	ni-shuu-kan	konsaato-o shimashita
Andoo	ha-isha	Indoneshia	go-ka-getsu-kan	
		Igirisu		eiga-o mimashita
Nomura	ueetaa			

Vocabulary: gaka (painter, artist), haiyuu (actor/actress), hisho (secretary), Kankoku (Korea),
Igirisu (England)

PART 2

❶ Kakimashoo! 🖊

During this activity each student will work as a pair with two different クラスメート to
check Assignment #2 from Part 1. The goal of the activity is to have two students
carefully check the sentences in your description, mark and discuss with you any errors
found, and sign off on your assignment. Form your first pair and exchange assignments
with your partner. Both partners independently check and neatly mark errors for the
entire assignment.

❷ Intabyuu 📄 & ✎

Do this interview activity as an entire class. If you have a large class, form groups of six. Then form pairs and interview each other asking about your partner's vacation. Ask the questions in the box below. Refer to the sample questions and answers as needed. When you have finished, find a new partner to interview. Before you begin, decide what you are going to say. **Use your imagination.**

SAMPLE QUESTIONS AND ANSWERS

Doko-ni ikimashita-ka?	**Kosutarika***-ni ikimashita. *Costa Rica
Dare-to ikimashita-ka?	**Tomodachi**-to ikimashita.
Kosutarika-ni dore-gurai imashita-ka?	**Ni-shuu-kan** imashita.
Kosutarika-de nani-o shimashita-ka?	**Gorufu-o shimashita.**

QUESTIONS

- Where did your partner go?
- Who did your partner go with?
- How long did your partner stay there?
- What did your partner do there?

L. 57 電話で 話しましょう

れんしゅう A: Your Future Plans

Your Japanese friend's older brother/sister is asking you about your future.
Answer his/her questions.

れんしゅう B: Where did s/he go? How long did s/he stay?

しつもん: (a) went where?　(b) did what?　(c) how long in ~?

(Ex.)

ボブ
for 2 weeks

(1)
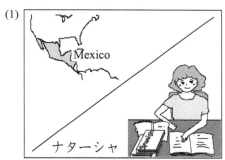
ナターシャ
for 6 weeks

(2)
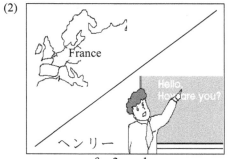
ヘンリー
for 3 weeks

(3)
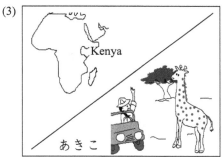
あきこ
for 1 week

441

れんしゅう C: What has Nodoka done in the past three years?

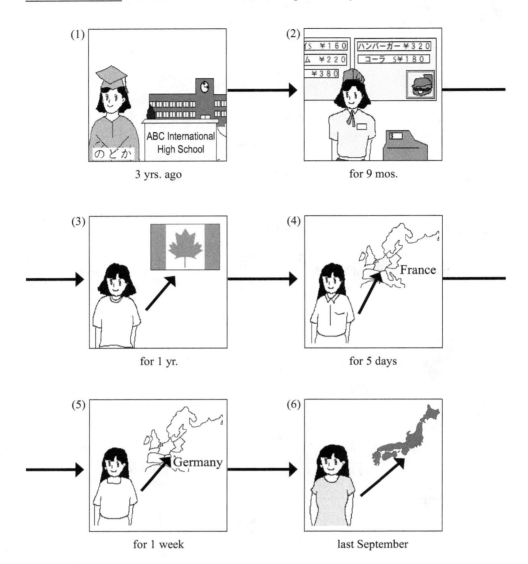

(1) 3 yrs. ago

(2) for 9 mos.

(3) for 1 yr.

(4) for 5 days

(5) for 1 week

(6) last September

442

LESSON 58
Travel Schedules

OBJECTIVES　　　　　　　　　　　　　　　　目標

At the end of this lesson you will be able to:

☑ Talk about travel schedules

☑ Read the *kanji*: 時 and 分

VOCABULARY　　　　　　　　　　　　　　　単語

Words

deru (demasu/dete)	leave
tsuku (tsukimasu/tsuite)	arrive
gozen	a.m.
gogo	p.m.

Other words and expressions you will hear in this lesson

hayaku	quickly
mizugi	swimsuit
Wasuremono-o shinai-de kudasai.	Please don't forget anything.

VOCABULARY NOTES　　　　　　　　　　単語ノート

1. Gozen and gogo ごぜん (午前) ごご (午後)

Gozen and *gogo* are expressed in English as *a.m.* (ante meridiem) and *p.m.* (post meridiem), respectively. The first syllable *go* means *noon*. *Zen* means *before*, and *go* (the second syllable) means *after*. Unlike their English counterparts, *gozen* and *gogo* are said before the clock time.

Gogo san-ji-ni tsukimasu.	I will arrive at 3:00 *p.m.*
Miitingu-wa *gozen* juu-ji-kara desu.	The meeting starts at 10:00 *a.m.*

2. Mizugi みずぎ (水着)

The Japanese word for *swimsuit* is composed of *mizu* (water) and *gi* (wear). The syllable *gi* is a phonetic variant of *ki* which appears in the word *kimono* ("wear-thing" or clothing).

KEY GRAMMAR POINTS　　　　　　　　文法ポイント

Date/time-ni demasu/tsukimasu でます (出ます)・つきます (着きます)

Both *demasu* (leave) and *tsukimasu* (arrive), when used with a date and/or time require the use of the particle *-ni*. If you say both the date and the time, insert the particle *-no* between them.

Roku-gatsu mikka-*ni* demasu.	I will leave on June 3.
Juu-ji-*ni* demasu.	I will leave at 10:00.
Roku-gatsu mikka-*no* juu-ji-*ni* demasu.	I will leave at 10:00 on June 3.
Gogo roku-ji-*ni* demashita.	We left at 6:00 p.m.
Suiyoobi-*ni* tsukimashita.	We arrived on Wednesday.
Gozen go-ji-han-*ni* tsukimasu.	She'll arrive at 5:30 a.m.
Itsu tsukimasu-ka?	When do you arrive?

```
DATE/DAY/TIME + ni + demasu/tsukimasu
```

In Lesson 60 you will learn how to talk about arriving in and departing from a country, city, or other place.

でる・でます・でて	leave
つく・つきます・ついて	arrive
ごぜん (午前)	a.m.
ごご (午後)	p.m.
ひこうきは 何時に でますか。	What time does the airplane leave?
六月三日の 十時に でます。	It leaves at 10:00 on June 3.
いつ でますか。	When do you leave?
いつ つきましたか。	When did she arrive?
何日間の ツアー ですか。	How many days is the tour?
りょこうに 何が いりますか。	What do I need for the trip?
はやく	quickly
みずぎ (水着)	swimsuit
わすれものを しないで ください。	Please don't forget anything.

できますか。

Can you unscramble these 単語, all of which appear in the 読みましょう section above? Then write the meaning in えい語. Check your answers with your クラスメート.

1. うこりょ
2. やはく
3. いすまり
4. すきまつ
5. うひきこ
6. まです

KANJI NOTES 漢字ノート

In this lesson you will learn to read two *kanji*: 時 and 分. Be sure that you know the readings of each *kanji* and can tell what the *kanji* means. The readings which are marked by an asterisk are for your reference only; you do not need to learn them at this time. You also do not have to learn any new words which are given in the examples. The correct stroke order for these *kanji* is given in the Optional Writing Practice section.

時 **JI; toki [doki]** (time, *counter for clock hours*)

何時	nan-*ji*	what time
三時	san-*ji*	three o'clock
何時間	nan-*ji*kan	how many hours
五時間	go-*ji*kan	(a period of) five hours
時々 *	*tokidoki*	sometimes
時計	*to*kei	watch, clock
大学生の時	daigakusei-no *toki*	when (I was) a college student

*The symbol 々 means that the *kanji* before it is read again, sometimes with a sound change.

すみませんけど、明日時間がありません。	Sumimasen kedo, ashita *ji*kan-ga arimasen. (I'm sorry, but tomorrow I don't have time.)
今日、何時頃学校に行きますか。	Kyoo, nan-*ji*-goro gakkoo-ni ikimasu-ka. (About what time are you going to school today?)
ニューヨークから東京まで十四時間です。	Nyuu-Yooku-kara Tookyoo-made juu-yo-*ji*kan desu. (It's 14 hours from New York to Tokyo.)
大学生の時、友達と四国に行きました。	Daigakusei-no toki, tomodachi-to Shikoku-ni ikimashita. (When I was a college student, I went with friends to Shikoku.)

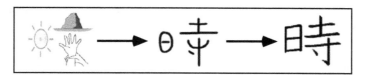

The *kanji* 時 was created from the *kanji* 日, 土, and 寸 (a Japanese unit of measure). *Hours* are a *measure* of the *sun* moving across the *land*.

分 **FUN [PUN]** (minute, *counter for minutes*), **BUN*, BU*** (part, share); **wa(keru)*** (divide, separate), **wa(karu)** (understand)

二分	ni-*fun*	two minutes
八分	hap-*pun*	eight minutes
一分	ip-*pun*	one minute
何分	nan-*pun*	how many minutes
自分で	ji*bun*-de	by oneself (with no help)
分かります	*wa*karimasu	understand

東京行きの電車は何時
何分に出ますか。

Tookyoo-yuki-no densha-wa nan-ji nan-*pun*-ni
  demasu-ka?
(What time does the train bound for Tokyo leave?)

後、二分です。

Ato, ni-*fun* desu.
(There are two minutes left.)

自分で書きました。

Ji*bun*-de kakimashita.
(I wrote it myself.)

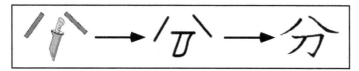

The *kanji* 分 was derived from a picture of wood being cut into pieces or parts. In addition to the meanings *part* and *divide*, it also came to mean *minutes* which are parts of an hour.

KANJI REVIEW

上	名	二	見	今	万	大	中	時	年	八	元	土	口	前
目	才	六	日	木	四	気	分	七	人	国	十	何	三	水
子	金	百	語	月	行	田	一	小	学	高	川	本	千	校
火	五	下	天	九	来	書	生	父	読	山	間	耳	母	聞
先	言	話	私	円										

How do you read them? What do they mean?

INTERACTIVE ACTIVITIES

PART 1

❶ Yomimashoo!

During this activity each student will work as a pair with two different クラスメート to check Assignment #1 from Part 2 in Lesson 57. The goal of the activity is to have two students carefully check your answers, mark and discuss with you any errors found. Form your first pair and exchange assignments with your partner. Both partners independently check and neatly mark errors for the entire assignment.

❷ Fukushuu-o shimashoo!

Do this review activity with a クラスメート. Using the chart in the 文法ポイント section of Lesson 57 (-kan), take turns testing each other on the use of -kan with **days**, **weeks**, **months**, and **years**. Do one column at a time, from one to 10.

❸ Nihon-ni dore-gurai imashita-ka?

In this fast-paced pair activity, Partner A asks Partner B the same question (*Nihon-ni dore-gurai imashita-ka?*) five times in a row. Partner B taps out the answer with a pencil, touching first a number box and then a -kan box. Each time Partner A responds by saying, "*A, (length of time) deshita-ka? Ii desu-ne.*"

1	**6**	日間	しゅう 週間
2	**7**		
3	**8**		
4	**9**	か月間	年間
5	**10**		

PART 2

---

❶ Kakimashoo! 🖊

During this activity each student will work with a クラスメート to check Assignment #2 from Part 1. Have your partner carefully check your answers, mark and discuss with you any errors found.

❷ Itsu tsukimasu-ka? 📄 & 🖊

In this pair activity take turns asking and answering questions to exchange the information you and your partner need to complete your charts. Look only at your own chart. The finished chart will show the itinerary of Mrs. Ikeda, an extremely wealthy individual who will be taking a 16-month tour around the world. Included are where she will go, when she will arrive, how long she will stay, and when she will depart. Ask all of the questions in the same order as in the example. Then switch roles. Fill in the lines of the chart in order from the top. After you have finished, compare the charts.

SAMPLE QUESTIONS AND ANSWERS

Ikeda-san-wa doko-ni ikimasu-ka?	**Rondon**-ni ikimasu.
Itsu tsukimasu-ka?	**Shi-gatsu mikka**-no **ku-ji juu-go-fun**-ni tsukimasu.
Rondon-ni dore-gurai imasu-ka?	**Go-shuu-kan** imasu.
Itsu demasu-ka?	**Go-gatsu kokonoka**-no **hachi-ji han**-ni demasu.
Sono ato, doko-ni ikimasu-ka?	**Rooma**-ni ikimasu.

PARTNER A

DOKO	TSUKIMASU	DORE-GURAI	DEMASU
Rondon	4 月 3 日 9 時 15 分	go-shuu-kan	5 月 9 日 8 時 30 分
	5 月 日 時 分		月 日 4 時 分
Isutanbuuru	6 月 9 日 5 時 15 分	ni-shuu-kan	6 月 24 日 6 時 00 分
	月 日 1 時 分		月 日 3 時 分
Bonbei	8 月 30 日 6 時 30 分	san-shuu-kan	9 月 19 日 9 時 10 分
	9 月 日 時 分		月 日 10 時 分
Taipei	10 月 5 日 4 時 00 分	yon-ka-getsu-kan	2 月 4 日 7 時 00 分
	月 日 3 時 分		2 月 日 時 分
Fijii	2 月 20 日 9 時 30 分	san-ka-getsu-kan	5 月 18 日 8 時 15 分
	5 月 日 時 分		月 日 時 00 分
Ankarejji	5 月 29 日 8 時 20 分	kokonoka-kan	6 月 6 日 9 時 15 分
	6 月 日 時 分		7 月 日 時 分

Rondon = London; Rooma = Rome; Bonbei = Bombay; Ankarejji = Anchorage

PARTNER B

DOKO	TSUKIMASU	DORE-GURAI	DEMASU
Rondon	4 月 3 日 9 時 15 分	go-shuu-kan	5 月 9 日 8 時 30 分
Rooma	5 月 11 日 2 時 00 分	ik-ka-getsu-kan	6 月 8 日 4 時 20 分
	6 月 日 時 分		月 日 時 00 分
Kairo	6 月 26 日 1 時 25 分	ni-ka-getsu-kan	8 月 23 日 3 時 15 分
	8 月 日 時 分		月 日 9 時 分
Manira	9 月 25 日 9 時 10 分	is-shuu-kan	10 月 1 日 10 時 45 分
	10 月 日 時 分		月 日 時 00 分
Tookyoo	2 月 7 日 3 時 45 分	tooka-kan	2 月 16 日 5 時 30 分
	2 月 日 時 分		月 日 8 時 分
Honoruru	5 月 22 日 7 時 15 分	muika-kan	5 月 27 日 11 時 00 分
	5 月 日 時 分		月 6 日 時 分
Otawa	6 月 10 日 10 時 45 分	roku-shuu-kan	7 月 22 日 1 時 25 分

Rondon = London; Rooma = Rome; Bonbei = Bombay; Ankarejji = Anchorage

LEARNING TIP
See if you and your partner can complete this entire activity by speaking only in Japanese. The more you speak in Japanese, the more rapidly your speaking skills will develop.

L. 58 電話で 話しましょう

れんしゅう A: Departure/Arrival Schedules

しつもん: (a) When is it leaving?　　(b) When is it arriving?

(1) L.A. Airport　1:00 p.m.　to Tokyo　スコット　Tokyo Airport　4:00 p.m.

(2) New York　11:00 a.m.　to Washington D.C.　チェルシー　Washington D.C.　12:45 p.m.

(3) Denver　8:20 a.m.　to Salt Lake City　マイケル　Salt Lake City　3:40 p.m.

れんしゅう B: Let's converse!

Dialogue:
A: Excuse me. Do you have a <u>Paris</u> tour?
B: Yes. We have a <u>6-day</u> tour.
A: When does it leave (here)?
B: It leaves (here) at <u>10 p.m.</u> on <u>July 6th</u>.
A: When will it arrive (there)?
B: It'll arrive (there) at <u>2:00 a.m.</u> on <u>the 7th</u>.
A: Oh, really.

At a travel agency

Sample Dialogue:

A: すみません。<u>パリ</u>のツアー
がありますか。

B: はい。<u>6日間</u>のツアーがあり
ます。

A: いつ でますか。

B: <u>7月6日</u>の<u>ごご10時</u>にでます。

A: じゃ、いつ つきますか。

B: <u>7日</u>の<u>ごぜん2時</u>につきます。

A: そうですか。

Sample Dialogue:

A: Sumimasen. <u>Pari</u>-no tsuaa-ga
arimasu-ka?

B: Hai. <u>Muika-kan</u>-no tsuaa-ga
arimasu.

A: Itsu demasu-ka?

B: <u>Shichi-gatsu muika</u>-no <u>gogo
juu-ji</u>-ni demasu.

A: Jaa, itsu tsukimasu-ka?

B: <u>Nanoka</u>-no <u>gozen ni-ji</u>-ni
tsukimasu.

A: Soo desu-ka.

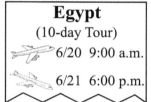

Egypt
(10-day Tour)
6/20 9:00 a.m.
6/21 6:00 p.m.

London
(1-week Tour)
7/4 9:30 p.m.
7/5 4:00 a.m.

Cape Town
(9-day Tour)
5/8 11:00 a.m.
5/10 5:00 a.m.

<u>れんしゅう C</u>: Where do you want to go?

Congratulations! You won a trip to the destination of your choice. You are
leaving this winter.

Singapore
80°F
*Feast on
exotic cuisine!*

Anchorage
15°F
*See gigantic
glaciers!*

Sydney
54°F
*Come see
koalas!*

Cancun
90°F
*Enjoy
water sports!*

Whistler
40°F
*Ski on
scenic slopes!*

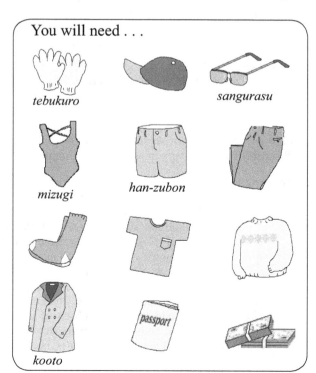

You will need . . .

tebukuro   *sangurasu*

mizugi   *han-zubon*

kooto   passport

LESSON 59
Famous Tourist Sights in Japan

OBJECTIVES   目標

At the end of this lesson you will be able to:
- ☑ Identify some famous tourist sights in Japan
- ☑ Read the *kanji*: 雨 and 雪

VOCABULARY   単語

Phrases and expressions

shashin-o toru (torimasu/totte)   take a picture

Other words and expressions you will hear in this lesson

onsen	hot spring
hikooki-no chiketto	airline ticket
Tookyoo Tawaa	Tokyo Tower

CULTURE NOTES   カルチャーノート

Famous tourist sights in Japan

Most tourists making their first trip to Japan have only one to two weeks to see as much as they can of the country. Although Japan's land mass may be small compared to that of many other nations, there is much to see and do in this vibrant and fascinating country. If you wish to learn more about the sights described below or the thousands of other interesting places to visit, check some books out of your school or local library. For the most current information, use the Internet!

TOKYO

Tokyo is the capital of Japan and is like Washington, D.C., New York, Los Angeles, and San Francisco all rolled into one. It is the political, financial, commercial, entertainment, and educational capital of the country. Originally known as Edo, the city had a population of approximately one million by the early 1700's. Today Tokyo is home to approximately 12 million people, making it one of the largest cities in the world.

Tochoo (Tokyo City Hall)

Tokyo City Hall is located in the western part of Tokyo in an area known as Shinjuku and was completed in 1991. In the 1960's, a massive revitalization and development project was launched in Shinjuku in an effort to relieve congestion in the central part of Tokyo. Since 1970, a large number of skyscrapers have been constructed, giving this part of Tokyo a very modern and well-organized look.

Tookyoo Tawaa (Tokyo Tower)

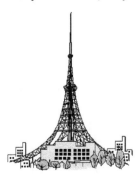

Tokyo Tower is approximately 1,000 feet high and includes two observatories. The highest observatory is at an elevation of 850 feet and affords a magnificent view of the entire city. Built in 1958 to serve as the radio communication center for the country, it symbolized Japan's emergence from the total devastation of World War II into a new era of peace, growth, and prosperity. For many years, Tokyo Tower reigned majestically over the city, but over the past 20 years it has gradually become obscured as an increasing number of tall buildings have been added to Tokyo's constantly changing skyline. Tokyo Tower is, however, still the tallest structure in Tokyo.

Kookyo (Imperial Palace)

The Imperial Palace is located in the heart of central Tokyo and is home to the Japanese Imperial Family. Until 1868, it was the home of the Shogun, the supreme military commander of Japan whose family line had held complete political control over the country since the early 1600's. The palace, with its surrounding moats and impressive stone walls and gardens, constitutes one of the largest green areas in Tokyo. Although most of the original palace buildings have long since been destroyed by fires, the magnificent stone walls, the moats, the reconstructed guard houses, and the huge number of neatly tended pine trees still create a unique sense of majesty and provide a powerful visual connection to Japan's feudal past.

Kokkai-gijidoo (National Parliament Building)

Japan's National Parliament Building was completed in 1936 and since that time has housed both the upper and lower houses of Parliament.

Meiji-jinguu (Meiji-jinguu Shrine)

Meiji-jinguu Shrine is dedicated to the Emperor Meiji (1852-1912) who, beginning in 1868, guided the nation out of the feudal period and into the modern industrial age. He was an extraordinary individual with exceptional vision and a historic sense of purpose. His shrine is located in the western part of Tokyo in the heart of a magnificent forested park and provides a welcome refuge from the hustle and bustle of life in the capital city.

KYOTO

Kyoto is located in the heart of Western Japan approximately 300 miles southwest of Tokyo. With a population of about 1.5 million, it is one of Japan's largest cities. Kyoto was the nation's imperial capital for over a thousand years (794-1868) and was modeled after the Chinese city of Chang-an (Xian). It was laid out in a grid-like pattern with broad streets running east and west intersecting with large avenues running north and south. Kyoto is the cultural heart of the country with hundreds of Shinto shrines, Buddhist temples, and a magnificent imperial palace within the city precincts. Although Kyoto is a modern city with all of the services and amenities one might expect, the city's unique cultural heritage is well-preserved and highly accessible.

Kinkakuji (Kinkaku-ji Temple/Temple of the Golden Pavilion)

Kinkakuji Temple was originally built in 1397 as a villa for the Shogun (supreme military commander). It is said that when he retired from public life, he used this villa as a place for spiritual meditation. After his death, his son had the villa converted to a Buddhist temple. The original building remained intact until it was destroyed by an arsonist in 1950. Five years later, an exact replica of the pavilion was constructed on the original site. Like the original, the current temple is covered with very fine sheets of gold foil which give it its distinctive glow and make its reflection in the adjacent pond truly striking.

Heian-jinguu (Heian-jinguu Shrine)

Heian-jinguu Shrine is located in Eastern Kyoto and was constructed in 1895 in honor of the 1,100th anniversary of the founding of the city by the Emperor Kammu. The temple is a replica (on a smaller scale) of the original imperial palace in Kyoto that had been destroyed long before. The shrine precincts contain a magnificent garden which evokes powerful images of what Kyoto must have been like when the city was at its cultural and political peak in the ninth and 10th centuries.

Kiyomizu-dera (Kiyomizu-dera Temple)

Kiyomizu-dera Temple is located in Eastern Kyoto on the side of a mountain overlooking the city. It was first built in 798. The present structure dates back to 1633 and is particularly unique because of the elaborate system of supports which allow the temple to extend over the cliff. This extraordinary engineering feat has stood the test of time very well.

Ryooanji (Ryooan-ji Temple)

The garden of Ryooanji Temple is one of the most famous temple gardens in Japan. Consisting of only sand and 15 carefully arranged stones, the garden has long been the subject of considerable speculation as to what the sand and stones represent. Some have thought that the sand represents the ocean and the stones, islands. Others have speculated that the sand represents

the clouds and the stones, the peaks of mountains visible above the clouds. The garden has an aura of absolute calm which can still the mind and soul of those who take the time to sit and contemplate its austere beauty.

YOMIMASHOO!　　　　　　　　　　　　　　　　　　読みましょう

しゃしんを とる・とります・とって	take a picture
しゃしんを たくさん とりました。	I took a lot of pictures.
日本の どこに 行きますか。	Where in Japan are you going?
ちずを 見て ください。	Please look at the map.
ここは ゆう名な まち です。	This (place) is a famous town.
とうきょうに 何が ありますか。	What's in Tokyo?
とうきょうで 何を したい ですか。	What do you want to do in Tokyo?
何を 見たい ですか。	What do you want to see?
きょうとに ゆう名な おてらと	In Kyoto there are a lot of famous
じんじゃが たくさん あります。	temples and shrines, aren't there?
りょこうは 何日間 ですか。	How many days is the trip?
何日間 とうきょうに いましょうか。	How many days shall we stay in Tokyo?
その あと、はこねに 行きますか。	After that, are you going to Hakone?
おんせん	hot spring
ひこうきの チケット	airline ticket
とうきょう タワー	Tokyo Tower

KANJI NOTES   漢字ノート

In this lesson you will learn to read two *kanji*: 雨 and 雪. Be sure that you know the readings of each *kanji* and can tell what the *kanji* means. The readings which are marked by an asterisk are for your reference only; you do not need to learn them at this time. You also do not have to learn any new words which are given in the examples. The correct stroke order for these *kanji* is given in the Optional Writing Practice section.

雨   **U*; ame, ama*** (rain)

雨	*ame*	rain
大雨	oo-*ame*	heavy rain
雨戸	*ama*do	storm door
雨雲	*ama*gumo	rain cloud
雨量	*u*ryoo	rainfall
梅雨	tsuyu	rainy season

今日は雨です。   Kyoo-wa *ame* desu.
                           (It's rainy today.)
先週は大雨でした。   Senshuu-wa oo-*ame* deshita.
                           (Last week there was heavy rain.)
夜、雨戸を閉めます。   Yoru, *ama*do-o shimemasu.
                           (At night we close the storm doors.)

The *kanji* 雨 was derived from a picture of rain falling from a cloud.

 雪   **SETSU*; yuki** (snow)

雪	*yuki*	snow
大雪	oo-*yuki*	heavy snow
雪山	*Yuki*yama	*family name* [snow-mountain]
雪子	*Yuki*ko	*female given name*
雪国	*yuki*guni	snow country*
積雪	seki*setsu*	snowdrift

*Japan's *yukiguni* (snow country), a region to the northwest of Tokyo in Niigata Prefecture, receives heavy snowfalls in the winter.

雪で遊ぶのが大好きです。	*Yuki*-de asobu-no-ga daisuki desu. (I really like playing in the snow.)
先週は大雪でした。	Senshuu-wa oo-*yuki* deshita. (Last week there was heavy snow.)
中山雪子さんは雪国に住んでいます。	Nakayama *Yuki*ko-san-wa *yuki*-guni-ni sunde-imasu. Yukiko Nakayama lives in the "snow country."

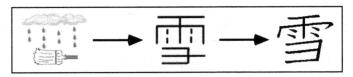

The *kanji* 雪 was derived from a picture of a broom added beneath the *kanji* 雨. Like rain, snow falls from the clouds, but it can be swept with a broom.

KANJI REVIEW														
上	名	二	見	今	万	大	中	時	年	八	元	土	口	前
目	日	木	四	気	分	七	人	国	十	何	三	水	子	金
百	語	田	一	雨	小	学	高	川	父	千	校	火	五	下
天	九	来	書	読	山	間	耳	母	聞	先	私	円	雪	本
話	才	六	月	行	言	生	How do you read them? What do they mean?							

INTERACTIVE ACTIVITIES

PART 1

❶ Kakimashoo!

During this activity each student will work as a pair with two different クラスメート to check Assignment #1 from Part 2 of Lesson 58. The goal of the activity is to have two students carefully check your answers, mark and discuss with you any errors found, and sign off on your assignment. Form your first pair and exchange assignments with your partner. Both partners independently check and neatly mark errors for the entire assignment.

❷ Hai, soo desu.

Using the reading passage in Assignment #1 in Part 2 of Lesson 58, Partner A makes a true/false statement for Partner B. Partner B scans the passage as quickly as possible and responds with *Hai, soo desu* or *Iie, chigaimasu*. If the statement is false, Partner B corrects it. Continue changing roles as long as you have time.

PART 2

❶ Yomimashoo!

Work with a クラスメート to check Assignment #2 from Part 1. Have your partner carefully check your answers, mark and discuss with you any errors found, and sign off on your assignment.

❷ Doko-ni ikimashoo-ka?

In this activity, you and a クラスメート will plan the itinerary for a two-week trip to Japan for your entire class. Decide where you will go (four or five places), how many days you will spend in each location, and what you want to do. If you select places from the カルチャーノート section of this lesson, you may use their English names. Otherwise, speak only in Japanese and use sentences such as those given below. Record your itinerary.

SAMPLE SENTENCES

Kyooto-ni ikimashoo-ka?	Shall we go to Kyoto?
Kyooto-ni ikimashoo!	Let's go to Kyoto!
Kyooto-ni ikitai desu-ka?	Do you want to go to Kyoto?
Kyooto-ni nani-ga arimasu-ka?	What's in Kyoto?
Yuumei-na jinja-to o-tera-ga takusan arimasu.	There are many famous shrines and temples.
Kyooto-de nani-o shitai desu-ka?	What do you want to do in Kyoto?
Kinkakuji-ni ikitai desu.	I want to go to Kinkakuji.
Nan-nichi-kan Kyooto-ni imashoo-ka?	How many days should we stay in Kyoto?
Mikka-kan-wa doo desu-ka?	How about three days?
Ii desu-ka?	Is that O.K.?
Sono ato, doko-ni ikimashoo-ka?	Where shall we go after that?
Tookyoo-wa doo desu-ka?	How about Tokyo?
Tookyoo-to Hakone-wa chikai desu-ne.	Tokyo and Hakone are close, aren't they?

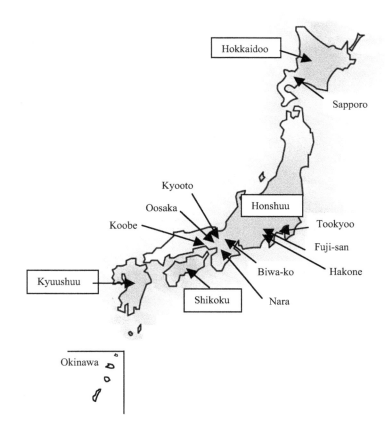

L. 59 電話で 話しましょう

れんしゅう A: Tokyo and Kyoto's Web Sites

Are the following tourist spots (a) ~ (d) in Tokyo or Kyoto? Complete the charts by filling in the blanks on the Web page.

(a) Meiji Jingu Shrine (b) Kiyomizu Temple (c) Kinkakuji Temple (d) Imperial Palace

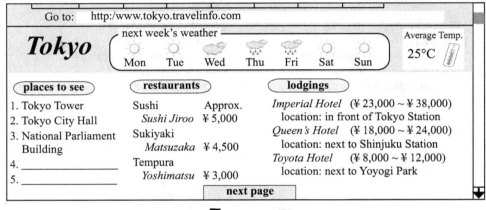

Go to: http:/www.tokyo.travelinfo.com

Tokyo

next week's weather

| Mon | Tue | Wed | Thu | Fri | Sat | Sun |

Average Temp. 25°C

places to see	restaurants	lodgings
1. Tokyo Tower	Sushi Approx.	*Imperial Hotel* (¥ 23,000 ~ ¥ 38,000)
2. Tokyo City Hall	*Sushi Jiroo* ¥ 5,000	location: in front of Tokyo Station
3. National Parliament	Sukiyaki	*Queen's Hotel* (¥ 18,000 ~ ¥ 24,000)
Building	*Matsuzaka* ¥ 4,500	location: next to Shinjuku Station
4. _____	Tempura	*Toyota Hotel* (¥ 8,000 ~ ¥ 12,000)
5. _____	*Yoshimatsu* ¥ 3,000	location: next to Yoyogi Park

next page

Go to: http:/www.kyoto.travelinfo.com

Kyoto

next week's weather

| Mon | Tue | Wed | Thu | Fri | Sat | Sun |

Average Temp. 27°C

places to see	restaurants	lodgings
1. Heian Jinguu Shrine	Toofu Ryoori Approx.	*Grand Hotel* (¥ 25,000 ~ ¥ 39,000)
2. Ryooanji Temple	*Ryooan* ¥ 4,000	location: in front of Kyoto Station
3. _____	Tempura	*Yasaka Hotel* (¥ 16,000 ~ ¥ 28,000)
4. _____	*Ikeda* ¥ 3,500	location: next to Yasaka Shrine
	Kamo Ryoori (duck)	*Heian Hotel* (¥ 7,000 ~ ¥ 13,000)
	Kamoyoshi ¥ 8,000	location: next to Heian Shrine

next page

<u>れんしゅう B</u>: Jonathan's Hobby

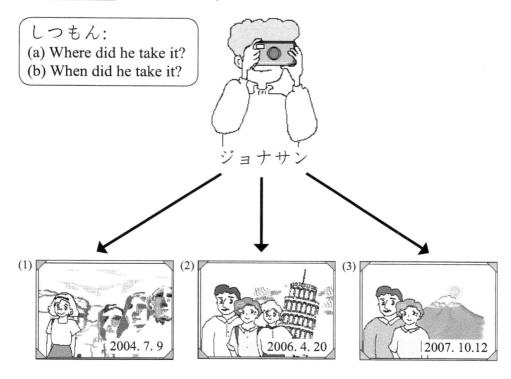

しつもん:
(a) Where did he take it?
(b) When did he take it?

ジョナサン

(1) 2004. 7. 9

(2) 2006. 4. 20

(3) 2007. 10.12

<u>れんしゅう C</u>: 読みましょう。こたえましょう。

(1) 今、何時何分ですか。

(2) きのうの天気は雨でしたか。

(3) おんがくは何を聞きますか。

(4) なつやすみは何か月間ぐらいですか。

(5) がい国語は何ができますか。

(6) シェークスピアの本を読んだことがありますか。

LESSON 60
Transportation Arrangements

OBJECTIVES

At the end of this lesson you will be able to:
- ☑ Make transportation arrangements
- ☑ Read the *kanji*: 東　京　駅

VOCABULARY   単語

Words

shinkansen	"bullet train"

Phrases and expressions

____-ni ikitai-n desu-kedo . . .	I want to go to ____. [at ticket window]
____-made otona/kodomo #-mai kudasai.	# adult/child ticket(s) to ____, please.

Other words and expressions you will hear in this lesson

kippu	ticket
kuukoo	airport
Kansai	*a region in Western Japan which includes Osaka, Kyoto, and Kobe*

VOCABULARY NOTES   単語ノート

Shinkansen しんかんせん (新幹線)
English speakers commonly refer to the high-speed *shinkansen* trains, which travel at speeds of 200 kilometers (125 miles) an hour or higher, as the *bullet trains*. The word *shinkansen* literally means *new trunk line*.

KEY GRAMMAR POINTS   文法ポイント

1. *Place*-ni tsukimasu つきます (着きます)
With the verb *tsukimasu*, use the particle *-ni* after the place where you arrive(d) and after the time and/or date. If you say both the date and the time, insert the particle *-no* between them.

Otawa-*ni* tsukimasu.	We will arrive in Ottawa.
Tookyoo-eki-*ni* tsukimasu.	She'll arrive at Tokyo station.
San-gatsu mikka-*ni* Bosuton-*ni* tsukimashita.	I arrived in Boston on March 3.
Go-gatsu muika-*no* juu-ji-*ni* Koobe-*ni* tsukimasu.	I'll arrive in Kobe at 10:00 on May 6.

2. *Place*-o demasu でます (出ます)
With the verb *demasu*, use the particle *-o* after the place you leave/left and the particle *-ni* after the time and/or date. If you say both the date and the time, insert the particle *-no* between them.

Roku-gatsu tsuitachi-ni Tookyoo-*o* demasu.	I will leave Tokyo on June 1.
Gogo san-ji-ni Atoranta-*o* demashita.	We left Atlanta at 3:00 p.m.
Ashita-no nan-ji-ni Shikago-*o* demasu-ka?	What time tomorrow will you leave Chicago?

しんかんせん	"bullet train"
バスていは どこ ですか。	Where's the bus stop?
なりたくうこうから 東京まで 何で 行きますか。	How do you get from Narita Airport Tokyo?
なごやに 行きたいん ですけど。	I want to go to Nagoya. [at ticket window]
つぎの しんかんせんは 何時に でますか。	What time does the next "bullet train" leave?
なごやまで 大人一まい ください。	One adult ticket to Nagoya, please.
ご前 十一時に 東京を でました。	I left Tokyo at 11:00 a.m.
ごご 一時五分に なごやに つきました。	I arrived in Nagoya at 1:05 p.m.
きっぷ	ticket
くうこう	airport
かんさい	*a region in Western Japan which includes Osaka, Kyoto, and Kobe*

> できますか。
>
> Can you unscramble these 単語, all of which appear in the 読みましょう section above? Then write the meaning in えい語. Check your answers with your クラスメート.
>
> 1. までたし　　　3. かせんんんし　　　5. しきたまつ
> 2. さいくだ　　　4. うこくう

CULTURE NOTES　　　　　　　　　　カルチャーノート

Japan's international airports

The two largest international airports in Japan are located outside of Tokyo and Osaka. Narita International Airport, also known as the New Tokyo International Airport, is located about 40 miles northeast of Tokyo in Narita. Kansai International Airport is built on a man-made island in Osaka Bay and holds the distinction of being the world's first ocean airport. Both airports have train terminals. From Narita International Airport to central Tokyo is about one hour by limited express train. From Kansai Airport there is equally convenient rail service to Osaka, Kobe, and Kyoto.

KANJI NOTES　　　　　　　　　　　漢字ノート

In this lesson you will learn to read three *kanji*: 東, 京 and 駅 . Be sure that you know the readings of each *kanji* and can tell what the *kanji* means. The reading which is marked by an asterisk is for your reference only; you do not need to learn it at this time. You also do not have to learn any new words which are given in the examples. The correct stroke order for these *kanji* is given in the Optional Writing Practice section.

TOO; higashi (east)

東	*higashi*	east
北東	*hokutoo*	northeast
東京	*Tookyoo*	Tokyo [eastern capital]
東洋	*tooyoo*	the East, the Orient
東京行き	*Tookyoo-yuki/iki*	Tokyo-bound [train]
東山	*Higashiyama*	*family name, place name* [east-mountain]

京都の東山はとても　　　　Kyooto-no *Higashi*yama-wa totemo kirei-na yama desu.
　きれいな山です。　　　　(The mountains of eastern Kyoto are very beautiful
　　　　　　　　　　　　　　　mountains.)

私の家は東京の東に　　　　Watashi-no uchi-wa *Too*kyoo-no *higashi*-ni arimasu.
　あります。　　　　　　　(My house is in the eastern part of Tokyo.)

父と母はアメリカの　　　　Chichi-to haha-wa Amerika-no hoku*too*bu-ni sunde-
　北東部に住んでいます。　　imasu.
　　　　　　　　　　　　　　(My father and mother live in the northeastern U.S.)

The *kanji* 東 was derived from a picture of the morning *sun* rising in the *east* behind a
tree.

 KYOO, KEI* (capital)

東京	Too*kyoo*	Tokyo
京都	*Kyoo*to	Kyoto
京浜	*Kei*hin	Tokyo-Yokohama (area)
上京する	joo*kyoo* suru	go (up) to the capital

昔は京都が日本の都　　　　Mukashi-wa *Kyoo*to-ga Nihon-no miyako deshita.
　でした。　　　　　　　　(Long ago Kyoto was the capital of Japan.)

横浜は東京に近いです。　　Yokohama-wa Too*kyoo*-ni chikai desu.
　　　　　　　　　　　　　(Yokohama is near Tokyo.)

The *kanji* 京 was derived from a picture of a stone *lantern*, which, in ancient times, was
placed outside the gates of the *capital*.

 EKI (station)

駅	*eki*	station
駅前	*eki*mae	in front of the station
駅長	*eki*choo	stationmaster
駅員	*eki*in	station employee
東京駅	Tookyoo-*eki*	Tokyo Station

駅前の本屋で友達を　　　　*Eki*mae-no honya-de tomodachi-o matte-imashita.
　待っていました。　　　　(I was waiting for my friend at the bookstore which is in
　　　　　　　　　　　　　　front of the station.)

東京駅の東口で五時に　　　Tookyoo-*eki*-no higashi-guchi-de go-ji-ni Higashiyama-
　東山さんに会います。　　　san-ni aimasu. (I will meet Mr. Higashiyama at the east
　　　　　　　　　　　　　　exit of Tokyo Station at 5:00.)

大阪駅に行った事が　　　　Oosaka-*eki*-ni itta-koto-ga arimasu-ka?
　ありますか。　　　　　　(Have you ever been to Osaka Station?)

The *kanji* 駅, which was derived from a picture of a *horse*, referred to stage coach stations before trains came into use.

KANJI REVIEW

上	生	二	耳	見	今	万	大	中	時	年	八	元	土	口
前	目	東	日	木	四	気	分	七	人	国	十	何	三	水
名	金	百	語	田	一	雨	小	学	高	川	父	千	校	火
五	下	天	九	来	書	京	駅	読	山	間	母	聞	先	私
言	話	円	雪	本	才	六	月	行	子					

How do you read them? What do they mean?

INTERACTIVE ACTIVITIES

PART 1

---

❶ Kakimashoo! ✏️

During this activity each student will work as a pair with two different クラスメート to check Assignment #1 from Part 2 of Lesson 59. The goal of the activity is to have two students carefully check the sentences in your description, mark and discuss with you any errors found, and sign off on your assignment. Form your first pair and exchange assignments with your partner. Both partners independently check and neatly mark errors for the entire assignment.

❷ Yomimashoo! 📄 & ✏️

This pair activity provides you with an opportunity to review many of the *kanji* which you have learned to read. Partner A masks the *roomaji* side and reads the vocabulary in the left column in order. Partner B responds after each with either *Hai, soo desu* or *Iie, chigaimasu. Moo ichido yonde kudasai.* Partner A writes down those which need to be studied. Switch roles and repeat.

漢字	ローマ字
1. 上田さん	1. Ueda-san
2. 千百五十一円	2. sen hyaku go-juu-ichi-en
3. 十万人	3. juu-man-nin
4. 中国語で話す	4. chuugokugo-de hanasu
5. お父さんのお名前	5. otoosan-no o-namae
6. 母のお金	6. haha-no o-kane
7. 元気な子ども	7. genki-na kodomo
8. 来年の四月三日	8. rainen-no shi-gatsu mikka
9. 日本の大学	9. Nihon-no daigaku
10. 今日の天気	10. kyoo-no tenki
11. 小学校の先生	11. shoogakkoo-no sensei
12. 下に行く	12. shita-ni iku
13. 一年生	13. ichi-nen-sei

漢字

14. 目と耳
15. 言います
16. 六年前
17. 雨と雪
18. 読みました
19. 聞きます
20. 見ました
21. 東京駅
22. 私の高校
23. 書きます
24. 何時何分

ローマ字

14. me-to mimi
15. iimasu
16. roku-nen-mae
17. ame-to yuki
18. yomimashita
19. kikimasu
20. mimashita
21. Tookyoo-eki
22. watashi-no kookoo
23. kakimasu
24. nan-ji nan-pun

PART 2

❶ Kakimashoo!

Work with a クラスメート to check Assignment #2 from Part 1. Have your partner carefully check your answers, mark and discuss with you any errors found, and sign off on your assignment.

❷ Make a sentence!

Do this sentence building activity with a クラスメート. Partner A begins a sentence with a place name and a particle (*-ni* or *-o*). Then Partner B adds the next word or phrase of the sentence. Continue taking turns until you have created a grammatically correct and meaningful sentence. Each sentence must include a form of one of these verbs: *tsukimasu, demasu,* or *imasu*. Read the examples aloud with your partner before you begin.

EXAMPLES

1. San-gatsu . . . mikka-ni . . . Oosaka-ni . . . tsukimashita.
2. Go-gatsu . . . muika-no . . . juu-ji-ni . . . Koobe-ni . . . tsukimasu.
3. Gozen . . . hachi-ji yon-juu-go-fun-ni . . . Shikago-ni . . . tsukimasu-ka?
4. Roku-gatsu . . . tsuitachi-ni . . . Tookyoo-o . . . demasu.
5. Gogo . . . san-ji-ni . . . Atoranta-o . . . demashita.
6. Shi-gatsu . . . itsuka-no . . . ku-ji-ni . . . Nagoya-o . . . demasu-ka?
7. San-shuu-kan . . . Hawai-ni . . . imashita.
8. Ik-ka-getsu-kan . . . Otawa-ni . . . imasu.

> **NOTE**
> *Date/Time*-**ni** *place*-**ni** tsukimasu/tsukimashita.
> *Date/Time*-**ni** *Place*-**o** demasu/demashita.
> *Place*-**ni** imasu/imashita.

L. 60 電話で 話しましょう

れんしゅう A: Travel Schedules

しつもん: (a) When leaving?　(b) When arriving?

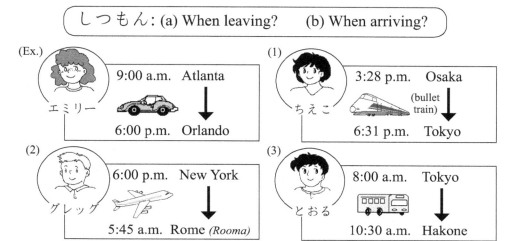

(Ex.) エミリー
9:00 a.m.　Atlanta
↓
6:00 p.m.　Orlando

(1) ちえこ
3:28 p.m.　Osaka
(bullet train) ↓
6:31 p.m.　Tokyo

(2) グレッグ
6:00 p.m.　New York
↓
5:45 a.m.　Rome *(Rooma)*

(3) とおる
8:00 a.m.　Tokyo
↓
10:30 a.m.　Hakone

れんしゅう B: Let's converse!

> **Dialogue:** (at a ticket window at Tokyo station)
> A: Please give me <u>one</u> adult ticket to <u>Nagoya</u>.
> B: What time do you prefer?
> A: <u>10:02</u>, please.　How much is it?
> B: It is <u>10,500</u> yen.

Sample Dialogue:

A: なごやまで、大人、<u>1</u>まいください。

B: 何時のがいいですか。

A: <u>１０時２分</u>の、おねがいしますいくらですか。

B: <u>１０,５００</u>円です。

Sample Dialogue:

A: <u>Nagoya</u>-made, otona, <u>ichi</u>-mai kudasai.

B: Nan-ji-no-ga ii desu-ka?

A: <u>Juu-ji ni-fun</u>-no, o-negai-shimasu. Ikura desu-ka?

B: <u>Ichi-man go-hyaku</u>-en desu.

東京	名古屋 (Nagoya) (10,500円)		京都 (Kyooto) (13,000円)		大阪 (Oosaka) (15,000円)		広島 (Hiroshima) (19,000円)	
着	着	発	着	発	着	発	着	発
10:02	12:04	12:06	13:01	13:04	13:07	13:10	15:00	15:03
10:34	12:36	12:38	13:33	13:36	13:39	13:42	15:32	15:35
11:05	13:07	13:09	14:04	14:07	14:10	14:13	16:03	16:06
11:29	13:31	13:33	14:28	14:31	14:34	14:37	16:27	16:30

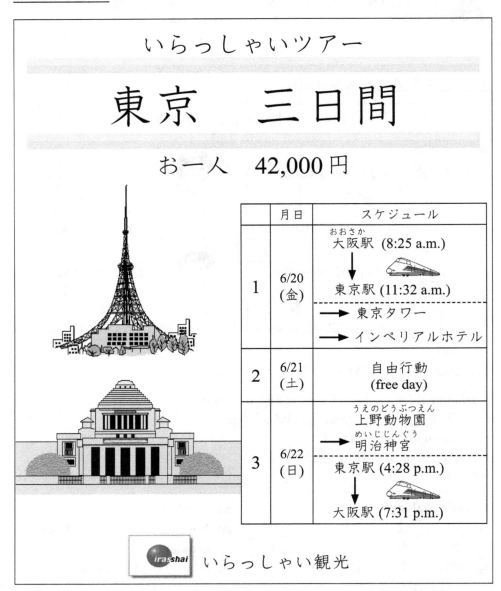

いらっしゃいツアー

東京　三日間

お一人　42,000円

	月日	スケジュール
1	6/20 (金)	大阪駅 (8:25 a.m.) ↓ 東京駅 (11:32 a.m.) --- → 東京タワー → インペリアルホテル
2	6/21 (土)	自由行動 (free day)
3	6/22 (日)	上野動物園 → 明治神宮 --- 東京駅 (4:28 p.m.) ↓ 大阪駅 (7:31 p.m.)

irasshai　いらっしゃい観光

LESSON 61
Describing Lost Items

OBJECTIVES 目標

At the end of this lesson you will be able to:
- ☑ Describe a lost item

VOCABULARY 単語

Words

sagasu (sagashimasu/sagashite)	look for
naku-naru (naku-narimasu/naku-natte)	be(come) lost, be missing, be gone

Other words and expressions you will hear in this lesson

pasupooto	passport

KEY GRAMMAR POINTS 文法ポイント

1. *Item*-ga naku-narimashita.

To say that an item is *lost* or *missing*, use the name of the item followed by the particle *-ga* and the verb *naku-naru*.

Watashi-no megane-*ga naku-narimashita.*	My glasses *are missing*.
Chichi-no kaban-*ga naku-narimashita.*	My father's briefcase *is lost*.

2. *Place*-ni *item*-o wasuremashita.

Use this sentence pattern to tell where you left something behind. Use the particle *-ni* after the place and the particle *-o* after the forgotten item.

Kissaten-ni megane-o wasuremashita.	I left my glasses at the coffee shop.
Kooen-ni kamera-o wasuremashita.	I left my camera in the park.
Otooto-wa takushii-ni kaban-o wasuremashita.	My brother left his bag in the taxi.

YOMIMASHOO! 読みましょう

さがす・さがします・さがして	look for
なくなる・なくなります・なくなって	be lost, get lost, be missing, be gone
私の めがねが なくなりました。	My glasses are missing.
今、パスポートを さがしています。	I'm looking for my passport now.
どんな かばん ですか。	What does your bag look like?
中に 何が はいっていましたか。	What was in (the bag)?
田口さんは 何を わすれましたか。	What did Mrs. Taguchi forget?
どこに わすれましたか。	Where did she leave it?
きっさてんに かばんを わすれました。	I left my briefcase at the coffee shop.
パスポート	passport

INTERACTIVE ACTIVITIES

PART 1

❶ Dekimasu-ka?

Work with a クラスメート to check Assignment #1 from Part 2 in Lesson 60. Have your partner carefully check your answers, mark and discuss with you any errors found, and sign off on your assignment. Share your sentence with other クラスメート. Who incorporated the largest number of "excluded" *kanji* in a grammatically correct sentence?

465

❷ **Dialogue**

With a partner, practice the dialogue following the usual procedure. Make sure you understand the meaning of each line before you begin. As you practice the dialogue, use gestures and facial expressions. After you have memorized the dialogue, perform it for another pair. If you have time, change roles and learn the other part.

Yamaguchi-san (山口さん) is reporting a missing item at a lost-and-found office. Nakagawa-san (中川さん), who works at the office, is asking 山口さん questions.

山口: Sumimasen. Kaban-ga naku-narimashita.
中川: Soo desu-ka? (pauses) Donna kaban desu-ka? (picks up pen to make notes)
山口: Eeto . . . (showing approximate size with hands) Ookiku-te kuroi kaban desu.
中川: Ookiku-te kuroi kaban desu-ne. (writes it down) Naka-ni nani-ga haitte-imashita-ka?
山口: Kamera-to pasupooto desu.
中川: Kamera-to pasupooto! Sore-wa taihen desu-ne.

For greater reading practice, use the Japanese equivalent of the dialogue.

山口: すみません。かばん が なくなりました。
中川: そう ですか。(pauses) どんな かばん ですか。(picks up pen to make notes)
山口: ええと、(showing approximate size with hands) 大きくて くろい かばん です。
中川: 大きくて くろい かばん ですね。(writes it down) 中に 何が はいって いましたか。
山口: カメラと パスポート です。
中川: カメラと パスポート！それは たいへん ですね。

PART 2

❶ **Changing the dialogue**

During this activity each student will work as a pair with a クラスメート to check Assignment #2 from Part 1 of this lesson. Have your partner carefully check your version of the dialogue (making sure that you followed the directions), mark and discuss with you any errors found, and sign off on your assignment. Then read both of the "new" dialogues with your partner.

❷ **Donna kaban desu-ka?**   📄 & ✏️

Do this activity with a クラスメート. Use the dialogue above. Many items, including those shown in the chart on the next page, have been turned in to the lost-and-found office. Partner A (Yamaguchi-san) selects an item in the chart and writes it down. After completing the dialogue (with either a *kaban* or *bakkupakku* as the lost item), Partner B (Nakagawa-san) points to the item in the chart and asks, "*Kore desu-ka?*" Partner A confirms or denies it. Continue changing roles and repeating the activity.

ITEM	SIZE	COLOR	WHAT'S INSIDE?
kaban	ookii	kuroi	saifu-to pasupooto
kaban	chiisai	chairoi	kamera-to pasupooto
kaban	ookii	aoi	o-kane-to pasupooto
kaban	chiisai	aoi	o-kane-to pasupooto
kaban	ookii	chairoi	kamera-to pasupooto
kaban	ookii	chairoi	kamera-to saifu
kaban	ookii	aoi	saifu-to pasupooto
kaban	chiisai	aoi	kamera-to o-kane
kaban	chiisai	chairoi	kamera-to saifu
kaban	ookii	kuroi	saifu-to kamera
bakkupakku	ookii	akai	nooto-to o-kane
bakkupakku	ookii	shiroi	hon-to pen-to kamera
bakkupakku	chiisai	shiroi	hon-to nooto-to kamera
bakkupakku	ookii	akai	hon-to nooto-to saifu
bakkupakku	ookii	shiroi	nooto-to hon-to saifu
bakkupakku	ookii	kiiroi	nooto-to hon-to saifu
bakkupakku	chiisai	shiroi	nooto-to pen-to saifu
bakkupakku	ookii	kiiroi	nooto-to pen-to kamera

L. 61 電話で 話しましょう

れんしゅう A: Winning a Free Trip

You have won a free trip! Your A.I. teacher is asking about details of the trip.
Answer his/her questions.

(1)
Istanbul
6 days

leave 6/25 2:00 p.m.
arrive 6/26 6:00 p.m.

(2)
Rome
4 days

leave 7/2 11:00 a.m.
arrive 7/3   9:30 a.m.

(3)
Hong Kong
5 days

leave 6/19 8:30 a.m.
arrive 6/20 1:00 p.m.

(4)
Kyoto
8 days

leave 7/12 12:00 p.m.
arrive 7/13   3:30 p.m.

(5)
Montreal
3 days

leave 8/7 11:45 a.m.
arrive 8/7   4:15 p.m.

(6)
Santiago
7 days

leave 9/1   5:30 p.m.
arrive 9/2 10:00 p.m.

れんしゅう B: Forgetful People

(Ex.)

レベッカ

(1)

ミッシェル

(2)

ブライアン

(3)

ジェフ

しつもん: (a) What is s/he looking for?   (b) Where did s/he forget it?

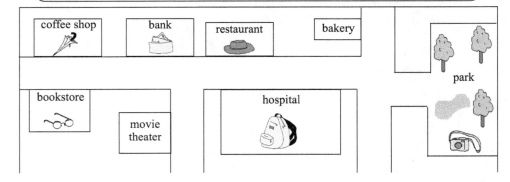

coffee shop   bank   restaurant   bakery   park

bookstore   movie theater   hospital

468

れんしゅう C: Let's converse!

Dialogue:
A: Mr. Tanaka, I lost my bag!
B: What kind of bag (is it)?
A: It's a <u>big, black</u> bag.
B: What was inside?
A: A <u>notebook</u> and a <u>dictionary</u>.
B: O.K. Let's look for it together.

Sample Dialogue:
A: 田中先生、私（ぼく）のかばん
　　がなくなりました。
B: どんなかばんですか。
A: 大きくて、くろいかばんです。
B: 中に何がはいっていましたか。
A: ノートとじしょです。
B: じゃ、いっしょにさがしまし
　　ょう。

Sample Dialogue:
A: Tanaka-sensei, watashi (boku)-no
　　kaban-ga naku-narimashita.
B: Donna kaban desu-ka?
A: <u>Ookiku-te kuroi</u> kaban desu.
B: Naka-ni nani-ga haitte-imashita-
　　ka?
A: <u>Nooto</u>-to <u>jisho</u> desu.
B: Jaa, issho-ni sagashimashoo!

れんしゅう D: Crossword Puzzle

Please choose the most appropriate *kanji* from the list below and fill in the blanks.

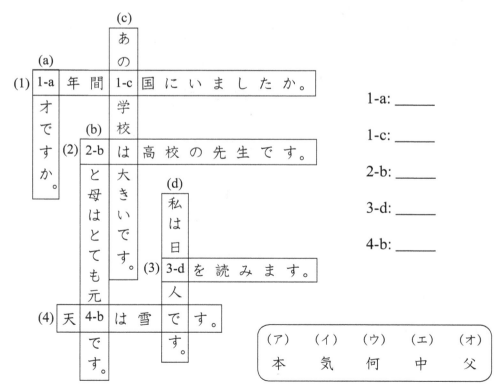

1-a: _____

1-c: _____

2-b: _____

3-d: _____

4-b: _____

469

LESSON 62
Review

OBJECTIVES 目標

This lesson reviews some key vocabulary, grammar points, and *kanji* from previous lessons.

KEY GRAMMAR POINTS 文法ポイント

1. Counters (Review)

In this course, you have learned some of the most important counters in Japanese. In the box below, mask the Japanese counters with a piece of paper. How many counters can you remember by looking only at the category descriptions? Check your answers line by line.

COUNTER	CATEGORY	EXAMPLE
-ban	numeric order	ichi-ban (number one)
-do	degrees	san-juu-do (30 degrees)
-doru	dollars	juu-go-doru (15 dollars)
-en	yen	hachi-juu-en (80 yen)
-fiito	feet	nan-fiito (how many feet)
-fun	minute	ni-fun (two minutes)
-gatsu	month	shichi-gatsu (July)
-hon	long, cylindrical objects	rop-pon (six)
-hyaku	hundred	san-byaku (300)
-ji	o'clock	yo-ji (four o'clock)
-ji-kan	hour (length of time)	go-ji-kan (five hours; a period of five hours)
-ka-getsu	month (length of time)	ni-ka-getsu (two months)
-kai	floor, story (in a building)	rok-kai (sixth floor)
-mai	thin, flat objects	nan-mai (how many)
-man	ten thousand	kyuu-man (90,000)
-meetoru	meter	go-meetoru (five meters)
-nen	year	juu-san-nen (13 years)
-nen-kan	year (length of time)	ni-nen-kan (two years; a period of two years)
-nichi	day of the month	juu-go-nichi (the 15th [of the month])
-nin	people	hachi-nin (eight people)
-sai	years old	is-sai (one year old)
-sen	thousand	yon-sen (4,000)
-shuu-kan	week	san-shuu-kan (three weeks)
-tsu	thing [general counter]	hitotsu (one thing)

2. Past adjectives (Review)

In Japanese, *i*-adjectives and *na*-adjectives form their affirmative and negative past tenses in different ways.

PAST TENSE (AFFIRMATIVE) OF ADJECTIVES		
I-ADJECTIVES	drop *i*, add *katta*	taka*i* desu - - - taka*katta* desu
NA-ADJECTIVES	change *desu* to *deshita*	shizuka *desu* - - - shizuka *deshita*

PAST TENSE (NEGATIVE) OF ADJECTIVES		
I-ADJECTIVES	drop *i*, add *-ku-nakatta*	taka*i* desu - - - taka*ku-nakatta* desu
NA-ADJECTIVES	add *ja nakatta*	shizuka desu - - - shizuka *ja nakatta* desu

470

How many of the following adjectives do you remember? Write down those which you need to review.

I-ADJECTIVES

Non-past affirmative	Non-past negative	Past affirmative	Past negative	English
furui	furuku-nai	furukatta	furuku-nakatta	old
atarashii	atarashiku-nai	atarashikatta	atarashiku-nakatta	new
chiisai	chiisaku-nai	chiisakatta	chiisaku-nakatta	small
ookii	ookiku-nai	ookikatta	ookiku-nakatta	big
hayai	hayaku-nai	hayakatta	hayaku-nakatta	fast, early
osoi	osoku-nai	osokatta	osoku-nakatta	slow, late
nagai	nagaku-nai	nagakatta	nagaku-nakatta	long
mijikai	mijikaku-nai	mijikakatta	mijikaku-nakatta	short
hikui	hikuku-nai	hikukatta	hikuku-nakatta	low
takai	takaku-nai	takakatta	takaku-nakatta	high, tall, expensive
yasui	yasuku-nai	yasukatta	yasuku-nakatta	cheap
tsuyoi	tsuyoku-nai	tsuyokatta	tsuyoku-nakatta	strong
yowai	yowaku-nai	yowakatta	yowaku-nakatta	weak
atsui	atsuku-nai	atsukatta	atsuku-nakatta	hot
samui	samuku-nai	samukatta	samuku-nakatta	cold
tsumetai	tsumetaku-nai	tsumetakatta	tsumetaku-nakatta	cold (to the touch)
chikai	chikaku-nai	chikakatta	chikaku-nakatta	close
urusai	urusaku-nai	urusakatta	urusaku-nakatta	noisy
isogashii	isogashiku-nai	isogashikatta	isogashiku-nakatta	busy
tanoshii	tanoshiku-nai	tanoshikatta	tanoshiku-nakatta	pleasant, fun
kitanai	kitanaku-nai	kitanakatta	kitanaku-nakatta	dirty, messy
ii (yoi)	yoku-nai	yokatta	yoku-nakatta	good
tsumaranai	tsumaranaku-nai	tsumaranakatta	tsumaranaku-nakatta	boring
omoshiroi	omoshiroku-nai	omoshirokatta	omoshiroku-nakatta	interesting
muzukashii	muzukashiku-nai	muzukashikatta	muzukashiku-nakatta	difficult
oishii	oishiku-nai	oishikatta	oishiku-nakatta	delicious
amai	amaku-nai	amakatta	amaku-nakatta	sweet
karai	karaku-nai	karakatta	karaku-nakatta	spicy, hot, salty
nemui	nemuku-nai	nemukatta	nemuku-nakatta	sleepy
kibishii	kibishiku-nai	kibishikatta	kibishiku-nakatta	strict
yasashii	yasashiku-nai	yasashikatta	yasashiku-nakatta	kind, easy-going
akarui	akaruku-nai	akarukatta	akaruku-nakatta	cheerful
kawaii	kawaiku-nai	kawaikatta	kawaiku-nakatta	cute

NA-ADJECTIVES

Non-past affirmative	Non-past negative	Past affirmative	Past negative	English
dame	dame ja nai	dame deshita*	dame ja nakatta desu*	bad, worthless
kantan	kantan ja nai	kantan deshita	kantan ja nakatta desu	easy, simple
suki	suki ja nai	suki deshita	suki ja nakatta desu	pleasing
joozu	joozu ja nai	joozu deshita	joozu ja nakatta desu	skilled
heta	heta ja nai	heta deshita	heta ja nakatta desu	unskilled
shizuka	shizuka ja nai	shizuka deshita	shizuka ja nakatta desu	quiet
iya	iya ja nai	iya deshita	iya ja nakatta desu	bad, terrible
kirei	kirei ja nai	kirei deshita	kirei ja nakatta desu	pretty
hen	hen ja nai	hen deshita	hen ja nakatta desu	strange
majime	majime ja nai	majime deshita	majime ja nakatta desu	serious
genki	genki ja nai	genki deshita	genki ja nakatta desu	energetic, healthy
yuumei	yuumei ja nai	yuumei deshita	yuumei ja nakatta desu	famous

*Deshita and desu are not part of the na-adjective but are used with it to produce a level of politeness equivalent to that of the -masu form of verbs.

3. Migi-kara #-ban-me desu./Ichiban ue desu. (Review)

You can express a range of spatial relationships by using the ordinal numbers such as *ni-ban-me* and *san-ban-me* with words such as *migi, hidari, ue, shita, mae,* and *ushiro,* such as second from the top, third from the right. Note that when something is first from the ~, just the phrase "*ichiban ~*" is used instead. Study these examples carefully.

Shita-kara san-ban-me desu.	It's *the third one from the bottom.*
Ue-kara ni-ban-me-no kukkii-o yon-mai kudasai.	Please give me four of the cookies that are *second from the top.*
Ichiban hidari-no doonattsu-o futatsu kudasai.	Please give me two of the doughnuts that are *furthest left.*
Ichiban mae-no hito-wa Saitoo-san desu.	*The first* person *in front* is Mr. Saito.

YOMIMASHOO!　　　　　　　　　　　　　　　　読みましょう

みぎから 三ばん目	the third from the right
中に 何が はいっていますか。	What's inside?
ようふくが はいっています。	There are clothes inside.
何も はいっていません。	There is nothing inside.
一ばん ひだりの えは へん ですね。	The picture on the far left is strange, isn't it?

INTERACTIVE ACTIVITIES

PART 1

❶ Kakimashoo!

During this activity each student will work as a pair with two different クラスメート to check Assignment #1 from Part 2 of Lesson 61. The goal of the activity is to have two students carefully check the sentences in your assignment, mark and discuss with you any errors found, and sign off on your assignment. Form your first pair and exchange assignments with your partner. Both partners independently check and neatly mark errors for the entire assignment.

❷ Yomimashoo!　　📄 & ✏️

This pair activity provides you with an opportunity to review many of the *kanji* which you have learned to read. Partner A masks the *roomaji* side and reads the vocabulary in the left column in order. Partner B responds after each with either *Hai, soo desu* or *Iie, chigaimasu. Moo ichido yonde kudasai.* Partner A writes those which need to be studied. Switch roles and repeat.

漢字	ローマ字
1. 田中さん	1. Tanaka-san
2. 書きます	2. kakimasu
3. 目と耳	3. me-to mimi
4. 中国語と日本語	4. chuugokugo-to nihongo
5. お父さんのお名前	5. otoosan-no o-namae

472

漢字	ローマ字
6. 雨と雪	6. ame-to yuki
7. 元気な子ども	7. genki-na kodomo
8. 来年の四月三日	8. rainen-no shi-gatsu mikka
9. 東京駅	9. Tookyoo-eki
10. 千百五十一円	10. sen hyaku go-juu-ichi-en
11. 私の小学校	11. watashi-no shoogakkoo
12. 上と下	12. ue-to shita
13. 四年生	13. yo-nen-sei
14. 十万人	14. juu-man-nin
15. 言いました	15. iimashita
16. 六年前	16. roku-nen-mae
17. 母のお金	17. haha-no o-kane
18. 読みました	18. yomimashita
19. 聞きます	19. kikimasu
20. 八つ	20. yattsu
21. 日本の大学	21. Nihon-no daigaku
22. 高校の先生	22. kookoo-no sensei
23. 今日の天気	23. kyoo-no tenki
24. 何時何分	24. nan-ji nan-pun

PART 2

❶ Hoteru-wa doo deshita-ka?

Do this activity with a クラスメート. Place the tip of a pencil on the dot in the center of the circle below with one end of a paper clip around the pencil tip. Use this as a spinner to select a number on the wheel. Partner A spins first and asks _____-*wa doo deshita-ka?* using the selected noun. Partner B always responds with an affirmative past tense adjective. If the same noun has been selected on a previous turn, try to describe it by using a different adjective. Refer to the 文法ポイント section of this lesson for a list of adjectives. Read the sample exchange aloud with your partner before you begin.

SAMPLE EXCHANGE

B: A-san-no ban desu. [ban = turn]
A: Hai. (*spins a 3*) **Hoteru**-wa doo deshita-ka?
B: **Takakatta** desu.
A: B-san-no ban desu.

1. Itoo-san-no wanpiisu*
2. sushi
3. hoteru
4. sono machi
5. Taniguchi-san-no kuruma
6. Nishiyama-san-no paatii
7. tomodachi-no atarashii konpyuutaa
8. Arasuka**-no fuyu-no tenki
9. keeki
10. tesuto
11. mae-no*** sensei
12. pianisuto****

*dress **Alaska ***previous ****pianist

❷ Migi-kara ni-ban-me-no doonattsu-o mittsu kudasai. 📄 & ✏️

Do this activity with a クラスメート. Partner A works as a salesperson in a doughnut shop. Partner B is buying <u>30 doughnuts</u> and has decided on <u>six kinds</u> of doughnuts shown below in the rack behind the salesperson. They are not labeled so Partner B must tell the salesperson which ones <u>and</u> how many of each. Partner B buys different numbers of the different kinds (but not more than nine of any one kind). Read the sample exchange with your partner before you begin. Both partners record the requested number of doughnuts.

A: O-kimari desu-ka?
B: Migi-kara ni-ban-me-no doonattsu-o mittsu kudasai.
A: Ni-ban-me-no doonattsu desu-ka?
B: Hai, sore desu.
A: Sorekara?

GENERAL COUNTERS	
hitotsu	muttsu
futatsu	nanatsu
mittsu	yattsu
yottsu	kokonotsu
itsutsu	too

							3	

Compare your answers when you have finished. Continue the activity, alternating roles.

ni-ban-me	second	go-ban-me	fifth
san-ban-me	third	roku-ban-me	sixth
yon-ban-me	fourth	nana-ban-me	seventh

ichi-ban migi/hidari-no doonattsu	the doughnut(s) on the far right/left

L. 62 電話で 話しましょう

れんしゅう A: Guess who my friend is!

One of the following people is a friend of your's. Choose which one, and describe him/her using the information below. Have your classmates guess which person it is. They will guess by describing that person's location on the chart.

	(1) age	(2) residence	(3) hobby	(4) personality
	16 yrs. old	Miami	cooking	serious and kind
	18 yrs. old	Detroit	soccer	cheerful and energetic
	18 yrs. old	Miami	travelling	quiet and serious
	16 yrs. old	Detroit	cooking	cheerful and energetic
	16 yrs. old	Miami	travelling	quiet and serious
	18 yrs. old	Detroit	soccer	kind and interesting
	16 yrs. old	Miami	cooking	kind and cheerful

<u>れんしゅう B</u>: Reviewing Counters

If these pictures illustrate the answers, try to think of the questions.

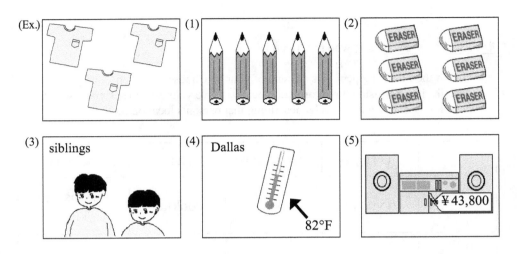

<u>れんしゅう C</u>: Absent-minded Kenji

しつもん: (a) went where? (b) forgot what?

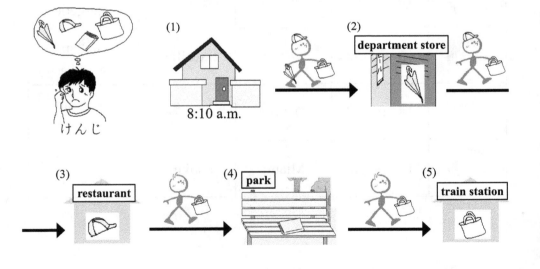

LESSON 63
Review

OBJECTIVES 目標

This entire lesson is devoted to a review of important vocabulary, grammar points, culture notes, and *kanji* in Lessons 21 through 61 of this book. When you identify an area where you need additional practice, you will want to return to the specific earlier lesson(s) for more information and activities. References to earlier lessons will help you to quickly locate the desired material. The key symbol (⚷) indicates that **after** you have completed the exercise, you can check your answers using the answer key at the end of this lesson.

VOCABULARY 単語

Write your answers in *hiragana* and *kanji* (where you can) as much as possible for your writing practice. 📄 & 🖋

TIME WORDS [L. 22 & 25]
1. Complete the chart below in Japanese.

	last	this	next
week			
month			
year			

2. Write the Japanese equivalents of the following. ⚷
a. the 12th of last month
b. this Tuesday
c. next year's winter vacation
d. this April

TELEPHONING [L. 24]
What do these expressions mean in English? ⚷
a. 田中さんは いらっしゃいますか。
b. 今、るす です。
c. 六時ごろ かえります。
d. 何時に おかえり ですか。
e. また あとで でんわ します。

SPORTING EVENTS [L. 27]
Write the Japanese equivalents of the following.
a. sporting match, game
b. practice
c. weak
d. # to # (a score)
e. Who won?
f. What was the score?

PARTS OF THE BODY [L. 41 & 42]
Write the Japanese equivalents of the following.
a. eye
b. nose
c. mouth
d. ear
e. hand, arm
f. foot, leg
g. tooth, teeth
h. throat

HEALTH CONDITIONS & TAKING MEDICINE [L. 42-44]
1. Write five different answers to the following question. ⚷
Q. どう したん ですか。　Ex.) あたまが いたいん です。

2. Write a sentence that you would probably say to someone who is sick. ⚷

477

3. What question would you ask to get the following answers? 🔑
a. のどの くすり です。
b. ごはんの 前に のんで ください。

DESCRIBING PEOPLE [L. 45 & 46]
Write the Japanese equivalents of the following.
a. strict
b. warm, kind, lenient
c. cheerful
d. serious
e. hair

f. short (opposite of long)
g. blond hair
h. tall (person's height)
i. short (person's height)

OCCUPATIONS AND GETTING A JOB [L. 52 & 53]
1. Write the Japanese equivalents of the following.
a. company
b. white collar worker
c. address

d. What is your job?
e. How much (money) per hour?
f. Can you drive a car?

2. Write three occupations that interest you. Refer to Vocabulary Notes of Lesson 52 if you need to.

GRADUATION AND PLANS FOR THE FUTURE [L. 49, 54 & 55]
Write the Japanese equivalents of the following.
a. graduation
b. after that
c. five years later
d. maybe, perhaps, probably
e. graduate from high school

f. future
g. famous
h. marriage
i. get married, marry
j. baby

OTHER VOCABULARY
Write the Japanese equivalents of the following.
1. umbrella [L. 21]
2. wind [L. 21]
3. strong [L. 21]
4. window [L. 21]
5. season [L. 22]
6. animal [L. 26]
7. zoo [L. 26]
8. adult [L. 26]
9. child [L. 26]
10. I'm hungry. [L. 26]
11. free time [L. 28]
12. we [L. 28]
13. go to play, go to have fun [L. 28]
14. come over (and have fun) [L. 29]
15. same [L. 31]
16. altogether, in all [L. 32]
17. which one (of two) [L. 32]
18. this one (of two) [L. 32]
19. that one (of two) [L. 32]
20. that one over there (of two) [L. 32]
21. next to, adjoining [L. 33]
22. vicinity [L. 33]

23. next to, adjoining [L. 33]
24. fruit [L. 36]
25. fruit store [L. 36]
26. anything else [L. 36]
27. already, yet [L. 38]
28. not yet, still [L. 38]
29. basement [L. 38]
30. sweet (taste) [L. 39]
31. spicy, hot, salty [L. 39]
32. cold (to the touch) [L. 39]
33. glasses [L. 47]
34. know(s) [L. 48]
35. I don't know. [L. 48]
36. alone, by oneself [L. 51]
37. grandmother [L. 51]
38. grandfather [L. 51]
39. (for) one day, all day [L. 57]
40. a.m. [L. 58]
41. p.m. [L. 58]
42. take a picture [L. 59]
43. bullet train [L. 60]

I. Verb forms 📄 & ✏️

Study the following verb forms and complete the chart. The rules of verb conjugation is given in the Appendix. (Aff. = Affirmative, Neg. = Negative)   🔊

-*u* verbs

Present Aff. (-*masu* form)	Present Aff. (plain)	Present Neg. (Plain)	Past Aff. (Plain)	English
arimasu	aru	1	atta	exist, be [inanimate]
aimasu	2	awanai	atta	meet, see
asobimasu	asobu	asobanai	asonda	3
chigaimasu	chigau	chigawanai	chigatta	be different
hairimasu	hairu	hairanai	4	enter, join
hajimarimasu	hajimaru	hajimaranai	hajimatta	(something) begins
hanashimasu	hanasu	hanasanai	hanashita	speak
ikimasu	iku	5	itta	go
iimasu	iu	iwanai	itta	say
irimasu	iru	iranai	itta	6
7	kaeru	kaeranai	kaetta	return
kakimasu	8	kakanai	kaita	write
kachimasu	katsu	katanai	katta	9
kaimasu	kau	10	katta	buy
kikimasu	kiku	kikanai	11	listen
moraimasu	morau	morawanai	moratta	12
13	naku-naru	naku-naranai	naku-natta	be(come) lost
14	naru	naranai	natta	become
nomimasu	nomu	nomanai	15	drink
owarimasu	owaru	owaranai	owatta	(something) ends
tsukaimasu	tsukau	tsukawanai	tsukatta	use
tsukimasu	tsuku	tsukanai	tsuita	16
tsukurimasu	tsukuru	tsukuranai	tsukutta	17
sagashimasu	sagasu	sagasanai	sagashita	18
sumimasu	sumu	sumanai	19	will live
utaimasu	20	utawanai	utatta	sing
wakarimasu	21	wakaranai	wakatta	understand
yomimasu	yomu	22	yonda	read

-*ru* verbs

Present Aff. (-*masu* form)	Present Aff. (plain)	Present Neg. (Plain)	Past Aff. (Plain)	English
akemasu	akeru	akenai	aketa	23
24	atsumeru	atsumenai	atsumeta	collect
demasu	deru	denai	deta	25
imasu	26	inai	ita	exist, be [animate]
makemasu	makeru	makenai	maketa	lose
mimasu	miru	27	mita	look at, see
misemasu	miseru	misenai	miseta	28
nemasu	neru	nenai	29	go to bed/sleep
okimasu	okiru	30	okita	get up
oshiemasu	oshieru	oshienai	31	teach
shimemasu	shimeru	shimenai	shimeta	32
tabemasu	taberu	tabenai	33	eat
umaremasu	34	umarenai	umareta	be born
35	wasureru	wasurenai	wasureta	forget

Irregular verbs

Present Aff. (-*masu* form)	Present Aff. (plain)	Present Neg. (Plain)	Past Aff. (Plain)	English
kimasu	36	konai	kita	come
shimasu	suru	37	38	do

II. -tai/-takunai desu [L. 25 & 26] 📄 & ✏️

To express the idea of *want to do something*, replace the *-masu* ending of a verb with *-tai desu*. The *-tai* form is actually an *i*-adjective. To form the negative, drop the final *i* and add *-kunai* just as you do for other *i*-adjectives.

1. Write a sentence about what you want to do this summer.
2. Write two sentences about what you want to do in the future. (want to live in Japan, want to get married, want to be a doctor, etc.)

III. Plain form + kara (desu) [L. 37] 📄 & ✏️

To answer questions with *dooshite*, use the plain form of a verb, an *i*-adjective, or *desu* followed by *kara* or *kara desu*. The plain form of *desu* is *da*.

Complete the following sentences.
Q: どうして フランスごの べんきょうを していますか。
A: _____、しています。(go to France)

Q: 山下さんは どうして パーティーに 来ませんか。
A: _____、来ません。(busy)

Q: どうして ハワイに すみたい ですか。
A: _____、すみたい です。(like the ocean)

IV. Past plain verb + -koto-ga arimasu (arimasen) [L. 39] 📄 & ✏️

This is used to ask and talk about past experiences – what one has or has not experienced.

1. Write the following in Japanese.
Q: Have you been to Japan?
A: Yes, I lived (there) when I was a child.

2. Write two questions that you can ask your classmates about their past experience.

V. Linking adjectives (-te form) [L. 45] 📄 & ✏️

To link adjectives, use their *-te* form. The *-te* form of *i*-adjectives can be formed by dropping the final *i* and adding *-ku-te*. The *-te* form of *na*-adjectives is formed with *-de* (do not use *-na*).

Link the following two adjectives and write the sentences in Japanese.
a. Person is serious and strict.
b. Person is cheerful and kind.
c. Person's hair is black and short.
d. Person's hair is blond and (he/she is) tall.

VI. *Article of clothing*-no *person* [L. 47] 📄 & ✏️

To describe people in terms of the clothing they are wearing, use the particle *-no* with the item of clothing.
Write the following in Japanese.
a. the man with glasses
b. the woman with the red shirt

c. the child with the white pants
d. the person with the big hat

VII. Particles 📄 & ✏️

Write the missing particles in the blanks. Write X if no particle is needed.　🔑

1. どっち＿＿＿ やすい です か。[L. 32]
2. この ちかく＿＿＿ ぎんこう＿＿＿ ありますか。[L. 33]
3. たん生日＿＿＿ あね＿＿＿ セーター＿＿＿ もらいました。[L. 35]
4. ばんごはん＿＿＿ あと＿＿＿ テレビ＿＿＿ 見ました。[L. 44]
5. 母＿＿＿ カリフォルニア＿＿＿ 生まれました。[L. 49]
6. 小学生＿＿＿ とき、アラスカ＿＿＿ すんでいました。[L. 50]
7. 五時はん＿＿＿ シカゴ＿＿＿ つきます。[L. 60]
8. ごご三時＿＿＿ アトランタ＿＿＿ でました。[L. 60]
9. 父＿＿＿ めがね＿＿＿ なくなりました。[L. 61]
10. きのう＿＿＿ こうえん＿＿＿ カメラ＿＿＿ わすれました。[L. 61]

CULTURE NOTES　　　　　　　　　　　　カルチャーノート

Irasshai is a course not only in Japanese language but also in Japanese culture. Through the various components of *Irasshai* – video lessons, audio interaction sessions, print materials, and the *Irasshai* website – you have already learned a lot about the Japanese culture. What are some of the interesting things you have learned about the Japanese people and their way of life? Make up some questions to ask your クラスメート. Be sure you know the answers. You may want to refer to the Culture Notes section of this book.

seasonal references in letters [L. 21]	Japanese medicine [L. 42]
important Japanese telephone numbers [L. 24]	giving flowers to a sick person [L. 43]
admission prices for adults and children [L. 26]	*o-miai* [L. 49]
personal pronouns [L. 29]	choosing a name for a child in Japan [L. 50]
addressing an envelope Japanese style [L. 33]	traditional Japanese calendar [L. 51]
Japanese vending machines [L. 34]	Japanese résumés [L. 53]
o-chuugen and *o-seibo* [L. 35]	owning and driving a car in Japan [L. 53]
fruit as a gift [L. 36]	religion in Japan [L. 56]
Valentine's Day [L. 40]	famous tourist sights in Japan [L. 59]
common expressions related to body parts [L. 41]	Japan's international airports [L. 60]

KANJI　　　　　　　　　　　　　　　　　　　漢字

1. Kakimashoo!　🔑

Write each of the following in Japanese. Use *kanji* for the underlined parts.

1. o-<u>mizu</u>
2. <u>kookoo</u>-no <u>sensei</u>
3. <u>Do</u>-yoo<u>bi</u>-ni eiga-o <u>mi</u>mashita.
4. Yamakawa-san-wa 45-<u>sai</u> desu.
5. Imooto-wa <u>chuugakusei</u> desu.
6. Kono nooto-wa 100-<u>en</u> deshita.
7. <u>Rainen nihon</u>-ni ikimasu.
8. Arubaito-wa <u>ka</u>-yoo<u>bi</u>-to <u>kin</u>-yoo<u>bi</u> desu.

2. Yomimashoo!　🔑

1. 上と下
2. 雨と雪
3. 二日間
4. 東京駅
5. 中国人
6. 聞きます
7. 言います
8. 本を読む
9. 一時八分
10. 今日の天気
11. 目と耳と口
12. 山本さんの学校
13. 五万六千七百円
14. 日本語で話しました。
15. 名前を書いて ください。
16. 中川さんは お元気 ですか。
17. 父と母は 三十九才 です。
18. 高田さんは 子どもさんが 四人います。

481

ANSWER KEY

This answer key does not include any answers to those exercises which you can easily find yourself by going back to the lessons given in brackets. For exercises where there are many possible answers, ask a number of your classmates to check your work. Also look at the examples given in lessons which covered that particular grammar point. All of the other answers are given in this section.

VOCABULARY
TIME WORDS
2. a. 先月の１２日
   b. 今しゅうの火よう日
   c. らい年の ふゆやすみ
   d. 今年の４月

TELEPHONING
a. Is Mr./Mrs./Ms. Tanaka there?
b. He/she is not at home now.
c. He/she will be back about 6:00.
d. What time will he/she be back (home)?
e. I'll call again later.

HEALTH CONDITIONS & TAKING MEDICINE
1. Part of the body が いたいん です。 (For the list of the body parts, see the VOCABULARY section of L. 41 & 42.)
   かぜなん です。/ ねつが あるん です。
2. お大じに。/ 大じょうぶ ですか。
3. a. 何の くすり ですか。
   b. いつ (これを/この くすりを) のみますか。

KEY GRAMMAR POINTS
I. Verb forms (-*u* verbs)

1. nai	9. win	17. make
2. au	10. kawanai	18. look for
3. play, have fun	11. kiita	19. sunda
4. haitta	12. receive, get	20. utau
5. ikanai	13. naku-narimasu	21. wakaru
6. need	14. narimasu	22. yomanai
7. kaerimasu	15. nonda	
8. kaku	16. arrive	

(-r*u* verbs)

23. open (something)	28. show	33. tabeta
24. atsumemasu	29. neta	34. umareru
25. leave	30. okinai	35. wasuremasu
26. iru	31. oshieta	
27. minai	32. close (something)	

(Irregular verbs)

36. kuru	37. shinai	38. shita

II. -tai/-takunai desu
(Sample Answers)
2. Place に すみたい/行きたい です。 けっこんしたい です。
   Occupation に なりたい です。 (For the list of occupations, see the VOCABULARY NOTES section of L. 52.)

III. Plain form + kara (desu)
<u>フランスに 行くから</u>、 しています。
<u>いそがしいから</u>、 来ません。
<u>うみが すきだから</u>、 すみたい です。

IV. Past plain verb + -koto-ga arimasu (arimasen)
1. Q: 日本に 行ったことが ありますか。
   A: はい、 こどものとき すんでいました。

V. Linking adjectives (-*te* form)
a. <u>Person</u> は まじめで きびしい です。
b. <u>Person</u> は あかるくて やさしい です。
c. <u>Person</u> は かみが くろくて みじかい です。
d. <u>Person</u> は きんぱつで せが 高い です。

VI. *Article of clothing-*no *person*

a. めがねの おとこの 人   c. しろい ズボンの こども
b. あかい シャツの おんなの 人   d. 大きい ぼうしの 人

VII. Particles

1. どっちが やすい ですか。
2. この ちかくに ぎんこうが ありますか。
3. たん生日に あねから セーターを もらいました。
4. ばんごはんの あとで テレビを 見ました。
5. 母は カリフォルニアで 生まれました。
6. 小学生の とき、アラスカに すんでいました。
7. 五時はんに シカゴに つきます。
8. ごご三時に アトランタを でました。
9. 父の めがねが なくなりました。
10. きのう X こうえんに カメラを わすれました。

KANJI

1. Kakimashoo!

1. お水
2. 高校の 先生
3. 土よう日に えいがを 見ました。
4. やまかわさんは ４５才 です。
5. いもうとは 中学生 です。
6. このノートは １００円 でした。
7. らい年 日本に 行きます。
8. アルバイトは 火よう日と 金よう日 です。

2. Yomimashoo! (English is given for your reference.)

1. ue-to shita (top and bottom)
2. ame-to yuki (rain and snow)
3. futsuka-kan (for two days)
4. Tookyoo-eki (Tokyo station)
5. chuugoku-jin (Chinese)
6. kikimasu (listen, hear)
7. iimasu (say)
8. hon-o yomu (read a book)
9. ichi-ji hap-pun (1:08)
10. kyoo-no tenki (today's weather)
11. me-to mimi-to kuchi (eyes, ears and mouth)
12. Yamamoto-san-no gakkoo (Mr. Yamamoto's school)
13. go-man roku-sen nana-hyaku-en (¥56,700)
14. Nihongo-de hanashimashita. (I spoke in Japanese.)
15. Namae-o kaite kudasai. (Please write your name.)
16. Nakagawa-san-wa o-genki desu-ka? (Is Ms. Nakagawa well?)
17. Chichi-to haha-wa san-juu-kyuu-sai desu. (My father and mother are 39 years old.)
18. Takada-san-wa kodomo-san-ga yo-nin imasu. (Mrs. Takada has four children.)

L. 63 電話で 話しましょう

れんしゅう A: Past Experiences

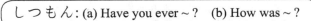
しつもん: (a) Have you ever ~ ?　(b) How was ~ ?

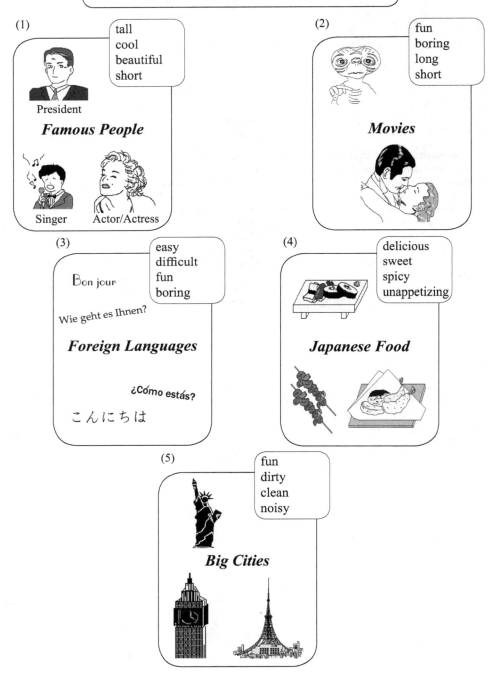

(1)
tall
cool
beautiful
short

President

Famous People

Singer　Actor/Actress

(2)
fun
boring
long
short

Movies

(3)
easy
difficult
fun
boring

Bon jour

Wie geht es Ihnen?

Foreign Languages

¿Cómo estás?

こんにちは

(4)
delicious
sweet
spicy
unappetizing

Japanese Food

(5)
fun
dirty
clean
noisy

Big Cities

れんしゅう B: What's wrong with you today?

Based on your condition today, choose the most probable cause from yesterday's activities (illustrated below).

(1) YOU

(2) YOU

(3) YOU

(4) YOU

Yesterday you did:

YOU — ice cream

YOU — 9:00 p.m. ~ 11:00 p.m.

YOU — math

YOU — friend — 4:00 p.m. ~ 8:00 p.m.

れんしゅう C: しりとり (*Shiritori* Game)

Think of a word that begins with the last syllable of the word you hear. The only rule is that you can't use a word that ends with "ん."

(Ex.) さか<u>な</u> → な<u>つ</u> → つまらな<u>い</u> → い.....

れんしゅう A: Year-end review

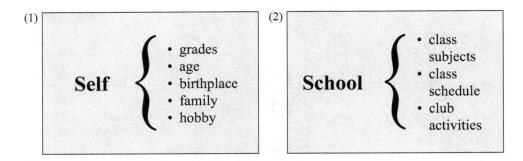

(1) **Self** { • grades • age • birthplace • family • hobby }

(2) **School** { • class subjects • class schedule • club activities }

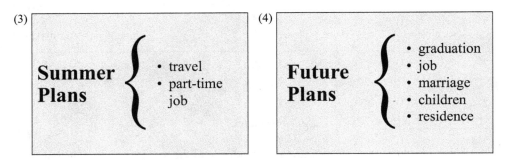

(3) **Summer Plans** { • travel • part-time job }

(4) **Future Plans** { • graduation • job • marriage • children • residence }

(5) **Past Experiences** { • food • sports • foreign languages • foreign countries }

<u>れんしゅう C</u>: よみましょう！こたえましょう！

1. さむい国に行ったことがありますか。

2. よく本を読みますか。

3. うんてんができますか。

4. なん年間、日本語をべんきょうしましたか。

5. らい年、そつぎょうしますか。

irasshai™
Welcome
to Japanese

Appendices

Verbs
Adjectives
Particles
Counter Words
Time-Related Words

VERBS

VERB GROUPS

Verb **conjugations** are all the different forms of a verb which show number, person, tense, etc. For example, the conjugation of the English verb to sing includes the forms *sing, sings, singing, sang,* and *sung*.

All Japanese verbs (with the exception of two irregular verbs, *suru* and *kuru*) belong to one of two different groups. These verb groups are usually referred to as

> (1) the **ru**-verb, or the **consonant** conjugation, and
> (2) the **u**-verb, or the **vowel** conjugation.

These two verb groups are different but regular. To be able to conjugate a Japanese verb correctly, you must know its **plain form**. The plain form is also called the **dictionary form** because verb entries in Japanese dictionaries are given in this form. Beginning in Lesson 47 (JPN I), both the *-masu* form and the plain form for each new verb are given in the Vocabulary section. The dictionary form consists of a root and an ending.

DICTIONARY FORM		TYPE	ENGLISH	ROOT		ENDING	
見る	miru	*ru*	see	見	mi	る	ru
食べる	taberu	*ru*	eat	食べ	tabe	る	ru
読む	yomu	*u*	read	読	yo	む	mu
聞く	kiku	*u*	listen	聞	ki	く	ku

1. *ru*-verbs
A verb which belongs to the *ru*-verb group generally has a plain form which ends in a syllable from the *i*-column (*i, ki, shi, chi, ni,* etc.) or the *e*-column (*e, ke, se, te, ne,* etc.) of the *hiragana* syllabary + *ru*. Verbs such as the following belong to the *ru*-verb group.

RU-VERBS			
mi**ru**	look at, see	tabe**ru**	eat
oki**ru**	get up	oshie**ru**	teach
ne**ru**	sleep, go to bed	atsume**ru**	collect
ake**ru**	open (something)	make**ru**	lose
shime**ru**	close (something)	mise**ru**	show
wasure**ru**	forget	de**ru**	leave

2. *u*-verbs
Verbs which are not in the *ru*-verb group belong to the *u*-verb group. The dictionary form of an *u*-verb ends in one of the syllables in the *u*-column of the *hiragana* syllabary (*u, ku, su, tsu, nu,* etc.)

U-VERBS			
hanas**u**	speak	nom**u**	drink
yom**u**	read	asob**u**	play, have fun
ka**u**	buy	uta**u**	sing
tsuka**u**	use	mora**u**	receive, get
ik**u**	go	ir**u**	need
kaer**u**	return	tsukur**u**	make
hair**u**	enter, join	kats**u**	win
kak**u**	write	kik**u**	listen

3. Irregular verbs

Unlike languages such as Spanish, French, German, and Russian, Japanese has only two irregular verbs: *suru* (do) and *kuru* (come). You will have to memorize the conjugations of these verbs. All compound verbs which include *suru*, such as *benkyoo suru* (study) and *ryokoo suru* (travel), form their conjugations the same way as *suru*.

THE -*MASU* FORM

Different forms of the same Japanese verb can indicate different levels of politeness. The -*masu* form, which is sometimes called the **non-past, polite form**, is used when speaking with people to whom you wish to show respect because they are older or more important than you or because you do not know them very well.

You can arrive at the -*masu* form from the plain form. For *ru*-verbs, drop the *ru*-ending and add -*masu*. For *u*-verbs, drop the *u* and add *i* and then -*masu*.

THE -*MASU* FORM			
***ru*-verb**	tabe **ru** →	tabe + masu	= tabemasu
***u*-verb**	kik **u** →	kik + **i** + masu	= kikimasu

In the conjugation of *u*-verbs, certain sound changes may occur.

SOUND CHANGE	PLAIN FORM	-*MASU* FORM	ENGLISH
su → shi	da **su**	da **shi** masu	take out
tsu → chi	ka **tsu**	ka **chi** masu	win

The -*masu* form of the irregular verbs **suru** and **kuru** are **shimasu** and **kimasu** respectively.

Te invitation -**masen-ka** (Would you like to ~?) form and -**mashoo** (Let's ~.) form can be made by replacing -**masu**. (I, L. 54)

VERB TENSES

Japanese verbs have two basic tenses: non-past and past. The **non-past tense** is used to talk about habitual, present actions and events as well as future actions and events. Use the -*masu* (affirmative) form or the -*masen* form (negative) for the **non-past tense**. The **past tense** is used to express actions and events in the past. Use the -*mashita* form (affirmative) or the -*masen deshita* form (negative) for the **past tense**.

	NON-PAST	PAST
AFFIRMATIVE	-masu	-mashita
NEGATIVE	-masen	-masen deshita

THE -*TE* FORM

The -*te* form is an important verb form since it is used in polite commands, in series of actions, in progressive tenses, and in other constructions.

Moo ichido *itte* kudasai.	Please *say* it again.
Uchi-ni *kaette*, ban-gohan-o *tabete*, terebi-o *mite*, nemashita.	I *returned* home, *ate* dinner, *watched* television, and went to bed.
Ima, *tabete-imasu*.	He *is eating* now.
Nani-o *shite*-imasu-ka?	What *are* you *doing*?
Shinbun-o *yonde*-imashita.	She *was reading* the newspaper.

491

To make the *-te* form of a *ru*-verb, simply replace the *ru* with *te*.

-*TE* FORM OF *RU*-VERBS			
mi **ru**	→	mi **te**	look, see
tabe **ru**	→	tabe **te**	eat
oshie **ru**	→	oshie **te**	teach
mise **ru**	→	mise **te**	show

Making the *-te* form of *ru*-verbs is more complicated because of a number of sound changes which occur. Although these changes are regular and follow certain rules, you may find it easier to simply memorize the changes shown in the chart below. Think of verbs you already know as you learn the sound changes.

PLAIN FORM ENDS IN	FORM -*TE* FORM BY SUBSTITUTING	EXAMPLES	ENGLISH
-ku	**-ite**	kaku → kaite	write
		kiku → kiite	listen
-gu	**-ide**	isogu → isoide	hurry
-tsu		matsu → matte	wait
-ru	**-tte**	hairu → haitte	enter, join
vowel + u		au → atte	meet
-mu		yomu → yonde	read
-nu	**-nde**	shinu → shinde	die
-bu		asobu → asonde	play, have fun
-su	**-shite**	hanasu → hanashite	speak

The *-te* forms of the irregular verbs **suru** and **kuru** are **shite** and **kite** respectively.

THE PLAIN FORM

The plain form is used instead of polite form (*-masu* form) in conversations between family members and close friends.

Mainichi, asa-gohan, *taberu*? Do you eat breakfast every day?
Uun, mainichi-wa *tabenai*. No, I don't eat every day.
Kyoo, *tabeta*? Did you eat (breakfast) today?
Uun, *tabenakatta*. No, I didn't.

All four conjugations of plain verbs and how to form them are shown in the chart below.

	PLAIN (NON-PAST)	HOW TO FORM	PLAIN (PAST)	HOW TO FORM
AFF	dictionary form (Ex.) ねる かう はなす		-ta/da form (Ex.) ねた かった はなした	Change the final *-te/de* of *-te* forms to *-ta/da*
NEG	**-nai** form (Ex.) ねない かわない はなさない	1. *ru*-verbs: change *ru* to *nai* 2. *u*-verbs: change the *u* sound of the final letter of the dictionary form to *a* sound (except when う becomes わ) and add *nai*. 3. irregular verbs: *suru* → *shinai*, *kuru* → *konai*	**-nakatta** form (Ex.) ねなかった かわなかった はなさなかった	Change the final *-nai* of *-nai* form to *-nakatta*

ADJECTIVES

All Japanese adjectives fall into one of the two following groups:
- (1) the *i*-adjectives
- (2) the *na*-adjectives

I-adjectives end in an *i* sound when preceding the noun it modifies. *Na*-adjectives end with *na* when preceding the noun it modifies.

Akai kaban-o kaimashita.	I bought a red bag.
Kirei-na sukaato-o moraimashita.	I received a pretty skirt.

I-ADJECTIVES

あかい	akai [red]	はやい	hayai [fast, early]
いい	ii [good]	おいしい	oishii [delicious]
おおきい	ookii [big]	ほしい	hoshii [desired]

NA-ADJECTIVES

きれい(な)	kirei(**na**) [pretty]	しずか(な)	shizuka(**na**) [quiet]
すき(な)	suki(**na**) [favorite]	だめ(な)	dame(**na**) [bad]

ADJECTIVE TENSES

Japanese adjectives have two basic tenses: non-past and past. *I*-adjectives and *na*-adjectives conjugate differently.

Tanaka-san-no uchi-wa *ookii desu.*	Mr. Tanaka's house *is big.*
Toshokan-wa *shizuka deshita.*	The library *was quiet.*
Yasai-ga *suki desu*-ka?	*Do you like* vegetables?
Iie, anmari *suki ja nai desu.*	No, I *don't like* them much.
Ima, mizu-ga *nomitai desu.**	I *want to drink* water now.

* [Verb: -*masu* form stem] + *tai* forms (-*tai desu*, -*takunai desu*, -*takatta desu*, -*takunakatta desu*) expressing one's desire have the same conjugations as *i*-adjectives.

I-adjectives conjugate as follows:

i-adjectives	non-past	past
affirmative	**-i desu**	**-i̶ katta desu**
negative	**-i̶ kunai desu**	**-i̶ kunakatta desu**

Na-adjectives conjugate as follows:

na-adjectives	non-past	past
affirmative	**-n̶a̶ desu**	**-n̶a̶ deshita**
negative	**-n̶a̶ ja nai desu**	**-n̶a̶ ja nakatta desu**

PARTICLES

Particle	Lesson	Note(s)	Sample sentence
ka	I-2	indicates a question	*Kore-wa nan desu-ka?* (What is this?)

Particle	Lesson	Note(s)	Sample sentence
ne	I-2	used to get one's agreement or confirmation	*Tanaka-san desu-ne?* (You are Mr. Tanaka, **aren't you?**)
wa は (not わ)	I-5	1) indicates the topic of the sentence	*Kenji-kun-wa kookoosei desu.* (Kenji is a high school student.)
	II-6	2) used when contrasting or distinguishing items	*Igirisu-de-wa eigo-o hanashimasu.Nihon-de-wa nihongo-o hanashimasu.* (They speak English in England. They speak Japanese in Japan.)
no	I-8	1) denotes affiliation	*Irasshai-no Timu desu.* (I am Tim **of** *Irasshai.*)
	I-12	2) indicates description or modification of the noun following it	*Kore-wa nihongo-no jisho desu.* (This is a Japanese dictionary.)
	I-15	3) expresses possession	*Kore-wa watashi-no hon desu.* (This is my book.)
	I-23	4) used to separate a string of numbers	*Denwa-bangoo-wa 685-no 2551* desu. (The phone number is 685-2551.)
de	I-10	1) language-*de ~ -to iimasu*; means "it is called ~ **in** (language)."	*Kore-wa nihongo-de denwa to iimasu.* (This is called *"denwa"* **in** Japanese.)
	I-47, I-67	2) indicates place where an action occurs	*Watashi-wa uchi-de terebi-o mimasu.* (I watch T.V. **at** home.)
	I-71	3) indicates a method or means	*Jitensha-de gakkoo-ni ikimasu.* (I go to school **by** bicycle.)
	II-9	4) denotes a place or category	*Fuji-san-wa nihon-de ichiban takai yama desu.* (Mr. Fuji is the highest mountain **in** Japan.)
	II-11, II-51	5) *jibun-de, hitori-de*; indicates an exclusive agent	*Jibun-de suugaku-no shukudai-o shimasu.* (I will do math homewok **by** myself.) *Ima, hitori-de sunde-imasu.* (I live alone now.)
	II-24	6) *ato-de*; indicates boundary of time	*Mata ato-de kimasu.* (I will come back later.)
yo	I-13	adds emphasis	*Dame desu-yo.* (It's bad!)
to	I-10	1) word-*to iimasu*; means "is called (word)."	*Kore-wa shitajiki-to iimasu.* (This is called *"shitajiki."*)
	I-15	2) connects nouns and means "and"*	*Asa sakana-to gohan-o tabemasu.* (I eat fish **and** rice for breakfast.)
	I-41	3) indicates the person one does something with	*Yoru kazoku-to tabemasu.* (I eat dinner **with** my family.)
ga**	I-18, I-20	1) ~ *-ga imasu, arimasu*; indicates the existence of persons/items or possessions	*Watashi-wa ani-ga imasu.* (I have an older brother.) *Kuroi pen-ga arimasu-ka?* (Do you have /Is there a black pen?)

Particle	Lesson	Note(s)	Sample sentence
ga**	I-38, I-52, I-55, I-56, II-36	2) ~ -**ga** *hoshii desu/suki desu/ dekimasu/joozu desu/irimasu*; indicates the object of desire, preference, ability/skill, and need	*Watashi-wa nihongo-ga suki desu.* (I like Japanese.) *Watashi-wa supeingo-ga dekimasu.* (I can speak Spanish.) *Supuun-ga 4-hon irimasu.* (I need four spoons.)
mo	I-18	indicates someone/something is the same sort as the one previously mentioned	*Kono hon-wa ii desu. Sono hon-mo ii desu.* (This book is good. That book is **also** good.)
o を (not お)	I-26, II-4	indicates a direct object	*Sakana-o tabemasu-ka?* (Do you eat fish?) *Sakana-o katte-imasu.* (I have fish as pets.)
	II-54, II-60	2) institution-**o** *sotsugyoo shimasu*, place-**o** *demasu*; indicates the starting point of a moving action	*Kotoshi, kookoo-o sotsugyoo shimasu.* (I will graduate **from** high school this year.) *Itsu koko-o demasu-ka?* (When are you leaving here?)
kara, made	I-26, II-7	time/place-**kara** time/place -**made**; indicates the time/date/ occasion when an action or process takes place	*Nihongo-no jugyoo-wa 8-ji -kara 9-ji-made desu.*(Japanese class is **from** 8:00 **to** 9:00.) *Dochira-kara desu-ka?* (Where are you **from**?)
ni	I-27, I-38	1) time/date/day-**ni**; indicates the time/date/occasion when an action or process takes place	*Asa 7-ji-ni okimasu.* (I get up **at** 7:00 in the morning.) *1-gatsu 15-nichi-ni paatii-o shimasu.* (We're having a party **on** Jan. 15.)
	I-32	2) noun-**ni** *shimasu*; indicates the result of one's deciding on something	*Watashi-wa koohii-ni shimasu.* (I'll have coffee.)
	I-35	3) noun-**ni** *narimasu*; indicates the result or final state	*Tanjoobi-ni 19-sai-ni narimasu.* (I'll be 19 yrs. old on my birthday.)
	I-40, I-47	4) place-**ni** *ikimasu/kimasu/ kaerimasu* (motion verb); indicates the purpose/place one goes to	*Ashita Nyuu Yooku-ni ikimasu.* (I will go **to** New York tomorrow.)
	I-69, II-14	5) place/location-**ni** *arimasu/ imasu/haitte-imasu*; indicates a place/location where someone/something exists	*Gakkoo-wa kooen-no mae-ni arimasu.* (The school is located **in** front of the park.) *Tenisu-bu-ni haitte-imasu.* (I belong **to** the tennis club.)
	II-18, II-20	6) person-**ni** *aimasu/kakimasu*; indicates the person who is the object of an action	*Nihongo-no sensei-ni aimasu.* (I will meet my Japanese teacher.) *Tomodachi-ni tegami-o kakimasu.* (I write letters **to** my friends.)

* NOTE: The "and" for sentence + sentence is **soshite**.
    Ex) Watashi-wa sakana-o tabemasu. *Soshite* ocha-o nomimasu.
        (I eat fish *and* drink Japanese tea.)
Sorekara meaning "and then" can be used when something happens after something else.
    Ex) Watashi-wa asa-gohan-o tabemasu. *Sorekara*, gakkoo-ni ikimasu.
        (I eat breakfast, *and then* I go to school.)

** NOTE: **Ga** changes to **wa** in negative statements.
    Ex.) Pen-*ga* arimasu-ka? Iie, pen-*wa* arimasen.
        (Is there a pen? No, there is no pen.)
    Ex.) Sakana-*ga* suki desu-ka? Iie, sakana-*wa* suki ja-nai desu.
        (Do you like fish? No, I don't like fish.)

COUNTER WORDS

	-nen-sei (grade)	-sai (years old)	-nin (people)	-do (degree)	-tsu (general counter)	-mairu (mile)
1	ichi-nen-sei	is-sai	hitori	ichi-do	hitotsu	ichi-mairu
2	ni-nen-sei	ni-sai	futari	ni-do	futatsu	ni-mairu
3	san-nen-sei	san-sai	san-nin	san-do	mittsu	san-mairu
4	yo-nen-sei	yon-sai	yo-nin	yon-do	yottsu	yon-mairu
5	go-nen-sei	go-sai	go-nin	go-do	itsutsu	go-mairu
6	roku-nen-sei	roku-sai	roku-nin	roku-do	muttsu	roku-mairu
7		nana-sai	nana-nin	nana-do	nanatsu	nana-mairu
8		has-sai	hachi-nin	hachi-do	yattsu	hachi-mairu
9		kyuu-sai	kyuu-nin	kyuu-do	kokonotsu	kyuu-mairu
10		jus-sai	juu-nin	juu-do	too	juu-mairu
20		hatachi	ni-juu-nin	ni-juu-do		ni-juu-mairu

	-hyaku (hundred)	-sen (thousand)	-man (ten thousand)	-en (yen)	-doru (dollar)	-sento (cent)
1	hyaku	sen	ichi-man	ichi-en	ichi-doru	is-sento
2	ni-hyaku	ni-sen	ni-man	ni-en	ni-doru	ni-sento
3	san-byaku	san-zen	san-man	san-en	san-doru	san-sento
4	yon-hayku	yon-sen	yon-man	yon-en	yon-doru	yon-sento
5	go-hyaku	go-sen	go-man	go-en	go-doru	go-sento
6	rop-pyaku	roku-sen	roku-man	roku-en	roku-doru	roku-sento
7	nana-hyaku	nana-sen	nana-man	nana-en	nana-doru	nana-sento
8	hap-pyaku	has-sen	hachi-man	hachi-en	hachi-doru	has-sento
9	kyuu-hyaku	kyuu-sen	kyuu-man	kyuu-en	kyuu-doru	kyuu-sento
10			juu-man	juu-en	juu-doru	jus-sento

	-mai (thin, flat object)	**-ban-me** (numeric order)	**-h/p/bon** (long, cylindrical object)	**-k/gai** (floor)
1	ichi-mai	ichi-ban-me	ip-pon	ik-kai
2	ni-mai	ni-ban-me	ni-hon	ni-kai
3	san-mai	san-ban-me	san-bon	san-kai
4	yon-mai	yon-ban-me	yon-hon	yon-kai
5	go-mai	go-ban-me	go-hon	go-kai
6	roku-mai	roku-ban-me	rop-pon	rok-kai
7	nana-mai	nana-ban-me	nana-hon	nana-kai
8	hachi-mai	hachi-ban-me	hap-pon	hachi-kai
9	kyuu-mai	kyuu-ban-me	kyuu-hon	kyuu-kai
10	juu-mai	juu-ban-me	jup-pon	juk-kai

TIME-RELATED WORDS

	-ji (kan) (hours)	**-jikan-me** (#th period)	**-pun/fun** (minutes)	**-nen (kan)** (years)	**-shuu (kan)** (weeks)
1	ichi-ji (kan)	ichi-jikan-me	ip-pun	ichi-nen (kan)	is-shuu kan
2	ni-ji (kan)	ni-jikan-me	ni-fun	ni-nen (kan)	ni-shuu kan
3	san-ji (kan)	san-jikan-me	san-pun	san-nen (kan)	san-shuu kan
4	yo-ji (kan)	yo-jikan-me	yon-pun	yo-nen (kan)	yon-shuu-kan
5	go-ji (kan)	go-jikan-me	go-fun	go-nen (kan)	go-shuu-kan
6	roku-ji (kan)	roku-jikan-me	rop-pun	roku-nen (kan)	roku-shuu-kan
7	shichi-ji (kan)		nana-fun	nana-nen (kan)	nana-shuu-kan
8	hachi-ji (kan)		hap-pun	hachi-nen (kan)	has-shuu-kan
9	ku-ji (kan)		kyuu-fun	kyuu-nen (kan)	kyuu-shuu-kan
10	juu-ji (kan)		jup-pun	juu-nen (kan)	jus-shuu-kan

	-gatsu (#th month)	**-ka-getsu** (months)		**-nichi-kan** (days)		**-yoobi** (day)
1	ichi-gatsu	ik-ka-getsu	1	ichinichi	Su	nichi-yoobi
2	ni-gatsu	ni-ka-getsu	2	futsuka-kan	M	getsu-yoobi
3	san-gatsu	san-ka-getsu	3	mikka-kan	Tu	ka-yoobi
4	shi-gatsu	yon-ka-getsu	4	yokka-kan	W	sui-yoobi
5	go-gatsu	go-ka-getsu	5	itsuka-kan	Th	moku-yoobi
6	roku-gatsu	rok-ka-getsu	6	muika-kan	F	kin-yoobi
7	shichi-gatsu	nana-ka-getsu	7	nanoka-kan	Sa	do-yoobi
8	hachi-gatsu	hachi-ka-getsu	8	yooka-kan		
9	ku-gatsu	kyuu-ka-getsu	9	kokonoka-kan		**weekend**
10	juu-gatsu	juk-ka-getsu	10	tooka-kan		shuumatsu
11	juu-ichi-gatsu	juu ik-ka-getsu	11	juu-ichi-nichi		
12	juu-ni-gatsu	juu-ni-ka-getsu	12	juu-ni-nichi		

now	**morning**	**noon/afternoon**	**night**	**AM**	**PM**
ima	asa	hiru	yoru	gozen	gogo

everyday	**yesterday**	**today**	**tomorrow**
mainichi	kinoo	kyoo	ashita

Ima, mainichi, kinoo, kyoo, and *ashita* do not take the particle *-ni* .

spring	**summer**	**fall**	**winter**
haru	natsu	aki	fuyu

	-nichi (#th day)		-nichi (#th day)		-nichi (#th day)
1	tsuitachi	11	juu-ichi-nichi	21	ni-juu-ichi-nichi
2	futsuka	12	juu-ni-nichi	22	ni-juu-ni-nichi
3	mikka	13	juu-san-nichi	23	ni-juu-san-nichi
4	yokka	14	juu-yokka	24	ni-juu-yokka
5	itsuka	15	juu-go-nichi	25	ni-juu-go-nichi
6	muika	16	juu-roku-nichi	26	ni-juu-roku-nichi
7	nanoka	17	juu-shichi-nichi	27	ni-juu-shichi-nichi
8	yooka	18	juu-hachi-nichi	28	ni-juu-hachi-nichi
9	kokonoka	19	juu-ku-nichi	29	ni-juu-ku-nichi
10	tooka	20	hatsuka	30	san-juu-nichi
				31	san-juu-ichi-nichi

	last	this	next
week	sen-shuu	kon-shuu	rai-shuu
month	sen-getsu	kon-getsu	rai-gesu
year	kyonen	kotoshi	rainen

The time words in the chart above also do not take the particle -*ni* .

Glossary English - Japanese

Egypt *Ejiputo* 6
elbow(s) *hiji* 41
elephant *zoo* 26
(something) ends, finishes
    owaru [owarimasu] 13
engineer *enjinia* 52
England *Igirisu* 6
enter, join *hairu [hairimasu]* 14
Europe *Yooroppa* 7
eye(s) *me* 41
eye doctor *me-isha* 52
F
face *kao* 41
famous *yuumei(na)* 55
farmer *noofu* 52
feet (unit of measure) *fiito* 9
fever *netsu* 43
(I have a) fever. *Netsu-ga aru-n desu.* 43
finger(s) *yubi* 41
fisherman *ryooshi* 52
flight attendant *furaito atendanto* 52
#th floor *#-kai, #-gai* 38
foot/feet, leg(s) *ashi* 41
foreign country *gaikoku* 57
foreign language *gaikokugo* 10
forget *wasureru [wasuremasu]* 15
France *Furansu* 6
free (time) *hima(na)* 28
fruit *kudamono* 36
fruit store *kudamono-ya* 36
funny *okashii* 45
future *shoorai* 55
G
game, sporting match *shiai* 27
garage sale *gareeji seeru* 37
Germany *Doitsu* 6
get married *kekkon suru [shimasu]* 49
Get well soon. Take care of yourself. (said to
    a sick or injured person) *O-daiji-ni.* 42
giraffe *kirin* 26
glasses *megane* 47
go to play, go to have fun
    asobi-ni iku [ikimasu] 28
Good-bye. (said to person leaving home)
    Itterasshai. 18
Good-bye. (said when leaving home)
    Itte-kimasu. 18
gorilla *gorira* 26
graduation (graduate)
    sotsugyoo (suru [shimasu]) 54
graduation ceremony *sotsugyoo shiki* 54
grandchild (honorific form) *o-mago-san* 51
grandchild (humble form) *mago* 51
grandfather (honorific form) *ojiisan* 51
grandfather (humble form) *sofu* 51
grandmother (honorific form) *obaasan* 51
grandmother (humble form) *sobo* 51
grapefruit *gureepufuruutsu* 32
Greece *Girisha* 6
guidebook *gaido-bukku* 57
gym, gymnasium *taiikukan* 13
H
hair *kami* 46
hand(s), arm(s) *te* 41
he *kare* 29
head *atama* 41

height *se* 46
Hello, I'm home! *Tadaima.* 17
hippopotamus *kaba* 26
hobby, pastime, interest *shumi* 19
Hokkaido *Hokkaido* 8
homestay *hoomusutei* 2
honest *shoojiki(na)* 45
honeymoon *hanemuun* 57
Honshu *Honshuu* 8
hospital, doctor's office *byooin* 43
hot spring *onsen* 59
how long? *dore-gurai* 10
how many:
    feet? *nan-fiito* 9
    months? *nan-ka-getsu* 49
    pencils, pens, etc. (long, cylindrical objects)?
        nan-bon 36
    stamps, sheets of paper, etc. (thin, flat
        objects)? *nan-mai* 33
    weeks? *nan-shuu-kan* 57
    years? *nan-nen-kan* 10
(I'm) hungry.
    Onaka-ga suita [sukimashita]. 26, 34
(very) hungry *pekopeko* 34
(My ~) hurts. I have a ~-ache.
    (~-ga) itai-n desu. 42
husband (honrofic form) *go-shujin* 51
husband (humble form) *shujin* 51
I
impatient *ki-ga mijikai* 46
India *Indo* 6
Indonesia *Indoneshia* 6
(~ is) inside *(~-ga) haitte-iru [haitte-imasu].* 31
Is (person's name) there? (on the telephone)
    (Person's name-wa) irasshaimasu-ka?
    24
island *shima* 8
Italy *Itaria* 6
J
journal, diary *nikki* 17
journalist *jaanarisuto* 52
K
kangaroo *kangaruu* 26
Kansai *Kansai* 60
keep/have (a pet) *katte-iru [katte-imasu]* 4
Kenya *Kenia* 6
kind *shinsetsu(na)* 45
knee(s) *hiza* 41
know *shitte-iru [shitte-imasu]* 48
(don't/doesn't) know *shiranai [shirimasen]* 48
koala *koara* 26
Korea *Kankoku* 6
Kyushu *Kyuushuu* 8
L
lake *mizuumi* 8
Laos *Raosu* 6
last month *sengetsu* 25
last night *kinoo-no yoru* 12
last week *senshuu* 22
last year *kyonen* 25
later *ato-de* 24
lawyer *bengoshi* 52
leave *deru [demasu]* 58
left hand *hidari-te* 42
leopard *hyoo* 26
letter *tegami* 20

501

relative(s) (honorific form) *go-shinseki* 51
remember *oboete-iru [oboete-imasu]* 16
résumé *rirekisho* 53
review *fukushuu(-o suru [shimasu])* 30
rhinoceros *sai* 26
right hand *migi-te* 42
river *kawa* 8
romantic *romanchikku* 40
room *heya* 16
Russia *Roshia* 6
S
salesman *seerusuman* 52
same *onaji* 31
score *sukoa* 27
seal *azarashi* 26
season *kisetsu* 22
see, meet *au [aimasu]* 18
serious *majime(na)* 45
serviceman (armed forces) *gunjin* 52
she *kanojo* 29
Shikoku *Shikoku* 8
shop clerk *ten'in* 52
short (opposite of long) *mijikai* 46
short (person's height) *se-ga hikui* 46
shoulder(s) *kata* 41
show *miseru [misemasu]* 35
sick, ill *byooki* 43
singer *kashu* 52
sleepy *nemui* 5
slowly, leisurely *yukkuri* 10
smart, intelligent *atama-ga ii* 10
sneakers *suniikaa* 38
someone, somebody *dare-ka* 18
something *nani-ka* 18
son (honorific form) *musuko-san* 51
son (humble form) *musuko* 51
south *minami* 7
South America *Minami Amerika* 7
Spain *Supein* 6
speak *hanasu [hanashimasu]* 6
spicy, hot, salty *karai* 39
(postage) stamp *kitte* 20
stomach *onaka* 41
strict *kibishii* 45
strong *tsuyoi* 21
stuffed animal *nuigurumi* 19
(go) surfing *saafin(-o suru [shimasu])* 23
Sweden *Suweeden* 6
sweet *amai* 39
swimsuit *mizugi* 58
Switzerland *Suisu* 6
T
Taiwan *Taiwan* 6
take a picture *shashin-o toru [torimasu]* 23, 59
Take care. Be careful.
    Ki-o tsukete kudasai. 43
take (medicine) *nomu [nomimasu]* 44
tall (person's height) *se-ga takai* 46
tall, high, expensive *takai* 9
teach *oshieru [oshiemasu]* 10
teacher *sensei, kyooshi* 52
ten thousand *-man* 35
terrible, difficult, awful *taihen(na)* 52
textbook *kyookasho* 15
Thailand *Tai* 6
that one (of two) *sotchi* 32

that one over there (of two) *atchi* 32
the #th *#-ban-me* 34
thief *doroboo* 47
this month *kongetsu* 25
this one (of two) *kotchi* 32
this week *konshuu* 22
this year *kotoshi* 25
throat *nodo* 42
ticket *kippu* 60
tiger *tora* 26
time *jikan* 14
to (a person) (particle) *-ni* 20
to # (a score) *# tai #* 27
toaster *toosutaa* 35
toe(s) *ashi-no yubi* 41
Tokyo Tower *Tookyoo Tawaa* 59
too bad *zannen(na)* 27
tooth/teeth *ha* 42
top, above, up *ue* 16
tour *tsuaa* 57
travel, (take a) trip
    ryokoo(-o suru [shimasu]) 19
turtle *kame* 26
U
umbrella *kasa* 21
uncle (honorific form) *ojisan* 51
uncle (humble form) *oji* 51
under, below, down *shita* 16
use *tsukau [tsukaimasu]* 15
V
Valentine's Day *Barentain-dee* 40
Venezuela *Benezuera* 6
vicinity, near, around *chikaku* 33
Vietnam *Betonamu* 6
W
waiter *ueetaa* 52
waitress *ueetoresu* 52
we *watashi-tachi* 28
weak *yowai* 27
wear glasses
    megane-o shite-iru [shite-imasu] 47
week(s), a period of # weeks *#-shuu-kan* 57
Welcome home. *O-kaeri(nasai).* 17
west *nishi* 7
what floor? *nan-kai* 38
what kind of (+NOUN)? *donna* 3
What time will s/he return?
    Nani-ji-ni o-kaeri desu-ka? 24
What's wrong? What happened?
    Doo shita-n desu-ka? 42
when ~, at the time when ~ *(~-no) toki* 50
Where are you from?
    Dochira-kara desu-ka? 7
which number (in a series)? *nan-ban-me* 34
which one (of two)? *dotchi* 32
which? where? *dochira* 7
white collar worker *sarariiman* 52
why? *dooshite* 37
wife (honorific form) *okusan* 51
wife (humble form) *kanai* 51
will live *sumu [sumimasu]* 55
win *katsu [kachimasu]* 27
wind *kaze* 21
window *mado* 21
work *hataraku [hatarakimasu]* 52
world *sekai* 6

wrist(s) *te-kubi* 41
write *kaku [kakimasu]* 17
writer *sakka* 52
X
Y
(a period of) # years *#-nen-kan* 10
you, honey *anata* 29
Z
zebra *shimauma* 26
zoo *doobutsuen* 26

Glossary **Japanese - English**

Japanese English Lesson Number

A

Afurika Africa 7
au [aimasu] meet 18
Ajia Asia 7
akachan baby 41, 49
akarui cheerful 45
akeru [akemasu] open (something) 21
amai sweet 39
anata you, honey 29
a(n)mari not really 32
Aruzenchin Argentina 6
asa-gohan breakfast 5
ashi foot/feet, leg(s) *41*
ashi-kubi ankle 41
ashi-no yubi toe(s) 41
asobi-ni iku [ikimasu]
       go to play, go to have fun 28
asobi-ni kuru [kimasu]
       come over (and have fun) 29
asobu [asobimasu] play, have fun 28
atama head 41
atama-ga ii smart, intelligent 10
atchi that one over there (of two) 32
ato-de later; after 24; 44
atsumeru [atsumemasu] 19
au [aimasu] meet, see 18
azarashi seal 26

B

ban-gohan dinner 5
#-ban-me the #th 34
Barentain-dee Valentine's Day 40
Benezuera Venezuela 6
bengoshi lawyer 52
(o)bentoo boxed lunch 14
Betonamu Vietnam 6
bokushi pastor, minister 52
-bu club (suffix) 14
Burajiru Brazil 6
burookaa broker 52
byooin hospital, doctor's office 43
byooki sick, ill 43

C

chika basement 38
chikaku vicinity, near, around 33
Chiri Chile 6
chizu map 6
Chuugoku China 6

D

Daijoobu desu-ka? Are you OK? 42

daiku carpenter 52
dake only 10
dare-ka someone, somebody 18
dare-mo no one, nobody 18
-de in; a place or category (particle) 9
-de exclusive agent (particle) 11, 51
-de boundary of time (particle) 24
deru [demasu] leave 58
dezainaa designer 52
dochira which? where? 7
Dochira-kara desu-ka?
       Where are you from? 7
Doitsu Germany 6
donna what kind of (+NOUN)? 3
Doo shita-n desu-ka? What's wrong?
       What's happened? 42
doobutsu animal(s) 26
doobutsuen zoo 26
dooshite why? 37
dore-gurai how long? 10
doroboo thief 47
dotchi which one (of two)? 32

E

e picture 19
-e to; direction of movement; the person
       addressed (in letters) (particle) 21
enjinia engineer 52
e-o kaku [kakimasu] draw a picture 19
Ejiputo Egypt 6

F

fiito feet (unit of measure) 9
Firipin Phillipines 6
fuku [fukimasu] play (wind instruments) 19
fukushuu(-o suru [shimasu]) review 30
furaito atendanto flight attendant 52
Furansu France 6

G

-ga object of desire, preference, ability/skill,
       need 36
gaido-bukku guidebook 57
gaikoku foreign country 57
gaikokugo foreign language 10
gaikookan diplomat 52
gaka painter, artist 52
gareeji seeru garage sale 37
ginkooin bank employee 52
Girisha Greece 6
-go after, in (+ LENGTH OF TIME),
       (LENGTH OF TIME +) later 54
gogo p.m., in the afternoon 58

gorira gorilla 26
-goro around, about (+TIME) 24
go-ryooshin parents (honrofic form) 51
go-shinseki relatives (honorific form) 51
go-shujin husband (honorific form) 51
gozen a.m., in the morning 58
gunjin serviceman (armed forces) 52
gureepufuruutsu grapefruit 32

H

ha tooth/teeth 42
hairu [hairimasu] enter, join 14
ha-isha dentist 52
haitte-iru [haitte-imasu] belong to 14
(~-ga) haitte-iru [haitte-imasu] (~ is) inside 31
haiyuu actor 52
hajimaru [hajimarimasu] (something) begins, starts 13
hana nose 41
hanasu [hanashimasu] speak 6
hanemuun honeymoon 57
hataraku [hatarakimasu] work 52
hayaku quickly 58
heya room 16
hidari-te left hand 42
higashi east 7
hiji elbow(s) 41
hiku [hikimasu] play (stringed and keyboard instruments) 19
hikui low 46
hima(na) free (time) 28
hiru-gohan lunch 5
hisho administrative assistant 52
hitori-de alone, by oneself 51
hito-tachi people 18
hiza knee(s) 41
hoka-ni anything else 36
hoka-no another 22
Hokkaidoo Hokkaido 8
#-hon, #-bon, #-pon long, cylindrical object(s) (counter) 36
hondana bookcase 16
Honshuu Honshu 8
hoomusutei homestay 2
hyoo leopard 26

I

ichiban (the) most ~, (the) ~est (+ ADJECTIVE) 9
ichi-jikan ~ ~ per hour 53
ichi-nichi all day, (for) one day 57
Igirisu England 6
Indo India 6
Indoneshia Indonesia 6
inu dog 4
(Person's name-wa) irasshaimasu-ka? Is (person's name) there? (on the phone) 24
iru [irimasu] need (verb) 36
isha doctor 44, 52
Itai! Ouch! 42
(~-ga) itai-n desu. (My ~) hurts. I have a ~-ache. 42
Itaria Italy 6
itoko cousin (humble form) 51
itoko-san cousin (honorific form) 51
Itte-kimasu. Good-bye. (said when leaving home) 18

Itterasshai. Good-bye. (said to person leaving home) 18
iyaringu earring(s) 35

J

jaanarisuto journalist 52
jibun-de by oneself, alone, without the help of others 11
jikan time 14
#-jikan-me class period (suffix) 13
jimuin office worker 52
joyuu actress 52
juusho address 53

K

kaba hippopotamus 26
kaeru [kaerimasu] go (home), leave (for home), return (home) 47
#-ka-getsu # months 49
#-kai, #-gai #th floor 38
kaikeishi accountant 52
kaisha company (place of work) 52
kaku [kakimasu] write 17
kame turtle 26
kami hair 46
Kanada Canada 6
kanai wife (humble form) 51
Kanbojia Cambodia 6
kangaruu kangaroo 26
kangoshi nurse 52
Kankoku Korea 6
kanojo she 29
Kansai Kansai 60
kantorii kurabu country club 18
kao face 41
-kara because 37
-kara from a time, place or person (particle) 7, 34, 35, 60
karada body 41
karai spicy, hot, salty 39
kare he 29
kasa umbrella 21
kashu singer 52
kata shoulder(s) 41
katarogu catalogue 32
katsu [kachimasu] win 27
katte-iru [katte-imasu] keep/have (a pet) 4
kawa river 8
kaze cold 43
kaze wind 21
Kaze na-n desu. (I have a) cold. 43
keikan policeman 52
kekkon (suru [shimasu]) marriage (get married, marry) 49
kekkon shite-iru [shite-imasu] be married 49
kenchikuka architect 52
Kenia Kenya 6
kibishii strict 45
ki-ga mijikai impatient 46
ki-ga nagai patient 46
kinoo-no yoru last night 12
kinpatsu blond, blond hair 46
Ki-o tsukete kudasai. Take care. Be careful. 43
kippu ticket 60
kirei(na) clean, neat 16
kirin giraffe 26
kisetsu season 22

kita north 7
Kita Amerika North America 7
kitanai dirty, messy 16
kitte (postage) stamp 20
ko child (humble form) 26
koara koala 26
kodomo child (humble form) 26
kodomo-san child (honorific form) 49, 51
kongetsu this month 25
konshuu this week 22
Koronbia Columbia 6
kotchi this one (of two) 32
kotoshi this year 25
kubi neck 41
kuchi mouth 41
kudamono fruit 36
kudamono-ya fruit store 36
kuma bear 26
kuni country 6
kusuri medicine 44
kuukoo airport 60
kyanpu(-o suru [shimasu])
        camping (go camping) 25
kyanseru cancelled 43
kyonen last year 25
kyooju professor 52
kyookasho textbook 15
kyooshi teacher 52
kyooshitsu classroom 13
Kyuushuu Kyushu 8
L
M
mada not yet, still 10, 38
-made until/to a time, place or person
        (particle) 60
mado window 21
mae-ni before 44
mago grandchild (humble form) 51
#-mai thin, flat object(s) (counter) 33
majime(na) serious 45
makeru [makemasu] lose 27
-man ten thousand 35
masshuruumu mushroom(s) 36
mayoneezu mayonnaise 36
me eye(s) 41
meetoru meter (unit of measure) 8
megane glasses 47
megane-o shite-iru [shite-imasu]
        wear glasses 47
mei niece (humble form) 51
meigo-san niece (honorific form) 51
me-isha eye doctor 52
Mekishiko Mexico 6
meron melon 32
migi-te right hand 42
mijikai short (opposite of long) 46
mimi ear(s) 41
minami south 7
Minami Amerika South America 7
miseru [misemasu] show 35
mizugi swimsuit 58
mizuumi lake 8
moo already, yet 38
Moo ichido yukkuri itte kudasai.
        Please say it again slowly. 10
morau [moraimasu] receive, get 35

Morokko Morocco 6
mune chest 41
musuko son (humble form) 51
musuko-san son (honorific form) 51
musume daughter (humble form) 51
musume-san (honorific form) 51
N
naasu nurse 52
naga denwa long telephone call 24
nagai long 9
naku-naru [naku-narimasu] (be) lost,
        (get) lost, (be) missing, (be) gone 61
nan-ban-me which number (in a series)? 34
nan-bon how many pencils, pens, etc.
        (long, cylindrical objects)? 36
nan-fiito how many feet? 9
nani-ka something 18
nani-mo nothing, anything 18
nan-ji what time? 24
Nani-ji-ni o-kaeri desu-ka?
        What time will s/he return? 24
nan-ka-getsu how many months? 49
nan-kai what floor? 38
nan-mai how many stamps, sheets of paper,
        etc. (thin, flat objects)? 33
nan-nen-kan how many years? 10
nan-shuu-kan how many weeks? 57
neko cat 4
nemui sleepy 5
#-nen-kan (a period of) # years 10
netsu fever 43
Netsu-ga aru-n desu. (I have a) fever. 43
-ni at, in, on; when an action occurs
        (particle) 35, 54, 60
-ni direction or stopping place of movement
        (particle) 60
-ni person who is the object of an action
        (particle) 18, 20
-ni place where someone or something exists
        (particle) 14, 50, 59
-ni purpose or place one goes to
        (particle) 28, 29
-ni result or final state (particle) 55
nigiyaka(na) lively 45
nikki journal, diary 17
ninjin carrot 36
nishi west 7
nodo throat 42
nomu [nomimasu] take (medicine) 44
noofu farmer 52
nuigurumi stuffed animal 19
O
-o direct object (particle) 4
oba aunt (humble form) 51
obaasan grandmother (honorific form) 51
obasan aunt (honorific form) 51
oboete-iru [oboete-imasu] remember 16
O-daiji-ni. Get well soon. Take care of yourself
        (said to a sick or injured person) 42
oi nephew (humble form) 51
oigo-san nephew (honorific form) 51
oji uncle (humble form) 51
ojiisan grandfather (honorific form) 51
ojisan uncle (honorific form) 51
O-kaeri(nasai). Welcome home. 17

(~en-no) o-kaeshi desu.
    (~yen) is your change. 34
okashii funny 45
okusan wife (honorific form) 51
o-mago-san grandchild (honorific form) 51
o-miai arranged meeting (for consideration
    of marriage) 49
onaji same 31
onaka stomach 41
Onaka-ga suita [sukimashita]. (I'm) hungry.
    [The stomach became empty.] 26, 34
ongakuka musician 52
onsen hot spring 59
Oosutoraria Australia 6, 7
oshieru [oshiemasu] teach 10
otona adult 26
owaru [owarimasu]
    (something) ends, finishes 13

P
pairotto pilot 52
panda panda 26
pasupooto passport 61
pekopeko (very) hungry 34
pen-paru pen pal 20
Peruu Peru 6
petto pet 4
pikunikku(-ni iku [ikimasu])
    picnic (go on a picnic) 2
Poorando Poland 6
poteto chippu potato chips 34
puuru (swimming) pool 2
puuru paatii(-o suru[shimasu])
    pool party (have a pool party) 2

Q
R
raigetsu next month 25
rainen next year 25
raion lion 26
raishuu next week 22
rakuda camel 26
rama llama 26
Raosu Laos 6
reinkooto raincoat 21
renshuu(-o suru [shimasu]) practice 27
retasu lettuce 32
rirekisho résumé 53
romanchikku romantic 40
Roshia Russia 6
rusu out, away, not in 24
rusuban denwa answering machine 24
ryokoo(-o suru [shimasu])
    travel, (take a) trip 19
ryoori(-o suru [shimasu]) cooking (cook) 19
ryooshi fisherman 52
ryooshin parents (humble form) 51

S
saafin(-o suru [shimasu]) (go) surfing 23
sagasu [sagashimasu] look for 61
sai rhinoceros *26*
sakka writer 52
sakura cherry blossoms 21
sarariiman white collar worker 52
saru monkey 26
se height 46
seerusuman salesman 52
se-ga hikui short (person's height) 46

se-ga takai tall (person's height) 46
seijika polititian, statesman 52
sekai world 6
senaka back 41
senchi centimeter 46
sengetsu last month 25
senkyooshi missionary 52
sensei teacher 52
senshuu last week 22
shashin-o toru [torimasu] take a picture 23, 59
shiai game, sporting match 27
shiidii CD 16
Shikoku Shikoku 8
shima island 8
shimauma zebra 26
shimeru [shimemasu] close (something) 21
shinkansen bullet train 60
shinsetsu(na) kind 45
shiranai [shirimasen] (don't/doesn't) know 48
shita under, below, down 16
shitte-iru [shitte-imasu] know 48
shokudoo cafeteria 13
shoojiki(na) honest 45
shoorai future 55
shujin husband (humble form) 51
shumi hobby, pastime, interest 19
#-shuu-kan # week(s), a period of # weeks 57
sobo grandmother (humble form) 51
sofu grandfather (humble form) 51
sono ato after that 54
sooji(-o suru [shimasu]) cleaning (clean) 13
sotchi that one (of two) 32
sotsugyoo shiki graduation ceremony 54
sotsugyoo (suru [shimasu])
    graduation (graduate) 54
Suisu Switzerland 6
sukoa score 27
sumu [sumimasu] will live 55
sunde-iru [sunde-imasu] live 50
suniikaa sneakers 38
Supein Spain 6
suuji number 33
Suweeden Sweden 6
T
tabun maybe, perhaps, probably 54
Tadaima. Hello, I'm home! 17
Tai Thailand 6
 # tai # # to # (a score) 27
taihen(na) terrible, difficult, awful 52
taiikukan gym, gymnasium 13
Taiwan Taiwan 6
takai tall, high, expensive 9
takkyuu ping pong 27
tataku [tatakimasu]
    play (percussion instruments) 19
te hand(s), arm(s) 41
tegami letter 20
te-kubi wrist(s) 41
ten'in shop clerk 52
(~-no) toki when ~, at the time when ~ 50
tonari (the place) next to, adjoining 33
Tookyoo Tawaa Tokyo Tower 59
toosutaa toaster 35
tora tiger 26
tsuaa tour 57
tsukau [tsukaimasu] use 15

tsuku [tsukimasu] arrive 58
tsukuru [tsukurimasu] make 29
tsumetai cold (to the touch) 39
tsuyoi strong 21
U
ue top, above, up 16
ueetaa waiter 52
ueetoresu waitress 52
umareru [umaremasu] (be) born 49
umi ocean, sea 8
unten (suru [shimasu]) driving (drive) 53
untenshu driver, chauffeur 52
V
W
-wa contrasting or distinguishing items
        (particle) 6
wasuremono lost thing(s) 30
wasureru [wasuremasu] forget 15
watashi-tachi we 28
X
Y
yama mountain 8
yoku often 20
yokunai not good 21
Yooroppa Europe 7
yowai weak 27
yubi finger(s) 41
yukkuri slowly, leisurely 10
yume dream (NOUN) 30
yuumei(na) famous 55
Z
zannen(na) too bad 27
zenbu-de altogether, in all 32
zoo elephant 26

Topical Index - JPN II

Find the lesson where a certain topic is discussed.
All entries are listed alphabetically by category.

Culture - Key Points from the Culture Notes

Etiquette / Home and Family

Holidays / Seasonal Events

Miscellaneous

Traveling in Japan

Function - Lesson Objectives (also includes some cultural points)

Grammar - Key Grammar Points

511

Other - Miscellaneous Entries

Reading and Writing Information - *hiragana, katakana, kanji*

HIRAGANA Review

KATAKANA Review

KANJI -

English Meaning(s)	Reading(s)	reading / writing
before, front	ZEN; **mae**	44 / optional
beginning, foundation	**GEN**, GAN; moto	21 / optional
big, large, great	**DAI**, TAI; **oo(kii)**	9 / 12
birth, life, be born, live, raw	SEI, SHOO, JOO; **u(mareru)**, i(kiru), nama	47 / 48
book, origin, source; counter - long, narrow objects	**HON**, BON, PON; moto	8 / 11
bottom, down, under, lower, hang, hang down, give me	KA, GE; **shita**, shimo, sa(geru), sa(garu), **kuda(saru)**	37 / optional
capital	**KYOO**, KEI	60 / optional
child	SHI, SU; **ko, go**	50 / optional
come	**RAI**; **ku(ru)**, ki(masu)	29 / optional
country	**KOKU**, **GOKU**; kuni, guni	54 / optional
day, sun; counter - days of the month	**NICHI**, JITSU; hi, **bi**, **-ka**	7 / 10
ear	JI; **mimi**	42 / optional
earth, soil	**DO**, TO; tsuchi	20 / 23
east	**TOO**; **higashi**	60 / optional
eight	**HACHI**; **ya(tsu)**	31 / optional
eye; ordinal suffix	MOKU; **me**	42 / optional
father	FU; **chichi, too**	49 / optional
fire	**KA**; hi, bi	20 / 22
five	**GO**; **itsu(tsu)**	30 / optional
four	**SHI**; **yon, yo, yo(tsu)**	30 / optional
go, bound for	KOO, GYOO; **i(ku)**, yu(ki)	27 / 28
gold, money	**KIN**, KON; **kane**	20 / 23
hear, listen to, ask, be heard	BUN; **ki(ku)**, ki(koeru)	57 / optional
high, expensive	**KOO**; **taka(i)**	14 / 35
hundred	**HYAKU, BYAKU, PYAKU**	40 / optional
I, privacy	SHI; **watashi**, watakushi	18 / optional
interval, space, room, time	**KAN**, KEN; aida, ma	57 / optional
learn(ing), science	**GAKU**; mana(bu)	13 / 34
middle, inside, within	**CHUU**; **naka**	14 / 35

minute, part, share, divide, separate, understand; counter- for minutes	FUN, PUN, BUN, BU; wa(keru), wa(karu)	58 / optional
month, moon	GETSU, GATSU; tsuki	7 / 10
mother	BO; haha, kaa	49 / optional
mountain	SAN, ZAN; yama	8 / optional
mouth, opening	KOO, KU; kuchi, guchi	42 / optional
name, fame	MEI, MYOO; na	44 / optional
nine	KU, KYUU; kokono(tsu)	31 / optional
now, the present	KON, KIN; ima	18 / 19
one	ICHI; hito(tsu)	30 / optional
person, people; counter - for people	NIN, JIN; hito, -ri	7, 8 / 11
previous, ahead	SEN; saki	47 / 48
rain	U; ame, ama	59 / optional
read	DOKU, TOKU; yo(mu)	55 / optional
rice field, paddy	DEN; ta, da	24 / optional
river	SEN; kawa, gawa	8 / optional
school	KOO	13 / 34
see, look at, watch	KEN; mi(ru)	27 / 28
seven	SHICHI; nana(tsu)	31 / optional
six	ROKU; mut(tsu)	30 / optional
sky, heaven	TEN; ame, ama	21 / optional
small, little	SHOO; ko, o, chii(sai)	9 / 12
snow	SETSU; yuki	59 / optional
speech, statement, word, expression, say	GEN, GON; koto, i(u)	53 / optional
spirit, energy	KI, KE	21 / optional
station	EKI	60 / optional
story, speak	WA; hanashi, hana(su)	53 / optional
talent; counter - for age	SAI	45 / 46
ten	JUU; too	31 / optional
ten thousand	MAN, BAN	41 / optional
thousand	SEN, ZEN; chi	40 / optional
three	SAN; mi(tsu)	30 / optional
time; counter - for hours	JI; toki, doki	58 / optional
top, up, above, over, upper, raise, rise	JOO; ue, kami, a(geru), a(garu)	37 / optional
tree, wood	MOKU, BOKU; ki, gi	8 / 11
two	NI; futa(tsu)	30 / optional
water	SUI; mizu	20 / 22
what, how many; prefix used to form questions	KA; nan, nani	17 / 19
word, speech, narration, tell, speak	GO; katari, gatari, kata(ru)	54 / optional
write	SHO; ka(ku)	56 / optional
year	NEN; toshi	29 / 36
yen, circle	EN	38 / 39

All **Writing Practice Sheets** for *hiragana* , *katakana* and *kanji*

can be found in the workbooks and online at: www.gpb.org/irasshai

for students → student notebook → R+W Support column → Writing Practice Sheets

Kanji Index

Find the lesson where the reading(s) and writing of a *kanji* are introduced.
All entries are listed alphabetically.

Reading	*Kanji*	reading / writing	Reading	*Kanji*	reading / writing
ame	雨	59 / optional	JUU	十	31 / optional
bi	日	7 / 10	-ka	日	7 / 10
BYAKU	百	40 / optional	KA	火	20 / 22
chi	千	40 / optional	kaa	母	49 / optional
chichi	父	49 / optional	ka(ku)	書	56 / optional
chii(sai)	小	9 / 12	KAN	間	57 / optional
CHUU	中	14 / 35	kane	金	20 / 23
da	田	24 / optional	kawa	川	8 / optional
DAI	大	9 / 12	KI	気	21 / optional
DO	土	20 / 23	ki(ku)	聞	57 / optional
doki	時	58 / optional	ki(masu)	来	29 / optional
EKI	駅	60 / optional	KIN	金	20 / 23
EN	円	38 / 39	ko	子	50 / optional
FUN	分	58 / optional	kokono(tsu)	九	31 / optional
futa(tsu)	二	30 / optional	KOKU	国	54 / optional
GAKU	学	13 / 34	KON	今	18 / 19
GATSU	月	7 / 10	KOO	校	13 / 34
GEN	元	21 / optional	KOO	高	14 / 35
GETSU	月	7 / 10	KU	九	31 / optional
GO	五	30 / optional	kuchi	口	42 / optional
go	子	50 / optional	kuda(saru)	下	37 / optional
GO	語	54 / optional	kuni	国	54 / optional
GOKU	国	54 / optional	ku(ru)	来	29 / optional
guchi	口	42 / optional	KYOO	京	60 / optional
guni	国	54 / optional	KYUU	九	31 / optional
HACHI	八	31 / optional	mae	前	44 / optional
haha	母	49 / optional	MAN	万	41 / optional
hana(su)	話	53 / optional	me	目	42 / optional
higashi	東	60 / optional	mimi	耳	42 / optional
hito	人	7,8 / optional	mi(ru)	見	27 / 28
hito(tsu)	一	30 / optional	mi(tsu)	三	30 / optional
HON	本	8 / 11	mizu	水	20 / 22
HYAKU	百	40 / optional	MOKU	木	8 / 11
ICHI	一	30 / optional	mut(tsu)	六	30 / optional
i(ku)	行	27 / 28	na	名	44 / optional
ima	今	18 / 19	naka	中	14 / 35
itsu(tsu)	五	30 / optional	nan	何	17 / 19
i(u)	言	53 / optional	nana(tsu)	七	31 / optional
JI	時	58 / optional	nani	何	17 / 19
JIN	人	7,8 / optional	NEN	年	29 / 36

Reading	*Kanji*	reading / writing
NI	二	30 / optional
NICHI	日	7 / 10
NIN	人	7, 8 / 11
oo(kii)	大	9 / 12
PUN	分	58 / optional
PYAKU	百	40 / optional
RAI	来	29 / optional
-ri	人	7, 8 / 11
ROKU	六	30 / optional
SAI	才	45 / 46
SAN	山	8 / optional
SAN	三	30 / optional
SEN	千	40 / optional
SEN	先	47 / 48
SHI	四	30 / optional
SHICHI	七	31 / optional
shita	下	37 / optional
SHOO	小	9 / 12
SUI	水	20 / 22
ta	田	24 / optional
taka(i)	高	14 / 35
TEN	天	21 / optional
toki	時	58 / optional
too	十	31 / optional
too	父	49 / optional
TOO	東	60 / optional
toshi	年	29 / 36
ue	上	37 / optional
u(mareru)	生	47 / 48
WA	話	53 / optional
wa(karu)	分	58 / optional
watashi	私	18 / optional
yama	山	8 / optional
ya(tsu)	八	31 / optional
yo	四	30 / optional
yo(mu)	読	55 / optional
yon	四	30 / optional
yo(tsu)	四	30 / optional
yuki	雪	59 / optional

All Writing Practice Sheets for *hiragana*, *katakana* and *kanji*
can be found in the workbooks and online at: www.gpb.org/irasshai
for students → student notebook → R+W Support column → Writing Practice Sheets